W9-AOQ-113

Maryhelen Vannier, Ed.D.

Professor and Director, Women's Division
Department of Health and Physical Education
Southern Methodist University

Hollis F. Fait, Ph.D.

Professor of Physical Education
The School of Physical Education
University of Connecticut

1975 W. B. SAUNDERS COMPANY

Teaching Physical Education

in secondary schools

fourth edition

Philadelphia   London   Toronto

W. B. Saunders Company: West Washington Square
Philadelphia, Pa. 19105

12 Dyott Street
London, WC1A 1DB

833 Oxford Street
Toronto, Ontario M8Z 5T9, Canada

Library of Congress Cataloging in Publication Data

Vannier, Maryhelen, 1915–

Teaching physical education in secondary schools.

Bibliography: p.

Includes index.

1. Physical education and training.   I. Fait, Hollis F.,
   joint author.   II. Title.

GV361.V28 1975   613.7′07′12   74–6693

ISBN 0–7216–8962–0

Teaching Physical Education in Secondary Schools   ISBN   0-7216-8962-0

Last digit is the print number: 9   8   7   6   5   4   3   2   1

This Book is Dedicated to the Memory of
Our Two Inspiring Major Professors

DR. JAY B. NASH
AND
DR. CHARLES H. McCLOY

For the Great Contribution Each Has Made
To the Profession of Physical Education
And to the Lives of Their Many Students

PREFACE

This book is first of all a presentation of physical education, its place in the modern secondary school, and the contributions it can make to education. Secondly, it is a book of techniques and methods for teaching students successfully through many well-conducted physical education activities.

It has been written mainly for four groups: (1) the college physical education major who is preparing to be a teacher; (2) the beginning teacher who often lacks efficient methods for teaching large groups or individuals productively; (3) the graduate student and others looking for the latest developments in the secondary school physical education field; and (4) the experienced teacher who is searching for newer and better ways to lead youth successfully.

This fourth edition is a major revision and contains many additions and changes. Briefly listed, these include:

1. The bringing up to date of all previous materials, including the list of suggested readings at the end of each chapter.

2. Added materials on techniques for teaching large groups effectively.

3. New program offerings, including lifetime sports and movement exploration.

4. A description of current trends and changes in the secondary school curriculum.

5. The problem of the crowding out of childhood and the pushing of adulthood upon youthful shoulders in our society, and what teachers can do in relationship to it.

6. New methods for increasing teaching-learning effectiveness, including the use of programed materials.

7. The use of paraprofessionals and other teacher aids.

8. The role the physical educator can play to help in reaching troubled youth and in combating rising juvenile delinquency.

9. Recent federal legislation that has directly affected secondary education.

10. The problem of teacher turnover and suggestions about how it can be avoided, as well as a discussion of teacher unions.

11. Ways for combating discrimination in our schools against the scholastically brilliant, the "hand-minded," the clerical- or machine-minded, the socially intelligent and the creative student.

12. A discussion of the problem of expanded leisure time, giving suggestions for helping youth to use free time constructively.

13. A listing of new kinds of teaching aids needed for an expanded physical education program.

14. The inclusion of administrative patterns for combining physical education with health education in the curriculum.

15. Ways in which teachers can avoid legal liability.

16. New ways for evaluating skill mastery, learning competencies and program effectiveness.

17. The growth of interscholastic competition for high school girls and guiding standards to follow.

18. Sources for charts and other kinds of teaching aids.

19. A physical fitness test for the mentally retarded.

20. A discussion of recently developed equipment and facilities.

21. Presentation of the problem-solving method and the traditional method, and the syntheses of the two as effective ways to teach.

22. A discussion of new designs in teaching independent study, elective activities, team teaching and contract teaching.

23. Strong emphasis on how to teach the handicapped.

24. A description of the many ways to enlarge program offerings through the use of community facilities.

The authors, both of whom have had wide experience as secondary school teachers and directors of teacher preparation programs in colleges, subscribe to the philosophy that good teaching methods can be mastered by those willing to learn. They believe also that, since teachers hold the keys which unlock the doors of success and happiness for tomorrow's adults, it is imperative that teachers discover and develop the best techniques possible to educate and inspire youth for their present and future life tasks. Like Diogenes, they contend that the foundation of every state lies in the education of its youth, and would agree with Seneca that the real duty of any school is to teach the art of living well.

The techniques of teaching all skills described in the book have been in reference to right-handed players. In general, left-handed students should perform these skills in the opposite direction from that given. Most left-handed students of secondary school age will automatically make these changes when directions are given or when they copy the teacher's demonstration of correct skill forms.

The authors have assumed that the reader has experienced basic preparation in mastering the skills presented in each activity. Consequently, emphasis throughout the text has been placed on techniques for productively organizing class groups for successful presentation and mastery of these skills.

The need for such a practical book has long been felt because of the widening chasm separating idealistic educational theories from realistic educational practices and because of the need to cope with rapidly changing school conditions, including large enrollments and crowded, inadequate facilities. Never have the problems been greater, with less prospect for improved conditions.

Each teacher must find his own best teaching methods by a slow process of carefully blending the ingredients of educational theory, the techniques used by former admired instructors, and his own trial-and-error attempts. He can profit greatly, however, from experimenting with the many suggestions and learning short cuts found in this book and by tailoring them to fit his own needs.

The authors are convinced that a good physical education program is one which is well balanced in content, valued by students, educationally sound, and conducted by capable teachers. Along with Joseph Addison, the famous seventeenth-century essayist, they believe that education can be to the human soul what sculpture is to a block of marble.

It has been estimated by leaders in the field that only approximately 42 per cent of all elementary school children have an adequate program in physical education and that only 58 per cent of all secondary youth receive what is considered to be adequate or better instruction in this field. In some schools, paraprofessionals with only a bare minimum of education have replaced the professionally prepared physical education teacher as an economy move by the school administration. In other schools, in spite of the many program innovations in operation today for high school youth, students are still "learning" to play only volleyball, basketball, football and baseball throughout their entire three or four years in physical education classes. In still others, the coach throws out the ball to his classes and then retreats to his office to plan practice plays for his football squad. In many more schools the students, administrators and other teachers regard physical education as a farce and rightly so, for too often that is exactly what it is.

Never, then, have the problems, challenges and opportunities for the professionally well prepared and dedicated, creative and productive physical education teacher been greater!

MARYHELEN VANNIER
HOLLIS F. FAIT

ACKNOWLEDGMENTS

The authors are indebted to many persons who have made this book possible. Especial gratitude is due to our families, students, professional colleagues and other friends for their suggestions and reactions to the materials in this book, and for their encouragement during its creation.

We wish particularly to acknowledge the fine contributions made by Dr. John Billing, who wrote the revised chapters on "The Teaching Process," "Tumbling and Gymnastics," and "Physical Fitness," and by Dr. Shirley Corbitt, who wrote the new enlarged section on interscholastic competition for high school girls. Mrs. Gladene Hansen Fait was particularly helpful in editing portions of the manuscript. Mrs. Dorothy Good typed the manuscript.

ACKNOWLEDGMENTS
FOR PHOTOGRAPHS AND OTHER MATERIALS USED IN THIS BOOK.

Star Owen
Gymknits By
Macmillan Ward, Inc.

E. S. Henderson
Director, Silver Spurs Dance Group
Spokane Public Schools

Eugene Suttman
American Biltrite, Inc.
Irving, Texas

Ewell Sessom
Division of Program Development
Texas Education Agency
Austin, Texas

James Galceran
Hargall All Sports Carryall Company
P.O. Box 1094
Wilmington, California

Nancy Rosenberg
AAHPER
Washington, D.C.

Charles Horvath
East Hartford Public Schools
East Hartford, Connecticut

Charles Aredisian
Darien Public Schools
Darien, Connecticut

Carl Angelica
Enfield Public Schools
Enfield, Connecticut

Raymond NcNeil
Instructional Media Coordinator
Enfield Board of Education
Enfield, Connecticut

Mario Gentile
Carol Albert
Lora Arnold
Robert Lyngeal
Enrico Fermi High School
Enfield, Connecticut

Dale Harper
West Hartford Public Schools
West Hartford, Connecticut

K. Cash Luck
Regina High School
Minneapolis, Minnesota

CONTENTS

Part Five
PUPIL AND PERSONAL ASSESSMENT

Appendices

PART ONE

BACKGROUND

The results of a good physical education are not limited to the body alone, but may extend even to the soul itself.

. . . . . Plato

CHAPTER ONE

THE CONTRIBUTIONS OF PHYSICAL EDUCATION TO SECONDARY EDUCATION

Today's rapidly shrinking world and fast-changing society are the direct results of our modern educational system; however, the strong confidence Americans once had in their educational system is beginning to weaken. Our founding fathers, like our own grandparents and parents, believed in, fought for, cherished, and supported education. The early pioneers first built a church, and then a school, when they at long last found a place where they wanted to settle down and raise their children. Today, although many adults still believe that education is the foundation upon which happiness, human dignity and success are built, there are large numbers of people who are becoming increasingly critical of our schools.

If education is to continue to shape the lives of those in our rapidly changing society, it too must greatly change. Efforts in education, however, are hampered by lack of financial support for the schools, the detrimental influence of discrimination, and difficulties in implementing new methods and techniques. The gravest problem teachers face today centers around the dilemma of large classes and the difficulty of making education meaningful to each student in the group. The problem of how to get more students into our schools has been solved. The greatest concern of educators now is to find ways to create and share educational experiences with youth that are potent enough and valuable enough that they will stay in school to reap fully the many benefits of an enriched educational experience.

GROWTH OF SECONDARY EDUCATION

Free public education is still in its infancy, yet within its short time span of less than 350 years, it has had a phenomenal growth. In the year 1919–1920, 32.3 per cent of all youth between the ages of 14 to

17 were enrolled in secondary schools. In 1969–1970, 91.5 per cent of this age group attended high school. This is an amazing growth record. Three out of every four students now finish high school, whereas three out of every four did not go beyond the eighth grade in 1929. The number of black youths who graduate from high school has increased two and one-half times from 1929 to 1968, and the number is increasing at an even more remarkable rate in this decade. More of these students are now enrolled in two- or four-year colleges than ever before in our history. This is also true of youth from other minority groups.[1]

The dropout rate today is declining, and job-seeking youths who had left school before graduating are now "dropping back in" or are going into trade schools. In 1970–1971, less than one fourth of all youth left school—a total of 720,000 students.[2] It is predicted that by 1975, 85 per cent of all who enter high school will stay until they graduate.[3] In spite of these facts, critics of secondary education are becoming more vocal and, like many parents and students, are claiming that the curriculum of the modern school is still too college-orientated and greatly outdated. Some believe that our schools are becoming "aging vats" and, because youth today is more explosive and vulnerable than ever before, that "teachers can't and aren't really doing much teaching when so many of their charges are raising hell in our schools."[4] Police or security guards are employed in 66 per cent of the schools in America at the present time.

In America, more high school graduates go on to college than anywhere else in the entire world. Although at present many college graduates are having difficulty finding employment in certain specialized fields, experts claim that this problem is only a temporary one. As our society advances technologically, many new kinds of professional careers will come into being. Because of the knowledge explosion, facts we learn today will soon become greatly outdated. It is estimated that in today's fast-paced society, most workers are likely to change their jobs three or more times and that most families will move from one geographical area to another at least seven times in their lifetime. The retirement age is predicted to be in the early fifties by the end of this century.[5] Consequently, educational offerings on every

---

[1]According to the *Digest of Educational Statistics of 1972*, p. 81, there were 680,000 black students enrolled in colleges or universities, and 134,000 students (1.7 per cent) from other minority or racial groups.

[2]Simon, Grant, and Grant, Vance: *Digest of Educational Statistics.* Washington, D.C., United States Government Printing Office, 1973, p. 49, Table 56.

[3]Silberman, Charles: *Crisis In The Classroom.* New York, Vintage Books, 1971, p. 18.

[4]Malloy, Michael: "U.S. High Schools: Just An Aging Vat?" *The National Observer.* October 13, 1973, Vol. 12, No. 41.

[5]MacLean, Janet: Leisure and the Year 2000. *Recreation in the Modern Society.* Edited by Marion and Caroll Hormacher, Boston, Holbrook Press, 1972, p. 324.

level, including colleges and universities, must be greatly restyled if individuals of all ages, including senior citizens, are to enroll in school and reap its many benefits. Youths and adults alike must continually be taught many new skills and "know how" in order that they may help the problems that will affect us today, as well as tomorrow, in our greatly overpopulated world and in our vastly crowded, decaying inner-cities.

In the many secondary schools throughout the land we find no single pattern, for they are as varied as the topography of America and the socioeconomic backgrounds of our many ethnic groups. Some are small and below standard both in leadership and curriculum offerings, others are serving hundreds of students in their beautiful modern buildings through highly skilled, productive teachers. Some stress vocational training, others the broad general curriculum; some few are primarily college preparatory in nature, while still others are subject centered in contrast to those which are experience centered. Some include work experiences, others scorn them. Our schools have made America the leader of the entire world. Henry Steele Commager, the great historian, has declared that in spite of criticism, half-hearted and inadequate financial support and conservative, uncreative leadership, our American Schools have, in less than 350 years, succeeded in preserving democracy, building national unity and developing our own cultural heritage. Our many schools have been established, maintained and supported because the people have faith in them and because they want and dream of a better tomorrow, not only for their own children, but also for those of all mankind.

ORGANIZATIONAL PATTERNS

Types of secondary schools are general, special and part-time. These include:

General schools
    The limited (general curriculum)
    The comprehensive (college preparatory)
Specialized schools
    Emphasis placed upon specialized training and general education in:
        Agriculture
        Commercial skills
        Technical skills
        Trade skills
Part-time schools (found largely in big cities)
    Continuation (for those who have not been graduated, or have dropped out, and return on a part-time daily basis)
    Evening (same as above except that students attend at night)

School administrative patterns[6] are:

1. The junior and senior high school combined with elementary school (the 6-3-3 or the 6-2-4 plan).
2. The elementary and senior high schools separated (the 8-4 plan).
3. The elementary, middle and senior high schools separated (4-4-4, 5-3-4 or 6-3-3 plan).

In the last of the pattern mentioned, the middle division is now called the middle school in many schools, a term that is replacing the older, more traditional junior high school. The middle school pattern of organization has much greater flexibility in staffing, programming and scheduling than has usually been found in those school grades beyond the elementary level. The curriculum can be more child-centered and less subject-centered, and the materials to be learned are less textbook oriented. The student attending a middle school has greater opportunities for creative exploration and self-direction than did his counterpart who attended the traditional junior high school in 1925.[7] (Physical education for grades 7, 8 and 9 is frequently taught by teachers trained in secondary school education; consequently these grades are included in the presentation of appropriate material in this book.)

THE CURRICULUM

The curriculum is, in reality, the total life and program of the school. Intramural and interscholastic athletics, clubs and musical activities are often as important to the development of youth as are the traditional subjects of English, French, or mathematics. Although "extracurricular activities" have been added to the school program only since the late nineteenth and early twentieth centuries, they are gradually gaining more status in the eyes of educators. However, in most schools, they are maintained on an after-school, noncredit, voluntary basis.

To provide more fully for the common needs of all youth, the school curriculum attempts to provide learning experiences around present and future needs that will enable students to solve best the problems of life and daily living. Increasingly a "core" curriculum made up of general subject areas is being used. Students are given opportunities to elect certain courses included in the "core" offerings;

---

[6]Many school systems include kindergarten and nursery school in addition to the 12 grades. A few also include two years of college.

[7]Bough, Max: The Intermediate School: The Junior High and Middle Schools. *The Education Digest*. October, 1973, pp. 24–27.

broad areas in this curriculum usually include:

English	Mathematics	Home economics
Social science	Science	Foreign languages
Commercial subjects	Industrial arts	Music
Art	Physical education	Health education

Current trends in curriculum development show that:

1. There is a break from the traditional curriculum in content, and teaching methods, and teachers are now placing emphasis upon the need for lifetime learning and ways for continually adapting to the changing world of work and increased leisure. Students are increasingly being given more responsibility for their own educational, personal, and social development, as guided by their teachers.

2. Teachers are taking an active part in planning and revising courses of study for their own use.

3. The curriculum is being integrated through cooperative planning by subject matter specialists.

4. The "tool" subjects are being integrated into all learning materials as a means of helping students gain greater understandings, appreciations and more favorable attitudes toward education and learning.

5. The focus of the curriculum has shifted from the past to the present and future, and many new kinds of instructional media are being used to individualize instruction. The focus is now on the student, and not so much upon the material to be learned, as it was in the past.

6. Controversial issues have been included in the curriculum and there is consideration of current problems for which there is no authoritative answer.

7. Students are being increasingly encouraged to show initiative and creativity, and are being given considerably more freedom in determining what is to be learned and how to go about learning.

8. Guidance programs are being made an inseparable part of the regular teaching process.

9. Extracurricular activities are increasingly becoming inseparable from the school curriculum.

10. Graded courses of study in each subject area are being planned from kindergarten through the twelfth grade.

11. Specific programs are being devised for the talented and highly skilled pupil, the average one, the slow learner, who often also has poor motor skills, and the potential school dropout. Career education is spreading rapidly across the nation. Skill in job training experiences, such as learning auto repair, secretarial procedures, and so forth, take place in actual job situations during part of each school day, and academic subjects are taught the rest of the day at the high school.

12. The educational approach to the curriculum is increasingly stressing throughout the curriculum problem solving, critical thinking, and the development of the ability to generalize from factual material.

PROBLEMS

All has not been smooth sailing for secondary education, however, in spite of its phenomenal growth and the above-mentioned trends. Although the most immediate problems to be faced are those of increased enrollment and classroom shortage, secondary schools must sooner or later find answers to the following questions raised by critical educational experts, parents, and even the students themselves:

1. What should be done to keep more youth in school until they graduate? If more than almost one half of those who enter drop out, why do they leave school?

2. How can the elementary school program dovetail more effectively into that of the junior and senior high school, and on into the junior and/or four-year college?

3. What subjects should be elective? What ones required? How can this best be determined? By whom?

4. How can teachers give individualized attention in increasingly large class groups? How can individual needs and capacities be discovered?

5. What realistic work experiences do youth need? How can the exploitation of youth's labor and talents be avoided? Should all students receive work training experiences or only those who do not plan to go on to college?

6. How can we get better teacher preparation programs into colleges? Often those conducting courses in teacher preparation are themselves poor and unproductive teachers. Sometimes they are in the lowest status group among their own colleagues.

7. What are the educational responsibilities of the home, the school and the church? How can we get each to accept its own? How can the contributions of each be blended into a united effort?

8. How can education be financed by a long-range plan, rather than from its present makeshift, bottom-of-the-collected-tax-dollar barrel?

9. How can we stimulate teachers to be more creative, to experiment and conduct research which will bring them better results in their own work?

10. What can be done with those teachers who are using out-of-date materials and teaching methods and who will not change with the times since they will soon be retired and "could not care less" about the educational growth of their students?

11. How large should schools and classes be in order to obtain the best results? How can this be best determined? Should there be an adopted standard for all schools and classes? How can this be made possible in light of ever-increasing school enrollment?

12. How can local, state and national governments best help schools?

Increasingly the general public is becoming concerned about our American school system. Critics of our secondary schools are, mainly, responsible, intelligent laymen and educators. Specific criticism centers around the curriculum, the school's objectives, teachers, lack of student discipline, pupil-teacher relations, modern methods of teaching, the school's organization and administration, the over-emphasis on athletics for a few and lack of concern for the development of an expanded intramural program for the majority, school buildings and lack of adequate, safe and clean facilities for increasing class and school enrollment.

The Dropout. Many schools do not meet the needs of all youth. Over one million youth physically drop out of school each year. Literally hundreds more attend but "drop out" mentally. Some later "drop back in" school after an early marriage and family responsibilities appear and job opportunities fail to materialize. Knowledge of increased competition for jobs in relationship to education and salable skills is beginning to keep youth in school longer. The fact is that our country is becoming more and more a "credential society," in which a person is judged, hired, and accorded social as well as economic status based upon his high school or college diploma rather than upon what he can accomplish on the job. Recent studies show that there is little correlation between work performance and school grades or the amount of education a person has had. However, the fact remains that many job applicants are refused jobs on the grounds of lack of education, and thus they cannot demonstrate their competence.

The average dropout is about 16 years old, does not take part in extracurricular school activities, has parents who are uninterested in the value of book learning, usually has less than average intelligence, is disinterested in school, has reading and personality problems and is anxious to taste the many forbidden fruits found in the thrilling "real" world away from school.

Some suggestions for reducing the number of dropouts are to:

1. Develop a curriculum adapted to the immediate needs, intellectual capacities and interests of these students.
2. Increase guidance and counseling services.
3. Provide work-study programs wherein students can be paid for part-time work.
4. Enforce and extend our present school compulsory attendance laws.
5. Develop closer teacher-student and teacher-parent-student rapport.
6. Provide "right" school opportunities that are largely vocationally oriented.
7. Enrich courses of study through many in-school and out-of-school activities, such as excursions and recognition assembly programs.
8. Provide more teachers who are skilled in working with problem children and who are free to experiment in order to find the best way in which to help each student who is or might become a dropout.
9. Consolidate small inferior rural schools with more attractive modern ones.
10. Follow a nongraded curriculum, allowing each pupil to progress at his own speed rate.
11. Provide bilingual teachers to teach immigrant students and to communicate with their parents.
12. Extend educational opportunities for migrant children and youth.

Disparaties in Financial Support and Leadership. There is a wide difference in the quality of education found in many states. Our schools are not the great equalizer envisioned by the famous educator, John Dewey, for today many schools actually perpetuate differences between people and need to do a much better job of educating those from minority groups and lower class homes, such as Blacks, Indians, Puerto Ricans, Latin Americans, and the Appalachian whites. Our schools seemingly are failing to teach these students how to make a decent living or how to break out of the chain of poverty. Many of these students are taught by inferior teachers in the worst possible kinds of overcrowded facilities, and are passed from grade to grade in spite of the fact that they cannot read, write, or speak well and greatly lack the computational skills needed in our modern society. Some students are barely literate; many are problem-ridden and lack self-discipline or the motivation to strive for self-improvement. Youth in many of our poorest schools are involved in a tugging and pulling conflict of values—their values versus those held by some of their better teachers and educational idealists. They are also our most vulnerable and gullible consumers of "things" (the souped up car, the newest fashions and so on) and are living in a world which is a glittering dream world far removed from reality.

In 1972 the state of New York spent $1669 per pupil, California spent $1049, and Mississippi $706.00.[8] In spite of the increase in the cost of living, teachers' salaries on the secondary level have increased meagerly. The average high school teacher's salary in 1971 was $9568 and $10,015 in 1972. School teachers' strikes are increasing. According to the National Education Association, 86 school districts in 14 states reported teachers' strikes in 1973. In a comparable period of 1972 there were 66 walkouts by striking teachers in 10 states. In the fall term of 1973, 72 local affiliates of the NEA, or a total of 52,000 teachers, walked out of school, affecting 1.2 million students.[9] Although generally the walkouts involved money, salary increases were not the only issue, but involved overcrowded facilities and increasingly disruptive students as well. Dr. James Conant's book, *The American High School Today*,[10] Dr. Max Rafferty's, *Suffer Little Children*,[11] and Dr. Charles Silberman's, *Crisis In The Classroom*,[12] have done much to shock laymen into awareness of the need for improving educational programs on a national basis.

Busing. Black and white, conservative and liberal, rich and poor, the American people are now increasingly critical of busing students from one school to another as many feel that urban students are being bused miles away from their own neighborhoods into educationally

---

[8]Simon, Kenneth, and Grant, Vance: *Digest of Educational Statistics.* Washington, D.C., 1972, p. 76.

[9]"Predictions Wrong—Teachers Strike Anyway." *Christian Science Monitor.* September, 1973.

[10]New York, Harper and Row, 1961.

[11]New York, Devin-Adair Publishing Co., 1962.

[12]New York, Vantage Press, 1970.

poor as well as economically poor environments. Although the purpose of forced busing was to end discrimination, in many cases it has actually resulted in even further polarization of white and black, and in low versus middle and upper income groups. On the other hand, individual students often report favorably on the experience of association with peers of different backgrounds and races.

Discrimination. Dr. Malcolm MacLean has pointed out that if we are ever to reach the democratic ideal of functional literacy, culture and occupational education for all, we must, among other things, obliterate our present practices of discrimination in our schools. As many experienced teachers know, discriminatory educational actions are often directed against those who are: (1) scholastically brilliant (because many instructors are unwilling to change or to find a way to cope with increased class size, and thus are gearing their teaching to the mediocre average), (2) "hand-minded" students who, although they are often slower academically, are exceptionally well skilled with their hands and bodies, (3) clerically intelligent students, who are adept at doing paperwork and using machines, (4) socially intelligent students, who shine in extracurricular, noncredit activities, and (5) artistically intelligent students, who are often the most neglected but the most gifted and creative of all.

In addition, there are prevalent in the educational system those forms of discrimination common in our society. This includes discrimination based on sex, race, and religion. Less obvious forms of discrimination are those relating to persons who are handicapped or who exhibit characteristics different from those of the largest segment of society.

Increased Delinquency. Further evidence that drastic changes must be made in secondary education comes from experts in the field of juvenile delinquency, who are aware that in our schools we now have no real place for the teenager who has personality problems or who could not possibly go on to college (making education for all a myth). Some of these experts even go so far as to claim that, since those of the low academic group are not being educated and because of our prohibitive labor laws which bar the semiskilled as well as the unskilled from entering the working world, such practices are major contributing factors to our soaring juvenile delinquency rates. Furthermore, although these experts, along with teachers who really care about students, are aware that one of the most successful methods of combating delinquency is to provide meaningful school apprenticeship work experiences for the many nonacademic students, they also are resigned to the fact that educational change does filter through and come about slowly. Consequently, many fine teachers quit their jobs in disgust because of public apathy, local politics and their long working hours, which include many nonteaching duties that keep them away from fruitful counseling and contacts with those whom they recognize as troubled youth.

Needed changes in American education are pressing and they are many. Corrections are now being contemplated or have been already incorporated in our better school systems. Many schools, for example, are now providing or will in the future provide under one curricular roof, courses of study which will better fill the needs of the non-academic as *well* as the academic student.[13] Such a revised curriculum will provide a common core of education needed by both groups, equip those who upon graduation will enter the work world to be educated and socially accepted citizens, and provide those going on to college with the necessary educational preparation.

THE PURPOSE OF SECONDARY EDUCATION

The aims, goals and purposes of secondary education have changed frequently. Many would agree with Alfred North Whitehead that there is only one subject matter for education, and that is Life in all its manifestations. Others would concur with Robert Hutchins and raise academic standards higher on all educational levels for the benefit of a select group, believing that the best education possible of the talented few leaders will bring society the richest gains.

Numerous educators, such as John Dewey, Harold Rugg, William Kilpatrick and E. L. Thorndike, as well as many nongovernmental organizations, have both contributed to and shaped American educational concepts and practices. All stress that the real purpose of education is to develop the individual so that he, in turn, will develop society for the betterment of all.

Widely followed educational objectives are the Cardinal Principles of Education, formulated in 1918. These include the belief that all youth should receive education in the following broad curriculum areas:

Health	Vocational education
Command of the fundamental processes	Citizenship
Worthy use of leisure time	Worthy home membership
Ethical character	

In 1938, The Educational Policies Commission reorganized the above principles into four general headings and urged that they be-

---

[13]See the chapter on Curriculum for recommendations for and needed changes in physical education and health education made by Dr. Conant and other educational experts.

come the revised objectives of secondary education:

Self-realization	Economic efficiency
Human realization	Civic responsibility

In 1945, the Commission on Life Adjustment Education for Youth recommended that, in order that all youth would receive benefit from school, the curriculum be broadened to include meaningful experiences for the students who do not go on to college. Supervised work experiences and increased emphasis placed upon vocational education were strongly recommended, along with improved course offerings for those preparing for college.

According to this committee, the school curriculum should be built around the *real* needs of youth. These include their need to:

1. Develop salable skills.
2. Develop and maintain good health and physical fitness.
3. Understand their duties and rights as citizens.
4. Understand the methods of science and the influence of science upon human life, as well as to gather scientific facts concerning the nature of the world and of man.
5. Learn how to purchase and use goods intelligently.
6. Develop capacities to appreciate beauty in literature, art, music and nature.
7. Understand the significance of family life.
8. Use their leisure time well.
9. Develop respect for others; to gain insight into ethical values.
10. Grow in the ability to think rationally, to express their thoughts clearly, to read and listen with understanding.

The present humanistic movement in education is bringing far-reaching reforms in most subject areas of the school curriculum. New ways are being found to help youth make value decisions, not only about themselves but about society, too, and about how they can serve mankind by living significant lives themselves. Cultural, aesthetic civic, health, family living, and other kinds of enriched learning experiences are now a vital part of the curriculum in our best schools.

THE CONTRIBUTION OF PHYSICAL EDUCATION

Every subject in the school curriculum has a unique contribution to make to the development of each student and, thus, to society. A strong, moral and vigorous America can only be made up of citizens who have these qualities. The aims, goals and purposes of physical education are the same as those of all other school subjects — to develop well-rounded, happy, healthy, skilled and productive individuals determined to perpetuate democracy. A sound mind in a sound body is more than the happy state of affairs John Locke believed in; it is a prime necessity for our increased hours of leisure and in our tense, rushed, economically highly competitive and war-threatened time!

The total school physical education program consists of four parts: class instruction for all students, the intramural program, the recreation program and interscholastic athletics. Although there is wide variance in the types of programs, leadership and facilities found in secondary schools throughout the country in this specialized field, educators, students and the general public are becoming increasingly aware that all youth *should* and *must* receive benefit from partaking in a graded physical education program based upon sound educational objectives directed by skilled, professionally well prepared teachers.

Physical education in schools is made up of those directed, purposeful activities which are centered around the total body, its movement, care and use. It stresses the development of physical, social and mental well-being. In secondary schools, emphasis in physical education should be on carefully planned instruction in a variety of activities in a graded program that will develop total fitness through

Figure 1–1. Classroom instruction is one of four parts of the total physical education program, which also includes intramurals, recreation, and interscholastic athletics. (Courtesy of *The Scholastic Coach.*)

the contribution physical fitness makes to such a state of well-being, increase movement skill range and accuracy, socialize the individual, increase knowledges, favorable attitudes and appreciations and foster better use of leisure time. A program that is built upon the attainment of these objectives will have in it a variety of activities to be learned and they will become increasingly more challenging to learn as well as being selected for the purpose of teaching the student sport and dance skills that can be used throughout life. A program that consists of four years of football, basketball and baseball for boys does not fit into the concept of today's physical education curriculum. Nor does one of four years of soccer, basketball, volleyball and softball for girls.

Just as in ancient Greece and Rome, so today in our better schools physical education is considered to have an important place in the school curriculum. Modern educators see the folly of trying to separate the mind from the body or of considering one as superior to the other, for they know that, since man is a unity, it is impossible to educate or develop either singly.

Literally, to educate means to "lead forth." The purpose of the secondary school curriculum should be to teach each youth in each new rising generation to understand, believe in and value democracy as a way of life, as well as to inspire each student to strive for personal distinction in order that he may contribute toward the advancement of a more highly cultured, productive, happier and meaningful life for himself and all people. Thus, education is primarily concerned with improving the *quality* of living. In today's world, we cannot afford to risk a single underdeveloped or uneducated American citizen.

The unique contribution physical education makes to general education is in the area of effective, efficient and purposeful movement. Such a contribution is of tremendous importance to adults when we realize the impact of the scientific truth that "the basic tool for performance of any task in life is the human body."[14] As Oberteuffer and Ulrich point out, "movement is really more than a basic physiological necessity—it is also our interpretation of self to ourselves and others. It is fundamental to life, to growth, and to development."[15]

OBJECTIVES

The goals of physical education, like those of all other school subjects included in the school curriculum, should be to develop all

---

[14]Broer, Marion: *Efficiency in Human Movement.* Philadelphia, W. B. Saunders Co., 3rd ed., 1970.

[15]Oberteuffer, Delbert, and Ulrich, Celeste: *Physical Education, A Textbook of Principles for Professional Students.* New York, Harper & Row, 1971, p. 1.

youth physically, socially, mentally and morally so that they become well-rounded, healthy, responsible, happy and intelligent human beings who are concerned about the well-being and happiness of others as well as themselves. However, physical education has a unique contribution to make to both the school program and each individual student through its teachers, program and facilities. It is the only subject in the school program that is concerned primarily with the physical development of the student.

Physical educators and coaches are usually extremely popular with students and their professional colleagues. Pliable youth often finds them worthy of emulation. Furthermore, most students are enthusiastic about taking part in the program if it is well planned and contains a variety of challenging activities. It has frequently been said, and rightly so, that physical education carries its own drive, especially with youth, for they crave activity, fun, challenges and adventure. The gymnasium, tennis courts, pool, playing fields and the stadium are perhaps the most used of all school facilities, not only by their own population but by numerous community members and civic groups. The community-school concept is spreading rapidly throughout our nation. In this time of "tight" money, taxpayers are increasingly seeing to it that school buildings are being planned and used for the community's benefit as well as for youth.[16]

The role of the teacher is to educate each student *through* physical education by helping him to develop as a totally functioning human being while engaging in carefully selected activities which are best suited for his needs, interests and capabilities.

Developing Total and Physical Fitness. Organic development and general well-being are the results of vigorous activities. The muscles of the body increase in strength, size and tonus through exercise. The heart and other vital organs are markedly affected through the right kinds and amounts of activity. Improved sleep and eating habits as well as accelerated energy result. Physical fitness results from regularity of exercise, good habits of waste elimination, sleep and rest, eating and recreation, and the maintenance of emotional well-being and balance. As such, it must be sought and worked for, developed and maintained. Physical education contributes greatly to the health, happiness and well-being of all who enjoy its many thrills, pleasures and challenges. Health habits formed early in life are most likely to carry over into adult patterns for living abundantly by those who have learned that gaining and maintaining good health is basic to success and happiness in life. Total fitness is made up of physical, mental and emotional fitness. Those who possess it are the

---

[16]For information about the community-centered school write to the Board of Education in Flint, Michigan or Milwaukee, Wisconsin.

"doers" in our society rather than the "watchers," for they have the vigor, enthusiasm and desire to live life to its fullest.

Increasing Movement Skill Range and Accuracy. Skills are the result of training. They are learned mostly through trial and error, plus imitation. Since it is often harder to unlearn faulty movement habits than to master new ones, those individuals who receive superior instruction from highly skilled teachers are fortunate, indeed. Youth are eager to sample many activities; their eagerness and determination *to do* are dynamic learning incentives and should be capitalized upon by every teacher. This can be done through the guidance of each individual into activities best suited for his own capabilities and limitations. Insistence upon skill mastery or staying on one skill area too long in a unit often leaves some students with unfavorable attitudes toward the program or teacher.

The instructor's role in skill development is that of detecting learning readiness, correctly demonstrating the movements to be tried and copied and assisting each student to master them. Correct timing, strength, speed, increased body flexibility and movement range will accrue through practice if the right ways to do these skills are understood and followed. Any student will learn to play a sport or game better, faster and with more pleasure if he is instructed from the beginning by someone who knows how to motivate and teach him to master the desired skills.

Socializing the Individual. It has been often claimed by physical educators that sports, games and dances are the best common denominator of people of all backgrounds, races, creeds, nationality or color. Just as families who play together tend to stay together as united groups so, likewise, boys and girls who are teammates or opponents in a game of friendly rivalry develop strong and lasting friendship bonds.

For many students there are few school experiences which equal those found in physical education for helping people belong, feel secure and wanted, or find affection. The teacher, however, must provide opportunities for these feelings to develop in every student, not just in those who are already highly coordinated, but in the awkward, and insecure, or in the hostile, would-be troublemakers as well. Here, too, are abundant opportunities to develop fellowship and leadership skills and to help youth learn the techniques of getting along with others.

Increasing Knowledges, Favorable Attitudes and Appreciations. The more a person knows about a field, the more apt he is to have a favorable attitude and deeper appreciation of it. Those who have taken part in a modern dance program best recognize and appreciate the great talents of a Martha Graham or José Limon. Adult spectators of sports events who have themselves played the game they are watching receive greater enjoyment and are often more enthusiastic about the event than someone who has never tried to master the basic skills involved.

Learning to judge and choose wisely and the meaning of signals and symbols, and how to use them as society expects, helps youth to move around with ease at home, school or in the community. It is through experiences alone, moving in and out of groups and sharing activities with others, that one learns best about himself, others and his society. Youth learns early "what it's all about," how to get along with others with the least effort or conflict, and to give back to adults the answers they expect. It is through class instruction that he learns, too, the right moment to swing the badminton racket in order to hit the bird, or games and skills which he later modifies for use in his own backyard or city street. He develops the technique of improvising equipment from discarded junk or scrap materials. Through activity, through experience, each learns about life itself and learns either to shy away from it fearfully or to welcome it joyfully.

Fostering Better Use of Leisure Time. Never before have Americans had so much free time. Although many foolishly sleep and laze these hours away, or become bored, restless and frantic because "there is nothing to do," many others (the truly fortunate ones) find pleasure and much happiness from utilizing fully this precious free time, turning it into meaningful leisure. These are the ones who have mastered a wide variety of activity skills which bring them deep satisfaction. Free time is a period free from responsibility; it is when we can choose to do what we really want to do. Oddly enough, we usually select those things which we can do well or have had previous experience in, either directly or indirectly. Youth craves adventure, to be on the go and to get "there" as fast as possible. But youth also seeks companionship, to serve others, to create beautiful things and to surpass others in as many ways as possible.[17] Schoolteachers have more than a golden opportunity to help boys and girls to develop skills beyond the novice stage in as many activities, rich in high carry-over value for free time and developmental use, as they can and want to master. Hobbies and relaxation techniques should also be included in the program for free-time use, for merely learning how to "blow off steam" through play would be forgetting that one will still be there after the steam has disappeared and that time may still remain as heavy as sodden dough.

Physical strength, stamina, body flexibility, quick reaction time, speed and accuracy of movement, rhythmic body coordination, body balance and good posture, a knowledge of the necessity for balance between work and play and the importance of exercise in the totality

---

[17]See the chapter on *Understanding the Students.*

of life, a wide range of leisure-time skills, the belief in and practice of good sportsmanship and fair play—these, then, are the unique contributions of the physical educator. These are the rich, truly splendored outcomes of a well-planned, well-conducted and well-directed physical education program. These are the valuable contributions which can be made through this subject area in the secondary school curriculum to a strong, vigorous and healthy America.

DISCUSSION QUESTIONS

1. What are the basic problems found in our schools? Give several examples of each in formulating your answer.
2. Should the secondary school curriculum have a college or vocational orientation? Which subjects in your high school could be listed in either category?
3. Why is the school dropout rate declining at the present time? It is true that many are "at school" physically but have dropped out mentally. How can our high schools do a better job of meeting the needs of all students?
4. The Seven Cardinal Principles of Education are considered the seven objectives of education. Which of these objectives do you believe are most important in our rapidly changing society? What other objectives do you think should be added to the list?
5. How can we educate youth to use their free time away from school well? What is the difference between positive and negative free time use? Between the meaning of free time and leisure?
6. What are the major contributions of physical education to total education?
7. From your own experience in schools you have attended, illustrate changes in your attitudes toward your teachers, classmates, and life. What were the chief causes of these changes?
8. How could you as a physical educator help the individual student who is maladjusted, poorly coordinated, unhappy, unpopular and dislikes physical education?
9. Some experts believe that since the mind and body of man are inseparable, there is actually no such thing as "physical fitness" or even "physical education." What are your reactions to this statement?
10. Summarize in ten brief sentences the most important things you learned from this chapter and discuss these statements in class. Were your statements similar to those of others in the class?

THINGS TO DO

1. Make a study of the number of high school dropouts in your community in order to learn why these students have left school. Report your findings to the class, along with your recommendations of how you think the dropout problem could be solved in your own school.
2. Read any two chapters in Reich's *Greening of America,* or Silberman's *Crisis In The Classroom,* or *Our Children Are Cheated* by Benjamin Fine. Write a short summary on your reactions to the ideas expressed therein.
3. Summarize any article on physical fitness that you read in the *Journal of Health, Physical Education, and Recreation.* List ways in which you can increase (1) your own fitness, (2) the fitness of a class of students enrolled in physical education.
4. Interview any ten adults in your community who are parents of secondary students and are not professional educators in order to learn what they think of the required physical education in the school their child attends. How do they value such a program? Why do they regard it as they do? Report your findings orally to the class. As a group, summarize your conclusions and make needed recommendations, if necessary.

SUGGESTED READINGS

Ames, Louise, Gillespie, Clyde, and Streff, John: *Stop School Failure.* New York, Harper & Row, 1972.

Arnold, Peter: *Education, Physical Education, and Personality Development.* New York, Atherton Press, Inc., 1968.

Glasser, William: *Schools Without Failure.* New York, Harper and Row, 1969.

Grieder, Calvin: Have The Schools Failed Society? *The Education Digest.* November, 1972, pp. 3–5.

Grobman, Hilda: Accountability For What? *Education Digest.* October, 1972, pp. 18–27.

Hellison, Donald: *Humanistic Physical Education.* Englewood Cliffs, N.J., Prentice-Hall, Inc., 1973.

Hendrick, Irving, and Jones, Ronald: *Student Dissent in the Schools.* New York, Houghton-Mifflin Co.

Klein, Jacob: *American Values and American Education: A Study in Contradictions.* New York, Exposition Press, 1973.

Kleinman, Seymour: Toward a Non-Theory of Sport. *Quest,* May, 1968, pp. 29–34.

Lessinger, Leon, (Ed.): *Accountability: Systems Planning in Education.* Homewood, Illinois, ETC Publications, 1973.

Morphet, Edgar, and Ryan, Charles: Designing Education for the Future. No. 1, *The Prospective Change in Society in 1980;* No. 3, *Planning and Effecting Needed Changes in Education.* New York, The Citation Press, 1967.

Myers, Donald: *Teacher Power—Professionalization and Collective Bargaining.* Lexington, Mass., D. C. Heath & Co., 1973.

Pollack, Jack Harrison: Physical Education: Are Our Children Being Cheated? *Family Health.* September, 1970, pp. 15–18.

Reich, Charles: *The Greening of America.* New York, Random House, Inc., 1970.

Siedentop, Daryl: *Physical Education: Introductory Analysis.* Dubuque, Iowa, William C. Brown Co., 1972.

Ulrich, Celeste: *The Social Matrix of Physical Education.* Englewood Cliffs, N.J., Prentice Hall, Inc., 1968.

Updyke, Wynn, and Johnson, Perry B.: *Principles of Modern Physical Education, Health and Recreation.* New York, Holt, Rinehart and Winston, Inc., 1970.

CHAPTER TWO

UNDERSTANDING THE STUDENTS

Junior and senior high school students go through a second birth. They emerge from the adolescent period bigger, brighter and, often, more beautiful. They do not change from the ugly duckling to the lovely swan overnight or painlessly. For some, this growth period is almost a death struggle; for others, changes occur so gradually and naturally they cause little difficulty. For many it is a period of friction with those of the opposite sex, parents and adults. A few go from one extreme behavior pattern to another. Some study little as freshmen and end up the best senior class students. The dirty-necked thirteen year old becomes the spotlessly clean Beau Brummell at seventeen. The majority of doubtful, wild, rebellious youth somehow simmer down into being religous, mild, cooperative adults.

Although this age group is often difficult for adults to endure, it is also one of the most fascinating of all to teach, guide and lead. Only those who have great patience, understanding, teaching skills and energy can work successfully with them. The successful teacher realizes that each student is unique—his creation blueprint destroyed, methods of teaching, guiding and directing must be as varied as the members of the group itself.

The complete adolescent period ranges from ages nine to 21. It includes:

> Preadolescent—ages 9–11
> Early adolescent—ages 12–15
> Middle adolescent—ages 16–18
> Late adolescent and young adult—ages 19–21

During this turbulent period growth and development are gradual, with few clear-cut indications that one has completely passed from one growth stage to another.

All human development can be measured in terms of socio-emotional progress, physical growth and mental development. Individuals best adjusted socially, physically and emotionally healthy, and able to solve their own life problems best, show progressive developmental marks in all three areas. Teachers, in order to lead youth successfully, need to know each student's developmental social, physical and emotional status and to assist each one to progress through all three areas at approximately the same developmental rate.

Statistics tell us that half of our population is 25 years old or younger. Certainly modern youth has more freedom and less adult control and discipline than ever before. It has been suggested by some authorities that many are having too many experiences too soon, plus too much money to spend. Baton twirlers at football games now start in some cities at the age of five. We now have 13-year-old swimming champions, 14-year-olds playing in rock and roll bands, youthful ballplayers receiving fantastic bonuses and national publicity and child actors and actresses making a fortune. One observer of the teen scene has observed that today's 14-year-olds can put the 18-year-olds of five years ago over a barrel. All this crowding out of childhood and pushing down of adulthood upon youthful shoulders makes growing up in our modern society more painful, confusing, speeded up and frightening than ever before. Since in our affluent society increasingly more youth are being neglected or rejected by their parents, teachers everywhere are going to have to serve as behavior models for youth. Many will or should also become parent substitutes in helping students develop self-understanding and self-discipline.

PHYSICAL GROWTH

Many boys and girls in the tenth grade have reached physical maturity. Mentally, emotionally and socially the majority of them remain childlike and self-centered in their thoughts, feelings and actions. Some authorities refer to this period as a time of temporary disorganization. It might best be likened to a struggling swimmer, swept along by rushing tides, who is midstream away from the island of childhood and the mainland shore of adulthood. Certainly no two teenagers are exactly alike in looks, actions, physical makeup, or in any other areas. Yet individual differences in the rate and pattern of growth are more striking during this period than at any other time in life. Nevertheless, certain generalizations can be made about them as a group. To know and understand *just how unique* is each student is perhaps the greatest task the teacher faces.

Youth longs for independence but shuns the accompanying responsibility such freedom entails. A single year can make a chasm of difference in their total growth picture. Ninth and tenth graders are more homogeneously grouped than seventh and eighth graders. Many boys become as interested in dating as girls were earlier; both become increasingly concerned about good grooming, manners and social customs as well as future goals. Periods of sudden energy spurts alternate with lassitude. The eventual realization that their figures at sixteen are more or less permanent in shape and size and are the ones they will retain for the remainder of their lives often calls for a major emotional adjustment. Each needs to accept his body structure as it is; each must be taught how to use best what he has with the maximum of energy output from a minimum of effort. Slow developers, who may not reach their growth peak until two or three years later than their peers, need special attention and encouragement. The slowly maturing girl is better off than her rapidly growing classmates in that she remains near the lagging developmental rate of boys. On the other hand, boys who are fast growers are more fortunate and usually are the most popular leaders among their peers of both sexes.

The developmental growth rate of girls is usually two years ahead of that of boys. Except for a brief period between 11 and 13, boys are slightly taller than girls. Teenagers are extremely conscious of being too short or too tall, too thin or too fat. Since arm and leg bones

Figure 2–1. Each youth must be taught how best to achieve maximum physical efficiency. (Courtesy of the President's Council on Physical Fitness.)

Table 2–1. PHYSICAL CHARACTERISTICS OF ADOLESCENT BOYS

AGES 9–10–11	AGES 12–15	AGES 16–18	AGES 19–21
1. Slow gain in height.	1. Rapid gain in height and weight.	1. Adult height reached at 18 years.	1. Voice change completed.
2. Slow, but steady, increase in weight.	2. Growth spurt in width of the shoulder girdle.	2. Rapid weight increase.	2. Primary and secondary sex characteristics completed.
3. Strength increasing gradually.	3. Stronger than girls.	3. Blood pressure rises slightly.	3. Slight increase in weight.
4. By age of 12 only 5% reach sex maturity.	4. Higher blood pressure, but lower metabolic rate than girls.	4. Basal metabolic rate drops slowly.	4. Has an adult figure.
5. Frequent body temperature changes. Complain of being too hot or too cold.	5. Head and face almost adult size.	5. Trunk reaches adult size.	
	6. Stomach becomes longer and wider. Craves food. Acne and pimple stage.	6. Still craves more food. Still troubled with acne and pimples.	
	7. Seventy-five per cent reach sexual maturity. Secondary sex characteristics present.	7. Sex maturity reached.	
	8. Voices change on an average at 13.4 years.	8. Secondary sex characteristics completed.	
	9. Breast enlargement occurs in some due to hormone action.	9. Strength doubles.	
	10. Pubic hair appears on an average at 13.6 years.		

Table 2–2.   PHYSICAL CHARACTERISTICS OF ADOLESCENT GIRLS

AGES 9–10–11	AGES 12–15	AGES 16–18	AGES 19–21
1. Speedy growth in height. 2. Gains in weight continuous, growth spurt between 11–12 years. 3. Slightly weaker than boys. 4. Sharp rise in blood pressure and metabolic rate. 5. Lungs and head almost reach final size. 6. Sexual maturity begun by majority and is completed by 38%. Secondary sex characteristics begin to appear.	1. Increase in height. 2. Weight increase slows after onset of menstruation. 3. Bones almost mature. 4. Increased hip size. 5. Strength increasing. 6. Gradual rise in blood pressure. Metabolic rate much slower than boys. 7. Head and face approach adult size. 8. Stomach becomes longer and wider. Craves food. Acne and pimple stage. 9. Ninety-five per cent reach sexual maturity. Menstrual cycles irregular. 10. Secondary sex characteristics develop. 11. Greatest growth spurt in strength between 12 and 13 years. 12. Pubic hair appears on an average at 13.6 years. 13. Nose enlarges, chin remains small.	1. Adult height. 2. Slow slight weight increase. 3. Blood pressure drops. 4. Basal metabolic rate drops slowly. 5. Trunk reaches adult size. 6. Less craving for food. Still troubled with acne and pimples. 7. Sexual maturity reached. Irregular menstrual cycles. 8. Secondary sex characteristics completed.	1. Primary and secondary sex characteristics completed. 2. No increase in weight. 3. Menstrual cycle less irregular. Flow duration ranges from 3 to 7 days. 4. Has an adult figure.

grow faster in proportion than the trunk, many are awkward and walk with a gangling shuffle. Voice changes, the appearance of secondary sex characteristics, increases in the amount of perspiration, growth of sex organs, the onset of menstruation or nocturnal emissions, the outbreak of skin eruptions and other startling changes are enough to throw emotionally unstable teenagers off balance, and they often do. Tables 2–1 and 2–2 show the physical characteristics of both boys and girls during this period.

Those teaching teenagers need to help them understand what is happening to them physically and emotionally as they are changing into adults. Some make the transition from childhood to puberty to adulthood successfully, but many do not.

Suicide, illegitimacy, mental illness and venereal disease are all increasing at alarming rates among today's teenagers. The use of alcohol and of marijuana, LSD, "speed" and other mind-expanding drugs by teenagers has become a problem of deep national concern. Changing sexual mores add to the confusion and conflict of adolescence and create their own special problems. Venereal disease, for example, has reached epidemic proportions. At the present time the illegitimacy rate is higher than the previous year. Some 50 to 80 per cent of tennage wives are pregnant at the time of marriage.[1] The number of girls who have babies out of wedlock before age 17 is especially high among non-whites, city dwellers and among the poor. However, recently there has also been a sharp increase in the number of illegitimate babies born to white, affluent teenage girls. In their claimed search for alternate values to replace intense competition, materialism and technology these desperate youth are waving a red flag warning to all adults, but especially to parents and educators.

MENTAL DEVELOPMENT

As shown in Tables 2–3 and 2–4, the mental characteristics of adolescents vary considerably between the sexes as well as with each age group. As the child increases in chronological age his ability to see meaning, gain insight, and reason also develops. His attention span grows along with his ability to concentrate for a longer time period. Boys place higher on mathematical tests than girls. However, this may be due as much to our conditioning cultural patterns as to difference of innate ability to solve mathematical problems.

As the child progresses in school he becomes increasingly concerned about future goals, choosing a vocation and a life mate. It is

---

[1]Willgoose, Carl: *Health Teaching in Secondary Schools,* Philadelphia, W. B. Saunders Co., 1972, p. 22.

Table 2–3. MENTAL CHARACTERISTICS OF ADOLESCENT BOYS

AGES 9–10–11	AGES 12–15	AGES 16–18	AGES 19–21
1. Steady growth in reasoning powers.	1. Steady growth in mental and mechanical abilities; reasoning, judging, imaginative powers increasing.	1. Mental growth near close.	1. Maturation level in many abilities reached.
2. Steady growth in ability to gain insight.	2. Dislike drill and memory work done without reason.	2. Increased ability to concentrate, reason, see hidden meanings.	2. Mental growth nearly or is completed.
3. Increased ability to concentrate.	3. Steady growth in hand-eye coordination.	3. Increased vocabulary.	3. Seek meanings. Resent pure memory and drill.
4. Fifty per cent reach adult mental status by 12 years.	4. Place higher on mathematics test scores than girls.	4. Interest in school work often increases.	4. Are more practical than girls.
5. Imaginative, but has difficulty expressing self.	5. Steady gain in bimanual coordination, with growth spurts at 12½ to 13 years and at 13½ to 14 years.	5. Begin to relate present output with future goals.	
6. Boys surpass girls in mathematics test scores; show better understanding of numbers.	6. Early maturity associated with higher mental scores.	6. Greater attention span.	
7. Few mental disorders in this age group.	7. Growth in manual precision uneven.		

Table 2-4. MENTAL CHARACTERISTICS OF ADOLESCENT GIRLS

AGES 9–10–11	AGES 12–15	AGES 16–18	AGES 19–21
1. Steady growth in reasoning powers.	1. Steady growth in mental abilities; reasoning, judging, imaginative powers increasing.	1. Mental growth near close.	1. Maturation level in many abilities reached.
2. Steady growth in ability to gain insight.	2. Dislike drill and memory work done without reason.	2. Increased ability to concentrate, reason, see hidden meanings.	2. Mental growth nearly completed or is completed.
3. Increased ability to concentrate.	3. Steady growth in hand-eye coordination, especially during 12½ to 13 years.	3. Increased vocabulary.	3. Seek meanings. Resent pure memory and drill.
4. Fifty per cent reach adult mental status by 12 years.	4. Steady gain in bimanual coordination, with growth spurts at 12½ to 13½ years and again at 14 to 15 years.	4. Interest in school work often increases.	4. Seek reasons for learning things.
5. Imaginative, can express self better than boys.	5. Girls place higher on test scores in English, history, and other similar subjects.	5. Begin to relate present output with future goals.	
6. Girls superior in English, history, and other similar subjects (better understanding of verbalism).	6. Growth in manual precision longer and steadier than in boys.	6. Have greater attention span.	
7. Few mental disorders.	7. Early maturity associated with high mental scores.		

of great importance for youth to see the relationship between where he is and where he wants to go. The selection of life goals, devising plans and moving toward attaining them, as well as periodic evaluation of progress, are the vital tasks of each high school student. The role of the teacher should be that of a patient adviser, listener and friend during this all-important time.

Secondary school teachers will have students ranging in I.Q. from the dull (between 80 and 90) to the average (90–110), the above average (111–119), the moderately gifted (120–137), and the highly gifted (above 137). Each youth should help to select and plan his course of study and class activities as well as be taught how to succeed in these selected tasks according to his ability. If he is engaged in school work in which success can be achieved and which has meaning and real value to him, his chances for being a happy, well-adjusted productive present and future citizen are great.

SOCIOEMOTIONAL ADJUSTMENT

Margaret Mead, the famous anthropologist, has discovered that the emotional anguish many American youth experience is due largely to our culture, and that it is not a characteristic found among primitive adolescents. In her studies of South Sea youth she was amazed to discover that childhood blended into adulthood so normally, gently and gradually that no clear-cut time could be blocked out such as the one Americans label adolescence and characterize as a period full of frustration, physical awkwardness, emotional roller coasting, rebellion and fear. She also found that juvenile delinquency and mental illness, two rapidly increasing major curses among the so-called civilized nations, did not exist. Dr. Mead has concluded that adolescence in the South Seas is a simple life period because life is unhurried. There are few choices to make and little adult pressure; everyone cares for everybody and all contribute to group welfare.

In contrast, in our affluent society far too many youth are pampered and given too much by their parents. Many have "too much too soon" and are emotionally unequipped to cope with the amount of freedom given them too early in life.

SPECIAL NEEDS OF YOUTH

The preadolescent has the following special needs:

Understanding of the physical and emotional changes about to come.
Skillfully planned school and recreation programs to meet the needs of those who are not themselves skilled.

Opportunities for greater independence and for carrying more responsibility without pressure.

Warm affection and a sense of humor in adults.

No nagging, condemnation, or talking down to them.

Sense of belonging, acceptance by peer group.

The special needs of adolescent youth are:

Acceptance by and conformity with others of own age.

Adequate understanding of sexual relationships and attitudes.

Kind, unobtrusive, adult guidance which does not threaten the adolescent's feeling of freedom.

Assurance of security. Adolescents seek both dependence and independence.

Opportunities to make decisions and to earn and save money.

Provision for constructive recreation. Some cause, idea, or issue to work for.

PROBLEMS

Many of the problems adolescents face seem minute to adults but gigantic to them. Although their perplexing questions are often not so serious or life-shattering as those solved by adults, the average teenager lacks the experience, patience and problem-solving skills to cope with them successfully. Small fears snowball rapidly. A minority seek adult help; others flee from reality through daydreams or exaggerated behavior; the majority succeed (largely through trial and error methods) in finding a satisfactory if often only temporary solution to their problems; some few become so gnawed by emotion and fear that psychiatric help becomes necessary.

In order to best help students, the school, through its curriculum, should strive to help youth achieve:

1. More mature relationships with peers of both sexes.
2. Fuller development of their masculine or feminine life role.
3. Emotional and financial independence from their parents.
4. Preparation for marriage and family life.
5. A set of socially-approved values and an ethical system as a guide to behavior throughout life.

The problems most teenagers face center around school, the future, peer acceptance, family, boy-girl relationships, health and finding a sense of values or working philosophy of life.

Based on a survey of 15,000 teenagers, the following Table summarizes the type of problems most of them face:[2]

TYPE OF PROBLEM		PER CENT
Related to the Physical:		
desire to gain or lose weight		52
improve my figure		24
improve posture, body build		37
get rid of pimples		33
About School:		
what courses will be most valuable		50
want practical work experience		49
wish I could study better		54
difficulty in concentrating on studies		53
With People:		
want people to like me better		54
want to make new friends		50
wish I were more popular		42
get stage fright before a group		53
want to develop more self-confidence		36
can't live up to expected ideals		23
Personal:		
trouble keeping my temper		33
worry about little things		35
feeling guilty		26
easily hurt		29
unsure of myself		23
no girl or boy friend	boys	41
	girls	30
Vocational:		
kind of work best suited for		56
what are my real interests		42
how much ability do I have		59
should I go to college		33
jobs open to high school graduates		40

Financial problems often become magnified with this age group. Many yearn for freedom from the "apron string" but must depend upon their parents for food, shelter and clothing—the basic elements of life. It is said that Americans have the longest period of adolescent dependence upon adults of any society in the history of mankind. Many young people find part-time jobs baby sitting, working as messenger boys or in service stations, clerking in stores, doing light factory work, or serving as bus boys or restaurant waitresses. However, few save much from their earnings or see the dangers in gambling, race betting, charge accounts or installment buying.

[2]Jenkins, Gladys, Shacter, Hellen, and Bauer, William: *Those Are Your Children,* 3rd Ed., Glenview, Illinois, Scott, Foresman and Co., 1966, p. 349.

Table 2–5. SOCIOEMOTIONAL CHARACTERISTICS OF ADOLESCENT BOYS

AGES 9–10–11	AGES 12–15	AGES 16–18	AGES 19–21
1. Steady growth in manly outlook.	1. Fears center around money, sex, and relationships with others. Often daydreams of own escape.	1. Fears still center around money, sex, and relationships with others. Have increased fear of failing to make grades or entrance requirements.	1. Heterosexual adjustment completed. Many marry.
2. Gang stage, strong attachment to member of own sex.	2. Love attachment with someone about own age of the opposite sex. Many trials and errors at love.	2. Fall in and out of love often. Still seeking their ideal.	2. Respond angrily largely to mechanical failures. Still kick and storm but less frequently.
3. Admire those who show defiance to adults or authority of any kind.	3. Angered mostly because of some mechanical failures. Kick and stamp when angry.	3. Still angered mostly by mechanical failures. React to anger in more grown-up way rather than throwing or kicking.	3. Fears center around failure to pass in school, find a mate or a good job.
4. Regard cleanliness and neatness as sissy.	4. Afraid enlarging organs can be seen through clothing. Disturbed about nocturnal emissions.	4. Have sharp line drawn between mature and immature behavior but regress back to childish ways to gain favor or recognition from family.	4. Mental and emotional disorders upset many due to conflict between ideals and reality.
5. Each strives hard to be best in games, has strong need to be admired by own sex and age group.	5. Brag about size of sex organs among boys; seek prestige by doing so.	5. Respond more readily to social discipline in order to get ahead or make an ideal marriage.	5. Prejudices and antagonisms intensified. Seek friends with like ideas and attitudes about others.
6. Play harder, noisier, and longer than girls. Are adventurous and destructive.	6. Interested in own body and that of opposite sex.		6. Less doubtful about God and religion.
7. Show temporary disapproval of all girls.	7. Adjustment problems center around abnormal growth and how they look. Acne becomes a big problem.		7. Less idealistic.
8. Have simple, personal fears. Often think about running away.			

9. Interested in changes in their own bodies and talk about them freely with boys.

10. Fear being called "chicken" or "yellow."

6. Prejudices and antagonisms intensified.

7. Desperately want independence.

8. Crowd stage with own and opposite sex.

9. Great loyalty to group leaders.

10. Talk and joke about girls and own "sex duties."

11. Adventurous, thrill-seeking.

12. Seeking ideals and meaning to life.

13. Cleanliness becomes all important.

14. Rebel against parental authority.

15. Strong attachment to teacher or older friend who likes and believes in them.

16. Seek dangerous activities more with forbidden friends.

17. Crave athletic competition; strive for group recognition by being best.

18. At the age of 12 are enthusiastic doers. By 13 are worriers, often painfully sad.

19. Become more religious. Often joins the church when 13.

20. At 14 adults become old-fashioned. Become girl and party conscious.

Table 2–6. SOCIOEMOTIONAL CHARACTERISTICS OF ADOLESCENT GIRLS

AGES 9–10–11	AGES 12–15	AGES 16–18	AGES 19–21
1. Steady growth in womanly outlook.	1. Fears center around wearing wrong clothes, sex, and relationships with others. Often daydreams of escape.	1. Fears center largely around being different or failing to get ahead in life.	1. Heterosexual adjustment completed earlier than in boys.
2. Gang stage, strong attachment to member of own sex.	2. In and out of love often with member of opposite sex of approximate age.	2. Fall in love often. Hurt often. Some enjoy tragic affairs. Experiment with love.	2. Responds to anger by tears.
3. Admire girls who are friendly, neat, attractive, popular, and show obedience and love to parents.	3. Strive harder to cover up body deviations, will wear high heels to be taller, diet to be thin, and so on.	3. Extremely conscious of looks, dress, and work to have a good figure.	3. Fears center around failure to pass in school, being an old maid, or unpopular with men.
4. Dislike rowdyness or someone who doesn't behave as he should.	4. Response to anger is crying.	4. Discuss their bodies or sex role in life less often with girls.	4. Mental and emotional disorder upsets due to conflict between ideals and reality.
5. Seldom refer to their own bodies; modest about changes.	5. Fear menstrual stains will come through clothing.	5. Accept feminine role in life, most of them gladly.	5. Prejudices and antagonisms intensified. Seek friends with like ideas and attitudes about others.
6. Tomboys gradually becoming more unattractive.	6. Prestige gained among peers by breast development and knowledge of reproduction.	6. Anxious to remake the world. Service-conscious.	6. Less doubtful about God and religion.
7. Play in smaller groups than boys, mostly with own sex.	7. Cleanliness becomes increasingly important. How a person "smells" is a vital concern.	7. Resent position in low economic or social group. Strive and daydream about improving their lot in life.	
8. Seek adventure and excitement.			
9. Fewer run away than boys.			

8. Frequent hair-do changes. Like to wear heavy makeup, want to attract older men.
9. Peer acceptance all-important. Have special cliques of own and opposite sex.
10. Giggle and rave over nothing and do so often.
11. Repeat pet phrases often.
12. Athletic competition more on a social basis.
13. Homosexual "crush" stage lasts longer than with boys.
14. Adventurous, thrill-seeking.
15. Seeking ideals and meaning to life.
16. Cleanliness becomes almost an obsession.
17. Seek dangerous, undesirable friends in search to find out about people.
18. Beginning at 14, school and home become places to gossip in and to telephone from.

7. More idealistic for a longer period than boys.
8. Become more tolerant of parents and adults.
9. Prejudices and antagonisms intensified.
10. Seek company of opposite sex more.
11. Strong identification with admired adult.
12. Ideas of right and wrong become more like those of parents.
13. Want to go their way and parents go theirs.

Tables 2–5 and 2–6 show the socioemotional characteristics adolescents face. It is interesting to note that both boys and girls have intensified problems in the 13 to 15 age bracket.

TEENAGE DRINKING AND ACCIDENTS

More and more teenagers are learning to drive at the same time that they are beginning to drink, now that the age for both has been lowered to 18 or 19 in 27 states, a law that had previously been in effect in six other states. The percentage of automobile accidents involving 18- to 20-year-old drinking drivers has increased drastically ever since. In Michigan this has meant a 112 per cent increase in car accidents involving teenagers and drinking, with a corresponding percentage increase in the number of teenage fatalities. In Wisconsin in 1971, 72 accidents involved people 18, 19 and 20 years of age. In 1972, after the drinking age was lowered, this number increased to 94 and is rising sharply at the present. In Nebraska and elsewhere throughout the nation the problem of teenage drinking is becoming increasingly serious. A recent statewide survey in Massachusetts showed a 92.7 per cent increase in the use of alcohol, and 59.4 per cent of the students questioned said they had been drinking within the past year.[3] Students from all over the nation in other recent surveys have said that alcohol is increasingly becoming the favorite drug of teenagers. Many parents are so relieved that their children are not on "hard drugs" that they tend to look the other way at alcohol indulgence. The sales to teenagers of "pop" wines have also increased rapidly, rising from 3 million gallons in 1968 to 33 million gallons in 1973. Even junior high and elementary schoolers are often getting drunk in some areas of the country. In America car accidents involving drunken teenagers in the 13- to 17-year-old age group are also increasing. Alcoholics Anonymous has reported a sharp rise in teenage membership as well as the fact that reported a sharp rise in teenage membership as well as the fact that some of its youngest members are 10-year-olds who are trying to remain sober.

JUVENILE DELINQUENCY

The sharp increase in juvenile delinquency in America during the past decade has been considered by many experts in the fields of sociology, psychology and education to be our most alarming, dangerous and puzzling social problem. Research discloses that this social

---

[3]Mouckley, Florence: Cars, Liquor and Youth—Lethal Trio. *Christian Science Monitor.* October 10, 1973, p. 1.

malady is due largely to:

1. Emotional disturbance caused by frustrated and thwarted drives.
2. Faulty environmental conditions, including slum areas and/or an unhappy home life among any income group.
3. Psychopathic personalities who cannot distinguish between right and wrong.
4. Poor use of leisure time.

Sheldon and Eleanor Glueck of Harvard University have concluded from their studies of hundreds of young criminals that the antisocial belligerent behavior of those who get into serious enough trouble to be arrested is due to many interlaced factors and that no single cause can be isolated. They have discovered the following definite traits and characteristics of delinquents:[4]

Physical—Mesomorphic (average) in build and constitution
Temperament—Restlessly energetic, impulsive, aggressive, destructive
Attitude—Hostile, defiant, resentful, suspicious, stubborn, socially assertive, adventurous, unconventional, nonsubmissive to authority
Intellect—More understanding of the direct and concrete rather than symbolic, less methodical in their approach to problems
Socioculture—Reared in homes of little understanding, affection, stability or moral fiber, most usually by unstable, unfit parents
School adjustment—Truant, disobedient, defiant, hatred toward school
Companions—Extreme gang loyalty, frequent companionship with those older

Legally, a juvenile delinquent in most states is usually one between the ages of seven and 18 who has broken a law and has been arrested for doing so. The most common offenses are auto theft, burglary, running away, sex offenses, truancy and incorrigibility. Of late, more thought and financial support have been given to prevention of, rather than to punishment for, youth crime. Numerous community authorities throughout the entire nation have been shocked into action upon learning that at the present time four out of every ten juvenile delinquents become hardened adult criminals. All experts agree that an attack on this rapidly spreading social cancer in only one or two areas will surely fail. More neighborhood parks, community centers or increased athletic competition for younger children will neither solve nor eradicate the problem. In fact, Los Angeles, Dallas and other cities have painfully discovered that gangs often used a new center as a clubhouse where future crimes were plotted and gang membership easily increased. Certainly a concentrated effort on the part of all leaders close to youth can do much to spot and save predelinquents. Since frequent and increased truancy is an early but sure

---

[4]Glueck, Sheldon, and Glueck, Eleanor: *Delinquents in the Making.* New York, Harper & Brothers, 1948, p. 141.

symptom of serious socioemotional maladjustment, these leaders and teachers should increase their efforts to help each student succeed, belong to groups, and find adventure and recognition in legitimate ways. In addition to school skipping, other signs easily detected amont those most vulnerable for delinquency are:

1. Hatred of school because of
   a. Failure to succeed.
   b. Lack of intelligence, aptitude or real interest.
   c. Repeating a grade or grades.
   d. Being put back a grade or grades.
2. Failure to belong to any supervised recreational character-building group.
3. Bad home conditions
   a. Alcoholic parent or parents.
   b. Broken home; a foster parent.
   c. Employment of both parents.
   d. Inconsistent home discipline ranging from indifference to extreme harshness.
   e. Home in a high delinquency area.
   f. Overcrowded living conditions.
   g. Frequently changed family residence.
4. Signs of hatred or deep resentment toward others
   a. Has extreme prejudices and shows violent dislike of others.
   b. Lacks security, belongingness, and cannot identify with any socially approved group.
   c. Face and posture show strain and stress marks; child looks much older than he is.
   d. Shows extreme withdrawal or aggressiveness. Shows fight or flight reactions toward life and society.

Certainly the wisest preventive measures of all are in helping all children to succeed according to their capabilities in assigned tasks at school, at play, and especially in the home, protecting those most vulnerable, and eradicating evil home and community influences. The school, church, home and state must unite to destroy costly social evils and to help youth have a real and meaningful place in society at all times — not just in time of war or when in serious trouble.

Recreational programs must be greatly altered for them to ever combat crime and delinquency.[5] Leadership is the key and it is important that the leader be of the highest caliber, but it is also important that he be assisted by employees and volunteers who may have a sparse formal education but, because they come from the same background, can communicate and more often effectively deal with people of all ages, especially youth. Teenagers in the inner-city are greatly in need of places to go and things to do that are constructive rather than

---

[5]Nesbitt, John, Brown, Paul, and Murphy, James: *Recreation and Leisure Service For The Disadvantaged.* Philadelphia, Lea & Febiger, 1970, p. 72.

destructive and antisocial. Many of the program activities at teen centers in different kinds of minority group and poor neighborhoods should center around self-development, job training and placement, educational skills and health services. They should be conducted on an informal basis and not be like school but rather be geared to provide youth with pleasurable experiences aimed at helping them master skills in many things, including themselves.

Guidance Techniques

Guidance is helping people to help themselves. It is not telling them what to do, nor threatening them with disaster should advice be disregarded. All youth need strong friendship bonds forged securely to adults who sincerely care about them and are concerned about their welfare. Ideally, this unbreakable link should be parent-joined; often among rebellious youth it is not. The coach, physical educator or other teacher often becomes a trouble sounding board, source of inspiration and comfort, parent substitute, ideal or friend.

According to our societal demands, youth is expected to:[6]

1. Accept his own physique and physical characteristics.
2. Learn new and satisfactory ways for getting along with peers of both sexes.
3. Learn new and satisfying ways of getting along with adults.
4. Achieve emotional maturity.
5. Achieve a measure of economic independence.
6. Achieve a degree of intellectual maturity.
7. Build a philosophy of life that is in harmony with values which our society upholds.

Many successfully learn these vital lessons without too much difficulty; more run into progress-retarding snags and shoals. Emotions, the motivating forces directing the activity of this age group, often are inconsistent and disorganized. These dynamic drives are detectible. Symptoms (loud talk, rowdyism, vandalism and so on) are indicators or unseen red warning flags that one is in great difficulty. Teachers should not punish students for displaying such distress signs; they must discover *why* the student did what he did. They must find causes, not penalize for the effect of maladjustment.

It is imperative for teachers who are sincere in their desire to understand individual students better to gather as much information

---

[6]Havighurst, Robert: *Developmental Tasks of Education.* Chicago, University of Chicago Press, 1948.

about each one as possible. These data may be gleaned from:

1. Cumulative records.
2. Tests (achievement, physiological, psychological, sociological).
3. Personal data blanks.
4. Observation.
5. Interviews.
6. Check lists.
7. Rating scales.
8. Case studies.
9. Self-appraisal forms.
10. Anecdotal records.

Each problem-burdened individual is overloaded with his own unique uncertainties. Frustrations and fears form in clusters. Infectious maladjustment in one life area quickly spreads to another. Many such fears have long painful incubation periods; few erupt suddenly. The role of the teacher working with a confused youngster is to help him to understand what his real problem is and to get it into proper focus (this requires the detection and differentiation of cause and effect), and to organize his talents and abilities to solve his own problem through constructive action.

Carefully planned interviews are most fruitful in helping those with more serious difficulties. Suggestions for obtaining the best results include:

1. Have all background information about the student well in mind.
2. Establish early a feeling of rapport and respect in a relaxed atmosphere.
3. Avoid preaching, cross examining, and hurry.
4. Keep things told in confidence; avoid gossip.
5. Help the student discuss his problem early. Leading statements such as "What did you wish to see me about?", "What can I do for you?", or "No doubt, you have a problem on your mind" are suggested conversation openers.
6. Talk less, listen lots. Be shockproof. Use conversational "hooks" to link what has been said before, inferred but unsaid, and to clarify thinking.
7. Answer all questions honestly in a direct way.
8. Use much empathy, less sympathy.
9. Make several suggestions of how the problem might be solved or how one similar to it has been solved in the past.
10. Make it clear to the counselee that it is *his* problem and *his* responsibility to solve it. Your role is that of a friend, listener, helper, "pepper-upper" and expediter.

It has been said that youth is a bank in which we deposit our most treasured possessions—our cultural heritage, ideals and dreams for a better world. Today's youth are tomorrow's leaders. Our future depends, then, to a greater extent than most adults realize, upon their ability to develop strong, capable, intelligent, emotionally stable and democratic citizens who can and will carry on our American way of life.

DISCUSSION QUESTIONS

1. What kind of a physical education program for high school boys and girls would you endorse in light of what you learned from this chapter? Intramural program? Club program? Interscholastic program?

2. How can teachers best help high school students to grow up successfully?

3. What should the role of the teacher be in planning and attending school functions? As club or project sponsor?

4. Contrast the philosophy of the hippies with that of five of your classmates and five adults in relationship to their attitudes toward school, work, sex and the use of drugs.

5. Which seems to you to be the best method for disciplining students? Why?

THINGS TO DO

1. Study your community. Do you have a delinquency problem? What causes it? In what way can physical education become a preventive measure of this spreading social cancer?

2. Through interviews with students and faculty members find out if your school sex education program needs improvement. List five ways in which it can be made more meaningful in the lives of your classmates, who will become parents.

3. Bring to class five newspaper or magazine clippings to share with your classmates on the rising crime rates or any aspect of juvenile delinquency in America.

4. Interview a dropout and his parents. Try to persuade him to return to school. Report your experiences to your classmates.

5. Write a one-page report on your life goals. Show how what you are learning today at school will help you attain these goals.

6. Visit a teenagers' recreation center or observe a recreational program for this group conducted by any youth-serving organization. Give a report to your classmates based on what you learned from this experience.

SELECTED AUDIO-VISUAL AIDS

One Quarter Million Teen-agers. Describes the rapid spread of venereal diseases among this age group and suggests preventive measures. Available from the Department of Instruction of the Los Angeles Public Schools and from the state or local health department in most areas.

The Mind Benders. Shows the vastness of the drug problems among teenagers. Available from the Federal Drug Administration in most large cities.

Human Reproduction. A new color film on human reproduction. Available from McGraw-Hill, by rental or purchase.

The World of Troubled Youth. A training-for-action program of four records, a participants' manual, and a discussion leaders' manual. Available for $29.95 from the Addison-Wesley Publication Company, Reading, Mass.

SUGGESTED READINGS

AAHPER: *The Growing Years: Adolescence.* Washington, D.C., 1962.

Bernard, Harold: *Adolescent Development.* Scranton, Pennsylvania, Intext Educational Publishers, 1970.

Hechinger, Grace, and Hechinger, Fred: *Teen-Age Tyranny*. New York, Fawcett World Library (Crest), 1964.

Jenkins, Gladys, Shacter, Helen, and Bauer, William: *These Are Your Children*, 3rd Ed., Glenview, Illinois, 1966.

Mussen, Paul, Conger, John, and Kagen, Jerome: *Child Development and Personality*. New York, Harper & Row, 1969.

Porter, Robert: "Sports and Adolescence," in *Motivation in Play, Games and Sports.* Edited by Ralph Slovenko and James Knight. Springfield, Illinois, Charles C Thomas, Publisher, 1967.

Stone, Joseph, and Church, Joseph: *Childhood and Adolescence*. New York, Random House, 1973.

Tanner, Daniel: *Schools for Youth*. New York, Macmillan Co., 1965.

CHAPTER THREE

LEARNING

Learning can be a thrilling adventure or dull drudgery. Teachers can help to make this vital life experience either positive or negative. Learning takes place wherever there is life. High school girls learning to play field hockey during the school intramural program under the direction of a respected mature and capable teacher, who is primarily concerned about their well-being and development, are learning positive behavior patterns that could not be learned elsewhere under less desirable leadership. Students learn best under the guidance of teachers who help them to develop desirable behavior patterns, a workable philosophy of life and a sense of values in harmony with the best of those our society cherishes. All learning is most lasting when it meets the needs the individual has, sees or feels.

In reality, learning is an endless process of adjusting to one's environment. The six major categories into which all human learning falls are:

1. Motor skills.
2. Concepts, meanings, generalizations.
3. Attitudes, interests, motives.
4. Social and emotional control.
5. Esthetic appreciations.
6. Ability to solve problems successfully.

LEARNING THEORIES

More is known about how to stimulate and increase learning than about what takes place in people when they learn. Acquiring knowledge is a complicated process involving the whole body. One cannot separate mental from motor learning, for they are as interdependent as nerve cell and brain, mind and body, blood and heart. Most of what we know comes through our senses of hearing, seeing, smelling, tasting and touching. Learning is mastery over experience; it is changed behavior. People are eye-, and ear-, and voice-minded. The more the senses are used in teaching to stimulate emotional drives, the greater the learning results. Positive learning is the discovery of how to do things in new, better ways. We learn when we:

1. Understand words or other symbols and their meanings.
2. Can communicate with others.
3. Develop and use new skills.
4. Form new habits.
5. Develop new attitudes.
6. Build new interests.
7. Gain new understandings.
8. Make generalizations and use learned facts.
9. Develop social skills.
10. Become more concerned about our environment and other people around us and develop a high sense of moral value.
11. Develop favorable attitudes toward self and others.
12. Show concern for the rights of others; have good conduct.
13. Have respect for and obey laws.

Although theorists vary as to the number of different kinds of learning there are, most agree that the various types are not wholly dissimilar and that some of the same factors operate in all. For instance, all stress that one learns by doing, profiting from experience. One learns when he can respond correctly, such as when he jumps a rope without missing, or recognizes "dog" when he sees d-o-g written out. The most frequently found types of learning are (1) *conditioned responses* (the result of forming a patterned reflex), (2) *autogenous responses* (the result of self-initiated actions), (3) *sociogenous responses* (the result of social stimulation), (4) *incidental learning* (the result of exposure to a set of stimuli or to a single stimulus), and (5) *insightful learning* (the result of suddenly seeing relationships and meaning in what is being learned).

Many educators feel that the central task of the teacher is to help each student develop self-discipline. Although this cannot be imparted directly from one person to another, it can often be instilled best by setting high standards and by example. A self-directed learner, who is strongly motivated to attain goals he has clearly in mind, can and usually does obtain them whether these be for good or evil use. It is the job of the teacher to provide the stimulus which sets off this magical process of self-education for positive personal as well as social gains. However, it is the school's task to provide time for learning, studying, developing concepts, reading, thinking and discussing ideas. Education, then, is a long, slow filtering process that lasts a lifetime. It is shared by the school, the home and the community. If in these places there is a real respect for learning, education becomes easier, more enjoyably and productively fruitful, for as Plato has said, "What a nation honors it will cultivate." Much of a youth's attitude toward school and his own ability as a learner is a reflection of those closest to him—his family, friends and members of the school and community.

There are four significant elements in the learning process: the *drive* (stimulus that triggers action), the *cue* (the stimulus that guides action), the *response* (the action itself), and the *reward* (the result of action). If the student is to learn, he must (1) *want something* (the drive), (2) *notice something* (pick up a cue and relate it to his past knowledge of similar words or experiences), (3) *do something* (the response), and (4) *get something* for his efforts (the reward). A skillful teacher uses positive motivation and is adept at providing learners with cues which they can readily pick up and use in their own learning attempts. Such an educator also provides the drill necessary for retention of what has been previously mastered and establishes a warm and friendly learning environment so that positive attitudes can be shaped and healthy emotional responses can be established.

The most widely known learning theories are conditioning, connectionism and field theory. Each has marked implications for the physical educator. The three are interwoven; all stress that one learns best through activity, actually doing, or from his own experience.

CONDITIONING

The simplest type of learning is conditioning, or setting a patterned reflex to the same repeated stimuli. The famous Pavlov dog experiment proved that the animal could be conditioned to salivate when a bell rang because food was expected. This type of simple learning is commonly found among conditioned human beings—the child who is afraid of bugs; the person with an aversion to certain foods; one's routine acts of answering the front door knock, automatically stopping at the red traffic light, or unconsciously going the same mazelike way to work or school each day. These and other automatic acts are repeated to the same stimuli until a behavior-patterned habit has been formed.

Conditioning has many uses and values for the physical educator. It saves both time and energy. Students can be conditioned automatically to:

1. Report to roll call at an appointed time (by squads, reciting numbers, turning their name or number over on a tag board, signing a roll sheet, responding to hearing their names called, etc.).
2. Dress in the required uniform.
3. Come to attention upon command.
4. Keep quiet when the instructor is speaking.
5. Turn in written absence excuses at the proper time.
6. Stop when the game official blows his whistle for rule infringements, time out, game completion or substitution.
7. Get into skilled drill formations (circle, line, square) upon command.
8. Shower after class.

Although some teachers now conduct classes on a more informal basis, it must be remembered that there are advantages and disadvantages to both methods of teaching. What is needed is quality instruction through which students learn how to use and take care of their bodies as part of their total selves throughout life.

CONNECTIONISM

This theory, which results largely from the work of Thorndike and his associates at Columbia University, stresses that human beings, as well as animals, will voluntarily select things which bring them the most pleasure and satisfaction and best fill their needs. Although this is similar to the theory of conditioning, connectionists contend that learning must be on a higher plane, for the purpose of education is *not* to create human vending machines who will give back to the teacher an answer upon demand, but to develop educated citizens who can solve their own as well as help to solve group problems intelligently in many ever-changing situations.

Simply, this concept, known also as the *S-R*-bond theory of learning, means that when a stimulus (*S*) brings about a response (*R*) which is accompanied by satisfied feelings, the connection between that stimulus and that response is reinforced (bond). The intensity of these positive feelings can produce either an advancing, positive response (choosing it again, joy, satisfaction) or a retreating, negative one (not choosing it again, anger, disappointment, frustration).

According to this theory, the greater the need and inner pressure for learning, the keener and more productive are the attempts to satisfy this need and relieve this pressure. All human beings have certain common needs. These drives make up the underlying cause of all human behavior:

1. Physiological needs (food, water, air, temperature regulation, rest, exercise).
2. Love needs (sex, mutuality, belongingness, affection).
3. Need for esteem (recognition, mastery, approval, status, adequacy, self-respect).
4. Self-actualization (desire to succeed at tasks for which one is best suited).
5. Need to know and understand.
6. Need for ambiance (balance between love and hate, between desire to destroy and to build).
7. Need for adventure (to seek ever-greener pastures).

A skillful teacher can and does capitalize upon these drives common to all.

Motivation is the key to all learning. The teacher's role is to get the student to try, to teach himself through trial and error, copying, or experimenting to find the way to accomplish a desired act. It is the pupil who learns to master the skill, who "teaches" himself to do this or that. On the other hand, it is the instructor who points out the quickest, most efficient way to obtain the desired results. He helps the learner to reach goals more quickly and with greater ease by helping him to eliminate needless errors or journeys down known dead-end streets. Learning is a self-activity. The teacher's role is to short-cut learning time. This is achieved by helping the student (1) to see his goal or learning task clearly, (2) to find the best ways to solve the problem of how to learn what he really wants to master, (3) to practice always in the right way from the very start, and (4) to judge the results realistically. Skill mastery begins with getting an idea or mental picture of what a skill should be like. For some this idea comes from being told what to do, others gain it by manually being guided through a movement pattern, and still others by being shown what a skill is and how to do it. The more the student understands what he is to do, the better he will do it.

Students will be more motivated to learn when they:

1. See meanings and relationships in what they learn. Overviews of study units or other materials can quickly accomplish this, as will skimming through a book before reading any part of it.
2. Are assigned tasks which are not beyond their abilities.
3. Know and understand what is expected of them in the way of assignments, behavior or other areas.
4. Can see clearly that what they do each day in class will bring them closer to their goals.
5. Participate in activities which are meaningful and important to them.
6. Are guided into developing good study habits.
7. Gain recognition for accomplishments.
8. Like and respect their teacher, and know that he, in turn, likes and respects everyone in the class.
9. Can relate what they are learning with what they are doing in the whole school program, at home, and in their community.

A child's natural urges of curiosity, to communicate, to engage in dramatic and physical play and to create often present an "open sesame" for learning. The purposes, ambitions, drives, and values of each learner should be channeled to help him to develop his natural abilities. Teachers must help youth value well-earned achievement. Marks and verbal rewards, as well as reproofs, can play a powerful role in the development of performance. It is imperative, however, that the teacher discover what motivates each student best, as well as what most whets his curiosity and sustains his efforts until he accomplishes his own desired goal.

The following principles will assist in motivating youth to positive action:

1. Become familiar with each student's drives and plan learning experiences that will arouse his interest.
2. Motivation is more potent when the learner sees the relationship between what he is learning and his own goals.
3. Motivation is more effective when students are involved in setting goals.
4. Students should be encouraged to set both short- and long-range goals for themselves as well as to help formulate group goals.
5. Negative motivation (fear of punishment) usually retards learning, whereas positive motivation (anticipation of reward) elicits more favorable responses.
6. One learns to do best what is the most satisfying to him. The teacher should help boys and girls to gain satisfaction from right responses and right conduct.
7. Students are ready to learn when they are healthy, well adjusted, mature enough, and interested.

Learning desires are checked or spurred on by:

Wants and needs	Emotions
Individual behavior traits	Rewards
Attitudes	Punishment
Interests	Group recognition
Progress reports	Adult and/or
Purposes	parental approval

Thorndike's three famous laws of learning will, if properly applied by the teacher, increase both the scope and depth of pupil learning. These are: (1) the Law of Readiness, (2) the Law of Exercise, and (3) the Law of Effect.

The Law of Readiness.   Students learn best when they are ready to learn—when they have reached the proper growth level (maturation) and have a keen desire to find out. All instructors need to learn to detect such readiness. The learner is ready when he can learn with ease, succeed and is spurred on by his own ambitious desire to master what he attempts. All three conditions must be present before the student is ready, or learning ripe.

High school students are skill hungry. This drives them to try many new things, to practice long and hard in order to gain prestige through skill superiority. It is vastly important that all youth have many opportunities to sample numerous new activity delights in high school, for these joyful experiences will lead to a richer, fuller use of leisure in adulthood. Just as patterns for adult happiness are laid down in childhood, what one enjoys doing as a grown-up during his free time will depend largely upon what he thrilled to do when he was a work-free youth!

The Law of Exercise.   We learn what we do. The more frequently we practice, the faster we will learn, but *only* if we practice the right

Figure 3–1. We learn what we experience. The more frequently we practice, the faster we will learn, but *only* if we practice the right way. (Courtesy of *The Scholastic Coach.*)

way. Disuse and skill weakness are as correlated as are practice and rhythmical, effective movements which accomplish their intended purpose. The learner, according to this law, must know *what* and *how* he is doing as well as *why* in relationship to what he wants to do. He must also have a clear picture of the correct way the skill should be done in comparison with how he is doing it.

Teachers seldom point out why students are required to take physical education, the purpose of the program, the real reason they should learn a certain activity, or the value of taking part in exercise, games and sports during one's entire life. Such instructors soon become discouraged because of lack of pupil interest and effort. Few realize there is a strongly intertwined relationship between disinterested students and uninformed, goal-mystified students.

Students will continue to try to master skills in spite of slow gain and some failure when they see real meaning and value in what they are attempting and as long as they are desire-driven to learn. The greater the drive, the greater the effort. Nothing succeeds like success. Likewise, nothing is as spirit-quenching as repeated failure. All teachers should inspire students and "egg them on" to keep trying, but they should also know what activities are best suited to the capacity and skill maturation levels of each learner. It is as ridiculous to assign any learner to repeated tasks in which he will surely fail as to try to hit a home run with a toothpick! It also is ego-damaging and can cause serious emotional maladjustment. Few adults would ever attempt to sail the ocean in a washtub, for such a journey would surely end in disaster. It is equally foolish to force students incapable of learning certain skills at a certain age to stay at the learning task until it is mastered. Layman, chief psychologist for the Children's Hospital in Washington, D.C., declares that:[1]

Repeated failure makes the individual feel inferior, inadequate, and worthless. In both the child and adult it may result in various patterns of behavior—defeatist behavior, in which the individual gives up in discouragement and fails to function up to his capacity level; over-compensation, in which the individual exaggerates and brags about his accomplishments in other lines, or tries to prove his superiority by means of antisocial activities; expression of a feeling of frustration through temper tantrums; or lying and cheating about mythical exploits.

It should be pointed out that success too easily gained can be as ego-damaging as repeated failure.

The Law of Effect. How the learner *feels* about what he is doing is as important as what he is doing, if not more so. Trial attempts will produce a positive reaction if the student has had a pleasurable experience that was difficult enough to challenge him and meaningful enough to have been considered important, even to be desired.

Physical educators often succeed in their attempts to keep everyone active during the entire class period but fail miserably in helping students to know and appreciate the value of physical education. Such instructors, as Dr. Jesse Feiring Williams once pointed out, are tradesmen, not teachers. The profession, unfortunately, has a few such members in it who are like:

1. The Top Sergeant—The big boss who tolerates no monkey business in his group, regards the students as robots; the whip cracker; the "1-2-3, you jump" type of leader.
2. The Do-It-Yourself Expert—The ball thrower-outer who teaches a class by remote control.
3. The Nurse or Doctor—The corrective specialist who conducts the entire program on the theory that all students deviate from normal structurally and that all need to be corrected.
4. The Public Speaker—The show-off who explains, or rambles on for thirty-five minutes of the forty-minute period, thus leaving five measly minutes for activity that has real educational value.
5. The Technician—The form-fussy expert who believes there is only one way to hit the golf ball—students either master it or fail the course.
6. The Bone Crusher—The famous college athlete, bruised and battered —but still rugged—whose class program for junior high school boys is a

---

[1]Layman, Emma McCloy: *Mental Health Through Physical Education and Recreation.* Minneapolis, Burgess Publishing Company, 1955.

college competitive athletic one only for those most skilled and physically fit. Blood, sweat and tears are produced—along with a bad taste for the program in the mouths of the majority of students and parents.

7. The Maker of Champions—Usually this is the once professional dancer, ball player or college basketball star who is determined to turn out carbon copies of himself. Nothing else in the total program has value except his specialty. Consequently, the total program consists of mostly his speciality, be it basketball or some other sport.

FIELD THEORY

This concept, developed first by Koffka and Koehler, and later advanced by Hartmann and Wertheimer, stresses that one learns best by grasping whole concepts. It holds that one learns by trial and error plus "insight"—suddenly "seeing" how to do something. Anyone who has ever tried to learn to ride a bicycle usually was battered and bruised before he suddenly found he could do it. The novice swimmer learning the crawl stroke has a great moment of triumph when he finds he can synchronize his arm, leg and head movements and can move rhythmically through the water using all of these coordinated actions. Insight is "getting the hang" of anything we are learning; it can only be the result of previous trial-and-error attempts. The task of the teacher is to encourage the learner to keep trying until this thrill of accomplishment comes. Here again, care must be taken not to nip learning struggles in the bud by being too much of a perfectionist, overly critical or impatient, for each student has his own rate of learning. For some, insight comes early; for the majority, however, it appears after many trial-and-error attempts.

This concept of learning, known also as "Gestalt psychology," places the emphasis in any learning experience upon the learner, and stresses that he knows more about his own values, desires, capacities and preferences than the teacher. The instructor should help the learner to set his own goals, determine his action plans and judge the results. This does not mean that the teacher is unnecessary but does imply that his main task is that of guiding and directing. Students gain much more from such skillful leadership than from being told what to do, for there will be less friction and more rapport, fewer failures and more success, less boredom and far more excitement in learning.

If the main purpose of education is to help each person increase the number of socially approved things he can do well which are beneficial to him and society, teaching is more than either an art or a science, for it becomes a combination of both. A skilled teacher will provide the best kind of learning atmosphere—warm and friendly, yet controlled, motivate pupils to desire worthy goals by making them as attractive as possible, make even disagreeable tasks seem agreeable and interesting to a bored, uninterested learner by changing negative attitudes to positive ones and help the learner to develop finer and deeper appreciation of himself, others, and what he is doing.

Gestalt psychology also stresses that the best learning will result when the learning environment is used to its fullest extent, and also that the learner can and will learn only when he has a need to do so, and that he will learn best when he can do so under the friendly, consistent guidance of a firm teacher who regards his as a unique human being. It also contends that learning will come about faster and be more lasting when large blocks of material are mastered. Educators call this the whole-part-whole method of teaching and learning. They agree that it is superior to piecemeal educational attempts, for it will bring desired results more quickly by stressing relationships.

KINDS OF LEARNING

The three kinds of learning are primary or technical, secondary or associated, and concomitant.

Primary learning means learning a specific skill such as kicking the soccer ball, hitting the baseball, or serving the tennis ball. Research evidence discloses that the whole-part-whole method for gaining skill perfection is often superior to other methods. Performing a skill in slow motion and/or through

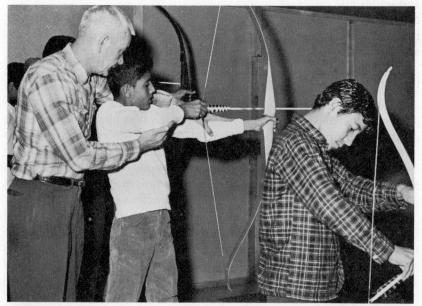

Figure 3–2. No two students have the same kind of learning problems—a fact skillful teachers recognize. (Courtesy of the Lifetime Sports Foundation.)

mimetics is considered inferior to learning it at normal speed or make-believe acted out substitutes. One learns rapidly after he gets the kinesthetic feel of what he is doing. Primary learning is often referred to as technical learning.

Secondary learning is marginal; it surrounds the mastery of skills. This type of learning consists largely of decision making, judging, the rules of games, body use, the selection and care of equipment as well as other numerous kinds of fringe knowledge. It can be illustrated by the skilled flycaster who has also gained much information about the breeding habits of fish, the best type of lures to use, when and where to go to catch trout, or other similar know-how tidbits surrounding his ability to use a rod and reel. Many adult hobbies center around game skills mastered in high school, as the bowling ball and archery bow maker well know.

Concomitant learning is primarily concerned with attitude-shaping and character development. It is derived from a Latin word meaning "come with." Skills should not be taught for their own sake. Game success or failure is rich in character-shaping possibilities. It has been said that character can be *caught* better than taught.

High school students have their sense of values well formed by graduation time. Their peers and all adults contribute to this; some do so much more than others. Leadership through examples is perhaps the best way to develop desirable behavior patterns of conduct as well as a basic philosophy of life.

MOTOR LEARNING

It has been said, in truth, that skills are *means* for the fulfillment of human purposes, and their development makes possible deeper and wider human experience. Functioning skillfully gives one a feeling of well-being and accomplishment. Although the capacity for learning is within each individual, teachers can help youth to gain needed self-discipline and the control necessary for skill growth.

Wells has classified motor activities man is called upon to perform throughout life, including those in physical education:[2]

> I. Skills of maintaining and regaining equilibrium.
> II. Skills of moving one's own body—
>   A. On land or other solid surface:
>   1. Arm, leg and trunk movements.
>   2. Locomotion.
>   3. Rotary movements of the body as a whole.
>   B. In the water:
>   1. Swimming.
>   2. Aquatic stunts.
>   3. Boating.
>   C. In the air:
>   1. Diving.
>   2. Trampoline and tumbling activities.

---

[2]Wells, Katharine: *Kinesiology*. 5th ed. Philadelphia, W. B. Saunders Co., 1971.

    D. In suspension:
       1. Swinging activities on trapeze, flying rings, etc.
       2. Hand traveling on traveling rings, horizontal ladder, etc.
  III. Skills of receiving impetus —
    A. Of own body:
       1. Landing from jumps and falls.
    B. Of external objects:
       1. Catching and trapping.
       2. Receiving with an implement.
       3. Receiving and spotting in stunts and apparatus events.
  IV. Skills of giving impetus to external objects:
    A. Pushing, pulling, thrusting, lifting.
    B. Throwing with hand or implement.
    C. Striking, hitting, kicking, etc.
   V. The selection and classification of skills related to prevention of injury:
    A. The maintenance of equilibrium.
    B. The range of motion.
    C. The intensity and duration of muscular exercise.
    D. The transmission of weight through the body segments and weight-bearing joints.
    E. The reception of one's own weight.
    F. The lifting and carrying of heavy objects.
    G. The impact of external forces.

Learning motor skills involves the whole human being, for in reality there is no separate kind of learning which is strictly "motor" in nature. While some individuals learn skills more easily than others, both sexes have the same sport skill learning potential within their structural and functional limits, for differences in learning most physical activities are actually largely due to cultural influences.[3] There is no true evidence that people of any one particular race can learn some sports more rapidly than others. The Eskimo youth may more aptly learn to throw the whale harpoon, the Australian child the boomerang, the African native the hunting spear, but each of these youths could also learn to use the equipment of another as well, but would need a longer practice time for doing so, largely because of lack of burning interest in learning that activity. Each individual in all of mankind's races learns motor skills in his own unique way and according to his own peculiar pattern. Some may make no apparent progress for some time, while others may learn quickly at first and then reach a leveling-off plateau, while still others may improve steadily and gradually until they can perform a skill well. Although people in their sixties can and do learn to play shuffleboard, golf or other sports, they do so more slowly than youth, for after the age of thirty an individual loses the ability to learn new physical skills easily. As seen in Figure 3–3, there are many prerequisites and controls involved in efficient movement.

_____

   [3]Oberteuffer, Delbert, and Ulrich, Celeste: *Physical Education, A Textbook of Principles for Professional Students.* 3rd ed. New York, Harper & Row, 1962, p. 282.

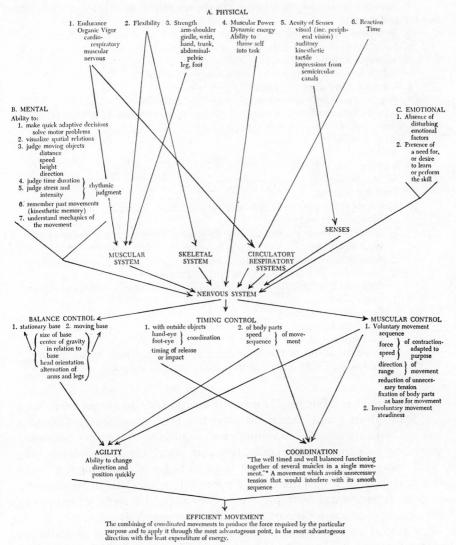

Figure 3–3. Prerequisites to efficient movement. Reproduced by permission from Broer, Marion R.: Human Movement.

McCloy discovered that a person has more motor educability if the following qualities are present:[4]

1. "Insight into the nature of the skill": "catching on" to what is expected.
2. Ability to visualize spatial relationships.

---

[4]McCloy, Charles: A preliminary study of factors of motor educability. *Research Quarterly.* May, 1946, pp. 28–39.

3. The ability to make quick and adaptive decisions.

4. Sensory motor coordination: as in the coordination of the eye with the head, hand, or foot.

5. Sensory motor coordination: the adaptation of weight and force.

6. Judgment of the relationship of the subject to external objects in relation to time, height, distance, and direction.

7. Accuracy of direction and small angles of error.

8. General kinesthetic sensitivity and control.

9. Ability to coordinate a complex unitary movement.

10. Ability to coordinate a complex series of combinations of movements which follow one another in rapid succession.

11. Arm control.

12. Balance.

13. Timing.

14. Motor rhythm.

15. Esthetic feeling.

16. The necessary prerequisites to effective motor learning including:

  a. Muscular strength.

  b. Dynamic energy—the ability to throw oneself into a performance with full vigor.

  c. Ability to change directions.

  d. Flexibility of muscles, joints and ligaments.

  e. Agility—the ability to move rapidly from one position in space to another.

  f. Peripheral vision.

  g. Good vision.

  h. Concentration.

  i. Understanding of the mechanics of the techniques of the activity.

  j. Absence of disturbing or inhibitory complications.

Movement is basic to all human life; when we no longer move we are dead. Throughout childhood there are the progressively difficult tasks of learning to walk, run, jump, and combined movement patterns involving coordination of hands, feet and body. The early adolescent "skill hungry years" are the best time to begin skill refinement. As one progresses through life there are more complex skills to be learned such as intricate dance steps, the hockey flick, the swan dive or, in old age, how to use a cane or manipulate a wheelchair.

Physical educators will find the following concepts regarding motor learning helpful when teaching students to develop new and to refine old motor skills:

1. *Each student has his own unique motor skill learning patterns and limitations.* These depend upon previous experiences, body build, heredity, depth, degree of interests and needs, as well as other factors. The teacher must know where each student is in his development in order to help him best learn movement skills. Some with previous limited physical education experiences may be in a twelfth grade class, but actually belong on the sixth grade level. These students must be taught skills at their development level before they can advance to where they should be.

2. *Beginners and advanced players in skill activities should be homogeneously grouped for the best results in skill teaching.* Pre-instruction testing is one of the more accurate ways to determine where each student should be grouped. (Care must be taken, however, because some students knowing their final grade will be based partly on improvement will, for example, in tennis begin playing left-handed, then switch to their normal right-handed use of the racket for the final exam skill test.)

3. *Errors should be corrected early in the learning process.* Practice does not make perfect unless one is practicing perfectly, but practice can make permanent. Although students teach themselves skills, those who are guided past sure-to-fail trial and error learning attempts learn more quickly. Incorrectly learned skills are more time-consuming to replace than is learning how to do a skill correctly from the beginning.

4. *The purposes of each student will influence their degree of motivation to learn skills.* High school students are a bundle of wants, for they want "to be a leader," "to be popular" or "to learn to dance." The teacher should know what these desires are in helping each devise self goals in learning activities.

5. *Students must set realistic goals for themselves, and if they have permanent handicaps learn to accept and work around them.* Those with cardiac conditions can be guided to select such beneficial activities as archery or billiards instead of football or track which would most likely prove to be harmful, for the learner's physical, mental and emotional condition deters or accelerates learning.[5]

6. *The class social climate will influence both the quality and quantity of learning.* Studies show that democratic leadership and a relaxed but controlled learning environment are by far more productive in learning than laissez faire and/or autocratic leadership in an insecure or tense learning environment that is uncontrolled or semicontrolled.

7. *Since not all students learn skills the same way, the teacher must use a variety of teaching methods.* Some will learn by imitation, others through perceptive methods (the learner through empathy with the teacher copies a skill as seen but is unaware of what she is doing, or how or why she succeeded in doing so), some kinesthetically (getting the "feel" of the movement) and still others by trial and error, insight or catching on to how to do it (which may come slowly or suddenly, or through conscious analysis of each part of the skill). Few students learn in just one of these ways; most do so by a combination of empathy, imitation, kinesthetic perception and conscious analysis.

8. *The maturation level of the learner will affect motor learning speed.* Just as there is reading readiness, there is also the right time for boys and girls to learn physical activities. Although generalizations concerning such "ripeness" can be made, much more experimentation is needed by each individual teacher in this area. Most students are "ready" to learn when they have the desire and capability for doing so. The learner must have more than a burning desire to learn a sport; she must also have the coordination and attributes needed for skill development.

---

[5]See Chapter 18, Adapted Activities.

9. *The learner must set his own immediate goals for achieving effective performance and use isolated skills learned in actual performance in dances, games or sports.* Thus, isolated game skills should be used as soon as possible in the actual activity being learned. In swimming, practicing skills in the water results in more lasting and faster learning than dry land practice.

10. *The learner's goals should change to become progressively more difficult to reach as each step is mastered.* A student may want to learn to swim, then want to swim for distance and speed, and finally to learn skin and scuba diving, thus building skill upon skill.

11. *Skills once learned will tarnish when neglected or unused.* A skill once learned is a person's permanent possession. Thus the student, who at fifteen learns to swim but does not do so again until he is a man of fifty in an emergency sink-or-swim situation, will "remember" how to do it again. Basic skills in any sport can become more valuable through frequent use. Although *we learn what we do, we must also do what we learn* if we are to become and to remain skillful.

12. *The learner teaches himself.* Oberteuffer and Ulrich declare "the game of hide-and-seek is never learned by the player who is never 'found.'" Each student must experience for himself how and when to swing the bat just at the right time in order to hit the ball, as well as all the other elements of skill perfection. Beginning teachers tend both to talk and to demonstrate too much, thus wasting much precious practicing and learning time needed for skill mastery.

SKILL LEARNING

Every learner is ready to learn a new skill when he has reached just the right stage in his development and can successfully go on to the next step. The right stage is reached when the student is learning and improving with ease, has some success, is motivated to keep trying, and has acquired some insight into the performance of the skill.

Feedback

Although the words reward, reinforcement, knowledge of results and feedback are often used interchangeably, feedback in motor learning refers to some kind of information related to the learning of the skill, that the performer receives during or after his performance. Thus feedback can motivate, speed up and reinforce learning. *Intrinsic feedback* is the result of the learner's actions, whereas *augmented feedback* comes from the teacher and is used to supplement what the learner did to point out what he should avoid or repeat doing in his trial and error attempts to learn. If a summary score is given after the student's performance it is called *terminal feedback,* in contrast to *concurrent feedback,* which is more continuous information that the learner receives about how he is progressing. Feedback may be received externally through the senses as well as internally by kinesthetic sense, or by the newer term, proprioceptive sense, which means getting the "feel" of the movement or by getting internal clues about how to perform a skill.

Individual Differences

Each person learns in his own unique way. The backgrounds and previous experiences of students in mastering skills, their adaptability to the particular skill, and even their mental attitude and body build, all effect the manner and the time of learning of the entire class and of each student in it. The student who can already run fast, change directions quickly, throw accurately, successfully kick a ball or hit it with a bat or racket will often progress more rapidly than the student who never learned these skills well. The teacher must begin where the learner actually is, not where the teacher thinks or hopes he is. If a student cannot move his body rhythmically to music, he will not be able to dance until he can feel and move to a rhythmic beat.

The Role of Practice

Practice is important when trying to do new skills, but it is no guarantee of learning them. *Practice makes permanent. It will make perfect only if one practices perfectly.* Game play will not lead to rapid skill acquisition or improvement. Practice without the intent to improve will result in inaccurate performance, as will practicing too long. Short periods of intense concentrated practice are far superior to lengthy ones.

Mechanical Guidance (Kinesthesis)

Done with the cooperative efforts of the learner, mechanical guidance often is the best teaching method to use to give the learner the gross framework idea of the skill. The teacher who "helps" the student swing the golf club correctly uses this method. Children, older people who have had little experience playing sports, the sensory handicapped, and the low-skilled all can learn best through the use of this method.

Visual Aids

Although the student learns fastest by doing, there are some who can be helped to gain movement ideas through the use of slow-motion movies, drawings and loop films. This technique may often be used best for those who have already acquired body-control skills.

The Beginner's Unit or Lesson Length

How much should be in a lesson and how fast to go on from learning a simple skill to a more complex one depends upon the previous things the pupil has learned. The unit or single lesson should also be strongly challenging, but it must be on the level of the low, middle, or highly skilled pupil or group. Those who are poorly co-ordinated often become thwarted and give up if learning tasks are too complicated, just as highly skilled students will quickly become bored and disruptive if their assigned tasks are "baby stuff."

The Use of Form and Creativity

Although golf and other sport champions develop a form that brings them success, the form or movement pattern the teacher selects should be one that has been used by many players successfully. The form should be simple for beginners. As each student learns the separate parts of every needed game skill, he will need to make adjustments according to his own unique structural requirements, either through self-analysis and experimentation or with the help of the teacher.

Knowledge of Mechanical Principles

Some, but not all, students will profit from knowing mechanical movement principles. This is especially true of those who are planning to become coaches, professional players, or physical educators. However, care should be taken that the use of mechanical movement principles is not overemphasized, for like excessive verbalization and having too many visual aids to show to a class, precious practice time can be lost. A good motto to have is, show and tell a *little* bit, have all students *do* a lot.

PRINCIPLES OF LEARNING

Principles are both basic beliefs and action guides. They are the end products of research, best experiences and expert opinion. The best learning will occur when the following principles are followed:

1. *All theories of learning are based upon the practice of developing good human relationships.* Here the learner is paramount. He is placed in situations in which he feels secure and is confident that mistakes can be made without undue penalty and are a vital part of learning. The learning climate should be warm, friendly and conducive to obtaining the best results.

2. *The learner's needs, interests and goals are the greatest factors in learning.* One learns best when he has a definite goal of his own well in mind, selects materials to be learned, plans his actions and judges the results in relationship to his clear picture and understanding of what successful performance is. Students cannot learn from superimposed needs, interests and goals set by the teacher.

We like to do things in which success expectancy is high. We all strive harder at tasks we think we can do. The role of the teacher is to build self-confidence in the learner to the extent that he will keep trying to obtain his own established goals until he reaches them. One major contribution a teacher makes is helping to determine the level and type of goals set by each of her students.

3. *Interrupted completion of the learning process leads to faster learning and longer retention.* Short practices are superior to long ones. All practice periods should vary in length according to the interest and fatigue levels of the learners. Such practices cannot successfully be confined always to the same time period. Practice is fruitful only if it brings satisfaction to pupil needs. One has practiced long enough when he can distinguish for himself the difference between wrong and right responses and can repeat the correct ones at will. Too much practice is as great an educational waste as not enough.

4. *The learner controls the learning situation.* The student is handicapped when dominated by adult control of what, when and how he is to learn. Knowledge of his progress in relationship to that of others will aid each student to learn more quickly. Care must be taken, however, not to cause embarrassment or feelings of inferiority by posting progress charts and graphs without warning or explanation. A posted list of students showing the most weekly or monthly progress is often a good class learning incentive.

5. *Each student is unique; each learns best in his own way.* Innate differences in body structure, coordination, motivated drive, capacity, emotional stability, personality and other factors exist in all human beings. Teaching each student is an individual matter. What and how one learns is also a single phenomenon. Each student develops his own unique learning curve. For the majority, this curve will be rapid at first, taper off to a plateau next and, finally, gradually rise as the student nears his goals. Some few individuals, however, are desire-driven to such a marked degree that a plateau level is rarely reached or may be so minute it remains undetected by the busy instructor.

6. *Longer retention results from overlearning.* Practicing a skill until it becomes rhythmical, effective and automatic will keep it more securely and longer in the body's memory storehouse. Overaccomplishment produces more securely fastened and pinned-down knowledges and skills. Experts believe that skills really learned are rarely forgotten or lost. It is not uncommon to see oldsters in their eighties swimming, fishing, sewing or performing other physical skills they learned when youngsters. The forty-year-old can still skate even though he has not done so from the time he successfully learned at the age of eight.

7. *Strong emotions retard or accelerate learning.* Fear and insecurity reign and check learning progress; enthusiasm and confidence spur and urge it on. Satisfaction and success are as related as frustration and fun are widely separated. Learning occurs more rapidly when it is a pleasurable, exciting and thrilling experience. *Those who receive the greatest joy from learning are those who are challenged and magically drawn to reach out and up to a longed-for goal and who succeed in grasping and keeping it as their very own.*

8. *Learning is a doing activity.* All discovery comes from searching. We learn what we do, things we experience. Although some information can be gleaned from seeing correct movement patterns, such as the golf swing, tennis serve or soccer dribble, from movies, slides, filmstrips, posters or other visual aids, students will master these skills only through their own efforts. If we would learn, we must do, see and discover things for ourselves.

9. *Transfer will occur only if sought in situations recognized to be alike.* Transfer of something learned in one area to another will result if one succeeds in making such duplication possible in a situation in which certain similarities are seen. All transfer obeys the law of configuration (the togetherness of isolated parts into a recognized form, concept, contour or outline). This is seen in the final mastery of the overhand throw in which the weight is transferred correctly, the correct grip, hand and arm positions used. This same movement can be repeated when throwing a rope to a drowning person, making an overhand tennis drive, or doing numerous other movements. In order for practices to transfer from one learning area to another, the student must clearly see the similarity between the two and continue to do in the second activity, with some modification, what he mastered in the first situation. Mastery of Latin grammar is no guarantee of speaking or writing flawless English. Good sportsmanship displayed by students who are victorious in one situation will not insure such desirable behavior when the same group is badly beaten. *Transfer occurs only when two situations are joined together, and one is aware that this union exists.* Many sorts of responses do, however, transfer. These include how one feels about himself and others, a particular environment or situation in which he finds himself, general movement skills and techniques, some specific facts, as well as conditioned action responses.

10. *Learning can be an adventure.* One has only to observe happy-faced youngsters learning to swim in a public pool, students' reactions when they hit the bull's-eye, or knock all the bowling pins over, or accomplish many similar goals, to realize the truth of the above statement. Life and learning are of the same parentage. Both can be happy, thrilling adventures!

11. *The learner reacts to a cluster of stimuli.* The teacher must eliminate those which are distracting, such as too much noise, jeering classmates who laugh at mistakes and poor lighting.

12. *The learner should be taught to see relationships.* He should be helped to understand the whole process before he drills on any specific parts, i.e., he should know the way a complete tennis serve is done and how it looks before beginning to practice on the correct grip, swing, toss or place of ball contact.

13. *The learner can learn only when he is ready to learn.* Each teacher should know "generalized" times for each age group in relationship to skill learning readiness as well as be able to detect readiness in a highly coordinated person in any age bracket. For example, most seven-year-olds cannot learn the badminton serve readily, but Craig, who is highly skilled, can do so at the age of six-and-a-half years.

14. *Since the learner is both an individual and a social being, he should be encouraged to work on educational tasks which will enhance his uniqueness as well as his value as a group member.*

15. *Evaluation is an essential part of learning.* We can avoid past mistakes only when we discover we have made incorrect responses, or ones that did not bring desired results. Evauation and improvement are inseparable. One decision difficult for teachers to make is *when* to step in to eliminate errors by pointing out mistakes, and to know *how critical he dare be* without destroying the student's zeal to continue trying to reach desired goals.

DISCUSSION QUESTIONS

1. Illustrate what is meant by conditioning, connectionism and the field theory of learning.
2. What is meant by the Laws of Readiness, Effect and Exercise as defined by Thorndike? Illustrate each law by relating your experience in learning a new skill in physical education.
3. What implications do each of these laws have to you as a physical educator?
4. Define the following terms: transfer, Gestalt psychology, configuration, feedback, learning plateau, goals, overlearning, maturation level.
5. Discuss the role of the teacher in helping students to learn.

THINGS TO DO

1. Write a short essay titled "Things I Want to Learn as a Teacher."
2. Try teaching any physical skill to a child 8–10, an adolescent 13–15 and a college student 19–21. Evaluate your results in relationship to Thorndike's three laws of learning, discussed in this chapter.
3. Illustrate the six major areas of human learning. Which seem to you the hardest to master?
4. Bring to class a conditioned pet and show how this pet was conditioned. Elaborate upon the role and methods you used as a teacher in conditioning.
5. Visit a school that has a good physical education program and evaluate how effectively students were motivated to learn. Report on the learning rate differences you observed.

SELECTED VISUAL AIDS

And No Bells Ring. (Illustrates team teaching, large and small group instruction, and independent study.) Sound, b. & w., 56 minutes. National Association of Secondary School Principals, Washington, D.C.

Children Growing Up with Others. Toronto, The National Film Board of Canada.
Children Learning from Experience. Toronto, The National Film Board of Canada.
Evaluating Physical Abilities. (Film shows a series of performance tests used to evaluate growth in strength, speed, endurance, coordination, flexibility, and agility). Available on rental and purchase basis from the Athletic Institute.
Facing Reality. New York, McGraw-Hill Book Company.
Lifetime Sports In Education. Shows the scope of this valuable program. Available on a loan basis from any state director of health, physical education and recreation of the department of education in all states.
Making Learning More Meaningful. New York, McGraw-Hill Book Company.
Meeting the Needs of Adolescents. New York, McGraw-Hill Book Company.
School Spirit and Sportsmanship. New York, Coronet Films.

SUGGESTED READINGS

Biehler, Robert F.: *Psychology Applied to Teaching.* Boston, Houghton Mifflin Co., 1971.

Broer, Marian: *Efficiency of Human Movement.* Philadelphia, W. B. Saunders Co., 1973.

Bucher, Charles: *Foundations of Physical Education.* 6th Ed., St. Louis, The C. V. Mosby Co., 1972.

Cratty, Bryant: *Movement Behavior and Motor Learning.* Philadelphia Lea & Febiger, 1967.

Crow, Lester D., and Crow, Alice: *Readings in Human Learning.* New York, David McKay Co., 1963, pp. 372, 9–11.

Gagne, Robert M.: Some New Views of Learning and Instruction. *Phi Delta Kappan,* Journal of Phi Delta Kappa, May, 1970, pp. 468–471.

Garry, Ralph, and Kingsley, Howard L.: *The Nature and Conditions of Learning.* 3rd Ed., Englewood Cliffs, N.J., Prentice Hall, Inc., 1970.

Havighurst, Robert J.: *Developmental Tasks and Education.* New York, David McKay Co., 1972.

Knapp, B.: *Skill In Sport, The Attainment of Proficiency.* London, Routledge and Kegan Paul Ltd., 1963.

Lawther, John: *The Learning of Physical Skills.* Englewood Cliffs, N.J., Prentice Hall, Inc., 1968.

Little Improvement Seen in Schools in Decade. *Education U.S.A.,* August 7, 1972.

National Association of Physical Education for College Women and National College Physical Education Association for Men: *A Symposium On Motor Learning, Quest.* Monograph VI, May, 1966.

Robb, Margaret: *The Dynamics of Motor-Skill Acquistion.* Englewood Cliffs, N.J., 1972.

Skinner, B. F.: *The Technology of Teaching.* New York, Appleton-Century-Crofts, 1968, pp. 15, 17, 93–96.

Smith, Leon (Ed.): *Psychology of Motor Learning.* Chicago, The Athletic Institute, 1970.

RECOMMENDED MOTOR ABILITY TESTS

Brace, David: *Measuring Motor Ability.* New York, A. S. Barnes, 1927.

Johnson, Granville: Physical skills tests for sectioning classes into homogeneous units. *Research Quarterly,* March, 1932.

McCloy, Charles: The measurement of general motor capacity and general motor ability. *Research Quarterly,* March, 1934, pp. 46–61.

McCraw, Lynn, and Tolbert, J. W.: Sociometric status and athletic ability of junior high school boys. *Research Quarterly,* 24:72–80, March, 1953.

Metheny, Eleanor: Studies of the Johnson Test of Motor Educability. *Research Quarterly,* 10:81–88, 1939.

Scott, Gladys: Measurement of kinesthesis. *Research Quarterly,* 26:325–341, October, 1955.

Stanbury, Edgar: A simplified method of classifying junior and senior high school boys into homogeneous groups for physical education activities. *Research Quarterly,* 12:765–776, December, 1941.

CHAPTER FOUR

THE TEACHING PROCESS

Teaching encompasses sharing, guiding, counseling, evaluating, directing, inspiring, and more. It is both an art and a science. As an art, it stresses experimentation, creativity and individuality. As a science, it is the application of knowledge gained from scientific research in all areas of learning, including what is known about human beings and how to help them learn most effectively and efficiently.

It is difficult to separate the process of teaching from the process of learning, and thus the teaching-learning process will be considered as one in this chapter. Although learning can occur without the influence of a teacher, it is hard to think of teaching without learning. The *raison d'etre* of teaching is to augment learning. Therefore it appears inappropriate to talk about teaching without continually linking it to learning.

Virtually all teaching acts are conceived to produce learning. Thus, the best test of effective teaching is the amount of student learning. Recognition of this fact helps to establish a proper perspective for teaching, which is that the most important person in the process is the student. The student is the very reason for the existence of the entire school experience. Teachers are present to enhance the student's experiences.

Superior teaching is probably the most significant variable in the learning environment. Many schools lack adequate facilities, equipment or supportive staff; however, quality leadership in the form of competent teachers can accomplish major achievements in student learning even in meager supporting environments.

POSITIVE TEACHER CHARACTERISTICS

Teachers deal with people, such as students, parents, other teachers, administrators and so forth. It is obvious then that teachers should like people in general and enjoy interacting with them. Although there is no established set of characteristics by which to identify good teachers, several studies indicate that the following qualities are exhibited by the more successful and respected teachers:

1. Enjoy being with people
2. Feel self-adequate
3. Have positive views of the worth of others
4. Have ability to see things from others' viewpoints
5. Have a sense of humor
6. Have broad interests
7. Are flexible in dealing with situations
8. Will experiment and try new approaches
9. Can "personalize" their teaching
10. Are knowledgeable in their subject matter
11. Praise others frequently

If teachers are to be effective in aiding the development of students, it appears that in addition to being well informed about the subject they teach, they must generally like themselves and others and enjoy engaging in the dynamic interaction of teaching.

TEACHING MOTOR SKILLS

The initial learning of all motor skills follows a sequential pattern. This sequence is basic to the learning process and thus occurs when any skill is acquired, whether it is in a highly structured class environment or in a singular performance. In attempting to enhance the quantity and quality of learning the teacher should first recognize the phases of the learning sequence and then identify the type of teaching behavior that is appropriate to facilitate each step.

The following diagram, adapted from Gentile,[1] depicts the critical events in the acquisition of a motor skill and the varying functions of the teacher as an augmenter of the learning process.

By viewing the learner and the teacher simultaneously we are able to identify the appropriate behavior sequence of each: (1) In sequence one the student must accomplish goal orientation; that is, he must clearly understand the task at hand and be motivated toward the achievement of this task. The teacher's role is to identify the task or problem, communicate its importance and attempt to induce a desire on the part of the student to achieve this specific goal. This may be done through either describing the goal or presenting a problem to be solved. (2) To solve a problem or reach a goal a general plan of attack must be developed by the student. Here he must see the skill

---

[1]Gentile, A. M.: A Working Model of Skill Acquisition with Application to Teaching. *Quest*, January, 1972, pp. 3–23.

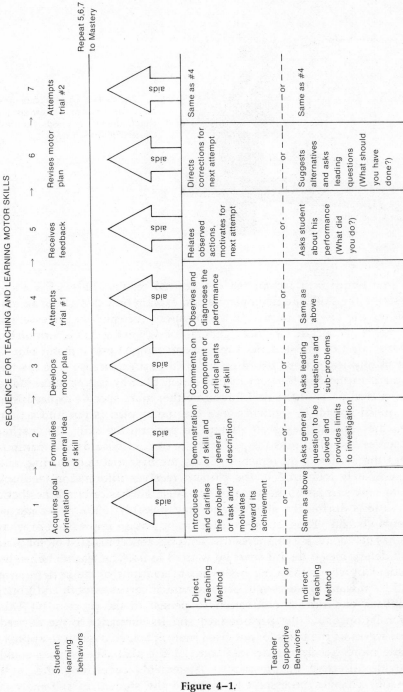

SEQUENCE FOR TEACHING AND LEARNING MOTOR SKILLS

Student learning behaviors	1	2	3	4	5	6	7	
	Acquires goal orientation	Formulates general idea of skill	Develops motor plan	Attempts trial #1	Receives feedback	Revises motor plan	Attempts trial #2	Repeat 5,6,7 to Mastery
Teacher Supportive Behaviors								
Direct Teaching Method	Introduces and clarifies the problem or task and motivates toward its achievement	Demonstration of skill and general description	Comments on component or critical parts of skill	Observes and diagnoses the performance	Relates observed actions, motivates for next attempt	Directs corrections for next attempt	Same as #4	
Indirect Teaching Method	Same as above	Asks general question to be solved and provides limits to investigation	Asks leading questions and sub-problems	Same as above	Asks student about his performance (What did you do?)	Suggests alternatives and asks leading questions (What should you have done?)	Same as #4	

Figure 4–1.

Figure 4–2. The teacher must help the student to understand clearly the task at hand. (Courtesy Darien Public Schools.)

as one which will accomplish the desired result. The teacher could describe the skill, and demonstrate and explain how this action accomplishes the task, or he may pose questions focusing on the essential elements of concern. (3) Once a general concept of the skill is formulated in the mind of the student, it must be developed into a motor plan, a set of physical actions based on his own past experience. The teacher can aid in the development of this action plan by calling attention to the critical parts of the skill through either more specific explanations or questions. (4) In sequence four the motor plan is put into action, i.e., the student makes an attempt to perform the skill. The teacher observes and diagnoses the performance or possibly aids and manipulates the student's movements. (5) As the first trial is occurring, and immediately following it, the student receives information feedback as to how successful the attempt has been. He has certain kinesthetic sensations during the attempt and may possibly follow other movements visually. Thus, at the conclusion he has an impression of what he has just done. He compares this with his conceptualized motor plan and determines if he did what he wanted to do. The teacher helps the student by communicating his own observations of the performance and by rewarding successful actions, which serves as both additional feedback and further motivation to persist in the process. (6) This information about the performance and its similarity to the desired goal serves as the basis for a revised motor plan, an attempt to approximate more closely the desired form of the skill. The teacher could provide directive or prescriptive statements concerning the most obvious changes necessary, or may aid the student in self-analysis by asking him questions about the performance. (7) The student is now ready for the second trial and the teacher functions again as in sequence four. Thereafter, sequences five, six and seven are repeated until the desired level of skill mastery is achieved.

The foregoing analysis of the teaching-learning process in the acquisition of a motor skill identifies several important aspects of good teaching inherent in the process. There is a logical order of events necessary for planning any instructional setting. It is the *student* who must do the learning: the teacher cannot learn for the student. Consequently, the function of the teacher becomes one of attempting to aid the student at each step of the process to enable the most rapid development possible. It should also be clear from the analysis that the functions of a teacher are varied and complex. The process requires diverse teaching skills, including motivating, demonstrating, explaining, questioning, critical observation and analysis, diagnosis of errors and directing corrections. All are necessary for effective teaching, each aiding the appropriate stage of the learning process.

The analysis of teaching motor skills thus far has focused on the initial phase of skill acquisition. Most school programs seek to achieve development beyond the basic acquisition of the motor movement. In the advanced phase of skill learning the concern is with fixation, refinement and diversification of the skill. The emphasis is on producing consistency, exacting control, or the ability to apply the skill in a variety of settings and game conditions. Appropriate teaching behaviors in this phase of skill learning are largely determined by the nature of the skills involved. Some skills put a high premium on consistency, and the settings in which they are practiced are highly similar. Bowling is an example of such a set of skills, often described as "closed skills," performed in a physical environment that is relatively consistent and where learning proceeds at the player's own pace. In contrast, an "open skill" is performed in an ever-changing setting and is often affected by the actions or pace of others. Basketball provides many examples of open skills, with the exception of foul shooting, which is more closed in nature. This differentiation between open and closed skills suggests that the teaching of closed skills is basically a problem of fixating a movement, of making it as exact as possible. The practice of such a skill should duplicate the exact conditions of the performance and should insure an opportunity for intensive repetition of the desired actions. The diagnosis of performance and the directions to the student should focus on specific movement patterns. Errors arising from deviation from good form should be identified and corrected, and the final form fixated by extensive practice.

In contrast, the teaching prescription for an open skill, such as the forehand drive in tennis, is quite different after the original skill acquisition phase is complete. In an open skill the environment is never quite the same; the shot is not attempted from the same position;

the ball is not coming with the same trajectory; and the opponent is in varying positions. Here circumstance calls for diversification of the skill, and the ability to produce a reasonable performance under a great *variety* of conditions. Hence, the teacher must provide practice situations which will be present in the game setting. Prolonged practice in any one set of conditions will detract from the concept of diversity. In this instance emphasis in the teaching diagnosis and directions is given to the existing conditions and the appropriateness of the technique selected by the learner in each attempt. The goal is not to produce one exact form but rather to consistently produce a desired outcome from a variety of settings.

TEACHING METHODS

Teaching methods are general procedures for promoting learning. In physical education the most frequently used methods are the traditional (direct) method, the problem solving (indirect) method and a synthesis of the two. The synthesis is the combination in varying degrees of the indirect and direct methods.

In any general method of teaching certain forms may be utilized. "Form" is the term applied to those special ways of structuring the activities or interactions between students and teacher within the general framework of the method.

THE DIRECT METHOD

The direct method of teaching offers great latitude in possible forms; however, the essential element of *direction* provided by the teacher permeates all the forms. It is characteristic of the direct method that the teacher initiates the learning activities and the students carry out the assignments as directed.

The most typical form of direct teaching in physical education is command and response. In this form the teacher closely controls all aspects of the learning environment and the students are basically treated equally, regardless of individual differences. Typical examples of the use of this form are group calisthenics performed to the instructor's commands, lines of students, with each student waiting for his turn at a task supervised by the teacher, and execution of a technique by the entire class in unison with the rhythm of the instructor's cadence. The form offers exacting control of behavior and presents a highly disciplined appearance. However, it relegates students to the role of obeying commands and treats them as if all had equal ability and experience. Moreover, it is a rather ineffective form from the standpoint of student activity time in that students must often wait in line for an opportunity to try their skill.

An alternative form of the direct method attempts to provide for individual differences in background and learning rates by supplying the student with a series of activities, tasks or drills. These are demonstrated and then a worksheet or task card is provided for the student to utilize in practicing the skills. This form allows students to progress as rapidly as their ability permits through the assigned tasks. Usually each activity has some quality or quantity measure inherent in it to enable the student to determine when he has reached the desired level and is ready to move on to the next task. (An example of such a work sheet is provided on page 259.)

In many instances it is not necessary that all students follow a specific order of tasks; thus, students can be working on different tasks simultaneously. This has obvious advantages in settings where facilities and equipment are limited. Gymnastics provide a good example: students can be working simultaneously on all the apparatus and the floor rather than everyone waiting for his turn at a stunt. Since the students each have a worksheet of the activities, the teacher is freed from the task of counting cadence or directing whose turn is next and

Figure 4–3. The use of worksheets is an alternative form of the direct teaching method that allows greater attention to individual differences. (Courtesy Enrico Fermi High School.)

may now move freely among the students to give individual help where it is most needed. This form offers the advantages of allowing the students to progress at their own optimal rate as well as freeing the teacher to work individually with students.

A third alternative form of the direct method is based on the organization of students into pairs or groups. Here, again, the group has a worksheet setting forth the tasks to be performed and the desired level of skills to be achieved. The difference is that members of the group alternate in the roles of performer and observer. The observer's role is to provide information feedback to the performer and to decide when the task has been satisfactorily accomplished. The worksheet for this form includes a listing of points to be checked during the performance of the task as an aid to the observer in his role as critic. The observer evaluates his partner's performance and offers suggestions based on the check points and the earlier demonstration of the activity. This form has the advantage of providing feedback to the learner on every trial and yet allowing the class to be doing various activities.

This relationship requires the observer to be far more cognitively involved in analyzing the skills than any other form. It also requires a different type of social interaction by the students. Admittedly, most students are not accustomed to this type of situation and will need time and direction in adjusting to it. The potential benefits, however, should outweigh this disadvantage. The teacher is able to work individually with the partners to aid them in execution of the tasks as well as reinforcing the relationship of performer and observer. It is important that the teacher not bypass the observer by working with the performer, rather, he should interact with the observer and thereby help him improve his ability to work with and relate to the performer.

In all forms of the direct method the teacher has three important functions: demonstration, diagnosis and direction. These are known as the three Ds of motor skill teaching.

DEMONSTRATION

Most of our learning comes through our eyes and ears. Although one picture is worth ten-thousand words, one experience is superior to many pictures. When students copy what they see, they learn from this experience through their mistakes. The teacher should be able to demonstrate all skills as perfectly as possible, for it is important that the students duplicate correct movement patterns. Mastery in a wide variety of sport and game skills should be required in the professional preparation period of all physical educators. Should the teacher be unable to do the skill well, however, a student leader can be trained to demonstrate it for the class.

DIAGNOSIS

Students in every class have some kind of skill-learning difficulties. There are many reasons for this, including emotional blocks, poor coordination or body structure and physical condition. The teacher must be an expert in diagnosing difficulties. Some excel in this and can direct and produce new movement patterns quickly with a few well-chosen words. These master teachers say, "*Press* your left arm closer to your body," or "*Glide* through the water," or give other simple directions, using key words to gain quick results. The novice instructor stumbles, is unsure of himself and often masks his uncertainty with a very positively stated but inaccurate diagnosis. Teachers should *know* or logically deduce what is wrong, not guess what the difficulty is. Ability to diagnose learning difficulty comes largely from knowledge of how to perform the skill correctly, knowledge of what each part of the correct movement pattern is, experience in analysis of motor performance and recognition of the fact that such detection is a vital part of the teaching-learning process which every educator must master.

DIRECTION

The teacher's next responsibility is to direct new movement patterns, for he must not only spot the learning snag but lead the

Figure 4–4. Assisting the student to discover his own most productive movement pattern is a function of the third D of teaching (direction). (Courtesy of the Youth Service Section of the Los Angeles Public Schools.)

student around it. Success quickens learning. Consequently, when the student follows the teacher's directions and then hits the bull's-eye, makes the basket or hits the ball, he is eager to repeat those new movements which led to success. However, each physical educator must realize that form is an individual matter and that each student should be assisted to discover his own most productive movement patterns.

It is impossible to isolate skill learning from attitude development or behavior change. Learning results from many simultaneous experiences. The teacher's presence, encouragement, patience and faith in the student's desire and ability to master what he sets out to do help longed-for goals become a reality.

In all of the various forms of the direct method, one common element occurs — teacher direction. The forms differ in the amount of student freedom in regard to pace of learning, the degree of inter-student contact and the availability of the teacher to work with individuals.

THE INDIRECT METHOD

The second general class of methods is termed indirect or problem solving. The major characteristic in all problem solving techniques is the posing of questions or problems rather than the giving of instructions or directions.

In the problem solving or indirect method the students will need to be given a rather extensive orientation into the nature of the problem solving approach in physical education if they have not previously experienced such an approach to learning motor skills. A sample problem can be given and alternatives may be shown as to how the problem may be solved. It is very important that the student understands the value he may gain from using the problem solving approach. After the students are familiar with the process of problem solving, the teacher presents a motor task to the students in the form of a problem. The nature of the problem is determined by the maturation level and past experiences of the students and the objectives of the program. These factors influence the degree of complexity of the problem presented. For example, a beginning student in basketball may experiment with the best technique in throwing an underhand pass. A more sophisticated problem for students more advanced in basketball might consist of discovering the angle at which the knee should be flexed in preparation for making a jump to recover a shot that missed the basket.

Effective use of the problem solving method requires careful preparation. The teacher must first decide upon the general area of motor learning that will constitute the major problem and, if there is to be a sequence of sub-problems, to formulate them. The selection of the problem is made from among those appropriate to the group in question. The basis for determining appropriateness is past experience in motor skill.

If the sub-problems are to take the form of a sequence leading to the solution of a main problem, they must be arranged logically. This requires careful analysis by the teacher of the activity to identify the step involved. If he will think through the progression of the movements required to accomplish the activity stated in the main problem, the steps into which the problem should be divided will usually become apparent. In planning the sequence, it is necessary to decide if each step constitutes a relevant problem; for example, does it lead to the discovery of information that has a direct bearing on the final solution? If not, it should be eliminated from consideration for inclusion in the sequence.

As part of the planning process, the teacher must give some thought to the possible solutions that the students may develop in response to the problems. The possibilities for solutions in most instances are numerous. Anticipation of possible solutions will enable the teacher to better accomplish a redefinition of the problem with a more limited scope, thereby reducing the number of possible solutions.

There are two basic forms which might be employed under the general heading of the indirect method. The major difference between the forms lies in the type of problems and questions utilized. A convergent or narrowing form of questioning poses increasingly more exacting questions which lead the student toward discovering the desired solution. This form basically follows the rules of deductive reasoning, progressing from a general statement or conclusion to a specific instance which falls under the general case. (An example of a series of convergent questioning appears on page 337.) This convergent form of questioning is planned to lead the student to a specific answer through a rational application of knowledge. If a response is inadequate, the teacher must ask another question which will point up the deficiency in the original response. However, the teacher must never tell the student the answer but rather ask pertinent questions which will cause him to discover the answer. At times this appears to be a tedious process which is much slower than simply supplying the answer. However, one must remember that the objective of the problem solving method is to involve the student cognitively. It aims at developing the student's ability to think and reason; the teacher cannot do that for the student and still expect the desired results.

The alternative to convergent questions in structuring a problem solving lesson is the divergent form. In this form of questioning the problem is posed in such a way as to invite a wide variety of alternative

Figure 4–5. In the problem-solving method the teacher asks pertinent questions that will cause the student to discover the answer. (Courtesy Enrico Fermi High School.)

solutions. Obviously, this means the question is much broader and implies that there are many acceptable responses. The problem is much larger in scope and may require the student both to structure and solve many sub-problems preliminary to his solving the major question. With this form the students must be allowed ample opportunity to consider the question and try out various possible solutions. (An example of divergent questioning used in teaching a skill is described on page 281.)

The nature of the divergent problem is such as to allow varying solutions; however, this does not imply that any answer is acceptable. As part of the form each proposed solution should be scrutinized by both teacher and other students to determine if the solution first, in fact, solves the problem and, second, if it is feasible and desirable. This process promotes the exposure to various answers and initiates an evaluation process on the part of the student. It would appear that divergent questioning results in even greater opportunity for a student's cognitive development.

The indirect or problem solving method in both the convergent and divergent forms puts a premium on discovering, understanding and evaluating the content of the lesson. Its advantage thus lies in the development of the cognitive—the thinking—process. Students must think in order to come up with answers. The direct method rarely requires cognitive involvement on the part of the student.

SYNTHESIS OF METHODS

It is usually assumed that the problem solving method and the traditional method of teaching physical education are philosophically in total opposition and therefore incompatible. While it is true that there is a basic difference in the philosophies of teaching upon which the two methods are based—the difference being between telling or showing students how and guiding them to self-discovery of how to perform—the two methods are not so incompatible as to require the teacher to make an absolute choice of either one or the other. Effective teachers who would be classified as users of the traditional method have always utilized certain aspects of problem solving. Recognizing that each child is an individual with certain abilities and certain limitations, these teachers have attempted to help the child discover how to achieve optimal performance without rigid adherence to the "correct" way. Although they may rely to a large extent upon telling and showing their students how to perform skills in patterns that have been proven to be the most efficient for most people, these teachers nevertheless recognize that not all children should be forced to adopt a particular pattern of performance or even that they should all be expected to attempt it. Within these classes, then, there has always been a certain amount of problem solving, arising from an effort to serve individual needs. Moreover, effective teachers of the traditional

Figure 4–6. After demonstrating the skill, the teacher breaks it down into its components to help students understand how the various parts of the skill are performed. (Courtesy Enrico Fermi High School.)

method have always understood that students frequently learn best when they have an opportunity to question, to examine, and to experiment; and they have, consequently, operated from much the same premise as those utilizing the problem solving method.

Further evidence that the two methods are not incompatible is found in the use of certain forms of teaching, usually associated with the traditional method, to increase the effectiveness of problem solving. Demonstration by the teacher or by a skilled student or through the use of films and other visual aids is frequently employed by the teacher to give students a better understanding of the nature of the movements involved in a certain motor task or to present them with a standard of performance against which to evaluate the solution they have achieved. For this purpose, the visual media are likely to be as provocative as the teacher's verbalization, and they offer the additional advantage of varying the usual presentation of problems to the class for solution.

On the basis of the above evidence for the compatibility of the two methods, Fait[2] suggests that an effective method can be achieved through a synthesis of the direct and indirect methods. This synthesis leaves the teacher flexible in the choice of method best suited to any specific situation.

There is no single best method of teaching, just as there is no single kind of student. However, the method utilized will affect the type of learning which occurs. Recall the basic difference between the direct and indirect approach in developing thinking ability. In selecting teaching methods and forms, consideration must be given to the primary objective of the lesson, the nature of the students and the available environment. The ability to vary instructional methodology to meet the appropriate needs of the individual class circumstances is part of the art of teaching. The extent to which the teacher is flexible in altering the approach depends upon his ability to analyze the situation at hand, to produce the various teacher behaviors and his willingness to try new approaches. The development of any technique or method is itself a learned skill which requires the same trial, feedback and alteration necessary in motor skill learning. Realization of this fact should aid the teacher in dealing with the dissatisfaction which often accompanies the first attempts to teach a new skill in a more creative way. The best possible teaching method may not prove entirely successful on the initial trial. Only practice and refinement can produce the wide repertoire of effective teaching procedures that all outstanding teachers possess.

---

[2]Fait, Hollis F.: *Physical Education for the Elementary School Child Experiences in Movement*. 2nd Ed. W. B. Saunders Co., Philadelphia, Pa. 1971, pp. 113–114.

NEW TEACHING DESIGNS

The age of stereotyped physical education programs offering a limited number of activities and organized in traditional ways is nearing an end. Every year more and more school systems are experimenting with new approaches to instructional physical education. Some of these, elective programs, independent study and individualized instruction, represent alterations in content while others, such as contract teaching, team teaching and the use of teacher aides, are changes in conduct of programs.

ELECTIVE PHYSICAL EDUCATION

The most popular redirection in the design of physical education programs has occurred with the concept of elective programs. Elective opportunities range from student selection of courses from among a few alternative offerings to a completely elective, nonrequired program in physical education. In some schools activities are selected from several broad groups, one course from each group being required. Common groupings include: team sports, individual lifetime sports, gymnastics/dance and aquatics. At the other extreme, some schools have constructed elective programs which simultaneously offer a variety of activities from which students can make daily selections. In this instance, instructors are available to assist students on an individual basis but there is little organized instruction. The concept of elective offerings has, if nothing else, served to expand the offerings in many schools and in this way provided students an opportunity to select activities suited to their individual needs and interests.

INDEPENDENT STUDY

The concept of an independent study option allows students to engage in sport, dance and exercise opportunities not possible within the confines of the existing school. This program enables students to gain physical education credit for experiences conducted away from the school complex. Typical possibilities include organized and approved instruction in skiing, ice skating, ballet, modern dance, tennis, fencing and so on. The idea is that, if a student has identified a legitimate activity selection which is not available in the school, is able to make the arrangements for professional instruction and can reach agreement with a regular faculty member as to an appropriate amount of work and a means of evaluating achievement, credit for physical education can be earned outside the regular school program.

Most schools do not allow students to meet the entire requirement in this manner but will approve one semester or a year of this type of extension work. Independent study offers the possibility for increased variety over and above what the school could ever offer. It also provides the opportunity for advanced instruction when an advanced class is not feasible.

In individualized instruction programs, students may be allowed to elect areas of study; however, once having selected an area each student is tested or diagnosed as to his current abilities. Based on this evaluation he begins with a prescribed set of experiences appropriate to his level. Most of his practice and study is self-directed in that he follows printed instructions and is provided with periodic means of self-evaluation through performance tests, audio-visual feedback devices and/or peer assessment. As he completes prescribed activities, he is re-evaluated by the teacher, who then recommends new activities or further attention to incomplete parts of past activities. This plan allows students to work at levels appropriate to their needs and for a class to be engaged in a variety of activities simultaneously.

TEAM TEACHING

Team teaching represents an effort to utilize the special talents of the faculty in a more productive way than the traditional arrangement of each teacher giving instruction in all phases of the course to each of his assigned classes. In one form of team teaching, the faculty member most qualified in a given unit conducts the major instruction of that unit, while the other teachers assist with the practice phase. In another form of this design, each teacher concentrates on his or her specialties and teaches them to all classes. Thus, Mr. X teaches all the advanced swimming, while Ms. Y teaches all tennis instruction. Students then have both Mr. X and Ms. Y for their respective specialities rather than both teachers instructing both activities for their group of students.

A number of schools are currently utilizing teaching teams that include noncertified personnel as well as professional teachers. Under this variation of the design, the former are known as teacher aides and work as clerks, lay readers and graders to relieve instructors of many nonteaching duties. This arrangement is particularly advantageous in that it enables teachers to make the best use of and to further develop their individual talents. There is a vast difference between *team* teaching and *turn* teaching, in which teachers do not plan together, but instead separately develop and teach single units or activities.

Teacher Aides. An increasing number of school systems employ teacher aides to assist the instructors. Since their work does not require the same degree of professional knowledge or skill development, the aides are utilized to free the teacher of such tasks as caring for and moving equipment and supplies, calling roll, grading objective tests and supervising routine activities. Being freed from these time-consuming tasks, the teacher has more time to study, plan and prepare lessons as well as give individual attention to students. Since the physical educators in any system usually work longer hours than most teachers, conducting after-school programs and coaching school teams, the use of teacher aides is particularly beneficial to them.

CONTRACT TEACHING

Contract teaching is a design that attempts to provide alternative routes to achieving grades in physical education. It involves selecting all feasible experiences for a given unit of instruction and assigning each a value. Grades for the unit are based on the total point value earned by the student. The student may earn the points for a grade through any combination of experiences. In this way both the teacher and the student are aware of exactly what amount of work and achievement will be required for each grade. They have made a contract that X units of achievement = Y grade. In most systems a variety of means for earning points is identified. This allows individuals to pursue various means toward achieving their grades. Certain students could earn a large percentage of their points through cognitive knowledge about the activities, while others might capitalize on skill development. Both are important learnings and should receive attention in the grading scheme.

The development of new, innovative approaches to physical education instruction should be regarded with favor since they encourage closer examination of our process and product. Traditional approaches are not necessarily the best possibilities. On the other hand, time-tested techniques should not be recklessly abandoned for any new idea presented.

LARGE GROUP INSTRUCTION

Although school enrollments appear to be decreasing, large classes continue to be a prevailing trend, resulting largely from budgetary pressures that preclude the hiring of additional teachers. Consequently, physical educators must be prepared to provide programs that will serve students effectively regardless of the number in their classes. Successful large group instruction requires careful planning, preparation and presentation on the part of the teacher. Flexibility and willingness to experiment are also essential.

Some types of instructional procedures can be used as easily in a large class as in a small one, including lectures, panel discussions, demonstrations, films and other types of visual aids, reviewing and writing examinations. All can be readily administered to a large class by a single teacher. Consequently, it is possible and feasible to present information about and to test knowledge of those portions of a course that are essentially factual, such as rules, strategy, historical development, health concepts and playing courtesies, utilizing a teaching procedure appropriate to a large group.

For the development of motor skills, however, there is a need for the number of students per teacher to be small enough to receive individual attention and assistance. A more desirable ratio can be effected through the use of some of the new designs described previously. Particularly effective for this purpose are team teaching and the use of teacher aides. Independent study and contract teaching are other examples that offer a means of providing individual development to students in a large class whom it might otherwise not be possible to serve as fully.

GUIDES TO EFFECTIVE TEACHING

The quality of teaching is directly related to the effectiveness of the planning and conduct of the learning experiences. The chart below outlines the important considerations that influence good planning and presentation of physical education activities and ultimately determine to considerable extent the effectiveness of the teacher.

CHART OF GUIDELINES

I. Planning Instruction
 1. Account for the readiness of the learners in question, their maturational level, prior experiences and motivation.
 2. Plan for instruction to progress from the simple to the complex, gross to refined, large to small. Adapt these to the individual levels of students.
 3. Allow sufficient time for overlearning of skills to enhance retention.
 4. Arrange for maximum opportunity for activity and equipment.
II. Early Skill Acquisition
 1. Clearly identify the goal or task to be achieved and make known its value.
 2. Attempt to motivate students toward the activity. They must see the activity as important, desirable and meaningful. The teacher's emotional involvement and obvious enthusiasm for the activity is contagious.
 3. Demonstrate a skill with the best possible form and at full speed before breaking it down into components or performing in slow

motion. This imparts the gross movement idea. Repeat demonstration several times, possibly from different angles or perspectives.

4. Keep verbal instructions and explanations to a minimum in early learning stages; focus student attention on the main objective. A few key phrases descriptive of the essential movements are valuable.

5. Provide frequent reinforcement in early attempts. Success is a powerful motivator.

6. Attempt to correct the most significant errors early in the learning. Small points and fine control can come later.

7. Do not overcorrect. One or two bits of information are about all the novice can process at one time.

8. Provide drills which focus on the one skill in question and which maximize student practice time.

9. Allow opportunity to use the new skills in the game or modified game situation even if not highly developed. This is usually self-motivating and helps students see the meaningfulness of the activity.

10. Keep competition to a minimum during early learning. The declaring of winners and losers as well as subjecting students to ridicule produces significant negative reinforcement in the activity. Competition causes anxiety in many students that interferes with the learning of complex skills.

11. Have the students verbally or mentally rehearse a skill. This is often helpful since early learning requires conscious control of movements. Simply having a student repeat the direction is a good check on what he has absorbed.

12. Keep practice on one specific skill short. Spaced practices are more effective than massed practices in the acquisition phase of skill learning. The optimal length of practice can be increased as the maturation, motivation and competency of the learner increase.

III. Later Skill Development

1. Attempt to involve the student intellectually; communicate the why of the skill form as well as the underlying mechanical principles and so on.

2. Encourage self-analysis of performance by the students. Ask them about what went wrong and why.

3. Provide more complex and detailed verbal instruction and corrections. After succeeding in the basic movement these now have meaning to the student.

4. Direct attention to specific parts and fine points of the movement pattern.

5. Schedule longer practice periods since students are now more conditioned to the activity and interest is presumably high at this skill level.

6. Use competition as a method of skill assessment to point up weaknesses in performance that require correction for continued improvement.

7. Provide for extensive directed practice for (a) closed skills, in which the movements should be highly repetitive and closely analyzed to perfect the exact movement pattern and (b) open skills, in which practice in a variety of conditions indicative of the ones occurring in the sport should be utilized to develop diversity in the use of the skill.

DISCUSSION QUESTIONS

1. What personal qualities do you believe are necessary for successful teaching?
2. What are the essential steps a student progresses through in learning a motor skill?
3. What are the characteristic differences between the direct and indirect methods of teaching?
4. Is there one best teaching method? Explain.
5. How might cognitive involvement aid motor skill development?

THINGS TO DO

1. Write a brief description of your understanding of how learning takes place.
2. Select a sport skill and indicate how the seven steps in the student behavior sequence (Fig. 4--1) would be accomplished.
3. Select one step of the motor learning sequence and explain in detail how the teacher can aid the student at that point.
4. Choose a step in the motor learning sequence and contrast how a teacher might accomplish it, using the direct method as opposed to the indirect method.
5. Observe a physical education class. Identify the predominant teaching method and form utilized. Give examples.

SUGGESTED READINGS

AAHPER: *Organizational Patterns for Instruction in Physical Education.* Washington, D.C., 1971.

Cratty, Bryant: *Movement Behavior and Motor Learning.* 2nd Ed., Philadelphia, Lea and Febiger, 1967.

Gentile, A. M.: A Working Model of Skill Acquisition with Application to Teaching. *Quest,* March, 1972.

Hamache, Don: Characteristics of Good Teachers and Implications for Teacher Education. *Phi Delta Kappan,* February, 1969.

Mosston, Muska: *Teaching Physical Education.* Charles E. Merrill Publishing Co., 1966.

Steeves, Frank: *Readings in the Methods of Education.* New York, The Odyssey Press, 1964.

CHAPTER FIVE

TEACHING AIDS

Physical education learning experiences become more memorable through the proper use of supplementary teaching aids. Each teacher should have a variety of good instructional materials but should remember that the mere exposure to them will not insure learning. All such materials should assist students to learn and should not be used as a means of entertainment. When properly used, such aids can increase the depth, permanence and speed of learning.

All carefully selected audio-visual aids should give a true picture of the idea they present, contribute more meaningful materials to the unit or sport for which they are used, be appropriate for the intelligence of the class, have eye and ear appeal, and be well worth the time, effort and expense of obtaining and using them.

There are many different kinds of teaching aids. Some of the best ones to use in teaching physical education include:

Scrapbooks	Diagrams	Microscopes
Specimens (live and preserved)	Charts	Mirrors
	Graphs	Comics
Pamphlets	Maps	Collections
Bulletin boards	Flashcards	Radio
Chalkboards	Mobiles	Templates
Flannel and felt boards	Flat pictures	Television
	Newspaper and magazine clippings	Recordings
Flip-it books	Filmstrips	Models
Posters	Photographs	Exhibits
Cartoons	Public address systems	Slides
Stick figures and drawings	Magnetic model board	Films
Opaque projector		Writing pads

MATERIAL SOURCES

There is an abundance of free and inexpensive materials in both health and physical education, and the problem for many teachers is to select, catalogue and find the best ways to utilize them.[1] The wise educator starts his own collection while still a college student, for such materials will help him to feel more secure in his first teaching experience. All teachers should subscribe to professional journals and daily newspapers and take several good magazines, as well as be ever on the lookout for supplementary materials and teaching aids they might use in their classes. Visiting suppliers' exhibits at conventions, on the local as well as the national level, will prove beneficial, especially for bringing one up to date on available new teaching aids.

Students should contribute even more than the teacher to the collection of materials, and will do so if encouraged to bring to class and share with the group things they have found outside of school which pertain to what they are studying. Friends and parents can also contribute many materials for class use but will need to be informed of the type of things needed.

The list of suggested readings at the end of this chapter will prove helpful to the teacher who wishes to make his own supplementary class materials for use with students.

RECOMMENDED MATERIALS

Each teacher should discover which type of supplementary materials can be used most profitably with each class. Regardless of which type of aid is selected, its use should be made as personalized as possible. Seeing one's own teeth in a magnifying mirror may be a splendid motivator for most youth, but not for all in each class. Gadgets which can be turned, buttons which can be pushed, and wooden flaps which must be lifted up in order to see what they hide, are all fascinating to students and might well be used in conjunction with each teaching unit.

TEXTBOOKS AND OTHER WRITTEN MATERIALS

Many schools have adopted textbooks for their physical education classes, such as *Physical Education For High School Students*, available from the AAHPER, or various booklets in sports, such as those available in the Saunders Physical Activities Series.[2] These cover more than 19 different sports, for instance, golf and swimming. Textbooks, like worksheets and task cards, can be a time saver of precious class periods,

---

[1]See the appendix for a list of sources of free and inexpensive audio-visual aids.

[2]Write to the W. B. Saunders Publishing Company, West Washington Square, Philadelphia, for more information about these materials.

for on their own students can learn game rules, safety requirements and so on outside of class and thus have more time in class for learning movement skills.

MOTION PICTURES

This communication medium can be one of the finest ways to stimulate interest in the field of physical education when used correctly. Although it is no doubt true that one picture is worth a thousand words, it must be remembered that one direct, purposeful experience is far superior to many pictures. Most state departments of education have a wide variety of health and physical education films which are available upon request and, increasingly, more are developing audio-visual aid branch libraries. The majority of our large school systems have their own film libraries and have stocked them with carefully

Figure 5–1. The use of well-selected films in schools can increase the whole climate of instruction, learning efficiency and retention, as well as reading ability and comprehension.

selected pictures suitable for students on each grade level. State universities, private colleges, city, county and state health departments, voluntary youth-serving agencies, commercial organizations and local libraries also have well-selected films which are available upon request. The U.S. Office of Education Film Library Directory lists free films that can be obtained for use in the classroom.

The use of well-selected films in the schools can increase the whole climate of instruction, learning efficiency and retention, as well as reading ability and comprehension.

Factors to keep in mind when selecting a motion picture to show to a class are that it must:

1. Be suited to the age level of the group and have high educational value.
2. Contain accurate, authoritative information.
3. Give pupils a more complete understanding of the activity they are studying than they could get elsewhere.
4. Be well organized, heard distinctly, and well photographed.
5. Fit the purposes, needs and interests of the students.
6. Be of suitable length.
7. Be up to date. (This is especially important in selecting films for secondary students.)

The pupils should see the film when they can most profit from this experience, and the teacher should preview it before showing it to the group so he can best direct the pupils' attention to the important things to look for in the picture. Likewise, he should give a brief résumé of the film content, doing so in a manner which will increase interest. He should be a skilled projectionist and know what to do when the film jumps or breaks or when any other kind of emergency occurs. Nothing destroys the effectiveness of a film more than these irritating mishaps. Certain interested students can be taught how to operate the projector. This is not only a good means for keeping truancy at a minimum on film-showing days but also can be a way to provide status-securing opportunities to those unskilled and mentally slower students who are attracted to machines and have an all-consuming desire to master their many mysteries. During the showing, the room should be well ventilated and darkened, and the viewers seated so that they can both see and hear well. The teacher should place himself in the best position to watch pupils' reactions to the picture.

After the film has been seen, the instructor should review the main features, either doing so himself or drawing out the entire group by asking pertinent questions, calling upon one student to summarize the main points emphasized, or by a simple paper and pencil objective test. It is recommended that such procedures be followed up with experiments, posters, bulletin board materials or creative activities devised around factual materials or concepts learned from seeing the film.

PROGRAMED MATERIALS AND TEACHING MACHINES

These materials are somewhat similar to workbooks. A mechanical device, often referred to as a teaching machine, is used to hold the material and advance framed questions when the student turns the knob. After the student writes the answer and turns the knob the correct answer appears. The student's answer is covered by a window and cannot be changed. The use of programed materials is based upon two important principles of learning: learning is more rapid when attempts to master material to be learned are rewarded, and students proceed from one learning task to another in learning graded materials at their own rate of speed, and, consequently, learn more effectively.

Although in its infancy, the use of programed materials in the fields of health and physical education have tremendous educational possibilities.[3] They are especially good for helping students become more responsible for their own learning progress. Studies show that some students make remarkable knowledge gains through this teaching method but this method is not suitable for all students, for some need more direct help as well as encouragement from the teacher, while they are struggling to learn.

FILMSTRIPS

These have many advantages over motion pictures in that they are less expensive, easily shown, and often made to supplement a particular textbook series or sports book. Many commercial companies have free filmstrips for classroom use.[4] Suggestions for making the best educational use of motion pictures also apply to the showing of filmstrips and slides.

Students can make their own filmstrips by cutting up old ones and rearranging the pictures. They can also create their own homemade cartoons by drawing pictures in a series on a long piece of paper, rolling it on a rod, and showing it by using a carboard carton with a window cut in the front for the screen.

---

[3]Patrick Suppes: "Computer-Based Instruction." *Education Digest,* October, 1967, p. 8.

[4]See the appendix for a list of companies handling filmstrips.

VIDEO TAPES AND CASETTES

Both of these are valuable teaching aids, if used correctly. It is important to plan well in advance when the best time is to use them in a unit. Both class discussions and individual conferences should be utilized during and after their use. Video tapes can give the learner instant feedback of movement errors and learning progress. Casettes are ideal for dance and rhythms classes but can also be used, if carefully selected, when teaching sports.

SLIDES

Although there is an abundance of slides available, the best ones are often made by the students themselves, for many have their own cameras and are skilled photographers. Commercial companies also have slides either for sale or for rent at a nominal fee. Students can also make their own pen and ink sketches on glass slides and see their own creative work on a screen. An automatic slide changer is recommended for classroom use, since it can be timed perfectly with any brief comments the teacher wishes to make about the slides being seen and it frees the teacher from the work of projectionist.

THE OPAQUE PROJECTOR

Newspaper clippings, charts, graphs, examples of student work or any other type of written or printed materials can be magnified and shown on a screen by the use of these inexpensive machines. Students respond quickly to having their own or a friend's best work shown to others in the group in this manner. The teaching of game rules is especially effective with this device.

DIAL ACCESS AND PUSH-BUTTON LESSONS

This new teaching tool, although expensive, has almost unlimited possibilities for self-instruction by students. Using a headset and sitting in a pentagon-shaped carrel, the student presses buttons or turns dials to hear and or see audio-video material, films, charts or other materials, while at the same time referring to guide sheets or workbooks to collect needed information. This technique is ideal for teaching the history, rules, and game strategy of sports.

TELEVISION

No other communication medium has grown so rapidly as television. As an educational device, it is powerful and potent—whether for good or evil—for it can and does produce positive as well as negative results. Increasingly in schools students and teachers are being given opportunities to see as well as hear master teachers conduct master lessons and sport champions play in national tournaments. Educational television is growing rapidly in all states at the present time. Teachers who work in schools without classroom sets can guide students to watch worthwhile and unique programs in their own homes or elsewhere and report back to the group things they have heard and seen that pertain to the areas they are studying in school. Television teaching in physical education has many possibilities but needs careful planning and direction.[5]

Closed circuit television programs are now being used successfully for educational purposes. In using this medium each student benefits from having two teachers, a live one and the studio teacher. Television makes it possible for more students to be taught by superior teachers. It is an ideal method for a teacher to demonstrate skills to a large group of students, who may be divided into small sub-groups assigned to various practice rooms rather than being part of a big class watching the screen in a large gymnasium. Using such a system, each smaller sub-group could then practice the skills they have seen demonstrated and be helped to learn them correctly by paraprofessional teaching aids or by their own classmates who are more skilled squad leaders.

RADIO BROADCASTS

In order that students may be guided to listen to worthwhile radio broadcasts, the teacher should obtain as much advance information about specific programs as possible. Assigning them to do some research before listening to any particular broadcast is highly recommended, as well as are follow-up assignments and class discussions of things heard either independently or in a group.

In order to retain broadcasting permits, all radio stations must devote a certain per cent of their total scheduled time to educational programs. Consequently, many local stations are now using school-sponsored broadcasts in which programs are planned and presented

---

[5]Department of Physical Education for Women, University of Illinois: *A Study of the Effectiveness of Televised Instruction in a Physical Education Activity Course.* Stipes Publishing Company, Champaign, Ill., 1962.

by the pupils themselves, assisted by their teachers. Such programs are not only an excellent means of maintaining a high level of pupil interest in health, fitness and physical education but also increase parental support of these activities.

RECORDINGS

Phonograph records and tape recordings can provide rich learning experiences. Records are especially ideal for classroom work, for the teacher can stop them in order to discuss or repeat certain passages heard previously; they can be played over and over again, can be preheard and evaluated, and can even be made by the pupils themselves assisted by their instructor. Making a tape recording of a class or panel discussion can be an enlightening experience, for hearing his own voice helps each youth become conscious of needs for improvement. Recording the talks given by visiting authorities or experts heard on a radio helps to motivate pupil interest and makes them more aware of the high regard well-known adults have for good health and physical education programs, and these tapes can be used for the benefit of both present and future classes.

The teacher using these recordings should prepare the listeners for the coming experience, sift out and refine what important things have been heard and relate them, insofar as possible, to the actual life of each listening student. There are numerous helpful guides and manuals, issued by leading manufactures of tape recordings, which the teacher should study carefully before using this type of equipment. Finding the best recording distances and speaker positions in relation to the microphone, having all speak in a clear but natural conversational manner, eliminating background noises as much as possible by recording in rooms where echoes can be reduced by drapes, screens or acoustical tile, and taping the entire program without interruptions will all improve the quality of any recording made at school.

Tape recorders are ideal for dance and synchronized swimming classes. They can also be used in calisthenic drills, for recording minutes of meeting, speeches for assembly and radio programs, convention talks, and a "talking" exhibit.

The record player has become standard equipment in most schools and the supply of available records is becoming more complete each year. The most satisfactory machine has a speed regulator and will play 16, 33⅓, 45 and 78 r.p.m. records.

Best use of records:
1. Buy records that carry six to eight rhymes, singing games or dances. Albums seem expensive but are actually economical because of the number of

recordings on each record. The playing time on a standard 78 record, although too long for the elementary grade children, is suitable for advanced groups.

2. Play record and clap rhythms lightly, accenting change of phrasing with a heavy clap.

3. Dance with prescribed steps. Listen to music. Do first step without music, then with music. Master and proceed to second step. Do first and second, etc.

PUBLIC ADDRESS SYSTEMS

These are found in most schools. They can be used at football, basketball and other games, swimming and wrestling events to increase spectator knowledge and enjoyment. Swimming instructors as well as playground leaders often find this device helpful in directing and controlling groups. Music and dance programs can be improved by having:

1. The machine ready to use beforehand. (Saying "testing 1-2-3" is better than blowing into the mike.)

2. The amplifier and turntable nearby.

3. The volume turned on correctly, realizing that the class will absorb some of the sound.

4. This equipment used in rooms which best absorb sounds.

5. The speakers placed so they do not face each other and are one or two feet above the heads of the audience.

6. The microphone far enough from the speaker to eliminate any squeaking or other distracting noises.

7. The volume greatly increased for outdoor use.

THE PIANO

The piano is excellent for accompaniment because the teacher can accent each beat, stop at any time, and take up again at the same place. The use of the piano requires special talent, aside from the ability to play, because instruction and demonstration must be interwoven with the accompaniment, requiring a great deal of change from piano to floor. It is ideal in schools where an accompanist is available.

PICTURES AND POSTERS

Pictures and posters should be pleasant to see many times over, have aesthetic appeal and power. There is a wealth of free posters now available for classroom use.[6] Even students unskilled in art can

[6]1966–67 National Safety Council: *Safety Materials Catalog and Poster Directory.* Single copies free. Available from the National Safety Council, 425 North Michigan Ave., Chicago, Illinois, 60611, Stock Number 5016-103.

cut out pictures and use them to make a poster, whereas those talented in this area can and should create a whole display themselves. Traced figures, cut out silhouettes, montages made from pictures, articles or newspaper headlines, stenciled or created lettering, the use of pipe cleaner stick figures, cotton, or other materials can be used effectively. Those who seemingly gain much from this type of experience should be encouraged to develop real skill in this medium of communication.

Commercial posters must be selected with care. Some schools have rules prohibiting the use of any visual aids or other supplementary materials which contain advertising. Many companies who supply free materials have obligingly printed their firm's name in small letters in a bottom corner so that, if necessary, this can easily be blocked out or covered over.

Effective posters, whether they be pupil created or obtained from other sources, are those which:

1. Contain a short, simplified idea or message.
2. Create a learning atmosphere.
3. Motivate action.
4. Give accurate, attention-getting information.
5. Emphasize the importance of doing a certain thing or developing a good health habit.
6. Possess eye appeal.
7. Create a lasting impression.

Photographs taken either by the teacher or pupils can provide meaningful educational experiences. Some teachers have discovered that the most effective way to motivate interest and a desire to develop good posture is to take an individual snapshot of each student as she stands before a wall, frontward and sideward. If this method is used, a conference should be held with each student and each asked to look closely at her own photograph as together she and the teacher pick out her postural assets and defects. Next, each should be shown ways to correct difficulties. The class can later select pictures of those in their group who had the best posture, and the photographs can be used for a bulletin board display on posture.

CARTOONS, COMICS, SKETCHES AND STICK FIGURES

Three kinds of simple drawings which can easily be made by most students are those that show faces, figures and objects. Each should be drawn with the definite purpose in mind of getting an important message across quickly and effectively. A cartoon should be used to exaggerate, to show the artist as being strongly opposed to or favorable toward a certain action or idea. Such pictures are especially fine to use with slow learners who need help in gaining understanding of needed information, especially when the teacher helps them to get the point of the drawing they are seeing. Carefully chosen comics or strip drawings which appear in newspapers or magazines can be used effectively with this group also, for often they can be strongly motivated to develop certain positive habits because sport or movie heroes or heroines urge them to do so.

CHARTS AND GRAPHS

A chart is a diagrammatic visual rearrangement of materials which is prepared so that one can see relationships or sequences of events more clearly and easily. The types of charts used most frequently are *time charts* (a traveler's itinerary), *tree or stream charts* (a genealogical tree), *organizational charts* (a line and staff personnel drawing), *and comparison or contrast charts* (height and weight tables). A chart should be simple, easily read and interpreted, and clearly labeled. Students can make their own charts and show them on an opaque projector by drawing or tracing them. To use charts effectively in teaching it is vitally important that the instructor help each learner to see the meaning of the chart in relationship to herself. For instance, a student will have this educational experience when she sees her own height and weight in relationship to a desired standard.

Although often confused with tables, graphs are diagrammatic methods of showing *numerical* data which show quantitative comparisons in forms of bars, geometric shapes or pictorial symbols so that one viewing them can quickly see relationships between figures. There are various ways to help youth grasp the significance of figures when comparing things. These include *bar graphs, figure graphs,* containing pictures of human beings, animals, birds or fish, with each one representing so many others of the same kind, *pie charts,* and *line or curve graphs.* These can be obtained commercially, collected from books or other printed sources, or a pupil can make his own.

Dale gives the following suggestions to teachers so that they might make the best use of statistical data when showing it in graph form.[7]

1. Each symbol should be self-explanatory.
2. Large quantities should be shown by a larger number of symbols and not by an enlarged symbol.
3. Only approximate quantities should be compared, not minute details.
4. Only comparisons should be charted, not isolated elements.

---

[7]Dale, Edgar: *Audio-Visual Methods in Teaching.* Revised edition. New York, The Dryden Press, 1964, p. 334.

Some possibilities for the use of graphs in physical education are to show:
1. Individual and/or group progress.
2. Attendance figures, individual height and weight recordings, student progress and achievement.
3. Tournament standings, number of participants and spectator attendance at various sport events throughout the year.
4. Physical fitness and motor ability test scores.

All secondary students should be taught carefully how to read and interpret graphs correctly. One of the best ways to do this is to have them make their own graphs using simple stick figures or lines. Give each one an assigned task such as making a series of stick figure drawings to show how many hours of out-of-doors play or sleep they had each day for a week and then showing this on a bar graph to the rest of the class. All will enjoy making pie charts or other types of graphs from reading assignments given them by their teacher and experimenting with different kinds of colors and materials in order to present accurate information and most successfully make use of their chosen medium.

FLASHCARDS

Flashcards used to gain quick pupil response should be 13" × 22" in size, eggshell color, easily read or seen, and attractive. They can be used for learning officiating hand signals, proper whistle use, reaction timing, rules for testing sports knowledges and for reviewing in preparation for final examinations.

SIMULATION AND GAMING

These are different from other methods of presenting information, for instead of the student being the receptor and the teacher the transmitter, the student, through trial-and-error, attempts to solve problems caused by interrelated actions, such as a series of errors made by his teammates that the quaterback must· rectify in a game.

Simulation games are used more in the social sciences than in other disciplines but do have great possibilities in the field of physical education. Such games, however, must be used as complements to other learning methods. Educational games can offer many opportunities for students to be involved in system analyses in which problems must be continually analyzed and restated as new information and situations occur. They are ideal for teaching students to analyze problems through creative thinking.

DIAGRAMS AND DRAWINGS

These help to inform students quickly and effectively. They can be prepared before as well as in class on chalkboards, writing and sketching pads, window shades or feltboards. They should be large and placed so that all students can see them. Diagrams are especially effective in teaching team play and tactics in sports.

MIRRORS

Mirrors enable students to see themselves and their movements. They are especially good as an aid in teaching posture and body mechanics, fencing, ballet and modern dance. They should be movable, and several full-length mirrors hinged together will permit viewing from various angles. By attaching one mirror to a wall and hanging another one 10 to 12 feet out from it face-to-face with the first and on a 20 to 40° angle, with the bottom edge the greater distance out, students can view their movement from the rear. The height and angle of the mirror can be adjusted by ropes and a pulley to the necessary height for the students using it.[8]

MAPS

These can also be used more effectively in the area of health education than in physical education and may be commercial maps purchased by the school or made by the students themselves. Drawing maps showing the route each student uses to come to school, locating playing field hazards on a map, showing traffic hazards on state highways or city streets in one's own town can be a profitable learning experience for youth. Such endeavors will help each to see his school, town or city as a whole, gain a clearer concept of where he lives in relationship to hospitals or fire stations, or become more cognizant of hazards or dangers found at school or while coming to or leaving there.

BULLETIN AND OTHER BOARDS

Modern classrooms usually have large, colorful bulletin boards on which examples of students' work can be attractively displayed. Such

---

[8]AAHPER: *Audio-Visual Materials for Physical Education.* Washington, D.C., 1964, p. 58.

boards can be used as a means of bringing new or current events to the attention of the class, showing parents and other adults what pupils are doing in school, as well as giving youth an area in the classroom or gymnasium that is their primary responsibility to use creatively and well. Class projects, which can be planned around a physical fitness or leisure time use unit, may take several days of classwork with pupils assigned to various committees. Such an educational adventure should be carefully thought through and the class should have definite objectives in mind as they determine how they can find out what they want to know. Wide reading, visits to places of importance to that particular project, interviews, and many other kinds of experiences can become a vital part of such units. A bulletin board committee should be responsible for displaying new materials or the final work of the class on any such project. The success of such a learning experience depends largely on the teacher's ability to spark student interest into a flame. The students will need as much guidance and encouragement as possible, and the teacher should assist them by showing how the bulletin board can be used most effectively and functionally in order to reach general and specific learning objectives. Shared evaluation, often called "action research," should be used throughout such projects and viewed as a means of "getting the lay of the land" in relationship to where the group wants to go educationally.

Any bulletin board can become a potently effective communicative device if it can:

1. Get an important message across through the means of well-selected and displayed materials.
2. Attract and hold attention in such a way that it becomes a living and frequently changed media for reaching others.
3. Stimulate thought, motivate action, and increase knowledge.

Bulletin boards can be used for announcements and for displaying student work, poster-type materials, short-term projects and mural-type art work. Since youth learns mostly from direct experiences, *they* should keep their class bulletin boards up to date and full of interesting and worthwhile materials which have esthetic, cultural and educational value.

THE CHALKBOARD

This can be used fully as a means of helping students to learn well when one keeps the following suggestions in mind:

1. Keep the board clean.
2. Be sure that all can see what is written or drawn on it.

3. Use class time to the fullest extent. Do not waste it by using half a period making a chart but rather do this before the class begins unless there is special value to be gained from having the pupils participate in its construction.

4. Get an idea or fact over to the students quickly. Accurate, time-consuming drawings done to scale can be a waste of time if a quickly drawn stick figure can accomplish the same purpose.

5. Prepare an entire board in advance, cover it and remove parts of the cover singly as a means of stimulating interest. Use such a trick sparingly, however.

6. Avoid putting too much on the board at one time.

7. Write key words, new words or key phrases on the board as you discuss things in class, remembering that what students hear *and* see becomes more meaningful to them.

8. Have your pupils use the board often and encourage them to discuss well what they have written or drawn there for the benefit of the group.

COLLECTIONS AND SPECIMENS

Encourage pupils to become experts in their chosen academic and leisure time interest fields, even though these may frequently change, for by doing so they can spur on the desire to learn and take part in positive and re-creative recreation and can often change awakening interests from a faltering step into a rollicking gallop.

Making a specimen collection can become an interesting and valuable education experience. Youth enjoys and profits from bringing to class real objects to supplement pictures found in textbooks. Since most of our learning comes through the senses, it is important that students touch and feel as well as see and hear about the many wonders of nature.

It is important that any collection be more than a gathering of dead things. Youth can be helped by teachers to see life and meaning even in a mounted fish or a stuffed owl. As Whitehead points out, a student should never be taught more than he can think and wonder about. Thus, a teacher should guide youth to well-presented and carefully selected learning aids which have been tailored to fit both their interest span and comprehension level. He, aided by a committee of pupils, should sort through, select and arrange well those collections and specimens students find and bring to class which can best serve as an educational aid for the entire group.

MODELS

Models are created as an imitation of a real thing and are usually made on a smaller or larger scale than the actual object they represent. A magnetic playing field board used in the teaching of hockey, football, basketball or soccer is a model, as is an enlarged replica of the human heart made of plaster of Paris. Such aids can be used for show-ing relationships which range all the way from the systems of the human body to the parts of the human brain. They serve chiefly, however, as a means of motivating interest and gaining a clearer understanding and appreciation of subject matter materials.

Magnetized playing field boards are invaluable in the teaching of court and field dimensions and boundaries, player position, game strategies, court and field maneuvers of each individual team member, rules, and for testing player understanding of team play.[9]

Many commercial firms now have splendid models available which show various parts of the human body. Some of these are available in cross sectional form, or in parts which fit together and can be separated so that each piece may be examined singly and relation-ships clearly seen. Cutaway models, or those which show what the "inside" of any body part looks like are also available and are relatively inexpensive.

Youths need opportunities to make their own models and experi-ment with clay, papier-mâché, soap carving, wooden blocks, plasticene, flour and water paste, plastics and other materials. The teacher must encourage them in as many ways as possible in their attempts to gain a clearer, better understanding of health, fitness, physical education and recreation and their importance to their daily lives, and aids should be used to the degree that this can be better accomplished. Caution must be exercised, however, since the mere making of a teaching aid can become an end in itself and "making things for class" can all too quickly become meaningless busy work. Likewise, the teacher needs to be sure that the learner's attention is directed from any model to the actual thing it was meant to represent and that he sees the relation-ship of that object to his own life and general well-being.

EXHIBITS

Exhibits can help spread the physical education message. They may be used to display school trophies won in athletic and intramural contests, various kinds of sporting equipment, uniforms, protective devices, first aid or other types of safety equipment, and pictures of outstanding students. Exhibits should be well placed (preferably at the entry of a building, near the gymnasium or pool), colorful and well lighted, and should express a single idea or theme. Tape recordings and phonograph records can be used as attention getters and for mu-sical background. Exhibits can also be set up in store windows, public buildings such as a library, and at fairs, meetings and conventions.

---

[9]Available from *Program Aids,* 550 5th Ave., New York, N.Y. 10036.

FIELD TRIPS

Trips taken by classes to see gymnastic meets, finals in tennis or golf matches, city recreational facilities or other events connected with classwork have high educational value but only when they are carefully planned, are an adjunct to what is being learned at school, are taken for a definite purpose which is clearly understood by the pupils and are evaluated carefully. The school should have written policies governing all out-of-school trips. Carefully planned field trips can:

1. Encourage exploration and interest.
2. Develop better student understanding.
3. Cultivate careful observational habits.
4. Provide accurate firsthand information.
5. Give more meaning to classwork experiences.
6. Provide opportunities for vocational and leisure time guidance.
7. Promote intelligent citizenship.
8. Strengthen community ties.
9. Increase parental interest in schools and in what students are doing in physical education.

IMPLICATIONS FOR IMPROVED INSTRUCTION THROUGH THE USE OF TEACHING AIDS

Learning is a teacher-student responsibility. It is one of the major tasks of the modern school to help youth gain an understanding of what good health and physical education are and their importance to each individual and society, along with an appreciation of their value and the skills necessary for developing total well-being. Neither good health nor physical education is easily taught, nor are they, for the most part, now being taught adequately or well. Consequently, teachers on all educational levels must first develop a deeply sincere desire to become efficient and effective instructors in these important fields. Supplementary teaching aids, created mostly by the learners themselves, can and will add much to the educational value of classes in these programs, but only when and if they are used intelligently for a definite and positive educational purpose that is kept well in mind.

THINGS TO DO

1. Learn how to operate a movie projector and an opaque projector. Show a film to your classes and other materials on the opaque projector.
2. Plan and record a panel discussion on a tape recorder in class on the subject of physical fitness or the problems of increased leisure.

3. Working with one other person, make an attractive exhibit on physical education for a store window.

4. Working with another person, make a bulletin board display on intramural activities or on any health-related topic, such as the value of exercise or good nutrition in relation to being physically fit.

5. Present by means of diagrams on the chalkboard game strategy to use for any play in a team game.

SELECTED VISUAL AIDS

Films
Audio-Visual Aids in Teaching. Coronet Films.
Bulletin Boards for Effective Teaching. Extension Division, University of Iowa.
Chalkboard Utilization. Young America Films.
Feltboards in Teaching. Audio-Visual Material Consultation Bureau, Wayne University.
Field Trips. Virginia State Board of Education.
Instructional Films, The New Way to Greater Education. Coronet Films.

Filmstrips
How To Keep Your Bulletin Board Alive. Teaching Aids Laboratory, Ohio State University.
Making Your Chalk Talk. Audio-Visual Material Consultation Bureau, Wayne University.
Slidefilms in Teaching. Young America Films.

Periodicals
Audio-Visual Instruction. AAHPER Dept. of Audio-Visual Instruction.
Educational Screen and Audio-Visual Guide. 2000 Lincoln Park West, Chicago, Ill.

Sources of Information
Sport and Dance Films. Educational Film Library Association, 345 East 46th St., New York, N.Y.
Sport Film Guide. The Athletic Institute.
Visual Aids in Safety Education. The National Commission on Safety Education, 1201 16th St. N.W., Washington 6, D.C.

SUGGESTED READINGS

AAHPER, 1201 16th St., N.W., Washington, D.C.:
 Audio-Visual Materials for Physical Education, 1957.
 Loopfilms on Artificial Respiration and Loopfilms on Diving.
 Materials for Teaching Dance.
 Sport Teaching Aids: Audio-Visual Card Catalog.
 Basketball Rules for Girls.
 Softball Rules for Girls.
 Loopfilms on Diving for Girls and Women.
 Loopfilms on Synchronized Swimming.
American Medical Association: *A List of Sources of Film on the Subject of Health.* 535 N. Dearborn St., Chicago, Ill.
Babcock, Chester: "The Teacher, TV, and Teaching Machines." *NEA Journal,* May, 1960.
 Educator's Index of Free Films: Randolph, Wisconsin, Educators' Progress Service.
 Filmstrip Guide; Educational Film Guide. H. W. Wilson Company, 950 University Ave., New York, N.Y.

Flanigan, Thomas: *Teaching Aids for Health, Physical Education and Recreation.* Teaching Aids Library, Box 27, Mokena, Ill.

Leonard, George B., *Education and Ecstasy.* New York: Delacorte Press, 1968.

Thomas, R. Murray, and Swartout, Sherwin: *Integrated Teaching Materials.* New York, David McKay Company, 1963.

Weisgerber, Robert A. (Ed.), *Instructional Process and Media Innovation.* Skokie, Ill.: Rand McNally & Company, 1968.

Wittich, Walter A., and Charles F. Schuller, *Audiovisual Materials: Their Nature and Use,* 4th ed. New York: Harper & Row, Publishers, 1967.

PART TWO

ADMINISTRATIVE
DETAILS

Blessed is the leader who knows where he is going,
why he is going, and how to get there.

. . . . . from the NEA Manual for Locals

CHAPTER SIX

CLASS PROCEDURES

Carefully planned, routinized class procedures save both time and energy. Superior teachers are those who make the best use of each precious class hour to obtain desired results according to standards devised by their professional association and leading experts in their field.

Effective teaching results in meaningful student learning. Although it is too often true that the poorest teaching done in an entire school system is in the physical education department, it is also true that in some schools the best teaching is found there. If physical education is to gain a secure place in the school curriculum, the quality of professional programs must be greatly improved and teachers must do a better job of teaching in this area. Careful planning and good organization are basic to effective teaching of every class, every day, in every school week, in this and all other fields.

Since instructional periods are short, the teacher must find short-cuts in order to be able to devote the major part of every class period to teaching.

Conditioning students to respond quickly and automatically to habits of undressing and dressing, roll call procedures, checking equipment in or out, as well as numerous other automatic movement patterns saves many minutes in each class hour. The teacher, likewise, should condition herself to perform numerous marginal tasks necessary for teaching each class efficiently and effectively.

ROLL TAKING

If roll is taken, it should be done quickly and accurately. Suggested methods for doing so include:

1. By squads—the squad leader is responsible for finding out who is absent from his squad.
    Advantage: Allows for leadership training. Roll is taken quickly.
    Disadvantage: Could allow for cheating. The teacher does not learn students' names and faces so quickly.

  2. Seating plan—the teacher marks down names or numbers of vacant
       seating or standing places.
     Advantage: Fairly quick method for taking roll. The teacher is
       better able to coordinate names with faces.
     Disadvantage: Does not allow for leadership training. Takes more
       time than squad method.
  3. Roll call—the teacher calls the roll with students answering if present.
     Advantage: Teacher may learn students' names with very little
       effort. Teacher may be assured about who is present
       or absent.
     Disadvantage: Too time-consuming. Allows for no leadership training.
  4. Random formation and checking the role at varying times—the students
     sit anywhere they wish or are doing activities by knowing everyone in
     class. The teacher can at anytime during the period, jot down the name
     of those who are missing.

Each teacher should develop his own system for recording absences, tardiness, excuses, from daily participation and unsuitable
costume. Roll should be taken at the beginning of each class period.
Requiring each pupil to wear a name tag will enable the teacher to
learn each child's name more quickly in large classes, which, in turn,
is a means of class control.

Individual record cards should be filled out the first day the class
meets and permanent record cards kept on each student. Grades, intramural points earned, physical fitness test scores, teacher's comments and other information should be recorded.

EXCUSES

There should be written policies regarding excuses from the required physical education classes. These policies should cover the
following items:

Excuses for Athletes.   Schools vary in their policies. Some do not
permit athletes to be excused from physical education classes, others
do. Some permit those engaged in athletics to return to their regularly
assigned class at the end of each sport season. This policy recognizes
that one purpose of education is to produce well-rounded citizens
skilled and interested in many activities.

Menstruation.   All girls should be required to dress in the regulation class costume. Each should decide for herself whether she will
merely observe the activities in progress, join some of them or take as
active a part in the class as possible. Having the girls watch the class
in their street clothes often encourages them to sit rather than take
part in some milder forms of activity as the medical profession recommends they do during this time. Although some few girls claim to be
menstruating when actually they are not, the majority of the group

School .... Address .... Phone ....

Physical Education Director .... Principal ....

To the Family Physician:

    The physical education program for both boys and girls is one which embraces a great variety of activities. It is hoped that this broad program fulfills the needs of the pupils in the areas of physical, emotional, and social growth and development. Physical education is a required subject and each pupil is encouraged to participate to the fullest extent of his or her capacity.

    Below are the various phases of activity offered. Please check the activities in which the pupil under your care *may not* participate.

☐ Archery	☐ Gymnastics	☐ Softball
☐ Badminton	☐ Jog and Walk	☐ Swimming
☐ Baseball	☐ Lacrosse	☐ Tennis
☐ Basketball	☐ Fitness Testing	☐ Touch Football
☐ Body Building	☐ Push Ball	☐ Track and Field
☐ Calisthenics	☐ Recreational Games	☐ Tumbling
☐ Dancing Activities	☐ Soccer	☐ Volleyball
☐ Field Hockey	☐ Speed Ball	☐ Walking
☐ Folk Dancing	☐ Square Dancing	☐ Weight Training
☐ Golf	☐ Social Dancing	☐ Wrestling

Name of Pupil .... Age .... Grade ....

Nature of Illness/Injury .... Limitation of Activity ....

Date of Return to Normal Activities ....

Signature of Physician .... Address ....

.... Telephone ....

Signature of Parent/Guardian .... Address ....

.... Telephone ....

Date ....

Figure 6–1. A suggested medical excuse form for the physician to use in recommending that a student take special physical education. (Courtesy of *Physical Education Newsletter,* Croft Educational Services, Inc., December 1, 1967.)

will be honest when asking to be excused. The teacher might well seek to discover the cause of any such student deceit, for it may be due to the program content or faulty teaching methods.

Religious Reasons. Teachers sometimes are asked through parent notes to excuse a student from phases of the program, such as social dance, for religious reasons. Caution in handling such cases is recommended.[1] The student could well be assigned to do individual exercises or sport activity during class. He should not be penalized for his beliefs by being required to read and report on outside reading assignments, nor should he be sent to the study hall during this phase of the program.

Make-up periods for classes missed are not usually endorsed by leaders in physical education, for it is often too difficult for all concerned to find a suitable free time for this purpose. Students returning to class after an illness or operation usually need additional rest and not increased activity. In rural areas where most of the pupils are transported to and from school by bus, after-school activities, including attending a make-up period, are almost an impossibility.

Students should be excused from classes in physical education in the same manner as for all other classes according to established school policies. It is highly recommended that no blanket excuse be given to any student, exempting him from the required program in physical education. If a program has a wide variety of activities and instructors who are capable of providing for individual differences, almost all students can participate in it to their advantage. No other activity such as ROTC, varsity sports or vocational subjects are effective substitutes for a well-rounded physical education program.

For those students with such serious disabilities that they cannot be served in the regular program, a special physical education program should be offered. An example of a letter and form to be used in assigning students to special physical education is shown in Figure 6-1. For a complete discussion of special physical education, see Chapter 18.

The school should have written policies regarding the State requirements for students' participation in physical education. These policies should be enforced and insuring that they are is one of the many responsibilities of the teachers. Although it is often argued that students in drill teams or marching bands are getting exercise, the purpose of physical education is to provide far more than exercise. There are those who also believe that athletes should be excused from physical activity classes for they, too, are getting enough exercise. However, few will continue to play team sports as they grow older and those on varsity sport teams usually know only how to play one or

---

[1]See the chapter on *Dance* for additional suggestions on how to meet this problem.

two individual sports well. Many schools excuse varsity athletes only during the season in which they are playing and after that is over, all must take physical education.

CLASS TIME

Classes are usually one hour long. This time should be utilized to its fullest extent in light of established objectives. A suggested time breakdown of the period includes:

Undressing	3 minutes
Roll call	2 minutes
Announcements	2 minutes
Mass calisthenics (teacher- or student-directed)	4 minutes
Teacher demonstration and instruction	8 minutes
Drill and practice of isolated skills	10 minutes
Team play, dance compositions, or other cumulating experiences	13 minutes
Dressing and showering	8 minutes
	50 minutes

Several total class periods, or major portions of time taken from a few, should be devoted to orienting the students to the purpose of the program, class planning and evaluation. Although classes are usually scheduled on an hourly basis, allowance must be made for showering and passing from one class to another.

Above all, class time should be instructional time when emphasis is placed upon skill development. The intramural and intrascholastic programs should provide laboratory experience in playing games and using learned skills. Many authorities in the area of motor learning are convinced that skills *per se* can only be perfected by hard and repeated practice, by drilling on isolated parts (hitting the bird on the badminton serve) and then by utilizing that single skill in a larger whole (playing a game of badminton).

COSTUMES

Customary clothing for boys are dark trunks, cotton tee shirts, high top tennis shoes and wool socks. Girls may wear regulation shorts and blouses, low cut tennis shoes and wool socks. One-piece uniforms are favored by some teachers. The regulation costume for both groups may be purchased locally or through leading manu-facturers, most of whom advertise regularly in the *Journal of Health, Physical Education, and Recreation*. Each school should devise a plan whereby students financially unable to buy the required costume may be assisted in obtaining it. Some teachers and school systems now are de-emphasizing conformity and uniformity and are allowing students of both sexes to wear gym costumes of their own choosing rather than requiring all to wear the same type of clothing. The costume may be prescribed: (1) only in terms of shorts and a blouse for girls and a T-shirt for boys, or (2) only in terms of specific color for shorts and blouse or T-shirt.

Justification usually given for requiring regulation clothing is that it is less expensive over a period of time, does not discriminate according to socioeconomic status, can help build class morale, leads to better appearance of the class, and provides for more comfort and safety. On the other hand, some teachers now claim that far too many students are "turned off" physical education by the required uniform policy (as well as by the showering requirement) and that it is what the student is and does that is important, not what he wears. There is merit in both arguments; consequently, whether or not to require standardized clothing is the individual teacher's decision.

If a costume is required, there are several ways students can buy it. The most common practice is for the physical education department to purchase the uniforms in large lots and then sell or lend them for a

Figure 6–2, A, B. Styles of regulation costumes. (Courtesy of Gym Knits, by Macmillan Ward, Inc.)

small fee to students. If this system is used, the issuing of the costume should be so well planned that excessive staff time is not required nor the handling of money made a problem.

Procedures for the maintenance of clean clothing are most frequently the responsibility of the students. Some schools do have laundry facilities and provide clean costumes periodically. Doing so, however, often requires equipment and personnel beyond the financial means of most public schools, especially today when money is scarce and taxpayers balk at having their school taxes increased except for top priority, pressing educational needs.

USE OF SPACE

Although the American Association for Health, Physical Education, and Recreation recommends that activity classes in secondary school not exceed 40 students, few teachers are fortunate enough to teach this ideally sized group. Chances are good that in the near future all classes will be even larger. Consequently, teachers must devise ways to use best all available teaching stations. Ths plan, coupled with use of squad leaders, will enable the teacher to rotate around space-assigned groups and to supervise them all adequately.[2] As is shown in Figure 6-3, a wide range of activities can be conducted in one gymnasium.

Locker Assignments. All locker assignments should be made during the first week of class. Locker numbers and lock combinations should be kept by the teacher on a separate form for each student or on a single master sheet.

Towel Service. In some schools each student furnishes his own towel and is responsible for providing a clean one periodically. Others have their own laundry system and furnish clean towels and clothing for all students. Still others have each student pay a small laundry fee

---

[2]See also the chapter on *Recreational Activities* for suggestion for establishing a Leaders' Club.

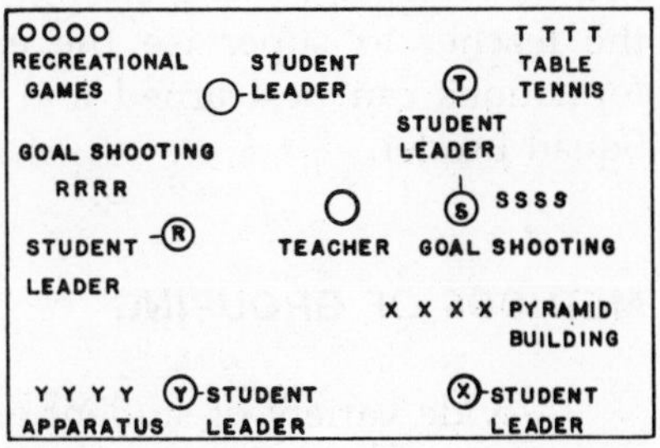

Figure 6-3. Diagram showing a wide range of activities that can be conducted in one gymnasium.

each semester and have local firms supply clean towels. Regardless of which type of procedure is used, a carefully recorded inventory must be made periodically.

CLASS ORGANIZATION

Physical education classes are often vastly overcrowded. Lack of sufficient time, poor facilities and inadequate equipment, coupled with large numbers of pupils, present many problems to the teacher. Careful planning for the best type of class organization possible will yield more fruitful results. Students should assist the instructor in planning, conducting and evaluating the program on each grade level.

Skillful organization and wise planning will assure that each period of instruction is meaningful to the learners, educationally sound and fruitful. The class should be conducted informally but should always be well controlled.

The teacher should have a definite beginning and ending to each class period. He should condition the students to listen automatically when he is talking, to form into a circle or squad formation when the class starting signal is given, or to sit in assigned groups at the end of each class for a short evaluative discussion of the period. Because students experiment with each new teacher in order to learn how far they can go or how much they can get away with, it is of primary importance that from the first class to the last one in each semester the teacher be *firm, fair* and *consistent* in his methods for controlling the group. Good class organization aids students to feel secure and ready for each new challenging experience.

FORMATIONS FOR INSTRUCTION

Far too much precious class time can be lost by reorganizing groups for relays, teams or skill drills. In order to eliminate such waste, students should be conditioned to form quickly into desired groups when directed to do so. Squads or teams of six to ten in number usually are best. Placing each group to cover the floor area fully allows the teacher to supervise the entire class effectively. The following formations can be learned and formed quickly. In each, S.L. means Squad Leader.

METHODS OF GROUPING

A wide variety of student groups should be used throughout the year. Providing opportunities for many students to be squad leaders

FAN

Players are spread before the leader in a fan formation. This is especially effective in skill drills for throwing, catching, and kicking balls of various sizes. The teacher works as a group supervisor.

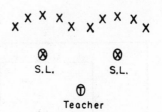

LINE

This is the easiest of all formations for beginners to learn. It is good for relays, basket shooting, and games wherein children take turns. Not more than five should be in each line if possible.

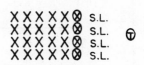

CIRCLE

Groups can get into a circle quickly from the line or fan formation by following their leader. This one is especially good for simple games and ball skill drills with the leader in the center throwing the ball to each player and correcting faulty movements when he throws it back.

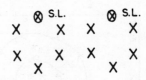

SHUTTLE

This grouping is best for ball passing or kicking skill drills.

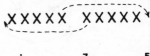

ZIGZAG

Two lines face each other. Player 1 throws to 2 who throws to 3, etc. This formation is best for soccer kicking, volleying, throwing and catching.

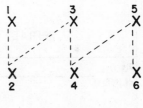

CORNER

The leader facing the line gives signal for 1 and 2 to form a V corner. The odd numbers go right; the even to the left. This grouping is ideal for skill drills and teaching response to command movements necessary for marching.

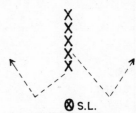

SQUARE

Have four groups form a square. Squad 1 forms West; 2 North; 3 East; 4 South. The leader stands to the left with his squad. This one is effective for ball-passing drills, and team games such as line dodgeball.

RANDOM

This is a formation in which students place themselves at random around the playing area. The informality of the arrangement is especially suited to the problem solving method but is also appropriate in any circumstance where a specific formation is not required by the nature of the game or activity.

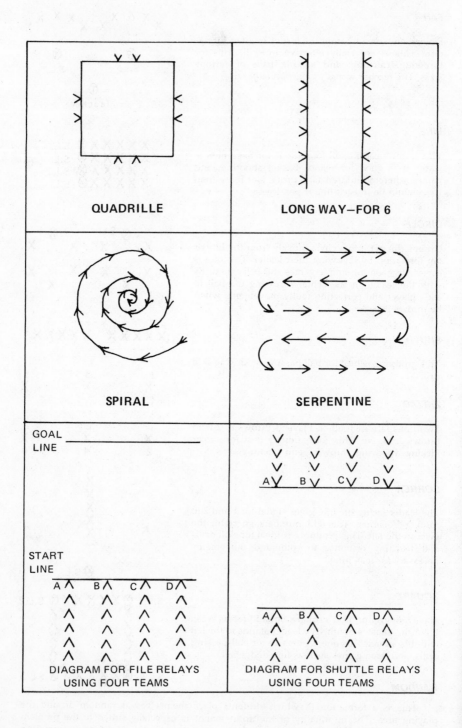

QUADRILLE

LONG WAY—FOR 6

SPIRAL

SERPENTINE

GOAL LINE

START LINE

DIAGRAM FOR FILE RELAYS
USING FOUR TEAMS

DIAGRAM FOR SHUTTLE RELAYS
USING FOUR TEAMS

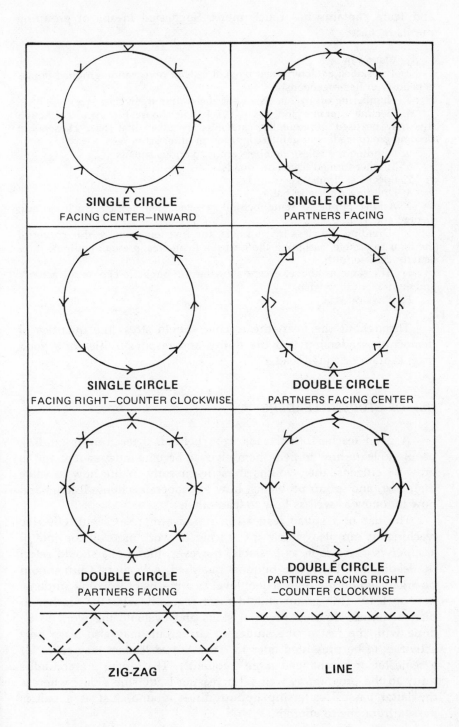

SINGLE CIRCLE
FACING CENTER—INWARD

SINGLE CIRCLE
PARTNERS FACING

SINGLE CIRCLE
FACING RIGHT—COUNTER CLOCKWISE

DOUBLE CIRCLE
PARTNERS FACING CENTER

DOUBLE CIRCLE
PARTNERS FACING

DOUBLE CIRCLE
PARTNERS FACING RIGHT
—COUNTER CLOCKWISE

ZIG-ZAG

LINE

and team captains has much merit. Suggested means of grouping pupils include:

1. Classes or age.
2. The skilled as determined by skill tests or observation grouped homogeneously or heterogeneously.
3. Numbering off by 2's, 3's, or 4's, depending upon class size.
4. Electing captains and having each one choose his team. (Although this may be used infrequently, care must be taken that those chosen last become group leaders or gain recognition in other activities.)
5. Dividing the tallest members among various squads.
6. Teacher-formed teams or squads.
7. Special skill practice groups.
8. Dividing a circle in half.
9. Asking pupils to stand behind selected team leaders, such as Jack, George and Tom.
10. Dividing the class by numbers, the first ten going to this corner of the floor to tumble, assigning the next ten to an area, piece of equipment, or activity, and so forth.
11. The same as above, except allowing the pupils to choose the activity and equipment they wish.
12. Physical size.

Throughout the year, the teacher should stress the qualities of democratic leadership and the duties and responsibilities of a good team captain or squad leader.

USE OF STUDENT LEADERS

A good teacher often leads from behind. If teaching is guiding people to learn how to help themselves to become independent and to grow as citizens, then youths must learn early in life how to solve their own and group problems, how to cooperate, choose leaders and how to follow as well as how to lead others.

The use of a squad leader can produce more efficient, effective teaching. It can also enable the teacher to work more in the role of a supervisor. As soon as possible, however, the pupils should select the leader they believe to be most qualified. A Leaders' Club should be organized on the high school level as a means of teaching students how to lead. This group should meet regularly with the teacher to plan activities, develop physical skills and evaluate the work to be done with the rest of the students. The group may also learn new activities to be presented later in class. Squad leaders may serve for a semester or be changed more frequently. The former method adds unity to the program as well as increasing leadership skills, whereas the latter passes leadership opportunities around, just as a ball is passed from one to another.

Youth tends to dominate rather than democratically lead others. All groups in our culture, regardless of age, must have additional training and experience in choosing leaders wisely, in leading and in following others. The school is the most logical place for youth to develop those traits necessary for good leadership.

TEACHER AIDES AND OTHER PARAPROFESSIONAL ASSISTANTS

Most states have programs for teacher aides who work with the certified physical educator as an assistant and are paid by the state government. They are classified in two categories: (1) educational and clerical materials assistant, and (2) an instructional assistant.

Aides who work under the supervision and in the presence of certified physical educators should not assume the educational responsibilities of the teacher. Also they may not be used by any school or district to replace teachers, to substitute for those certified as educators, or to change the pupil-teacher ratio.

BASIC QUALIFICATIONS*

1. High school diploma or equivalent.
2. Minimum age of 21 years (unless enrolled in college).
3. Interest in physical education.
4. Emotional maturity, dependability, sound character.
5. Completion of standard first aid course or equivalent.
6. Ability to do clerical work.
7. Ability to get along with people.
8. Good health.

Auxiliary personnel must comply with all general requirements applicable to other school employees, such as health records.

RESTRICTIONS

Teacher aides should not be permitted to perform the following duties of a certified teacher:

1. Administer tests.
2. Organize curriculum.

---

*These recommendations concerning teacher aids were made by a task force committee with representative numbers from the Society of State Directors of Health, Physical Education, and Recreation. They also incorporate suggestions from City Directors of HPER and members of the Texas Education Agency staff.

3. Evaluate students.
4. Interpret results of tests.
5. Order equipment.
6. Take charge of fire drills.
7. Instruct students unless directed to do so under teacher's supervision.
8. Assume teacher's responsibility.
9. Supervise intramural activities.
10. Assume complete coaching responsibilities.
11. Administer corporal punishment.

Teacher aides should be required to participate in preschool institutes and in-service workshops. Conferences between aides, teachers, and supervisors are also necessary.

DUTIES OF EDUCATIONAL AND CLERICAL MATERIALS ASSISTANT

An *educational materials assistant* should prepare materials for instruction, maintain bulletin board displays, and operate audio-visual equipment.

1. Keep locker room orderly.
2. Launder and distribute uniforms and towels.
3. Operate shower controls and oversee shower room conduct.
4. Take care of equipment room.
5. Make periodic safety checks and maintain and repair equipment.
6. Clean gymnasium and store equipment.
7. Set up gymnasium for various activities.
8. Mark instructional areas.
9. Help maintain indoor and outdoor instructional areas.
10. Help construct instructional materials.
11. Maintain timely and neat bulletin boards.
12. Procure, set up, operate, and return audio-visual equipment.
13. Be responsible for valuables checked by students.
14. Check doors and windows at the beginning and end of period.
15. Ensure proper lighting.
16. Mark uniforms and other supplies.

A *clerical assistant* should provide clerical assistance, duplicate materials, maintain student records, collect money, and perform some of the duties of an educational materials assistant.

1. Check attendance.
2. Check uniforms.
3. Check lockers, assign locks and lockers.
4. Unpack, count, and store new equipment.
5. Distribute and collect equipment.
6. Make periodic inventory of equipment.
7. Assist in initial health screening—check eyes, height, and weight and record health information.

8. Type and mimeograph stencils for tests.
9. File correspondence.
10. Transfer grades from record book to marking forms.
11. Take care of records for classes made up.
12. Compile credits for extracurricular attendance and awards.
13. Mimeograph, correct, change instructional material or curriculum outlines.
14. Record scores on physical fitness test forms.
15. Score objective test papers.
16. Type reports requested from the teacher by the administration.

The *instructional assistant* would demonstrate skills, assist individual students, and perform some of the assigned duties of a clerical worker or educational materials assistant.

1. Assist at fire drills.
2. Enforce safety rules.
3. Assist chaperone or sponsors and other student groups.
4. Help with first aid only when properly trained.
5. Assist at playdays, exhibitions, and sports days with publicity, tickets, and supervision of groups.
6. Supervise nonparticipating students.
7. Assist in swimming program. (Should hold Water Safety Instructor's Certificate or Red Cross lifesaving certificate.)
8. Assist with examinations.
9. Assist on field trips.

PROFESSIONAL PREPARATION OF TEACHER AIDES

School districts that use teacher aides should develop guidelines for professional preparation, such as:

1. Enroll in a physical education program at a two year or four year institution.
2. Complete a two year curriculum at a two or four year institution which is aimed at preparing physical education aides.
3. Participate in staff development workshops held before, during, and at the end of the school year that are especially prepared for teacher aides in physical education. This in-service program would be geared to achieving the maximum in assisting in the coordination and cooperation in the teacher-learning process.

STUDENT CLASS MANAGERS

These managers, who may be teacher- or class-elected, have the responsibility of issuing equipment to the entire class or to squad leaders and returning it to its proper storage place. They, as well as other student leaders, can also help mark playing fields and testing areas on the gymnasium floor.

THE WAYS TO DEVELOP STUDENT LEADERSHIP

One basic principle of good leadership is that a real leader makes more leaders. Master teachers apply this concept by providing increasingly more well-planned opportunities for students to demonstrate skills, by helping teach those having learning difficulties in mastering skills, leading class exercises, and so on. A good teacher guides students to learning how to become independent and grow in many ways as human beings. All youth can learn, if skillfully guided, how to cooperate, choose leaders, and how to follow, as well as how to lead others.

TEACHER CONDUCT

Teachers must not be meek mice, stalking tigers nor threatening bulls. Those who are alert, poised, calm, assured, enthusiastic and controlled develop student confidence in them. They should be models of cleanliness in appearance, physical fitness and attractiveness. Those who are greatly underweight or overweight, have faulty posture and lowered vitality set an example youth scoffingly shuns and refuses to copy. Traits necessary for good class leadership are appearance, dependability, forcefulness, promptness, instructional skill and good class control.

Before Class. The teacher should be dressed in a costume that allows freedom of movement. If possible, he should greet each pupil by name as he enters the gymnasium or locker room. (Requiring students to wear name tages will help here.) All needed equipment for the class should be ready and he should have planned well the activities he will teach.

Locker Room Regulations. Each pupil should know where he is to put his clothing when changing for class; each should lock his locker before coming into the gymnasium. A combination lock is recommended, and the teacher should have a master key for all combinations.

CHECKING EQUIPMENT IN AND OUT

If there is no custodian available to render this service, procedure for doing so should be established.[3] Assigning one student in each class to this responsibility is recommended. All equipment needed for each period should be ready before the class meets so that instruction

---

[3]See the chapter on *Equipment and Supplies* for additional suggestions for checking equipment in and out.

time is not lost. This should be readily accessible so that all needed items can be gathered at once. Large, strong laundry sacks are ideal for this purpose and are easily carried back and forth to playing fields.

MOVING TO OTHER AREAS

Groups should be moved quickly from indoor to outdoor play areas. Methods for speeding up the laggers are to require all to run to and from the assigned areas, to check roll at the area where the class is to meet, and to vitalize teaching and the activity to the extent that students are eager for class to begin. It has been said that the physical education instructional and after-school program should be like a state fair merry-go-round. If it is enjoyable, adventurous and satisfying enough, youth will want to jump on and keep going with the group.

SHOWERS

Many physical educators believe that students should be encouraged but not required to take showers. They should be given enough time for showering and dressing after class. Some few will find their greatest joy in this part of the program, especially those from low-income groups who do not have adequate bathing facilities at home.

The shower and locker rooms should be supervised, preferably at all times, by a custodian. If this is impossible, it is necessary that the teacher do so as each class enters, showers and leaves. Horseplay should be forbidden as a safety precaution. School rules regarding smoking, marking on walls or using obscene language must be obeyed throughout the entire building, and especially here during the after-school recreational period. The instructor should realize that he must assume the authority necessary to protect public property. Those who have gained experience in the field realize that sometimes they do their best teaching outside of the gymnasium class while talking informally to students in the locker room, or on the way to and from the playing field.

KEEPING RECORDS

Records should be functional and practical, and used as a means of evaluating student progress and program content, or for recording administrative details. They should not be time consuming or energy

draining for the teacher. Such records include essential health information, basket or locker master sheets, cumulative physical education
forms, grades, attendance records, inventory and accident reports.
Records and reports should be kept in a locked steel file. All recorded
information should be for present or future use and never assigned
busy work, for accurate and meaningful records and reports are as
essential to good teaching as efficient and effective class management.

PERMANENT RECORD FORMS

Grades, teacher's comments, intramural points earned, and other
information of value concerning each student should be recorded for
permanent use. A cumulative health record should also be filed for
each student that is easily accessible to all teachers and other authorized personnel for professional use.*

COMMUNICATIONS WITH PARENTS

Teachers must make a greater effort to publicize the physical
education program for all students—what its purpose is, what it consists of, how progress in it is evaluated, and the roles of individuals
who take part in it. Parents are especially pleased to know how their
children are affected by the program, each being more interested in
the progress of his own child.

Some schools have devised a descriptive handbook and have
found it to be an effective medium for interpreting the physical education program to parents. The handbook, provided by the Norfolk City
Schools of Virginia, is sent to 30,000 parents each year and is one
of the best available.

Other schools are now distributing brochures which have also
proved an effective way not only to inform parents of the program but
to gain their support for it. A brochure designed specially for parents
might well contain the following topics:

The purpose and educational significance of the physical education
program.
The objectives of the program, with brief explanation of each.
The need for directed physical activities for secondary school youth.
The value of the team and lifetime sports included in the program and
their relevance in our age of expanding free time.

*See *Teaching Health in Elementary Schools,* 2nd Ed., 1974, by Maryhelen Vannier,
available from Lea and Febriger Publishing Company, West Washington Square, Philadelphia, for a suggested cumulative health record form.

Sample forms of the seasonal program for the secondary school for boys and girls.

    Rules and regulations
    Grading procedures
        The physical fitness test forms
        Skill achievement tests
        Knowledge tests
    Excuse policies
    Showering policies
The student leader's program.
The intramural program for all students.
The competitive athletic program for boys and girls.

PARENT-TEACHER CONFERENCES

Whom. There may be times when the conference should involve parent, teacher and student. It is better if conferences can be parent-teacher conferences.

What. Planned meeting between parent and teacher to report on the student's progress and/or discuss mutual problems.

Why. To develop a closer relationship between teacher and parent so that through mutual understanding and cooperation they may work for the child's benefit.

When. Preferably at some permanently scheduled time—that is, at a time set aside by the teacher for conferences—after school, off-periods, and so on, particularly at the beginning of the year and when occasion demands.

Where. If possible in the home of the student as well as at the school.

How. The PTA might give special notices to all parents, informing them of the parent-teacher conference plan. The teacher might call each parent or write him a note, on the report card perhaps, giving the parent the teacher's schedule and issuing an invitation for a conference. The follow-up might be a phone call to each parent. The parent may be invited to call the school office and make an appointment with the teacher.

DO'S

1. Do plan conferences with *all* parents.
2. Do tell the parents the aim of the conference.
3. Do expect and welcome both mother and father at parent conferences, i.e., they should be parents-teacher conferences.
4. Do be very friendly, interested, relaxed and to the point.
5. Do accept and respect the personalities of the parents.
6. Do listen to what parents have to say.
7. Do try to find out all you can about the student without trying to pry.

8. Do be completely honest in matters of fact.

9. Do begin and end in a positive manner.

10. Do have representative material of the work done by the student. If possible, this should be a fair sampling containing examples of both good and bad work to show parents.

11. Do have physical test information in lay language to give to the parents.

12. Do have the student's cumulative record, or information contained therein, on hand for reference.

13. DO PLAN CONFERENCES IN ADVANCE

DON'TS

1. Don't try to confer with the parent when either the parent or teacher is emotionally upset.

2. Don't try to crowd a conference into too short a time.

3. Don't try to cover too much material.

4. Don't compare the student with others or with brothers or sisters in his family.

5. Don't try to "out-talk" the parent.

6. Don't quote capacity or mental ability (I.Q.) test scores to parents.

7. Don't make conferences too formal.

8. Don't alarm parents with "norms," "means," or other statistics of a professional nature that they may not understand, i.e., avoid use of professional jargon.

9. Don't repeat any personal material.

10. Don't sit behind the desk if at all possible.

11. Don't say anything to the parent that you would mind the child knowing.

The physical education teacher, in spite of large classes, often knows more about the physical and emotional problems that high school students face than any other teacher in the school. Many teachers do an excellent job of counselling students and some later go back to school to obtain certification in this specialized area, leaving the teaching field. Counselling is far more than being a good "listening," understanding friend and has nothing to do with "telling" people how to solve their problems. Consequently, many major departments preparing teachers and recreation personnel are now requiring that students take at least one course in guidance and counselling.

TEST RESULTS SENT TO PARENTS

Some schools send physical fitness test results to parents as a means of acquainting them with the fitness status of their child as well as helping them know more about his physical education program and the role the development of fitness plays in it. The following form is sent to all parents whose children are taking physical education in the Cedar Rapids, Iowa public schools.

TEACHER (Spring)

PRINCIPAL   TEACHER (Spring)

CEDAR RAPIDS COMMUNITY SCHOOLS

Physical Welfar Department

PUPIL PHYSICAL FITNESS REPORT

NAME _____ SCHOOL _____ DATE _____TEACHER (Fall)_____

PRINCIPAL _____TEACHER (Spring) _____

TO THE PARENTS: A series of physical fitness tests has recently been given to all pupils in grades 4--12. They are being given twice each school year. This is a report on the performance of your child. In each test you may compare your child's score with the performance score of other children throughout the state. The state scores are given in terms of percentile rank. For example, a percentile rank of 75 means that a child's performance surpasses that of 75 per cent of the children of the same grade tested through the state. The state norms were constructed on data obtained by testing boys and girls in 104 schools in Iowa during the 1960–61 school year. Thus, the percentile scores cannot necessarily be interpreted as the ultimate in achievement. They can be assumed to represent the achievements for the 1960–61 school year of those schools where attention was given to motor fitness.

If your child has a low performance score, it might be because of a particular height, weight or other physical characteristic. The important thing is for each child to show continued improvement in his own performance.

This department is making strenuous efforts to assist our young people to attain and maintain health and physical fitness. The physically underdeveloped youngsters are being identified and programs geared to individual needs. We are giving increased emphasis to the more vigorous type activities. It is recommended that parents encourage their children to participate regularly in physical activity.

TEST	WHAT IT TESTS	YOUR CHILD'S SCORE Fall Spring	PERCENTILE RANK Fall Spring	HOW TO INTERPRET THE RESULTS
SIT-UPS	Strength/endurance of abdominal muscles			The object was to do as many as possible in 1 min. (2 min. boys, Gr. 10–12)
STANDING BROAD JUMP	Power in the legs and coordination	in. in.		The greater distance jumped, the better the performance.
SHUTTLE RUN	Agility			The greater number of trips in a 15 second interval, the better the score.
FORWARD BEND	Flexibility	in. in.		The higher score (plus) measured in the nearest ½", the better the performance.
GRASSHOPPER	Endurance			The object was to do as many as possible in 30 sec. (1 min. boys, Gr. 7 & up.)
DASH	Speed	sec. sec.		The faster time the better the performance; 40 yd., Gr. 4--6; 50 yds., Gr. 7–12.
PULL-UPS (Boys) BENT ARM HANG (Girls)	Arm, shoulder and upper back strength			Boys—one point each time chin goes above the bar. Girls—the longer the time (in sec.) with arms fully bent, chin above bar, the better the performance.

ARNOLD SALISBURY
Superintendent of Schools

EMIL A. KLUMPAR
Physical Welfare Consultant

Physical fitness report form to be sent to parents. (Courtesy Cedar Rapids Community School District, Cedar Rapids, Iowa.)

DISCUSSION QUESTIONS

1. Should an activity be substituted for physical education, such as band or ROTC? Support your reasons as an educator.

2. Should students be required to wear a specified costume in their physical education classes? What factors are important in the purchase and care of required uniforms? Who should furnish them? Where can the best ones be obtained? (Consult the *AAHPER Journal* for advertisements of the leading uniform supply companies.)

3. Discuss the factors essential to good class management.

4. When is it more advantageous to use homogeneous grouping rather than heterogenous grouping?

5. Discuss the merits of each of the seven formations for instruction. List three activities best suited for each one.

6. How can paraprofessionals and student leaders become valuable teaching assistants? What should the in-service training program consist of for each of these persons?

THINGS TO DO

1. Describe three methods of taking roll in physical education. Give the advantages and disadvantages of each.

2. List three administration methods for each of the following.
   a. Providing towel service
   b. Requiring regulation costumes
   c. Handling excuses
   d. Absences from class

3. Outline a system of commands that can be used in the giving of commands for calisthenics and marching. Be prepared to give exercises to the class and direct the class in marching activities. Have commands well in hand so they can be given with dispatch and precision. Include in a notebook a description of ten different exercises. Be prepared to direct these in class and to tell the purpose of or benefit from each exercise.

4. List ten suggestions that will aid the teacher in preventing discipline problems and give suggestions for handling them when they do occur.

5. Since the best discipline is self-discipline, how can teachers help students develop this? Write a one-page paper giving your suggestions for doing so.

SELECTED VISUAL AIDS

Archery. A complete set of four filmstrip units in sound and color. Each shows techniques for arranging class groups and teaching methods. Available from The Athletic Institute.

Baseball. A complete set of seven filmstrips in sound and color. Each shows instructional methods and suggested ways for diagnosing movement faults. Available from The Athletic Institute.

Careers in Physical Education. A 27 minute color film showing what physical educators and coaches do on the job. Available from Association Films in most large cities on a rental basis.

SUGGESTED READINGS

Bucher, Charles: *The Administration of Health and Physical Education.* St. Louis, The C. V. Mosby Co., 1968.

Cowell, Charles and Schwehn, Hilda: *Modern Principles and Methods in Secondary Physical Education.* 3rd Ed., Boston, Allyn and Bacon, Inc., 1973.

Daughtrey, Greyson and Woods, John: *Physical Education, Programs.* Philadelphia, W. B. Saunders Co., 1971.

Insley, Gerald: *Practical Guidelines For The Teaching of Physical Education.* Reading, Massachusetts, Addison-Wesley Publishing Co., 1973.

Neilson, N. P., and Bronson, A. O.: *Problems in Physical Education.* Englewood Cliffs, N.J., Prentice-Hall, Inc., 1965.

Oberteuffer, Delbert, and Ulrich, Celeste: *Physical Education.* New York, Harper & Row, 1961.

Voltmer, Edward, and Esslinger, Arthur: *The Organization and Administration of Physical Education.* 4th Ed., New York, Appleton-Century.Crofts, 1967.

CHAPTER SEVEN

THE INTERRELATIONSHIPS OF HEALTH EDUCATION AND PHYSICAL EDUCATION

The total school health program is composed of three parts: healthful school environment, health services and health instruction. All are closely woven together; no one strand is more important than any other. Likewise, the physical education and the total health program of the school are two separate but closely related areas, each equally valuable in its contribution to the students, school, community and nation.

The primary function of the school in the area of health is to build and maintain a high health status in each student. All teachers make up a health team; each has a specific duty to perform in helping youth to develop a sense of well-being and good health habits which will promote efficient body functioning. Each has an important role to play through daily observations and day-to-day inventory of each student's general condition of health. Although individuals vary in appearance, posture and numerous other ways, each shows a unified picture of how he usually looks. Some appear pale when they are not feeling well, others are flushed; some are droopy, others overactive. Each teacher should be able both to recognize the usual appearance of each student and to detect deviations which would indicate some departure from normality.

Although one may look healthy and still be ill, there are, nevertheless, numerous indices of good health. These are seen in those who have:

1. Buoyant, free, joyous body movements.
2. Enough energy to do what he should do without undue fatigue.
3. A zest for life.
4. The ability to rest, relax and recover from fatigue.
5. A good appetite and enjoyment of eating.
6. No extreme weight variations from that which is normal for one's age, weight, height and body type.
7. No remediable defects that have not been corrected.

8. Good feelings about himself and toward others.
9. The ability to recover quickly from occasional illnesses.

Anderson claims that there are five health levels within which almost all students fall.[1] These are:

A Level of Health.   Those in this category have all of the above qualities, enjoy life, being with others, and participate wholesomely in many activities.

B Level of Health.   Although those in this group have no remedial defects, they lack the vigor and zest of those in the A Level.

C Level of Health.   Those who are neither completely sick nor completely well. They drag through life at low gear.

D Level of Health.   All individuals who are ill from a chronic infection or some concealed factor. They should not be in school until remediable defects are corrected.

E Level of Health.   Those who are obviously ill and should not be in school.

Health means more than absence of disease, for it is the degree of total body soundness compared with standards of good, poor and bad as determined by medical experts. It is that state of well-being which enables one to live joyfully and effectively. Our constitutional make-up is largely the result of the balance of body structure to hormone activity and is unique with each individual. Also, all persons can be classified as being: the short, stocky endomorph; the small, frail ectomorph or the average, athletically built mesomorph. The wiry, skinny person who has boundless energy may be, and often is, healthier than his heavier, slower moving friend. Looking healthy and being healthy may be two widely separated conditions. Teachers need not be medically trained experts to be able to detect illness or a person's inability to fulfill life's demands.

HEALTH SERVICES

Health services provided by the school should be geared toward keeping the health status of all students at the highest possible level, for those with low vitality, chronic infections or other such difficulties have little interest and success in schoolwork. Emotional as well as physical health protection should be included in the program.

The school should assist and supplement the home in providing health service. Students who come from low income groups often need more financial aid than others. Although it is questionable just how

---

[1]Anderson, C. L.: *School Health Practice*. St. Louis, The C. V. Mosby Co., 1972, p. 50.

far the school should go in providing remedial devices such as glasses or artificial legs for those financially unable to secure them, youth-serving organizations often supply such equipment as a community service.

The total health service program is made up of health appraisal, prevention and the correction of remedial defects. Included under each division are the following:

Health appraisal:
>Physical examinations
>Screening tests for hearing, vision, posture, dental defects, others
>Height and weight measurements
>Health guidance
>Teacher health
>Daily observation

Prevention:
>Safety
>Emergency first-aid care
>Communicable disease control

Correction of remedial defects:
>Correction of remedial defects
>Follow-up services

Increasingly, schools are adding physicians and nurses to their staffs. First-aid stations, isolation areas, a waiting and examination room are more frequently considered as being a necessary part of a modern school's facilities.

TEACHERS' OBSERVATIONS

Teachers play a vital role in a student's physical and emotional health and must learn how to observe deviations from the normal appearance and behavior of each student in the class. Unlike the parents, this educator has an opportunity to see the unique individual differences of each student in contrast to those of his many peers of approximately the same age and school grade.

The teacher can learn how to observe the daily health status of each person in the class by first being able to pick out just one or more deviations in the appearance of one student in each of his classes encountered daily. He should practice observation for the specific purpose of detecting departure from good health; it is imperative that he know how the student normally looks, whether she usually has a pale, pallid look, or if she ordinarily comes to school with a ruddy complexion and apparently is a happy, smiling youngster or a shy, withdrawn, timid one. The teacher must also be able to recognize abnormalities and know what constructive action to take when deviations occur.

The teacher should be aware of the following disorders in various parts of the body, as well as of behavior symptoms and emotional problems as he daily observes each child in the class.

Eyes
Sties or crusted lids
Inflamed eyes
Crossed eyes
Repeated headaches
Squinting, frowning or scowling
Protruding eyes
Watery eyes
Rubbing of eyes
Excessive blinking
Twitching of the lids
Holding head to one side

Ears
Discharge from ears
Earache
Failure to hear questions
Picking at the ears
Turning the head to hear
Talking in a monotone
Inattention
Anxious expression
Excessive noisiness

Teeth and mouth
State of cleanliness
Gross visible caries
Irregular teeth
Stained teeth
Gum boils
Offensive breath
Mouth habits such as thumbsucking

General condition and appearance
Underweight
Overweight
Does not appear well
Tires easily
Chronic fatigue
Nausea or vomiting
Faintness or dizziness

Growth
Failure to gain regularly over a three
   month period
Unexplained loss in weight
Unexplained rapid gain in weight

Glands
Enlarged gland at side of neck
Enlarged thyroid

Nose and throat
Persistent mouth breathing
Frequent sore throat
Recurrent colds
Chronic nasal discharge
Frequent nosebleeds
Nasal speech
Frequent tonsillitis

Skin and scalp
Nits on the hair
Unusual pallor of face
Eruptions or rashes
Habitual scratching of scalp or skin
Uncleanliness
Excessive redness of skin

Heart
Excessive breathlessness
Tires easily
History of "growing pains"
Bluish lips
Excessive pallor

Posture and musculature
Asymmetry of shoulders and hips
Peculiarity of gait
Obvious deformities of any type
Anomalies of muscular development

Behavior
Overstudious, docile, withdrawn
Bullying, overaggressive, domineering
Overexcitable, uncontrollable emotions
Unhappy and depressed
Stuttering or other forms of speech difficulty
Lack of confidence, self-denial, self-censure
Poor accomplishment in comparison with ability
Lying (imaginative or defensive)
Lack of appreciation of property rights (stealing)
Abnormal sex behavior
Antagonistic, negativistic, quarrelsome

HEALTH EXAMINATIONS

Although some school authorities believe in annual physical examinations, others contend that each student should have a minimum of four periodic examinations. These should be given when the child enters the first grade, once during the middle elementary experience, at the beginning of adolescence during junior high school years, and before leaving the senior high school. However, throughout a child's experience at school he should be referred to either the school physician or a specialist whenever the teacher's observation or the results of a screening test indicate the need. Each school district should determine how often, by whom, when, and where the physical examinations should be given.

The kind of medical examination given will, of course, vary from school to school. In general, however, the examination should include the following.

Nutritional status	Muscle tone
Eyes and eyelids	Posture
Ears and eardrums	Bones and joints
Skin and hair	Abdomen
Heart	Nose and throat
Lungs	Thyroid gland
Nervous system	Lymph nodes
Pulse rate when resting and after exercise	Teeth and gums

Teachers can and should make a great contribution to this phase of the school health program. Their chief contribution can be made in helping each student understand why he needs to be examined, what the doctor will do, and talking with each youth after the examination has been given so that he gains a clearer understanding of anything the doctor has told him.

PREVENTION AND CONTROL OF COMMUNICABLE DISEASES

Each school should have written policies concerning the exclusion and re-admission of students who have communicable diseases, the kinds of immunizations required for school admission, as well as procedures to be followed should an epidemic occur. Teachers, along with the school administrators, public health department, local physicians and parents, should work closely together in formulating such policies. Likewise, they should help enforce these policies once they have been adopted.

Signs of the early stages of most communicable diseases include:

Flushed or pale face, "glassy eyes," running nose
Excessive sneezing and coughing
Light blue or pale lips and fingernails
Rash, or other unusual skin conditions
Swollen glands
Body temperature above 99 F.
Listlessness or unusual overactivity

HEALTHFUL SCHOOL ENVIRONMENT

A clean, safe physical plant with proper sanitation, ventilation, lighting and heat control helps to provide a healthful learning environment. However, only those living in such an environment can keep it an attractive, safe and hygienic place. Teachers, students and administrators should work together to draw up procedures and rules for the lunchroom, passing to and from classes, custodial housekeeping, playground safety and other practices necessary for the safety and welfare of all. Teachers must provide a relaxed, friendly atmosphere and help each student in every class gain recognition, success, security, friendship and self-respect. Such safety measures as regular fire drills also are an important part of the healthful school environment program. In its entirety such a program includes:

The physical environment:
School site
Heating

Figure 7–1. Students have a right to enjoy their physical education program in clean, safe and attractive surroundings. (Courtesy of *The Scholastic Coach*.)

Ventilation
Water supply
Lunchroom facilities
Sewage and garbage disposal

The emotional-mental environment:
Pupil status
Pupil-teacher relationships
Curriculum provisions for individual differences
Classroom atmosphere

Administrative practices:
Class and teaching schedules
Provisions for balance between difficult and easy subjects
Rest and relaxation
Fire, water and light inspections
Housekeeping procedures

HEALTH INSTRUCTION

Although health education experts are being more frequently given the responsibility for the school health instruction program, every teacher should be concerned not only with imparting health knowledge at teachable moments but also with the shaping of student attitudes toward his own obligation, as both a citizen and an individual, to maintain his highest possible health status.

The aim of the instructional program from the primary grades through college should be to develop good health habits, teach those facts necessary for health promotion and shape attitudes and ideals as strong motivating forces for all to become and stay healthy. These valued aims are integrated and reciprocal, for without proper attitudes and well-developed health habits mere factual knowledge concerning hygiene is worthless.

Stress in health instruction on the secondary level should be placed on the *why* and *what*, for students of this age search for truth. Good health habits should be reinforced to the degree that each youth will continue them when out of school and into his own self-directed life. Methods for teaching health successfully include:

Small group discussions
The use of audio-visual aids
Individual health counseling and conferences
Field trips
Exhibits
Role playing
Dramatizations
Teacher- and student-led class discussions

Review, drills and examinations
Guest speakers
Laboratory experiments
Panel discussions
Projects
Health units
Research
Oral reports
Problem solving
Class recitation

Since schools have no monopoly on education, students should be aided in learning how to select highly commercialized and advertised health products wisely. Because they are entering independent adulthood, increased efforts should be made to equip each with enough background in health to find answers to his own problems and health needs, as well as how to utilize best the health services available in his own community and state.

Poor practices in the school health instructional program are both costly and injurious to society. Fortunately, schools are gradually giving more than mere lip service to the value and place of this subject in the school curriculum. In the better schools, signs of this newly found belief in the importance of good health instruction programs can be found in:

1. Health classes taught by those who have been adequately prepared. Good preparation usually includes a minimum of sixteen hours in personal health, community health, mental health, nutrition, school health services, first-aid, and methods and materials in health instruction.

2. Classes which are regularly assigned and required of all students. Massing groups in the gymnasium on rainy days to hear a "health lecture," or separating the boys and girls to hear "all about sex" are rapidly disappearing practices. Fortunately, so is the excusing of students from the required class in order to enroll in something else which is "more important."

3. The use of newer and better methods of teaching in which fear, dullness and the mere memorization of ever-changing health facts have been eliminated. Stress is now being placed upon a positive rather than a negative type of motivation.

The health instruction program on all education levels should include:

Planned instruction:
    Shaping attitudes
    Imparting knowledge
    Developing desirable health habits

Integrated learnings:
    Correlation with other subjects
    The life experiences of others
    Individual experiences
    Student-teacher relationships

Incidental instructions:
    Marginal experiences surrounding direct learning in other areas
    Direct learning in other areas
    School experiences and events
    Community happenings
    National and international events
    Current news
    Popular movies, television and radio programs

The contents of the secondary school health education program should be based upon both the general and specific health needs and interests of each individual student, the community, state and nation. Persistent health problems and concerns of adolescents include:

1. Inadequate nutrition.
2. Undetected and uncorrected visual, dental and auditory defects.
3. Inadequate information about communicable disease including syphilis and gonorrhea (both of which are increasing at an alarming rate among teenagers at the present time).
4. Undue fatigue due to faulty rest, exercise and sleep habits.
5. Needless accidents and injuries.
6. Getting along with peers and adults; self-direction and understanding.
7. Adjustment to rapidly changing bodies.

8. Preparation for an occupation and for marriage and parenthood.
9. Personal appearance, skin blemishes, weight control and cleanliness.
10. Teen-age drinking, smoking and narcotic addiction.
11. Health and safety protective insurance; how best to spend the health dollar.
12. Self-medication; consumer protection and education.
13. Mental health; personality and life value system development.
14. Prevention and control of chronic and degenerative diseases.

Ruggan suggests the following ways to improve secondary health education programs so that they can become more meaningful in the lives of adolescents:[2]

1. Obtain pertinent facts about the health status, concerns, problems, and interests of the teen-agers in their school and in their community.
2. Determine what health education has been taught, or is now being taught, or how it is organized.
3. Determine instructional policies and the philosophy, guiding principles, and general approach to curriculum improvement that prevail in the school and in the school system.
4. Define the framework within which the curriculum improvement for health education in the particular school or school system may take place.
5. Define specific objectives or behavioral goals to give direction to program development.
6. Define and select content, learning experiences, and materials.
7. Develop an acceptable organizational pattern for health education.
8. Consider ways of evaluating the health education program, stressing change in attitudes, behavior, use and application of knowledge, and the development of critical judgment.

Some of the poorest as well as some of the best teaching done in secondary schools is found in the area of health. Expert instructors in this area have capitalized upon youth's eager quest to *find out* about themselves and others and have directed these rapidly developing youngsters toward paths leading to truth, better understanding and

---

[2]Ruggan, Mabel: "Guidance in solving teen-age health problems." *Adolescence.* Washington, D.C., AAHPER, 1963, p. 73.

appreciation of health as one of life's values, as well as taught them how to become and remain healthy.

The best methods for teaching health are the same as those used in the effective teaching of any other subject. The basic aims of the program should be to teach others to live healthfully, acquire health knowledge, and develop positive reliable and accurate health attitudes. All educators with this aim in mind will develop their own best curriculum and teaching methods, guided by the abundance of health education and secondary education materials and teaching aids now available.[3]

Every physical educator has a contribution to make in the area of health and safety. Each can best do so by:

1. Helping students see the interdependent relationship between desirable health practices and total well-being, productivity and happiness.

2. Playing all games and sports according to rules.

3. Requiring all players to wear protective gear, such as catchers' masks or football helmets.

4. Instisting that all students, including athletes, use their own individual towels, toilet articles and drinking cups.

5. Having a physician present at all athletic contests in which health and safety hazards are increased.

6. Giving proper first-aid treatment when needed.

7. Protecting the health of each player, placing doing so above winning in athletic contests.

8. Honoring doctor's requests regarding recommendations for participation in physical education classes.[4]

9. Requiring all students to have an adequate physical examination before participating in physical education classes and athletics.

10. Giving students who desire it sufficient time for showering after their physical education class.

11. Providing opportunities for all students to participate in wholesome after-school recreational activities.

12. Helping students gain movement and sport skills they can use throughout life whether they are 16, 36 or 66.

13. Directing students to community agencies which have developmental and protective health and safety programs.

14. Conducting a well-rounded physical education program from which all students receive lasting benefit.

15. Maintaining a clean and sanitary shower room, locker room and gymnasium.

The Combination of Health and Physical Education Instruction

Increasingly, schools are combining health and physical education instruction, especially on the junior high school level. Such a

---

[3]See the *Suggested Readings* for recommended reference materials.

[4]See the *Appendix* for a sample medical examination blank on which the physician can check physical activities best suited for atypical students.

plan can only be successful if the teacher is certified to teach in both areas and if he is as interested in teaching health as he is in teaching physical education. Patterns for combining these two areas vary, as is illustrated here:

1. *The 3-2 Plan* — Two periods are given weekly to health education, or two to each and the fifth class meeting to corecreational activities.
2. *The 3-3 Plan* — Three weeks are given to instruction in each area.
3. *The 6-6 Plan* — Six weeks are given to instruction in each area.
4. *The Semester or Entire Year Plan* — A semester or even a whole year is given to each area, on a rotating basis.
5. *The Alternate Week Plan* — Instruction in the two areas for the two sexes is given on an alternate weekly basis; while girls have health, the boys have physical education.
6. *The Rainy Day Program* — Instruction in health is given when physical education classes must be held indoors.

Each plan, except the last one, which should *not* be used, has certain strengths and weaknesses. Any program is only as good as a skilled, enthusiastic teacher makes it. Certainly if physical educators are going to be required to teach in this area as well as in health, first aid and driver education, their professional preparation programs must include courses in teaching methods and materials in all of these areas. Health education in schools on all levels is greatly in need of a face lifting. (This is also true of physical education.) In spite of the dangers, there are many advantages to be gained from combining the two separate but related areas. Some feel that combining the two weakens both programs. This, however, is only true if physical educators are not interested in or prepared to teach health.

THE CONTRIBUTION OF THE PHYSICAL EDUCATOR TO SCHOOL HEALTH

All teachers have much to contribute to the school health program. The physical educator, however, is by the nature of his work in the most strategic position not only to detect early deviations from normal appearance but also to contribute greatly in helping students to find answers to their immediate pressing health problems. Usually his friendly informal relationship with students encourages them to come to him with their intimate problems, the majority of which center around physical or mental health. However, his greatest contribution to the total school health program is in developing physical fitness, promoting good health habits and providing safety protection and emergency care for all students.

DEVELOPING PHYSICAL FITNESS

The body develops best through exercise of the right kind in the proper amounts. Muscles increase in size, strength, tone and function through vigorous activity. The vital organs of the body are likewise affected. The rate and force of the heart beat, breathing depth and rhythm, energy and heat production, and more rapid elimination of waste products result from exercise obtained through strenuous calisthenics or playing rugged sports. All contribute to the health of the body and give one the needed zest and drive to work, play and live abundantly.

The specific benefits of exercise are that[5]

1. It builds a substructure of flexible, compact muscle which is strong and enduring.
2. It improves muscle tone and thus helps to promote an erect, balanced posture.
3. It trains the nerve centers in coordination, permitting muscle fibers to work together with less strain and more energy output. Relaxation and grace accompany good coordination.

---

[5]Frahley, Lester, Johnson, Warren, and Massey, Benjamin. *Physical Education and Healthful Living.* New York, Prentice-Hall, Inc., 1954, pp. 111–112.

Figure 7–2. Physical activity is essential to the development of a sturdy, healthful and physically efficient body. (Courtesy of the Physical Education Department, Los Angeles Public Schools.)

4. It promotes circulation, which relieves congestion in tissues and organs, stimulates cell nutrition and the destruction of foreign bodies and aids in elimination.

5. It tones up the temperature control mechanism, making the body better able to stand sudden change in temperature. It prods the sweat glands into activity and thus removes impurities from the skin.

6. It increases the thickness and strength of the heart muscle. A heart trained at overload works more efficiently at lower loads. Trained hearts pump more blood per minute with longer rest intervals between beats.

7. It increases the alkaline reserve, the glycogen and the phosphocreatin of the blood and tissues.

8. It forces the lungs to function more efficiently in supplying oxygen and in removing carbon dioxide. Better ventilation of the apices of the lungs accompanies vigorous activity, and these are the regions where tuberculosis begins.

9. It decreases the heart beat and blood pressure.

10. It stimulates total body growth.

In spite of the fact that Americans live in a land of abundant food and recreational opportunities, and that they have been exposed to or taken part in school health and physical education programs, there is much evidence that we are not so strong nor healthy as we should be. In our modern push-button age, machines, gadgets and robots increasingly do our work for us. Some claim we are becoming a "nation of onlookers," the victims of "spectatoritis." Basically, modern man's physical needs are the same as those of his far-removed ancestors. A sturdy, well-developed, useful body can only be created through activity. Now, more than ever before in our entire history, we need to take part in vigorous body-building play programs in order to compensate for activities that develop strength, stamina and health of which our "mechanical servants" are robbing us.

PROMOTING GOOD HEALTH HABITS

Because physical educators and/or coaches possess products greatly desired by youth, and because they keep prices high for obtaining them, these educators provide students with strongly motivated drives to accomplish their desired goals. Students will go to great lengths and spend much time and energy to make the first team in baseball, basketball or other sport.

Training rules regarding eating, sleeping, smoking and drinking, when enforced by the coach and vigorously followed by the student, have helped many boys and girls develop fine health habits which have carried over into their adult lives. These fortunate citizens would agree with Plato that "the results of a good physical education are not limited to the body alone, but they extend even to the soul itself."

President Eisenhower, recognizing the dangers of mechanization and soft living, while in office, appointed the President's Council on Youth Fitness which continues to function. He and other national leaders are concerned over the failure of American youth to pass basic minimum fitness tests which European youth breeze through with higher scores. The council has urged that a program of physical education and better health instruction be required of every youth, fitness programs be begun at home for adults as well as children, more adults be recruited to lead youth recreational programs, all existing recreational facilities be used more extensively and physical education programs be for all—the handicapped as well as the skilled athletes.

PROVIDING SAFETY PROTECTION AND EMERGENCY CARE

According to the National Safety Council, most school accidents which occur inside buildings happen in the gymnasium (one third of the total), with classrooms second (one fifth of the total). On the playgrounds and athletic fields, football and activities requiring running cause the most injuries. Accidents serious enough to require medical attention and school absence occur in the following places:[6]

At home	20 per cent
On school grounds	28 per cent
Inside buildings	24 per cent
Other (chiefly in public)	23 per cent
Going to and from school	5 per cent

Safety experts agree that most accidents are preventable and are caused by human failure. Teachers should be on the lookout for students who are accident prone, for often they are willing to take foolish risks and even to do bodily harm to themselves as a means of gaining recognition or group status. Since all behavior is caused, physical educators should recognize techniques used by emotionally maladjusted, accident-prone students, for they:

1. Complain of being picked on.
2. Usually are the group scapegoats.
3. Cannot or will not play according to game rules.
4. Often have poor posture, worry lines.
5. Constantly daydream (flight reaction) or are overly aggressive and rebellious (fight reaction).
6. Have annoying habits or tics, such as constant eye blinking, throat clearing and shoulder shrugging.
7. Do not succeed in school in spite of their ability to do so.
8. Often have inferior skills in playing games; are usually chosen last.

---

[6]National Safety Council: *Yearly Reports*. Chicago.

All students who show the above symptoms of maladjustment should be aided by the teacher to discover why they behave as they do. Healthier, happier and safer individuals will result when emotional stumbling blocks have been discovered, analyzed and eliminated.

PROTECTION

Although the gymnasium often contains equipment hazardous to students, and the program is filled with danger-laden activities, both attract youth because they help to satisfy their intensified need for adventure. Safety education means learning to take chances wisely in the world as it is. It would be educationally foolish to remove all hazardous activities from youth's environment, for to do so would deny them rich opportunity to learn caution, develop skills and certain protective fears. High school students are usually more attracted to danger than to safety. The instructor's approach, when stressing the importance of this health area, should be that when accidents are avoided one can play longer, or have a better chance to make the first team, than those who must lose precious practice days because of injuries. Most youth are anxious to participate in sports and games; the majority long for a first-string position. Teachers are wise to capitalize upon these dynamic desires.

Students have a right to enjoy their physical education program in clean, safe and attractive surroundings. Teachers are professionally obligated to provide them or to do their utmost to see that they are made available. Group-devised safety rules are best obeyed. The following suggestions may prove helpful for increased pupil protection in the gymnasium, pool and locker rooms, on the playground, sports field, or intramural area, and for those taking part in competitive athletics:

The Gymnasium, Pool and Locker Rooms:
1. Check to see that all equipment is in good condition. Discard and replace that which is not.
2. Avoid slippery floors.
3. Cover all exposed dangerous areas with protective pads or paint them bright yellow.
4. Have all doors open out.
5. Fountains should be in safe recessed locations.
6. Post, and strictly enforce, all rules regarding the use of the pool, running and horseplay in the showers, and use of equipment when the instructor is not present.
7. Require all students to be properly dressed for athletics; require all to wear socks and tennis shoes.
8. Stay with all assigned classes for the entire time of duty. Strive for close supervision of the whole class. Stand where you can see and be seen by the majority or the entire group.

Figure 7-3. The pool should be clean, sanitary, and well lighted and ventilated. (Courtesy of *The Scholastic Coach.*)

Playgrounds, Sports Fields and Intramural Areas:
1. Allocate space so that all teams and individuals can participate without danger to themselves or others.
2. Check all equipment. Discard and replace that which is dangerous.
3. Discover hazards with each class group; encourage them to point these out to you. Paint all immovable hazards bright yellow.
4. Mark fields and play areas; play according to official rules, for they have been made for safety of the players.
5. Place yourself on the field where you can best supervise all groups. Do not leave the area until your assigned duties are over.
6. Help all to assume responsibility for their own safety and that of others.

Competitive Athletics:
1. Lay out all playing areas from the standpoint of the best player and spectator safety protection.
2. Remove all hazardous obstructions.
3. Use only equipment approved and/or recommended by the governing association for secondary school competition in your locality.
4. Provide all players with properly fitting and safe protective clothing. Require them to keep it on while playing.
5. Receive medical approval for every participant.
6. Allow only those who have been properly trained and "warmed up" to play or enter games as substitutes.
7. Supervise all practices and competitive events; keep player safety uppermost in mind.
8. Supply proper first-aid treatment and needed medical care for all injured.

9. Insist upon adherence to training rules; avoid too frequent competition and long distance travel.
10. Make all players safety conscious.

In spite of all precautionary measures, accidents do occur in physical education classes, intramural programs and competitive interschool contests. Both their frequency and their degree of severity can be reduced by taking the following measures:

1. Play all games according to official rules.
2. Develop skills; it is the clumsy player who is most frequently injured.
3. Allow students to participate only in those activities which are suitable to their skill maturation levels.
4. Be on the lookout for fatigue, realizing that it is the tired student who is most apt to be injured. Know that fatigue levels differ with each individual.
5. Encourage students to report all injuries to you regardless of how minor they may seem at the time, and see that they receive proper treatment.

HEALTH RECORDS

Carefully kept health records provide the teacher with valuable information regarding each pupil. Contributions to these records should be made by school physicians, nurses, dentists, secretaries and teachers. They enable the instructor who studies them carefully not only to gain a greater understanding of each student in his class but they also serve as a guide in adjusting the school program to the limitations of those needing such an arrangement. The records should be cumulative, kept from the time the child enters the first grade until he leaves high school, and should follow him from one school to another. Most states have adopted standardized records. Each cumulative record should contain:

Name, age and correct address of each student
Name and address of the parents
Name of the family physician and dentist and the preferred hospital to which the child should be taken in case of an emergency
How and where the parents or guardian of the child can be reached in case of an emergency
Where the father works and type of work he does; if the mother works, where, and type of work she does
A health history, including that of all communicable diseases, operations, and other pertinent information
Immunization record
Allergies or other conditions which affect health
Height and weight records; body type (Wetzel Grid)
Remediable defects, recommended corrections and a follow-up record
Recommendations concerning nonremediable conditions (birth injuries, etc.) and suggestions concerning a modified school program, and a record of such adopted program

Dental examination results
Physical examination results
Physical fitness test results
Results of intelligence tests, personality inventories
Results of social tests in which children reveal how they feel about them-
selves and others
Record of emotional problems
Attendance reports

Individual cumulative health records should be filed in a central office and be easily accessible to all teachers and other authorized personnel for professional use.

HEALTH GUIDANCE

The health history, physical examination results and other valuable information contained in each student's cumulative health record are the basis upon which an adequate individual health guidance program should be built. In cases requiring that the school program be adjusted to meet the needs of a particular student, it is the duty of both the school nurse and teacher to see that such an adjustment is made. There are boundless opportunities for the development of a splendid program in health guidance to be built around the teacher's daily health appraisal of each student through observation, screening tests, and the physical examination. Such a guidance program should also reach the parents.

FIRST AID AND EMERGENCY CARE

Frequently, school accidents are referred to the physical educator for, unless the school has a nurse, he often is the only trained first aider on the staff. First aid is the first temporary treatment given to an injured person in an emergency by one trained and certified to do so by the American Red Cross. *Second aid* should always be given by a physician. All schools should have written policies concerning how accidents are to be handled, as well as emergency first-aid stations. It is recommended that first-aid kits be placed in every classroom and that each school have several well-stocked first-aid cabinets placed in strategic locations. Each should contain the following minimum of supplies:

ACCIDENT REPORTS

It is recommended that all accidents be reported to the proper authorities in written form. This should be filled out in triplicate. The principal should receive one copy, the director of the School Hygiene

FIRST AID CHART FOR ATHLETIC INJURIES

FIRST AID, the immediate and temporary care offered to the stricken athlete until the services of a physician can be obtained, minimizes the aggravation of injury and enhances the earliest possible return of the athlete to peak performance. To this end, it is strongly recommended that:

- ALL ATHLETIC PROGRAMS include prearranged procedures for obtaining emergency first aid, transportation, and medical care.

- ALL COACHES AND TRAINERS be competent in first aid techniques and procedures.

- ALL ATHLETES be properly immunized as medically recommended, especially against tetanus and polio.

Committee on the Medical Aspects of Sports
AMERICAN MEDICAL ASSOCIATION

To protect the athlete at time of injury,

FOLLOW THESE FIRST STEPS FOR FIRST AID:

STOP play immediately at first indication of possible injury or illness.

LOOK for obvious deformity or other deviation from the athlete's normal structure or motion.

LISTEN to the athlete's description of his complaint and how the injury occurred.

ACT, but move the athlete **only** after serious injury is ruled out.

EMERGENCY PHONE NUMBERS

Physician _____ Phone: _____

Physician _____ Phone: _____

Hospital _____ Ambulance _____

Police _____ Fire _____ Other _____

FIRST AID
FOR ATHLETIC INJURIES

First Aid, the immediate and temporary care offered to the stricken athlete until the services of a physician can be obtained minimizes the aggravation of injury and enhances the earliest possible return of the athlete to peak performance. To this end, it is strongly recommended that:

All Athletic Programs include prearranged procedures for obtaining emergency first aid, transportation, and medical care.

All Coaches and Trainers be competent in first aid techniques and procedures.

All Athletes be properly immunized as medically recommended, especially against tetanus and polio.

Committee on the
Medical Aspects of Sports
American Medical Association

FOLLOW THESE INITIAL STEPS FOR FIRST AID TO PROTECT THE ATHLETE AT THE TIME OF INJURY.

STOP play immediately at first indication of possible injury or illness.

LOOK for obvious deformity or other deviation from the athlete's normal structure or motion.

LISTEN to the athlete's description of his complaint and how the injury occurred.

 The American Medical Association designed this symbol to be a universal sign indicating the presence of information important to the life and health of the wearer. The first aider should know when people have special health problems.

BONES & JOINTS
Fracture—Never move athlete if fracture of back, neck, or skull is suspected. If athlete can be moved, carefully splint any possible fracture. Refer to physician at once. Never force protruding bones back into place.

Neck—Maintain traction on the neck, and maintain the neck in the plane of the body, neither flexing nor hyper-extending to correct.

Dislocation—Support joint. Apply ice bag or cold cloths to reduce swelling, and refer to physician.

Bone bruise—Apply ice bag or cold cloths and protect from further injury. If severe, refer to physician.

Broken Nose—Apply cold cloths and refer to physician.

MUSCLES & LIGAMENTS
Bruise—Apply ice bag or cold cloths, and rest injured muscle. Protect from further aggravation. If severe, refer to physician.

Cramp—Athlete stretches gently the affected muscle while helper massages it. If during hot day, give sips of dilute salt water. If recurring, refer to physician.

Strain and Sprain—Elevate injured part and apply ice bag or cold cloths. Apply pressure bandage to reduce swelling. Avoid weight bearing and refer to physician.

CARDIAC ARREST
Cardiac Arrest—does occur, though rarely, in coaches, players, spectators and officials. When definite cardiac arrest can be determined, a sharp blow with the fist to the chest area overlying the heart will sometimes initiate regular rhythm. If this does not occur, external cardiac massage is necessary. Mouth-to-mouth resuscitation should then be initiated. A physician should be summoned immediately.

Mouth-to-Mouth Resuscitation
(1) Victim face-up.
(2) Tilt head back and clear airway.
(3) Take a deep breath and pinch victim's nose.
(4) Blow in double-stemmed airway (if available) until chest rises.
(5) Remove your mouth and let victim exhale.
(6) When victim has exhaled, replace your mouth on his, pinch his nose and repeat.
(7) Repeat 15 times per minute.

0138-590K.8/74—3M

External Cardiac Massage
(1) Place heel of one hand on victim's lower half of middle chest.
(2) Place other hand on top of first.
(3) Keep elbows straight and exert firm downward pressure using upper half of body to do work.
(4) For adult, compress chest bone 1½ to 2" and hold for ½ second.

1. **This illustration depicts simultaneous mouth-to-mouth resuscitation and cardiac massage executed by a single person. In this case, 15 heart compressions are alternated with 2 lung ventilations.**

2. **With two persons, cardiac compression is executed by one person every second continuously and the second individual ventilates the lungs after every 5 heart compressions.**

IMPACT BLOWS
Head—If any period of disorientation, loss of memory, dizziness; headache, incoordination, or unconsciousness occurs, refrain from any further activity and refer to physician at once. Keep athlete lying down; if unconscious, give nothing by mouth. If there is inequality of the pupils or drift of the outstretched hand with the eyes closed, this is an emergency situation.

Teeth—Save teeth if completely removed from socket. If loosened, do not disturb; cover with sterile gauze and refer to dentist at once.

Solar Plexus—Rest athlete on back and moisten face with cool water. Loosen clothing around waist and chest. Do nothing else except refer to physician if needed.

Testicle—Rest athlete on back and apply ice bag or cold cloths. Refer to physician if pain persists.

Eye—If vision is impaired, especially on upward gaze, refer to physician at once. With soft tissue injury, apply ice bag or cold cloths to reduce swelling.

HEAT ILLNESSES
Heat Stroke—Collapse WITH DRY WARM SKIN AND RAPID WEAK PULSE indicates sweating mechanism failure and rising body temperature. THIS IS AN EMERGENCY: DELAY COULD BE FATAL. Immediately cool athlete by the most expedient means (spraying or sponging with cool water is a good method). Refer to physician at once.

Heat Exhaustion—Weakness WITH PROFUSE SWEATING AND RAPID PULSE indicates state of shock due to depletion of salt and water. Place person flat on his back in the shade with head on the ground, level or lower than body. Give sips of dilute salt water, if conscious. Refer to physician at once.

Sunburn—If severe, apply sterile gauze dressing; refer to physician.

OPEN WOUNDS
Heavy Bleeding—Apply direct pressure to the wound with pressure bandage if available. Elevate the part if possible. Cold application will further restrict bleeding. Refer to physician at once.

Cut and Abrasion—Hold briefly under cold water, then cleanse with mild soap and water. Apply sterile pad firmly until bleeding stops, then protect with more loosely applied sterile bandage. If extensive, refer to physician.

Puncture Wound—Handle same as cuts, and refer to physician.

Nosebleed—Keep athlete sitting or standing; cover nose with cold cloths. If bleeding is heavy, place small cotton pack in nostrils and then pinch nose. If bleeding continues, refer to physician.

OTHER CONCERNS
Blisters—Keep clean with mild soap and water and protect from aggravation. If already broken, trim ragged edges with sterile instrument. If extensive or infected, refer to physician.

Foreign Body in Eye—Do not rub. Gently touch particle with point of clean moist cloth and wash with cold water. If unsuccessful or if pain persists, refer to physician.

This chart in poster size is available from the AMA Department of Health Education. (Reproduced by permission.) *Source:* Prepared by the AMA Committee on the Medical Aspects of Sports in cooperation with the National Athletic Trainers Association and the National Federation of State High School Athletic Associations. All rights reserved. Copyright 1965, American Medical Association.

SUGGESTED FIRST AID SUPPLIES[1]

For open wounds or dry dressings for burns; these are packed sterile so do not try to make your own

First Aid Item	Use
1. Sterile first aid dressing in sealed envelope 2″ × 2″ for small wounds	Finger bandage
2. Sterile first aid dressing in sealed envelope 4″ × 4″ for larger wounds and for compress to stop bleeding	
3. Small sterile compress with adhesive attached in sealed envelopes	
4. Roller bandage 1″ × 5 yds.	To hold dressings in place
5. Roller bandage 2″ × 5 yds.	To hold dressings in place
6. Adhesive tape, roll containing assorted widths	
7. Triangular bandages	For sling; as a covering over a larger dressing
8. Mild soap	For cleaning wounds, scratches, and cuts
9. Absorbent cotton, sterilized	Swabs or pledgets for cleaning wounds
10. Applicator sticks	For making swabs
11. Tongue blades	For splinting broken fingers and stirring solutions
12. Scissors with blunt tips	For cutting bandages or clothing
13. Tweezers	To remove stingers from insect bites or to remove splinters
14. Splints ¼″ thick, 3½″ wide, 12–15″ long	For splinting broken arms and legs
15. Table salt	For shock—dissolve 1 teaspoon salt
16. Baking soda	and ½ teaspoon of baking soda in 1 quart of water
17. Hot water bottle with cover	Local relief of pain
18. Ice bag	Local relief of pain and to prevent or reduce swelling Burns
19. Tourniquet. Wide strip of cloth 20″ long, and a short stick	For use in severe injuries when no other method will control bleeding
20. Eye dropper	For rinsing eyes

---

[1]SOURCE: *Joint Committee on Health Problems in Education of the National Education Association and the American Medical Association*, School Health Services (*Chicago: National Education Association and American Medical Association, 1964*), *p. 228.* Reproduced by permission.

or Health Department, the second, and the first aider should keep the third one. A sample accident blank report is shown in Figure 7–4.

LIABILITY

Few school boards can be sued for negligent acts of omission or commission because of their common-law immunity. This theory states that because the "king can do no wrong" and the state represents him, the state cannot be sued. Consequently, since each school district is a division of government, the school board is immune to lawsuits. Because school districts conduct nonprofit governmental functions they also are nonliable. In contrast, all organizations which carry on profit-making or proprietary functions can be held liable. Teachers, on the other hand, as well as activity directors in profit-making organizations, can be sued for proven acts of negligence. Legally, negligence is defined as either conducting an act which any reasonable person would have known to be too unreasonable and risky for others to do or failing to perform an act necessary for the protection of others.

Physical educators should be keenly aware that the possibilities of accidents occurring in their classes are greater than in any other area of the school program. They must be greatly concerned with the accident potential of every activity they teach. As Daughtrey points out:[7]

When teachers leave their classes unattended, attempt to supervise groups that are too large, or allow students to participate in too many activities at the same time, accidents are most liable to occur. The importance of quality instruction as a deterrent to accidents cannot be over-emphasized.

Physical educators can be held liable for proven negligence for the following reasons:

1. Pupil injuries where playground or gymnastic equipment is defective. (Physical educators should check and periodically report in *written form* to their administrators known defective, dangerous equipment and hazardous areas. They should keep a carbon copy of this report.)
2. Injuries which occur to pupils who attempt to do exercises or activities beyond their skill, such as handstands, running-jump somersaults, etc. (Teachers should not permit students to attempt exercises or activities for which they have not developed the necessary skills or been warned about inherent dangers.)
3. Injuries caused by the negligence of another pupil. The other pupil's misconduct must be foreseeable. (All teachers should know about what to expect of each student in behavior as well as performance.)

---

[7]Daughtrey, Greyson: *Effective Teaching in Physical Education for Secondary Schools.* Philadelphia, W. B. Saunders Co., 1973, p. 316.

ACCIDENT REPORT

Name of the school ....

This report must be sent immediately, (a) original to School Principal, and (b) Director of School Hygiene, Health Department, and (c) keep a copy of this yourself.

1. Name of injured ....
   Age .... Sex .... School attended .... Grade ....

2. Date of injury .... Exact time ....

3. School employee in charge at time of accident ....

4. Where did accident occur? (Be specific) ....

   ....

5. Describe the accident fully. (What was person doing? How did accident occur?) ....

   ....

   ....

   ....

   ....

6. Kind of injury (Broken arm, cut finger, etc. Be specific) ....

   ....

7. Was first aid given? .... By whom? ....
   What kind? ....

8. Accident caused by another person .... Name ....
   Address .... How? ....

9. Name and address of person giving facts as to time, nature, and manner of injury ....

10. Eyewitnesses present at time:
    Name .... Address ....
    Name .... Address ....

11. Where was injured taken? ....
    How? .... By whom? ....

    ....

12. Name and address of doctor handling case ....

13. Parent or guardian notified? .... By whom? ....
    How? ....

14. Other pertinent facts ....

    ....

15. How could accident have been prevented? ....

    ....

16. Was injury attributable to any defect in construction or improper maintenance of the building or equipment? ....

    ....

    ....

Signature ....

Date ....

Figure 7–4. A sample accident report.

Figure 7-5. Both the students and teachers must always be safety conscious. (Courtesy Enrico Fermi High School.)

4. Leaving assigned groups, even though temporarily, to get a drink of water, go to the bathroom or answer a phone call. (Physical educators who teach class by throwing in the ball and leaving or other such types of instructing by remote control are *asking for trouble*.)

Accidents sometimes happen in spite of precaution, safety education programs, adequate emergency measures, or routinized habits drilled into students of what to do in case of fire or an air raid. Periodic surveys should be made and carefully studied to determine the real effectiveness of the school safety program. Only when comparative figures show a reduction in the number of school accidents and a lessened severity of individual injuries can progress be claimed or the program said to be of value.

HOW TO AVOID LIABILITY

Teachers can help safeguard pupils from injuries and avoid liability if they:

1. Check all equipment periodically and report in writing to supervisors all deficiencies. Be especially on the lookout for defective playground and other kinds of apparatus, worn out equipment and unattached lockers or other items that could fall on someone.
2. Be sure all students in the required programs and athletes have recent physical examinations and for the latter that all parents sign yearly permission play forms.

3. Do not send an injured student or player back into a class or game without clearing with the school physician or other medical personnel.

4. Remove overly and easily fatigued students or players from too strenuous class activity or game play. Work individually to help each student develop physical stamina and strength.

5. Never allow a student to try a stunt or other physical activity until he has been taught the lead-up skills needed to do it safely.

6. Be sure all students have mastered needed skills and game techniques before they are allowed to play in games.

7. Play all games according to their rules and have the required number of players on each team. Avoid matching an unskilled player with a highly skilled one in events in which chances of injury are greatly increased (e.g., wrestling and pole-vaulting).

DISCUSSION QUESTIONS

1. What health services should the school provide?
2. How can courses in health education be improved?
3. What are the signs of emotional maladjustment? How can teachers best help students who show these signs?
4. How can accidents best be prevented?
5. What is the legal difference between governmental and a proprietary function? Why are most school boards immune from lawsuits, while teachers are not?
6. What constitutes negligence? How can it be avoided?
7. How can students be taught good safety precautions in any three team sports, three individual sports and in aquatics? Give specific suggestions for each of these activities.

THINGS TO DO

1. Visit any health class in any school. Report to your classmates what you learned from this experience.
2. Make a survey of your own school environment with a classmate for health and accident hazards. Report your findings in class.
3. List the advantages and disadvantages for each of the six patterns for combining health instruction with physical education instruction given in this chapter. Which plan do you most endorse?
4. Take any physical fitness test. Evaluate your own fitness status in written form.
5. What training rules should a coach have? How can these best be enforced? Discuss these two questions in class.

SELECTED VISUAL AIDS

First Aid. Encyclopaedia Britannica Films. Stresses all aspects of first aid.

The Safe Diving Series. Coronet Films. Teen-agers especially will be interested in this film, which stresses all aspects of being a good and safe diver.

Guide to Good Eating. National Dairy Councel. Stresses the value of a balanced diet in relationship to good health.

SUGGESTED READINGS

Aaron, James, Bridges, Frank, and Ritzel, Dale: *First Aid and Emergency Care: Prevention and Protection of Injuries.* New York, Macmillan Co., 1972.

AAHPER: *Sports Safety.* Washington, D.C., 1968.

AAHPER: *School Safety Policies With Emphasis on Physical Education.* Athletics and Recreation, Washington, D.C., 1968.

Alexander, R., and Alexander, K.: *Teachers and Torts, Liability for Pupil Injury.* Middletown, Kentucky, Maxwell Publishing Co., 1970.

Appenzeller, Herbert: *From Gym To Jury.* Virginia, Michie Co., 1970.

Daughtrey, Gregson, and Woods, John: *Physical Education Programs: Organization and Administration.* Philadelphia, W. B. Saunders Co., 1971.

Grimsley, J. D.: "Legal Liability of the Injured Pupil." *The Physical Educator,* 26:104, 1969.

Hafen, Brent, Thygerson, Alton, and Peterson, Ray: *First Aid: Contemporary Practices and Principles.* Minneapolis, Burgess Publishing Co., 1972.

Henderson, John: *Emergency Medical Guide.* New York, McGraw-Hill Co., 1969.

Klafs, C. E., Arnheim, D. D.: *Modern Principles of Athletic Training.* 3rd Ed. St. Louis, C. V. Mosby Co., 1973.

Klafs, Carl, and Lyon, M. Joan: *The Female Athlete, Conditioning, Competition, and Culture.* St. Louis, C. V. Mosby Co., 1973.

Leebee, Howard: *Tort Liability for Injuries to Pupils.* Ann Arbor, Michigan, Campus Publishers, 1965.

National Commission on Safety Education: *Who Is Liable for Pupil Injuries?* Washington, D.C., National Education Association, 1963.

Resick, Mathew, Seidel, Beverly, and Mason, James: *Modern Administrative Practices in Physical Education and Athletics.* Reading, Mass., Addison-Wesley Publishing Co., 1970.

Van Der Smissen, Betty: *Legal Liability of Cities and Schools of Injuries in Recreation and Parks.* Cincinnati, W. H. Anderson Co., 1968.

Vannier, Maryhelen: *Teaching Health in Elementary Schools.* 2nd Ed. Philadelphia, Lea and Febriger, 1974.

CHAPTER EIGHT

FACILITIES

As was pointed out earlier in the discussion of the aims and objectives of physical education, the many objectives of physical education can be more readily achieved for a greater number of students if the program presents a wide variety of activities. Different types of activities require different facilities; consequently, any limitation of facilities creates difficulties in presenting the desired variety of activities. In the "ideal" environment for conducting a superior physical education program, these facilities would be available: administrative and staff offices, locker, shower and dressing rooms, a gymnasium, outdoor play fields, storage space, pool, room for adapted activities, dance studio, recreation room and classroom. Few schools have sufficient financial resources to provide all of these facilities. To overcome their lack of space and facilities, more and more schools are utilizing appropriate public and private facilities in the community, ranging from golf and bowling to roller skating and horseback riding, for the instruction of physical education activities.

INDOOR FACILITIES

Effective utilization of indoor facilities, whether in the school or community, is determined by the number of teaching stations desired and the types of activities which are to be presented. *Teaching station* refers to a separate teaching space of sufficient size to accommodate a group in a specific activity. The number of teaching stations required in any school situation is determined by the total number of students enrolled, the size of the classes, the frequency of class meetings, the number of periods in the school day, and the activities to be provided. For optimum teaching, class size should not exceed 40 students. The formula that follows is useful in determining the number of teaching stations needed for each class period.[1]

---

[1]Daughtrey, Greyson and Woods, John B.: *Physical Education Programs: Organization and Administration.* Philadelphia, W. B. Saunders Co., 1971, p. 67.

$$\frac{\text{Students enrolled in physical education}}{\text{Class size}} \times$$

$$\frac{\text{Number of periods class meets weekly}}{\text{Number of class periods in school week}} = \text{Number of stations needed}$$

Number of periods class meets weekly × periods in one day = Number of class periods in school week

Students enrolled in physical education = 1200
Class size = 40
Number of periods class meets weekly = 5
Number of periods in one day = 6

$$\frac{1200}{40} \times \frac{5}{6 \times 5} = \frac{6000}{1200} = 5 \text{ stations needed}$$

THE GYMNASIUM

The recommended size for a school gymnasium which will be used by senior high school students is 65 feet × 102 feet floor space with a 22 to 24 foot high ceiling. A gymnasium with this much floor space will accommodate one official basketball court or two smaller basketball courts running the width of the floor; three volleyball courts of less than official size; and 12 badminton courts of less than official size. The gymnasium may be equipped with a folding partition which divides the space into two areas. When the folding partition is in use, there are available on each side six badminton courts or one volleyball court.

For the safety of the students as well as for ease of instruction, the gymnasium should have a smooth, nonslippery floor, good lighting

Figure 8–1.

and a soundproof ceiling, adequate heat and ventilation thermostatically controlled, recessed radiators, wall or hanging apparatus, folding bleachers, recessed water fountains, floor plates for standards and apparatus, a wire-covered clock, electrical outlets, a scoreboard and player benches. Floor markings for playing areas may be painted on permanently, or temporarily with liquid chalk or tempera paint. Preferably, the gymnasium should be located in a separate wing that is easily accessible to the public for community as well as school use.

The American Association for Health, Physical Education, and Recreation has listed several important factors to keep in mind when planning the gymnasium.[2]

1. Hard maple flooring is resilient and nonslippery, and should be used.
2. Interior walls should be smooth to a height of 10 or 12 feet.
3. Upper walls need not be smooth.
4. The ceiling should reflect light and absorb sound, and there should be at least 22 to 24 feet from the floor to exposed beams.
5. Windows should be 10 to 12 feet above floor and placed on long side of room.
6. Heating should be thermostatically controlled and radiators should be recessed with protecting grill or grate if placed at floor level.
7. Sub-flooring should be resistant to moisture and termites and be well ventilated.
8. Prior consideration must be given to the suspension of apparatus from the ceiling and the erection of wall-type apparatus.
9. Mechanical ventilation may be necessary.
10. Proper illumination meeting approved standards and selectively controlled for various activities must be designed.
11. Floor plates for standards and apparatus must be planned, as well as such items as backboards, electric clocks and scoreboards, public address system and provisions for press and radio.
12. Floor markings for various games should be placed after prime coat of seal has been applied and prior to application of the finishing coats.

POSSIBILITIES FOR ADDITIONAL TEACHING STATIONS

Only in rare instances can the size of the gymnasium be altered to increase the amount of space. Consequently, when more teaching stations must be developed, it is necessary to utilize other available spaces with activities appropriate to the size and capacities of these spaces. Unused classrooms, hallways, storage areas, and the stage offer possibilities for teaching weightlifting, wrestling, gymnastics and recreational activities. Within the community there may be public or privately

---

[2]American Association for Health, Physical Education, and Recreation: *Administrative Problems in Health Education, Physical Education, and Recreation*. Washington, D.C., 1953, The Association, p. 83.

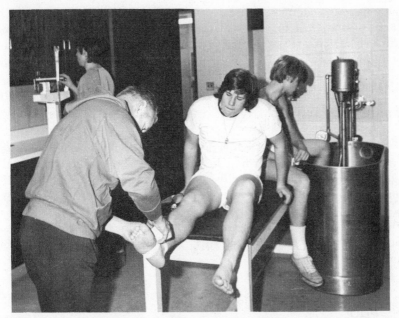

Figure 8–2. The training room provides a place for such activities as preventive taping of athletes. (Courtesy Enrico Fermi High School.)

owned buildings with large floor spaces or with athletic facilities of various types. These may often be leased by the school for use during the day when the buildings are ordinarily not in use. Such utilization of community resources is an excellent means of providing additional space for teaching stations and for broadening the physical education opportunities for students. The only significant disadvantage occurs when the facility is located beyond easy walking distance from the school and transportation of the students by buses is necessary, creating financial and administrative problems. Consideration of such problems has prompted Ezersky and Theibert[3] to suggest that future construction of community sports facilities, such as basketball, aquatic, gymnastic and tennis centers, be located in close proximity to schools that may wish to utilize the facilities.

The possibility for actual expansion of indoor space for added teaching stations exists in several kinds of recently developed structures that can be erected economically and rapidly on available school ground. Two of the more promising structures are the geodesic dome and the air-supported structure. The former is constructed from aluminum tubing bolted together in a geodesic form. One style, with the

[3]Ezersky, Eugene and Theibert, Richard P.: "City Schools Without Gyms." *Journal of Health, Physical Education, Recreation.* April, 1970, pp. 26–29.

trade name of Dome-Gym, has built-in gymnastic equipment.[4] The air-supported structure is a large plastic bubble, the ceiling and sides of which are supported by continuous air pressure provided by an air pump.[5]

SPECIAL AREAS

Ideally, the physical education facilities would include a classroom where discussions could be held, films shown and written tests taken and a room in which the adapted physical education activities could be conducted. However, one room can serve for both the classroom type activities and the adapted physical education activities. With very careful planning, the same room may also be utilized as another teaching station for such activities as weightlifting and tumbling.

THE POOL

The size, shape and depth of the pool which is most satisfactory for a school swimming program are determined by the nature of the pool's use. For example, the requirements for a pool used for competitive swimming and diving are different from recreational swimming requirements. For nearly all purposes the rectangular pool with varying depths is the most satisfactory.

Recommended water depths for a pool used for educational purposes are: 5 feet 8 inches, 3 feet 9 inches to 5 feet deep, and a shallow area 2 feet 10 inches to 3 feet 8 inches. The separate water depth areas may be identified by buoy markers. The pool should be equipped with ladder and steps; ideally these are built into the pool during its construction. Also, so there is no discrimination against the handicapped, the pool should be equipped with a hydraulic lift to enable those with lower limb disabilities to enter and leave the pool.

The pool should be kept at temperatures ranging from 75 to 80° for mass recreation, between 80 to 86° for beginners and for therapy or adapted work, and be not less than 70° for competitive swimming. The walls and ceiling should be painted in a soft color that will reflect light evenly over the swimming area. The room must be well heated and ventilated. Adequate space needs to be provided for dressing rooms,

---

[4]American Association for Health, Physical Education, and Recreation: "Products Parade." *Journal of Health, Physical Education, Recreation.* May, 1972, p. 93.

[5]Puckett, John: "Two Promising Innovations in Physical Education Facilities." *Journal of Health, Physical Education, Recreation.* January, 1972, pp. 40–41.

spectators, storage and the instructors' offices. Hair dryers should be made available in the dressing areas, as well as lavatory and toilet facilities.

For information about pool design, see the "Suggested Readings."

SHOWER, LOCKER, TRAINING AND RESTROOMS

There should be one shower head for every three or four students, all spaced at least 4 feet apart. It is desirable that there be several cubicle type showers, in addition to the gang showers, for use by those students who prefer privacy. Soap, properly controlled water and room temperature, and good ventilation should be supplied in the shower area.

The locker room should be large enough to accommodate each class and contain an average of 4 square feet per student at peak load. Long lockers made of wood or metal are considered more satisfactory than wire baskets.

Increasingly, secondary schools with interscholastic sports programs have training rooms, special areas for first aid treatment, preventive taping and padding, and so on. Standard equipment for this facility consists of one or two padded tables, scales, whirlpool tub and storage cabinets.

Adequate, well-lighted, ventilated restrooms should be provided. These must be kept clean and sanitary at all times. Soap and towels are usually furnished by the school.

All of these facilities should be arranged so they are readily accessible to handicapped students, including those in wheelchairs.

THE INSTRUCTOR'S OFFICE

The teacher needs some private space for keeping records and doing his desk work, preferably near the areas used for his classes. The office space should be large enough to accommodate a desk, file cabinet, bookcases and chairs. If the office is shared with other teachers, special arrangements should be made for conferring privately with students.

OUTDOOR FACILITIES

Ideal outdoor facilities include a football field encircled by a running track, spectator seats, baseball and softball diamonds which can be superimposed over other areas, if necessary, playing fields for

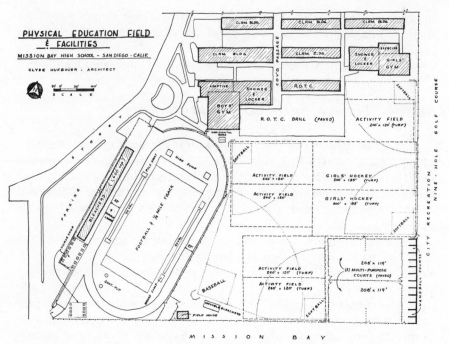

Figure 8–3. Mission Bay High School in San Diego, California, has well-planned field and physical education facilities for both girls and boys. (Courtesy of *The Scholastic Coach.*)

various other sports and games, archery lanes, a golf pitch and putt or driving range, tennis courts, a swimming pool and an area for recreational games. Adjacent to the track there should be areas for the broad jump, pole vault and high jump pits.

The playing field area should be approximately 150,000 square feet and marked for multiple use for volleyball, hockey, soccer, softball, speedball, football, touch football, baseball and recreational games. The areas may be lined with white tape or lime.

Secondary schools should have a minimum of 40 acres for outdoor activities. All outside play areas should be fenced. Outdoor lighting will greatly increase the use of all areas and is relatively inexpensive when costs are viewed in relation to the number of people served.[6]

In cities where land for outdoor playing fields is limited, some schools are utilizing the roofs of their buildings for those physical education activities that can be accommodated in this space. Often the roof surface can be used just as it is, but in some cases it must be covered with suitable material. Synthetic turf is considered

[6]National Electrical Manufacturers Association: *Standard Floodlight Layouts for Floodlighting Sports Areas.* 155 E. 44th Street, New York, N.Y. 10017.

Figure 8–4. As many as six teams can play basketball at one time on the three outdoor courts. The goals are specially constructed to provide regulation basketball playing areas. (Courtesy of *The Scholastic Coach..*)

the most desirable cover because of its effectiveness, durability and attractive appearance.

Synthetic turf surfacing is also being used by some schools for playing areas that traditionally required turf. The synthetic turf is relatively expensive and to date has been used chiefly on stadium football fields at universities and colleges. A recent survey of athletic directors whose schools were using artificial turf[7] indicated that the synthetic surface increased the actual time that the field could be used and also increased the number of activities that could be scheduled in the activity program.

The surfacing around all fixed outdoor equipment should be of air-cell materials like rubber, cork and sponge, and be under as well as around hanging ropes, chinning and turning bars or other kinds of apparatus.

MULTIPLE-PURPOSE COURTS

All hard surfaced areas should be constructed and marked for multiple-purpose use. Such courts can be used for tennis, badminton, volleyball, handball, shuffleboard, boccie, basketball, deck tennis,

[7]Lashbrook, Lynn: Artificial Turf," *Journal of Health, Physical Education, Recreation.* November–December, 1971, pp. 28–29.

roller and ice skating, fly and bait casting, mass calisthenics and recreational games. Dimensions for some of the courts whose boundaries can be marked permanently on a hard surface are given in the Appendix.

INCREASED USE OF FACILITIES

School facilities are paid for by the public and should serve this group by being used to their best advantage. Rooms or fields that are used only a few hours of the day by a few students become very expensive per exposure hour. (The exposure hour for any facility is de-

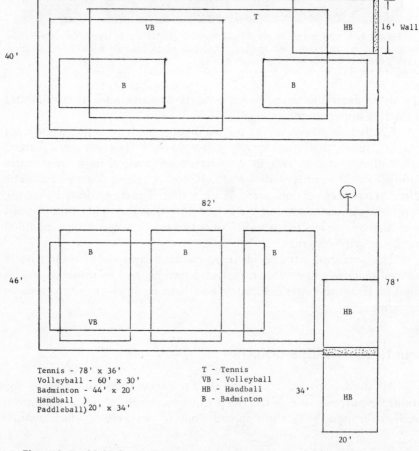

Figure 8–5. Multiple-use sport areas. (Reprinted from *Intramurals for the Senior High School,* courtesy of the AAHPER.)

Figure 8-6. All outdoor facilities, including handball courts, should be used to their fullest extent in class and after-school programs. (Courtesy Los Angeles Unified School District.)

termined by the number of hours it is used multiplied by the number of participants involved.) Facilities such as special varsity athletic fields and adapted physical education rooms which are not used for any other purposes become extremely expensive when the exposure hours are calculated, because of the limited number of students using them. If ways can be devised to provide for more extensive use of facilities of this kind by more students without detracting from the facilities' original intent, the total education cost will be spread and the cost per person lowered.

THE COMMUNITY-CENTER SCHOOLS

The per person cost of educational facilities can be further reduced by opening the schools when the majority of people are free from work and are searching for places to go for positive recreation. Since schools belong to the people in the community, all should be served by them and school properties opened for public use after school hours, during summer months and vacation periods, subject to regulations necessary for safeguarding this public property. A planning and administrative council, representing the school, the local recreation leaders of youth-serving agencies, and community government, should be formed to work out detailed operational codes and other necessary regulations carefully. These should include:

1. Regulations regarding the hours the facilities will be available.
2. Leadership source and salary scales.
3. Financial details.
4. Equipment source, use, repair and replacement.
5. Program offerings for all age groups.
6. Summer recreational plans.

An operational principle which might well govern the planned use of school facilities by the public is that the school exists for education (and in most cases for a specific age group), and the "recreational uses" should in no way detract from the "educational uses" of the school.

DISCUSSION QUESTIONS

1. How is the achievement of the established objectives of physical education influenced by the type of facilities available? Illustrate with examples.
2. What other information is needed to answer the question: How many teaching stations are needed for a school with an enrollment of 500?
3. What facilities are considered as special areas? What are their purposes and could they be easily dispensed with?
4. Discuss how additional teaching stations could be established for a school with limited facilities. For your own school.
5. What are the advantages of having the school serve as a community center? Can you name some disadvantages?

THINGS TO DO

1. Prepare a diagram and descriptive notes showing the kinds and amount of outdoor space needed to conduct a good physical education program for a high school of 1500 students.
2. Design an outdoor multiple-use facility and describe how night lighting will affect both the cost and use of it.
3. Read and summarize any article in the *Journal of Health, Physical Education, and Recreation* on facilities for physical education or recreation.
4. Visit any secondary school in your area. Write a summary of your visit in light of this chapter.
5. Outline a community-school recreation program for a specific group. Elaborate on one phase of it, e.g., leadership, activities, finances, needed equipment, areas and facilities.

SELECTED VISUAL AIDS

The El Paso Story. A color film showing how federal funds were used to build facilities for school physical education and community recreation use. Available from the El Paso, Texas, Public Schools.

Country and Community in Action. Shows the organization and development of three community recreation programs in Indiana. Available on a rental basis from the Audio-Visual Center, Indiana University, Bloomington, Indiana.

A Chance to Play. A 20 mm., b & w, free loan film stresses the importance of lighting in relationship to night recreational programs. Available from the Apparatus Department, General Electric Company, Schenectady, N.Y.

SUGGESTED READINGS

Dressing Rooms and Related Service Facilities for Physical Education, Athletics, and Recreation. AAHPER, 1972.

Planning Areas and Facilities for Health, Physical Education and Recreation. The Athletic Institute and AAHPER, 1966.

Bucher, Charles: *Foundations of Physical Education.* 6th Ed. St. Louis, The C. V. Mosby Co., 1972.

Butler, George: *Introduction to Community Recreation.* 4th Ed. New York, The McGraw-Hill Book Co., 1967.

Castaldi, Basil: *Creative Planning of Educational Facilities.* Chicago, Rand McNally and Co., 1969.

Daugherty, Greyson, and Woods, John B.: *Physical Education Programs: Organization and Administration.* Philadelphia, W. B. Saunders Co., 1971.

Gabrielsen, M. Alexander *et al.: Aquatics Handbook.* 2nd Ed. Englewood Cliffs, New Jersey, Prentice-Hall, Inc., 1968.

CHAPTER NINE

EQUIPMENT AND SUPPLIES

Equipment for the physical education program consists of all durable materials such as flying rings, badminton nets and standards used in the various activities of the program; supplies are those items such as tennis balls and baseball bats which are expendable and need to be replaced more frequently. Equipment and supplies implement the teaching of physical education, and the activities to be taught should determine the equipment needed rather than the equipment determine what will be taught.

The amount and kinds of equipment and supplies needed are dependent upon the number and sex of the students to be served, available community facilities, skill level of groups, geographical location, and method of teaching. In general, one piece of equipment such as a basketball or softball bat for every eight students should be adequate when the traditional method is used in teaching the class. However, when the problem solving method is used, it is often necessary for each student to have his own piece of equipment.[1] Equipment and supplies needed for specific activities in the secondary school physical education program include:

Body Building, Physical Fitness and Figure Control
Calisthenics—mats
Figure Control—mats, full-length mirror, scales
Weightlifting—weights, bars, collars, head harnesses
Isometric contractions—head harnesses, straps, hooks on the wall, floor and ceiling
Combative activities—mats
Relays—stop watch

Individual Sports
Archery—bows, arrows, arm guards, finger tabs, ground quivers, targets
Badminton—birds, nets, standards, racquets
Bowling—bowling balls, pins, alley or plastic balls and pins with backstop

---

[1]AAHPER: *Administrative Problems in Health, Physical Education and Recreation.* 1201 16th Street, N.W., Washington, D.C., 1953, pp. 86–87.

Golf — balls, iron and wood clubs, driving range or cage
Tennis — balls, nets, standards, racquets, backstop, tennis ball throwing machine
Wrestling — mats, head gear
Croquet — balls, mallets, wickets
Deck tennis — rings, nets, standards
Handball — official handballs and gloves or soft handballs
Horseshoes — horseshoes, stakes, pits
Shuffleboard — cues, disks

Track and Field
Track events — batons, hurdles, stop watch, starting blocks
Field events — tape measure, jumping pits, jumping and vaulting standards, shot put, vaulting poles, javelin, discus

Aquatics
Swimming — flutter boards, life-saving equipment, hair dryers
Diving — life-saving equipment, diving boards, hair dryers
Water polo — balls, goals, hair dryers

Team Sports
Basketball — balls, goals, backboards
Field hockey — balls, goals, sticks, shin pads, goalie pads
Football (tackle, touch, flag) — balls, goalposts, protective equipment, flags
Soccer — balls, goals, protective equipment
Softball and baseball — balls, bats, bases, gloves, protective equipment, backstop
Speedball — balls, football goalposts
Volleyball — balls, nets, standards

Dance
Folk, square, social, modern — piano, records, record player, percussion instruments, full-length mirror

Tumbling and Gymnastics
Tumbling and rebound tumbling — mats, tumbling belt, trampoline
Gymnastics — horizontal bar, ladders, rings, side horse, parallel bars, ropes, vaulting buck, Swedish box, springboard, balance beam

A list of general equipment and supplies necessary for the conduct of many of the activities usually found in the program includes: lime and marker, first-aid equipment, tape measure, whistles, timer, stop watches, eyeglass protectors, portable blackboard, chalk, eraser, floor tape, lockers, locks, air pumps, marking and stenciling equipment.

There are many skill development devices currently on the market that can aid the secondary school student to develop ability and skill in physical education activities. They include such aids as the automatic pitching machine for development of batting skills, a tennis ball throwing machine for individual practice on specific strokes, rebound nets for practicing tennis strokes and also throwing and catching skills, kicking cage for improving football kicking skills, and golf cage for

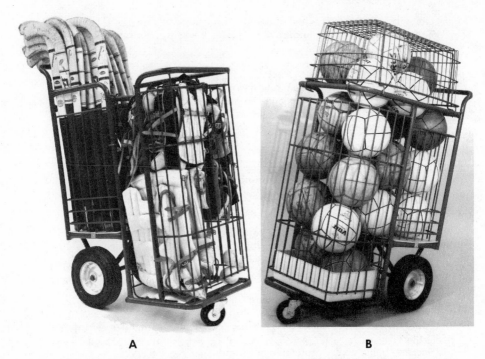

A   B

Figure 9–1. A, B. There are many types of commercial devices now on the market that will help teachers move equipment quickly and with ease. (Courtesy of the Hargal All-Sports Carryall Company.)

practicing the swings. In addition, there are a number of devices available for aiding the development of physical fitness. These range from wall pulleys, bicycle ergometers and motorized and nonmotorized treadmills to weightlifting machines.

Many of these items can enhance a physical education program but they are often very expensive and can be used only by a limited number of students at a given time. If purchase of such a machine is planned, careful consideration must be given to the value received in relation to the cost. For information concerning new equipment both for the development of skills and of physical fitness, see "Product Parade," a feature appearing frequently in the *Journal of Health, Physical Education, Recreation.*

INVENTORY

An inventory of the supplies and equipment on hand should be made at the end of each school year. A teacher in a new position, finding that no recent inventory has been made, should make one at the beginning of the school year in order to have some useful basis of comparison for the end of the year inventory. From the yearly inventory a teacher is able to gain helpful information for planning future equipment needs and for determining whether equipment and supplies are being lost or worn out at an unreasonable rate. These assessments can then be used to develop an adequate and realistic budget for the following year and to set up procedures to ensure proper care of the supplies and equipment if this need is indicated.

BUDGET

Traditionally, budgets in public schools focus mainly upon the costs of the equipment, supplies, services, salaries and so forth required to carry out the functions of the school. The amount to be budgeted for each need is determined by the administrative officers of the school after considering the requests and recommendations of the faculty. Before submitting their budget requests the teachers of physical education are well advised to develop a statement of explanation and justification of the request.

Such a statement might first list the objectives of the present program and identify the activities of the program that meet these objectives and the equipment and supplies required to teach these activities effectively. Deficiencies in the amount of equipment and supplies are pointed out. Next, desirable expansion of the objectives and programs are presented with good evidence to support the need. The equipment and supplies required for the new activities are listed. If the new items are so numerous or so costly that there is little likelihood of their being purchased on one year's budget, the items may be given priority ratings for purchase over several years. This kind of long-range planning is often the most satisfactory way of ensuring an expanded program.

A new concept in budgeting, Planning-Programming Budgeting Systems (PPBS), offers the possibility of planning a budget based on the cost of achieving the educational objectives. The first step in this budgeting approach is to establish the goals or objectives that are to be accomplished. The next step is to identify all the programs that constitute the school's activities, e.g., instruction, administration, service, and then define the objectives of each of these programs. After these objectives have been established, the possible approaches that may be used to achieve them are examined and several alternative approaches are determined. In the next step, the various approaches are carefully analyzed for feasibility, effectiveness, and costs, and the best approach is selected and its cost included in the budget. An important part of this system is an evaluation at the end of the time which the budget covered to determine how well the expenditures have allowed the stated objectives to be achieved.

The role of the individual teacher in PPBS is to develop the objectives and identify the possible approaches to be utilized in achieving them. The evaluation procedure is also largely a teacher responsibility.

It is generally accepted that the money for the physical education budget should come from the same source as funds for other educational endeavors. Dependence of the physical education program—and this includes interscholastic sports—on gate receipts to finance the program is likely to jeopardize its educational values. When any portion of the physical education program is forced to be a moneymaker, the emphasis in that activity is almost certain to be placed elsewhere than on the education of the participants.

PURCHASING EQUIPMENT

School systems employ different procedures in purchasing equipment and supplies. In some schools the physical educator is himself responsible for ordering and purchasing the supplies and equipment needed by the school. Elsewhere, usually in the larger systems, the items are secured through centralized purchasing. Most schools request that the suppliers submit bids and make their purchases from the company that has the lowest selling price. When the physical educator is preparing the list of items to be purchased either through centralized purchasing or by the bidding procedure, he must be extremely careful in the description of the items to avoid the possibility that inferior supplies will be purchased.

In the selection of equipment and supplies, consideration must be given to these factors: design and safety factors, material, quality of workmanship, cost of maintenance in both time and money, and the actual cost. The design of the item to be purchased should be practical, that is, it should serve the purpose for which it will be used. The design of sports apparel should provide comfort and safety for the wearer. Appearance should be a consideration but utility should not be sacrificed for looks. The quality of the material and the workmanship greatly influence the length of service one may expect from the product. The material should be durable and appropriate for the uses to which the item will be put. The quality of the workmanship is attested to by the way the product is sewn or put together. Regardless of the superiority of its design or material, a product lacks quality if it has not been constructed with expert workmanship.

Research is constantly developing new designs and materials for physical education supplies and equipment. Because it is difficult for the buyer to keep up with the new developments, he must provide himself with certain safeguards against unsatisfactory purchases. One of the better safeguards is to purchase only from reputable manufacturers who stand behind their products. Another is to purchase un-tried newly developed products in small quantities and test them in actual use before securing a large number.

The ease with which the supplies and equipment can be cared for is important not only for the actual dollars and cents which may be saved in maintenance but in the expenditure of time. Quality, design and material are the factors which chiefly influence the amount of care which must be given to preserving and repairing a given item. Gadgets or "extras" on equipment which make it difficult and costly to main-tain should be avoided.

In the consideration of the actual cost of an item, it is necessary to weigh all of the above mentioned factors. As a general guide for the purchaser, it may be said that in buying from a *reputable firm*, the highest priced items are the best quality.

The following suggestions, if followed, will be an aid in obtaining the most value from allocated funds:

1. In buying sportswear consider appearance, comfort, wearing quality of the fabric, stability, safety, guarantee, frequency of use, climatic conditions, and amount of laundering or cleaning needed.
2. Buy the best quality possible. Shop around and place orders with several companies.
3. Buy multipurpose equipment.
4. Provide for left-handed players.
5. Avoid accepting gifts from salesmen, for they usually entail obligations of some kind.
6. See what you are buying. Test it carefully in order to learn if it will fit your needs. Do not order trophies or other awards from a catalogue or have them engraved before actually seeing them.
7. Buy early. Football equipment can be ordered in December, delivered in late August, and billed for in October.

EQUIPMENT ROOM

The equipment room should be an area which can be shut off from general use. It must be well ventilated and securely locked. If the school does not have such a room, it might convert a storage room, or a section of the dressing room or of a nearby classroom could be parti-tioned off with caging wire to provide an adequate equipment room.

The entrance door to the equipment room may be cut in half to allow the upper section to swing open while equipment is being issued. Such a door is functional, but does not always prevent students from swinging open the bottom section and helping themselves. This can be prevented by installing a small window through which to issue the equipment. If outside windows are easily accessible, these should be barred to discourage thieves.

MARKING EQUIPMENT

It is recommended that the name or initials of the school appear on all athletic uniforms, physical education costumes and gear. The size (or designation of small, medium or large) should be labeled on the garments. For example, a pair of warm-up pants, size 28 and the first to be numbered, would be stenciled with "1–28". The second pair, size 30, would become "2–30" and so on.

As a check on durability, it is well to mark the year of purchase on the equipment. All equipment purchases prior to the time of marking for which the purchase date is not known may be marked with some code number such as "P–74" (prior to 1974). The marking on the size 28 pants mentioned above might then become "1–28–P74."

Balls, bats, racquets and equipment of similar nature should be numbered consecutively. The year of purchase or the code number described above should also appear on the equipment.

CHECKING OUT EQUIPMENT

Some system for issuing equipment should be established. Although it is very desirable to develop in every student a sense of re-

Figure 9–2. The equipment should be arranged so that it is readily accessible. (Courtesy of Enrico Fermi High School.)

sponsibility for the proper use and return of equipment, it is generally necessary to appoint certain students to be responsible for checking out varsity and class equipment.

Sheets listing the description of the article, as described in "Marking," can be easily prepared. Equipment room personnel can then jot down names opposite the items issued and check as it is turned in. Any article that is damaged or lost can then be traced to the responsible party. It is a wise, effective practice in most situations to compel students who damage or lose equipment to make restitution or be denied further use of any more equipment.

CARE OF EQUIPMENT

Taking the best possible care of the equipment can prove to be the greatest single money-saving procedure. A well-organized program for the care of equipment will pay off in increased longevity of balls, bats and racquets and in fewer replacements of jerseys, sox and towels. The result: Money saved, which can be allocated to the purchase of more sports equipment.

A well-organized program for the care of athletic equipment should follow this general pattern: (1) An adequate room for the storage of equipment; (2) a good marking system; (3) efficient issuance of equipment; (4) proper care of equipment; (5) a positive program for educating the students to respect and care for the equipment.

Leather Goods. Cleanliness is the first order in the preservation of leather goods. Leather balls such as footballs, baseballs, softballs and basketballs can be cleaned adequately by wiping with a damp cloth. Preservatives and cleaners may be used on other leather equipment but are not advised for balls as they may affect the "feel" of the ball in the hands of highly skilled players.

Proper drying of leather goods which have become wet may mean the difference between a stiff, harsh piece of equipment which grows old before its time and a piece which returns to normalcy without undue shortening of its life. Such goods should be dried as soon as possible at room temperature. Leather should never be forced dry. It should, of course, be thoroughly cleaned. After the leather is dried, neat's-foot oil should be applied to keep the leather from becoming harsh and hard. The oil can be applied with a cloth. However, when much oiling is to be done, it is more convenient to pour the oil into wide-mouthed jars and apply it with small paint brushes. Shoes and gloves should be worked into normal shape before being allowed to dry. Balls should be kept inflated to normal pressure while drying. Before being stored, balls should be sufficiently inflated to hold normal shape. They should not be folded or crushed.

Leather and Rubber Balls. Balls should never be overinflated, as this will cause them to lose shape and resiliency. The amount of required pressure will be stamped on all new balls. As an added precaution, a card indicating the correct pressure for each type of ball might be posted over the pump.

Volley balls and soccer balls should be clearly labeled to avoid inflation errors, since soccer balls require a higher air pressure. Labeling will also help to prevent the misuse of the volley ball as a soccer ball.

Since excess pressure will damage the ball, guesswork can be dangerous. Balls should be filled with a hand pump which shows the pressure in the ball between strokes. It is a good practice to allow only persons who have been fully instructed in proper filling to perform this job. The pump can be kept in the equipment room so that it will not be available to unauthorized persons.

When inserting the needle for filling a ball, the needle should first be moistened with glycerin. Wetting the needle with saliva is an unsanitary procedure and will cause the needle to rust which, in turn, may cause damage to the rubber valve of the ball.

Wooden Equipment. Heat is the enemy of wood. It is therefore important to keep wooden equipment away from excessive amounts of heat. To help preserve all types of wooden articles, they may be wiped with a cloth soaked in boiled linseed oil.

Whenever the varnish cracks or peels, the unprotected wood rapidly absorbs or loses moisture (depending upon the humidity), causing it to crack. For this reason, it is important to keep all wooden equipment well varnished. This includes bats, racquets, javelins, discuses, cues and sticks.

All wooden equipment that is long and has a heavy end, such as a javelin or shuffleboard cue, should be hung vertically with the heavy end downward. A couple of feet of garden hose tacked vertically to the wall will provide an excellent holder for the javelin. Racquets should always be stored in presses, never hung by their strings.

Textiles. Athletic garments and items such as body pads and helmet linings are subject to mildew unless properly cleaned and stored in dry, well-ventilated rooms. Improper cleaning of textiles often causes shrinkage and fading; recommended methods for cleaning various items of athletic clothing may be obtained from the manufacturer.

Some schools have their own laundry facilities. If the washing is done at the school, the following instructions should be considered. Wash whites alone. Never mix differently colored garments in the same wash. Tumble drying causes more shrinkage than other methods. High water level holds down mechanical action in machine washing and reduces injury possibilities to garments. Temperatures lower than 100° F. reduce cleansing ability and will not remove perspiration residues, heavy soiling and surface stains. Wash temperatures between 100 and 120° F. are recommended, unless special cold water washing powder is used. Heavy grass stains and ground-in soil may still remain after using 120° F. washing temperature, but most coaches prefer to have grass stains rather than lose the color or have the numerals and stripes become illegible. As temperatures increase, so do color and shrinkage problems.[2] Bleach should not be used. Any piece of athletic equipment that contains some wool should be treated as a wool garment. Never use cleaning fluids on items containing rubber.

Mats. Nothing destroys mats faster than dragging across the floor. Mat carts for transportation purposes can be purchased from many sports equipment companies. However, a cart can be readily constructed from two by fours with rollers (purchased from any hardware store) attached to the bottom. If the mats are of the small light-weight variety that is joined together by velcro or zipper fasteners, they can be easily carried by one or two people.

Mats of plastic or foam rubber should be cleaned as directed by the manufacturer.

Towels. A good way to increase the life of towels is to prevent students from abusing them and leaving them lying around on the floor. An efficient checking-out system which demands that everyone turn in a soiled towel before receiving a clean one will usually take care of this problem.

Nets. Most important in the care of nets is loosening to relieve the tension when not in use. Nets used outside should be taken in during bad weather and stored in a dry place.

Nets should be repaired at first sign of wear to prolong their usefulness. Canvas tops and binding which receive the hardest wear can be replaced.

Metal Equipment. Metal equipment must be kept oiled or painted to prevent rusting. Equipment such as metal shots, steel tapes and discuses can be kept from rusting by cleaning and periodic application of a thin layer of oil. Other metal equipment such as jumping and vaulting standards can be painted.

Rubber Goods. Soap, water and "elbow grease" are the necessary agents for keeping rubber goods clean. Oil and grease deteriorate rubber and should, therefore, be promptly removed. For this reason, too, cleaning fluids should not be used on rubber equipment. Avoid excessive exposure to heat.

Plastic Equipment. Many pieces of equipment are currently made entirely or partially of plastic. These items may be cared for very

---

[2]Athletic Goods Manufacturers Association: *How to Budget, Select and Order Athletic Equipment.* Chicago, 1962.

simply by cleaning with a damp cloth, using soap if necessary on stubborn soil.

Phonographic Equipment. Record players must be handled carefully to protect the delicate mechanisms. Records, too, require care in use to prevent scratches and breakage. Consequently, it is wise to provide a special cabinet with rollers for safe housing and transporting of the machine and with space for secure storage of the records. Such a cabinet could be constructed from wood by students or the teacher.

STOLEN AND BORROWED EQUIPMENT

The problem of stolen equipment cannot be solved without an educational program aimed at the student. Many times goods taken from the athletic department are not considered "stolen." The department should use every opportunity to break down this concept and replace it with the idea that stealing athletic goods is a criminal act.

Damaged or lost equipment is another headache. An efficient checking system which points the finger at the student responsible will do much to reduce losses of this kind.

Coaches and physical education instructors should make it part of their classroom activity to instruct students in the proper use and care of the athletic equipment they handle. Students must be instilled with a healthy respect for the school's property. This cannot be done if they are not given the proper kinds of instruction for care and use.

Making the equipment inaccessible will reduce theft, just as teaching the best use and care of equipment will reduce loss and damage. But building desirable attitudes will do the job in a more positive manner.

Students must be shown that money spent to replace lost or stolen equipment cannot be used to buy extra types of equipment for their pleasure; it cannot be used for better dressing room facilities or for new gym lights or a new scoreboard.

REPAIR

The repair and reconditioning of equipment should be done by highly trained specialists who can frequently save institutions hundreds of dollars. There are numerous firms throughout the nation who specialize in this type of service. It is wise to repair all articles following each sports season, for such prompt attention will add to the length of usefulness of all such equipment.

Teachers can make minor repairs such as replacing broken arrow of badminton feathers, or can train a group of students to assist with this task. Local shoe repair firms can sew seam rips or make other needed repairs for leather goods.

IMPROVISED EQUIPMENT

Creative teachers have learned to improvise and use things in their environment for their program. Unfortunately, few have been trained to build or make equipment which could be used as a substitute for a desired or needed article. In almost every phase of the physical education program, however, certain pieces of inexpensive equipment can be made either by the school mechanical arts or home economics departments, by the teacher, or by an interested and carefully supervised group of students. The following items are some that can be improvised for class use; each can be made from scrap or inexpensive materials.

Archery. Finger tabs from tire inner tubes; arm guards from heavy cardboard and rubber bands; quivers from mailing tubes.

Baseball. Homeplate, a pitcher's box, backstops from scrap lumber and heavy wire; batting tees made with a heavy wooden base and a hard rubber tube; bases from flattened heavy fire hose held together in base form by nuts and bolts and covered with a heavy material.

Basketball. Goals from heavy metal rings and heavy string nets.

Bowling. Pins from milk cartons, filled with sand and sealed; to be used with lightweight balls.

Dance. Music for accompaniment from barrel kegs covered with leather, shakers from rock-filled cans; tambourines from tin plates and metal bottle tops; wind and string instruments.

Football. Gaolposts from scrap lumber.

Golf. A miniature course, with tin cans driven into the ground for holes and the game played with hockey or broomsticks with varying size balls. (Also see Figure 9–3.)

Gymnastics. A balance beam, Swedish box, chinning bar and ladder walk from scrap lumber; wands for stick stunts and balancing from handles of old brooms.

Physical Fitness. Pull-up bars and measuring boards for the vertical jump from scrap lumber; weights for use in leg lifts from used inner tubes or burlap sacks filled with sand.

Recreational Activities. Box hockey, dart boards and darts, ring toss equipment, tilting spears, quoits, toss boards and rings, checker board and disks from scrap lumber of appropriate sizes and pieces of used tires and rope.

Shuffleboard. Cue sticks and disks from scrap lumber.

Soccer, Hockey, Speedball. Goalposts from scrap lumber and heavy chicken wire.

Swimming. Buoys from rope and wood.

Tennis, Badminton, Volleyball. Net posts of wood or iron pipes driven into the ground; nets from rope or chickenwire; tennis backboards from scrap lumber.

Figure 9–3. A triangle and a piece of carpet are used for an improvised putting green. (Courtesy of the Lifetime Sports Foundation.)

Tether ball. Paddles from scrap lumber; poles from tree limbs or scrapped metal poles.

Track. Starting blocks, jump standards, broad jump take-off board, indicators of broad and high jumps, pole vault standard, shot-put toe circle and toe board from scrap lumber.

Tumbling. Mats from bed mattresses that have been discarded or secured from army surplus stores.

Imaginative teachers can easily add to this suggested list. No physical education program need be limited because of lack of equipment or supplies, for the continued growth in the number of different activities to be included in the curriculum as well as needed materials with which to learn to do them safely and skillfully depends solely upon each professional worker's ability to obtain or create them.

DISCUSSION QUESTIONS

1. Discuss the values of the equipment-marking system described in this chapter.
2. What determines the amount and kinds of equipment needed?
3. Discuss the problems the teacher may anticipate in securing equipment and supplies for a new activity in the program.
4. Describe briefly the "Planning-Programming Budgeting Systems."
5. What are the best methods for cleaning and storing fabrics, leather, wooden and rubber goods, racquets, plastics, and equipment made of light metals?

THINGS TO DO

1. List the advantages and disadvantages of early buying, quantity buying, buying through a purchasing agent, buying on "bids," and having each instructor order or purchase his own needed equipment.
2. Make a list of all program activities you hope to include in your school. Add under each one listed the kinds of equipment you will need if each is to be a part of your desired program.
3. Design an equipment storage room.
4. Add to the list of improvised equipment on page000. Give a brief description of how each item is improvised.
5. Write to several sporting goods manufacturers for information about their products and their proper care. Save the materials for your future use as a teacher.

SUGGESTED READINGS

AAHPER and the Athletic Institute: *Equipment and Supplies for Athletics, Physical Education and Recreation*. 1201 16th Street, N.W., Washington, D.C., 1960.

Athletic Goods Manufacturers Association: *How to Budget, Select and Order Athletic Equipment*, 805 Merchandise Mart, Chicago, 1962.

Bucher, Charles A.: *Administration of and Physical Education Programs Including Athletics*. 5th Ed., St. Louis, The C. V. Mosby Co., 1971.

Daughtrey, Greyson, and Woods, John B.: *Physical Education Programs: Organization and Administration*. Philadelphia, W. B. Saunders Co., 1971.

Forsyth, Charles E., and Keller, Irvin A.: *Administration of High School Athletics*. 5th Ed., Englewood Cliffs, N.J., Prentice-Hall, Inc., 1972.

PART THREE

THE ACTIVITY PERIOD

If we work upon marble, it will perish; if we work upon brass, time will efface it; if we rear temples, they will crumble into dust; but if we work upon immortal minds, if we imbue them with principles, with the just fear of God and love of our fellow men, we engrave on those tablets something that will brighten to all eternity.

. . . . . Daniel Webster

PLANNING THE PROGRAM

In its entirety, the school physical education program consists of the required class instructional program, the adapted program for atypical students, the intramural and extramural programs and the interscholastic program. There is more lack of uniformity in required physical education programs throughout the nation than in any other subject in the public school curriculum. Although this has its disadvantages it also has certain advantages, for it allows for elasticity and experimentation, calls for greater teacher initiative, and provides increased opportunities for students to learn activities best suited for them and that are most popular in their local communities. In some schools, teachers are fortunate enough to have the standard recommended number of pupils per teacher recognized by the profession, namely, a total of 240 students weekly in their physical education classes in the elementary schools and 190 weekly on the secondary level. Unfortunately, in others, assigning teachers to as many as 120 students per class for five daily periods, making the total number of students per day per teacher total 600, is common practice. Most states require a minimum 140 minutes weekly in physical education for each student for the four years of high school. In some areas classes meet five times weekly, while in others this time is divided between physical and health education. It is regrettable that there are still some few schools which do not offer any class instruction in physical education, although they may conduct a makeshift after-school athletic program for a few select boys. In the best schools, however, strong emphasis is being placed upon physical education and state time requirements are being met. At these schools, too, a graded program has been established from the first through the twelfth year, with a wide variety of balanced activities offered at each grade level. Generally speaking, throughout the country the amount of instruction time for physical education is increasing, program content is improving, instructors are being better prepared and are doing a better job of teaching this subject.

The total secondary physical education program should consist of the required or core instructional program and the elective sports

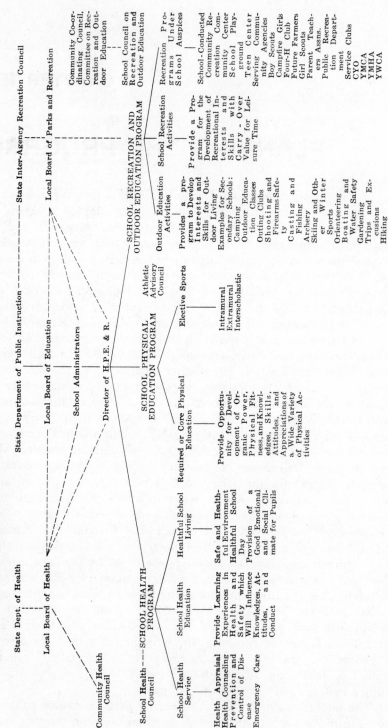

AN ORGANIZATIONAL CHART OF THE SECONDARY-SCHOOL PROGRAMS OF HEALTH EDUCATION, PHYSICAL EDUCATION, RECREATION, AND OUTDOOR EDUCATION

Figure 10–1. Reproduced by permission from AAHPER: *Fitness for Secondary School Youth.* Washington, D.C., 1960.

program (intramurals, extramurals, and interscholastic competition). This program should be closely related to school programs in health education, school recreation, and outdoor education as is seen in Figure 10–1.

PRINCIPLES OF PROGRAM PLANNING

The required physical education program in the middle, junior and senior high school must be built upon sound educational principles. These stress that the program should be:

1. Based upon the age, sex, needs, capabilities and interests of the students.
2. Related to the physical, mental, social and emotional characteristics of each individual and group.
3. Planned in light of the objectives, aims and goals sought by the teacher and class.
4. Established to make the best use of all available resources, including teacher qualifications, facilities and equipment available at the school and in the community.
5. Wide enough in scope to be of present and future value to each individual, the community, state and nation.
6. One which can be participated in safely and will lead to an improved status of health.
7. Rich in opportunities to develop desirable social and moral behavior.
8. A learning laboratory for democratic group living.
9. Flexible, with provision for student elective choice of activities.
10. Coeducation in part.
11. Planned to foster all degrees of skill—beginning, intermediate and advanced.

BEHAVIORAL OBJECTIVES

The writing of objectives is an essential function in planning the program, since the objectives provide a guide for the entire implementation of the teaching-learning experience. Objectives are concise statements of desired outcomes. They describe what learnings are sought as the final results of the unit of instruction.

Significant attention has recently been directed by many educators toward the writing of objectives. Teachers have probably always utilized some form of objectives, either stated or implied; however, these objectives have often been conceived of in such general or all-encompassing terminology as to make precise evaluation of the outcomes difficult. Increasing pressure to make educators more accountable for the learning of their students has led to a re-examination of the traditional way of expressing objectives. To determine accurately how students have changed as the result of their instruction, one must first know rather exactly what it is he wishes them to learn. It seems only logical that the more specifically the desired outcomes can be stated, the more appropriately experiences can be tailored toward their achievement and the more exact can be the teacher's evaluation of a student's accomplishments. This movement toward specific expression of learning objectives has resulted in the development of a form of objective writing termed "behavioral objectives." Behavioral objectives are explicit statements of behaviors expected of the student at the conclusion of the unit or course. The objectives are worded in a manner to describe both the observable behavior expected and the way in which it will be demonstrated. Thus, the behavioral objective attempts to answer the questions of "What shall we teach?" and "How will we know we have taught it?"

A behavioral objective states specifically the desired student behavior in terms of measurable performance. It is thus necessarily limited in scope to a particular type or class of behavior. A good example can be drawn from the American Red Cross Swimming

Figure 10-2. A behavioral objective for the table tennis may be to strike the ball with the backhand stroke five consecutive times using correct form. (Courtesy Enrico Fermi High School.)

Program. The general goal of the program is to develop swimming skills; however, such a broad statement is not very informative as to the types of skills students are expected to learn. Consequently, the expected results are precisely spelled out, as in this example: an advanced beginner swimmer shall be able to perform a front dive into deep water, swim 15 feet underwater, surface and tred water for half a minute and swim the crawl stroke for 20 yards. This statement of the behavioral objective for advanced beginners describes specifically *what* behaviors the student should be able to exhibit. It offers little room for variability as to *how* to measure the performance. Most importantly, it identifies very concisely for both teacher and student exactly what the desired results of the learning experience are. Similar precise statements of desired behavior can be constructed for any desired learning. The following examples contrast the characteristics of broad, imprecise objectives with behavioral objectives:

to develop physical fitness	to be able to exhibit muscular endurance of the arms and shoulders by performing 25 consecutive push-ups
to expose students to the game of basketball	to be able to list four situations in the conduct of a basketball game when possession of the ball must be relinquished to the opposing team
to develop sportsmanship	to demonstrate self-control in tense situations by refraining from making derogatory comments after a referee's controversial decisions in competitive soccer games

Broad objective statements, as exemplified in the first of each pair of statements above, lack the quality of precision necessary to provide guidance as to program content or means of determining achievement. Exactly what is expected of the students in each case? What do we want them to know about basketball? Which skills do we expect them to possess? At what skill level? How do we know when they have reached the desired level? What qualities are included in sportsmanship? What actions are examples of "good" or "bad" sportsmanship? What qualities of physical fitness are we interested in? How will we know when they are developed? These questions remain unanswered in the broadly stated objectives. Contrast them with the behavioral objectives stated as the second choice of each pair. Although providing some direction the broad objectives are not sufficiently specific to enable clear identification of the intention of the program.

The listing of behavioral objectives for a unit will thus constitute a content outline of the skills and abilities sought and provide a statement of how to determine if these skills have been achieved. The list will of necessity be more detailed than broad, goal-type statements. The value of behavioral objectives lies in the clarity of the expressed expected outcomes. Once we know rather precisely what the desired learnings are, it is not too difficult to select effective means for developing or measuring the achievement of these behaviors.

CLASSIFICATION OF ACTIVITIES

Activities included in the required program are (1) the fundamental movement skills incorporated into individual and team sports, (2) formal activities and gymnastics, (3) aquatics, (4) self-testing activities, (5) dance and (6) recreational activities including hiking, camping and hosteling.

PROGRAM FOR UPPER MIDDLE OR JUNIOR HIGH SCHOOL

Although the program for the upper grades of the middle school and for the junior high school is similar to that of the secondary school, here major stress should not be placed upon the mastery of basic sports techniques; rather a wide variety of these skills should be introduced which are suitable to the maturation level of the students. Lead-up games learned during the fourth, fifth and sixth years, such as kickball, newcomb, or hitpin baseball, might well be reviewed and serve as a starting point for teaching beginning sport skills such as the football punt, tennis serve, or the swimming swan dive in the seventh and eighth grade.

Suggested activities for the program include:

Basic skills in sports and games:

> Basketball
> Fieldball for girls
> Golf
> Soccer
> Softball
> Skiing
> Speed-a-way
> Speedball
> Tennis
> Touch football for boys
> Track and field
> Volleyball

Formal activities and gymnastics:

> Beginning fundamental skills
> on the stationary and fly-
> ing rings, parallel bars,
> horse, buck and Swedish
> box
> Body mechanics
> Conditioning exercises
> Marching

Dance

> Folk—beginning skills and
> simple patterns
> Modern dance—basic exer-
> cises, movement tech-
> niques, simple composi-
> tion problems
> Social—foxtrot, waltz and
> rhumba
> Square—elementary skills and
> simple figures

Aquatics:

> Basic diving skills
> Basic strokes of swimming
> Junior lifesaving
> Water games

Stunts and tumbling:

> Backward handsprings
> Backward roll to handstand
> Cartwheels in series
> Couple stunts
> Dives for distance
> Forward and backward rolls
> Handsprings
> Hand walks
> Pyramids
> Rebound tumbling
> Roundoffs
> Running forward somersaults
> Shoulder stand
> Stomach balance

Recreational games:

Active and passive games of
   low organization
Archery, tincan, pitch and putt
   golf
Billiards
Bowling—lawn and duckpin
Carom
Goal shooting
Hiking and camping
Horseshoes
Ice skating
Relays
Roller skating
Table and paddle tennis

Major emphasis in the program for this age group should be placed on rigorous physical activity and cooperative group activities. At each grade level the program should include at least four team games, tumbling and gymnastics, track and field events, at least three individual sports, rhythms and dance, as well as first aid and health instruction.

THE JUNIOR HIGH SCHOOL ELECTIVE PROGRAM*

At Theodore Roosevelt Junior High School, Eugene, Ore., the entire school curriculum operates on the elective basis. Every nine weeks students elect those courses which they wish to take for the next quarter of the school year.

This approach began to take shape in the spring of 1969 when a group of teachers representing every department in the school sat down to discuss ways of making the junior high school experience more exciting and meaningful for students. As the teachers began to arrive at agreement on a philosophy for change, they involved the administration, parents, and students in their discussions. What evolved was a set of beliefs, ideals, and expectations about people, students, and schools in which the importance of individual choice and the need to feel successful was stressed.

When the drafting of the school philosophy and an accompanying program was devised, it was a committee composed of the principal, teachers, and parents which successfully presented it to the school board for approval as an experimental program for three years.

Five basic departures from tradition which make Roosevelt different from most junior high schools are:

1. Nongraded classes (no 7th, 8th, 9th levels).

2. Written evaluations of student performance (no letter or number grades).

3. Totally elective classes which change every nine weeks.

4. House-Advisor program for 30 minutes each day.

---

*"Conducting a Junior High School Elective Program in all Areas of the Curriculum." From the *Physical Education Newsletter*, Nov. 1, 1973. Courtesy of Lowell A. Klapphof.

5. Alternate A-B day schedule with classes meeting for blocks of 40 or 80 minutes.

Says Shareen Young, who serves as the coordinator for the physical education department: "There are no requirements in any area including physical education. However, about 85% of the student body does elect physical education every nine weeks, which I feel is an excellent percentage. Each course a student elects to take within the physical education curriculum has its own class requirements or behavioral objectives, but other than that there are no set requirements for physical education."

The physical education program is arranged to enable each student to become physically educated through participation in activities in six major areas. They are team sports, individual sports, dance, fitness, recreational games, and swimming.

Team Sports. The following team sports, with quarters offered in parentheses, are included in the program:

1. Basketball (2,3)
2. Floor Hockey (1,3)
3. Fundamental Skills (1). This is a very advanced class in basketball drills, fundamentals, and conditioning for boys who have had at least two years of basketball.
4. Touch Football (1)
5. Soccer (1,4)
6. Softball (4)
7. Volleyball (1,2,3)

Individual Sports. Individual activities, with quarters in which they are offered in parentheses, include:

1. Archery (1,4)
2. Beginning Net Sports—Tennis and Badminton (1,4)
3. Bowling (1,2,3,4)
4. Golf (1,4)
5. Gymnastics (2,3)
6. Intermediate Net Sports—Tennis and Badminton (1,4)
7. Nets To You (3). This course includes three weeks of instruction in each of three net sports—badminton, volleyball, and basketball.
8. Track and Field (1,4)
9. Wrestling (2).

Dance. The curriculum includes three major dance forms, folk dance which represents dances and cultures of many nations, and modern dance in which the student's imagination and creativity is translated into movement are stressed. The dance program consists of Folk Dance I offered every quarter, Folk Dance II offered during the second, third, and fourth quarters, Modern Dance offered during the second quarter, and "Oldies but Goodies" stressing dancing to "now" and "old" beats and rhythms which is offered every quarter.

Fitness. The fitness courses are designed to help students develop and maintain their physical fitness, with special emphasis on strength and endurance. Individual courses, with quarters offered in parentheses, include:

1. Advanced Weights (3,4)
2. Beginning Weights (1,2)
3. Conditioning (4). This course features cycling, jogging, endurance sports, and exercises.
4. Cycling (4). Youngsters participate in cross country cycling every period this class meets, rain or shine.
5. Jogging (1,3,4)
6. Physical Fitness (2,3) Activities include running, weight lifting, calisthenics and exercises, and endurance testing.

7. Slimnastics (1)
8. Yoga (1,2,3,4)

Recreational Games. Individual courses, with quarters offered in parentheses, are:

1. Table Tennis (4)
2. Pot Pourri (2,3). This course emphasizes low organized games and team sports ranging from relays to games and contests.
3. Prison Ball (2,3)
4. Recreational Games (1,4). Class activities include badminton, table tennis, shuffleboard, horseshoes, tennis, volleyball, and softball.
5. Roller Skating (2,3). This activity course includes instruction in basic skating skills, games such as hockey, relays, and races.

Swimming. The swimming curriculum consists of two courses. The first, offered during the first and fourth quarters, is called Red Cross Junior Lifesaving and Water Sports. It is designed for students who have earned a Red Cross Swimmer's card or have equal ability. Students electing this course are expected to know the front crawl, side stroke, and breast stroke. The major emphasis is on review of basic strokes, acquiring the endurance needed for distance swimming, and learning lifesaving skills. Some time is devoted to water sports. The second course, offered during the fourth quarter, is called Water Sports and is recreational in nature. The activities include races, water polo, water volleyball, and water basketball.

"Our elective program is set up so that 13 to 15 activities are offered each quarter or nine-week period." Miss Young says. "In this way every student has an opportunity to elect a great variety of activities during his or her junior high career. By careful guidance, both in physical education and in other areas of the curriculum, we can usually see that students sample a great number of activities and take courses that they need to prepare themselves for future educational experiences and life itself."

For each course, the physical education staff has established specific requirements, including performance or behavioral objectives. Below is a sample of requirements for the Beginning Net Sports course.

Terminal Goals. The following behavioral objectives have been set up for the Beginning Net Sports course:

1. The student will be able to execute the basic tennis skills (forehand, backhand, and service strokes) with proper technique.
2. The student will be able to score a game of tennis while playing.
3. The student will be able to obtain a score of 90% on a written test of scoring and rules in tennis.
4. The student will demonstrate the skills mentioned in (1) above while participating in a class tennis tournament.
5. The student will be able to execute the basic skills (overhead clear, underhand clear, short serve, long serve, and drive shots) in badminton.
6. The student will be able to obtain a score of 90% on a written test of scoring and rules in badminton.
7. The student will be able to score a game of badminton while playing.
8. The student will be able to demonstrate the skills mentioned in (5) above while participating in a class badminton tournament.

Rationale. Dual sports such as tennis and badminton are widely used as recreational past-time activities in our society. They require hand-eye coordination, quick movement, skill, and knowledge of strategy and rules.

Analogous Experiences. As part of the program, students will:
• Spend part of each day learning the basic skills through instruction provided by the teacher.

Sample Evaluation

Theodore Roosevelt Junior High School
  1973-1974   Advisor   _____

Progress Report of _____
                        Student's name   Teacher's Name   _____

  Beginning Net Sports   Physical Education   4th — Credit — Incomplete
      Course Title   Department   Quarter

Beginning Net Sports offers the student a chance to learn the individual sports of *tennis* and *badminton*. Approximately one-half of the classtime is spent in tennis, learning the basic skills and playing the game. The other half of the time is spent in badminton, learning the basic skills and playing the game. Students are evaluated on their improvement in skills and their class participation.

	Skill Test Score	Accept-able	Needs Improvement	Comment
Tennis A. Skills—10 possible on each Skill Test 1. Forehand 2. Backhand 3. Serve				
B. Scoring and Rules Test ____ points possible				
C. Doubles Team and Tournament Play				
Badminton A. Skills 1. Drive shot 2. Overhead clear 3. Underhand clear 4. Short and long serve 5. Drop shot 6. Hair pin shot				
B. Scoring and Rules Test ____ points possible				
C. Doubles Team and Tournament Play				

• Spend part of each day drilling on the basic skills.
• Spend the latter part of each unit in tournament play.
• Demonstrate their knowledge of the games of badminton and tennis by taking written quizzes on the rules and strategy of the games.

Expectations. Students participating in this course are expected to dress down for activity each day, participate in all activities, pass a written test on the rules of each game with a score of 85 or higher, demonstrate cooperative behavior when working with others.

Evaluation. Students are evaluated on improvement by skills tests, are observed on their use of skills in actual game and tournament play, and must pass written quizzes. A detailed evaluation form is shown in the box above.

Speaking of evaluation, Miss Young notes that the program has been most successful and that the word "experimental" has been dropped by the administration and board of education.

THE SENIOR HIGH SCHOOL PROGRAM

The senior high school program should be more advanced, with stress placed upon sports and games, dance, and other areas high in carryover values for leisure time use. Coeducational classes should be considered an important part of the program and held frequently. Although some activities included in the curriculum may be modified for this purpose, social and square dance, volleyball, swimming, tennis, badminton, golf and bowling can be incorporated with the least amount of difficulty. Such coeducational classes are often best taught jointly by both a man and a woman teacher. This is especially true of social dance, for although the boys may long to learn how to do the latest steps so that they can go to dances with girls, they often are shy or reluctant about accepting an opportunity to learn because they fear being taunted by their peers and being called a "sissy." The male teacher's presence and encouragement in such a class often helps these boys to rid themselves of needless fears and to learn how to dance more quickly.[1]

Senior high school students should be given many opportunities to help plan, conduct and evaluate the program. Stress should be placed on helping them to gain an understanding of the importance of physical education, assisting each to learn as many leisure time skills beyond the novice stage as possible, and aiding all to build the highest degree of physical fitness possible. As future citizens, parents and community leaders, those who have enjoyed a meaningful and pleasurable physical education experience can be great supporters of and believers in a good school physical education program and will be more likely to work toward securing such a program for all students in schools throughout the nation.

Suggested activities for the senior high school program include more advanced skills and requirements in each of the following areas:

Individual:
  Archery
  Badminton
  Bait and fly casting
  Bowling
  Skating, ice and roller
  Skiing
  Squash racquets
  Tennis
  Track and field
  Wrestling
  Snow shoeing

---

[1]See the chapter on *Learning* to review the role that emotion plays in learning speed and retention.

Figure 10–3. Winter outdoor activities should be included in the school physical education as well as the recreational program. (Courtesy of the Youth Service Section of the Los Angeles Public Schools.)

Dance:
 Acrobatic
 Folk
 Modern
 Rhythms
 Social
 Square
 Tap

Team:
 Baseball
 Basketball
 Field ball for girls
 Field hockey
 Football
 Lacrosse
 Lead-up games
 Soccer
 Speed-a-way
 Team handball
 Fencing
 Golf
 Handball
 Lead-up games
 Paddle tennis
 Racket ball
 Speedball
 Touch football
 Volleyball

Self-testing activities:
  Acrobatics
  Apparatus
  Gymnastics
  Obstacle course
  Rebound tumbling
  Rope climbing
  Stunts
  Trampoline

Formal activities and gymnastics:
  Body mechanics
  Calisthenics
  Gymnastics
  Marching

Aquatics:
  Boating and canoeing
  Diving
  Senior lifesaving
  Skin and scuba diving
  Swimming
  Synchronized swimming
  Water games
  Water safety
  Water ballet

Recreational activities:
  Box hockey
  Camping and outing
  Card games
  Checkers
  Chess
  Croquet
  Dart ball
  Duckpins
  Games of low organization
  Hiking
  Horseback riding
  Horseshoes
  Shuffleboard

Campcraft skills:
  Orienteering
  Back packing
  Survival camping
  Tracking and trapping
  Fly and bait casting
  Outdoor cooking
  Use of camping tools

In the senior high school, the program should consist of the refining of skills previously learned and the addition of as wide a variety of individual-dual sports as possible, coeducational experiences in dance and other activities, senior first aid and water safety, and an increased health instruction program.

Increasingly, senior high schools are devising either complete or partially elective programs for their high school students. Throughout the nation in our better schools increased emphasis is being placed on including far more elective lifetime sports in the program. It is only in our weakest schools that inferior teachers are still conducting programs built largely around baseball, softball, volleyball, basketball, stunts and tumbling.

Questions each teacher must ask himself are what materials should be taught and what are the most important ones to select from the above list to fit individual and societal needs. Every educator must find the answers to these perplexing problems for himself, although he can be guided by curriculum experts, medical authorities connected with the school, leaders in the field, the pupils themselves, governing agencies, parent group representatives, outside consultants, and his own experience. All activities chosen to be included in the yearly program should be selected upon their recommendations and judged by established selective criteria. These are to determine if these activities reach the objectives of the program, are of the greatest value in the students' present and future life, are geared to their previous background and present ability levels, can better be taught in the class than at some other place in the community and do not endanger the health or safety of students.

COEDUCATIONAL CLASSES

Coeducational physical education classes should be offered on all educational levels. Certain social competences which accrue from such experiences, however, may be greater on the secondary level, because the need for such skills becomes intensified with this age group. Members from each sex in such classes, through carefully planned educational experiences, receive mutual benefit, for the boys tone down and become less competitive, while the girls perk up and become more interested in sports, games and exercise. Each sex also gains a new appreciation and understanding of the special aptitudes, skills and contributions made by members of the opposite sex. Equally important, the sharp distinction between the roles of the sexes in sports and other motor activities is greatly diminished.

The success of coeducational classes involving two or more teachers or departments requires close cooperation and mutually shared responsibilities. Policies and procedures, as well as course content of each instructional unit included and means of evaluating the results, should be written out. The specific objectives of each class should be devised by both the teacher and the class members, as well as certain basic rules for social behavior in class. Boys and girls who are highly skilled should be placed in homogeneous groups. However, poorly coordinated boys should not be placed in a dancing class with highly skilled girls. In such team games as volleyball, soccer, speedball, or speed-a-way, the boys and girls may be given separate class instruction but be encouraged to play these sports coeducationally in after-school recreation programs or in planned coeducational classes at the end of each teaching unit. Most team games in which strength and previous playing experience are major factors in the enjoyment of the game can be played coeducationally with a slight modification of rules or by having the boys play according to girls' rules (with the exception of touch football, which some few schools are now including in the program). In softball, teams should be equalized, with skilled boys scattered throughout each coeducational team. To meet the social and emotional needs of all students in such classes, the teacher must give special help to those who are shy and immature. Skill mastery should be emphasized only to the extent it will lead to increased player enjoyment, and the development of social skills and knowledges should be emphasized. The men and women teachers should be worthy of emulation by pupils of both sexes. Activities suitable for coeducational instruction are: swimming, diving, volleyball, softball, badminton, racketball, table tennis, paddle ball, tennis, aerial tennis darts,

Figure 10–4. Coeducational physical education classes should be offered on all educational levels. (Courtesy of the Physical Education Department, Los Angeles Public Schools.)

croquet, billiards, horseshoes, deck tennis, archery, golf, bowling, all kinds of dance activities and recreational games.

An instructional plan should be so devised that each teacher can best use her and his abilities in a teaching team of two. For example, in teaching a unit on badminton, the woman instructor might concentrate on basic skills and the man on team play and game strategy, or in swimming, the former on form swimming and the latter on racing and other types of competitive events. Coeducational classes can be organized on any instructional pattern or on a sport unit basis. Preferably the classes should be held throughout the school year. Regardless of the plan used, the students should be drawn into the planning and evaluation of the course as much as possible.

NEW PROGRAM ACTIVITIES

The Lifetime Sports Program. The Lifetime Sports Education Project, a part of the American Association For Health, Physical Education and Recreation, strongly recommends that schools include such activities as badminton, bowling, golf and tennis in their programs.

The Lifetime Sports Foundation, organized in February 1965, is doing outstanding work in promoting clinics and workshops in individual sports throughout the country. These are geared to instruct teachers how to go about teaching sports with high carryover value to large class groups and how to make the best use of the existing facilities and equipment that they now have for doing so. Excellent guides and other materials for teaching tennis, golf and bowling skills on only a basketball court or football field are available at nominal cost from the Director, Lifetime Sports Education Project, 1201 Sixteenth Street, N.W., Washington, D.C., 20036. All teachers are urged to obtain and use these materials as well as attend the local and state clinics and workshops.

Movement Exploration. Although best suited in many ways to the elementary level, movement exploration is used with success in the secondary school, particularly in the teaching of dance activities. The problem solving method, which is used in movement exploration, is applicable in the teaching of many types of motor skills. (See Chapter 3 for a comprehensive discussion of this method of teaching.) Most of the activities that can be included in the program should be of a self-testing nature and give each student opportunity to discover how to best use his body in relationship to time and space problems. The kinds of activities most suited for this aspect of the program center around:

1. Basic movement skills and body control.
2. Developmental exercises and movement sequences.

A Four-year Rotation Plan

All students in a four-year high school are scheduled in one class. A well-balanced and complete program is assured by arranging the units of instruction for each of four years so that undesirable repetition is avoided, variety in activities is maintained, and provision is made for appropriate progression. All students in the ninth grade and new students in the tenth, eleventh and twelfth grades participate in an orientation unit for six weeks at the beginning of each year. During this period the other students participate in recreational activities and certain ones assist with the orientation unit.

WEEKS	FIRST YEAR	SECOND YEAR	THIRD YEAR	FOURTH YEAR
6	Orientation and recreation activities	Orientation and recreation activities	Orientation and recreation activities	Orientation and recreation activities
8	Speedball	Hockey	Speed-a-way	Choice of field games and of officiating
6	Coeducational folk and square dancing	Rhythms	Coeducational folk and square dancing	Modern dance
6	Skiing	Recreation leadership	Skiing	Coeducational court games (indoors)
6	Basketball	Volleyball	Tennis or badminton	Softball
6	Swimming	Tennis or badminton	Swimming and lifesaving	Golf or archery

Figure 10–5. Reprinted by permission from *The Teachers' Guide to Physical Education for Girls in High School.* Sacramento, California State Department of Education, 1957, pp. 25 and 26.

3. Stunts, tumbling and gymnastics.

4. Activities using small equipment such as balls, ropes, hoops and boxes.

5. Activities on large apparatus, including the balance beam and other kinds of gymnastic apparatus.

Proponent of this new approach from the teacher's instructional command to the student's educational discovery of how to use his own body in solving movement problems on the secondary level is Dr. Muska Mosston of Rutgers State University of New Jersey. His approach to the teaching of physical activities in all sports is based on self-insight, as is shown in a unit in guided body capabilities discovery in the gymnastics shown below.[2]

Gymnastics

1. The role of the center of gravity in the performance of the turns on the balance beam.

2. The role of momentum in maintenance of balance on the balance beam.

3. The relationship between the trunk and the appendages in developing balance.

4. The factors affecting stability in positions on the balance beam.

5. The factors affecting stability in motion on the balance beam.

6. The factors affecting the "smoothness" of connecting elements on the balance beam to a continuous sequence of movements.

7. Can you suggest a phase concerning the mounts on the balance beam that you would like to teach by guided discovery?

8. Can you suggest a phase concerning the dismounts?

9. Can you suggest any topic in any phase of teaching balance that could be taught by guided discovery?

10. A lesson to discover the possibilities that exist in the variety of rolls in tumbling.

11. A lesson to discover the principles that relate the variety of rolls to one another.

12. The relationship between directions and postures in movements in tumbling.

13. In teaching the kip principle, the relationship between the length of the lever, produced by the legs, and success in performing the kip.

14. The relationship between the kip principle learned on the mat and the kip used for various mounts on the parallel bars.

15. The role of the lever (the whole body) in producing various degrees of momentum in swinging on the parallel bars.

16. Do you have any suggestions for other aspects of the parallel bars performance?

17. Are your suggestions specific to the parallel bars, or can they lead to discovering the application to other apparatus?

18. In vaulting, the various phases involved in a vault.

19. The assets and liabilities in each phase of a vault. Discovery of a generalization!

---

[2]Mosston, Muska: *Teaching Physical Education—From Command To Discovery*. Columbus, Ohio, Charles E. Merrill Books, Inc., 1966, pp. 176–177.

20. Application of the generalization to a specific vault.
21. The variables affecting changes in the form of a given vault.
22. Any suggestions for other aspects of vaulting?
23. Can you suggest two consecutive aspects to be taught by guided discovery?
24. Three consecutive aspects?
25. Any other proposals?

MODULAR SCHEDULING

Some schools have found that modular scheduling is useful in improving both teaching and learning in physical education. In this type of scheduling each student takes physical education for three consecutive 20-minute teaching modules (or one hour) three times weekly, instead of having class for 45 minutes daily. This arrangement, it has been found, gives the students and teachers more time for instruction and the practicing of skills in each class period and reduces the time spent in showering, dressing and taking roll.

At the Township High School in Evanston, Illinois, where this type of scheduling is used, class periods are arranged so that all freshmen have physical education together, as do the sophomores, juniors, and seniors, with half the students in each grade scheduled for class either in the morning or afternoon. In a typical period, 300 freshmen boys report to the gymnasium, play field, or to other teaching stations and are then sub-divided into groups so that each of the ten teachers on the staff works with 30 boys. Each instructional unit is grouped according to ability, homeroom, or other means as determined previously by the instructors. The instructors work together to plan and conduct the graded curriculum used throughout the entire four years students are enrolled in the high school.

It has been found that scheduling each grade together for a longer period has many advantages, especially when a professional athlete comes to give a demonstration to an entire class group, or on any other occasions which require more time than a single class period, such as interclass tournaments at the end of a teaching unit. Under this type of scheduling, instructors can provide competitive tournaments among each of the ten separate class groups, be it a freshman or senior group, during the same period.

THE STUDENT COMPETENCY-BASED CURRICULUM

Much is being written today about educational accountability (what exactly is the teacher really accomplishing in his classes?) and student competencies (what specific skills are the students really learning?). Many college physical education departments are now utilizing a competency-based curriculum for those students who are preparing to become teachers.

Although there is merit to be found in the competency-based physical education curriculum for middle and high school students, there are also disadvantages to it. It is advantageous to conduct a program based upon the teaching of specific skills and the student's attainment of them. Just how to determine the degree level of such skill attainment for each student in the many large classes teachers have today in far too many of our schools is quite another matter. Doing so could only be accomplished by a largely subjective judgment in an enlarged testing program. This would require increased time and effort on the part of the teacher, thus leaving little time for actual teaching and mastering by the students of the various skills being taught. Thus, the instructor in such a program would become more of a tester than a teacher. Consequently, many leaders in the field see that there are serious problems in the competency-based curriculum.

On the other hand, there are many authorities who would argue that the preparation and use of a competency-based program establishes clear-cut objectives that are absolutely essential before effective teaching can occur. The clearly defined objectives readily suggest ways of teaching to insure their accomplishment, while more vaguely conceived objectives do not. Moreover, with the more imprecise objectives a teacher is likely never actually to know when an objective has been fulfilled or exactly how it was accomplished. Another group favoring this type of curriculum includes those physical educators who are alarmed by the increase in the use of teacher aides having little or no professional preparation. They believe that the adoption of the competency-based program will counteract this growing practice of employing untrained personnel, particularly when used for budgetary reasons to replace available men and women who are highly qualified by education and experience in physical education.

GREATER USE OF COMMUNITY RESOURCES

Increasingly, schools are using facilities belonging to the general public or semiprivate agencies in order to bring new program offerings into their physical education curriculum. Some are paying nominal fees collected from students in these new special classes or the fee is paid solely by the school for the use of off-campus facilities. Others are exchanging various services as a token payment for their use, such as allowing a community service group to schedule meetings in certain school classrooms during off-hours in exchange for the use of community-owned swimming pools. Arrangements with local stables

Figure 10–6. Many schools are now adding ice skating to their program. (Courtesy Los Angeles Unified School District.)

have enabled some schools to add horseback riding to the curriculum. Others include camping activities, using summer camp facilities usually closed during the winter. Still others are offering ice and/or roller skating at community rinks, and there are even those schools which have arrangements with local farmers for their classes to use hilly farm areas for the teaching of skiing fundamentals, horseshoeing, or other parts of the area for campcraft activities, including backpacking, orienteering, survival camping, and other basic outdoor education skills.

Any teacher today who confines his program solely to the gymnasium and playing or athletic fields of his own campus is selling his program short. Taxpayers are no longer willing to let themselves be taxed to build school facilities and then be taxed again to provide duplicate facilities for community recreational purposes. Thus, the community-centered school has come into being, and in such cities as Flint, Michigan, and Milwaukee, Wisconsin, all school facilities as well as some personnel are mutually shared for educational and recreational purposes all year for people of all ages. Since our schools belong to the people who have paid for and own them, we can no longer open

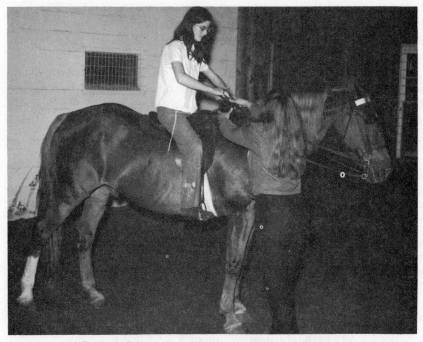

(Courtesy Regina High School. Minneapolis, Minnesota.)

(Courtesy Regina High School. Minneapolis, Minnesota.)

their doors only to and for the education of children and older youth. Nor can any community-owned recreational facility located away from the school close its doors to children and older youth, for both of those groups are a vital part of each community, too.

In such cities as Los Angeles and Anaheim, California, in Cleveland, Ohio, and in increasingly more cities throughout our nation, the school district and city work closely together to plan, finance and share educational and recreational personnel, facilities and administrative talents. As one authority has said:

The elementary school is an ideal neighborhood recreation center because of its central location in the neighborhood. The secondary school is also an ideal community recreation center, taking in a larger area. Then the junior college ideally, could become a regional recreation center. This is a concept we should consider more thoroughly. One thing agreed upon was that there is no one way to do the job, that each individual community must determine what its resources are, and these differ. Then the power structure decides what, and who, and how the job is to be done. The determining factor in deciding who should administer the program is who can best do it with the cooperation of the others. Teamwork in planning and operating the program is essential.[3]

---

[3]American Association For Health, Physical Education and Recreation: *Planning and Financing School-Community Recreation*. Washington, D.C., 1967, p. 103.

COMPUTER MONITORED PROGRAMS

Students taking coeducational physical education classes at the Simmons Junior High School in Aurora, Illinois progress at their own skill developmental rate through self-directed learning of activities. Each student is given print-out materials showing both his movement problems and his correction of them through trial and error attempts. Each student also has individual conferences with a teacher concerning his own unique learning rate and difficulties. Since the skills learned in this program are supplemented by cognitive concepts, students learn both the "how" and "why" of each activity they are learning. Such cognitive concepts are "why" and "how" various spins can be put on tennis balls, or why the triangular head placement is the superior one to use when learning the headstand, or how to regain quick body stability after doing the back flip on the trampoline, and so on. The student goes through eight minutes of a physical fitness circuit of activities planned for his own level of fitness and then spends the rest of the period learning the skills of an activity of his choice. Students may work singly or with others, and each is well aware of the objectives he is striving to reach. Each progresses at his own rate, and those having learning difficulties receive constant positive reinforcement as they strive to master their own performance objectives. Students check out audio-visual materials such as sound pages, cassette tapes, transparencies and wall charts to help them learn as much as possible about each activity of their choice.

In this program all students are required to take tumbling, two team sports, three individual sports and boating safety as well as work to improve their own fitness level. There are 28 different activities offered in the curriculum from which each student may choose. The faculty plans to include 12 other activities in this program in the near future. These will include ice skating, jogging combined with cycling, cross-country running, still rings, fencing, and swimming. All classes are coeducational and in this unique program students not only are given increased freedom of choice and assume greater responsibility for their own learning progress but they also work more closely together than in a traditional physical education class to help each other learn. The teacher, likewise, gains increased opportunity to work more closely as a helpful learning motivator and guide to each student.

INDIVIDUALIZED PROGRAMS

Some schools are now designing individualized physical education programs for their students that include both on- and off-campus electives during the school year and summer. At the Regina High

School in Minneapolis, Minnesota, girls in grades 10 to 12 may select on-campus electives each quarter from the following activities:

Recreation leadership activities	Tennis
Power volleyball	Physical fitness
Gymnastics	Archery
Recreational games	Campcraft
Soccer and speedball	Trampoline
Floor hockey	Balance beam
Bike hiking	Track
Volleyball	Creative Dance
Basketball	Softball

In order to encourage better use of leisure time, community recreation facilities are used in a large portion of the program. Specialists in each sport, assisted by a physical education teacher or paraprofessional, are hired to conduct activities in the off-campus program.

A fee is charged to pay for transportation, use of facilities, and specialized instruction received by each student choosing to enroll in the off-campus elective program. These activities and fees are:

Activity	Fee
Horseback riding	$ 34
Bowling	$ 8
Downhill skiing	$ 28
Cross country skiing	$ 10
Roller skating	$ 11

Other off-campus electives offered on a rotating year-to-year basis include golf, swimming, lifesaving, and a whale class for outstanding swimmers with diversified aquatic interests.

In this individualized program junior and senior students can earn one-quarter physical education credit during the summer months for taking part in one of the following activities:

Participating in individualized ice skating activities.

Taking part in an Outward Bound program, including writing a paper on it.

Winning a belt in a karate program.

Taking snowmobiling safety courses and spending two weekends snowmobiling.

Coaching a softball team in a summer recreation league.

Serving as counselors in training.

Acting as a counselor at a day camp.

Participating in bike hiking every day during the summer and completing the project by taking a supervised 50-mile bike hike.

Taking part in a family camping project which involved, among other things, reading about birds, fish, trees, orienteering, and flowers, and being able to identify a specified number of birds, fish, trees, wild flowers, stars and constellations and animals.

Undertaking a fishing project and learning such things as boating safety and fishing laws, how to bait a hook, how to filet fish, and how to become proficient in a variety of fishing skills.

Taking horseback riding lessons and learning to ride western style and how to jump.

Teaching swimming lessons in a program scheduled and conducted for young children.

Earning a junior lifesaving certificate.

Earning a Red Cross First Aid Certificate.

Participating in a "Weight Watchers" program in which girls must reach and maintain the weight suggested by their doctors.

Taking a two-week wilderness canoe trip in the Boundary Waters.

In order to receive credit for the summer course elected, the student must sign a contract with the teacher that spells out what must be done in the program. Each individualized study project is goal oriented. Parents take an active interest in their child's individualized projects and in activities which involve fishing and camping; the family also takes part in these leisure time activities together. Thus, the students in this exciting and creative high school program are gaining far more than skill mastery, for they are also attaining those other objectives of a physical education program many teachers pay only lip service to — namely, developing total fitness, self motivation to do physical activities, socializing the individual, increasing knowledge, fostering favorable attitudes and appreciations, and encouraging better use of leisure time for the present as well as the future.

TYPES OF PLANNING

PLANNING WITH OTHER TEACHERS

If the department has a chairman, each instructor should be included in curriculum planning and policy making, as well as in selecting desired goals, teaching methods and evaluative tools. In smaller schools where one man and one woman teacher are responsible for the entire program, their pooled ideas should be formulated into curriculum plans with the assistance of the school administrator and other teachers. Those primarily concerned with physical education should welcome this rich opportunity to educate their colleagues concerning the nature, scope, purpose and value of the program. Likewise, they should be grateful for the opportunity to work with other teachers to help them plan and fit their subject's contribution into the total school curriculum. Teachers who are real working partners on an educational team have gained an understanding and respect for the contribution of each member.

TEACHER-PUPIL PLANNING

The program should also be teacher-student planned, conducted and evaluated. Although this is often time-consuming, it is the necessary educational foundation upon which the entire program must rest if it is to be of value. Since youth learn best when and if they wish, a feebly sparked desire to find out or to do can be fanned into a flame by helping each select individual and group goals, choose activities through which these can be reached, and then aid him to evaluate the results. The chief values of teacher-pupil planning are that it assists youth to gain democratic leadership skills and an understanding of their importance, increases interests and motivates learning attempts, helps in making each feel responsible for his own chosen actions, develops insight into the nature of the whole program by working through each integral part, and develops good group rapport through friendlier teacher-pupil relationships.

The ability to be democratic is a skill learned largely through practice. Youth is often domineering, impulsive and impatient and will replace selfish "I" drives slowly and often painfully with the higher valued "We" concepts. Just as one cannot run without first learning how to walk, youth groups cannot plan alone for the greatest good for the greatest number without gradually being given opportunities to make initial choices with the help of mature adults. Secondary school groups should gradually be given a stronger voice in determining what they wish to do as well as in their own governing rules. It is suggested, therefore, that the teacher begin joint pupil planning by asking each class for suggestions for solving certain problems that have arisen which affect group welfare, such as students talking while he is giving class instruction to the degree that precious instructional time is wasted. Other ways for establishing good democratic class procedures are to let each group set their desired goals, choose activities they are to do by gradually increasing the number of days in each semester when they are given this privilege, select their own squad leaders, representatives, officials, team captains or teams, check attendance, obtain and return their own supplies and equipment, determine how much class time will be used for skill drills and playing, and draw up and conduct their own class tournaments.

In permitting students to select their own goals and activities to be learned, the teacher should realize that the wrong approach is asking the class what they want to do, for very few know what things are available that they can learn, the majority will cling to old favorites and rebel against anything new, and only one or two will have even the vaguest notion of any desired goals, for these often remain submerged and must be brought to light. Since teaching is guiding, and all those who enter the profession should be masters of patience with a full knowledge of the value and use of the wares they sell, teacher-student planning should be practiced, not student-teacher, especially on the secondary level. Learning to be democratic is not an easy task to master, for it takes much time, great patience, and the deepest kind of understanding of people and what makes them behave as they do. Teacher and pupil goals need not be the same, even though both may be formed around the same activity. The former might have as his chief aim the development of good sportsmanship and honesty among the members of a class basketball team which has been known to cheat; whereas this same group may set as its own desired objective the winning of the class tournament and may realize that to do so all must work hard to master basic skills taught in class. Although class planning will vary with the nature of the problems to be solved, generally speaking, all planning which involves carefully made explorations and decisions can best be done in a regular classroom or in the teacher's office by student-selected representatives and the instructor. Such a group should not exceed ten in number; ideally, it may be composed of six students and one teacher. Minor matters, such as choosing class teams, can best be done during the regular class period by the entire group. It has often been said that working with people is like bowling — get the kingpin first and you have the rest. All school groups, regardless of age, need practice in learning how to select their group leaders wisely and in reaching decisions which will be of value and benefit to all concerned. One basic technique of good democratic leadership is to lead through elected subleaders. High school students are more peer- than adult-conscious, and some have strong leadership qualities, but like Hitler, lead the wrong way.[4] Each school physical education class can be a lucrative learning laboratory for democracy and the development of future positive adult leaders of great worth.

THE SCOPE OF PLANNING

Types of program plans are the closely related long-term, yearly, unit and seasonal plans, which differ little except that some cover longer periods than others, and the much shorter weekly and daily plans. All are closely related, yet each has its own unique characteristics.

LONG-TERM PLANS

These are also known as vertical plans, and are found in a graded program for physical education from grades one through twelve.

---

[4]See the chapter on *Understanding the Students* to review the role the herd instinct plays at this age.

A Four-year Required and Elective Program

Students in the ninth and tenth grades work together in one class through a series of units in physical education that requires two years to complete. Students in the eleventh and twelfth grades work together in the class and are given opportunity to choose the units they wish to complete from a series of units covering two years' work.

PHYSICAL EDUCATION UNITS FOR THE NINTH AND TENTH GRADES			PHYSICAL EDUCATION UNITS FOR THE ELEVENTH AND TWELFTH GRADES		
FIRST YEAR	WEEKS	SECOND YEAR	FIRST YEAR	WEEKS	SECOND YEAR
Orientation and fundamentals of body movement in stunts and tumbling	8	Orientation and fundamentals of body movement in modern dance	Coeducational tennis or badminton	10	Coeducational archery or golf
Basketball	6	Volleyball	Speedball or hockey and officiating	10	Basketball or volleyball
Speedball or speed-a-way	8	Hockey			
Social and folk dancing (coeducational)	6	Square dancing (coeducational)	Coeducational folk dance or modern dance	10	Coeducational recreational games or coeducational tennis
Softball	6	Archery or golf			
Swimming	6	Tennis or paddle tennis	Recreational leadership or social recreation	10	Swimming and lifesaving or sports officiating

ᴇNIOR HIGH SCHOOL

Fall Program

10ᴛʜ ɢʀᴀᴅᴇ	WEEKS	11ᴛʜ ɢʀᴀᴅᴇ	WEEKS	12ᴛʜ ɢʀᴀᴅᴇ	WEEKS
Organization/		ᴏnization/		Organization/	
Orientation	1	ᴏntation	1	Orientation	1
Touch Football	4	Tᴏ Football	2	Touch Football	2
Soccer/Speedball	3				
Volleyball	2	Volleyᴏ	2	Volleyball	2
Gymnastics/		Gymnaᴏ /		Gymnastics/	
Apparatus	2	Apparᴏ	2	Apparatus	2
Basketball	4	Basketbalᴏ	3	Basketball	3
		Tennis	2	Tennis	2
		Golf	2	Golf	2
Health Instruction		Health Instrucᴏ ᴏ		Health Instruction	
		Badminton/		Badminton/	
		Handball	2	Handball	2
TOTAL	16	TOTAL	16	TOTAL	16
Exercises: 3-7 minutes daily					

Spring Program

10ᴛʜ ɢʀᴀᴅᴇ	WEEKS	11ᴛʜ ɢʀᴀᴅᴇ	WEEK	12ᴛʜ ɢʀᴀᴅᴇ	WEEKS
Track and Field	4	Track and Field	3	ᴏack and Field	3
Softball	4	Softball	4	ᴏ ᴏtball	4
Gymnastics	2	Gymnastics	2	Gᴏ ᴏnastics	2
Wrestling	2	Wrestling	2	Wᴏ ᴏling	2
Handball	1	Archery	2	Arcᴏ ᴏy	2
First Aid	1	First Aid	1	First ᴏ ᴏd	1
Health Instruction		Health Instruction		Health ᴏstruction	
Volleyball	2	Volleyball	2	Volleybaᴏ	2
TOTAL	16	TOTAL	16	ᴏTAL	16
Exercises: 3-7 minutes daily					

Figure 10–8. Los Angeles City Schools: *Boys' Physical Education, ᴏ ᴏching Guide for Junior and Senior High Schools.* Los Angeles Division of Instructional Seᴏ ᴏices, Publication No. SC-585, 1960, p. 8.

Often valuable teacher time is lost when it becomes necessary to rᴏ ᴏer back to records in order to review what has been taught two or thrᴏ ᴏ weeks previously. These plans are of greatest value when they arᴏ broadly outlined and kept flexible. Note in the sample monthly program (Table 10–3) that additional materials are listed to be taught in each period, should there be enough time left to do so.

Table 10–2 lists a coeducational program from the ninth to the twelfth grades that is based upon another type of commonly used weekly planning.

DAILY PLANS

Beginning teachers should make detailed written daily lesson plans in order to use best each class period and to gain security as

Table 10–2.   WEEKLY PROGRAM IN PHYSICAL EDUCATION
FOR BOYS AND GIRLS FROM GRADES 9 THROUGH 12

NUMBER OF WEEKS	9TH GRADE	10TH GRADE	11TH GRADE	12TH GRADE
First 6 weeks	Soccer	Speedball	Touch football for boys Advanced speedball for girls	Advanced touch football for boys Hockey for girls
Second 6 weeks	Elementary square dance	Intermediate square dance	Beginning social dance	Intermediate and advanced social dance
Third 6 weeks	Intermediate aquatics	Intermediate aquatics Junior lifesaving	Advanced aquatics and diving	Advanced aquatics and diving Junior lifesaving Comparative meets for boys Synchronized swimming for girls
Fourth 6 weeks	Formal gymnastics Recreational games	Formal gymnastics Volleyball	Formal gymnastics Intermediate basketball	Formal gymnastics Advanced basketball
Fifth 6 weeks	Elementary track and field events	Intermediate track and field events	Advanced track and field events	Tennis Golf
Sixth 6 weeks	Lead up team games to softball and baseball Basic skills in throwing and catching Recreational games	Beginning softball and baseball Recreational games	Intermediate baseball for boys Intermediate softball for girls	Advanced baseball for boys Advanced softball for girls Elective archery or badminton

educators. As they grow in experience and confidence it is often not necessary to plan in such detail, although outline planning is still needed. Daily planning saves time and energy and prevents much frustration. Students quickly lose respect for teachers who lack confidence and seemingly do not know what they are doing and for those who fail to provide variety or a challenging class program.

Daily lesson plans should include objectives, needed equipment, techniques for linking previously learned materials through review to the present lesson, the new activities to be taught and techniques for evaluating progress.

Regardless of which type of planning the teacher adopts, the program should be well balanced. Sports alone or free play periods cannot lead to total body development, nor should overemphasis be placed upon any one part of the program at the expensive exclusion of others. Conditioning exercises and warm-ups should be a part of every period. All activities in the program should be included because they can best reach desired objectives. No activity should be repeated in

Table 10-3.   A SAMPLE MONTHLY PROGRAM FOR TWELFTH GRADE GIRLS

	MONDAY	TUESDAY	WEDNESDAY	THURSDAY	FRIDAY
First week	*Tennis* Forehand, backhand, (Serve)	*Tennis* Review Volleying Serving (Flat serve)	*Tennis* Review Lob, chop strokes (Doubles play)	*Tennis* Review Chop Smash New play Singles play (Twist serve)	*Coed square dance* Basic figure, mixers, Red River Valley (Oh, Suzanna!)
Second week	*Tennis* Review Doubles play-up and back (Back court play)	*Tennis* Review Doubles play Parallel system (Advanced net play)	*Tennis* Review Doubles play Rotation system (Singles strategy)	*Tennis* Review Class play entire period (Individual instruction)	*Coed square dance* Review Texas Schot- tische, Road to the Isles (Heel-and-Toe Polka)
Third week	*Tennis* Review Class play entire period (Individual instruction)	*Tennis* Wall skill test (Rotate students tested while others play)	*Tennis* Types of tournaments Written objec- tive test (Class evalua- tion by discussion)	*Tennis* Test questions gone over in class (Play tennis remainder of period)	*Coed square dance* Review Yaller Gal Dive for the Oyster (Forward Six)
Fourth week	*Stunts and tumbling* Orientation and safety rules Rolls, forward, backward, double (Headstand)	*Stunts and tumbling* Warm-ups Review Forward, backward somersaults Couple stunts (Headspring)	*Stunts and tumbling* Warm-ups Review Cartwheel Round off Dives (Partner balance stunts)	*Stunts and tumbling* Warm-ups Review Pyramids (Tumbling routines)	*Coed square dance* Review Star by the Right Birdie in a Cage Jessie Polka (Lili Marlene)

Figure 10-9. Warm-up exercises should be included as part of the activity plan for the daily lesson. (Courtesy of the Youth Service Section of the Los Angeles Public Schools.)

the same way in each lesson nor at each grade level, for skill must be built upon skill, and the entire program for each year must be interesting, challenging and meaningful. As much of it as possible should be conducted out of doors. All sport activities should be taught in season and followed up with a well-planned intramural program in which all students are encouraged to take part.

THE DAILY LESSON PLAN

Each day's lesson should be carefully planned. A suggested form for doing so is found below:

A DAILY LESSON PLAN

Grade_____ Class_____ Title of Unit_____ Lesson Number_____
Length of Period_____ Number in Class_____

Primary Objectives:
    1._____
    2._____
    3._____
Secondary Objectives:
    1._____
    2._____

References:
    1._____
    2._____

Class Procedure:	Equipment needed:
1. Roll call by	1.
2.	
	Organizational Plan:

Evaluation: (Suggestions and improvements)

SELECTED VISUAL AIDS

Beginning Badminton Series. Six filmstrips in color with records. Shows the game, serve, overhand, forehand, backhand strokes and the game. Available rental from the Athletic Institute.

Speedball For Girls. 16 mm., 11 min., sd, b & w, color. Demonstrates skills, players' positions, rules, and ways to develop team play. Available for rental from Coronet Instructional Films.

Beginning Swimming. 11 min., b & w, sd, rental. Shows land and water drills involving breathing, kicking, floating, paddling and stroking for the crawl, back float, back stroke and breast stroke. Available from Coronet Instructional Films.

Beginning Track and Field. Five filmstrips with record. Shows starts, sprints and hurdles, middle and long distance running, and jumping events. Available for rental from the Athletic Institute.

SUGGESTED READINGS

AAHPER: "The Now Physical Education," *The Journal of Health, Physical Education and Recreation.* Washington, D.C., September, 1973, pp. 23–29.

AAHPER: *Organizational Patterns for Instruction in Physical Education.* Washington, D.C., 1971.

AAHPER: *Physical Education For High School Students.* Washington, D.C., 1970.

Bucher, Charles: *Foundations of Physical Education,* 6th Ed., St. Louis, C. V. Mosby Co., 1972.

Daughtrey, Gregson, and Woods, John: *Physical Education Programs: Organization and Administration.* Philadelphia, W. B. Saunders Co., 1971.

Insley, Gerald: *Practical Guidelines For The Teaching of Physical Education.* Reading, Mass., Addison-Wesley Publishing Co., 1973.

Irwin, Leslie: *The Curriculum in Physical Education.* Dubuque, Iowa, William C. Brown Co., 1969.

Kraus, Richard: *Recreation and Leisure in Modern Society.* New York, Appleton-Century-Crofts, Inc., 1971.

Kroll, Walter: *Perspectives in Physical Education.* New York, Academic Press, 1971.

Mosston, Muska: *Teaching Physical Education—From Command to Discovery.* Columbus, Ohio, Charles E. Merrill Books, Inc., 1966.

Nixon, John, and Jewett, Ann: *Physical Education Curriculum.* New York, The Ronald Press, 1964.

Oberteuffer, Delbert, and Ulrich, Celeste: *Physical Education,* 4th Ed., New York, Harper and Row, Publishers, 1970.

Resick, Mathew, Seidel, Beverly, and Mason, James: *Modern Administrative Practices in Physical Education and Athletics.* Reading, Mass., Addison-Wesley Publishing Co., 1970.

Seidel, Beverely, and Resick, Mathew: *Physical Education: An Overview.* Reading, Mass., Addison-Wesley Publishing Co., 1972.

Siedentop, Daryl: *Physical Education, Introductory Analysis.* Dubuque, Iowa, William C. Brown Publishers, 1972.

Taba, Hilda: *Curriculum Development: Theory and Practice.* New York, Harcourt, Brace and World, Inc., 1962.

Texas Education Agency: *Suggestions For Planning The Secondary Physical Education Program.* Bulletin 625, Austin, Texas, 1963.

Vannier, Maryhelen, Foster, Mildred, and Gallahue, David: *Teaching Physical Education in Elementary Schools.* 5th Ed., Philadelphia, W. B. Saunders Co., 1971.

Willgoose, Carl: *The Curriculum in Physical Education.* Englewood Cliffs, N.J., Prentice-Hall, Inc., 1969.

DISCUSSION QUESTIONS

1. Discuss the advantages and disadvantages of long-term planning, seasonal plans, weekly plans, unit plans and daily lesson plans.

2. In what ways can students assist in program planning? What are the chief advantages to this practice?

3. Read any of the suggested readings for this chapter. Discuss any new ideas you gained from your reading regarding curriculum and lesson planning.

4. How can teachers and students best be guided in the selection of program activities?

5. The physical education program should help prepare students for the totality of life. Discuss the Lifetime Sports Program in light of this principle. How can your school develop such a program, perhaps in spite of high enrollment and limited facilities?

THINGS TO DO

1. Outline a six-week teaching unit for a physical education class in tumbling for high school boys and one in tennis for high school girls.

2. Make daily lesson plans for a two-week teaching unit for folk dance and for a class in archery.

3. As a member of a debate team, discuss the pros and cons of modular scheduling or the pros and cons of an elective choice program versus the same required course for all students.

4. Which of the suggestions given for having a good program did you see practiced when you visited a high school physical education class in any school in your area? Report your findings to your classmates.

5. List the advantages and disadvantages of coeducational classes rather than separate classes for each sex throughout the entire physical education program.

6. Give a five minute oral report on the importance of secondary school physical education experiences in relationship to the totality of life, taking into account changes which must be made if physical education is to make a meaningful contribution.

7. Summarize in outline form your reading of "Educational Changes in the Teaching of Physical Education," Quest, Monograph 15, (January, 1970).

CHAPTER ELEVEN

PHYSICAL FITNESS

CALISTHENICS, WEIGHT TRAINING, ISOMETRICS, JOGGING AND WEIGHT CONTROL

Students generally are aware of the necessity for physical conditioning for sports participation, but they often fail to realize the importance of increasing the physical efficiency of their own bodies to meet the demands of everyday living. Consequently, it becomes one of the most important tasks of the physical educator to give students an understanding of the nature of physical fitness and to impress upon them the health benefits of physical fitness activities.

Physical fitness refers to the ability of the body to perform maximally as well as to work as efficiently as possible. This implies a general well being of the body and a capacity for vigorous activity. Optimal physical fitness enables one to work and play without undue exertion, and without excessive fatigue, and with sufficient reserve to meet any reasonable physical emergency.

Common usage of the term physical fitness varies greatly. As a result much confusion exists as to exactly what is meant by physical fitness. For purposes of simplification, those qualities relating more closely to neurological aspects or skill mastery than to physiological capacities of the organism will be termed motor fitness, while those aspects that appear to be more nearly related to physiological capacities will be termed physical fitness. Therefore, such qualities as coordination, agility, balance and speed will be included in the classification of motor fitness. Combinations of the various motor fitness elements result in specific movement patterns termed skilled movements. Thus skill in serving a tennis ball, shooting a basketball or doing the butterfly swimming stroke is dependent primarily on motor fitness elements, not on physical fitness elements. Physical fitness elements are identified with the maximal functional capabilities of one or several systems. In the classification described above, the qualities comprising physical fitness are muscular strength, muscular endurance, flexibility and

Figure 11-1. A special device called the milking machine develops arm strength. (Courtesy of Russell Bondt of the La Sierra High School, Carmichael, California.)

cardiorespiratory endurance. Development of these four functional qualities serves as a necessary basis for many sport skills and is primary to others. For example, strength is far more important in the shot put than in a basketball shot, where it is only a basis on which skill must be built. However, these four physical fitness qualities are so universally evident in sport activities that development of all of them warrants special attention. In addition, the health implications of physical fitness are extensive. Much current literature has been devoted to the liabilities associated with poor physical fitness levels.

This chapter will be concerned with identification of the means of enhancing those physical fitness qualities which are of importance to both sport participation and health. The conducting of programs to develop these qualities is simultaneously emphasized.

FITNESS QUALITIES

A primary quality in many activities is muscular strength. Strength is defined as the maximal amount of force which a particular muscle can exert. It is normally measured in pounds of pull. Strength is specific to the various muscles or groups of muscles which work together. Nevertheless, it has been established that there is some relationship between the strength of sets of muscles of the body. This does not preclude the possibility of a given individual having several strong muscle groups and also several which are relatively weak, particularly if the sets of muscles have been exposed to different workloads. Total strength is estimated by sampling a variety of commonly used muscle groups throughout the body. However, research has indicated that the best single measurement by which to estimate total strength is the hand grip.

Muscular endurance is the capacity to sustain a submaximal contraction or to repeat rapidly a series of contractions. Endurance implies the ability to persist or continue in the effort and is thus measured by time or by repetitions of the movement completed. Common tests of the number of push-ups and sit-ups that can be done and the amount of time in that the bent arm hang can be maintained are examples of measures of muscular endurance. Muscular strength and muscular endurance are not totally independent qualities in that increased strength can aid endurance; however, one can possess exceptional muscular endurance without exhibiting extraordinary strength. The student who can lift the heaviest weight is not always the one who can do the most chin-ups. As is true of strength, muscular endurance is specific to a muscle or functional muscle group. However, all things being equal, the stronger muscle has the greater amount of endurance.

The quality of flexibility refers to the range of motion possible. It is best measured in degrees of rotation possible within the joint. Although less publicized than the other physical fitness qualities, flexibility contributes to effective performance in many activities by affording the participant greater latitude of mobility in his joints. He can reach objects and make movements which other less flexible persons are incapable of performing. In some activities, such as dance, gymnastics, ice skating and diving, flexibility in specific joints is especially valuable.

The fourth quality of physical fitness is cardiorespiratory endurance. It is a general quality concerned with the body's ability to process oxygen for supplying energy for muscular work. It includes the combined functioning of the lungs, heart and vascular system. The greater the amount of oxygen these combined systems are capable of supplying, the higher the level of muscular work the body can sustain over a period of time. As is true of muscular endurance, cardiovascular endurance is measured by how long strenuous activity of the whole body can be maintained. Tests are usually timed distance runs. This type of total system endurance is advantageous in most fast-moving sports as well as being primary in all distance race events.

PRINCIPLES FOR DEVELOPMENT

All physical fitness development results from the body's adaptation to the stresses of conditioning programs. The general concept which underlies all scientific conditioning programs is the "SAID" principle.[1] This acronym stands for *Specific Adaptation to Imposed Demands.* The principle states that the body adapts rather specifically to the demands which are imposed upon it. In practice this means that if we are desirous of increasing the strength of a particular muscle group we must require it to contract with a force greater than that which it is normally accustomed to performing. The muscle will adapt to this demand by becoming larger and stronger. The SAID principle is also valid in cases where we reduce the normal load by ceasing the training period. In this instance the muscle adapts to the new demands by atrophying and becoming weaker. The SAID principle applies to all the qualities of physical fitness. In the above example, the body specifically adapted to the strength demand; it changed little in flexibility, muscular endurance or cardiorespiratory endurance. To effect these qualities we must specifically apply stress to achieve them, i.e., cause the body to work through above-normal stresses of range of motion, sustained muscular contraction or repeated total body movements. The development of one quality is rather specific unto itself and does not, in most

---

[1]Wallis, Earl L. and Logan, Gene: *Figure Improvement and Body Conditioning Through Exercise.* Englewood Cliffs, N.J., Prentice-Hall, Inc., 1964, p. 1.

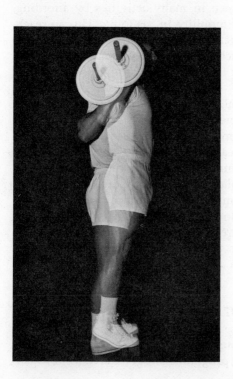

Figure 11–2. In the toe raise the SAID principle is applied to develop the legs.

cases, automatically or appreciably aid the development of the others. If all qualities are important, physical education programs must provide demands sufficient to cause each quality to improve.

A corollary to the SAID principle is the progressive overload principle. This concept states that, if continued development is desired, the system in question must be progressively stressed by greater and greater demands. In accordance with the SAID principle, as a system is stressed it will adapt and become more capable. If we wish to continue to improve, we must increase the demand incrementally as the adaptation to the first increase is achieved. In this manner demand is always kept ahead of adaptation and the system continues to increase in its functional ability.

The SAID principle is thus the underlying concept explaining all changes in the status of the fitness qualities of an individual. It is the basis for predicting what changes will occur from participation in any planned conditioning program as well as the results of inactivity.

COURSE CONTENT

Units of instruction in physical fitness are generally of two types: (1) a specific unit directed only at physical fitness or (2) a distributive unit in which physical fitness activities form a portion of the daily lesson over the entire year, i.e., 10 minutes of exercise at the beginning of every class session regardless of the content of the unit. Most distributive units utilize calisthenics or running as the physical fitness activity and so often serve the dual purpose of fitness development and warm-up for the day's class. Specific units in physical fitness may utilize calisthenics, weight training, isometrics, jogging or a combination of these activities to make up their content. The content of any unit should be carefully planned through the application of the SAID principle to assure proper selection of exercises for development of the qualities desired.

In addition to the selected developmental activities, knowledge of the "how" and "why" of fitness development should be included. Students should understand the benefits which may be obtained from the selected activities and how each enhances health and sport performance. Specific topics concerning physical fitness development that might be included are:

1. The SAID principle.
2. The importance of the physical fitness elements in sport performance and everyday living.
3. Methods of evaluating one's fitness status and needs.
4. Appropriate activity selection for achieving and maintaining fitness.
5. The role of sport participation in producing fitness.

Figure 11-3. An outdoor exercise unit, consisting of pegboard, climbing poles and cables, makes possible interesting variety in physical fitness activities. (Courtesy of Russell Bondt, of the La Sierra High School, Carmichael, California.)

6. The modification of certain exercises as one grows older.
7. The misconception of muscle boundness.
8. The effects of exercise on the figure.
9. The value of exercise in weight control.
10. The relationship of body weight to sport performances.

CLASS ORGANIZATION

Class designs for physical fitness development can be accomplished in a variety of ways, including en masse directed calisthenics, circuit training programs, sequential activity stations or individually designed programs. Regardless of the design, instructors must remain aware of the need for total development of all the physical fitness components. Often the component which is most lacking in a student is the very one he will least likely engage in voluntarily. An unconscious personal bias of this kind also affects teachers in their selection of activities.

Whichever method of organization is utilized, it should provide for the potential development of students of both high and low physical fitness alike. Some form of recording student progress is highly desirable. The demonstration of improved capabilities is a strong motivating factor.

TEACHING PROCEDURES

The activities and organizational scheme selected for inclusion in the unit of instruction must be explained and demonstrated to the students. Each exercise, its potential contribution and the correct form of execution, should be presented. Since the manner in which exercises are performed greatly affects the developed qualities, emphasis on the proper technique is important. Simultaneously, students should be made aware of any safety considerations, such as forcing a joint too far and proper handling of equipment. This concern is paramount when one student relies on another for spotting or providing resistance in dual exercises.

Since many exercises involve some degree of unpleasant feelings associated with fatigue, it is advantageous to provide outside motivation from the instructor or fellow students. This can be accomplished through the enthusiasm the instructor demonstrates for the unit, the manner in which he controls the group and the amount of verbal reward he provides to the class members. Often the pride and enthusiasm which the instructor can generate in a class make the difference between a favorable or unfavorable attitude on the part of students toward exercise in general.

CALISTHENICS

Calisthenic exercises are one means by which the fitness factors of strength, body flexibility and endurance can be increased. Such activity produces especially effective results because it provides a good total body work out in a short period of time.

Two formations are frequently used to organize the class for the presentation of calisthenics. In one, the class is lined up in rows with arms' distance between the students, with one exercise instructor in charge. The other formation involves dividing the class into groups of eight to ten students who are under the direction of a student leader. These small groups may each form a circle with the leader in the center, or he may face the group, which is lined up before him.

If the exercises are being chosen to supplement the activity of a sport, the teacher must give some consideration to the needs which have been left unfilled by the activity. For example, in gymnastics there will be a deficiency of leg activity because work on the apparatus is largely limited to shoulder girdle and arm movements, so supplementary formal exercises for the legs will make a better total work out. During the basketball unit the teacher may wish to include formal heavy resistance exercises to develop strength, which is not greatly increased by playing basketball. When table tennis and shuffleboard

Figure 11–4. The random formation may be used for physical fitness exercises. (Courtesy Enrico Fermi High School.)

are being taught to the class, exercises to increase endurance and stimulate the cardiovascular system may be included to round out the activity; the side-straddle hop and the squat thrust are two types of supplementary exercises which are frequently used.

For a unit of body conditioning in which calisthenics are an integral part, three different procedures may be followed: the set drill pattern, the core exercise pattern and the ever-changing pattern. The set drill consists of utilizing a fixed set of exercises through an entire unit, while the core exercise pattern consists of starting the program with a core of exercises and then, as the unit progresses, adding others. In the ever-changing pattern there are no set exercises; rather, the teacher introduces new exercises each period or revises the old ones.

The military manner has greatly influenced the method of instruction in calisthenics. First, the exercise is demonstrated by the leader, then it is executed by the group to the counting cadence of the leader. Some teachers prefer to use music instead of counting. Performing to music would have some value as a lead-up activity for the unit on rhythms and dance, and it adds enjoyment to the exercise.

The length of time that a specific exercise should be given is dependent upon the type of exercise and the physical condition of the students. In general, students just starting such exercises should begin with short periods and light work loads which are gradually increased.

The teacher may wish to perform the exercises with the class, at least until he is able to estimate the work output required to perform the exercise a certain number of times. He will then be better able to judge the amount of increase necessary in work load and in duration.

The variety of calisthenic possibilities is practically endless. However, the selection of any program should probably contain activities designed both to work all the major muscle groups and to cover the various physical fitness areas of strength, endurance and flexibility. A core program of exercises consistent with these guidelines might be composed of the following:

  1. *Warm-up* — side straddle hop or running in place
  2. *Shoulder and Neck* — neck circling; arm circling
  3. *Arms* — push-ups
  4. *Abdominal* — sit-ups
  5. *Legs* — squat and jump
  6. *Flexibility* — trunk rotations; toe touching and overhead reach
  7. *Cardiorespiratory* — continuous (2 to 5 minutes) squat thrust, running in place, side straddle hop or combination

Most students of physical education have had exposure to a variety of calisthenic possibilities in instructional classes, sport programs or through their own interests. For this reason, no attempt at an explanation or listing of calisthenics is attempted here. Readers seeking this information should consult one of the appropriate references listed at the end of this chapter.

Pull-ups, dips and rope and peg board climbing are exercises

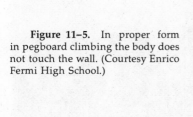

Figure 11–5. In proper form in pegboard climbing the body does not touch the wall. (Courtesy Enrico Fermi High School.)

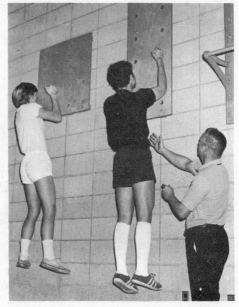

that have proved popular with boys. They are especially good for developing the arm and shoulder muscles. Pull-ups, rope climbing and peg board climbing exercise the same muscles, the flexors of the arm, so that in planning the exercises for any given period duplication of these activities need not be made. Dips on the parallel bars, however, work the opposite muscles, the extensors of the arm, and may be included with one of the other activities for more complete exercise of the areas involved, without producing undue fatigue in the arms and shoulders.

Because of the enthusiasm peg board climbing usually engenders among boys it can be used as a voluntary participation activity, if the shoulder girdle has been sufficiently strengthened previously by such exercises as the pull-up. Before allowing free participation, however, the proper use of the peg board and safety procedures to be observed should be explained thoroughly to the entire class.

Pull-ups and dips are difficult to present in a program unless several high bars and parallel bars are available. However, even with a limited number of bars, a class rotation system can be set up so that two or three students are working on the bars while other groups are doing different exercises in other parts of the gymnasium.

For whatever reasons, calisthenics are probably the least popular form of exercise with high school students. This may be due in part to the militaristic methods often utilized in these programs as well as to a lack of information and motivational concern on the part of instructors. To conduct an entire unit, which may cover several weeks, with calisthenics as the only activity would prove very unpopular in most high school settings. The following sections suggest other forms of physical fitness activities which are more appealing to a majority of students.

Figure 11–6. Specially constructed parallel bars enable large numbers of students to participate in physical fitness activities at one time. (Courtesy of Russell Bondt, of the La Sierra High School, Carmichael, California.)

WEIGHT TRAINING

Weight training is distinguished from weight lifting in that the former implies the use of weights for resistance in a wide variety of exercise movements, while the latter is a sport concerned with lifting maximal weights by three specific techniques. The concern in this chapter is the use of weight training procedures in the production of physical fitness.

Weight training has become a very popular activity for both boys and girls. Girls typically use lighter weights and perform more repetitions, seeking muscle toning and shaping. Many boys look to weights as a means of greatly increasing muscular strength. Both are possible outcomes, depending upon the structure of the program, and have been popularized by the development of "health spas." Although few girls are desirous of large muscular development, the use of weight training for figure control has become increasingly acceptable.

In the past, work outs with weights had been discouraged by some because they believed weight training destroyed speed and coordination. Experimentation, however, demonstrated these fears to be false and established weight training exercises as an excellent method of enhancing the physical fitness components without having detrimental effects upon neuromuscular actions.

COURSE CONTENT

Many different exercises are possible with weights. Outlined below is a core of exercises that can be used as a guide in developing a program. The total time for the performance of these exercises is approximately 50 minutes, if 10 repetitions of each exercise are performed and the entire set is repeated twice. Other lifts may be added if class time permits. It is possible to substitute other lifts for the ones included; however, in making substitutions it should be remembered that the total core must exercise all areas of the body. Advanced students can do approximately the same exercises but should use more weight and variations in movements.

Unit for Beginners	*Unit for Advanced Students*
High pull-ups (warm-up)	Alternative forms of exercises, i.e.,
Two arm curls	variations in grips, hand spacing,
Two arm presses	performed in front or in back of
Stiff leg dead lift	head, etc.
Supine press	
Sit-up	
Supine pull-over	
Supine lateral raise	
Front raise	
Lateral raise	
Three-quarter knee bend	
Toe raise	

Figure 11–7. Homogeneous grouping for weight lifting is desirable because it reduces the time consuming need for changing the weights. (Courtesy Enrico Fermi High School.)

CLASS ORGANIZATION

The class members may work in pairs or in small groups. Homogeneous grouping is best since it will necessitate less changing of the weights. Each group of two should have plenty of space so that there will not be interference with other lifters. A central supply area should be established for the weight plates. Students should go here directly to pick up the weights and then proceed immediately to an assigned station. Organizing this part of the class carefully and enforcing this routine will save time and reduce confusion.

TEACHING PROCEDURES

The unit should be introduced by showing students the value of weight training as an exercise. They should be given some idea of what they may expect from a specific amount of exercise in terms of additional strength and muscle size. These safety precautions should be defined explicitly:

1. Never work above anyone.
2. Tighten all collars well and then double check them.

Figure 11–8. The weight selected for a lift should be one that can be lifted ten times before fatigue sets in. (Courtesy Enrico Fermi High School.)

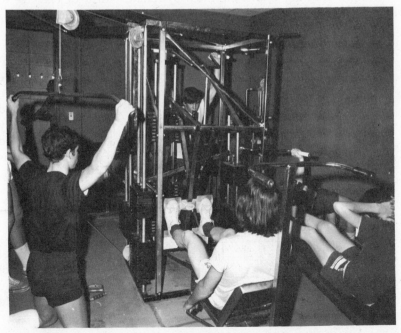

Figure 11–9. The weight training machine is a compact unit that enables several students to work out at one time. (Courtesy Enrico Fermi High School.)

3. Always warm up before attempting heavy lifts.

4. Avoid lifts employing deep knee bends. (A recommended substitution is a heavier load with three-fourths knee bends, assured by placing a bench or stool under the lifter.)

In determining the weight that should be used for each exercise the student should select one that he can lift about ten times before becoming fatigued. If he chooses a weight which he cannot lift this many times without tiring, he should reduce the weight for his next attempt. Should he choose a weight and then discover that he is able to lift it many times beyond ten without tiring, his weight is not sufficiently heavy and should be increased. The sincere student will be mindful always that as his strength increases, the weight must be increased in order to attain the desired results. Lazy students go on using a weight long after they are able to progress to a heavier load.

In the beginning, the specific exercises should be done in one set consisting of ten repetitions. After the second week they should include three sets with a few minutes of rest between each set. It is usually recommended that heavy resistance exercises be done every other day. If the class meets every day, other activities should be interspersed. These activities should be those which emphasize running so that the total program for the week is complete in the body conditioning it provides.

Weight training offers the most systematic form of exercise for physical fitness development, since the intensity of exercise can be

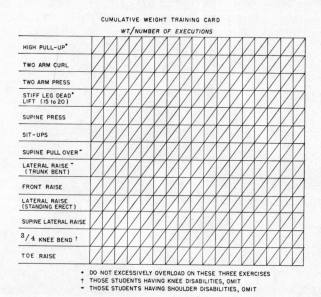

Figure 11–10. Cumulative weight training card. The date is entered above each column. On that date the weight lifted for a specific exercise is entered above the diagonal line and the number of repetitions below the diagnonal line. (Fait, Shaw, Fox and Hollingsworth: A Manual of Physical Education Activities. 2nd ed.)

accurately adjusted by changing either the weight lifted or the number of times it is lifted. In this manner, progressive overloading can be accomplished and an accurate record of development kept.

Recently, new resistance exercise devices have been marketed and utilized in both physical education and athletic programs. These include weight training machines, which offer the advantages of rapid load adjustment, increased safety and reasonably little problem with loss or storage of weights. Another popular type of exerciser, the exergenie has been developed to allow adjustable resistance to a variety of body movements. This device consists of a rope which runs through a control unit that provides a braking force against slippage of the rope. The resistance is increased by increasing the breaking force. A series of exercises for the major muscle groups has been developed utilizing this device. Specific developmental exercises for many sports movements have also been devised.

ISOMETRICS

Isometric contractions is a term given to a special technique for developing strength in which a muscle pulls against a stationary object. Research evidence has demonstrated that strength can be developed just as rapidly using isometrics as in isotonic contractions, which occur when muscles move weight. These gains in strength, however, appear to be greatest at the angle at which the joint is positioned during the isometric exercise and decrease the farther one moves from that position. Thus, development throughout the range of a muscle's possible movement requires isometrics at several positions. The benefits of isometrics to muscular endurance, flexibility and cardiovascular endurance have not been as favorable as those benefits to strength. It appears that the other fitness qualities are better obtained through different means. One significant advantage of isometrics is that they allow a particular weak point in a movement to be specifically worked without necessitating the use of the entire range of motion. A limitation to the use of isometrics comes in determining the work done; no actual weight is moved so there is no guide to the effort expended by the student and no viable means of measuring progress. This difficulty can be resolved, however, if a dynamometer is available to attach to the object against which force is exerted.

Isometric techniques have become popular among athletes because of the minimal time they require and because they avoid the need for specific equipment. The equipment can be easily improvised. It consists of ropes, towels or straps which can be hooked to the wall or wrapped around the body. Adjustable bars or stall bars can also be used for different isometric exercises. Commercial isometric exercise devices are currently on the market. As an alternative, many isometric exercises can be designed to utilize other parts of the body to resist the movement. Examples of this would include pulling up with one arm while resisting with the other, using the hands to resist head movements, or holding a foot with the leg bent to the rear while attempting to straighten the leg.

COURSE CONTENT

All lifts used in weight training can be simulated in isometric contractions. The exercises mentioned in the beginning unit on weight training (page 235) are all suitable for use. The lifts may be simulated with the use of an adjustable strap attached to an immovable object.

CLASS ORGANIZATION

The organization of the class will depend upon the nature and amount of equipment. Students will need to be rotated after certain time intervals so that all will have an opportunity to use the different pieces of equipment. Those using belts may work individually, progressing from one exercise to the next at will, or they may exercise in unison.

TEACHING PROCEDURES

To introduce this unit, the nature of isometric contractions and their value may be explained. When work begins, it is recommended that contractions be no longer than 10 seconds in duration. During the count from 1 to 10 the span from 1 to 3 should be used to develop maximum tension, 4 to 7 to hold that tension and 8 to 10 to decrease the tension. Students can count for themselves, or the teacher may give the commands for starting and stopping.

After the first week the students should perform three sets of 10-second exercises. It is recommended that other activities be presented in the same class period. An activity which emphasizes running should be included to provide an opportunity to develop other aspects of fitness. Isometrics can also be utilized in conjunction with calisthenics or weight training.

JOGGING

The popularity of jogging as a means of enhancing physical fitness has mushroomed in recent years. The publication of several popular books along with increased concern by medical and exercise specialists have made jogging a fashionable activity. The potential of this activity for developing cardiorespiratory fitness is outstanding. Its benefits, however, are limited to this one area, with the exception of building muscular endurance for the leg muscles used in jogging.

The purpose of any jogging program is to provide sustained (between 10 to 60 minutes) exertion on the oxygen transport system (heart, lungs, circulation). Regardless of the level of physical fitness of the participant, the jogging must be maintained for at least 10 minutes. It takes approximately this long before significant gains will begin to be made. This requires that the load be adjusted by altering the speed to permit a continuous performance at a constant pace.

COURSE CONTENT

Concept of aerobic activity
Cardiorespiratory fitness determination through jogging
Jogging technique
Track jogging
Cross country jogging
Care of feet and legs in jogging
Safety in jogging on highways
Setting reasonable goals

CLASS ORGANIZATION

After the introductory information on jogging concepts, values and methods has been completed, some form of cardiovascular development test is usually administered. This could consist of the step test, timed distance running or maximal distance running in a set time. Once a determination has been made of the level of development of the class, homogeneous groups can be constructed and appropriate work outs scheduled. Most work will then be carried out individually or in groups. Group leaders can be assigned stop watches or the instructor can record the starting and finishing times of each student. Often a central clock can be utilized, with the teacher calling out the times and student recorders writing down the elapsed time of runners. Progressive overload can be provided for by reducing the time or increasing the distance of the run.

TEACHING PROCEDURES

The major teaching functions entail setting up the program, explaining the program to the students, providing for record keeping and continually motivating the participants. Varying the distances, changing the course or even introducing some competition between equal groups are methods of stimulating continued interest. One of the basic functions should be provision of an accurate record of the student's improvement and identification of new target times. In many instances, jogging will be used as only part of a total unit on physical fitness that employs other exercises designed to enhance other fitness components.

CIRCUIT TRAINING

Circuit training is not a different exercise technique but rather a unique concept of organization which can be utilized with any set of exercises, whether they involve calisthenics, weight training, isometrics or jogging. It has gained increasing popularity in Europe and the United States. Its major advantage is that by performing exercises in a sequence, with the goal being to complete the entire circuit in a specified time period, stress is placed on the cardiorespiratory system in addition to the stresses of the specific exercises selected.

Table 11–1. A SAMPLE CIRCUIT

EXERCISES	WHAT THEY EXERCISE	COLOR GROUP		
		Item Repetitions:		
		Green	*Blue*	*Red*
1. Pull-ups (bar)	Upper arm and shoulder	3	5	7
2. Squat thrusts (floor)	Body extensors; cardiovascular system	6	10	14
3. Arching back (floor)	Lower back	6	10	14
4. Side risers (stall bars)	Hip and trunk abductors (each side)	3	6	9
5. Leg raising from hanging position (stall bars)	Hip and abdominal flexors	4	7	10
6. Step-ups (bench)	Hip, knee and trunk extensors; cardiovascular system	10	16	22
7. Jumps to bench (bench)	Leg and hip extensors; cardiovascular system	8	12	16
8. Alternate presses (15# dumbbells)	Elbow extensors; shoulder flexors (each side)	5	10	15
9. Sit-ups (floor)	Abdominal and hip flexors; cardiovascular system	12	18	24
10. Dips (parallel bars)	Elbow extensors, shoulder flexors	4	6	8

INSTRUCTIONS TO THE STUDENT:

After practicing each item for perfect form in execution, not for speed, proceed as follows:

1. Go through the circuit twice, using green group item repetitions.
2. Note time at start and finish (do not neglect form for speed; record total time for two circuits).
3. Next class your target time will be three-fourths the initial total time of green group.
4. When you reach target time, advance to the next color group, performing the required number of repetitions, recording the time, and so forth, as for previous color group.
5. Your new target time will again be three-fourths the total time of new color group.

Circuit training (both name and idea) originated in England. It is a method of providing a series of exercises to a large number of students, while at the same time allowing each to work at his own pace and level of physical fitness. The exercises in the circuit are selected to accomplish a specific objective. For example, the sample circuit which follows is designed to provide a total body work out with the objective of improving physical fitness. If the objective is warm-up for class participation or conditioning for a specific sport, other appropriate exercises should be selected for that objective.

Stations for each exercise are designated on the gymnasium floor, and any equipment needed for the exercise is placed at the appropriate station. Students move from one station to the next, completing the entire circuit in accordance with the instruction. (See Table 11–1 for an example of a circuit.)

WEIGHT CONTROL

Most adolescents are figure conscious. They are at a stage of development when they are beginning to approximate their adult body forms. Consequently, they are keenly interested in learning how

Figure 11–11. Rope jumping is a suitable activity for physical fitness and weight control. (Courtesy Los Angeles Unified School District.)

to develop attractive body proportions. Young males are concerned with being too fat or too skinny and desire a reasonably muscled physique. Young females usually abhor excessive body fat and are desirous of shapely body contours. The contribution which exercise can make in controlling body dimension is an important topic.

Although weight control is not directly related to physical fitness, it has important ramifications to health, appearance, physical fitness levels and sport participation. For many students and adults a primary motivator for participation in physical fitness activities is improved body weight.

COURSE CONTENT

Any unit in weight control must be carried out with an individual focus. It should begin with an analysis of present body proportions, weight and posture, followed by a determination of desired and realistic goals. Suggested topics to be included in each unit for beginners and advanced students are:

Beginners Unit	*Advanced Unit*
Body type analysis	Individualized analysis of needs
Ideal and target body weight	and program development
Caloric balance in weight control	Alternative forms of exercises
Role of exercise in weight control	Role of sports in weight control
Role of exercise in physique shaping	Exercise as a therapeutic device
Spot reduction	Exercise for relaxation
Exercises to remedy postural problems	Adult society and weight control

CLASS ORGANIZATION

A unit specifically on weight control may not be necessary, since much of the content parallels that of general fitness. However, some treatment of the topic should be planned, either as a special unit or as a section of a broader unit. The general organization will be similar to that suggested for the specific exercises presented earlier, since any of these might be appropriate techniques for altering body proportions.

TEACHING PROCEDURES

The basic procedures for a unit in weight control will follow closely the format recommended earlier under the type of exercises to be selected. It is highly recommended that the program be treated on as individual a basis as possible. Students must feel that the program allows them to work on their specific needs. The greater the opportunity for setting individual goals and producing appropriate programs, the more meaningful the program will be to each student. Those portions of the early classes devoted to basic concepts or possible exercise activities and analysis of problems may be advantageously presented to large groups. For active class work it is probably better to group students according to similarity of needs. Methods of recording progress should be available and periodically required.

With respect to students who wish to lose weight, it is necessary to recognize that before weight reduction can occur, the output of energy must surpass the input. Consequently, attention must be given to caloric intake. Each individual should work out the food intake and work output balance he must achieve to lose weight. The home economics teacher might be willing, if called upon, to help the students work out this balance.

EVALUATION

To determine if the objectives of physical education are being achieved, it is necessary to evaluate. To measure the degree of success in attaining the objective of improved physical fitness, certain tests of the various components of physical fitness are given. It is recommended that these tests be given also before work begins on the program, in order to determine the needs of the individual students as well as to provide a statistical basis for determining the amount of improvement over a period of time.

Physical fitness tests that are brief enough to be utilized during the physical education class generally are limited by necessity to certain factors of physical fitness. Good tests evaluate those factors that contribute greatly to the total physical fitness of the student, can be readily measured and can be improved by a good physical education program. Furthermore, physical fitness tests that are utilized in physical education classes test only certain "spots" of physical fitness, again by necessity. For example, in measuring factors of strength only certain muscles of the arm are tested by a specific test. It can be assumed that the strength of one set of muscles is an indicator of the total body muscle strength. Studies have shown that there is a relatively high correlation between the strength of one muscle and the other muscles of the body. However, if the arm strength has been increased by specific exercises, the strength relationship between the arm and the rest of the body is unbalanced, and so arm strength could not be used as an indicator of total body strength in such a situation.

Exercises for the Shoulders, Chest, and Upper Arms

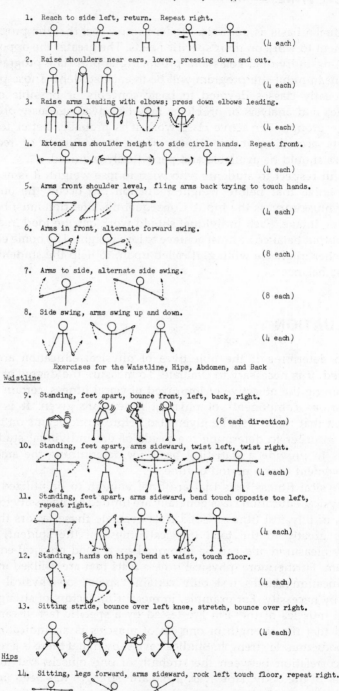

1. Reach to side left, return. Repeat right.

(4 each)

2. Raise shoulders near ears, lower, pressing down and out.

(4 each)

3. Raise arms leading with elbows; press down elbows leading.

(4 each)

4. Extend arms shoulder height to side circle hands. Repeat front.

(4 each)

5. Arms front shoulder level, fling arms back trying to touch hands.

(4 each)

6. Arms in front, alternate forward swing.

(8 each)

7. Arms to side, alternate side swing.

(8 each)

8. Side swing, arms swing up and down.

(4 each)

Exercises for the Waistline, Hips, Abdomen, and Back

Waistline

9. Standing, feet apart, bounce front, left, back, right.

(8 each direction)

10. Standing, feet apart, arms sideward, twist left, twist right.

(4 each)

11. Standing, feet apart, arms sideward, bend touch opposite toe left, repeat right.

(4 each)

12. Standing, hands on hips, bend at waist, touch floor.

(4 each)

13. Sitting stride, bounce over left knee, stretch, bounce over right.

(4 each)

Hips

14. Sitting, legs forward, arms sideward, rock left touch floor, repeat right.

(4 each)

Figure 11–12. On this and the following page are suggestions for body conditioning exercises that students can practice daily at home as well as in class.

15. Sitting, legs forward, supported by hands, bend left leg, extend, bend and return to starting position. Repeat right leg.

(4 each)

Abdomen

16. Lying on back, raise chest to sitting position, roll back to floor. (Keep legs flat).

(4 each)

17. Lying, lift left leg, lower, repeat right, lift both legs.

(4 each)

18. Lying, raise legs and chest to jack knife position, swinging arms to assist.

(4 each)

Back

19. Lying on face, resting on elbows, lift left leg, lower, repeat right.

(4 each)

20. Face down, arms stretched, lift legs and chest.

(4 each)

21. Sitting, legs front, touch toes and return (like rowing boat).

(4 each)

22. Sitting stride, arms behind head, twist left then right.

(4 each)

Exercises for the Legs and Ankles

23. Kneeling, hands on hips, lean back keeping back straight, return.

(4 each)

24. Lunges front, swinging arms overhead, return; alternate left and right leg. Lunges side, swinging arms in direction of lunge and pointing toe in direction of lunge, return. Alternate left and right.

(4 each)

25. Kick front, alternating left and right. Kick side, alternating left and right. Kick back, alternating left and right.

(4 each)

26. Deep knee bends, alternating with rising to tip toe. Hands on hips.

(4 each)

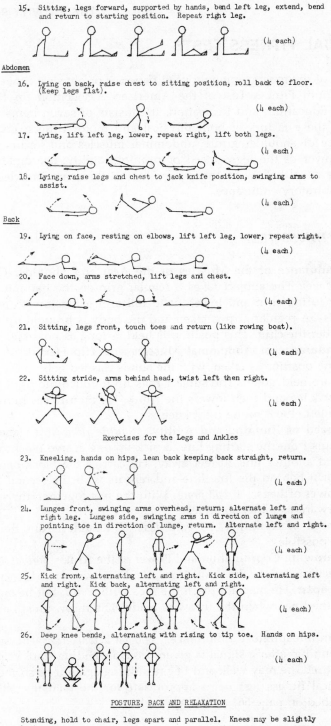

POSTURE, BACK AND RELAXATION

Standing, hold to chair, legs apart and parallel. Knees may be slightly bent.

a. Tuck under the hips rounding back on the slow count of six to music.
b. Release hips and straighten back on the slow count of six to music.

Figure 11-12. *(Continued.)*

PHYSICAL FITNESS TESTS

One of the most commonly used batteries of physical fitness tests is the Youth Fitness Test of the American Association for Health, Physical Education, and Recreation. It consists of seven items which measure these factors of both physical and motor fitness: muscular endurance of shoulder girdle, abdominal muscles and flexors of the trunk; power of the legs; speed of running; agility; coordination in throwing a softball with the power of the throwing muscles; and cardiorespiratory endurance.

YOUTH FITNESS TEST[2]

1. **Endurance of the Muscles of the Arm and Shoulder Girdle.** *Pull-up (boys):* The subject takes a regular grip on the bar and raises the body to the chin and lowers it to full arm extension. *Flexed arm hang (girls):* A regular grip is taken and the body is brought up so the bar is under the chin. This position is held as long as possible.
2. **Endurance of Abdominal Muscles and Hip Flexors.** *Sit-ups:* The supine position is taken, with the hands clasped behind the head. The feet are held down. The subject rolls up to touch the right elbow to the left knee and then lowers the trunk. He then raises himself to touch the left elbow to the right knee.
3. **Speed of Running and Agility.** *Shuttle run:* At a signal, the subject runs from the starting line to pick up one of two blocks which are behind another line 30 feet away. He carries the block back and sets it down behind the first line and repeats with the second block.
4. **Power of Legs.** *Broad jump:* With the feet together, the subject jumps forward as far as possible.
5. **Speed of Running.** *50 yard dash:* The subject runs the dash as fast as possible.
6. **Throwing Coordination and Power of the Arm.** *Softball throw:* The subject must make the throw from an area between two lines which are 6 feet apart. He may approach the area with a run, but he must be between the lines when the throw is made. The throw must be over-hand.
7. **Cardiorespiratory Endurance.** *600 yard walk-run:* The subject begins running, after a signal is given, from a standing start. When he becomes tired, he may walk and begin running again if he so chooses.

Physical fitness test items appropriate for the mentally retarded are described on page 564 in the Appendices.

---

[2]Established norms are published in AAHPER *Youth Fitness Test Manual.* See Suggested Readings.

Another cardiorespiratory test gaining in popularity is Cooper's 12 Minute Run Test.[3] In this test students run for 12 minutes, attempting to cover as much distance as possible. Distance is most easily measured by counting completed laps to the nearest quarter lap on a measured track and converting to miles. The chart below shows how to convert distance in miles to fitness level. The figures are for adults 17 to 30 years of age.

	Miles Covered	
Category	*Males*	*Females*
Very Poor	<1.0	<.95
Poor	1.0 –1.24	.95–1.14
Fair	1.25–1.49	1.15–1.34
Good	1.5 –1.74	1.35–1.64
Very Good	1.75 +	1.65 +

DISCUSSION QUESTIONS

1. What is physical fitness?
2. In what way can the physical fitness of the students in the physical education class be increased?
3. Discuss the specific physiological benefits which result from participation in strenuous activity. Consult a textbook on the physiology of exercise.
4. What factor or factors govern the amount and length of time strenuous activities should be engaged in at a given time?
5. What are the basic considerations in developing a figure control program?

THINGS TO DO

1. Make a list of exercises that might be added to or substituted for those suggested in the course content for any one of the activities in this chapter.
2. Review several textbooks of tests and measurements in physical education and select a test to demonstrate and discuss in class. Indicate which items would be classified as motor fitness and which as physical fitness and explain why.
3. Select several calisthenic exercises and demonstrate them to the class. Explain what specific contribution each exercise makes to physical fitness.
4. Make a list of the different ways physical fitness is defined in the literature. Comment on the significance of the differences and likenesses in the definitions.
5. Using the sample circuit on page 242, create a circuit of your own.

SUGGESTED READINGS

AAHPER: *AAHPER Youth Fitness Test Manual.* Rev. ed., Washington, D.C., 1965.
Cooper, Kenneth H.: *The New Aerobics.* New York, Bantam Books, Inc., 1970.
Fox, Edward L. and Mathews, Donald K.: *Interval Training:* Conditioning for Sports and Physical Fitness. Philadelphia, W. B. Saunders Co., 1974.

---

[3]Cooper, Kenneth H.: *The New Aerobics, p. 30.*

Johnson, Perry B., et al.: *Physical Education: A Problem Solving Approach to Health and Fitness.* New York, Holt, Rinehart and Winston, 1966.

Mathews, Donald K.: *Measurement in Physical Education.* 4th ed., Philadelphia, W. B. Saunders Co., 1973.

Olsen, Edward: *Conditioning Fundamentals.* Columbus, Ohio, Charles E. Merrill Books, Inc., 1968.

President's Council on Physical Fitness: *Adult Physical Fitness.* Superintendent of Documents, U.S. Government Printing Office.

Roby, Frederick B. and Davis, Russell: *Jogging for Fitness and Weight Control.* Philadelphia, W. B. Saunders Co., 1970.

Scholtz, Alfred E. and Johnson, Robert E.: *Body Conditioning for College Men.* Philadelphia, W. B. Saunders Co., 1969.

Sorani, Robert P.: *Circuit Training.* Dubuque, Iowa, William C. Brown Co., 1966.

Vannier, Maryhelen: *Body Conditioning and Figure and Weight Control for Girls and Women.* Belmont, Calif., Wadsworth Publishing Co., 1971.

Wallis, Earl L. and Logan, Gene: *Figure Improvement and Body Conditioning Through Exercise.* Englewood Cliffs, N.J., Prentice-Hall, Inc., 1964.

CHAPTER TWELVE

INDIVIDUAL SPORTS

Individual sports is a term given to all games and activities in which one person participates alone, with one opponent, or with a partner and a pair of opponents, although games played with a partner or an opponent are sometimes called dual sports. Such activities have great importance in the secondary school physical education program; they not only help to meet the immediate physical education needs of youth but, because they are easily adapted or modified in accord with individual physical capacity and stamina, they provide carryover skills for use in adulthood and even into the senior citizen years. (For this reason, they are often referred to as life-time sports.) Because adults do tend to continue to participate in the individual sports in which they have acquired proficiency as youngsters, the school should give full support to the inclusion of as many individual sports as possible in its physical education program.

The teacher may encounter difficulties in trying to present a variety of individual sports because of the lack of facilities. Many schools do not have courts, ranges and areas for individual activities or do not have them in sufficient number to permit all members of a class to engage in play at one time. However, by careful organization and scheduling, the fundamentals of the games can be taught successfully even though the amount of time spent playing the game on a regulation playing area must necessarily be limited.

The individual sports most frequently presented in the secondary school physical education program are: archery, badminton, bowling, croquet, deck tennis, golf, handball, horseshoes, shuffleboard, table tennis, lawn tennis and wrestling. The discussions of these sports in the pages that follow are uniformly designed to present ideas and suggestions for (1) course content, (2) class organization, (3) teaching procedures and (4) evaluation. Because of space limitations, no attempt has been made to include in the discussion of each sport all of the varied choices and possibilities open to the teacher. Rather the aim has been to present varied examples to illustrate what may be included in the teaching unit and how it may be taught. It is emphasized that the particular class organization and teaching procedures described for one sport are applicable to other sports as well.

ARCHERY

Archery is a popular activity in the physical education program for high school girls, but it will prove equally popular with the boys if included in their program. It is suited to both girls and boys because the fundamentals can be learned in a relatively short time, but the activity continues to be challenging even to those who become highly skilled and experienced archers. This sport is especially rich in carry-over values for leisure time use in later life.

Archery is most frequently taught as an outdoor activity because of the greater amount of space which is usually available. When selecting an outdoor area for archery instruction, it is essential to give consideration to the freedom of the area from buildings, trees, shrubs and pedestrian traffic. If possible, the targets should be placed in front of a hill or elevation in the terrain so that arrows which overshoot the target will come to rest in this area. If there is no such raised terrain, a greater distance of unobstructed area behind the targets will be needed, or a backstop composed of bales of hay may be set up. Hay bales are particularly effective for wheelchair archers, who would have difficulty moving the chair up an incline to retrieve arrows.

Figure 12–1. Mastery of the correct form is basic to becoming a skilled archer. (Courtesy Los Angeles Unified School District.)

Archery may also be taught inside. For indoor shooting it is necessary to hang a canvas behind the targets to stop the arrows which go beyond the targets. Frequently high schools have large canvases which are used to close the field from view during athletic events, and these would make fine backdrops for the targets.

To learn the techniques of archery it is essential that each student shoot as often as possible. For this reason it is recommended that each person be provided with a bow and at least 12 arrows; but, when there are more students than equipment, it is, of course, necessary to have two or more alternately using the bow and arrows. Ideally, one target should serve no more than three students. Additional targets can be easily improvised by a resourceful teacher, who can use heavy cardboard cartons for a target and painted oilcloth for a target face.

The use of finger tabs and wrist guards protects against possible injury by the string and is highly recommended for beginners because of the fear and apprehension about shooting which may develop following an injury to the fingers or arm.[1]

COURSE CONTENT

Suggested course content for beginning and advanced students in archery includes:

Unit for beginners	*Unit for advanced students*
Brief history	Discussion of archery clubs and
Selection of equipment	tournaments
Care of equipment	Review of safety and courtesies
Safety and courtesies	Review of fundamental skills
Fundamentals:	Instinctive shooting
Stringing	Field archery
Nocking	Flight shooting
Pulling	Clout shooting
Releasing	Hunting skills
Point of aim and use of range	Evaluation
finder and use of bow sight	
Scoring	
Evaluation	

CLASS ORGANIZATION

Some teachers prefer to group their students homogeneously with respect to ability, although such grouping is probably less necessary in archery than many other activities. The nature of the sport is such

---

[1] See the chapter on *Equipment and Supplies* for suggestions for making finger tabs and arm guards out of scrap materials.

that the more experienced and more skilled are constantly competing against themselves and so they are not greatly hindered by those less adept. Students who are extremely skilled and have mastered the techniques may be used to assist the teacher in watching for and correcting form faults in individual performers, and for demonstration purposes. However, advanced skill learning experiences must be provided for these students, too.

If the students must be paired because of the lack of tackle for everyone, it will usually work out well in the early practice sessions to have a more skilled archer with a less skilled one. Later on, it will prove more stimulating to the archers if they are more evenly matched.

TEACHING PROCEDURES

Assuming the direct method is being used to teach the archery unit, instruction for the beginners may commence with an explanation of the parts of the bow and arrow and a brief description of the other equipment which may comprise the complete archery tackle. This could be followed with a discussion of the factors which govern the selection of the proper weight of bow and length of arrow. The students should begin shooting the first day in order to establish a need for learning as well as to satisfy their desires to "try it."

The class members should also be impressed with the necessity of caring properly for the equipment they use. It is essential to demonstrate early in the course the correct procedures for stringing and un-

Figure 12–2. Early in an archery unit students should be given instruction on how to remove arrows correctly from the target. (Courtesy of the Youth Service Section of the Los Angeles Public Schools.)

stringing the bow and the proper way to retrieve arrows from the target and the ground. The dangers of overdrawing the bow must also be emphasized. The first lesson must impress upon the students that the arrow shot irresponsibly from the bow is a threat to human life, and this fact should be emphasized repeatedly throughout the teaching of the archery unit.

The teacher must stress form from the very first for it is essential to accurate shooting. Demonstration is helpful for presenting a vivid visual image of the correct stance and form for nocking, drawing and releasing. If the teacher feels insecure about his own performance and has no student who may be counted upon to perform with perfection, he would be wise to demonstrate the techniques without a bow. He might also make use of some of the excellent films and filmstrips which are now available to illustrate the techniques he cannot demonstrate adequately. Mimetic practice, however, will prove far more important to the learner than viewing these materials.

Following the demonstration, the students attempt the skills. Regardless of the size of his class, the instructor should watch each individual nock the arow, draw the bow and release the arrow at least once to make sure he understands the proper techniques before he begins to practice shooting at the target.

The students are checked constantly on their shooting form to prevent errors which may become movement habits, for these are hard to correct or eradicate. Finding a faulty technique early will save time spent in relearning and will add to the over-all pleasure derived from the activity.

The students will now be ready to learn how to find the point of aim and to be instructed in the use of a range finder or the use of the bow sight if their bows are equipped with sights. Instinctive shooting may be introduced to the more advanced students. This group will also want to learn more about the various types of skills required in flight shooting, field archery, clout shooting and hunting with the bow and arrow.

To stimulate interest in classes of either beginning or advanced students, archery contests and tournaments may be organized, the level of organization depending upon the abilities of the students. Mail and telegraphic matches, elimination or round robin tournaments, flight shooting, interclass competition, clout shooting, and archery golf are all possibilities for lively class participation.

EVALUATION

To measure the results, an objective test on the factual material may be given and an evaluation made of each student's performance with the bow and arrow. The latter may consist of a subjective evaluation based upon the correction chart. A perfect score is 100 points; four points are subtracted for each error.

As a measurement of actual shooting ability, a test consisting of the following procedures may be given: two ends (six arrows per end) shot at a regulation target from 10 yeards and repeated at 20 yards. For boys, include a third try at 30 yards. The scores achieved at each distance are added together for the final score, which may be evaluated using the score sheet shown.

SELECTED VISUAL AIDS

Archery for Beginners. United World Films, Inc.
Archery for Girls. Coronet Films.
Archery Fundamentals. Bailey Films, Inc.
Beginning Archery. Athletic Institute.

PUBLISHED SKILL TESTS

AAHPER: *Archery Skills Test Manual* (Boys and Girls). Washington, D.C., 1967.
Hyde, Edith I.: An achievement scale in archery. *Research Quarterly, VII,* No. 2, May, 1937, p. 109.
Reichart, Natalie: School archery standards. *Journal of Health and Physical Education, XIV,* No. 2, February, 1943, p. 81.

SUGGESTED READINGS

AAHPER: *Archery—Riding.* Washington, D.C., Division for Girls' and Women's Sports. Published biennially.
Broer, Marion R.: *Individual Sports for Women.* 5th ed. Philadelphia, W. B. Saunders Co., 1971.
Fait, Hollis F., et al.: *A Manual of Physical Education Activities.* 3rd ed. Philadelphia, W. B. Saunders Co., 1967.
Pszczola, Lorraine: *Archery.* Philadelphia, W. B. Saunders Co., 1971.
Vannier, Maryhelen, and Poindexter, Hally Beth: *Individual and Team Sports for Girls and Women.* 3rd ed. Philadelphia, W. B. Saunders Co., 1974.

Periodicals
Archery, P. O. Box H, Palm Springs, California.
The Archer's Magazine, 1200 Walnut Street, Philadelphia, Pa.

BADMINTON

Because of the pleasure and physical benefits which may be had from a vigorous game of badminton, the game deserves to be taught in every secondary physical education program. Badminton may be played indoors or outdoors by youths and adults alike.

In addition to the net and standards which hold it, badminton equipment consists of a racquet and a shuttlecock. Frequently, steel racquets and plastic birds are used for class instruction because they are more durable than wooden racquets and feather birds. Respect for the equipment must be instilled in the students, however, regardless of which type is used. Careful handling of equipment should include proper placing of the standards upon the gymnasium floor, for rolling or dropping the heavy metal standards can do considerable damage to the floor. A demonstration of how to move the standards properly often sets the stage for further discussions of how to protect the floor when other activities are being played.

COURSE CONTENT

Topics which the teacher should plan to cover in the units for beginning and advanced badminton players are:

Unit for beginners	*Unit for advanced students*
Brief history	Discussion of tournaments and
Care of equipment	clubs
Game courtesies	Selection of personal equipment
Fundamental strokes:	Review of game courtesies
Serving	Review of fundamental skills
Forehand	Advanced skills
Backhand	Advanced strategy and bird
Flights	placement
Footwork	Officiating
Rules	Evaluation
Strategy in doubles and singles	
Evaluation	

CLASS ORGANIZATION

The task form of the direct method of teaching is well suited to beginning badminton skills, although other forms may be used. The task form allows students to progress at their own optimal rates and, therefore, to be engaged in different activities, making the most effective use of the equipment and space available.

Instruction begins with a description of the various tasks or stations appearing on the written task work sheet. A demonstration of each activity is also provided for the purpose of pointing out the critical elements of the skill. The students begin with the first task and, as each achieves the level of performance required by the task, he goes on to the subsequent activity. When a student finishes all tasks on Card #1, he receives Card #2 and continues. Each day, or perhaps every few days, it

Figure 12–3. A new skill is introduced by the teacher to ensure clear understanding of its performance by the students before they begin work on specific tasks. (Courtesy of the Physical Education Department, Los Angeles Public Schools.)

will be necessary to introduce, demonstrate and explain the new tasks prior to students' engaging in them.

TEACHING PROCEDURES

A major teaching function of the task form is the systematic planning of the progression of tasks. The work of planning tasks and preparing them in printed form for all students must be done outside of class. Although this is a time-consuming activity, once done it provides a basis for future teaching of the same unit. The majority of the actual class time is available for the teacher to work with students, since organizational concerns have been taken care of through the work sheets. The teacher observes the students, identifies and diagnoses problems, corrects errors and provides encouragement on a personal, one-to-one basis. The teacher also spot checks students on completed tasks to determine if the desired level has been reached.

An example of a task card for beginning badminton appears in Figure 12–4. Similar cards for all the skills to be included in the unit must be prepared and ready for students as they complete the initial set of cards.

It is desirable to introduce the game of badminton to a class by

<table>
<tr><td>Starting date</td><td>Beginning Badminton
Task Card No. 1
Basic Racket Control</td><td>Name</td></tr>
</table>

Completion date

Check after completing each task

_____ 1. Grip the racket with the "shake hands" style. Check for proper alignment of the **V** formed between thumb and fore finger. Without looking at the racket spin it in your hand and regrip with the proper racket face alignment 10 times in succession. If you miss grip, observe your fault and begin the count again.

_____ 2. Using the proper grip, with the racket held to your forehand side, cock your wrist back and then snap the racket forward, utilizing only the action of the wrist. Repeat 20 times. Check to see that you use only the wrist.

_____ 3. Same as #2, only on backhand side of body.

_____ 4. Hold the racket in front of you with the palm of the hand up. Bounce a bird about 2 feet into the air 10 times in succession. If you drop bird, begin count again. Repeat 3 times.

_____ 5. Same as #4 but with palm-down grip. Concentrate on the wrist providing the movement.

_____ 6. Same as #4 but alternating palm up and palm down on consecutive shots.

_____ 7. Staying in an area approximately 4 feet square, attempt to hit the bird straight overhead to a height of about 7 feet over your head, using both palm-up and palm-down strokes. Keep the bird within your area and in the air for 10 consecutive hits. Repeat 3 times.

_____ 8. Stand 4 feet from a wall and volley the bird from racket to wall, using only a forehand stroke for 8 consecutive trials. Repeat 2 times.

_____ 9. Repeat #8 but all hits must be above the 5 foot line on the wall.

_____ 10. Pick out the previous task which gave you the most trouble and repeat it.

When you have completed all tasks on this card, turn it in at the desk and pick up the next card in this set.

Figure 12–4. Sample worksheet of tasks for beginning badminton.

giving the students a concept of the total game. This can be effectively accomplished by a demonstration game between two good players accompanied by commentary by the teacher to point out the various flights and their use. A total grasp of the game will not result from a single demonstration, so the teacher's comments should be directed toward establishing the basic fundamentals and their importance.

If skilled players are not available to demonstrate, a movie may be substituted (see _Selected Visual Aids_). Film strips may be used for showing specific skills later in the unit when the students have had a chance to gain enough information and appreciation of the game to view the showing with understanding.

All the basic rules can be presented to the class at one time, but they will need to be repeated often when the students actually begin to play. Usually they will ask enough questions about rules in relation to their game situations to assure that all the necessary information will be reviewed.

A discussion of strategy is in order as soon as the students demonstrate some mastery of the game. Because of the lack of sufficient courts to accommodate singles, most of the playing will be doubles. For this reason, the strategy for the doubles game should be explained first. The up and back system or the side by side system are the easiest for beginners to comprehend. The rotating system can be introduced most successfully to advanced players.

The flights should be introduced and the situations in which they are used explained, accompanied by demonstration. The flights may be practiced best with specific drills in which two players deliberately send the bird to each other so that one of the flights must be employed. For example, in practicing the smash, the receiving player stands near the net and his partner directs the bird to him so that he can execute the

TECHNIQUES	COMMON ERRORS	EVALUATION	
		DOES	DOES NOT
Grip	Gripping too high up on the handle		
Serve	Failure to watch the bird while serving	——	——
	Failure to use the wrist in stroking	——	——
	Serving to the same spot repeatedly	——	——
	Moving the feet during the serve	——	——
	Holding the bird too close to the body; this causes the bird to go into the net	——	——
	Setting up the bird for the opponent which may be caused by holding the bird away from the body or by not using enough or too much wrist in the stroke	——	——
Strokes in general	Standing too close to the bird while stroking	——	——
	Failure to use the wrist in the stroke	——	——
	Failure to place the shot away from the opponent	——	——
	Telegraphing shots or using strokes in a specific pattern	——	——
Overhead stroke	Allowing the bird to drop too low before stroking	——	——
Forehand stroke	Failure to hit the bird up when it has dropped lower than the net	——	——
Backhand stroke	Failure to abduct the wrist in the backswing and snap the wrist forward as the swing comes forward	——	——
Net shots	Hitting net shots too high	——	——
Drives	Hitting up on the bird	——	——
Court positions	Failure to return to the proper position after stroking the bird	——	——
	Encroaching on partner's court area	——	——
	Backing up for deep shots instead of pivoting and running back	——	——

Figure 12–5. Chart for evaluating badminton skills.

smash. After receiving the bird for a specified number of times, the partners reverse the procedure. This same type of drill may be used advantageously to overcome specific stroke difficulties.

EVALUATION

Evaluation of the performer in an actual game situation is one of the best ways of determining how well the skills have been mastered. A chart similar to Figure 12–5 may be used by the teacher to evaluate the student's game performance. The student's standing in a class tournament may also serve as a basis for evaluation. Such contests have the additional advantage of being good motivators as well; all types of tournaments can be used.

The Miller Badminton Wall Volley Test may be used to measure general achievement. The test consists of three trials of volleying a bird against the wall for 30 seconds. The student stands ten feet from the wall. The score is the number of volleys. Similar tests of serving accuracy and deep clearing may be devised by marking the court into areas of appropriate point values. Either a subjective or objective test may be given to test knowledge of the rules, history and factual material about badminton.

skill test

SELECTED VISUAL AIDS

Fundamentals of Badminton. All American Productions.
Good Badminton. Teaching Film Custodians.
How to Improve Your Badminton. Athletic Institute.
Tips on Better Badminton. Sport Tips and Teaching Aids.

PUBLISHED SKILL TESTS

French, Esther, and Stalter, Evelyn: Study of skill tests in badminton for college women. *Research Quarterly,* XX, No. 3, October, 1940, p. 257.
Lockhart, Ailleen, and McPherson, F. A.: The development of a test of badminton playing ability. *Research Quarterly,* XX, No. 4, December, 1949, p. 402.
Miller, Francis A.: A Badminton Wall Volley Test. *Research Quarterly,* XXII, No. 2, May, 1951, p. 208.

SUGGESTED READINGS

AAHPER: *Official Tennis and Badminton Guide, Selected Tennis and Badminton Articles.* Washington, D.C., Division of Girls' and Women's Sports. (Published biennially)
Broer, Marion R.: *Individual Sports for Women.* 5th ed. Philadelphia, W. B. Saunders Co., 1971.
Fait, Hollis F., et al.: *A Manual of Physical Education Activities.* 3rd ed. Philadelphia, W. B. Saunders Co., 1967.

Johnson, M. L.: *Badminton*. Philadelphia, W. B. Saunders Co., 1974.

Vannier, Maryhelen, and Poindexter, Hally Beth: *Physical Activities for College Women*. 3rd ed. Philadelphia, W. B. Saunders Co., 1974.

Varner, M.: *Badminton*. Dubuque, Iowa, William C. Brown Co., 1966.

Periodicals

Bird Chatter. American Badminton Association. Mary Moran, Pine Street, Dover, Mass.

BOWLING

For the teaching of a complete unit of bowling skills it is necessary that the school have available a regulation size bowling alley. If there is a local commercial bowling alley, it is usually possible to work out an arrangement whereby the alleys may be rented for a nominal fee for use during school hours when the establishment would ordinarily not be doing business. Some schools include the rental fee in their budgets; others assess the students to defray this cost. If it is not possible to secure the use of a commercial alley, the teaching of the skills may be accomplished through the use of substitute equipment. There are now available on the market plastic and rubber bowling pins and bowling balls which may be used on the gymnasium floor without fear of damage to the floor's surface. Most of the basic bowling skills can be taught with this substitute equipment. Portable bowling alleys which may be set up on any available floor space are also available.

Figure 12–6. With the use of rubber bowling balls some of the skills of bowling can be taught in the gymnasium. (Courtesy of the Lifetime Sports Foundation.)

If the above equipment is too costly for the school to purchase, the resourceful teacher can still have a successful program of bowling with improvised pins and balls. Indian clubs encased in flannel to prevent their chipping the floor when knocked down make excellent pins, and softballs or any large rubber balls can be used as substitutes for the bowling ball.

COURSE CONTENT

Suggested topics to be included in the units for beginners and advanced students are listed below:

Unit for Beginners	*Unit for advanced students*
History	Discussion of tournaments
Ball selection	Review of safety and courtesies
Importance of proper shoes and clothing	Review of fundamentals
Courtesies and safety	Advanced skills:
Rules	Hook ball delivery
Grip and holding the ball	Curve ball delivery
Four-step approach	Back-up ball delivery
Aiming	Five-step approach
Straight ball delivery	Picking up spares
Picking up spares	Team strategy
Scoring	Evaluation
Evaluation	

CLASS ORGANIZATION

The organization of the class for the learning of the bowling skills will be dependent upon whether the teaching is to be done with actual bowling equipment or entirely with improvised equipment. If an alley is available, the class instruction period should be long enough for each student to bowl one game after he has acquired the skills. It is possible to plan for four students to use one alley during the 40 to 50 minutes of playing time.

Even when there is an alley available, some teachers prefer to teach the early lessons on the gymnasium floor. The nature of the game, the proper stance and the four-step approach can be taught and practiced effectively on the floor. If using the direct method, the teacher has the class assume a line formation to practice the stance and approach in unison without balls while he observes and makes suggestions for corrections as necessary.

Having become familiar with these fundamentals, the students are ready to use balls. If the class is using "nonbowling" balls and Indian club pins, the difference in gripping the ball must be pointed out; however, the grip will have much in common with that used for duckpins or candlestick bowling. Three or four students may be assigned to each improvised alley; one student bowls, one keeps score, and the remaining one or two set the pins and return the ball. After several frames the students rotate, with the scorer going to the pit, the one from the pit coming to bowl, and the bowler becoming the new scorer. Organization of the class for bowling in alleys need not follow this pattern unless the establishment does not have automatic pin setters. Those who are not bowling may be assigned to help the scorer with his work and to watch for form faults in the one who is bowling.

TEACHING PROCEDURES

It is well to begin the bowling unit with some of the interesting highlights from the history of the game. This will lead into a discussion of the nature of this activity, how equipment is selected, and the courtesies and essential safety measures. Important considerations which are introduced at this time should be re-emphasized whenever the occasion arises in the course of teaching the unit.

The teaching procedures described in the following paragraphs utilize the direct method. It should be understood that other methods could also be used effectively.

If the class is working without regulation bowling balls, the grip cannot be taught. However, the proper stance and approach can be simulated and practiced. The grip, stance and approach should be taught by a demonstration accompanied by clear explanations of the movements. The class should then attempt the skills under the close supervision of the teacher.

The four-step approach is recommended for beginners. The approach should be demonstrated, followed by student practice without a ball. Marking the steps on the floor may help those to achieve success who are having difficulty making a smooth approach.

It is well to allow the student to practice the approach with a ball as soon as he understands the rhythm of the steps in the approach, for the release is an integral part of the entire movement. Some teachers even prefer to introduce the release first and have the students practice it without the ball six or seven times. Then the approach is learned and practiced, followed by synchronizing the two movements. When the students are able to move smoothly through the approach and release, they try it with the ball.

The method of scoring in bowling may be presented following the instruction of the above skills and before the students begin to practice on their own. Because the scoring is difficult for students to

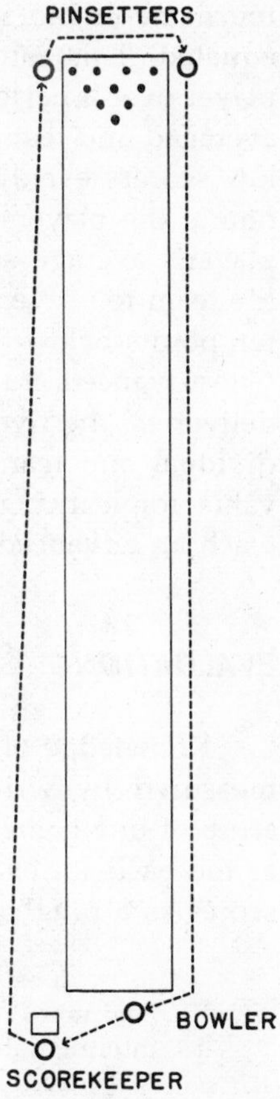

PINSETTERS

Figure 12-7. Rotation plan for four students bowling on an improvised or regulation alley.

BOWLER

SCOREKEEPER

comprehend from an oral explanation, it is suggested that a score sheet be reproduced in large size on a blackboard or on a piece of heavy paper for the class to view as the teacher keeps score of a real or imagined game. A lesson in picking up spares may well follow scoring. Diagrams, slides and films may be used to supplement or substitute for actual demonstrations.

If instruction is being given in the gymnasium because no alley is available, or if for some reason the class is not going to the alley during a certain class period, there is a number of bowling games which may be introduced to vary the class routine and to provide additional activity. Among the games recommended are soccer bowling, skittles, tire bowling, lawn bowls, miniature bowling, arch bowls, bowl spot ball, cocked hat bowling and square five bowling (see *Suggested Readings*).

After students have achieved a reasonable degree of skill bowling on an alley, various types of tournaments may be set up during the class periods. Pyramid and ladder tournaments are popular. Team tournaments can also be used in class work if the competing units are equated. This can be done by computing the average score of each player over a period of several days. Next, the total score of the team is averaged and teams adjusted accordingly by distributing the high and low scorers evenly among the groups. In the event of an absence of one of the players during tournament play, the team may receive the player's average score or, to discourage absences without penalizing the team too severely, the score which the team receives can be five or ten points below the absent player's average score.

Advanced students may be taught the hook, curve and back-up deliveries, the five-step approach, and advanced strategy for both individual and team play. Because improvised equipment has limited value for learning advanced skills, the teacher probably should not teach an advanced bowling unit unless a regulation alley is available.

EVALUATION

Knowledge of rules, strategy and safety skills in bowling may be measured by written tests. To grade the skill achieved, the actual score of one game or the average score of several games may be used as the basis for evaluation. The teacher may wish to use the following scores as a rough guide to ability for secondary school students:

	Boys	Girls
Beginner	110 or under	88 or under
Intermediate	111 to 134	89 to 109
Advanced	135 and over	110 and over

SELECTED VISUAL AIDS

A Life Timer of Bowling. AAHPER.
Bowling. Brunswick Corp.
Bowling, A Woman's World. American Machine and Foundry Co.
Bowling Fundamentals. International Film Bureau, Inc.
Coed Champions Bowling. Brunswick Corp.
Duckpin Bowling—Everybody's Game. DUCKPIN Bowling Council.
Free Bowling Clinic. American Machine and Foundry Co.
How to Improve Your Bowling. Athletic Institute.
Learn to Bowl. Brunswick Corp.
Pin Games. RKO Radio Pictures, Inc.
Splits, Spares and Strikes. Official Films, Inc.

PUBLISHED SKILL TESTS

Martin, Joan L.: Bowling norms for college men and women. *Research Quarterly XXXI,* No. 1, March, 1960, p. 113.
Phillips, Marjorie, and Summers, Dean: Bowling norms and learning curves for college women. *Research Quarterly, XXI,* No. 4, December, 1950, p. 377.

SUGGESTED READINGS

AAHPER: *Bowling-Fencing-Golf*. Washington, D.C., Division for Girls' and Women's Sports. (Published biennially).

AAHPER: *Physical Education for High School Students*, 2nd ed. Washington, D.C., 1970.

Barsanti, Rena A.: *Bowling*. Boston, Allyn and Bacon, Inc., 1973.

Bellisimo, Lou: *The Bowler's Manual*. Englewood Cliffs, N.J., Prentice-Hall, Inc., 1969.

Fait, Hollis F., et al.: *A Manual of Physical Education Activities*. 3rd ed. Philadelphia, W. B. Saunders Co., 1967.

Shaw, John, et al.: *Individual Sports for Men*. 3rd ed. Dubuque, Iowa, William C. Brown Co., 1964.

Vannier, Maryhelen, and Poindexter, Hally Beth: *Individual and Team Sports for Girls and Women*. 3rd ed. Philadelphia, W. B. Saunders Co., 1974.

Periodicals

Bowling. American Bowling Congress, 1572 E. Capital Drive, Milwaukee, Wisconsin.

Woman Bowler. Women's International Bowling Congress, 4319 W. Irving Park Road, Chicago, Illinois.

GOLF

Because of the increasing popularity of golf, more and more high schools are adding instruction in this sport to the physical education curriculum. It is a game which continues to be challenging to players of all degrees of skill and experience as well as one which can be played by most people throughout their lives.

While the initial cost of setting up a program of golf instruction may seem prohibitive, there are many ways in which expenses can be cut. By carefully planning the classwork, a limited number of golf clubs may be made to serve a large group. Because of the interest local golfers will have in the success of the school's program, they may be willing to donate used clubs and balls to the school. Then, too, there is now on the market a club with interchangeable heads which is comparable to an entire set. It is inexpensive and ideal for school use.

If the school is unable to supply balls to the students, they must furnish their own. There are two ways in which to handle the balls furnished by students for class use. The students may be asked to contribute two or more balls to a class stockpile from which the balls are distributed as needed for each class period or they may be asked to bring two or more initialed balls to each class session. The former method is more time-saving since the balls do not have to be sorted out and redistributed to the owners at the end of each session. It is also more satisfactory because it avoids the problem of students forgetting to bring their balls.

Golf may be taught inside or outside. Because considerable space must be allotted each student when practicing the swing, this phase of

Figure 12-8. The physical education program should include individual sports instruction for leisure time use, both in youth and later adulthood. (Courtesy of the Youth Service Section of the Los Angeles Public Schools.)

the instruction is usually more conveniently held outside. However, with careful planning, the entire instructional unit can be taught inside. If golf cages are not available for inside shooting, a canvas backdrop suspended from the ceiling or supported by uprights will be necessary to stop the balls. If the canvas is long enough, it is well to have it folded forward at the bottom to keep the balls from bouncing as they fall to the floor after hitting the canvas. Cocoa or rubber mats should be placed on the floor to prevent possible damage to the floor and to the club when swinging. Putting greens may be simulated by strips of carpet placed on the floor, while chip shots may be practiced by shooting into wastebaskets or similar receptacles.

Usually, golf courses will be pleased to open their facilities to high school classes. In most instances the use of the course for teaching golf will be impractical because of the time involved in traveling to and from the course; but some arrangements should be made to enable students to play on the fairway some time during the course of instruction because of the valuable experience it gives the beginning golfer. At the very least, the teacher should plan a field trip to a local golf course. The teacher may also be able to arrange for students to practice at local public driving ranges, which are comparatively free of customers during school hours, although here again the time and transportation problems may negate the advantages of their use.

COURSE CONTENT

Suggested topics to be included in the unit for beginning golfers are listed below. For advanced players the instruction must, because of the nature of the game, be based entirely upon the specific problems of the individual player.

Unit for beginners	*Unit for advanced students*
Brief history	Review of previously learned skills
Nature of the game	Specific individual skill and playing
Safety	problems
Fundamental skills:	Intentional hook
Grip and stance	Intentional slice
Swing	Handicap procedures
Use of different clubs	Tournament play
Various types of shots	
Rules and courtesies	
Evaluation	

CLASS ORGANIZATION

The class organization described here is that which is used when the direct method is employed. For instruction on the grip, the class is formed into a line or lines facing the instructor. The line formation permits all to see the demonstration and enables the teacher to pass rapidly along to check everyone's grip and to motivate learning.

If the class is using a miscellaneous assortment of clubs, as may well be the case if clubs have been donated to the school, the class organization must be carefully planned in advance. Students having the same number of wood or iron should be grouped together to receive instruction and to practice swinging. The students should also

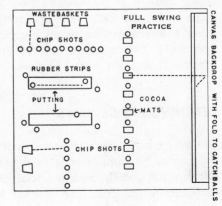

Figure 12-9. Class organization for teaching golf indoors.

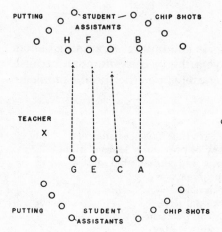

Figure 12–10. Class organization for outdoor golf instruction. Groups rotate.

understand when the club is used in actual play. After sufficient practice with a particular club, the clubs should be rotated so that each group will have an opportunity to work with all the different types of clubs available. In this type of class organization it is extremely helpful to the teacher to have the aid of advanced golf students in directing the instruction within the groups.

Class instruction is more easily organized if the school has furnished the basic clubs for each student, as this permits explanation and demonstration to the entire class at once. Usually instruction is given first on the mashie (No. 5 iron), although some teachers prefer to begin with the driver. This is followed by teaching the woods, the short irons, the putter and the long irons, in that order. As the class progresses, the teacher may wish to divide the class into groups practicing skills with different clubs.

The use of plastic and cotton balls makes class practice easier both inside and out. Because there is no danger in being hit by these softer balls, it is possible to pair the students off at some distance apart to hit the balls back and forth (Fig. 12–10). At the same time, other students can be practicing putting and chip shots with regular golf balls. This organization of the class makes possible the most practice in a given period of time.

TEACHING PROCEDURES

It is usually recommended that beginners be taught the overlapping grip. The importance of developing the proper grip cannot be overemphasized. In addition to demonstrations, posters may be used to illustrate the grip. The teacher should continually check the grip throughout the instruction period to make certain that no student is deviating from the proper form.

Although the square, opened and closed stances are all used by some golfers for various shots, it is often recommended that beginners be taught the square stance for all shots. Other stances may be taught to advanced players.

Because success in golf is largely dependent upon developing correct form and a relaxed swing, considerable time should be spent on this phase. The explanation of the swing should be kept simple enough that the student will not be confused and tense when he attempts it. The following teaching techniques may be useful in helping the student to overcome common difficulties:

To help the student to develop a slow backswing, have him pause slightly at the height of the backswing
To help to solve the problem of keeping the left elbow straight, have the student swing the club with only the left arm.
For developing the cocking of the wrist, the student should swing the right arm alone.
To correct the fault of moving the head during the swing, hold the student's head stationary during the swing.
For trouble in keeping the right elbow close to the body, place a tennis ball under the right arm socket during the swing.
To help a student to "groove" his swing, encourage him to practice the swing occasionally with his eyes closed.

Much can be done to promote the playing skills and the interest in the game in the gymnasium or on the play field, but real enthusiasm is engendered by playing an actual game. If it is not possible for the class to play on a regulation course, the high school athletic field can be converted to serve as a substitute. The actual game situation may be used to introduce the basic rules, scoring, the types of tournament play and golf etiquette.

EVALUATION

Knowledge of rules, scoring and other factual material may be tested by objective or subjective tests. To evaluate the student's overall progress in the skills of golf, the best score for 18 holes may be used.

In testing driving ability, plastic balls may be substituted for regular golf balls. A plastic ball will travel about 10 per cent the distance of a regular ball.

Chipping and putting accuracy are easily assessed by constructing appropriate targets for scoring.

SELECTED VISUAL AIDS

Beginning Golf. National Golf Foundation.
From Tee to Green. National Film Board of Canada.

Golf Techniques. Connecticut College for Women.
Group Golf Instruction. AAHPER.
Nine Bad Shots of Golf. McGraw-Hill Book Company, Inc.
The Rules of Golf Etiquette. National Educational Films, Inc.
How to Improve Your Golf. Athletic Institute.
Winning Golf. National Collegiate Film Service.

PUBLISHED SKILL TESTS

Clevett, Melvin: An experiment in teaching methods of golf. *Research Quarterly, II,* No. 4, 1931, p. 104.

McKee, Mary E.: A test for the full swinging shot in golf. *Research Quarterly, XXI,* No. 1, March, 1950, p. 40.

SUGGESTED READINGS

AAHPER: *Bowling-Fencing-Golf.* Washington, D.C., Division for Girls' and Women's Sports. Published biennially.

Cheatum, Billye Ann: *Golf.* Philadelphia, W. B. Saunders Co., 1969.

Fossum, Bruce G. and Dagraedt, Mary: *Golf.* Boston, Allyn and Bacon, Inc., 1969.

National Golf Foundation: *Golf in Physical Education.* 407 S. Dearborn St., Chicago.

TENNIS

Tennis is one of the fastest growing sports in America. Its value as a recreational activity, the availability of facilities and the social opportunity of play between the sexes have all contributed to its popularity. Currently, tennis ranks high in the selection of desirable sport activities by high school students of both sexes.

As with golf, the essentials of tennis can be taught without elaborate facilities. Most schools have access to at least a few courts or areas where courts can be marked out. Practice of essential tennis skills can be conducted in regular gymnasiums, surfaced outdoor play areas and against interior or exterior walls. By rotating students between available facilities, a very few courts can accommodate even large class enrollments.

Ideally, the school should furnish rackets and balls. However, students tend to play more consistently if they use one racket exclusively, so it is desirable for them to have their own racket when possible. Lost balls are a perpetual problem in tennis instruction. Necessity may dictate that students bring their own, well-marked balls or be responsible for turning in issued balls at the end of class. Developing student attitudes of courtesy and conscientiousness in the use of all school equipment may help alleviate this problem.

Figure 12–11. Tennis is one of our fastest growing sports among teenagers and adults. (Courtesy Los Angeles Unified School District.)

COURSE CONTENT

Material which may be included in the tennis units includes:

Unit for beginners	*Unit for advanced students*
History	Review of courtesies
Selection and care of equipment	Selection of personal equipment
Sport courtesies	Review of fundamentals
Fundamentals:	Advanced skills:
Grip	Smash
Footwork	Lob
Forehand	Chop
Backhand	Advanced strategy for singles and
Serve	doubles
Volley	Tournament play
Rules and regulations	Individual skill problems and skill
Scoring	development
Strategy:	Elimination and round robin tour-
Singles	nament play
Doubles	Evaluation
Evaluation	

CLASS ORGANIZATION

The skills of tennis lend themselves to instruction by the partner form of the direct teaching method, although other forms may be used. In the partner form, students are divided into pairs or small groups, depending on the available equipment and space. Every student must have at least one partner so that there will be at least one observer for each performer. The observer's major responsibility is to analyze the technique of the performer and offer encouragement and suggestions for improvement after each trial. To aid the observer a worksheet or task card is provided to each student. This sheet or card is similar to the one utilized in the task form of teaching but differs in that, in addition to describing the task, it identifies specific points of execution for which the observer should watch. Thus the task card both identifies the activity and becomes the basis for the observer's analysis of the performer.

As in the task form, the items appearing on the worksheet are first introduced and demonstrated by the instructor. The critical points which the observer is to look for are identified on the card and are also illustrated by both correct and common incorrect examples by the instructor.

After the initial instruction is concluded, the student groups begin to work on the activities described, with one student performing and the other analyzing the performance in terms of the provided critical points of the skill. After each trial the observer discusses the execution with the performer, reinforcing correct actions and identifying observed faults. When the first member of the pair has completed the task satisfactorily, the partners change roles and the second member becomes the performer.

This form allows students to progress at different rates, while at the same time receiving an evaluation of their performance from an outside source. The role of observer and critic also requires students to develop an ability to analyze the movements and become conversant with correct and incorrect skill execution. This not only increases their own knowledge of the skill but possibly helps them in directing their own performance.

As students complete one task card, they move on to the next. It will be necessary for the teacher to introduce and demonstrate new tasks every few days. In certain instances homogeneous pairings are advantageous in that the partners will advance at a similar pace. However, it is not necessary that partners be working on the same skill at the same time, and often a highly skilled performer can aid a more poorly skilled student. Identical groupings need not be maintained for an entire unit, offering chances for both homogeneous and heterogeneous pairings.

Worksheets are generally collected at the end of each period to assure availability at the next class meeting and to allow the teacher to monitor the progress of individual students and of the class as a whole.

TEACHING PROCEDURES

As in the task form, a great amount of the teacher's work is accomplished prior to meeting the class in that the worksheets or task cards

Tennis Forehand Task Card No. 1

Starting date_____

Completion date _____

Performer's name
_____

_____
Observer's name

Task 1. Without using a ball, mimic at least 5 forehand strokes at: (1) waist level, (2) shoulder level and (3) knee level, beginning from the ready position. Stop after each stroke and listen to your partner's comments.

	Complete at Waist level	Complete at Shoulder level	Complete at Knee level

Observer check points:
(A) Begins from ready position
(B) Pivots to side position as arm is brought back in backswing
(C) Keeps elbow close to body during backswing
(D) Takes weight on back leg as opposite foot moves forward to make pivot
(E) Hesitates slightly at the end of the backswing before starting forward swing
(F) Steps forward into swing
(G) Swings racket level with the ground when ball is hit
(H) Makes backward and forward swing without wrist action
(I) Turns racket head slightly forward prior to contact with ball
(J) Continues to turn racket head as ball is hit and during follow-through
(K) Continues to follow-through after ball is hit

Performer must satisfactorily complete three consecutive attempts at each level before moving on to the next task.

Task 2. Drop and hit 10 balls with the forehand stroke against the fence, stopping after each to listen to your partner's analysis of your performance.

	Incomplete	Complete

Observer check points:
A. Uses side to net position
B. Swings racket level on backswing
C. Hits ball on "up" bounce
D. Shifts weight forward prior to hitting
E. Swings level, not up or down
F. Makes adjustment in height of arm to height of approaching ball
G. Swings racket level with the ground when ball is hit
H. Makes backward and forward swing without wrist action
I. Turns racket head slightly forward prior to contact with ball
J. Continues to turn racket head as ball is hit and during follow-through
K. Continues to follow-through after ball is hit

Do not move on to next task until performer can complete five consecutive shots without errors.

Task 3. At a distance of 25 feet from a wall, drop a ball and then hit 5 successive forehand shots. Consult with your partner and repeat five times.

	Incomplete	Complete

Observer check points:
(A) Returns to ready position after stroke
(B) Positions body so ball bounces in front of it
(C) Keeps elbow close to body during backswing
(D) Takes weight on back leg as opposite foot moves forward to make pivot
(E) Hesitates slightly at the end of the backswing before starting forward swing
(F) Steps forward into swing
(G) Swings racket level with the ground when ball is hit
(H) Makes backward and forward swing without wrist action
(I) Turns racket head slightly forward prior to contact with ball
(J) Continues to turn racket head as ball is hit and during follow-through
(K) Continues to follow-through after ball is hit

Do not go on to the next task until completing three consecutive five-shot trials without errors in A to K above.

When you have completed all tasks on this card, turn it in at the desk and pick up next card in this set.

Figure 12–12. Sample worksheet for partner form of direct method.

must be prepared and ready for student use. After distribution of the task cards to the students, all activities should be demonstrated and explained fully, with special emphasis given to critical skill points indicated on the card. In essence, what the teacher is trying to do is educate the observers, i.e., make them competent at detecting the performance points outlined on the card.

As the students begin working on the activities, the teacher circulates through the class, working with groups who are experiencing problems. An important function of the teacher is to reinforce the partner relationship; therefore, the teacher usually directs his comments and instructions to the observer, asking him to look closer at a particular part of the skill, and so on. He does not work directly with the performer, since this excludes the observer and destroys the reliance of the performer on the observer for verification of correct skill technique.

An example of a task card prepared for use in the partner form of direct teaching appears in Figure 12–14. The task card in this case is for the forehand stroke. Upon satisfactory completion of the tasks on this card, the student turns it in to the teacher and receives another. The new task card may contain items related to perfecting skill development

Figure 12–13. There are many kinds of commercial products now available for the increased effectiveness of tennis instruction. (Courtesy of the Youth Service Section of the Los Angeles Public Schools.)

in the forehand stroke, or they may be related to the next skill to be learned, e.g., the backhand stroke.

Rules, sport courtesies and strategy, including kinds of shots and when to use them, can follow as the class is ready. This should occur as early as possible because student interest will wane quickly without the thrill of playing. While some students are playing, others can practice their strokes periodically on the backboard. The instructor should encourage those who have specific stroke weaknesses, such as a faulty backhand, to practice that stroke on the backboard or to have a partner drop balls for him on which he practices the backhand.

Visual aids can be utilized for instructional and motivational purposes. It is recommended that detailed films be shown only after the students have had some information given them so they are better able to understand the instruction given in the film. It is often valuable to show detailed films or filmstrips several times during the unit because these visual aids contain too much information to be grasped fully from one showing.

Class tournaments are good motivators for participants. Single and double elimination tournaments may be used to best advantage in large classes; round robin and ladder tournaments are more suitable for smaller groups. The time available governs the choice of tournament. A round robin tournament is recommended for beginners because it increases skill, practice and interest.

EVALUATION

Written tests may be given to evaluate tennis knowledge. The Dyer Tennis Test may be used for evaluating general tennis ability. (See Published Skill Tests.) For measurement of specific skills the student may be evaluated in an actual game situation by scoring him on a point system such as the one given below. For each item the player is awarded ten points or a portion of ten points, depending on the degree of success.

Watching the ball at all times
Keeping the body at right angles to the net while stroking the ball
Shifting the body forward while stroking
Getting good body position before stroking
Hitting the ball rather than just pushing the ball
Correct angle of the face of the racquet while hitting the ball (improper angle will cause the ball to go into the net or go high and out of bounds)
Proper amount of speed for the stroke made
Using the backhand when necessary rather than running around the ball to make a forehand
Sufficient backswing to make an effective stroke
Backswing started in sufficient time so it is not hurried

Starting in time to reach the ball to make stroke
Sufficient follow-through
Tossing the ball accurately and sufficiently high in the serve
Slow and easy backswing in the serve
Failing to transfer body weight during the backswing of the serve

In addition, specific skill competency may be evaluated by utilizing tests of timed wall volleying, serving accuracy and consistency and stroking accuracy.

SELECTED VISUAL AIDS

Beginning Tennis. All American Productions.
Beginning Tennis. U.S. Lawn Tennis Association.
Fundamentals of Tennis. Young American Films, Inc.
How to Improve Your Tennis. Athletic Institute.
Technique of Tennis. Teaching Film Custodians, Inc.
Tennis Tactics. Association Films.

PUBLISHED SKILL TESTS

Broer, Marion R., and Miller, Donna M.: Achievement tests for beginning and intermediate tennis. *Research Quarterly, XXI,* No. 3, October, 1950, p. 303.

Dyer, Joanna T.: The backhand test of tennis ability. *Supplement to the Research Quarterly, VI,* No. 1, March, 1935, p. 63.

Scott, Gladys: Achievement examinations for elementary and intermediate tennis classes. *Research Quartery, XII,* No. 1, March, 1941, p. 40.

SUGGESTED READINGS

AAHPER: *Tennis—Badminton.* Washington, D.C., Division for Girls' and Women's Sports. Published biennially.

Fait, Hollis, et al.: *A Manual of Physical Education Activities.* 3rd ed. Philadelphia, W. B. Saunders Co., 1967.

Gensemer, Robert E.: *Tennis.* 2nd ed. Philadelphia, W. B. Saunders Co., 1975.

Plagenhoef, Stanley: *Fundamentals of Tennis.* Englewood Cliffs, N.J., Prentice-Hall, Inc., 1970.

Vannier, Maryhelen, and Poindexter, Hally Beth: *Individual and Team Sports for Girls and Women.* 3rd ed. Philadelphia, W. B. Saunders Co., 1974.

WRESTLING

Most physical education programs include some type of combative sport. It is held that such an activity offers an experience that is difficult to obtain elsewhere. It provides, first of all, training in physical contact of a competitive nature. Moreover, it fosters an understanding and appreciation of vigorous contact in sports. Finally, it encourages the mastery of the fear that may arise from the anticipation of participating in violent personal contact.

Wrestling is perhaps the easiest of the combative sports to introduce into the physical education program because of its popularity as a sport with teenagers and because it requires only a single piece of major equipment. The only absolutely essential equipment needed to teach wrestling is a mat. However, if they can be had, it is worthwhile to provide the students with wrestling headgear to protect the ears from bruises. Such injuries are such a common occurrence in wrestling that many professional wrestlers develop ear deformities commonly called "cauliflower ears." While there is little danger of extensive and repeated bruising of the ears in the wrestling done in physical education classes, nevertheless, it is recommended that headgear be worn as a safety measure. It is also recommended that the wrestlers wear wrestling trunks or long sweat pants to protect their knees from possible mat burns. Nothing dulls the enthusiasm for wrestling so rapidly as continually nursing a painfully skinned knee.

COURSE CONTENT

The information and skills which might be covered in the wrestling units are:

Unit for beginners *(mat wrestling only)*	*Unit for advanced students*
Brief history	Review of the safety regulations and
Safety regulations and	courtesies
courtesies	Take downs from standing position
Referee's position	Additional holds
Techniques of eight	Counters for each hold
maneuvers	Advanced strategy
Two break downs	Officiating
Two reversals	Evaluation
Two escapes	
Two pinning holds	
Counter for each hold	
Rules of wrestling	
Strategy	
Evaluation	

CLASS ORGANIZATION

The organization of the class that is described below is representative of how the teaching of wrestling might be approached utilizing the indirect method, divergent form.

Figure 12–14. Practice sessions can be made more interesting by setting up controlled wrestling situations.

The class should be divided into pairs of approximately equal size and strength. If mat area is limited, half of the class may observe while the other half works, switching after a few minutes to give everyone equal mat time.

The instructor begins by defining the situation and directing the students' attention to the problem or question under consideration. This is usually done en masse with the entire class. After the problem has been presented, each pair of students takes a place on the mat to work out a solution. The teacher moves about the class, aiding students in getting started, restating the problem and its restrictions and encouraging student exploration of possibilities. As students figure out possible solutions, they try them out with the partner. Both partners should be actively engaged in solving the problem. After sufficient time for exploration of the problem has elapsed, the class is called back together and individual pairs are asked to demonstrate their solution to the problem. The entire class then tries several of the proposed solutions and evaluates each. After several workable solutions have been demonstrated by students, the entire class is asked to generalize about common elements in the solutions. These common elements underlie all solutions. Having identified them, students can then utilize these in developing additional solutions of the same type.

The format for class organization, then, involves presentation of a problem or question to the entire class, followed by students working on their own to solve the problem, then discussion and evaluation of their solutions with the entire class, and finally application of the generalized solution elements in creating new solutions to the problem.

TEACHING PROCEDURES

The following example describes an appropriate procedure for identifying qualities underlying all breakdowns. Concepts appropriate to pinning, escaping or specific skill techniques could be similarly approached.

After having experienced the referee's position, the entire class is presented with the problem confronting the offensive wrestler, that is, "How can the offensive wrestler break his opponent down from all fours?" Partners find a place on the mat and experiment with ways of getting the defensive man off his hands and knees and down to the mat. The teacher encourages students to try out their solutions with their partners providing some resistance. During the experimentation the teacher is available to assist pairs having trouble understanding the problem or its limitations. The instructor should not be too anxious to "help" the students find an answer, for it is the nature of this teaching method to cause the student to come up with his own answer to the problem. The teacher may, however, clarify or redirect students who for some reason are completely off the question under consideration. After sufficient time has been allotted for each student to have dealt with the problem and experimented with his solution, the class is called back together to observe and evaluate the solutions developed by various pairs of students. Students may be asked to volunteer their solutions, or the instructor may call upon those pairs whom he has observed trying various techniques. As each technique is demonstrated, the remainder of the class should observe and mentally evaluate its utility in solving the problem. Specific proposed solutions can then be tried by the entire class and evaluated.

After several alternative solutions have been identified and tried by all, the class is asked to determine what general qualities seem to be important in all breakdowns. Here the desired responses would include: destroy the partner's balance by removing a supporting limb and pushing him toward it, or blocking a limb and pulling him over it. In addition, more specific ideas, such as performing the movements rapidly and forcefully as well as maintaining continuous contact with the opponent, might be suggested. At this point the students could be asked to use these ideas to develop new solutions, or the instructor could demonstrate some common breakdowns and ask the students to identify how each utilizes the qualities determined to be characteristic of all breakdowns. After students understand the essentials of all breakdowns and after several examples have been identified, the class should spend some time perfecting these techniques. The identification of essential components serves as a method of checking basic errors in the execution of the techniques.

This problem solving method will obviously be slower than

simply telling the students *what to do*. But the gains in knowledge, understanding and problem solving ability should make this method worthwhile in the long run, since students are now better able to analyze and direct their own future learning. The excitement of being actively involved in the solving of problems has an added benefit in the motivation and self-direction of the learners.

Practice sessions can be made more interesting by setting up controlled wrestling situations. Each wrestler is told which moves he may and may not use. The partners then wrestle for 15 seconds, observing the stipulations with respect to the moves. This type of practice directs attention to particular skills and ensures the development of the skill in the competitive setting.

As the boys become more proficient, a class tournament may be set up. Such an activity provides a unique opportunity to discuss the rules which govern competitive wrestling. Safety regulations can also be discussed in this connection. It is a particularly effective procedure for the instructor to demonstrate the illegal holds and explain their dangers. In connection with safety measures, the necessity for removing rings, watches and identification bracelets and for keeping the nails short should be stressed.

Unless the school is fortunate in having more than one mat, the instructor will be faced with the difficulties arising from limited mat space. In such circumstances he must make the watching of the performing wrestlers an educational experience by evaluating the bout step by step. Employing a student as referee for each class bout also helps to promote the value derived from this class procedure.

After the students have become familiar with the holds, it is possible to have three or four groups of partners practicing on a mat. The practice in this situation requires moving at less than full speed. After the students have once developed this technique, they can continue practicing a longer period of time without fatigue and gain more insight into the methods of putting on holds and breaking them than is possible when wrestling at full speed.

General wrestling strategy may be introduced as soon as the students have become well acquainted with the holds and counters. Then, during practice sessions the instructor may help each student to develop an individual strategy based upon the holds which he performs most effectively.

At this stage some students will begin to experiment with different holds. The instructor should encourage those who demonstrate this interest to read books in which more advanced holds are described. These students can then demonstrate and explain some of the holds about which they have read to the rest of the class. Some may even be able to teach these new holds to the class. This sharing technique is usually extremely helpful to a teacher who is inexperienced in wrestling.

The methods of instructing advanced wrestlers are substantially the same as for teaching beginners. The material which is presented will be of a more advanced nature; this applies to strategy, rules and regulations, and officiating as well as holds and counters. Advanced wrestlers are usually interested in officiating, and a significant portion of the teaching time may well be devoted to this phase of the sport. It is also useful to the teacher to have everyone in the class capable of refereeing a match because, with the aid of student referees, several matches can proceed in orderly fashion during the class period.

EVALUATION

Knowledge of factual material can be tested by either a subjective or objective test. To measure the motor learning which has taken place during the unit, the best method is to evaluate performance during actual combat. This is a rather slow process, but the bouts can be shortened to as little as three minutes and still offer a valid basis for evaluation. In order to make the evaluation a better measurement of how well the holds and counters have been mastered, a point system similar to that given below can be devised.

Number of holds attempted with a reasonable degree of success	10 points per hold
Violation of the following principles	−5 points for each violation
Moving so that body balance is not maintained	
Failing to follow up opponent's mistake with offensive maneuver	
Failing to keep the body perpendicular to the opponent's body when the opponent is on his back and the wrestler is on top	
Keeping a hold on the opponent's head while he is on the top and wrestler is on his back	
Failing to make the opponent carry the weight of the wrestler's body when he is on top	
Number of holds blocked	10 points for each block
Number of holds countered and turned into an offense	20 points

As an alternative, students may be asked to perform various skills for evaluation of their technical execution. For such testing, the opponent should not be aware of the move to be executed and should be instructed to resist being scored upon without countering or initiating a hold of his own.

SELECTED VISUAL AIDS

How to Improve Your Wrestling. Athletic Institute.
Wrestling Fundamentals and Techniques. University of Michigan.

PUBLISHED SKILL TESTS

McCloy, Charles Harold, and Young, Norma Dorothy: Seevers wrestling test. *Tests and Measurements in Health and Physical Education.* New York, Appleton-Century-Crofts, Inc., 1954

SUGGESTED READINGS

Amateur Athletic Union of the United States: *Official Wrestling Guide.*
Dratz, John P., et al.: *Winning Wrestling.* Englewood Cliffs, N.J., Prentice-Hall, Inc., 1966.
Fait, Hollis, et al.: *A Manual of Physical Education Activities.* 2nd ed. Philadelphia, W. B. Saunders Co., 1961.
Seaton, Don Cash, et al.: *Physical Education Handbook.* 6th ed. Englewood Cliffs, N.J., Prentice-Hall, Inc., 1974.
Umbach, Arnold, and Johnson, Warren: *Wrestling.* Dubuque, Iowa, William C. Brown Co., 1967.

CROQUET, DECK TENNIS, HANDBALL, HORSESHOES, SHUFFLEBOARD AND TABLE TENNIS

A great many high schools do not have sufficient courts and equipment to present a unit to the entire class in handball, table tennis and shuffleboard. However, if the school does have one hand-ball court (or a smooth wall surface to accommodate a one-wall hand-ball court) and one or more tables and shuffleboard courts, it is often desirable to combine the three activities in one unit. If it is necessary to add other activities to have enough stations for everyone, croquet, deck tennis and horseshoes may be included also.

Shuffleboard courts can be laid out on any smooth floor space approximately 52 feet long and 6 feet wide. Hallways, aisles along the gym floor, and dressing room space may be utilized, if necessary, for the courts. Tables for table tennis may be placed in areas where there is at least 25 feet by 8 feet of unobstructed floor space. Frequently areas such as the space under balconies, unsuitable for other activities because of low ceilings, can be used for this purpose. In lieu of a regulation handball court, a one-wall court may be laid out using a smooth wall 20 feet wide by 16 feet high with adjacent floor space 20 feet wide by 34 feet long.

If the floor is not marked for deck tennis courts, badminton courts may be utilized. The badminton court is slightly large for the singles game but serves very well for doubles. Croquet and horseshoes are outdoor activities which can best be taught outside; however, lessons on the nature of the games, rules, safety and courtesies can be included in an indoor program. Rubber horseshoes and stakes are available for inside use, and students can learn the game fundamentals using them.

COURSE CONTENT

The items which should be included in the teaching of each of the activities are:

Croquet
History and nature of game
Game courtesies
Grip
Stance
Hitting the ball
Rules
Strategy

Handball (four-wall and one-wall)
History and nature of game
Safety regulations
Serves
Returns
Footwork
Proper court positions
Rules
Strategy:
Singles
Doubles

Deck tennis
History and nature of game
Game courtesies
Serve
Throwing and catching
Rules
Strategy

Shuffleboard
History and nature of game
Game courtesies
Grip
Aim and delivery
Rules
Strategy

Horseshoes
History and nature of game
Sport courtesies
Grips
Stance
Throws
Rules
Strategy

Table tennis
History and nature of game
Safety regulations
Game courtesies
Volleying
Serves
Returns
Rules
Strategy

CLASS ORGANIZATION

All of the activities, or any portion of them, may be included in the unit, depending upon the objectives of the program and the available facilities and equipment. The class should be divided into groups of workable size for each activity. The students should be so distributed that they will be participating in some activity rather than waiting around for their turn. In large classes with limited facilities, playing doubles will be more satisfactory than singles. In croquet and horseshoes several players may play at the same time.

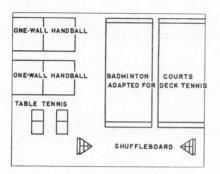

Figure 12–15. Class arrangement for teaching a combination of individual sports.

TEACHING PROCEDURES

It is desirable to begin playing the game as soon as possible in each of these activities since the game situation can be used to develop the skills. Anyone who has extreme difficulty in performing a skill and is unable to master it sufficiently to start playing an elementary game may be placed by himself or with another student having similar difficulty to drill on the skill or with a fellow classmate who can help him to learn it. For example, a student who cannot hit the ball satisfactorily in handball or table tennis may be assigned a station on any available wall space (not necessarily regulation size) to practice hitting

Figure 12–16. Extra practice in the basic skills of table tennis can be provided by utilizing a table pushed against the wall. (Courtesy Enrico Fermi High School.)

the ball up against the wall, working either with someone else who is having trouble or with someone who has mastered the desired movements.

The teacher should rotate from group to group, giving individual instruction whenever the need arises. He must remain generally alert to what is happening in other sections of the gymnasium, even though he is working specifically with one group, in order to deal with any instructional or discipline problem which might disrupt a group.

EVALUATION

Since the instructor will have a limited amount of time in which to watch individuals perform, it will be difficult to evaluate the class members using the subjective methods. Records of wins and losses in class play show individual ability as compared with other class members, and in some situations will demonstrate the progress achieved by individuals. If such records are to be used for evaluation, it is necessary to establish a rotation system whereby the players have new partners frequently through the course of the unit.

In the games of shuffleboard, croquet and horseshoes, progress is better ascertained by comparing the scores recorded at intervals throughout the unit. In shuffleboard the average score of several rounds may be taken to measure the level of achievement. In croquet, the number of strokes required to complete the course without competition, and in horseshoes the number of ringers or close shoes in a specified number of throws, may be used to measure the skills in the respective sports.

To evaluate general knowledge of the games and the skills involved, a short written test may be given.

SELECTED VISUAL AIDS

Horse Shoes. Teaching Films Custodians, Inc.
Ping-Pong. Teaching Films Custodians, Inc.
Table Tennis. Teaching Films Custodians, Inc.
Table Tennis. United World Films.

DISCUSSION QUESTIONS

1. What is the place of individual sports in a physical education program?
2. How can a teacher determine which individual sports to include in the physical education program?
3. In what ways may a class in any specific individual sport be organized to accommodate students of varying degrees of ability?

4. How can a teacher promote a lasting interest in a sport so that the students will continue to play it outside the physical education class and beyond their school years?

5. Of what importance is it for the students to have some knowledge of the history of a sport?

THINGS TO DO

1. Develop class organization and teaching procedures for a specific skill required in any of the sports in this chapter. Use a different method or form from the one described in the text for teaching that skill.

2. Diagram a possible organization of a class of 35 students for instruction in three or four of the individual sports simultaneously. Assume that this organization is necessary because of limited supplies of equipment for these sports.

3. Make an objective test for factual knowledge of one of the individual sports.

4. Devise a drill for practice of a skill needed in one of the individual sports.

5. Analyze the skills of a player in a class that you have arranged to observe or of one of your classmates who agrees to "perform" for you. Suggest ways in which he may improve his skills.

SUGGESTED READINGS

Fait, Hollis, et al.: *A Manual of Physical Education Activities*. 3rd ed. Philadelphia, W. B. Saunders Co., 1967.

Haslam, Charles: *The How to Book of Shuffleboard*. St. Petersburg, Florida, Great Outdoors Association, 1955.

Seaton, Don Cash, et al.: *Physical Education Handbook*. 6th ed. Englewood Cliffs, N.J., Prentice-Hall, Inc., 1974.

Stanley, Dennis K., et al.: *Physical Education Activities Handbook for Men and Women*. 3rd ed. Boston, Allyn and Bacon, Inc., 1974.

Vannier, Maryhelen, and Poindexter, Hally Beth: *Physical Activities for College Women*. 3rd ed. Philadelphia, W. B. Saunders Co., 1974.

CHAPTER THIRTEEN

TRACK AND FIELD SPORTS

Track and field activities provide opportunities to develop the basic skills of running, jumping and throwing, which are fundamental to many sports activities and to the activities of everyday life. A unit of track and field events is frequently included in the girls' physical education program as well as in the boys', particularly if a unit in body mechanics does not include running and jumping skills.

COURSE CONTENT

The contents of the teaching unit in track and field are often limited to the events listed. The javelin and discus throws and the pole vault are not usually presented in physical education classes because of their inherent dangers. However, they may well be included in the advanced unit if the group is small, plenty of space is available, and each student has demonstrated a sufficiently mature regard for the rules of safety.

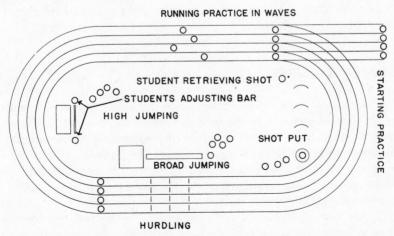

Figure 13–1. Organization of the class for the teaching of track and field events.

Unit for beginners

Sprints:
  50 yard dash
  Shuttle relay
  100 yard dash
Field events:
  High jump
  Long jump
  Triple jump
  Shot put
Low hurdles
Baton passing and 440 yard relay

Unit for advanced students

Sprints:
  220 yard dash
Middle distance:
  440 yard run
Cross country
High hurdles

CLASS ORGANIZATION

Track and field instruction should be organized with the purpose of introducing all members of the class to a variety of events. Opportunities for specialization should be provided for interested students in intramural and interscholastic meets. Some specialization may well form a part of the classwork for advanced students, but it should follow rather than precede the introduction to the various events.

The class can best be organized for teaching the field events and hurdles by dividing the group into small units of five or six students. Each group will learn and practice a different event, and in this way the best possible use can be made of facilities and equipment.

The running events can be taught to the complete group at one time. If it is a very large class and the number of running lanes or running areas is limited, the class may be lined up in several different lines to run in "waves" for the sprints and middle distances. Because the time it takes for one wave to complete the sprints and the middle distance runs is relatively short, the next wave of runners will not need to start until the previous wave is finished. In running the longer distances each wave may follow within a few minutes.

CLASS PROCEDURES

The students should be informed of the scope of the class activities and the objectives of the unit. To stimulate interest in the class the discussion may include some of the interesting achievements of the school's varsity team. A discussion of the records established for the school or past class records and a comparison of these with conference, national and world records in the same events often proves an interesting introduction to the unit.

Track and field events are competitive by nature. Students are either in competition with themselves to better their own time or distance or are competing with others to better them in a contest. The interest of the students in their running time and the distances achieved in the field events may be used in motivating the development of the skills. The natural desire for competition may find outlets in races and contests held during class periods. Such competitive events engender student enthusiasm as well as provide additional practice on newly acquired skills.

During the early part of the unit, a record of the times and distances of each student should be made. At intervals throughout the unit new times and distances should be recorded so that the student and the teacher will have evidence of the progress which is being achieved throughout the course.

The advanced class in track and field will continue in the development of the skills of the events which they learned as beginners. Although the skill techniques vary somewhat, methods of presenting and practicing the skills do not differ appreciably.

Distance and cross country running require a different technique from that used in sprinting. The success of a distance runner is dependent upon his endurance; however, good technique in running conserves energy. The same criteria used to judge sprinting skill may be used to check good form in distance running. The chief differences will be that the runner is not up on his toes, his stride is shorter, his arm action is less pronounced, and the elbow is usually held at a greater angle.

TEACHING PROCEDURES

The examples of teaching procedures presented in this chapter are of the command-response form of the direct method. Other forms of the direct method as well as the indirect method could be readily utilized for track and field instruction.

SPRINTS

Running form should be the first skill presented to beginners. A large percentage of each class will have failed to learn to run efficiently and will profit from correction of their running form faults. Before the teacher makes the actual evaluation of each student's running skills, he should point out to the class that efficient running is a complicated skill and that many of them who have learned to run without instruction have not developed a form which will give them the greatest speed with the least possible effort. Such an explanation is usually necessary for it will never have occurred to most students that the way they run is not the best possible way for them to run, and they will not be especially receptive to the idea of changing patterns of long standing.

For the evaluation of the running techniques, the class can be lined up four or five students abreast. At a given command, each line runs at full speed toward the teacher, who stands at a distance of 40 or 50 feet from them. He should check each runner against a list containing the following items:

1. Does the runner lean forward at an angle of approximately 65 degrees?
2. Are the hands brought back and forth alternately with the legs rather than brought across the body?
3. Is the head held in line with the body?
4. Is the upper body aligned with the lower part of the body?
5. Is the stride the correct length for the build of the runner and the potential power of the leg drive?
6. Are the toes pointing straight ahead?
7. Are the legs brought straight forward and backward?
8. Is the body brought forward of the lead foot when it comes in contact with the ground?

Those who deviate from the above criteria will require further work to correct their form faults in running. These students may be placed in a group together for instructional purposes. If only a few students demonstrated good form in the evaluation test, they may be used to assist in the instruction of the others; otherwise, they may be placed in a group to work on some other skill.

CORRECTION OF FORM FAULTS

In correcting form faults the following methods are helpful:

Improper Angle of the Body. Most runners who do not run at the proper angle throw their heads back and hold their bodies too erect. To correct this fault, the teacher has each student assume the correct angle by supporting himself against a wall. He stands the necessary distance from the wall and then leans toward it, leaning forward from the ankles, and places his hands upon the wall. This gives the student a kinesthetic feeling of the correct angle at which to carry the body. He will need to understand that only when he is driving hard with his legs will he be able to assume this angle while running.

The running which the student does after the above instruction should be carefully checked by the teacher and further suggestions offered as needed. Some students will attempt to attain the correct angle by bending at the hips. This is incorrect, for the lean must come from the feet.

Improper Use of the Arms. The improper use of the arms is a frequent error in the running form of many students. If the arms are carried too low, the students should be instructed to raise them until the angle at the elbows is about 90 degrees.

If the student is crossing his arms over the chest in running, a rotation of the upper part of the body will be produced. This, of course, hinders top performance in running. To correct this fault, the student may practice the proper form with exaggerated movements of the arms while jogging around the track. Early in the re-education of the arms, it may be helpful for the student to visualize mentally that he is reaching forward to grasp something elastic; he pulls it back and then lets it go before reaching for it again with the other hand. After the arm movement is well established with conscious exaggeration, the student will usually find himself using the proper form with just the required emphasis as he reaches full running speed.

Faulty Use of the Head. There are two form faults which beginners will demonstrate in the use of the head while running. The head will either be permitted to flop back and forth or it will be thrown back too far.

The first of these faults is frequently the result of incorrect use of the shoulders and arms. Correction of these movements will stop the flopping movements of the head.

Correction for throwing the head too far back consists of establishing the proper body angle. Frequently, when a runner is throwing his head back, he is doing so because of his excessively erect position.

Improper Body Alignment. An improper alignment of the body is caused by crossing the arms in front of the body, which produces trunk rotation, or by the runner's attempting to establish the proper lean by bending at the hips. The methods already discussed in connection with these two faults should be used to achieve proper body alignment.

Faulty Stride. The errors made most frequently in the stride are: overstriding, failing to stride far enough, toeing out and throwing the legs out to the sides. The last error in the list is committed more commonly by girls than by boys.

A runner is overstriding when the center of the weight of his body is behind the foot when he places it on the ground. The remedy is to practice with a shortened stride. A stride that is too short produces a choppy uneven gait. The student should be encouraged to strive continually to increase the length of his stride.

Toeing out actually cuts down the length of the stride. To correct this difficulty the runner should practice consciously toeing straight ahead while jogging. When the correct movement begins to feel familiar, he may increase the speed of his running while continuing the conscious effort to toe ahead.

When the runner's fault is that of throwing the legs out behind or throwing them to the sides, he must practice with extreme effort on the correct movement while running at a slow pace. When the new movements no longer feel strange, the student may increase the speed of the run.

STARTING

The start in running the dashes is an important factor in racing. There are three types of crouch starts: the bunch, the medium and the elongated. The elongated is the easiest to learn because the position is less strange and for this reason is the one first taught to beginners. The start is first demonstrated to show the placement of the feet and hands, the angle of the hips, and how the head and back are held. With the class in line formation the teacher can move up and down the line to check the crouch as it is assumed by each student. When the students have some mastery of the stance, they may begin practicing the start with a short run. Two or three students can start at one time and run for 10 or 15 yards under the supervision of the instructor. The runners should be checked for these possible errors:

1. The stride is too short or too long in the first step.
2. The runner is too erect on the first step.
3. The runner toes in on the first step.

To remedy the first error, a mark may be made at the spot where the first step should be made; and the students may practice several starts stepping on this mark. Frequently, overstriding in the first step

Figure 13–2. The runner takes the elongated position for the start. (Courtesy of Cheryl Cohen.)

will cause the runner to straighten up more than he should during the first step. Shortening the stride may help him in overcoming this difficulty. Toeing in on the first step will cause the runner to falter slightly on the first step. Overcoming this error will require conscious effort while practicing at half speed; the speed may gradually be increased as the runner becomes more accustomed to pointing the foot straight ahead.

Starting a run from a crouch position is limited almost entirely to race running. The running which is done in games and everyday life situations will be started from an upright position. Consequently, students should receive some instruction in how to start effectively while standing erect. The factors which contribute to an efficient start in running in these circumstances are:

1. The slight lean forward in the direction of intended movement.
2. The length (20 to 40 inches) of the first step.
3. Attaining full running stride within two or three steps.

HIGH JUMP

Many track and field coaches recommend that the western roll be taught first to beginners and that the straddle form be held in reserve until after a year or so of experience jumping with the western roll. No matter which style the jumper begins with, he should stay with it until it is thoroughly learned. The techniques of the style should be explained and demonstrated to the students. Still or moving pictures may be put to good use in giving the class the proper concept of the correct techniques.

Before actually attempting the jump, students should practice bounding into the air with one leg and swinging the other leg upward as high as possible. After this practice and after sufficient warm-up, the students may make a few attempts at jumping the bar which is set at waist height. As soon as the degree of skill will permit, the bar should be raised to the greatest height that the student can clear with success in at least some of his attempts. This will necessitate appointing students to take turns adjusting the bar for the jumpers. To limit the number of adjustments, the students who jump the same heights can be grouped together at one bar, if there are several bars, or follow each other successively when using only a single bar.

LONG JUMP

The style of long jumping recommended for beginners is the "sit in the air" style. It is the most easily learned and just as effective in performance as the others. In long jumping the ability to sprint with good form is an important contributing factor to making a good jump. Any deviation in good running form which decreases speed will result in a shorter jump than could otherwise be achieved.

Demonstrations, still pictures and movies of the correct form in jumping will help the students to visualize the proper form. The students must be shown how to establish check marks for the steps in the approach and how to adjust the last step to hit the board properly. Attention must also be directed toward gathering the body for the jump on the next to the last step, the stamp down on the take-off foot, the coordination of the arms and legs on the take-off, and the proper landing. It is recommended by some coaches and teachers that a length of yarn be stretched between the take-off board and pit at a height of about 3 feet to encourage beginners to obtain sufficient height.

TRIPLE JUMP

This jump incorporates two additional movements, a hop and a step, with the long jump. The successful performance of the combined movements requires that the landings after the hop and the step be made with the body sufficiently forward to permit projection of the body into the next phase of the jump without loss of momentum. In presenting the skills of the triple jump, the teacher must particularly emphasize the proper method of landing for utilization of the speed attained for the next movement. Students may drill on each phase of the triple jump separately before practicing the combined movements.

SHOT PUT

Before a student attempts to put the shot he must realize that it is a *put* and not a throw. An attempt to throw the shot as if it were a baseball may result in injury to the arm. A demonstration by the teacher or by an expert in the shot put should be given or movies should be shown to emphasize the nature of the action.

Students' first practice on the form should be done without a shot. They should assume the putting position with the correct lean of the body with the shot carried in the hand against the jaw and with the back leg bent about 60 degrees. Actual putting should begin with practice in putting from this position without moving across the ring. Crossing the ring may be introduced as soon as the students demonstrate their skill in putting from the stationary position. First attempts in crossing the ring should be made without the shot.

LOW HURDLES

The low hurdles should not be introduced until the latter part of the beginning unit in track. Before attempting to run the hurdles, the students should have at least two weeks of running and preliminary work in the form of exercises. Chief among the exercises which are used is the hurdler's exercise performed on the ground. The hurdles that are used for classwork should be the type that serve to protect the hurdler against ankle and knee bruises and against unnecessary falls.

The usual procedure in teaching hurdling is to have the students practice a short time with one hurdle and then proceed to three or more hurdles. This is recommended because of the importance of a definite rhythm in the steps between successive hurdles.

The techniques of hurdling may best be shown by demonstration. Students can get a good idea of the feel of the position in hurdling by assuming the position while seated on the ground. The number of steps that should be taken to the first hurdle and the subsequent steps between hurdles must be worked out with the students. They should practice the steps along the sides of the hurdles until the correct number is ascertained.

The runner may choose either leg as the forward leg. If he cannot determine which leg he prefers to use, he may jump over the hurdle from a standing position in front of it. The leg that he leads with in this informal jump will be the more comfortable as the lead leg. Short-legged runners may have difficulty developing the proper number of steps between the hurdles. They may need to add one more step; this will necessitate changing the lead leg every other hurdle. This is permissible for those with an especially short stride but is not recommended for those with a sufficiently long stride.

RELAY RACING

The important factor in relay racing is successful passing of the baton; in a good pass little or no speed is lost during the exchange, the chain of contact is smooth and unbroken and the exchange is made between the designated lines. A successful pass depends, first, on the receiver correctly anticipating the speed of the oncoming runner and adjusting his start to match the speed at the moment of exchange, and, second, on the passer placing the baton correctly in the hands of the receiver, whether the method used is the blind or open pass. Considerable practice is usually necessary to achieve a successful pass.

To practice passing the baton, students may be paired off and stationed with one runner 10 to 20 yards in front of the other. The rear

Name of Event... Class.......................... Section.................

NAMES OF STUDENTS	DATE OF TRIAL 1	DATE OF TRIAL 2	DATE OF TRIAL 3	DATE OF FINAL TRIAL	REMARKS
		Times and distances recorded here			

Figure 13–3.   Sample record sheet for scoring track and field events.

runner advances at full speed while the front runner adjusts his speed so that it is the same as that of the other runner at the moment of passing the baton. The front runner shifts the baton to his other hand on the first stride after receiving it, without breaking his stride.

EVALUATION

The times and distances of each event may be utilized in the evaluation of the track and field skills. The amount of improvement in the marks attained would be especially significant in determining the learning which has taken place and the amount of body conditioning achieved. A sample record sheet for the teacher's use in keeping class marks is shown in Figure 13–3. One record sheet would be required for each different event taught in the unit.

Written tests could include knowledge of techniques, rules and conditioning appropriate to each of the various events.

DISCUSSION QUESTIONS

1. Why are the skills that are learned in track and field important in the total education of the individual?

2. By what means might students be motivated to want to take part in track and field events?

3. Describe possible ways of class organization that would be advantageous to the teaching of running techniques.

4. Describe a teaching situation in which the unit on jumping might be more closely related to jumping in everyday life situations, such as jumping a puddle or a stream.

5. Discuss the safety precautions which should be emphasized in a unit of track and field and enumerate ways in which they might be impressed upon the students.

THINGS TO DO

1. Draw a diagram to show a way in which one teacher might instruct 40 students in track and field skills.

2. Set up a procedure for teaching a specific skill in track and field using some other form than command-response.

3. Secure several stop watches for class practice on correct timing techniques.

4. List the organizational steps necessary for an intersquad track meet within a class.

5. Observe another class or members of your own class as they practice running. Analyze their errors and suggest ways of correcting them.

SELECTED VISUAL AIDS

The Broad Jump. United World Films, Inc.
Distances. United World Films, Inc.
How to Improve Your Track and Field. Athletic Institute.
The High Jump. United World Films, Inc.
The Hurdles. United World Films, Inc.
Middle Distances. United World Films, Inc.
Skill Builder Loop Films. Athletic Institute. (A series of loop films on track and field events for both boys and girls.)
The Relays. United World Films, Inc.
The Sprints. United World Films, Inc.

PUBLISHED SKILL TESTS

McCloy, Charles Harold, and Young, Norma Dorothy: The Sargent Jump and the McCloy Classification Index. *Tests and Measurements of Health and Physical Education.* New York, Appleton-Century-Crofts, Inc., 1954.

SUGGESTED READINGS

AAHPER: *Track and Field.* Washington, D.C., Division for Girls' and Women's Sports. Published biennially.

Cretzmeyer, Francis, et al: *Bresnahan and Tuttle's Track and Field Athletics.* 7th ed. St. Louis, The C. V. Mosby Co., 1969.

Kennedy, Robert E.: *Track and Field for College Men.* Philadelphia, W. B. Saunders Co., 1970.

Parker, Virginia and Kennedy, Robert E.: *Track and Field for Girls and Women.* Philadelphia, W. B. Saunders Co., 1969.

CHAPTER FOURTEEN

AQUATICS

Increasingly, instruction in aquatics is being included in the physical education curricula of the nation's secondary schools. Many recently constructed high school facilities include swimming pools. Likewise, schools are increasingly sharing community recreational and educational facilities.

Numerous schools sponsor a program of water activities through the cooperation of local clubs or organizations which have swimming pools. The Y.M.C.A. and Y.W.C.A., boys' clubs and similar organizations often open their pools to the school for the teaching of aquatics during school hours when their facilities are normally not in use. Portable pools which can be moved from school to school have been utilized with success in large school systems.

SWIMMING

In addition to the benefits it provides as recreational and physical activity, swimming is a survival skill. A person with swimming skills may save his life and that of others in unexpected water disasters. Because the development of these skills cannot be duplicated by participation in any other activity, it has been argued by some physical educators that swimming is the only activity which can legitimately be required of everyone.

COURSE CONTENT

Students who report to swimming classes in high school almost always demonstrate such a wide variance in skill achievement that the swimming unit is commonly divided into three segments. Suggested topics to be included in each unit for beginners, intermediates and advanced students are as follows:

Unit for beginners	*Unit for intermediates*	*Unit for advanced students*
Pool safety	Pool safety	Pool safety
Adjustment to the water	Crawl	Breaststroke
	Sidestroke	Dolphin
Breathing	Elementary backstroke	Lifesaving skills
Tuck float (jellyfish float)	Surface dive	
Face float	Underwater swimming	
Back float		
Leg kick and glide		
Dog paddle		
Finning and sculling		
Treading		

CLASS ORGANIZATION

The simplest and most time-conserving method of classifying students on the basis of their skill for the purpose of class organization is to hand out a simple questionnaire for them to fill out. This can be done during the first class period or prior to it, if such arrangements are possible. The questionnaire in Figure 14–1 illustrates the type of questions which might be included.

It is strongly recommended that there be an instructor or qualified swimmer for each 20 students. As an added safety measure, the buddy system may be employed. This is an arrangement whereby two students work together and are responsible for each other's safety in the water. It is probably better to permit beginning students to make their own selection of a partner than to appoint them arbitrarily because the feeling of security will be greater in working with a friend than with a stranger. This is particularly so if the beginner has fear of the water.

Activities for nonswimmers should be conducted in waist deep water. The limits of their area should be roped off, just as those used by the intermediate and advanced swimmers must also be clearly defined in the interest of group safety.

A large class of swimmers always presents problems in class organization. One of the most effective means of organizing a large group to ensure maximum practice during a class period is to divide the students into rows stationed behind each other. Swimmers in the first row take to the water to swim across the pool with the designated stroke. They are followed at intervals of 10 feet by each of the succeeding rows.

The temperature of the water should be at least 80°F. to provide

Name.. P.E............. Section.......... Classification............
    Last   First

The following questions are for the purpose of acquiring information about your ability in water. In case the wrong classification is made as a result of these answers, you will be changed to the appropriate class when you take swimming. Therefore, please calculate the answers as closely as you can. Answer YES or NO.

SWIMMING

.... 1. Can you swim across a 20-ft. pool?
.... 2. Can you do rhythmic breathing in water 20 times (breathe in above water and breathe out under water in an even rhythm)?
.... 3. Are you at ease in deep water?
.... 4. Can you swim 60 feet with the crawl stroke in good form (using rhythmic breathing and a definite flutter kick)?
.... 5. Can you swim the side stroke (lie on your side, use a scissor kick, keep arms and legs under water)?
.... 6. Do you glide for a whole count after each side stroke?
.... 7. Do you use the crawl stroke more than any other stroke?
.... 8. Have you swum 1/8 mile (660 feet)?
.... 9. Have you swum with instruction for more than one lesson from a regular swimming instructor?
               .... more than 10 lessons?
               .... more than 20 lessons?
               .... more than 30 lessons?
               .... more than 50 lessons?
.... 10. Are you afraid of the water?

DIVING

.... 11. Do you enter the water hands and head first?
        If you answer "yes" to No. 11,
.... 12. Do you enter water within 6 feet of where you take off?
.... 13. Do you spring UP into the air for a moment when diving?
.... 14. Do you feel yourself in the air for a moment when diving?
.... 15. Do you enter the water beyond 6 feet of where you take off?
.... 16. Do you lean forward when attempting to spring?
.... 17. Do your legs relax during the dive?
.... 18. Do you use the standing board to do other than standing dive?
.... 19. Do you take longer steps in your approach than you do in walking?

KEY TO CLASSIFICATION

Swimming:

a. Beginners will answer NO to 3.
b. Intermediates will answer YES from 1 through 8.
c. Advanced will answer YES from 1 through 9.

Diving:

a. Beginners will answer NO to 11.
b. Intermediates (if answers are different from b and c in swimming).
c. Intermediates will answer YES to 11, 12, 13, 14; NO to 15, 16, 17.
d. Advanced will answer YES to 11, 12, 14, 18; NO to 15, 16, 17, 19.

Figure 14-1. Questionnaire for use in classifying students in swimming skills. A key for the instructor's use is shown also.

Figure 14-2. One of the most effective means of organizing a large class to insure maximum practice during a class period is to divide the students into rows behind each other. (Courtesy of the Physical Education Department, Los Angeles Public Schools.)

the comfortable environment required for relaxed enjoyable activity in the water. The success of the teaching is reduced when the students are sitting around the edge of the pool shivering and dreading to get into the cold water.

TEACHING PROCEDURES

The first class period of the swimming unit should open with a clearly and emphatically stated lesson on the rules and regulations to be observed in the interest of pool safety. Among the points to be discussed should be:

1. The reasons for showering before entering the pool.
2. The wearing of bathing caps.
3. The use of the foot bath.
4. The prohibition against running on the deck and in the shower room.
5. The importance of being in the water only in the assigned areas and when the instructor is present.

The specific teaching procedures described for instruction of swimming and diving are usually classified as the direct method. With some modification, they can be readily utilized with the indirect method.

Beginners will need a period of orientation to the water. It should be remembered that some will have a genuine fear of the water resulting either from total lack of experience or from early unfavorable experience. Simple water play may be used by the teacher to aid these students in overcoming fright. This should occur in waist-deep water, where students can really begin to experience the *feel* of the water moving about their bodies. The group should be encouraged to splash the water over themselves and to bob up and down, ducking to chin depth. This will be followed by a series of simple activities which can be performed by joining hands in a circle formation or by holding hands with a buddy. The activities should include ducking, kneeling and sitting on the bottom of the pool.

Simple water games are suggested below;[1] the resourceful teacher will devise others as the teaching situation demands.

1. **Ball tag.** The players are scattered around in the shallow end of the pool. The one who is "It" has the ball. The object is to hit another player with the ball who then becomes "It."

2. **Walking race.** The players are lined up at one side of the pool in the shallow area. At a given signal, they walk as fast as possible through the water to the opposite side. The first one to arrive is declared the winner.

3. **Head tag.** Players are scattered around in the shallow end of the pool. The one who is "It" attempts to tag another player who will replace him in being "It." To avoid being tagged, the player must submerge until his head is completely under.

4. **Poison tag.** This game is played like head tag except that to avoid being tagged the player must be floating, finning or sculling.

5. **Corks.** A large number of corks are thrown into the pool. Players attempt to collect the greatest number in a given time.

6. **Retrieving.** Objects such as smooth clean rocks, lead washers, tin pans and pucks are placed in the pool. Players gather as many of these as possible in the prescribed time.

7. **Water dodge ball.** This is played like regular dodge ball with the substitution of ducking for dodging.

8. **Tunnel ball.** The class is divided into teams to pass the ball under water between the legs.

9. **Can you do it.** The class is divided into two groups, and a leader is selected for each group. The leader of one group performs a stunt. If the opposing team cannot do it, he receives a point for his team. Teams alternate in performing stunts.

10. **Drop the puck.** The players form a circle and "It" drops the puck behind a player who must retrieve it and try to catch the player before he returns to the vacant place. If he does not catch him, he becomes "It."

When these students begin to evidence enjoyment of the water

---

[1]See also the chapter on recreational swimming in Vannier's *Methods and Materials in Recreational Leadership,* and Smith's *Water Games.*

play, they are ready for trial attempts at holding the breath and putting the face in the water. Holding the nose and closing the eyes may be permitted in very early trials, but the student should soon begin to practice submerging the face with the eyes open and without holding the nose.

As soon as the students are able to keep the face in the water for about fifteen seconds, they are generally ready for instruction and practice in exhaling under water. After a few experimental attempts on their own, the class may line up in the water along the sides of the pool to practice rhythmical inhaling and exhaling. Students may be permitted to grasp the gutter with one hand during the exercise.

The beginners are now ready to try a stunt which will give them a realization of the buoyancy of the body while building confidence in the ability to regain the standing position in the water. The stunt combines the tuck float and stand. The teacher should make an oral explanation of the technique and demonstrate it several times in the water and then have the students practice it in water which is less than chest depth. He should observe the entire group and give aid and instruction as needed.

The beginner should now be ready to try the face float with a glide. Propulsion for the glide comes from a push off from the side or bottom of the pool. This skill enables the beginner to get something of the feel of moving across the water with the body supported by the water. A greater distance should be aimed for with each glide. The teacher should watch each student execute the glide several times; those who tend to roll from side to side during the glide should be instructed to spread the arms and legs farther apart.

In learning the back float, the buddies may help one another. As the student lies back in the water, the partner may give support to the neck and the small of the back. The support is gradually removed. The partner may also assist in the initial attempts in the recovery to the standing position.

The teacher can introduce the leg kick with a demonstration, emphasizing the relaxed knee and ankle. Students may practice holding on to the pool gutter or using a flutter board. Buddies may also pull each other by the hands while one is practicing the kick. The same type of kick is used on the back, and the teacher can introduce kicking in the back float position at this time. Many students will practice more diligently from this position because the face is out of the water all the time. Strength in the kick will be developed only through repeated practice, so the teacher should plan to devote some time to kicking practice each class meeting.

Arm movements may now be added to the beginner's growing list of swimming skills. The dog paddle stroke is demonstrated for the students, who attempt it first while standing in the water. It is then combined with the glide. The kick is added, and the student is swimming. It is recommended that students practice with heads up and without holding the breath. As efficiency is gained in the stroke, the face may be submerged and the breath exhaled under water.

Sculling and finning may be introduced as soon as the student can propel himself through the water on his back by means of the leg kick. A careful explanation will need to accompany the demonstration because the arm movements are so distinctly different from the arm movement in the dog paddle.

Treading is the final skill to be taught in the beginning unit. After students have been shown the technique, they may be divided into pairs to assist one another in practicing.

Beginners should receive as much individual attention as possible. However, if the instructor is also directing intermediate and advanced students during the same period, his time is necessarily limited. Because beginners will need occasional rest periods, the teacher can plan to move on to the other groups during these periods.

Crawl. The intermediate swimmers will be ready to work on the crawl. This stroke requires successful coordination of the arm movement, the leg kick and breathing. It is recommended that each of these phases of the crawl be drilled upon separately before putting them together. Methods for practicing each skill are outlined below. If space permits they may be practiced simultaneously by the entire group of intermediates; otherwise, some of the students may practice on the deck of the pool while others drill in the water.

To practice the arm movement:
1. The students stand on land with the upper body bent forward and the arms hanging. The shoulders are alternately raised and lowered. Gradually the arm is lifted with the shoulder until the elbow is high. The forearm and hand are then moved forward until the arm reaches straight ahead. The hand is then pulled directly down under the shoulder, and the movement is repeated. *No rotation of the body should accompany the lifting of the arm.*
2. Standing in waist deep water, the students lean forward from the waist with the arms extended forward and practice the arm movement, either in the standing position or while walking in the water.
3. The students anchor their feet in the gutter of the pool, extend the body forward, and move the arms alternately in the stroke. If there is no place to anchor the feet, the partners may hold each other's feet.
4. In the water the arm movement can be practiced while gliding in a face float position. Keeping the eyes open during the glide will enable the swimmer to watch the placement of the hands and enable him to execute a more accurate stroke.

To practice the leg movement:
1. Students lie on the deck with the legs extended over the edge of the pool.
2. Students lie on a stool or bench.
3. Holding on to the gutter of the pool, students kick in the water.

Figure 14–3. The use of the flutter board is effective in developing correct leg movement. (Courtesy Enrico Fermi High School.)

4. The students assume a face float position and propel themselves with the kick only.

5. Flutter boards may be used and held with the arms extended; they may be relayed from group to group for practice.

To practice breathing:

1. On land inhaling and exhaling may be added to the arm movement (Drill 1 above) or to Drill 2 in the water.

2. Students bend forward to place the face in the water and rhythmically *inhale* and *exhale. The head should be turned for breathing, not lifted.*

Having practiced the three skills separately, the student is ready to put them all together. Better body balance can be had by pushing off from the side or bottom of the pool. The swimmer should be as flat in the water as possible. Music in waltz time may be played to encourage rhythmical performance of the stroke.

Backstroke. The elementary backstroke is introduced next in the intermediate unit. The movements of the arms and legs should be drilled upon separately before being coordinated into the total movement. The class may be divided into groups to practice on land or in the water at the discretion of the teacher.

To practice the leg movement:

1. The students sit on land and lean back with the upper body, supporting it with the hands or forearms.

2. Students lie on their backs in the water while holding on to the pool's gutter.

3. A floating position is assumed with arms held straight out to the sides or the hands placed on the hips.

To practice the arm movements:
1. The students go through the motion while standing on the deck.
2. In the water, one partner supports the feet of the other who executes the arm movement lying on his back.

To practice breathing:
1. The proper timing of the inhalation and exhalation is added to any of the above drills on land or in the water.

The students are now ready to put the skills of the stroke together in one coordinated movement. They should be instructed to push off on their backs with their feet together and their arms at their sides. For some students, practice in coordinating all the movements on land may be necessary.

Sidestroke. The sidestroke should be introduced with some explanation of its value as a rest stroke and in lifesaving accompanied by appropriate demonstration. Some land drills as well as practice in the water on the arm and leg movements will be necessary before the swimmers attempt the whole stroke.

To practice the leg movement:
1. Students lie across a bench or stool.
2. Students lie on the deck with or without the legs extended over the edge of the pool.
3. While holding on to the side of the pool, students turn on the side for the kick.
4. After pushing off, students practice leg movement only while maintaining side balance.

To practice the arm movements:
1. Students stand on land while executing the movements.
2. Students stand in neck-deep water and practice by leaning to the side.
3. After pushing off, students use the arm movements only while maintaining side balance.

To practice breathing:
1. Proper breath control may be practiced in connection with any of the above drills on land or in the water.

The teacher should stress the importance of the glide as part of the sidestroke. Those students who find it difficult to maintain balance while on the side in the water should be given additional opportunities to work on the glide by pushing off from the side. While the students first put the movements together for a coordinated execution of the sidestroke, they will find it helpful to do it to a count of *1-2-3-glide* by the teacher. The teacher may draw out the last count to force the students to hold the glide longer than they are likely to do when practicing on their own.

Surface diving and underwater swimming conclude the intermediate unit described here. The teacher should explain and demonstrate

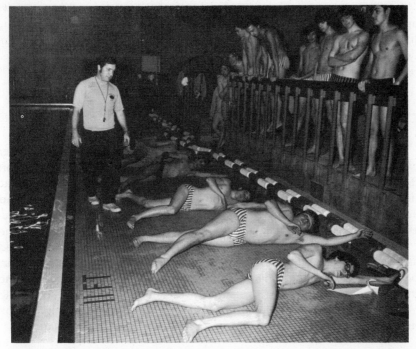

Figure 14–4. The leg movement for the sidestroke may be practiced on the deck of the pool. (Courtesy Enrico Fermi High School.)

the techniques and then let the students practice in groups of two, with one helping and criticizing while the other performs. Students who are having difficulty must receive individual help from the teacher or advanced students who are assisting the teacher.

Advanced students may be taught the breaststroke and dolphin. Because these are largely variations of the basic strokes in which these students will already be proficient, nothing more will be required than a demonstration and explanation of the techniques. However, land drills may be helpful in correcting form faults.

Lifesaving may be introduced into the unit for advanced swimmers because of its importance to all swimmers. Acquiring skills in lifesaving also has strong motivation value. Before lifesaving instruction begins, the student should be able to perform the following:

1. Make a shallow dive in good form.
2. Swim a quarter mile without resting.
3. Keep afloat for ten minutes by floating, sculling, finning or treading.
4. Swim either the crawl or trudgeon and the breaststroke.
5. Swim on the back using the legs alone for 20 yards.
6. Make a surface dive.
7. Swim a short distance under water.

Class instruction may be divided into these areas: the take-off, approach, blocking and parrying the victim's hold, carrying a victim, lifting from the water, and artificial respiration. The teacher should devote some time to discussing the circumstances in which drownings occur and what procedure to follow in each situation.

EVALUATION

The teacher can construct either a subjective or objective test to evaluate the understanding and insight into the skills which the students have attained. The test could include questions on the historical development of swimming and the safety precautions essential to the activity as well as knowledge of the competitive events and related events, such as water polo.

Speed in swimming the strokes may be clocked with a stop watch as one measurement of skill in the specific strokes. To evaluate general performance in swimming the progressive swimming skills tests of the American Red Cross are highly recommended.[2] The AAHPER Youth Fitness Test includes three aquatic tests to appraise the level of fundamental ability of the student to handle himself in the water.[3]

SELECTED VISUAL AIDS

Advanced Swimming. Associated Films.
Aquatics Technique Charts. Division for Girls' and Women's Sports, AAHPER.
Elementary Tactics of Life Saving. Motion Picture Bureau.
Fundamentals of Creative Swimming. Colburn Film.
Life Saving and Water Safety. All American Productions.
Swimming. Athletic Institute.
Swimming for Beginners. Gallagher Film Service.
Swimming Instruction Series. United World Films.

PUBLISHED SKILL TESTS

AAHPER: *Youth Fitness Test Manual.* Washington, D.C.
Hewitt, Jack E.: Achievement scales for high school swimming. *Research Quarterly,* XX, No. 2, May, 1949, p. 170.

SUGGESTED READINGS

AAHPER: *Aquatics.* Washington, D.C., Division for Girls' and Women's Sports. Published biennially.

---

[2] These tests may be obtained from the National Office in Washington, D.C.
[3] AAHPER: *Youth Fitness Test Manual.* Washington, D.C.

American Red Cross: *Instructor's Manual, Swimming and Diving Courses.* Washington, D.C., Latest edition.

Armbruster, D. A., et al.: *Swimming and Diving.* 6th ed. St. Louis, The C. V. Mosby Co., 1973.

Councilman, James E.: *The Science of Swimming.* Englewood Cliffs, New Jersey, Prentice-Hall, Inc., 1967.

Gabrielsen, M. Alexander, et al.: *Aquatics Handbooks.* 2nd ed., Englewood Cliffs, New Jersey, Prentice-Hall, Inc., 1968.

Midtlyng, J.: *Swimming.* Philadelphia, W. B. Saunders Co., 1974.

DIVING

Learning to enter the water head first requires courage even on the part of students who have become accustomed to water and are fairly proficient in the skills of swimming. For this reason it is recommended that some of the early fundamentals be introduced as soon as the beginning swimmer is past the orientation stage. Confidence can then be built up gradually through the learning stages to the more difficult dives.

COURSE CONTENT

The skills basic to diving and the dives which are taught at each level of the swimmer's progress are divided into units below:

Unit for beginners	Unit for intermediates	Unit for advanced students
Coming to the surface	Sitting dive	Running front jackknife
Breath control	Kneeling dive	Back dive
Form	Dive from one leg	Backward somersault
Dive standing in shallow water	Dive from both feet	Back jackknife
	Standing dive from side of pool	Half twist
	Standing dive from board	Half gainer
	Running front dive or swan dive	Running forward somerault

CLASS ORGANIZATION

When using the command-response form of the direct method, an effective way in which to organize the class for instruction in diving is to give instruction and demonstration to the entire group while they are seated around the edge of the pool. If the dives which are being taught involve practice from the side of the pool, the students will be in place to practice as soon as the teacher gives the signal. For a very large group it may be beneficial to organize the class into couples who will help each other with the dive.

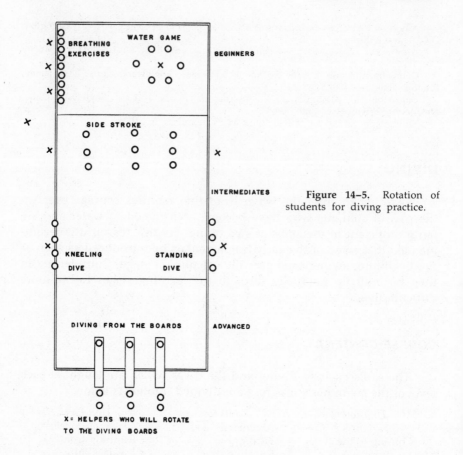

Figure 14–5. Rotation of students for diving practice.

Dives from the board may be practiced in line formation. If there are so many students that the line will be unduly long and will force students to stand around for long periods before their turn arrives, some may be assigned to practice swimming skills or to assist the beginners and intermediates. After a specified time they trade positions with those practicing on the board.

TEACHING PROCEDURES

The beginner may become acquainted with diving by doing a dive from a standing position in shallow water. He does this by extending the arms over the head with the thumbs locked together, bending forward from the hips, and pushing off from the bottom. In addition to emphasizing good form in executing this dive, the teacher must explain breath control during the dive and the way in which the swimmer comes to the surface by lifting the head and thrusting the hands upward.

When the student can accomplish these things satisfactorily in the water, he is ready to try a sitting dive. From this the student progresses through the series of dives, each slightly more difficult from the previous one, until he is diving from the standing position on the side of the pool (Fig. 14–6). To aid the student in acquiring the push-up for the standing dive these two exercises are helpful:

1. The student practices an easy spring jump in place. The arm movement may be added later.

2. The student places his hands at shoulder height on the wall and practices an easy spring jump in place.

Having acquired the skills of diving from a stationary take-off, the student is ready to dive from the springboard. Some instruction on the use of the board to achieve height and balance is necessary as is instruction on essential safety measures in the use of the board. To practice attaining balance on the board, the student jumps up and down on the diving end of the board about 4 inches from the end. The arm movement is coordinated with the push from the feet. The objective of the exercise should be balance. Later the same exercise may be used to attain height. When the diver has acquired some height in this jumping exercise on the board, he may add jumping into the water feet first and then entering the water head first as the climax to the jump.

The running dives require an approach of at least three steps and

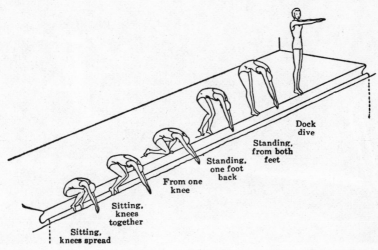

Figure 14–6. Diving progression. (Ainsworth, et al.: *Individual Sports for Women*, 4th ed.)

a jump or hurdle. The diver should pace out the steps from the end of the board and start from this place each time when making the dive. Practice in the approach can be done off the board before it is tried on the board. The teacher should watch each diver for such common faults as overthrowing the legs, not lifting the arms well, and going out too far.

The teaching procedure for each of the advanced dives is outlined here for quick reference. The teacher should explain and demonstrate each dive, drill the divers in land practice, and then watch their performance on the board for correction and improvement.

Running front jackknife.   Land practice consists of standing erect with the knees straight and bending the upper body forward and reaching down with the hands until they touch the instep. The head is held up.

Back dive.   Diving with the back to the water may be practiced first from the edge of the pool. On the board the diver may be supported by a helper at the hips until the upper body is pointing down over the water. Then the support is removed and the diver drops into the water.

Backward somersault.   The somersault in diving is similar to the somersault used in tumbling. To gain confidence and feeling for correct form on the board, this tumbling stunt may be used as a land drill on a mat. The student assumes a squat position, grasps the front of the legs and sits back, pulls the knees up to the chin, and rolls over in a backward somersault.

Figure 14–7. The back dive is attempted after first practicing jumping up and back from the board. (Courtesy Enrico Fermi High School.)

Back jackknife. The same land drill used for the front jackknife may be given for this dive. On the board, the diver may first practice jumping up and back from the board before attempting the full back jackknife.

Half twist. To get the feel of the movements of the arms and upper trunk in the twist, the twist may be practiced on land by extending the arms over the head and lowering the right arm and turning the head to the right (for a right twist).

Half gainer. Preliminary land practice for this dive consists of having the student do the following: With the weight on one foot, swing the other leg forward and upward with the knee straight. At the same time bend back from the hips and move the arms up and back over the head. Alternate in the use of the legs. A one-foot take-off employing this drill may be used for early practice from the board. With the weight on one foot the diver jumps out over the water and proceeds as described above to enter the water head first. When the diver is ready to use both feet in the take-off, the teacher may hold a cane pole out in front of the diver for him to aim at with his feet.

Running forward somersault. Land drill for the forward somersault consists of practicing the forward roll on a mat. From a squat position the student grasps the front of the legs with the arms, brings the chin well in and the head forward, and rolls forward. Next, the diver practices rolling in this manner from the side of the pool into the water. Finally, it is combined with a running approach on the board.

EVALUATION

A subjective evaluation of diving skills may be based upon these elements of good diving form:

1. The approach starts at least four steps back from the end of the board.
2. In the last step the spring is made off the back leg while the forward leg is bent sharply at the knee and both feet are brought together as they come down near the end of the board.
3. The take-off from the board is timed with the spring of the board.
4. The angle of the body is nearly straight at the moment of take-off from the board (in the somersault there will be a slightly forward lean at take-off).
5. As the body leaves the board, the arms are swung forward and upward.
6. The height of the flight is sufficient to allow for a straight entry into the water.
7. The entry into the water is near the end of the board.

Knowledge testing could include items related to types of competitive dives, scoring, elements of proper form and conduct of diving contests.

SELECTED VISUAL AIDS

Diving Fundamentals. Association Films.
Diving-Springboard Techniques. Coronet Instructional Films.
How to Improve Your Diving. Athletic Institute.
The Sport of Diving. United World Films.

PUBLISHED SKILL TESTS

Bennett, L. M.: Diving ability on the spring board. *Research Quarterly,* XIII, no. 1, March, 1942, p. 109.

DISCUSSION QUESTIONS

1. What is the best division of a physical education class for swimming instruction?
2. List and discuss the safety regulations that must be observed in most class swimming situations.
3. Discuss ways to help beginners overcome their fear of the water.
4. What are the values of land drills and how may they be used?
5. Describe the diving progression for teaching beginning divers.

THINGS TO DO

1. Make a file of water games to use with beginning swimmers.
2. List the organizational steps necessary to hold an intersquad swimming meet within a class.
3. Read the American Red Cross swimming skill tests and discuss in class their use in evaluating swimming skills.
4. List the progression in teaching a beginner the dive from the dock.
5. Develop procedures for teaching a specific skill in swimming using some other form than the command-response form.

SUGGESTED READINGS

AAHPER: *Aquatics.* Washington, D.C., Division for Girls' and Women's Sports. Published biennially.

Armbruster, D. A., et al.: *Swimming and Diving.* 6th ed. St. Louis, The C. V. Mosby Company, 1973.

Broer, Marion: *Individual Sports for Women.* 5th ed. Philadelphia, W. B. Saunders Co., 1971.

Fait, Hollis, et al.: *A Manual of Physical Education Activities.* 2nd ed. Philadelphia, W. B. Saunders Co., 1961.

Fairbanks, Anne R.: *Teaching Springboard Diving.* Englewood Cliffs, N.J., Prentice-Hall, Inc., 1963.

Midtlyng, Joanna: *Swimming.* Philadelphia, W. B. Saunders Co., 1974.

Vannier, Maryhelen, and Poindexter, Hally Beth: *Individual and Team Sports for Girls and Women.* 3rd ed. Philadelphia, W. B. Saunders Co., 1974.

CHAPTER FIFTEEN

TEAM SPORTS

The team sports form an important and vital core of the secondary school physical education curriculum. It is acknowledged that the team sports contribute to the health and fitness of youth through big muscle activity in a way that cannot be duplicated in other sports and games. To engage in the play of any of them, students must learn not only the skills of the game but how to be a *member of a team* and all the desirable social interactions implied in that phrase.

The team sports most frequently offered at the secondary school level are basketball, field hockey, soccer, softball and baseball, speedball, touch football and volleyball. The discussions of these team sports in the paragraphs below are uniformly designed to present ideas and suggestions for (1) course content, (2) class organization, (3) teaching procedures and (4) evaluation. Because of space limitations, no attempt has been made to include in each section all of the varied choices and possibilities open to the teacher. Rather the aim has been to present varied examples to illustrate what may be included in the teaching unit and how it may be taught. It should be understood that the specific class organizational procedures and teaching methods described for one sport are applicable to other sports as well.

BASKETBALL

Until recently girls' and boys' basketball were played with distinctly different rules. However, today the two sets of rules do not vary to any great extent, and the procedures for teaching both games are the same.

The floor on which the basketball court is laid out is a costly piece of equipment and requires a considerable amount of care if it is to be kept in good condition for playing. An attitude of pride in the floor's appearance and a desire to protect it should be developed in students through skillful direction by the teacher whenever the opportunity presents itself.

COURSE CONTENT

Suggested topics to be introduced at the beginning and advanced levels are:

Unit for beginners	Unit for advanced students
History	Review of courtesies
Safety and courtesies	Rules and regulations
Catching	Review of fundamental skills
Passing:	Variations of fundamental skills
Two-hand chest pass	Advanced skills:
Overhand pass	Pivot shot
Bounce pass	Hook pass
Two-hand underhand pass	Backward pass
Dribbling	Screening
Shooting:	Playing the backboard
Two-hand set shot	Advanced defense play
One-hand push shot	Strategy and team tactics
Lay-up shot	Tournament play
Underhand foul shooting	Officiating
Pivoting, jumping, feinting,	Evaluation
dodging	
Defense play	
Basic rules	
Strategy	
Spectatorship	
Evaluation	

CLASS ORGANIZATION

Basketball instruction characteristically includes drills to practice specific skills and playing the game to utilize the skills in response to the demands of the situation. Drills by their very nature dictate that the command-response form of the direct teaching method be used. Four or five different drills can be organized and carried on during a class period on a basketball court of regulation size. Ten to twelve players can be accommodated in each drill.

If basketball hoops can be placed along the two long sides of the gymnasium, the floor space can be divided into several small playing courts to make possible greater participation in team play. If the available baskets are limited to one at each end of the court, more students can be accommodated if two teams of three to four players are assigned to each half of the court, with both teams using the same basket. If possible, students should be allowed to play the entire court with those not playing engaged in drill in free areas, if space permits, or watching and evaluating the game or certain players. The teacher must be careful to rotate the players often enough so that all class members have an opportunity to play a game and to work in different positions. The teacher must also plan to make the watching of the game an educational experience through discussion and evaluation of the game.

TEACHING PROCEDURES

Interest in playing basketball will usually be high among students of both sexes. However, some students frequently need to be motivated to learn the skills which will improve their playing ability and increase their pleasure from the game. A discussion of interscholastic play and prominent players on the local and national sport scene will often arouse interest in skill development. Such a discussion can often be directed to highlight safety precautions and the courtesies required of players and spectators. Since basketball spectators are notoriously undisciplined and discourteous, the teacher should take every opportunity he can to stress proper conduct for spectators.

Because many of the skills are effectively taught through drills, the command-response form is commonly utilized in basketball instruction. The procedures discussed below are examples of the use of this form.

Ball handling is an important factor in developing skills in basketball. Drill in ball handling is as essential for the advanced player as for

Figure 15–1. Interest in playing basketball is high among most high school students of both sexes. However, students frequently need to be motivated to learn the skills which will improve their playing ability. (Courtesy of the Physical Education Department, Los Angeles Public Schools.)

the beginner, but there is a distinction in the degree of complexity of the drills.

Catching should be the first skill of ball handling to be introduced to beginners. It is also worthwhile to review catching skills with those who have had basketball experience because in so many instances the skills have been learned improperly. Before setting up drill work on catching, the techniques should be demonstrated, with special emphasis placed upon fingertip control. During this demonstration some throwing techniques may be introduced since throwing is an integral part of any catching drill. The two-hand chest pass may well be introduced first. For watching the demonstration the class may be formed into two lines facing each other, as this will put the students in formation for preliminary attempts at passing and catching under the supervision of the teacher. When the students are ready to drill, no time will be lost getting into formation.

The drill itself consists of passing the ball back and forth down the lines. It is wise, where the supply of balls permits, to have one ball to every eight to ten students in order to avoid much of the confusion which results from attempting to keep several balls going in a long line. As skills improve, the distance between the lines should be increased. This drill will not sustain interest for long periods of time and should, therefore, be used only for short durations. A variation of the drill includes moving while passing. The first player in Line 1 passes to the first player in Line 2 (Fig. 15-2) who passes to the next player in Line 1 and so on through the lines. After each player has passed the ball, he assumes a position in the opposite line. Play continues in this manner until all the players have changed sides.

Dribbling may be the next skill introduced to the class. The skill should be thoroughly explained and demonstrated, with repeated emphasis on the use of the fingers. A simple preliminary drill in dribbling can be had by forming several lines of equal length at one end of the gymnasium. The first person in each line dribbles the length of the gymnasium and back to the starting position where the

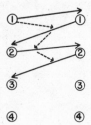

Figure 15-2. Passing and moving drill.

→ PATH OF PLAYER
------→ PATH OF BALL

ball is handed to the next in line. The dribbler then takes his place at the rear of his line. After several trial runs, the students will be ready to compete against each other to determine which line can execute the drill in the shortest time.

A more intricate dribbling drill will be enjoyed by the class after they have become more proficient in dribbling. Chairs or Indian clubs are placed in a line on the floor, with intervals of 5 feet between them. The dribbler is obligated to dribble back and forth between the obstacles. The competitive element can be introduced by having several lines of students run against each other to complete the drill in the shortest possible time.

Most students enjoy shooting at the basket more than any other activity in basketball. Shooting drills may be devised to include practice in dribbling, pivoting, passing, feinting, dodging and recovery from the backboard. Figure 15–3 illustrates some recommended drills for both boys and girls.

The whole class may be assigned to practice one skill either as one large group and/or as several small groups, depending upon the available space and class size; or the class may be divided into groups practicing different skills. The latter plan is especially desirable when a wide range of basketball abilities is evident in the class, for the highly skilled can practice more advanced techniques in groups by themselves while those who need more practice on the basic skills can drill in homogeneous groups.

The easiest method for dividing the class according to abilities is the Shuttle Run Test. Since testing is time-consuming it is important that students be informed of the ways in which it will benefit them, for in this way the testing program takes on real significance for the learner.

Although drills are valuable teaching aids, it is in playing the game itself that the greatest learning occurs, for it is in participation as a team member that the skills are brought together into a functioning unit and the necessity for team strategy makes itself felt. Because interest is high and the desire to succeed as a team member is great, this part of the instructional unit requires less motivation than practicing drills.

The teacher should not make the grave error of thinking that after *having brought his students to the point of actual game participation, he can relax his vigil for errors and retire to the sidelines to enjoy the game.* He must be ever alert to form, tactics and attitudes demonstrated by the class in play. Sometimes he may wish to stop the game and make an explanation to the entire group; at other times he may give instructions to a single player who needs individual advice or correction.

Advanced students may be taught the variations of the funda-

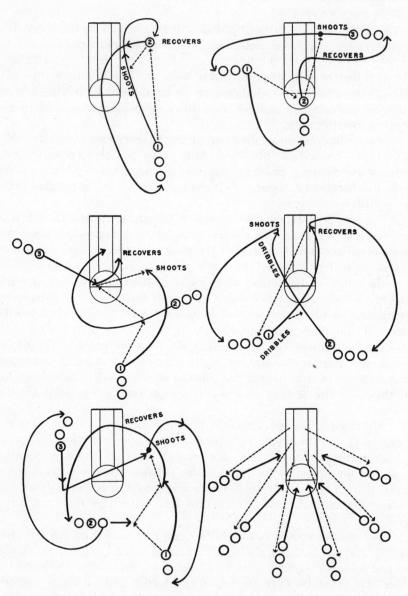

Figure 15–3. Shooting drills. → = Path of play; ⋯→ = path of ball; *1* passes to *2*; *2* passes to *3*; *3* shoots, *1* goes to end of line *2*; *2* to line *3*; and *3* to line *1*.

mental skills and the more complicated skills of passing, shooting, screening and playing the backboard. The same types of drills as were used in perfecting the beginning skills may be used for drilling on these advanced techniques, with the more complex skill substituted for the basic one. Advanced strategy may be taught with the aid of diagrams or other visual aids.

Most of the instructional unit for advanced players should be spent playing the game. Some students may be used as officials in order to involve the entire class in active participation, for learning to officiate gives students greater insight into the game and makes them more appreciative spectators.

EVALUATION

General knowledge may be tested by means of written tests containing questions on the history, sport courtesies, care of facilities, safety precautions, strategy and spectatorship. The teacher may wish to make a subjective evaluation of each student's playing ability as demonstrated during a game. Tests may also be given on each or all of the fundamentals of the game. For example, skill in shooting may be measured by the number of baskets the student can make in a given period of time. Other common skill tests include foul shooting accuracy, timed dribbling around obstacles, accuracy passing and field goal accuracy.

SELECTED VISUAL AIDS

Ball-Handling in Basketball. Encyclopaedia Britannica Films, Inc.
Basketball Coaching Kit (24″ × 36″ steel playing court and magnetic pieces). The Program Aids Co., Inc., 550 Fifth Avenue, New York.
Basketball Is Fun. Baily Films, Inc.
Girls' Basketball for Beginners. Paul Burnford, Film Production.
How To Improve Your Basketball (girls and boys). Athletic Institute.
Illustrated Sports Charts (Packet of 11″ × 17″ wall charts). University of Colorado Book Store, Boulder, Colo.
Shooting in Basketball. Encyclopaedia Britannica Films, Inc.

PUBLISHED SKILL TESTS

AAHPER: *Skills Test Manual Basketball for Boys.*
AAHPER: *Skills Test Manual Basketball for Girls.*
Lehsten, N.: A measure of basketball skills in high school boys. *The Physical Educator,* V, No. 4, December, 1948, p. 103.
Voltmer, E. F., and Watts, T.: A rating scale of player performance in basketball. *Journal of Health and Physical Education,* February, 1940, p. 94.

SUGGESTED READINGS

AAHPER: *Official Basketball Guide; Selected Basketball Articles.* Washington, D.C., Division for Girls' and Women's Sports. Current edition.

Barnes, Mildred J.: *Women's Basketball.* Boston, Allyn and Bacon, Inc., 1972.

Cousy, Bob and Power, Frank Jr.: *Basketball.* Boston, Allyn and Bacon, Inc., 1970.

Ebert, Frances H., and Cheatum, Billye Ann: *Basketball—Five Player.* Philadelphia, W. B. Saunders Co., 1972.

Hanson, Dale: *Basketball.* Englewood Cliffs, N.J., Prentice-Hall, Inc., 1972.

National Federation of State High School Athletic Associations: *Official Basketball Rules.* Chicago, Published annually.

FIELD HOCKEY

Field hockey is played almost exclusively by girls now, but at one time it was played only by boys. The game is still tremendously popular with boys in many foreign countries, from which the conclusion might be drawn that American boys would enjoy the sport if they were introduced to it in their physical education classes.

Each student should wear shin guards when playing hockey. As an additional safety measure, the goalkeeper should be provided with special protectors for the chest and the instep. The sticks should be checked each time before use for splinters and possible breaks. It will be necessary for team members to wear some kind of identification in the form of jerseys or "pinnies."

COURSE CONTENT

The teaching of field hockey to either boys or girls may be organized into lessons as suggested in the units below.

Unit for beginners	*Unit for advanced students*
History	Review of fundamentals and rules
Safety and courtesies	Advanced skills:
Dribble	Scoop
Carrying position of stick	Left job
Passing:	Right cut
Push pass	Right hand lunge
Drive	Advanced strategy
Flick	Officiating
Tacklings:	Evaluation
Left hand lunge	
Circular tackle	
Straight tackle	
Goalkeeping	
Fielding	
Roll-in	
Bully	
Rules and regulations	
Strategy	
Evaluation	

CLASS ORGANIZATION

The class may be organized into squads of ten to twelve on the basis of ability for practice on the hockey skills. Some teachers recommend that the assignment to a squad be made permanent for the duration of the hockey unit, for this enables the class to progress smoothly from watching a demonstration or receiving instruction to practicing the skill without the delay necessitated by forming new drill squads each time. However, the teacher should not hesitate to regroup when it is evident that new groupings on the basis of ability will work to the greater advantage of all.

A line or circle formation (whichever provides greater visibility to the students) may be used to show the class a specific skill. On rainy days the class may drill inside, employing the same formations used outdoors. Covering the ball with tape will slow down its action suitably for inside use. Class meetings which must be held inside may also be used to advantage for discussions of rules and strategy or for viewing many of the splendid visual aids now available in this sport. Inside classwork must be planned just as carefully as outside work.

TEACHING PROCEDURES

An informal short but interestingly presented discussion of the historical development of field hockey may be used to introduce the unit. In the unit for beginners a brief description of the nature of the game and the safety precautions and courtesies common to the game should also be given. Magnetized boards on which disks representing each player can be moved are excellent for teaching player's duties and team positions. The orientation period should be limited to those items of information which are needed for understanding what field hockey is all about; they can be re-emphasized and enlarged upon as the occasion arises in the course of the unit. The command-response form of direct teaching is frequently employed in the instruction of field hockey. Examples of its use are described below.

Usually the first skill to which beginners are introduced is the dribble. The technique is demonstrated and explained, and then the class tries to dribble slowly in a straight line. As they begin to show some progress in this, the students are directed to increase the speed. To insure that they are dribbling in a straight line, each squad of students may be assigned to dribble one behind the other along one of the lines which marks the field. The teacher should watch the class closely for any deviations from good form.

When the class is proficient enough to attempt dribbling around objects, an obstacle drill may be set up. Indian clubs or similar obstacles are placed in a column on the field about 5 feet apart. The players form a line facing the first obstacle and 10 feet from it. The first person in the line dribbles in and out between the obstacles and returns to the starting position to give the ball to the next in line before moving to the rear of the line. This drill may be used for competition between the squads to determine which one can complete the drill in the shortest time.

At the next lesson the class may be instructed in carrying the stick properly. A brief part of the class period should be devoted to practice in running while carrying the stick and in bringing the stick into action from this position. The teacher will have ample opportunity to check on students as they drill and play.

Beginners may be taught the push pass, drive and flick; the scoop may be held in reserve for advanced students. These passes should be carefully demonstrated and thoroughly explained. An introductory drill on any of the passes may be had by having each squad line up with one of the members about 10 feet in front of the squad (Fig. 15–4). Player 1 directs the pass toward each one in the row in turn. When the activity has been completed, Player 1 goes to the end of the line and the first person at the head of the line assumes the position of Player 1.

To combine any one of the strokes with dribbling, a drill may be set up as follows: Each squad forms a line facing a marker 10 to 15 feet away. The first person in the line dribbles to the marker, turns, and passes to the next player in the line before going to the end of the line. The drill may be used to practice only the pass specified by the teacher, or it may be used to give practice on all the passes by instructing the students to use any pass he wishes.

The tackles taught to beginners should include the left hand lunge, the circular tackle and the straight tackle. The left jab, right cut and right hand lunge may wait until the advanced unit. The drill formations shown in Figure 15–5 are effective for practicing the skills involved in tackling.

As soon as their skills allow, the students should be permitted to play a game. In preparation for this, some time must be devoted to the duties and techniques of goalkeeping, the skills of fielding, the procedures in the roll-in and the bully, and the general outline of defensive

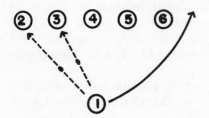

Figure 15–4. Introductory drill for passes.

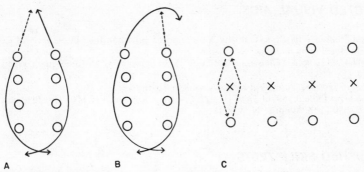

Figure 15–5. Formations for practicing tackles. *A,* Left hand lunge; *B,* circular tackle; *C,* straight tackle.

and offensive strategy. Giving the students a chance to play the game provides a change from constant practicing and has the additional education value of pointing up those skills on which the students need more practice.

For actual playing, the class may be divided into as many teams as the field will accommodate. Extra students after the teams have been chosen can be assigned to drill in the areas around the playing fields. The teacher must work these students in as substitutes on the teams whenever possible so that all will have equal opportunity to play. The team members should also interchange positions frequently so that everyone will have a chance to play every position.

Because of their greater skills, advanced players can spend a greater portion of the unit in actual play. Officiating should be introduced so that any extra students can participate as officials for the games. These students should change with the players often enough to give everyone an opportunity to work both as an official and as a player.

EVALUATION

An objective test may be used to measure the students' knowledge of rules, courtesies, strategy and other factual material presented in the unit. An obstacle course which requires the use of several different field hockey skills may be designed by the teacher as a skills test. An illustration of such an obstacle course may be found in the first reference under *Published Skill Tests.* Specific skill tests for dribbling ability, passing accuracy and shooting speed and accuracy can also be devised.

SELECTED VISUAL AIDS

Field Hockey Filmstrips. Dorothy Yonesch and Jean Landis, State Teachers College, West Chester, Pennsylvania.
Field Hockey Rules Filmstrips. Teaching Aids Service, 31 Union Square West, New York, N.Y. 10003
How to Improve Your Field Hockey. Athletic Institute.
Magnetic Bulletin Board Field Hockey Coaching Kit. No. PM-600. The Program Aids Co., Inc., 550 Fifth Avenue, New York.

PUBLISHED SKILL TESTS

Fait, Hollis F., et al.: *A Manual of Physical Education Activities.* 3rd ed. Philadelphia, W. B. Saunders Co., 1967.
Friedel, Jean: The development of a field hockey skill test for high school girls. *Microcard,* University of Oregon, 1956.

SUGGESTED READINGS

AAHPER: *Field Hockey, Official Guide.* Washington, D.C., Division for Girls' and Women's Sports. Current edition.
Fait, Hollis F., et al.: *A Manual of Physical Education Activities.* 3rd ed. Philadelphia, W. B. Saunders Co., 1967.
Haussermann, Caroline: *Field Hockey.* Boston, Allyn and Bacon, Inc., 1973.
Meyer, Margaret, and Schwarz, Marguerite: *Team Sports for Girls and Women.* 4th ed. Philadelphia, W. B. Saunders Co., 1963.
Poindexter, Hally Beth, and Muskier, Carol: *Coaching Competitive Team Sports for Girls and Women.* Philadelphia, W. B. Saunders Co., 1973.
Vannier, Maryhelen, and Poindexter, Hally Beth: *Individual and Team Sports for Girls and Women.* 3rd ed. Philadelphia, W. B. Saunders Co., 1974.

Periodicals
The Eagle. Official Publication of the United States Field Hockey Association, 30 Lamont Avenue, Glenolden, Pa.

SOCCER

Soccer is a game which for unexplained reasons has attained greater popularity in some sections of the country than in others, but it deserves significant attention in the physical education programs of both boys and girls regardless of locality. It requires the use of the head, body and feet as in no other game with the exception of speedball in which these skills were adapted from soccer.

The rules by which girls play differ somewhat from boys' rules. The chief difference is the rule against body contact. Because this rule tends to reduce the number of injuries, it is often used in boys' physical education classes, particularly where there is a wide range of playing abilities. While it is not absolutely essential that shin guards be worn by boys in physical education classes, it is recommended that they do so as a safety measure.

COURSE CONTENT

Suggested topics for the units in soccer include:

Unit for beginners	*Unit for advanced students*
History	Review of courtesies, safety and
Safety and courtesies	rules
Dribbling	Review of fundamental skills
Kicking:	Variations of body trapping:
Inside of foot	Leg trapping
Outside of foot	Heading
Top of instep	Kicking
Heel	Strategy
Toe	Attacking and evading
Trapping:	Officiating
Inside of one leg	Evaluation
Inside of both legs	
Front of both legs	
Sole of foot	
Heel	
Blocking or body trapping	
Heading	
Tackling:	
Front	
Side	
Hook	
Split	
Punting	
Rules and regulations	
Strategy	
Evaluation	

CLASS ORGANIZATION

The suggestions that follow for organizing a class for teaching soccer are based on the command-response form of the direct method. The class should practice each new soccer skill upon the completion of its demonstration and explanation. Initial drills should consist almost entirely of having each student handle the ball as required by the skill, although some of the drills may use kicking the ball against the wall for indoor practice. Later, competitive games using the drills can be used to motivate interest in developing certain skills. When the class demonstrates sufficient skill, lead-up games can be introduced and a part of the class period devoted to playing a regular game.

When organizing the class for drills the groups should be kept as small as the supply of balls will permit. Small groups afford each student greater experience in learning to control the ball; moreover, the drill can move along more rapidly and interest be maintained over a longer period. Early in the instructional period, before students

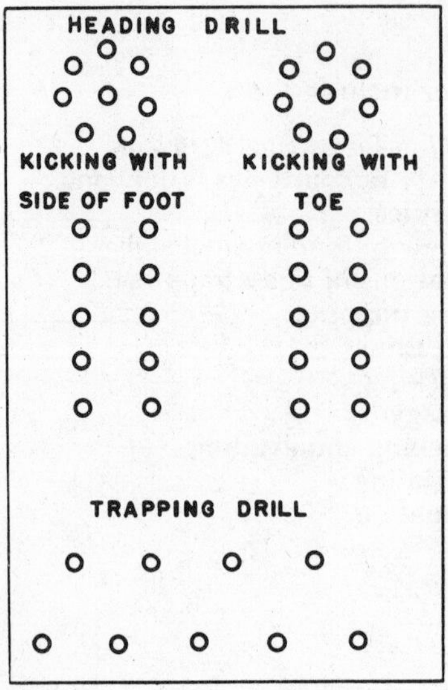

Figure 15–6. Class organization for practicing soccer skills.

have acquired several different skills, it will be necessary to have each drill group practicing on the same skill. As the repertoire of skills increases, the groups may be assigned to practice different drills. Figure 15–6 shows a possible division of the class for drilling on different skills. This type of practice session is especially useful in providing additional practice on specific individual weaknesses.

A student gains greater insight into the game if he is assigned to play different positions on the team. It must be pointed out, however, that in rotating positions frequently he is less likely to develop the skills to a high level of proficiency. The teacher must try to reach a compromise on the basis of what will benefit the student and class most.

Rainy days may be used to advantage for discussion of rules and strategy. Interest and variety may be achieved by films and chalkboard talks. Drills on the gymnasium floor may be used to provide a workout for part of the period. Dribbling, heading, tackling, charging and kicking can all be practiced inside. Some of the lead-up games may also be played, depending upon the space available.

TEACHING PROCEDURES

If the game of soccer is being introduced for the first time in a locality where it is virtually unknown, the presentation of a good action-packed movie is suggested to develop some understanding and appreciation of the nature of the game. A discussion of the history of soccer, in which its relationship to football is emphasized, may also be included in the orientation. Safety measures, the importance of warming up, and the game courtesies should be stressed.

The teaching of kicking should progress from the inside of the foot through outside of foot, top of instep, heel and toe. Using the command-response form of direct teaching, the instructor demonstrates each skill to the class; this is followed by group practice of the kick in a stationary position. The teacher must watch each student to correct form faults during these preliminary trials.

The class may be lined up with from five to six players to a line for practicing the various kicks from a stationary position. The lines may face each other for kicks with the top of the instep and the toe, but for kicks with the heel one line must turn its backs to the other line. Students form into double columns for kicks with the inside or outside of the foot. A circle formation may also be employed for practicing kicking. Players are spaced around in a circle at 10 foot intervals, and the ball is passed around the circle. The passes are made clockwise around the circle when kicking with the inside of the right foot or the outside of the left foot and counterclockwise when using the inside of the left foot or the outside of the right foot.

The recommended teaching progression of trapping skills is: with the inside of one leg, with the inside of both legs, with the front of both legs, with the sole of the foot, and with the heel. After the class has watched the demonstration of each trap, they should attempt this skill on a slowly moving ball. As skill increases, the trap should be practiced, followed by a kick and by a dribble. Practice should also include the trap on a fast moving ball.

For preliminary drills in trapping, the class may be divided into groups which form two lines facing each other about 10 feet apart at staggered intervals (Fig. 15–7). The first player in Line 1 passes to the first person in Line 2 who traps the ball and then passes to the next person in Line 1. A slightly more difficult drill in trapping requires a shuttle formation. Students line up behind two people who face each other 15 feet apart. The first person in Line 1 passes to the first person in Line 2 who immediately traps the ball and passes to the second person in Line 1. As each player makes the pass, he goes immediately to the rear of the opposite line. This drill may be used as a contest to

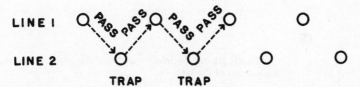

Figure 15–7. Staggered interval formation for passing and trapping drill.

determine which of several groups can complete the drill in the shortest possible time.

For a lead-up game employing trapping skills the students, standing 4 feet apart, form a circle with one player in the center. The center player attempts to kick the ball out of the circle while those forming the circle attempt to prevent it by trapping or blocking the ball. When the ball goes out, the player on whose right the ball passed takes the center position. Kicks must be below shoulder level to be legal.

Instruction in blocking or body trapping should include chest blocking and blocking with the thighs or abdomen. A drill in blocking may be devised from the same shuttle formation suggested for practicing trapping. The toss of the ball to the blockers may be made for the special type of block which is being practiced; for variety, the students may be allowed to toss the ball for any type of block so the blockers will not have a chance to anticipate the block.

For a slightly more difficult drill, the following one which simulates a game is useful. The class is divided into groups of three, with one member of the group standing about 10 feet away from the other two (Fig. 15–8). Number 1 tosses the ball between the two who attempt to gain control of the ball by blocking or trapping. Positions are rotated after several repetitions in each formation.

Heading the ball is introduced with a demonstration, followed by practice heading on a tossed ball. For this the class may be placed in short lines or in circles with a leader tossing the ball to each person in turn. The first practice on heading should be kept short. It is recommended that volleyballs be used in place of the harder soccer balls for heading until the techniques are well mastered.

The order in which tackling is taught should proceed from the front tackle through the side, hook and split tackles. After a tackle has been explained and demonstrated, students practice it on a rolling ball, then on a player dribbling slowly down the field and, finally, on a player dribbling at full speed.

To practice on a rolling ball, the class may be divided into units of twelve to fourteen players. The players face each other in lines 15 feet apart. The first player in Line 1 kicks the ball slowly toward the first player in the opposite line who advances to tackle the imaginary opponent in possession of the ball. He then kicks the ball toward the

Figure 15–8. Formation of three students to practice gaining control of the ball.

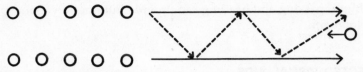

Figure 15–9. Drill formation for passing and tackling.

second person in Line 1, and in this manner the ball is played back and forth down the lines.

The formation for a drill which offers excellent practice in timing the tackling and in passing to avoid the tackle is shown in Figure 15–9. The lines are 10 feet apart. The first two players advance dribbling and passing the ball toward the player who is stationed about 15 feet out. This player attempts to tackle while the other two try to avoid being tackled. If the number of players in the formation is small, the rotation of players can wait until the end of the line; otherwise, they may be shifted after several attempted tackles.

Timing is the most important factor in successful punting; therefore, the teacher should stress the rhythmic pattern of the punt when demonstrating it for the first time. Simple line formations with the two lines facing each other 25 yards apart may be used to practice punting back and forth from stationary positions.

As the skills in punting increase, the teacher may introduce this exciting game which offers practice in punting plus blocking and trapping practice. The game is played by teams of from ten to twenty players. Two goal lines are marked on the field 50 to 75 yards apart. The ball is put into play with a punt from the goal line and must be advanced down the field by punting. A player catching a punt is permitted to advance three running strides before punting. A ball which is not caught must be blocked or trapped without the use of hands and punted from the point of contact. The team which first crosses the opponent's goal line is declared the victor.

EVALUATION

Evaluation of the student's knowledge of the factual material of soccer may be made from the results of an objective or subjective test or a combination of the two. Evaluating general team playing ability requires careful subjective analysis of each player in a game situation. The volleying test may be used as the best single measurement of soccer ability. This test consists of volleying the ball against the wall with the foot as many times as possible during a specified time period and is scored on the basis of successful tries. The player must stand 10 feet from the wall. In addition, teacher-constructed tests of shooting, dribbling, passing and heading can provide information about specific development.

SELECTED VISUAL AIDS

AAHPER: *Soccer Technique Chart*. Washington, D.C., Division for Girls' and Women's Sports.
Fundamentals of Soccer. All American Productions.
Great Game. British Information Service.
How to Improve Your Soccer. Athletic Institute.
Soccer for Girls. Coronet Instructional Films, Inc.

PUBLISHED SKILL TESTS

Fait, Hollis F., et al.: *A Manual of Physical Education Activities*. 3rd ed. Philadelphia, W. B. Saunders Co., 1967.

SUGGESTED READINGS

AAHPER: *Official Soccer—Speedball Guide*. Washington, D.C., Division for Girls' and Women's Sports. Current edition.
Bailey, C. Ian, and Teller, Francis: *Soccer*. Philadelphia, W. B. Saunders Co., 1970.
Goldman, Howard: *Soccer*. Boston, Allyn and Bacon, Inc., 1969.
Meyer, Margaret, and Schwarz, Marguerite: *Team Sports for Girls and Women*. 4th ed. Philadelphia, W. B. Saunders Co., 1963.
Moore, A. C., and Schmid, M. R.: *Soccer Anthology*. Chiefland, Fla., Citizens Publishing Co., 1965.
Nelson, Richard: *Soccer*. Dubuque, Iowa, William C. Brown Co., 1966.
Vannier, Maryhelen, and Poindexter, Hally Beth: *Individual and Team Sports for Girls and Women*. 3rd ed. Philadelphia, W. B. Saunders Co., 1974.

SOFTBALL AND BASEBALL

Because softball was patterned after baseball the games are very much alike. The softball diamond is smaller and a game consists of seven innings as compared to nine in baseball. A smaller, lighter bat and a larger ball are used in softball. The ball is pitched with a different type of delivery, and the rule regarding base running differs, but these are the major differences in playing regulations.

In secondary schools, baseball is often given varsity sport status and rarely taught in the physical education programs. Softball, on the other hand, is a popular physical education activity for both boys and girls. The units in softball can be handled in identical manner for both sexes because the only difference in the game is the shorter pitching distance for girls. If baseball is included in the physical education program, it may be taught along the same general pattern outlined

Figure 15–10. Students may be assigned to squads to work on specific skills. (Courtesy of *The Scholastic Coach*.)

below. Regardless, however, of whether the sport being taught is softball or baseball, the teacher should use the unit to develop a healthy attitude toward the game and its officials whether the students participate as players or as spectators.

COURSE CONTENT

All players in baseball must have gloves; the catcher will need added equipment for his protection. In softball it is recommended that the catcher wear a mask and a glove. Girl catchers should wear a chest protector in addition to this equipment.

Unit for beginners	*Unit for advanced students*
History	Review of courtesies and safety regulations
Courtesies and safety regulations	Review of rules
Catching and throwing	Review of fundamental skills
Pitching	Catching and throwing variations
Batting	Pitching variations
Fielding	Strategy
Base running	Offensive: hitting, bunting, signals, double
Rules	steel, squeeze play
Strategy	Defensive: player placement on field
Evaluation	Tournament play
	Evaluation

CLASS ORGANIZATION

The teaching method that is used to illustrate one possibility for presenting the softball unit is the convergent form of the problem solving method. For individual experimentation by students attempting to resolve the problems a random class formation is both functional and appropriate. If groupings or formations are desired (see *Teaching Procedures*), the class may be divided into squads, the number depending upon the size of the class and the size of the playing area. The groups may be assigned letters so that in referring to a squad, the instructor may simply designate it by A, B and so on. Having students stay in their assigned group for the entire unit does away with the necessity for reorganization every time new groups are needed and is a great timesaver.

The squads may also be assigned stations on the playing field. After individual experimentation, the students should go to their assigned squad in its designated area for group work on problems or for group practice on skills. If enough experienced students are enrolled in the class to provide student leadership for each squad, they should be assigned this responsibility. The teacher should attempt to spend some time with each squad to watch the development of the skills, even though the student in charge may be extremely competent.

Early in the softball unit the squads may work on the same skills of throwing, catching or batting. For base running and fielding, it may be necessary to assign one or more squads to the diamond to work on these skills while the other squads are engaged in pitching, throwing and catching skills. Figure 15–11 shows a possible plan for class organization under these circumstances.

The class may be divided into teams when the students are ready to put their newly acquired skills to use in a game. If the group is larger

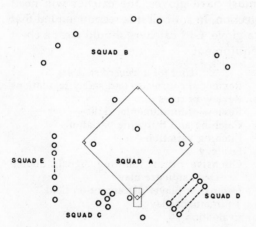

Figure 15–11. Class organization for drills on the diamond.

than the 18 team members required, three more outfielders may be permitted on each team. Other possibilities for handling extra students include using them as base coaches, as umpires and other officials, and putting them in the space beyond the diamond to practice throwing, catching, pitching and batting. Rotation of assignments should occur after several innings of play.

TEACHING PROCEDURES

Most students will have become familiar with softball or baseball either through active participation or through watching the game being played. Because of this, good introduction to the sport may be an oral question and answer period on some of the interesting historical facts, the rules, game courtesies, techniques and strategy. Such a quiz session usually points up the fact that students are much less informed about the sport than they thought. As a follow-up, utilizing the problem solving method, specific questions could be developed during the discussion for the students to research and report back on at a future class meeting.

In teaching the motor skills of softball by the problem solving method, a set of questions must first be constructed about each specific skill that is to be learned by the students. The following procedure is offered as a guide for developing the problems for a beginning unit in softball; however, the procedure is applicable to other sports as well.

A major problem is set up for each of the important skills to be acquired, and the wording of the problem is determined by the nature of the skill. Then, if it is necessary in order for the major problem to be resolved by the students, sub-problems are developed. For example, a major problem in softball may be how best to catch a fly ball. To help students in their attempts to resolve this problem, a number of sub-problems can be offered. These are developed through examination of the basic skill components, in this case fielding a fly ball. The major components would be found to be: (1) positioning the body in relation to the ball; (2) placement of the feet; (3) positioning the arms, hands and body for contact with the ball; and (4) movements of the arms and body after contact with the ball. The sub-problems, then, are set up in such a way that the student examines each of the components. Possible ways in which the sub-problems might be structured are presented in these questions:

1. Where is the body positioned in relation to the ball as it comes toward the hands?
2. How are the feet placed in readiness to catch the ball?
3. How are the arms and hands held when the ball is over the head? Below the waist?

4. How are the hands and arms held when contact is made with the ball? How is the body held?

5. What do the arms do when the ball is caught?

For the inexperienced problem solver, it may be necessary to suggest ways that the problem may be attacked or to provide assistance in the form of more highly refined sub-problems. As an example of the former, the teacher may suggest to the student that he start his experimentation in how to position his body by tossing the ball into the air at various heights and distances and catching it. Examples of more refined sub-problems are presented in such questions as the following: What part do the eyes play in positioning the body? When does the body start moving to get into position to catch the ball? How are the running steps taken in order to get the feet in the most effective stance for making the catch? How are the arms held while running for the ball? When are the hands brought into position for catching the ball? Where do the eyes focus during the contact with the ball? How are the fingers held during contact? What happens to the fingers, wrist and elbows during the catch?

The problems and sub-problems may be presented verbally by the teacher, or they may be distributed to each student in printed form. The students may work separately or in pairs or groups to solve the problems. For group work, it is possible to utilize the kinds of formations often employed for drills when the traditional method is used to present the softball unit. Because of the nature of problem solving, the formation is more informal and student-centered than is the case when it is used for a traditional drill. For example, in the experimentation with the overhand throw and base touch, a formation like that in Figure 15–12 may be used. The first person in Line 1 throws to the first person in Line 2 who catches the ball and touches the base before throwing it to the next person in Line 1. As each person makes his throw, he goes immediately to the rear of the opposite line.

A formation for a game type of drill in the overhand throw employing the base touch is shown in Figure 15–12. The first person in Line 1 throws to the first person in Line 2 who catches the ball and touches the base before throwing it to the next person in Line 1. As each person makes his throw, he goes immediately to the rear of the opposite line.

For throwing and catching practice on the regulation diamond, students may be placed 5 or 6 feet deep at each base, including home plate. They may throw around the bases or may follow any one of a number of assigned patterns devised by the instructor. As soon as the circuit has been completed, the players involved should go to the rear of their respective lines.

Pitching skills may be practiced between partners within the squads until the students become fairly competent. Then the squad can be divided into groups of three to work with a plate—one student

Figure 15–12. Formation for overhand throw and base touching drill.

pitches, another catches, and the third calls the balls and strikes. After several pitches positions should be rotated.

The demonstration and discussion of batting techniques should stress the position in the batter's box, the position at the point of contact with the ball, the follow-through and the dropping of the bat. For batting practice each squad should select a pitcher, catcher, three or four fielders and several batters. A pitching plate and a home plate will need to be established for each squad. The pitcher should send five easy strikes across the plate before positions are rotated. As the batting skill increases, the speed of the pitches can be increased.

For practice in fielding and placing hits, fungo hitting is excellent. A batter and five or six fielders are required. The batter tosses the ball and hits it to various fielders either as a fly or ground ball. After a designated number of hits, positions are rotated. Techniques of base running may be included with this drill. As the ball is batted by the batter, another student runs the bases while the fielders attempt to put him out.

Work-up is a modification of the regulation game which offers practice in all positions. Players are assigned to each position on the field with three or four in the batting line-up. If the first batter strikes out or is put out, he takes a position in right field and all players move up one position. If he hits and gets on base, the next batter in the line-up comes to bat. Work-up makes a good exercise when there are not enough players in the class to make up two full teams for competitive play. In large classes on a large playing field two or more games of work-up might be held simultaneously.

Where the facilities and size of the class permit, play between teams can be a regular part of the teaching program. Discussions of rules, strategy and play situations can be held as the need arises. Such discussions can be illustrated with diagrams on a portable chalkboard brought out to the playing field or inside the gymnasium when inclement weather forces the class indoors. Films on fundamentals of pitching, catching, base running or other skills may be used to make an indoor lesson interesting and educational.

Advanced students should be introduced to the finer points of team strategy and the responsibilities of individual players in play situations. They should also concentrate more heavily on variations of the pitch and on place hitting. Drills for advanced plays may well utilize the same formations suggested for practicing the beginning skills.

EVALUATION

Paper and pencil tests will enable the teacher to evaluate knowledge of rules, strategy and other factual material. Fungo batting may be used as a test for evaluating the batting ability of beginning and intermediate players. The subject tosses the ball into the air and bats it. Scoring is as follows: ball lands in the outfield, 5 points; ball lands in the infield, 3 points; foul, 1; miss, 0. Other specific softball skill tests could include base running for time, repeated throw and field of ground balls against a wall, throw for distance and throw and pitch for accuracy.

SELECTED VISUAL AIDS

How to Improve Your Softball. Athletic Institute.
Fundamentals of Softball. Audio Film Center.
Girls, Let's Learn Softball. United World Films, Inc.
Softball for Beginners. Mary Beth Timm, 2232 W. Alabama, Houston, Texas.
Softball for Boys. Coronet Instructional Films, Inc.
Softball for Girls. Mary Beth Timm, 2232 W. Alabama, Houston, Texas.
Softball Rules for Girls. (Six unit filmstrips with captions and color.) AAHPER, 1201 16th St., N.W., Washington, D.C. (Purchase.)

PUBLISHED SKILL TESTS

AAHPER: *Skill Test Manual Softball for Boys.*
AAHPER: *Skill Test Manual Softball for Girls.*
Fox, Margaret G., and Young, Olive G.: A test of softball batting ability. *Research Quarterly.* XXV, No. 1, March, 1954, p. 26.

SUGGESTED READINGS

AAHPER: *Official Softball Guide.* Washington, D.C., Division for Girls' and Women's Sports. Current edition.
Kneer, Marian, and McCord, C. L.: *Softball.* Dubuque, Iowa, William C. Brown Co., 1966.
Litwhiler, Daniel: *Baseball.* 4th ed. Englewood Cliffs, N.J., Prentice-Hall, Inc., 1967.
Meyer, Margaret, and Schwarz, Marguerite: *Team Sports for Girls and Women.* 4th ed. Philadelphia, W. B. Saunders Co., 1963.
Vannier, Maryhelen, and Poindexter, Hally Beth: *Physical Activities for College Women.* 3rd ed. Philadelphia, W. B. Saunders Co., 1969.

SPEEDBALL

Speedball is a unique game combining the skills of basketball, soccer and football. In teaching this game it is often possible to capitalize on the intense interest of portions of the class in one or more of these parent games. In some areas, speedball is taught as a lead-up game to soccer.

The game is played by both girls and boys, with few differences in the rules. Boys may play the game on the football field using identical markings to those used in playing football; for girls, the penalty kick mark must be added.

COURSE CONTENT

The skills which are presented in the speedball units will be dictated by the games which have preceded it in the physical education program. If any of the parent games (basketball, soccer, football) have been taught prior to this unit, little or perhaps no time will need to be spent on the duplicating skills.

Unit for beginners

History
Courtesies and safety
Soccer skills:
 Dribbling with feet
 Instep kick
 Inside of foot kick
 Outside of foot kick
 Punt
 Body trap or block
Basketball skills:
 Catching and passing
 Overhead juggle (girls)
Football skills:
 Drop kick
 Sole of foot trap
 One leg trap
 Two legs trap
 Tackling
Speedball skills:
 Pick-up with two feet
 Pick-up with one foot on stationary ball
 Pick-up with one foot on moving ball
 Lifting the ball to teammate
 Overhead juggle (men)
 Guarding
Rules
Strategy
Evaluation

Unit for advanced students

Review of rules and courtesies
Review of fundamentals
Advanced basketball skills
Advanced soccer skills
Advanced speedball skills
Variations of the body trap or block
Variations of the leg trap
Advanced strategy
Officiating
Evaluation

CLASS ORGANIZATION

As with other team sports, the direct method is readily applied to the teaching of speedball. The examples given here for class organization and in the section on teaching procedures are of the command-response form. Because speedball employs so many skills which may already be familiar to many of the students, the teacher is almost certain to have able assistance from highly skilled students in teaching the class. In this event, he will wish to divide the class into groups to review and practice different skills under the supervision of student assistants. When introducing a completely unfamiliar skill, the entire class should be instructed at one time, with the students arranged in a circle or in a line formation where all can easily see the skill demonstration.

Drills on specific skills related to basketball, soccer and football may be organized as suggested elsewhere in this chapter in connection with these sports. Skills which are peculiar to speedball may be drilled and the class organized with several groups practicing different skills, or each squad may drill the same skills. In organizing drills it should be remembered that skill potential is increased more rapidly if the groups are kept small enough for each student to have many opportunities to practice the desired technique.

Because student interest will ebb if too much time is spent in drilling, the class should be permitted to play as soon as they have sufficiently mastered the fundamental skills. If the class is small, it is likely that all students can be assigned to the teams in starting positions or as substitutes. However, if the class enrollment is far in excess of the necessary 22 players, some students must be organized into groups for drills along the side lines. Figure 15–13 suggests a possible arrangement for a class of 45 students. Occasionally, four teams might

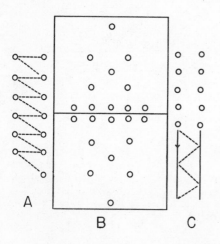

A

B

C

Figure 15–13. Class organization with some students playing a game and others drilling on skills along the side-lines. A, Pick-up drill; B, team play; C, dribble and lift-up drill.

be organized to play across the width of the playing field without use of field markings or goals.

On days when inclement weather necessitates staying indoors, the class can practice basketball, soccer and speedball skills in the gymnasium. The occasion might be utilized, also, for showing films and discussing game strategy.

TEACHING PROCEDURES

The introductory lesson in the speedball unit can well be given over to a discussion of the historical development of the game and the manner in which it utilizes skills from three of our most popular sports. Some of the rules and game courtesies might also be introduced at this time. It is usually a good teaching procedure with high school students to point out some of the basic elements of the game (rules, courtesies, strategy, and so on) prior to actual participation, and then to re-emphasize and enlarge upon these as occasions arise during play.

The next lessons will be determined by the amount of experience the class has had in football, basketball and soccer. Unless one of these sports was taught immediately before the current unit, a review of all the skills from these parent sports which are involved in speedball will be necessary. Punting a speedball requires a somewhat different technique than that used in kicking a football because of the different shape of the ball. However, if the football skills are already familiar to the class, the teacher will not need to plan on spending much time teaching this phase of the game.

Instruction in speedball should emphasize footwork, for most students have become more skilled with hands than feet. So few of our games demand skill in handling a ball with the feet that many will find this an entirely new and awkward experience. Since soccer is one of the games which does require ball handling with the feet, the basic skills of this game should be taught first in the unit; the amount of time spent on this depends upon the previous soccer experience of the group. Drills for practicing the soccer skills, as well as the basketball and football skills, are presented in the discussion of these sports elsewhere in this chapter.

Several drills and lead-up games may be used by the teacher to practice the skills unique to speedball. A drill for the pick-up with one foot on a moving ball may be devised by dividing the class into several groups composed of two lines of students facing each other 15 feet apart. The first person in Line 1 rolls the ball on the ground to the first person in Line 2 who picks it up with his foot and then rolls it to the next person in line on the opposite side. The drill continues in this manner to the end of the line; it may be repeated as often as desired.

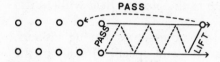

Figure 15-14. Formation for foot pass and lift drill.

Lifting the ball to a teammate may be practiced in the same formation described above. The first person in Line 1 rolls the ball to the first person in Line 2 who lifts it to the second person in Line 1. He rolls the ball to the second person in Line 2. The drill continues in this manner to the end of the line when the lines change to permit those who rolled to lift. Drill on pick-up on a stationary ball may be arranged by assigning a group of students to every available ball. The students take turns doing the pick-up.

Introducing lead-up games which combine practice on several skills plus an element of competition is always a wise procedure when the class begins to tire of other drills. One such game requires two lines of any desired number of students. At a signal the first person in each line dribbles around a series of obstacles such as Indian clubs which have been arranged in a row on the field. When he has successfully reached the end, he must execute a pick-up and then return to the starting line, doing the overhead juggle. The next person in line receives the ball and repeats the dribble, pick-up and overhead juggle; each player attempts to perform in the shortest possible time so that his line may win.

Another lead-up game involves foot passing, passing and lift-up skills. Each team of any desired even number is divided into two lines. The lines stand approximately 10 feet apart (Fig. 15-14). At a given signal the first two pass the ball to each other with their feet down the field to a designated point 25 yards away; each player must handle the ball at least twice. Upon reaching the designated marker one player lifts the ball to his partner who passes it to one of the next two people in line. The object is to complete the game in the shortest possible time.

EVALUATION

Written tests may be used to evaluate general speedball information. Kicking skill may be tested by having the subject kick the ball from a distance of 15 feet toward a goal on the wall. The goal consists of three concentric circles, one, two and three feet in diameter. A hit in the small circle scores 5 points; in the middle circle, 3 points; and in the outer circle, 1 point.

SELECTED VISUAL AIDS

Speedball for Girls. Coronet Films.
Portable Speedball Field. AAHPER, Soccer-Speedball Guide, 1950–52.

SUGGESTED READINGS

AAHPER: *Physical Education for High School Students.* Washington, D.C., 1970.
AAHPER: *Soccer-Speedball.* Washington, D.C., Division for Girls' and Women's Sports. Published biennially.
AAHPER: *Speedball for Men.* Washington, D.C., 1967.
Meyer, Margaret, and Schwarz, Marguerite: *Team Sports for Girls and Women.* 4th ed. Philadelphia, W. B. Saunders Co., 1963.
Vannier, Maryhelen, and Poindexter, Hally Beth: *Individual and Team Sports for Girls and Women.* 3rd ed. Philadelphia, W. B. Saunders Co., 1974.

TOUCH FOOTBALL

Because of the great popularity of football as an interscholastic sport, touch football is generally received with great enthusiasm by boys in physical education classes. In some schools girls are learning this game, too. In others, girls and boys make up teams to compete in this sport in intramurals.

The safety of the participants must be given careful consideration before launching the touch football unit. It is highly desirable to play on a turfed field. If a dirt playing field must be used, it should be thoroughly checked for holes, stones and other obstructions. Players should not be permitted to wear spike shoes or headgear and shoulder pads because in touch football these become hazards rather than safety measures.

COURSE CONTENT

Topics which may be included in a beginning and an advanced unit in touch football include:

Unit for beginners	*Unit for advanced students*
History	Relationship to eleven-man
Relationship to eleven-man	football
football	Review of fundamental skills
Safety and courtesies	Advanced strategy
Rules and regulations	Officiating
Passing and receiving	Evaluation
Kicking	
Centering	
Blocking	
Ball carrying	
Strategy	
Evaluation	

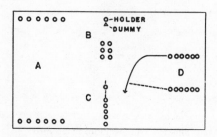

Figure 15–15. Class organization for teaching touch football skills. A, Kicking drill; B, blocking drill on dummy; C, centering drill; D, passing drill.

CLASS ORGANIZATION

The nature of touch football is such that much of the instructional time for beginners can be devoted to playing the game. Actual game situations will give rise to discussions about playing regulations, game courtesies and strategies. However, some instruction will be necessary to develop the skills sufficiently to avoid injuries and to receive the greatest possible enjoyment from playing.

The class may be organized so that instruction and demonstration of a skill are made to the entire class at one time, after which the class is divided into groups to practice it. Early in the unit it may be necessary for all groups to practice the same skill. Later, as definite weaknesses in skills are evidenced, it will be of more value to the students to be placed in groups in which the skill in which they are most deficient is being practiced. Under this plan one group of students might be working on passing while another improves kicking skills and yet another perfects the skills of blocking (Fig. 15–15).

TEACHING PROCEDURES

The unit may begin with the interesting historical development of football, the parent game of touch football. A discussion of the similarities and differences between the two games would logically follow. Courtesies as they pertain to the playing field and to the stands should receive strong emphasis enforced with assignments which will make the students more aware of their grandstand manners and will, at the same time, make the watching of football play a more enjoyable experience. The specific suggestions that follow for teaching procedures are based upon the command-response form of direct teaching.

Before participation begins, the student should be given some physical conditioning exercises. All types of running activities may be used to increase endurance. Specific exercises should be offered for increasing the strength of the muscles of the neck, shoulders, legs and ankles. (See Chapter 11 for specific exercises.)

The instruction in the skills can easily begin with passing and receiving, since these phases of the game prove the most fascinating to most of the students. The explanation and demonstration of the grip for passing should be presented first. Then everyone should have an opportunity to take the grip. Because there will probably not be enough balls for everyone to have one, several students may be assigned to use one ball. If there are varsity football players in the class who pass well, they may assist the teacher in checking the students' grips. In using these players, the teacher should keep in mind that varsity play is highly specialized and that a hero on the line may not know much more about the techniques of passing than the least informed student in the physical education class. Students who have never handled a football should be allotted time for tossing the ball into the air and catching it until they acquire the feel of giving with the hands when the ball is caught.

For drill in passing, the class may form two lines facing each other 20 to 30 feet apart. The first person in Line 1 begins by passing to the first person in Line 2 who catches it and passes it back to the second person in Line 1. The ball is passed back and forth down the line until all have had a turn. The drill is more satisfactory if the number in each line is kept to six or eight students using one ball rather than a large number using several balls. After several turns at passing at this distance, the lines may be moved back 10 to 20 feet farther for throwing long passes. The teacher can check the skills by watching the path of the ball as well as the actual throw. If thrown with good form, the ball will travel straight and will spiral through the air.

For additional practice in passing and receiving the ball in what approximates a game situation, the following drill is excellent. Two lines are formed at one end of the field 10 to 15 feet apart (Fig. 15–16). The one who will center the ball is placed in front of Line 1. The first student in Line 1 receives the ball from center and throws it to the first player in Line 2 who has run down the field to receive the ball on the run. The receiver then throws the ball back to the center and takes his place at the end of Line 1. The passer moves immediately to the end of Line 2. Eventually, all the passers will have an opportunity to be receivers and vice versa. The center should be changed frequently to allow everyone an opportunity to play this position. Several balls should be put into play in this drill to keep the action at a lively pace.

Figure 15–16. Drill formation for passing, receiving and centering.

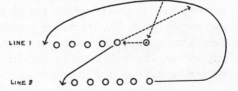

This passing, receiving and centering drill may be utilized to practice stance at the line, running, cutting and faking in addition to the skills of passing, receiving and centering. Before going down the field to receive the ball, the player assumes the stance. As he runs, he practices the maneuvers of cutting, faking and feinting against an imaginary opponent. After a degree of skill in passing has been attained by a majority of students, it is wise to put those having the most difficulty in passing into the line which is passing. This is contrary to customary class procedure, but the extra practice which it affords to the less skilled passers is not only its justification but also its recommendation. In like manner, those who are less skilled in centering can be placed in the centering line when this skill is added to the drill.

It is generally recommended that the blocking in touch football be limited to blocks in which the blocker remains on his feet throughout and immediately following the block. If the blocker stays on his feet, he must carry his body higher, thereby exerting less force against the opponent; this is considerably less dangerous to both the blocker and the one whom he is blocking. Two methods of blocking may be introduced to the class: one on one and two on one. In the former, one player blocks an opposing player while in the latter two players work shoulder to shoulder to block one opponent. Both methods may be practiced on dummies.

Blocking can be practiced effectively and with far greater safety on dummies than on other players. For dummy practice one or two students are appointed to hold the dummy while the others form a line facing it. Each student moves forward to execute a block. The holders should be changed at intervals to give them a chance at blocking. The intervals should be spaced far enough apart so that the drill will not be unduly delayed by the changes.

An excellent drill for centering the ball may be had by dividing the class into groups of four or less, if enough balls are available. Each student takes a turn centering the ball to another person in his group. The drill should be practiced at 10 feet from the receiver, at 5 feet, and from the T formation.

For practice in punting and punt receiving, the class may be organized into two lines facing each other at a distance of 25 to 30 yards. The first person in Line 1 punts to the first person in Line 2 who catches it and punts it to the second person in the line opposite. Punting continues back and forth down the lines.

A punting exercise with a competitive element is a kicking game between two teams in which the objective is to kick the ball over the opponents' goal. The teams are stationed at either end of the playing field. One team is elected to put the ball into play by punting it to the opponents. The ball must be kicked by the member of the opposing team who catches it at the point of contact. If the ball is not caught, it must be kicked from the point at which it was recovered. Any team member who catches the punt is awarded three steps forward; he may use them at the time of his return punt or he may elect to save them until a more crucial point in the game.

As often as possible the major portion of the class period should be devoted to playing the game. Touch football is played under many different sets of rules. The recommended size of the team varies from six to nine players; however, there is some evidence to indicate that teams composed of more than seven players have a higher rate of injuries. Rules regarding touching vary also. The rule most generally used is the one-hand touch any place on the body as long as the toucher remains on his feet. In selecting the rules for class competition the teachers should give first consideration to the safety and welfare of his students and second consideration to the rules which provide the greatest amount of fun in the particular class situation.

Plays are easily introduced in the general discussion of team strategy. It is a good procedure to present two or three simple plays with which everyone in the class can easily become familiar. The explanation of the plays can be clarified by diagramming them on the blackboard. When possible, it is highly desirable to have the plays mimeographed for class distribution so the students will have them for reference later as they plot their own team plays.

In organizing teams for class competition it is well to put players of equal ability on a team and to have teams of equal ability play each other. If the small size of the class limits the division to two teams, the distribution of skilled and less skilled should be made as evenly as possible.

EVALUATION

A subjective or objective test may be given to evaluate the mastery of football knowledge. General ability in touch football as well as the specific skills of catching, passing, kicking, centering and running may be evaluated subjectively in game situations. The skills of passing and kicking may be measured by the distance achieved by the subject in the forward pass and the kick. A test of skill in pass catching may be set up in this way: The subject runs down the field 20 yards and cuts to either the left or right to receive a pass from the thrower who remains at the starting line. Each subject has 10 tries and scores one point for each successful catch. Failure to catch a pass that was not within reach or was below the waist does not count against the receiver.

SELECTED VISUAL AIDS

Ball Handing in Football. Encyclopaedia Britannica Films, Inc.
Catching a Football. Coca-Cola Co.
Football Fundamentals. Coronet Instructional Films, Inc.
Football Today. Official Sport Film Service.

PUBLISHED SKILL TESTS

AAHPER: *Skill Test Manual Football.*
Borleske, S. C.: A study of achievement of college men in touch football. *Research Quarterly,* May, 1937, p. 73.
Brace, D. K.: Validity of football achievement tests as measurement of motor learning. *Research Quarterly,* Dec., 1943, p. 372.

SUGGESTED READINGS

AAHPER: *Physical Education for High School Students.* 2nd ed. Washington, D.C., 1970.
Fait, Hollis F., et al.: *A Manual of Physical Education Activities.* 3rd ed. Philadelphia, W. B. Saunders Co., 1967.
National College Physical Education Association: *Official National Touch Football Rules.* Chicago, The Athletic Institute, 1963.
Stanely, Dennis K., et al.: *Physical Education Activities Handbook for Men and Women.* 3rd ed. Boston, Allyn and Bacon, Inc., 1973.

VOLLEYBALL

Most high school students will have played some volleyball and may approach the instructional unit in the game with an attitude of "we know all about this game." Usually, however, all they know about the game is that the object is to hit the ball over the net. Many still have a great deal to learn about the various skills demanded by the game; it is upon this lack of playing skills and failure to appreciate the complexities of game strategy that the teacher must build his volleyball unit.

Regulation playing courts are 30 by 60 feet in size so that it is possible with careful planning to lay out several courts on the basketball floor. Slight deviations from standard size do not greatly affect the game. However, it is important to the development of correct skills in playing the ball that the net be at regulation height. For high school girls this is 7 feet; for boys it is 8 feet. When teams composed of both girls and boys are playing, the net may be placed at the regulation height for girls.

Figure 15–17. Volleyball can be played out of doors if indoor facilities are inadequate. (Courtesy of the Youth Service Section of the Los Angeles Public Schools.)

COURSE CONTENT

The topics suggested for units for beginners and advanced students in volleyball include:

Unit for beginners	*Unit for advanced students*
History	Review of rules and courtesies
Courtesies	Review of fundamental skills
Volleying the ball	Advanced skills:
Serving	Incurve
Setting up	Outcurve
Spiking	Drop curve
Blocking	Overhead serve
Retrieving the spike	Retrieving the ball from the net
Rules and regulations	Advanced strategy
Strategy	Officiating
Evaluation	Evaluation

CLASS ORGANIZATION

Utilizing the command-response form for teaching volleyball, the teacher introduces each new skill to the entire class at one time. After

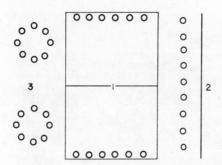

Figure 15–18. Class organization for teaching volleyball skills. *1,* Serving drill; *2,* volleying against wall; *3,* setting up drill.

the introduction of the skill, the class may be divided into groups for drills on the skill.

A good method of organizing the class into groups for drills on serving, volleying and setting up is shown in Figure 15–18. Here the students in Group 1 are practicing the serve while Group 2 is engaged in volleying the ball against the wall. At the same time Group 3 is working on setting the ball up to another player. This method is especially effective in giving drill on specific weaknesses.

When the students are ready to practice the spike and block, they are again divided into small groups. Figure 15–19 shows a drill formation that affords practice in the pass, set up, spike and block. For maximum effectiveness the groups should be no larger than nine students.

Actual play should begin as soon as possible. The rules state that there must be six boys and eight girls to a side. When court areas are limited, as many as nine or even twelve players may be placed on a side in order to accommodate the entire class. However, it is recom-

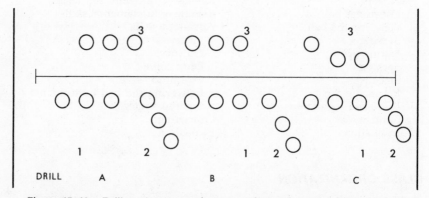

Figure 15–19. *Drill A–1* tosses perfect set-up for 2, who spikes ball retrieved by 3. *Drill B–2* tosses ball to 1, who sets up for 2, who spikes, and 3 retrives. *Drill C–1* tosses to 2, who passes to 1, who sets up for 2, who spikes and is blocked by 3.

mended that teams be kept as small as possible. One reason many students dislike the game is that at some grade level they were one of forty or more on a side for the game and rarely, if ever, handled the ball more than once during the entire class period.

TEACHING PROCEDURES

Interest in volleyball may be encouraged by starting the unit with a discussion of the interesting highlights of the sport's development and its significance in family, school and community play. To develop a better attitude about drills and practicing skills, which are commonly utilized in the direct method of teaching, it may be pointed out to the class how the enjoyment of the game is increased when skills are sufficient to open up numerous possibilities in strategy. A movie of a fast thrill-packed game played by two highly skilled teams shown during the first or second class period often helps to point up this lesson. This may be followed by a discussion of game courtesies, with possible examples observed in the film.

Ball handling is the basis of good volleyball, and this skill is best developed by repeatedly handling the ball. All types of drills can be used toward this end. The effectiveness of any drill lies in giving everyone a chance to work the ball many times rather than waiting around for an opportunity to play it, which is so often the case in game situations.

Early in the unit a ball handling drill can be devised by lining the class up 8 to 10 feet from the wall to volley the ball against the wall as rapidly as possible. This drill is especially effective if there are plenty of balls and large areas of unobstructed wall surface. To add spice to this routine drill, contests may be held to determine the individual or team who can volley the ball the most number of times during a specific period.

Another drill formation that is effective but does not require the use of wall areas is the circle volleying drill. For this six to eight players form a circle. One of the players begins by tossing the ball into the air to the player beside him who retrieves it and plays it to the next person. This is repeated around the circles as many times as desired. At different times each of the types of retrieve (head high, shoulder high and waist high) may be practiced.

To maintain interest in practice a running drill is useful. The formation for the drill consists of two lines facing each other. The first player in Line 1 tosses the ball high into the air to the first player in Line 2 and then runs to the end of his line. The player who has just received the ball plays it to the one who is now standing at the head of Line 1. As soon as he has played the ball, he runs to the rear of his line.

Play continues in this manner. The speed at which the players must move and handle the ball can be controlled by the number of players in the lines; reducing the number results in a faster game.

For beginners the straight underhand serve should be taught first. This serve is the easiest to master and is, at the same time, extremely effective. Following the explanation and demonstration of the serving techniques, the class may be divided into two lines facing each other about 30 feet apart to practice the serve. The ball is served back and forth from one side to another with each player having an opportunity to serve. After the skills are developed sufficiently, the distance between the lines can be increased to 55 to 60 feet, which approximates the serving requirement in game situations.

The introduction of the competitive element often rescues practice sessions from routine. A contest employing the serving skills may be arranged by dividing the class into two or more teams. A court is marked as shown in Figure 15–20. Each team serves a designated number of balls and the score is determined by the number of points of the areas in which the balls land.

Beginning players rarely see the great possibilities in the set-up, so when discussing team strategy the importance of setting up the ball to the spikers should be emphasized. Practice in setting up may be had in circles of six to eight players. The ball is played high into the air from one player to the next around the circle, simulating the set-up.

Another set-up drill combines practice in spiking and in blocking. It requires a formation of four players near the net, two on each side. One player tosses the ball high into the air in order to play it as a set-up to his partner who spikes it. The two players on the other side of the net go up together to block the spike. Each player takes a turn at setting up, spiking and blocking on both the left and right sides.

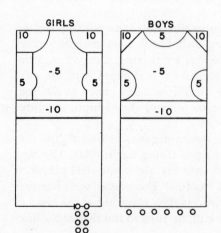

Figure 15–20. Court markings for lead-up game in volleyball.

It is recognized that the best way to stop a spike is to use a multiple block against it. However, beginning players seldom attain sufficient mastery of the multiple block to apply it effectively. If the ball is not blocked successfully at the net, it should be retrieved in the back court by the underhand scoop technique. Some drill will be necessary on the underhand scoop before it can be used with success in play. A set-up player and a spiker are situated on one side of the net to drive the ball down into the opposite court. Three or more players are stationed back from the net on the opposite side to scoop up the ball and put it into play. It should be emphasized that the ball must not be carried in making this play. To avoid carrying, it is recommended that the fists be closed.

For advanced players the teacher should emphasize the triple block which is the most difficult to execute but the most effective against expert spikers. In setting up drills for this, three players are used on each side of the net. One player starts the drill by tossing the ball to the set-up player who sets it up to the spike who, in turn, spikes the ball. The three players on the other side execute a triple block against the spike.

The drills mentioned in connection with beginning skills are applicable for teaching advanced techniques. For example, the formation used for drilling on the underhand serve may be used for practicing the overhand and curves by advanced players. Much more time can be given over to playing the game in the advanced unit, but drills should not be neglected. Many students tire quickly of drills and their enthusiasm is dampened by the overuse of drill practice. Ending a class period which has consisted largely of demonstration and drill with a short game is especially effective in keeping interest at a high level.

The ability to retrieve a ball knocked into the net can be readily attained by those students who have acquired skill in ball handling. Practice of this skill may be arranged by having two players work together. One stands back from the net while the other stands close to the net and makes the retrieve after his partner has thrown the ball into the net.

EVALUATION

Knowledge of rules and playing strategy may be tested by an objective test. General subjective questions may be used in checking general understanding of the entire subject of volleyball.

Volleying the ball against the wall as many times as possible during a specified time constitutes a good measurement of general volleyball ability. Either overhead or underhand contacts may be

Figure 15-21. Practicing hitting the ball against a wall is one of the fastest ways to develop skill in ball handling in the game of volleyball. (Courtesy of the Physical Education Department, Los Angeles Public Schools.)

specified. For this test the subject should stand three feet from the wall and the ball hit at least 7 feet up on the wall. Serving accuracy can be determined by markings on the court.

The teacher can also evaluate general playing ability and use of strategy by students while playing a game. All the students should be evaluated against the same standard such as the one suggested below:

1. The player stays in his own area and covers other players' areas when they are not in position.
2. Net players stay within an arm's length of the net.
3. Back players, when receiving the ball, play it high to the front line.
4. Players play the ball so that the best spiker makes the final play.
5. The ball is played three times by a side.
6. The net players respond fast enough to retrieve the ball from the net.
7. The ball is always played on the fingers, not with the whole hand.

SELECTED VISUAL AIDS

Fundamentals of Volleyball. All American Productions.
How to Improve Your Volleyball. Athletic Institute.
Volleyball Drills and Techniques. All American Productions.
Volleyball Skills. All American Productions.

PUBLISHED SKILL TESTS

Bassett, Gladys, et al.: Studies in testing volleyball skills. *Research Quarterly*, VIII, No. 4, Dec., 1937, p. 61.

Lamp, Nancy: Volleyball skills of junior high school students as a function of physical size and maturity. *Research Quarterly*, XXV, No. 2, May, 1954, p. 189.

SUGGESTED READINGS

AAHPER: *Physical Education for High School Students*. 2nd ed. Washington, D.C., 1970.

AAHPER: *Volleyball*. Washington, D.C., Division for Girls' and Women's Sports. Published biennially.

Fait, Hollis F., et al.: *A Manual of Physical Education Activities*. 3rd ed. Philadelphia, W. B. Saunders Co., 1967.

Slaymaker, Thomas and Brown, Virginia: *Power Volleyball*. Philadelphia, W. B. Saunders Co., 1970.

Vannier, Maryhelen, and Poindexter, Hally Beth: *Individual and Team Sports for Girls and Women*. 3rd ed. Philadelphia, W. B. Saunders Co., 1974.

DISCUSSION QUESTIONS

1. What criteria should be used to determine which team sports to include in the physical education program?

2. How can a teacher determine how much a class should drill on skills and how much time should be spent actually playing the game?

3. What is the teacher's responsibility while the squads are playing the game?

4. In what ways may a teacher introduce a sport in the physical education class that is entirely new to the students and unknown in the community?

5. How may the discussion of the history of a sport help to establish the concept that sports are definitely a part of our cultural heritage?

THINGS TO DO

1. Make a list of the safety precautions that need to be observed in each of the team sports.

2. Devise an objective test on rules and playing strategy for one of the team sports.

3. Develop a lead-up game that emphasizes certain skills in one of the team sports.

4. Make up a drill for the practice of a skill in one of the team sports.

5. Develop the teaching procedures for a specific skill of any sport in this chapter (using a form other than the one presented in the text as an example of a way in which that skill can be taught).

CHAPTER SIXTEEN

DANCE

All secondary students should take part in dance and rhythmical activities. Coeducational classes taught jointly by a man and woman instructor are highly recommended. The program in its entirety includes folk, square, social and creative or modern dance.

FACILITIES, EQUIPMENT AND SUPPLIES

Facilities and equipment needed to teach all of the above mentioned forms of dance are:

1. Gymnasium, recreational room or a creative dance studio.
2. Floor space free from obstructions, with a smooth, clean, nonslip waxed surface.
3. Piano.
4. Record player and record carrying case.
5. Hand or stationary microphone.
6. A full-length mirror.
7. Reference books.
8. Bulletin board and materials to post.

OBJECTIVES

Objectives of dance and rhythmical activities are:

1. To teach the terminology and skills in the fundamental figures of folk, square and modern dance.
2. To teach students an activity which they may recreate with joy and vigor.
3. To teach an appreciation of dances of one's own land as well as of other countries and as many different types of dances as possible.
4. To develop an appreciation of the people, cultural heritage and geography of other countries from which the dances are taken.
5. To develop a strong, well-coordinated and flexible body.
6. To develop ability to create dance patterns and original dance compositions.

FOLK DANCE

CONTENT

Beginning unit
Gie Gordons (Scotland)
Rumnjsko Kolo (Yugoslavia)
Miserlou (Greece)
Finnish Spinning Waltz
My Man Is Away in the Hay
    (Germany)
Gypsy Wine (Rumania)
Danish Schottische (Denmark)
Little Brown Gal (Hawaii)
Troika (Russia)
Sicilianella Tarantella (Sicily)
Road to the Isles (Scotland)

Advanced unit
Kalvelis (Lithuania)
Meitschi Putz Di—"Lassie Wash
    Your Face" (Swiss)
Oyda (Russia)
Oxen Dance (Sweden)
La Jesucita (Mexico)
Potku Mazurka (Finland)
Eide Rotos (Estonia)
Tancuj (Czechoslovakia)
Cherkessia (Jewish)
Totur (Denmark)

PRESENTATION

Folk dances may best be introduced to class groups by playing the music to them and having the students clap out the rhythm, and then showing a demonstration done to the music by the teacher and a partner or telling the story of the dance itself and the country from which it came. A combination of all three is ideal for motivating interest. This introduction should be brief but well presented.

It is best to begin a folk dance unit with a simple circle dance. Here the teacher can quickly note the skill level of each participant and gain a concept of what his previous dance experience has been. Next, he should progress to a simple couple dance. Praise, used as a means of group motivation, will help bring desired results quickly. Other suggestions are:

1. If the dance is short, use the whole teaching method. If it is longer, teach in the largest learning wholes possible. Teach with the music as a means of speeding learning.

2. Have the class walk through the pattern with you. Stand as part of the circle, or with your back to the group; have them in a straight line (or lines depending upon number) behind you.

3. Demonstrate and give directions at the same time. Have each repeat these with you, for by so doing each tells himself what to do. (All say and do, "step, hop, step, hop," and so on.)

4. Start the dancers and music together at a signal such as "ready, begin" or "and *start*," and so on.

5. Repeat previously learned patterns with the music each time you add a new one.

6. Change partners often. Place those who "get it" with those having difficulty.

7. Help slow learners analyze their errors; have them walk through and say the patterned steps with or behind you.

SINGLE CIRCLE, FACING CENTER

SINGLE CIRCLE, FACING CLOCKWISE

SINGLE CIRCLE, FACING
COUNTERCLOCKWISE

SINGLE CIRCLE, PARTNERS FACING

DOUBLE LINE FORMATION, PARTNERS FACING

Dance formations showing the correct positions for boys and girls.

LARGE CIRCLE, SQUARE DANCE

QUADRILLE, SQUARE DANCE

(From E. Benton Salt, Grace I. Fox and B. K. Stevens: *Teaching Physical Education in the Elementary School,* Second Edition. Copyright © 1960 The Ronald Press Company, New York.)

Figure 16–1. Indian dancing is one type of rhythmical activity which often appeals to high school boys. (Courtesy of the Board of Education, Spokane, Washington.)

8. Progress as fast as the class learns. Use praise (in the right amounts and frequency) as a means of motivation.

9. Review previously learned steps or complete dances each time before introducing something new.

10. Select dances which are fun, currently popular and challenging to the class.

TEACHING PROBLEMS

One problem which usually arises in teaching folk dance is that of suitable music. Records are considered superior to piano accompaniment. Most of these records can be purchased through leading music stores. Michael Herman is one of the best sources for securing outstanding folk music. The address is: Community Folk Dance Center, Box 201, Flushing, New York. Although orders are often delayed, they are well worth the long waiting period. *The Methodist World of Fun Folk Dance Record Albums,* secured from the Methodist Publishing House, Nashville, Tennessee, are excellent. The music is well recorded, and a valuable, well-written instruction book comes with each order. Generally speaking, albums are cheaper in the long

Figure 16–2. Folk dance, such as this Bamboo Dance from the Orient, helps students to gain a new understanding of people in other lands. (Courtesy of *The Scholastic Coach*.)

run than single records. Often dance directions are included. If one does not have access to a record player, piano accompaniment can be used. It is necessary, however, that the pianist be able to keep good time and play well. Ideally, the teacher should not accompany the class.

EVALUATION

Suggested skill tests for evaluating pupil progress and teacher effectiveness in folk dancing are largely subjective. Each student may dance alone or with a partner and be graded on his ability to dance well.

Written tests should be largely objective. Sample test questions are:

Part I. *True (+) or False (O):*

___+___ 1. "Kanafaska" means a full skirt or apron worn by a peasant woman.

___+___ 2. The "Swedish Varsovienne" is very likely to be the source of the American "Put Your Little Foot."

___O___ 3. "My Man Is Away in the Hay" is a dance from England.

___+___   4. In the dance "Potku Mazurka" the word "Potku" means
          "kick."

___+___   5. The heavy foot shuffle is a characteristic step of Jewish
          dances.

*Part II. Write in the provided blank the name of the dance learned in
          class for each principal step pattern given below:*

1. Step, point, sweep, turn   (Miserlou)
2. Schottische, step-hop   (Danish Schottische)
3. March, star, sleeves   (Green Sleeves)
4. Two-step, grapevine   (Gypsy Wine)
5. Schottische, dip, grapevine   (Road to the Isles)

*Part III. Identify the name and country origin of each dance learned in
          class as you hear the music for it played:*

Name of Dance	Country	Record Played
1. La Raspa	Mexico	(La Raspa)
2. Green Sleeves	England	(Green Sleeves)
3. Little Brown Gal	Hawaii	(Little Brown Gal)
4. Gypsy Wine	Rumania	(Sparkling Wine)
5. Rumnjsko Kolo	Yugoslavia	(Rumnjsko Kolo)

Essay type questions regarding the origin, customs of the people
or other types of marginal learnings can also be used. The teacher can
gain insight and guides for better material selection for future classes
by having the students answer questions such as the following:

1. What dances did you most enjoy learning?_____

2. What dances did you least enjoy learning?_____

3. Which class did you consider the best in the term? Why? _____

4. What to you was the most interesting information you learned in
   class about foreign people and their land? _____

SELECTED VISUAL AIDS

The Conchero Dancers of Mexico. **Perry-Mansfield.**
Dances of the Kwakiutl. **Brandon.**
The Fable of the Peacock. **Brandon.**
Folk Dances. **Brandon.**
Indian Dances. **Encyclopaedia Britannica Films.**
Norwegian Folk Dances. **American Film Registry.**
Russian Ballet and Folk Dances. **Brandon.**
Yoshi No Yama. **Brandon.**

MUSIC – RECORDS

Name	Country	Source
Bridge of Athlone	Irish	Imperial 1040
Cherkessia	Israeli	Israel 116; Kismet 130B
Czardas	Hungarian	Folkcraft F1121A+B
Danza	Italian	Imperial 1053B
Danish Schottische	Danish	World of Fun M102
Danish Sextur	Danish	Folk Dancer MH1021
Highland Fling	Scotch	Victor 45–6179
Horah	Israeli	Folk Dancer MH1052
Janoska	Slovak	Imperial 1090-B
Jarabe Tapatio (Mexican Hat Dance)	Mexican	Folkcraft F1119; Imperial 1002A
Kalvelis	Lithuanian	Folkcraft F1051A; World of Fun M101A
Kolo	Balkan	Folk Dancer MH3020; Folk Dancer MH1008
Korobushka	Russian	Imperial 1022A
La Bamba	Mexican	Imperial 1083
La Cucaracha	Mexican	Imperial 1082
La Jesucita	Mexican	Imperial 1082A
La Jota	Spanish	Imperial 1016
Lili Marlene	German	World of Fun M113
Los Camotes	Early California	Bowman 1118
Meitsche Putz Di	Swiss	Folk Dancer MH1019
Pas d'Espagne	Spanish	Imperial 1021
Philippine Mozarka	Philippine	Imperial 1184
Road to the Isles	Scotch	Imperial 1005A; Folkcraft F1095
Senftenberger	German	Imperial 1101
Sixteen Hand Reel	Irish	Imperial 1040B
Skaters Waltz	American	Victor 42–0144
Spanish Circle	Early American	Folkcraft F1047; World of Fun M105B
Sudmalinas	Latvian	Imperial 1038B
Swedish Varsovienne	Swedish	Folk Dancer MH1023
Tantoli	Swedish	Victor 45–6183
Trip to Helsinki	Finnish	Victor 45–6183
Tropanka	Bulgarian	Folk Dancer MH1020
Vandra Polska	Estonian	Imperial 1035B
Waltz of the Bells	American	World of Fun M113
Waltz Quadrille	American	Folkcraft F1046; Imperial 1095
Weaving	Danish	World of Fun M105; Folkcraft 1172
Weggis	Swiss	Folk Dancer MH1046; Imperial 1008B
Windmueller	German	Imperial 1103
Zahradnicek	Czechoslovakian	Imperial 1091B

SQUARE DANCE

CONTENT

Beginning unit	*Advanced unit*
Oh! Johnny	Waltz of the Bells
Arkansas Traveler	Trilby
The Girl I Left Behind Me	My Pretty Little Girl
Glory, Hallelujah	Milagro Square
Sioux City Sue	Cowboy Loop
Sentimental Journey	Texas Star
Cotton-eyed Joe	Alabama Jubilee
Jessie Polka	Spanish Circle
Black Hawk Waltz	Oklahoma Star
Ting-A-Ling	Forward Six and Fall Back Six
California Schottische	Five Foot Two
Patty Cake Polka	Josephine
Birdie in the Cage	Lili Marlene
Catch All Eight	Wagon Wheels
Split the Ring	
Shoot the Owl	
Wagon Wheel	

Mixers
Grand March
Herr Schmidt
Paul Jones
Progressive Schottische
Whistle Waltz
Oh! Johnny

PRESENTATION

Square dancing is fun both to teach and to do. A wealth of materials is available. These include an abundance of splendid records with or without calls, a wide assortment of clearly-written and easy-to-follow references, many films and attractive bulletin board materials.

When presenting a square dance unit, the following suggestions will prove helpful:

1. Begin with teaching a smooth, shuffling step done with knees flexed. Remind students that square dancing is done with easy gliding steps with the least expended energy possible. This will come as a great surprise to some (usually boys) who think square dancing is a run, a leap and a 20-yard dash done simultaneously with several fast partner twirls.

2. Explain and demonstrate the position of couples, partner, corner, home position, head and foot couples.

Figure 16–3. Square dancing is a popular activity in coeducational classes and for demonstrations in programs for the public. (Courtesy The Silver Spurs, Spokane Public Schools.)

3. Teach that calls are directed to men; walk through the following: circle left, allemande all, do-si-do, grand right and left sashay, promenade, pivot swing, form a star, and other basic patterns.

4. Have each square join hands and make a circle. Call all the above figures to music, mixing them freely. Endeavor to teach the group to follow called directions quickly.

5. Explain that each dance has an *opener*, then a *figure* which the first or head couple will dance with every couple and that this is repeated by the second, third and fourth couples, followed by a *filler* or *mixer*, and that the last call is the *close* or *ending*.

6. Walk through all dances first without the music, then dance to the music.

7. Review dances already learned before teaching a new one.

8. When teaching a new dance have each set walk through it once, then watch one set demonstrate. Stop and review again if the dancers become too confused.

9. Cover a wide variety of skills and types of square dances. Encourage your groups to practice later elsewhere what they learn in class.

10. Do your utmost to get a good record player and square dance record collection if you have only a piano for accompaniment. Records are superior

in every way and your class will enjoy square dancing much more when they are used.

11. Add to your collection of dances by making a card file.

12. Share your collection, skills and records with others.

SUGGESTIONS FOR SQUARE DANCE CALLING

1. Learn the dance *first*, then memorize the call. It is impossible to read a dance from notes and expect it to sound like a call; you will lose face with your students if you have to refer to notes or a book.

2. Practice listening to the rhythm of square dance music and repeating the call to yourself until you have the timing that is necessary.

3. Learn, explain and demonstrate several openers, fill-ins or mixers, and closes or endings.

4. Be sure that you can analyze, explain and demonstrate all calls that you include.

5. Practice calling into a microphone, if possible. Do not lean on the microphone or shout into it. Turn up the volume rather than yourself. Stand at least six inches away from the microphone so that your words will not be muffled.

6. All words must be clear and distinct. Singing calls are rarely as clear as spoken calls.

7. Give the dancers time to dance the figure, but remember that the call precedes the beginning of a figure. Since the dancers must hear directions before they can follow them give each call during the last part of the preceding figure.

8. When one set is slightly behind the others, give them time to catch up. The other sets can clap hands during this pause. If, however, several sets are behind the call, stop the dance to walk through the pattern again. Then start over.

9. As soon as the group has passed the beginners' stage, use fill-ins and mixers for the element of surprise.

10. Call the dance as though you are telling the dancers when to do each pattern. Keep your voice pitched as low as is comfortable.

11. Have another person listen at the other side of the dance area to help you adjust the tone and volume of the microphone properly.

12. When the group of dancers is large, stand on a platform so that you can be seen and heard.

13. Add your own personality to your calling. Make up your own fill-in patter. Use every opportunity to become more expert as a square dance teacher and caller.

TEACHING PROBLEMS

There are few problems in teaching square dance. The students are usually most enthusiastic to learn as many dances as possible, so perhaps the biggest difficulty the teacher has, other than securing good records and a record player, is satisfying this hungry desire for materials and skill mastery. Other difficulties which may be encountered are:

The Community's Disapproval of Dancing. Although this is not so great a problem now as previously, there are still some few communities or citizens who frown upon dancing. The teacher should not introduce this activity too quickly among such groups. Rather, he should work through established and recognized community leaders to secure assistance in solving this problem. It is not uncommon for the people to approve of folk dancing and to disapprove of other types of dancing, especially social dancing. In such areas, since the citizens object to the word "dance," the activity is often called "rhythms" or "play party games." Perhaps the best policy to follow in regard to this matter was once expressed by Alexander Pope, who held that only fools will rush in where angels fear to tread.

Lack of Male Partners. Often when this problem arises it can be solved by having certain girls dance the part of boys. Each should wear a "pinnie" or armband so that others in the set can quickly distinguish the girl dancing a male's part. It is important that those assuming these roles be changed frequently and that all girls learn to dance their own parts.

Students Stomping, Running and Behaving Wildly. There is something about square dancing that brings out frenzied actions. Perhaps it is a desire to recapture the spirit and gusto of the "Wild West." The teacher often encourages this type of behavior, especially by shouting instead of singing the calls. Both his voice and the class should be kept under control. One good way to do this is to stress the importance of naturalness in calling as well as in dancing.

EVALUATION

Subjective evaluation can be made of each student's progress by watching him as he dances in a square, or with a partner in a couple dance. He should be judged upon his speed and accuracy of response to calls, as well as his ability to dance skillfully.

Objective evaluation should include true and false, matching, fill-in-blanks and multiple test questions. Sample test questions follow:

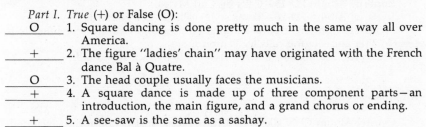

Part I. True (+) or *False* (O):

O	1. Square dancing is done pretty much in the same way all over America.
+	2. The figure "ladies' chain" may have originated with the French dance Bal à Quatre.
O	3. The head couple usually faces the musicians.
+	4. A square dance is made up of three component parts—an introduction, the main figure, and a grand chorus or ending.
+	5. A see-saw is the same as a sashay.

Part II. Explain the following terms:
1. Promenade_____
2. Allemande left _____
3. Do-si-do _____
4. Form a star_____
5. Outside track_____
6. Honor your corner_____
7. Dos-a-dos_____
8. Balance _____
9. Break_____
10. Corner lady _____

Written and practical tests can be given the same day, if desired.

Music — Records

Cowboy Dances (calls by Lloyd Shaw)	Decca, A-524
Honor Your Partner (calls by Ed Durlacher)	Square Dance Associates, 102 N. Columbus Ave., Freeport, N.J.
Soldier's Joy	Victor, 45–6184
Virginia Reel	Victor, 20447
Possum in the 'Simmon Tree	Columbia, 36021
Down Yonder	Capitol, 79–40161
Alabama Jubilee	MacGregor, 640
Red Wing	Imperial, 1009
Sally Goodin	MacGregor, 637
Cotton-eyed Joe	Imperial, 1069
Rye Waltz	Imperial, FD-9
Oh Susanna!	MacGregor, M-7
Oh! Johnny	MacGregor, M-7
Red Wing	Imperial, 1009
Spanish Waltz	Imperial, 1093
Black Hawk Waltz	Imperial, 1006
Put Your Little Foot	Folkcraft, F-1034

Albums with Calls

Decca Album 734 — Eastern style, Al MacLeond's Country Square Dance Band, calls by Ed Durlacher.
Folkcraft Album F-1 — Eastern style, calls by Hal Brundage.
Folkcraft Album F-15 — Texas style, calls by Rickey Holden of San Antonio.
Imperial Album FD-15 — Calls by Carl Myles.
Imperial Album FD-26 — Texas style, calls by Lee Bedford.
MacGregor Square Dance Albums (4 albums) — California style, calls by Les Gotcher and singing calls by Fenton Jones.
Victor Album No. 36 — Eastern style, calls by Jack Woodhull.

Albums without Calls

Capitol Album CDN 4009 — By Cliffie Stone, instruction record included.
Folkcraft Album F-6 — Texas couple dances and singing quadrilles.

Four Star Album FS 107—Couple dances.
Imperial Album FD-9—Includes written instructions and American folk dances.
Imperial Album FD-227—American folk dances.
Imperial Albums FD24 & FD25—Music by Bill Mooney and his Cactus Twisters.

SELECTED VISUAL AIDS

American Square Dance. Coronet Films.
Promenade All, Western Square Dancing. Gateway.
Skip to My Lou. Indiana University.

SOCIAL DANCE

CONTENT

Beginning unit	*Advanced unit*
The foxtrot	Advanced skills in the waltz, foxtrot, and waltz combinations
The waltz	
Simple waltz combinations	The jitterbug
The conga	The samba
The rhumba	The merengue
	The cha-cha

PRESENTATION

Students are usually eager to learn to dance by the time they reach secondary schools, for they realize that their lack of knowledge may affect their popularity. Homogeneous classes should be made available for beginners, intermediates and advanced students and should be coeducational.

Teaching suggestions include:

LEADERSHIP HINTS

1. Begin with a small nucleus of those interested in learning to dance or improving their skills.
2. Plan with the group what they want to learn.
3. Use advanced class members to demonstrate and give assistance to those having difficulty.
4. Know each dance, the steps, the records to be used, and how to teach it before you begin.
5. See that the record player is in order and have the records you need available.
6. Organize the group into some formation that is best for teaching.

Figure 16–4. Dance positions. *Upper:* The closed positions. Partners face each other. The boy laces his right arm around the girl with his hand at the small of her back. The girl lightly places her left arm on his right shoulder. They hold free hands with palms down. Each looks slightly over the other's right shoulder. The boy starts leading by stepping forward; the girl follows by moving backward.

Lower left: The open position. The boy turns the girl until they are facing the same direction. Hand and arm positions remain the same as for the closed position. Both step forward (the boy on left, girl on right) at the same time.

Lower right: The conversation position. The boy leads into an open position; then drops the girl's right hand. Their outside arms and hands remain at their sides.

7. Introduce the dance walk as the basis of social dance; demonstrate the differences between "walking" and the dance walk. Use stick figure drawings on a chalkboard or posters to show the difference.

8. Discuss the closed social dance position. First, teach the men to lead and then the women how to follow. (Leading and following techniques will need to be taught over and over.)

9. Progress through the foxtrot and the waltz, then go on to the Latin dances. If they are appropriate, include the Lindy and the Charleston or other special dances.

10. Encourage the dancers to learn, practice and go to dances.

11. Use key words to describe a step pattern. Review the patterns with the same key words. The group will learn faster if they repeat your directions as they do them.

12. Demonstrate each step.

13. Use mixers frequently to provide opportunity for each person to dance with many partners.

14. Enjoyment should be the primary objective. Improvements will come from a desire for improvement coupled with correct practice.

GROUP ORGANIZATION

1. Informal group, everyone facing in the same direction.

2. Lines facing each other. Men in one line, ladies in the other, so that each can practice his or her own part.

3. Double circle. Partners facing each other, hold hands. Ladies step backward, men forward, moving counterclockwise.

4. Single circle, everyone facing the center of a circle. Move into the center then out again.

The informal group is the best method of organizing a class which is all of one sex. "Pinnies" or armbands may be used if the dancers want to identify themselves as leaders or followers.

LEADING AND FOLLOWING

When dancers realize that the man must give the lead indication and that the lady follows an instant later, the couple will have an excellent start toward good dancing. Other suggestions are:

1. Know the basic steps and the variations of a dance.
2. Be conscious of the rhythm and the tempo of the music.
3. Begin on the proper foot; man steps forward, left; lady, backward, right.
4. Support your own weight. Have perfect balance at all times.
5. The lead indication is given immediately before the step is taken. It should be strong and definite. Timing is more important than method.
6. The man leads, then steps. The lady recognizes the signal, then steps. Therefore, the lady steps immediately *after* her partner transfers his weight into the step.
7. The lady must wait for her partner to step *first* if she is to follow successfully.
8. Lead indications are given through pressure of the hand, the arm or the upper part of the body. They are given by the man.

To move:

directly forward — press the upper body forward to begin moving in the line of direction.

backward-pull the right hand (and your partner) toward you.

into open position — turn partner away from you; press with the heel part of the right hand.

to the left — lower left shoulder slightly, press with right hand.

to the right — lower right shoulder slightly, press with fingers of the right hand.

MIXERS

Dance games, or change-partner dances and elimination dances, should be an integral part of both dance classes and scheduled dance sessions. They serve to motivate the group to practice a particular step, emphasize important points to remember and add interest.

Success of any mixer depends entirely upon the leader. He must constantly note the atmosphere as the game progresses and should keep each moving in tempo with the reaction of the dancers toward it. Elimination dances should not be used too often.

TEACHING PROBLEMS

Lack of Male Partners. Rather than have girls dance with girls too frequently in an effort to solve this problem, assign each boy to a "harem," made up of several girls. He is to dance with each of his group at least once every period. You will find that boys really go for this approach!

Reluctance to Change Partners. Teen-agers cling to their chosen boy or girl friends. Mixers,[1] establishing rules regarding changing partners, and letting the class solve this problem are suggested solutions.

Administrative Disapproval. Some administrators, fearful of community pressure groups, frown upon social dance instruction in school. Since the teacher's problem is to win their support and friendship as well as that of the local citizens, he should work toward this accomplishment slowly, or eliminate "social" dancing and increase folk "rhythms."

Poorly Coordinated Students. All who teach any form of dancing run up against the problem of the student with two left feet who has about as much grace and rhythm as a dinosaur. One should replace his occasional urge to throw up his hands in horror with a patient endeavor to do the best he can with him, and should strive for his enjoyment of several simple steps rather than insist that he master one before moving on to the next. It is also wise to let the best dancers in the class help to teach those having the most difficulty, for often these peer classmates can accomplish more with these unfortunates than anyone else. The instructor must keep his total program objectives uppermost in mind, realizing that social, emotional and attitude development are as important as skill mastery.

EVALUATION

Grade students subjectively on their ability to dance well with a partner or the girl's or boy's steps. Grade several boys or girls at the same time by having them dance toward or away from you in a straight line. Such grouping will aid in quickly spotting the good, poor and average dancers. Have the class assist in grading others.

Objective test questions can be based on identifying the type of a dance as records are played, as well as specific questions on rhythm or basic steps. Both the skill and practical examinations may well be given in one class period.

Music—Records

The Cha-cha:

Me Lo Dijo Adele	Victor 23—6232
Por Que	Victor 23—6206
Palmera	Victor 23—6563

---

[1]Vannier, Maryhelen: *Recreation Leadership*. 3rd ed. Philadelphia, Lea and Febiger, 1975.

Foxtrots:

Arthur Murray Favorites	Capitol CO-258
I'll See You in My Dreams	Capitol 5271
Blue Moon	Coral 60424
Dry Bones	Victor 20–3523A
Josephine	Victor 42–0023A
Ida	Victor 20–2510B

Waltzes:

Waltzes by Guy Lombardo	Decca A-509
Waltzes You Saved for Me by Wayne King	Victor P-70
Arthur Murray Favorites	Capitol CD-262
Tennessee Waltz	Decca 27336

Mambos:

Arthur Murray Favorites	Capitol CO-261
Sambo Mambo	Capitol 261, 15684

Rhumbas:

Rhumba with Cugat	Columbia C-54
Rhumbas by Poncho	Decca A-868
Rhumba Fantasy	Columbia 37939
The Peanut Vendor	Decca 25082

Sambas:

Sambas by Poncho	Decca A-457
Tico, Tico	Victor 28–0493A
Brazil	Capitol C-36651
Come to the Mardi Gras	Columbia 37556

Tangos:

Arthur Murray Favorites	Capitol CD-263
10 Famous Tangos by Poncho	Decca A-455
Tango	Victor 28–0403A
Valentino Tango	Decca 27511

Congo:

One-Two-Three Kick	Victor 27479
Tiger Rag Conga	Coral 60084

MODERN DANCE

CONTENT

Modern dance offers an exciting new physical education activity. The person learns established dance patterns and creates his own version of a mood, color, play, poem, word, etc. The leader who underestimates his influence in getting a dance group off to a good start is forgetting the single most important principle of leading—that enthusiasm is contagious.

His role is that of guiding rather than of showing the group what to do to music after they have learned basic movement techniques. The leader should provide opportunity for experience in a variety of movements done to rhythm. Point out how these movements may be incorporated into a dance.

Creative dance is not limited to one sex or age or to those already dance-minded. Anyone will usually be an enthusiastic participant if he joins a group voluntarily and is encouraged.

Dancers may be grouped according to age, sex, interests, level of skill or according to any other standard suggested by the group. Small groups of from four to eight dancers are ideal for creative purposes. All should change groups often. When one group develops something interesting and valuable, this should be shown to the others.

The leader-teacher of creative dance should make a reference file of approaches that may be used. Include sheet music, poems, songs, records, words that suggest themes and recordings. List the name of each on a separate card with such information as where to find it, the skill level for which it may best be used, and any notes that will be valuable in planning. Know the basic elements of music, such as measures, time, note symbols, where accents fall. Review these for yourself immediately before discussing them with a group, then make explanations clear. Move from the known to the unknown, trying to relate all

Figure 16–5. The teacher of creative dance should provide many opportunities for students to experience a variety of movements done to various kinds of rhythm. (Courtesy Los Angeles Unified School District.)

Figure 16–6. Modern dance is especially appealing to high school girls. (Courtesy of the Youth Service Section of the Los Angeles Public Schools.)

dance techniques in some way to everyday living. Discussions, practice and creative activity will thrive in an informal atmosphere. Again in creative dance, as in every other phase of recreation, increased enjoyment is the main objective.

Dancers have the whole world and all that is in it from which to choose background or accompaniment as approach to a composition. An idea, a song, a drumbeat, and an interpretation of a single work are good to use at first. The group may choose to experiment with a series of movements then make a pattern and compose a particular rhythm to complement the pattern. In any case, knowledge of basic movement skills is necessary.

In creative dance there are locomotor movements, axial movements and a combination of these two. Locomotor movements are done forward, backward or sideward through space. Combinations of these forms are known as the traditional dance steps. Axial movements are those in which all action takes place around a fixed base, as in a body swing, with the feet remaining stationary during the movement.

The three types of movement include:

Locomotor movements	Axial movements	Traditional dance steps
Walk	Flexion and extension	Waltz
Run	Bending and stretching	Polka
Leap	Swinging	Schottische
Hop	Twisting and turning	Mazurka
Jump		Two-step
Skip		
Slide		
Gallop		

These movements may be used in the following ways:

Beginning unit	*Advanced unit*
Warm-up exercises and techniques of rotation, bouncing, stretching, extension, flexion	Advanced techniques in all items listed on the left
Forms of locomotion	Composition forms: movement themes, two-part songs, three-part songs, rondo forms, theme and variation, voice forms, preclassic forms
Axial movements	
Aspects of movement: focus, direction, level, range, floor patterns	
Movement quality: swinging, sustained, percussive, staccato, vibratory, collapse, suspended	Advanced composition (both group and individual)
Traditional steps	
Elementary composition	

PRESENTATION

Begin with warm-up movements (largely stretching axial movements done to music) and gradually build larger movement exercises for the upper body and legs; finish with vigorous locomotor movements. Begin each class with a review of these activities. Suggested warm-up techniques are:

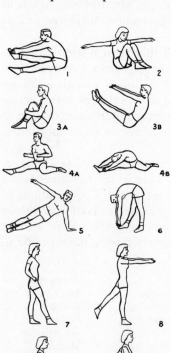

Figure 16-7. Warm-up movements for modern dance. (See text for explanation of exercises.)

1. Feet apart, sitting position. Extend arms, palms joined. Bounce four counts over left toe, sit erect. Same to the right.

2. Sit tall, bend knees to chest with feet on the floor. Extend arms to side, back to side, up, back to side.

3. Sit tall, bend knees and hold them with clasped hands. Count 1, extend legs and arms to a jack-knife sitting position. Count 2, back to place. Repeat.

4. Hurdle sitting position. Bounce forward to touch head to knee; reach for toes with both hands, bounce 4 counts. On 5 sit erect; on counts 6, 7, 8, 9 reverse legs; back to place on 10.

5. Counts 1, 2, 3, swing body and free arm up to the side while in a side hand-supported sitting position. Counts 4, 5, 6, back to place. Reverse sides. Repeat.

6. Stand tall, feet apart. Counts 1, 2, 3, 4, reach for left toes, stretch and bounce with knees straight. Count 5, back to place; 6, 7, 8, 9 to right toes, up on 10.

7. Stand tall. Extend left leg and toes. Count 1 and 2, bring leg in to meet right, back on 3. Change; count 4 and 5, bring right to left leg, back on 7. Repeat.

8. Stand tall with weight on one foot. Leg swing forward, backward, sideward.

9. Run to music in long strides.

10. Skip to music naturally, skip to music with higher movements, thrust head and body toward the ceiling.

The modern dance unit might well include the following:

Locomotor movement combinations
> Step, hop, step, hop
> Run, run, leap
> Run, run, run, run, walk, walk, walk, walk, run 4 steps, walk 4
> Hop on right foot 4 times; hop on left 4
> Hop 4 times, jump 4 times in place, hop forward 4 times
> Left foot: step, hop, slide to the left
> Right foot: step, hop, slide to the right
> Four small running steps, 4 long running steps
> Gallop with heavy step, then light step

Axial Movements
> Swinging:
>> Arm swings
>> Body swings—1, 2 or 3 beats
>> Leg swings
> Sustained motion—smooth, even release of energy:
>> Arm and torso movement
>> Sitting, stride position, raise slowly to knee. Support weight on knee and one hand
> Percussive—sudden explosion of energy with a definite beginning and a definite ending
> Vibratory—staccato movements in rapid succession
> Falls and recovery:
>> Back fall—recovery to knees; to feet
>> Side fall—recovery to knees

Rhythm (move in any of the above-mentioned ways to the following rhythms)
> Even and uneven
> Increase and decrease tempo

Constant slow tempo; fast tempo; twice as fast
Intensity — contrast loud and soft; heavy and light

Space

Moving forward, backward, sideward — diagonally, in a circle, zig-zag
Change of direction — start one way, change and go a different way
Levels — standing, kneeling, sitting, lying
Focus — (direction of the gaze) up, down, sudden change from right to left, constant even as body turns.

Force

Pulling
Repelling
Striking

Accompaniment

Music — piano, record, radio, voice
Words — meaning or mood (party, sailing, miniature, holiday, New Year's Eve, giant)
Poems — interpretation may set the mood for a dance and may suggest particular movement
Rhythm of poetry may be analyzed then used as dance rhythm
Songs — words or theme may suggest type of composition (folk songs, Christmas carols, spirituals)
Percussive instruments:
  Drums
  Maracas
  Gongs
  Triangles
  Two or more of these instruments
  Sticks

After teaching several warm-up techniques, progress to the locomotor movements below:

Activity	Rhythm	Tempo	Description
Walk	Even	Moderate	Series of steps. A step is a transference of weight from one foot to another.
Skip	Uneven	Moderate	A step and hop completed on one foot, repeated on the other.
Run	Even	Fast	Series of steps rapidly done.
Leap	Even	Slow	Series of steps with height and momentum.
Hop	Even	Any	Springing from one foot to the same foot.
Jump	Even	Any	Springing from one or both feet and landing on both.
Slide	Uneven	Moderate	Two steps; one foot is brought up to the other foot and the weight transferred to it.
Gallop	Uneven	Fast	Resembles a slide but differs in execution in that there is a decided knee action as transference of weight occurs.

Next, teach the following traditional steps based on the above locomotor movements:

Activity	Rhythm	Time	Mood	Description	Foot Pattern
Waltz	Even	3/4	Slow and smooth or fast and vivacious	Step-step-close	1 2 3 St St Cl
Two-step	Uneven	2/4	Lively	Step-close-step	1 & 2 St Cl St
Schottische	Even	4/4	Stately or gay	Step-close-step-hop	1 2 3 4 St Cl St Hp
Polka	Uneven	2/4	Lively	Hop-step-close-step	& 1 & 2 Hp St Cl St
Mazurka	Even	3/4	Vigorous	Step-close-hop	1 2 3 St Cl Hp

Develop an understanding and appreciation of rhythm by having the group listen, then clap or beat on instruments to the *underlying beat* (notes that have same time value), *primary rhythm* (duple meters of 2/4 and 4/4 time, triple meters of 3/4 and 6/8 time, and unusual ones of 9/8, 5/4, 12/8, 3/8 time), *secondary rhythm* (units or phrases which are repeated), and *contrapuntal rhythm* (a third rhythm superimposed upon a combination of primary and secondary rhythms as in the tango).

The students will enjoy moving to these different beats. Have one group move to the primary rhythm, the other to the secondary. Use

Figure 16–8. Modern dance is an ideal activity for creative youth. (Courtesy of the Girls Physical Education Department, Long Beach, California, Public Schools.)

rounds such as "Row, Row, Row Your Boat"; have group 1 clap the primary rhythm, group 2 the secondary, group 3 clap either rhythm. Another pattern is to divide the group in two facing lines. Group 1 moves toward group 2 on the primary, group 2 toward 1 on the secondary, group 3 is seated clapping to the primary while group 4 sits and sways to the secondary. Change groups so that each has the four types of experiences.

Approach composition gradually. Begin with a single group problem such as a group of four composing movements to a nursery rhyme. Have the class as a whole evaluate their work. Change group membership frequently. Move about the floor helping each group. Gradually assign students to select their own movement themes and enjoy watching them develop their own creative media for self-expression.

A RECITAL

Plan a recital for presenting compositions to the public and set a definite time limit toward which the group may work. Schedule the recital for evening since more spectators can come at this time and special lighting adds much to the effectiveness of the program. The same surface that is used for the class can be the recital stage. Cheesecloth, sheeting, or some other cotton material makes suitable inexpensive curtains and backdrops. Tack one edge of this along a wooden pole three or four inches in diameter. Use clothesline to hang the pole horizontal to the floor from the rafters of the building. A tennis court or softball backstop covered with paper or cloth makes a suitable backdrop for outdoor demonstrations.

Use steps or risers, if possible, so that audience chairs will be graduated and all can see. Secure spotlights or light the stage area, and turn off all other lights. Speakers of a public address system should be placed primarily so that the dancers can hear the music or narration.

Simple costumes, such as a long skirt over a leotard or a scarf tied at the waist, may be designed and provided by the group. To add special lighting effects for costuming, cover the face of the spotlight with cellophane of the desired color.

The show must have plenty of helpers. Select or have the group elect a person to be responsible for each of the following tasks:

Operate spotlights	Be responsible for costumes
Arrange for and set properties	Read the script
Print the program	Play the records and operate the
Usher and distribute programs	public address system

In order that the audience may recognize and understand the techniques and qualities of movement used in the compositions, present a brief demonstration in which simplified versions of the techniques are explained.

Publicize this and other dance programs in local papers, on posters or by other means. Add momentum to your efforts by enlisting volunteer leaders to help build a real dance program for all.

TEACHING PROBLEMS

It is often more difficult to teach modern dance than any other dance form. The chief problems usually encountered are:

Fear of Creativeness on the Part of the Student. Many high school youths have developed marked inferiority feelings toward their ability to create anything of real value. This results, unfortunately, from earlier educational experiences wherein their attempts were judged according to standards of the perfectionist or the artist. This problem can be overcome by the gradual "before you know it you're doing it" approach, encouragement expressed through praise, and a friendly teacher-student relationship.

Accompaniment. The best accompaniment is the piano played by one skilled in the ability to improvise melodies to movement. The teacher should do her utmost to find such a person. Records, if one must use them, are available which have been made by such well-known artists as Freida Miller, accompanist and composer for Doris Humphrey and Charles Weidman. Sheet music is also available.[2]

Lack of Teacher Preparation. This problem can be solved by one willing to experiment who will attempt to teach something for which he has had inadequate preparation. Such a teacher can gain courage by remembering the adage, "If you want to learn something, *teach* it." Attending summer school, taking extension courses, or enrolling in classes held at a Y.W.C.A. or Y.M.C.A. are all suggested training sources.

Confusion Over What Modern Dance Is. This is especially prevalent among administrators and male physical educators. Even some students are confused; many sincerely believe that when they enroll in the class they will learn the latest social dance steps. The teacher has a real selling job ahead of him when he introduces this dance form, especially in a small community or school. He needs not only to eliminate confusion regarding creative dance but to sell others on its value, and to do both without hopping on a soapbox or becoming hostile toward those who scoff and see little value in this creative art.

---

[2]AAHPER: *Materials for Teaching Dance* (3 pamphlets). Washington, D.C., National Section on Dance.

EVALUATION

A. Skill Test:
1. Grade on the basis of 10 points, divided as follows:
   Proper execution of activity—4 points.
   Rhythm—2 points.
   Coordination—2 points.
   Quality or finish to performance—2 points.
2. Method of organization:
   a. Alphabetical in 4's across gym. Start at the west side, letter toward east. Leave space for any absentees.
   b. Each four should be up and ready to start on signal with phrase, so it will not be necessary to stop and start record each time.
   c. Have them remain at the other end and be ready to return in the same order.
   d. If necessary, have them repeat the activity on the return.
3. Skills to be tested:
   a. Locomotor movements: walk, skip, run; jump; 4 slides and 4 gallops in combination.
   b. Traditional steps: waltz, two-step, schottische, polka.
   c. Axial movements: 2-beat swing, 3-beat swing, fall (back, forward, side), leg and arm swings.
   d. Combinations—any taught in class.
4. Group project:
   a. Use original groups and allow them five or six minutes to compose.
   b. Use all movement possible.
   c. Use any rhythmic 4/4 pattern new to the group.
5. Individual or group composition prepared outside of class.
B. Written Test

Objective test questions on identifying rhythmic patterns and materials covered in class or posted on the bulletin board should be used. Efforts should also be made to secure the students' reactions to and attitudes toward their own efforts in dance.

MUSIC

Records

America Singer Series. Decca, AL-AS.

Childhood Rhythm Records. Ruth Evans, Springfield College, Springfield, Mass.

Freida Miller Records for Dance. Freida Miller, 131 Bayview Ave., Northport, Long Island, N.Y.

Music for Modern Dance. Evelyn Lohoefer, Dean Records, 1139 New Hampshire Ave., N.W., Washington, D.C.

Misic for Modern Dance. Cameron McCosh, Dance Records, Inc., Waldwick, N.J.

Music for Rhythms. Hazel Johnson, 128 W. 13th Street, New York, N.Y.

Rhythmic Play. Sally Tobin Dietrich, 134 Sherman Avenue, Rockville Centre, N.Y.

Studies and Sketches for Modern Dance. Kathleen Merrill, 6484 S.W. 25th St., Miami, Florida.

Sheet Music

Horst, Louis: *Music for Dance Technique.* Write to *Dance Observer,* 55 West 11th Street, New York, N.Y.

O'Donnell, Mary P., and Dietrich, Sally T.: *Notes for Modern Dance.* New York, A.S. Barnes & Co., Inc., 1946.

Walberg, Betty: *Accompaniment for the Modern Dance.* Betty Walberg, 213 East 51st Street, New York, N.Y.

SUGGESTED RECORD SOURCES AND PIANO MUSIC

Dance Records, Inc., Waldwick, New Jersey.
David McKay Co., 119 W. 40th St., New York, New York.
E-Z Records. Merrbach Record Service, 323 W. 14th St., Houston, Texas.
Folkraft Records. Folkraft Record Co., 1159 Broad St., Newark, New Jersey.
Hoctor Records. Hocktor Dance Records, Inc., Waldwick, New Jersey.
Israeli Music Foundation, 731 Broadway, New York.
Kimbro Records, Kimbro—U.S.A. Records, Box 55, Deal, New Jersey.
Lloyd Shaw Recording Company, Box 203, Colorado Springs, Colorado.
Rainbow Rhythm Records, Box 15116, Atlanta, Georgia.
RCA Victor Educational Records, 155 E. 24th (Dept. 300), New York, New York.
The Methodist Church, World of Fun Series, Nashville, Tennessee.
Victor Educational Sales, 155 East 24th Street, New York, New York.
Windsor Records, 5530 N. Rosemead Blvd., Temple City, California.
World of Fun Records, 150 Fifth Avenue, New York, New York.

SELECTED VISUAL AIDS

A Dancer's World (Martha Graham and Company). One of the most beautiful films made on the preparation of a professional modern dancer. Dance Films, Inc., 120 W. 57th St., New York, N.Y.

Appalachian Spring. (Martha Graham and Company). Beautifully photographed, this film is a classic. Contemporary Films.

Body Mechanics and Fundamental Movement. Perry Mansfield.

Lament and the Moor's Pavance (danced by José Limon). A dancer's interpretation of Othello's tragedy. Contemporary Films.

The Shakers (danced by Doris Humphrey, Charles Weidman, José Limon and group). This is a hauntingly beautiful, classic film. Bouchard Films.

The Singing Earth (danced by Kurt and Grace Graft to Whitman's "Leaves of Grass"). Museum of Modern Art.

Steps to the Ballet. Shows the basic movements of classical ballet. Encyclopaedia Britannica Films.

THINGS TO DO

1. Plan on paper a folk dance festival for 200 high school students.
2. Collect several pictures for a bulletin board on a social, folk, square or modern dance unit. Share these with your classmates and give them your best source information.
3. Teach a social dance to your classmates. Evaluate your results as a prospective physical educator.
4. Demonstrate the step patterns of the waltz, tango, schottische, mambo, polka and two-step.
5. Teach and call a square dance to an upper elementary or a junior high school group. Evaluate your results as a prospective physical educator.

SUGGESTED READINGS

Hall, J. Tillman: *A Complete Guide To Social, Folk and Square Dancing.* Belmont, California, Wadsworth Press, 1963.

Harris, Jane, Pittman, Anne, and Swenson, Marlys: *Dance Awhile.* 4th Ed. Minneapolis, Burgess Publishing Company, 1968.

Kraus, Richard: *Folk Dancing, A Guide For Schools, Colleges and Recreation Groups.* New York, The Macmillan Company, 1962.

Kraus, Richard, and Sadlo, Lola: *Beginning Social Dance.* Belmont, California, Wadsworth Publishing Company, 1964.

Lidstir, M. D., and Tamburini, D. H.: *Folk Dance Progressions.* Belmont, California, Wadsworth Publishing Co., 1975.

Mynatt, C., and Kaiman, B.: *Folk Dancing for Students and Teachers.* Dubuque, Iowa, William C. Brown Co., 1968.

Spiesman, Mildred: *Folk Dancing.* Philadelphia, W. B. Saunders Co., 1970.

Vannier, Maryhelen, Foster, Mildred, and Gallahue, David: *Teaching Physical Education in Elementary Schools.* 5th ed. Philadelphia, W. B. Saunders Co., 1973.

Periodicals

Dance Magazine. 268 West 47th St., New York, N.Y.

Ballroom Dance Magazine. 268 West 47th St., New York, N.Y.

The Dance Observer. 55 West 11th Street, New York, N.Y.

Theatre Arts. 130 West 56th Street, New York, N.Y.

Viltis. (A folk dance magazine.) Box 1226, Denver, Colorado.

Country Dances. 31 Union Square West, New York, 10003.

Let's Dance. Folk Dance Federation of America, 1604 Felton St., San Francisco, California, 94134.

Sets In Order. 462 N. Robertson Blvd., Los Angeles, California, 90048.

CHAPTER SEVENTEEN

GYMNASTICS

Gymnastics and gymnastic-type activities are undergoing a resurgence of interest as a physical education offering. They are currently popular in both boys' and girls' programs because of the exciting nature of the events, which also offer a chance to express individuality through the selection and arrangement of stunts into routines. Gymnastic activities are especially appealing to students who are often at a disadvantage in other activities because of their body size, since height and weight are not important to successful performance.

As an individual sport gymnastics offer the chance for competitive experiences and the development of self-confidence through the self-testing nature of the activities. Gymnastic activities also contribute to several aspects of general physical and motor fitness, including upper body and abdominal strength, flexibility, balance and general body control.

Competitive gymnastic events recognized in international competition include, for men, floor exercise, side horse, parallel bars, still rings, horizontal bar and long horse vaulting; and for women, floor exercise, uneven parallel bars, balance beam, and side horse vaulting. In addition to these events, instruction and competition in related activities, such as tumbling, trampolining, rope climbing and swinging rings, are often included in school programs.

Because of a lack of equipment, many schools must limit their instructional units to tumbling and stunts. Even when this is not the case, schools often conduct separate units in tumbling prior to exposure to the apparatus, since many of the stunts performed on the apparatus are adaptations of basic tumbling stunts. For these reasons the areas of tumbling and floor stunts will be discussed separately from apparatus stunts.

TUMBLING AND FLOOR STUNTS

COURSE CONTENT

Tumbling and floor stunts are generally divided into three broad categories: tumbling, balance and flexibility. Competitive events in tumbling utilize three or four runs down a 40-foot strip of mats. In each run a series of tumbling moves are linked into a routine. The purpose of the routine is to display the diversity and difficulty of the tumbling stunts that have been mastered. In international gymnastic competition, tumbling is not a separate event but is incorporated into a floor exercise routine that includes stunts from all three categories.

Basic stunts for suggested inclusion in a secondary school program for both boys and girls are listed below. There are innumerable combinations of stunts which could be constructed into suitable routines.

Unit for Beginners	**Unit for Advanced Students**
Tumbling:	*Tumbling:*
tuck forward roll	review all beginning stunts
tuck back roll	diving forward roll
straddle roll back	back pike roll
straddle roll forward	back extension
cartwheel	one-hand cartwheel
jump and full turn	roundoff
headspring	kip
handspring	walkover
	back handspring
Balance:	*Balance:*
V-seat	review all beginning stunts
front scale	L-seat
side scale	forearm balance
squat stand	hand balance
headstand	backroll to headstand
straight legs to headstand	
kick to handstand-rollout	
two-arm lever	
Flexibility:	*Flexibility:*
straddle scale	review all beginning stunts
single leg circle	half split
tuck through arms from a	low straddle
push-up	front split
jump and straddle	pike through arms from a
stag leap	push-up
back bend	
Floor Exercise:	*Floor Exercise:*
combinations of several stunts	combinations of several stunts
from each group	from each group

It is beyond the scope of this text to describe the above skills or to comment on specific spotting techniques. Sources for this information are listed at the end of the chapter under Suggested Readings.

Figure 17–1. Suggested placement of equipment for teaching tumbling and gymnastic activities.

CLASS ORGANIZATION

Tumbling is often taught at the same time as gymnastics, which makes possible the use of a rotation plan in class organization. In the rotating system the class is divided into groups to work on the mats and the apparatus for a specified period before rotating to the next activity. A class rotation plan for several activities in tumbling and gymnastics is shown in Figure 17–1.

When tumbling is taught as an entirely separate unit, the line formation is the most effective method of organizing the class. If the class is very large, the group working on each mat may be divided into two lines which approach the mat at the center and work toward opposite ends of the mat to avoid contact between the performers (Fig. 17–2).

Tumbling is an example of an activity which lends itself well to coed classes. The stunts are virtually the same for both boys and girls, and there is not a great difference in beginning ability or rate of improvement between the sexes. Coed classes also foster an appreciation for the abilities of the opposite sex. Girls tend to be more flexible and conscious of form and grace in their movements than boys, while boys demonstrate more strength and speed than girls.

Introduction to the skills and beginning instruction may, if necessary, be presented to a large group, using the direct method. However, after the initial attempts by the class, smaller groups will be more effective as they permit more efficient utilization of all available mats and also enable students to aid each other in performing and improving the skills. On the advanced level, greater amounts of individual time should be provided in which students can construct and experiment with routines.

Figure 17–2. Line formation for safety in mat work.

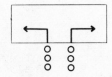

Figure 17–3. Students should never be allowed to attempt a stunt for which they have not learned the fundamental skills. (Courtesy Darien Public Schools.)

Figure 17–4. The resurgence of interest in tumbling and gymnastics is a reflection of the current emphasis on physical fitness and body trimness. (Courtesy Los Angeles Unified School District.)

TEACHING PROCEDURES

The first lesson in the tumbling unit should be given over to a discussion of the values of tumbling as a vigorous physical activity and as an activity which implements body control to avoid injury in everyday situations. This will lead to the explanation of the safety techniques so essential to the success and enjoyment of tumbling. Major emphasis should be placed on the technique of spotting, in which the beginner receives an assist from a helper until he has acquired some of the skill necessary to perform the feat. Demonstration by the teacher will be valuable at this point to show the class the necessity for the spotter to keep close to the performer he is spotting.

In presenting the tumbling stunts the teacher must plan the proper progression from the less difficult to the more difficult stunts. *Students must never be allowed to attempt a stunt for which they have not learned the fundamental principles.* The use of variations of the stunts has the double advantage of keeping the interest high and stressing the fundamentals.

An early lesson should include a description of the basic gymnastic positions of tuck, pike and layout. Great emphasis should be given to form, since in gymnastic events the exactness of form is the most important element. Difficulty and combination are both less important in the total score of a gymnastic performance than is form.

Regardless of the level of the students' ability in gymnastics, they should be encouraged to construct sequences of stunts into routines, for this is the nature of gymnastics. As soon as the rudimentary stunts are acquired, they should be made into combinations. Early combinations may be provided by the instructor, but soon thereafter students should be encouraged to express individually their unique skill abilities.

The stunts itemized under "Unit for Beginners" and "Unit for Advanced Students" are grouped according to similarity and are also listed in progressive order, going from easy to difficult. Stunts should be taught in progressions which assure that students have the necessary body control before advancing to new skills. As an example, many aspects of the headstand add to the ability to perform a handstand and thus should be taught first. This progressive teaching assures greater success for students and minimizes the chances of injury from trying a stunt far beyond the ability of the student.

Conscientious spotting is a must when students are working on difficult or dangerous stunts. Spotting must be taught and demanded of the students when working in small groups. This requires that the teacher identify the specific spotting procedure, including location of spotter, hand placement and desired result of the spot.

UNITS IN TUMBLING

The following teaching tips are offered in reference to the tumbling skills included in the beginning unit. The stunts themselves are not described; a comprehensive text on gymnastics should be consulted for this purpose.

Rolls. A demonstration of the stunt should precede student practice. The demonstration and explanation should stress the desired body position, use of the hands in taking the weight of the body and proper tuck of the head. All rolls should be practiced to reasonable proficiency on the mats before attempting them as floor exercise stunts. When working on stunts such as the rolls which require no run, students can work sideways on the mats, allowing many students to be active simultaneously.

Cartwheel, Roundoff. The cartwheel is introduced by a demonstration that emphasizes having the body in a straight line during the performance. Students may first "walk" through the cartwheel and roundoff by placing the hands on the floor and lifting the legs up and around. Subsequent practicing of the cartwheel and roundoff should follow a straight line. Chalk lines may be drawn on the mat for this purpose.

Headspring, Handspring, Kip. These stunts all rely on the rapid extension of the hips and back from a flexed to a hyperextended position. Practicing these stunts from atop a rolled mat creates more height and thus allows more time to achieve the arched position. The extension of the arms also achieves height in these stunts. Student attention must be directed at attaining an extended body position rather than the characteristic sitting error of the early learner.

Scales. Scales are held balance positions, usually performed on one foot. Attention should be given to fixing the eyes on a stationary point, and concentration directed to controlling the balance with the muscles of the foot and leg supporting the body. In the beginning, movements by the non-supporting limbs may be used to aid in keeping balance. As skill is developed, these motions should be eliminated and the static position held.

Squat, Head and Handstands. For these stunts, students should be made aware of the importance of the placement of head and hands to provide the most efficient base of support. Keeping the legs stiff and straight as they are raised allows balance to be controlled with greater

Figure 17–5. The three-man shuffle diagramed here can be done sideways on the mat, enabling more students to perform simultaneously.

Figure 17–6.   Flexibility stunts may be done on the apparatus as well as on the floor.
(Courtesy Darien Public Schools.)

accuracy. Students' attention should be directed toward perceiving as
soon as possible when balance is being lost and correcting it quickly
to keep from falling. When balance is lost, a quick tuck of the head and
legs enables the student to go into a forward roll rather than a fall. In
the learning of these stunts, practice against a wall is often helpful.

Flexibility Stunts.   The purpose of flexibility stunts is to demonstrate extreme range of movements. Specific flexibility required for the
various stunts can be developed by stretching the joints involved
through either calisthenic or static means. Practice of the stunts themselves will also increase flexibility and allow greater ease of performance. Most flexibility stunts can be performed on the gym floor and do
not necessitate a spot. Flexibility work can be practiced in an activity
area which does not have mats or apparatus, thus providing an additional teaching station. Improvement in flexibility also aids many of
the other gymnastic activities, such as straddle rolls, cartwheels, vaulting and various apparatus stunts.

Advanced Tumbling Stunts.   Before beginning the teaching of
the advanced unit, the fundamentals presented in the beginning unit
should be thoroughly reviewed. Spotting for the advanced stunts
should be carefully planned and explained so that students will understand exactly what is expected of them when they are spotting. The
teacher may wish to employ spotting belts as an added safety measure
and to inspire confidence while students learn the more difficult

stunts. The use of foam-filled landing pads, "crash pads," offers added safety and security during the early trials of more dangerous stunts.

Progressions and spotting for more advanced tumbling should be carefully reviewed (by consulting a text on gymnastic techniques if necessary), since correct lead-up activities and exacting spotting are required to insure the safety of students.

APPARATUS STUNTS

COURSE CONTENT FOR APPARATUS STUNTS

The following stunts are proposed for units consisting of apparatus stunts. If a unit in gymnastics comprises both tumbling and apparatus work, stunts should be selected from the previous groups as well. The following stunts are not arranged into beginning and advanced units but are listed in order of progressive difficulty. The instructor should select from these a number that is reasonable in terms of student ability, equipment and unit length.

Unit for Beginners (Boys)	Unit for Beginners (Girls)
Horizontal Bar:	*Uneven Bars:*
Skin the cat	Jump to support on low bar
Cast to a swing	Between bars swing to straddle
Rear dismount	seat
Cross turn grip change	Squat on low bar
Single leg mount	Scale on low bar
Pullover	Swan balance
Back hip circle	Pull-over
Single leg circle	Hang on high bar to seat on
Back hip circle	low bar
Kip	Single leg mount
	Single leg circle
	Back hip circle
	Underswing dismount
	Stem rise to high bar
	Kip
Rings:	*Balance Beam:*
Inverted hang	Crotch seat mount
Skin the cat	Walks-skips-jumps
Hanging L	Low turn
Single leg cut	High turn
Double leg cut off	V-seat
Muscle-up	Scale
Kip	One-leg squat
Shoulder stand	Leap off dismount
	Backroll
	Forward roll
	Cartwheel
	Roundoff

| Unit for Beginners (Boys) | Unit for Beginners (Girls) |

Unit for Beginners (Boys)

Side Horse:
  Jump to support
  Squat through to rear support
  Pivot to rear support
  Single leg cut
  Single leg circle
  Single leg travel
  Flank vault dismount

Parallel Bars:
  Jump to support
  Swing in support
  Swinging dips
  Straddle travel
  Front dismount
  Rear dismount
  Shoulder roll
  L-seat
  Back uprise

Vaulting:
  Squat vault
  Straddle vault

Trampoline: (Same as for girls)

Unit for Beginners (Girls)

Side Horse Vault:
  Flank vault
  Squat vault
  Straddle vault

Trampoline:
  High bounce
  Half turn
  Knee drop
  Seat drop
  Full turn
  Swivel hips
  Front drop
  Back drop
  Turntable
  Knee front somersault
  Back drop pullover
  Front somersault
  Back somersault

CLASS ORGANIZATION

If the equipment for gymnastics includes several pieces of the same apparatus, or if the class is small in size, it will be possible to organize the class on an all-at-one-time basis; that is, the entire group will receive instruction in the skill and will practice it simultaneously. With classes of average to large size, greater benefits will be derived from the use of the rotation system of class organization.

Under this system groups of four or five students work on each piece of apparatus for a specified period of time before rotating to another apparatus. The rotation must be carefully scheduled by the teacher so that everyone will have equal opportunity to acquire the skills of performance on each type of apparatus, and also so that those having difficulty with certain skills will have the additional drill they require. In the latter instance, it may be useful to reorganize the groupings after several class periods to place those with the same difficulties in one group which can then be allotted more class time for drilling on specific weaknesses.

Figure 17–7. Stunts performed by girls on the uneven bars require skills similar to those needed by boys performing on the parallel bars.

When it is necessary to teach a large group on a single apparatus, it is suggested that the group be lined up parallel to the apparatus for greater visibility than is possible if the group is lined up one student behind the other.

As students progress, more opportunity to work on routines or on specific weaknesses may be provided by allowing time at the end of the period for concentration on individual problems.

If the class is to set up the equipment at the beginning of the period, the teacher should institute a workable system to avoid confusion and undue delay. Probably the simplest way to handle the problem is to divide the group arbitrarily into squads of equal number, giving each a specific assignment. The teacher should supervise the moving of the equipment and should check each piece of apparatus to see that it has been properly set up for safe use. The group assignment for moving equipment should also include storing the apparatus at the end of the class period. It is best to have an assigned area for the storage of each item to keep this as orderly as possible. Printed or stenciled cards on the wall, indicating the specific places for the respective pieces, are very helpful.

TEACHING PROCEDURE

There are some precautions which, because of their importance in safeguarding the participants from accidental injury, constitute a major item in the teaching procedures for gymnastics. The safety factors which the teacher must present and repeatedly emphasize are:

1. Breaking a fall correctly.
2. Correct procedure in spotting.
3. Drying the hands with magnesium carbonate to reduce the chance of slipping on the apparatus.
4. Placing an ample number of mats under and around the apparatus.

To initiate the rotation system in the class, the teacher will need to explain and demonstrate the elementary skills of each apparatus to the class during the first instructional period. Then class division into groups for practice may be made. This means, of course, that on each apparatus there will be a group of largely inexperienced students attempting to perform one of the demonstrated stunts. Consequently, it is a good procedure to appoint responsible squad leaders (preferably with some skill in gymnastics) who can take charge of the unit while the teacher is occupied with other groups. The teacher should have, if possible, one or more meetings with the group leaders prior to the first class session to instruct them in the skills of the first lesson on the apparatus and to stress the essential safety measures.

All stunts should be introduced with an explanation and demonstration. If the teacher is unable to perform these adequately, he may be able to secure a varsity team member or an especially skilled class member to do the demonstrations. It is also possible to use a series of still photos and/or filmstrips for demonstration purposes.

APPARATUS ACTIVITIES

Specific stunts will not be described; however, several general considerations will be made concerning teaching the various apparatus stunts listed in the *Unit Content* section. The boys' apparatus activities are discussed first.

Horizontal Bar. Initial instruction should introduce the palms up and palms down grips, stressing in both cases the thumbs around the bar. The use of chalk is essential and all rings, watches, and so on should be removed before performing on the high bar. For many stunts the bar can be lowered to chest height to reduce fear and enhance spotting of the students. Some students, because of a lack of arm strength or because they are overweight, will have great difficulty on the high bar. In working with these students the necessity for upper body strength should be stressed and specific exercises such as chin-ups or modified chin-ups, should be required along with the high bar practice. Practice on the high bar should be limited to short periods to reduce the tendency to tear the skin on the hands. Spotting is generally done from directly below the bar on either side. Often it is advantageous to practice two or three stunts together, one as a mount, one while on the apparatus and one as a dismount. Often an easy stunt can be alternated with a strenuous one to allow sufficient rest between the very vigorous activities.

Rings. Most of the comments concerning the high bar are equally appropriate to the rings. Competitive gymnastics involve work only on the still rings. If work on the swinging rings is planned, it should be delayed until the stunts are first mastered on the still rings. If groups are moving among various stations, the sequence should separate the rings and the high bar, since both these events are very strenuous, involve similar musculature and produce great wear on the palms of the hands. As with the high bar, adjustable rings lowered to chest height will enable more rapid learning and easier spotting of many stunts.

Side Horse. Work on the side horse probably requires less spotting than the other events; however, mats must be provided and should surround the horse to cushion any falls. Spotting can help the student to "get the feel" of the particular movements. Stunts learned on the horse should be practiced first on the pommels, then on the neck and croup. As a general rule of balance, any time the legs are moved in one direction, the upper body must move in the opposite direction to maintain the center of gravity over the hands. Failure to observe this requirement is responsible for the majority of instances when balance is lost.

Parallel Bars. Good support ability should be developed with the bars lowered to below shoulder height. This allows the feet to contact the floor before the shoulders if balance is lost in swinging or if the arms collapse. Support work should be learned before attempting stunts that involve hanging from the upper arms or hands. During the early stages of instruction, when students are working exclusively at the end of the bars, two students can work simultaneously—one at each end. However, as movement from the end begins, only one student should be allowed on the apparatus at any time.

A set of floor parallel bars or parallets can be used to advantage in practicing many above-bar moves and balances.

Vaulting. Vaulting should never be performed with the pommels in place. The chance of injury is very high if the grip is missed. The holes for the pommels should be covered with tape when vaulting. Beginning vaulting should be done with the horse low and turned sideways. Only after the basic vault has been mastered should it be attempted over the long horse. When the long horse is first introduced, students should review the progression of the vault by putting the feet on top of the horse for several trials. Attention to placement of the hands in the correct area of the horse is an essential concern when changing to long horse vaulting. The learning of some long horse vaults may be improved by the use of a mini tramp until the proper body position is acquired.

Trampoline. The trampoline is covered under girls' events.

GIRLS' APPARATUS

Uneven Bars. Many of the stunts performed on the uneven bars are similar to boys' stunts on the high bar. If an adjustable high bar is available an additional teaching station can be utilized for the learning of many basic stunts. Girls often lack sufficient upper arm strength to experience early success with many of the more vigorous stunts on the uneven bars. For this reason, spotting should be carefully provided and developmental exercises recommended to those needing additional strength. In general, any bar movement should first be learned on the low bar before it is attempted on the high bar. During early stages, held movements involving standing or sitting on the low bar should

Figure 17–8. Balance beam activities are especially challenging to high school girls. (Courtesy of the President's Council on Physical Fitness.)

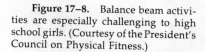

predominate. As strength increases, a series of one mount, one movement and one dismount allows efficient practice of skills, with minimal loss of time. Consideration should be given to the type of grips and care of the hands discussed under *Boys' high bar.*

Balance Beam. All stunts should be practiced first on a line on the gym floor, then on a low beam and finally on the regular beam. This greatly increases available practice time. In early learning, walks, jumps and simple turns should be stressed. After basic balance has been developed, the more difficult stunts can be introduced. When performing on the beam, the eyes should focus on the far end of the beam to provide a reference point in maintaining balance.

Side Horse Vault. See *Boys' vaulting.*

Trampoline. A minimum of six spotters should be provided during any trampoline work, two on each side and one at each end. They must be instructed that their role is to keep the performer on the trampoline bed. To maintain interest and allow all students an opportunity to practice, the number of bounces by each student should be limited. This is a good safety precaution as well, since often the student is more fatigued than he realizes.

In teaching the stunts, it is desirable to have the entire group practicing the same stunt and only that stunt. This allows effective

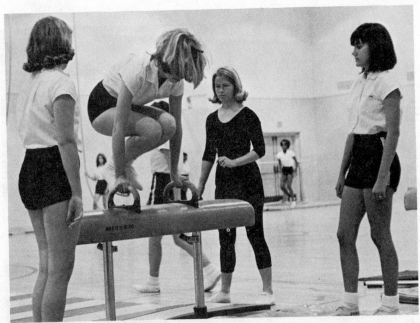

Figure 17–9. Stunts learned on the horse should be practiced first on the pommels. (Courtesy of the Youth Service Section of the Los Angeles Public Schools.)

Figure 17–10. Before students attempt to spot a performer on the trampoline, they should be thoroughly instructed in the techniques of spotting. (Courtesy Penny High School.)

Figure 17–11. The descent should be taught at the same time as the ascent in rope climbing. (Courtesy Enrico Fermi High School.)

control of the stunts attempted and prevents students from doing something for which the teacher or spotters are unprepared. Early practice with bouncing, killing a bounce and various landing positions should precede all other instruction. Safe methods of mounting and dismounting must also be taught. No more than one student should be allowed on the trampoline at any one time. An overhead spotting belt is of great help in assisting the learning of any somersault stunt. Spotting from the bed of the trampoline should only be done by the experienced instructor.

Supplementary Gymnastic-type Activities. In addition to the typical gymnastic stunts, many schools have found activities such as rope climbing, rope stunts, dual stunts and group stunts to be popular, challenging and useful in developing qualities similar to those developed through tumbling and apparatus stunts. The following material is provided for supplementary use in conjunction with gymnastic instruction.

Ropes. Mats should be piled several deep under the ropes before teaching of rope stunts begins. Students, except for those spotting or holding the rope, should not be permitted in the area under the ropes when others are climbing. A special warning should be made by the teacher about the possibility of rope burns to the hands when the student does not descend properly.

To familiarize the beginning student with the feel of rope climbing, the following activities are used:

1. The student lies on his back and grasps the rope with his hands at the height of his reach from this position. He then pulls his chest up to his hands and lowers again. This may be repeated several times.
2. From a standing position the student performs a chin-up on the rope.
3. From a standing position the student executes a chin-up and half lever.

The descents should be taught at the same time as the climbs. The beginner should climb only 5 or 6 feet from the floor and then descend with the correct techniques. At this height the teacher is able to help the student by placing his feet correctly on the rope. Students should not be allowed to climb to the top of the rope until skill has been demonstrated in the descent.

Dual Stunts. Tumbling stunts which students can perform in pairs are a special challenge. They may be introduced any time after the basic skills of the stunts have been learned well by the class, or they may be presented as a complete lesson in themselves, following the teaching of the individual stunts.

Knee-Shoulder Balance. The student selected for the top should have sufficient strength to hold the top man. A third man may aid the top man to attain his position.

Swan Balance and Back Balance. To get into the swan position, the bottom performer bends his legs and hips and lowers his feet. The

Figure 17–12. Knee-shoulder balance.

Figure 17–13. Foot to hand balance.

Figure 17–14. Double roll.

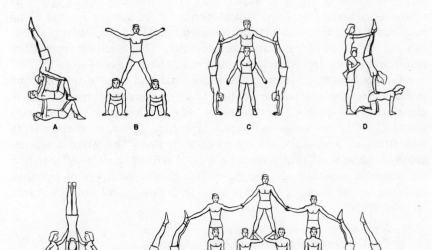

Figure 17–15. Balancing stunts for three or more students.

top performer then places his hips on the bottom man's feet. The bottom man then straightens his legs. In the swan balance the top man holds on to the lower man's arms until the balance is secured. In the back balance the bottom man may help the top man to secure his balance by placing his arms on the other's shoulders.

Foot to Hand Balance. For this stunt the bottom man must be strong enough to hold the top man. Smaller students should be used for the top man. A third person may assist the top man until balance is acquired.

Double Roll. For beginners it must be emphasized that the partner's feet take the weight off the head when the roll is made. The head comes down after the partner's feet are placed on the mat.

Elephant Walk. To assume the position for this stunt, one performer jumps up to encircle the other's waist with his legs. He then bends backward to place his head between his partner's legs and grasps his ankles. The other bends over forward and places his hands on the mat.

Back to Back. To assume the position the two performers stand back to back and lock elbows. One bends forward at the hips and hoists the other on his back.

Rocking Chair. This stunt is performed in the same way as the back to back, with the partners alternately lowering and lifting each other.

The balance stunts listed in the advanced unit are combinations of the elementary balance stunts and the individual tumbling stunts discussed previously; they would generally be taught by the same methods. The pitches and tosses are very similar to the lead-up activities for the handspring and somersaults. The teaching procedure would follow the procedure explained in teaching the lead-up activities.

Group Stunts. Many of the individual and dual stunts may be worked into group stunts involving three or more performers. This is especially true of the balance stunts. The teacher may suggest such possibilities to the class as shown in Figure 17–16, or the students may think up and work out others of their own. The latter is recommended because it offers creative group activity in a way that few activities do. The teacher should review these principles of pyramid building before turning the class loose to organize and practice stunts on their own:

1. A sound base prevents collapse.
2. The heaviest students should form the base.
3. The weight must be distributed properly.
4. The lightest students must be at the top.
5. Every student should understand exactly what is expected of him.
6. Each student must have confidence in his fellow performers.
7. Each student must cooperate fully in his particular assignment.
8. Simplicity of design is essential to success and safety.
9. Building and dismounting should be performed smoothly.

EVALUATION

A scorecard on which the student's achievements in tumbling and in stunts on each apparatus are recorded may be used as the basis for evaluation. A sample scorecard is shown. A paper and pencil test might also be used to evaluate knowledge of the skills of performance and spotting and the conduct of gymnastic competitions. Permitting the students to diagram the skills rather than writing a description of them will save time in writing the test and grading it.

Scorecard for Tumbling and Gymnastic Stunts.

Record the numbers of the stunts which can be performed by the student in the blanks beside the activity or apparatus.

Tumbling.............................. Side Horse ....
Horizontal Bar .... Rings....................................
Parallel Bars........................... Trampoline...........................
Ropes ....

1. Headstand
2. Upper arm or forearm stand
3. Handstand
4. Forward roll
5. Backward roll
6. Shoulder roll
7. Dive roll
8. Cartwheel
9. Kip
10. Headspring
11. Handspring
12. Roundoff
13. Backward handspring
14. 10 chin-ups
15. Skin the cat
16. Knee mount
17. Hip circle backward
18. Knee or leg circle
19. Squat vault, stand or hang
20. Inverted hang
21. Dislocate
22. Monkey hang
23. Bird's nest

24. Rear vault or dismount
25. Front vault or dismount
26. Straddle vault or dismount
27. Stride seat
28. Swing rise
29. Inside swing turn
30. Outside swing turn
31. Knee bounce
32. Seat bounce
33. Back bounce
34. Hand-knee bounce
35. Front bounce
36. Front bounce turn table
37. Foot and leg-lock climb
38. Stirrup climb
39. Stirrup descent
40. Cross leg climb
41. Cross leg descent
42. Make fast
43. Stand and seat mount
44. Rocking chair

DISCUSSION QUESTIONS

1. What are the chief points that should be presented to the students in a discussion of the value of tumbling and gymnastics?
2. What forms of the methods of instruction could be used so that students would be well qualified to spot each other in the performance of new stunts?
3. What are the values of presenting several variations of each stunt?
4. Discuss the advantages and limitations of teaching gymnastics as a coed activity.
5. Discuss the contributions of tumbling and gymnastics to physical fitness.

THINGS TO DO

1. Devise a unit of tumbling or gymnastic skills for beginners, using those stunts which you would be capable of demonstrating and explaining to the class. Make certain that the skills are within the realm of the abilities of secondary school students and that the fundamentals and lead-up skills are presented.
2. Outline possible ways of introducing a new stunt.
3. Using stick figures, diagram several group balance stunts or pyramids employing some of the basic balance stunts.
4. Devise a workable set-up for trampoline instruction that will give each student maximum time to practice.
5. Demonstrate how you would teach breaking a fall correctly.

SELECTED VISUAL AIDS

Gymnastic Loop Film Series, Athletic Institute.
Beginning Tumbling. Coronet Instructional Films.
Trampolining. Athletic Institute.
Tumbling for Beginners. State University of Iowa.
Tumbling for Physical Fitness. Castle Films Division.
Up in the Air; Whatever Goes Up. Nissen Trampoline Co.

PUBLISHED SKILL TESTS

Wettstone, Eugene: Tests for predicting potential ability in gymnastics and tumbling. *Research Quarterly,* IX, No. 4, December, 1938, p. 115.

SELECTED READINGS

AAHPER: *Selected Gymnastic Articles.* Washington, D.C., AAHPER Publications, 1971.
AAHPER: D.G.W.S. *Gymnastics Guide.* Washington, D.C., AAHPER Publications, 1974.
Baley, James A.: *Gymnastics in the Schools.* Boston, Allyn & Bacon, Inc., 1965.
Cooper, Phyllis: *Feminine Gymnastics.* Minneapolis, Burgess Publishing Co., 1973.
Edwards, Vannie: *Tumbling.* Philadelphia, W. B. Saunders Co., 1969.
LaDue, Frank, and Norman, Jim: *Two Seconds of Freedom.* Cedar Rapids, Iowa, Nissen Trampoline Co., 1960.
Loken, Newton C., and Willoughby, Robert J.: *Complete Book of Gymnastics.* Englewood Cliffs, New Jersey, Prentice-Hall, Inc., 1959.
Roys, Betty M.: *Gymnastics for Girls and Women.* Philadelphia, W. B. Saunders Co., 1969.
Vincent, William J.: *Gymnastic Routines for Men.* Philadelphia, W. B. Saunders Co., 1972.

Periodicals
Amateur Athletic Union Gymnastic Yearbook. 233 Broadway, New York 7, N.Y.
Athletic Journal. 1719 Howard Street, Evanston, Ill.
The Modern Gymnast. P.O. Box 425, Santa Monica, Calif.
Scholastic Coach. 33 W. 42nd St., New York 36, N.Y.

CHAPTER EIGHTEEN

SPECIAL PHYSICAL EDUCATION: ADAPTED, CORRECTIVE AND DEVELOPMENTAL

The provision of educational opportunities that will enable each individual to develop to his optimum is a basic tenet of democracy. Each year more and more children with physical or mental disabilities are receiving the increased attention they deserve. A very great contribution is being made by physical educators through special programs which enable these exceptional youngsters to participate in physical activities within the limits of their capabilities. As a result, many who are extremely underdeveloped and lacking in even the rudiments of muscular control are being given the benefits of an organized physical education program designed for their special needs.

The special physical education programs encompass three types of physical education activities: adapted, corrective and developmental. The nature and teaching procedures of each type are discussed in separate sections in the pages that follow.

ADAPTED PHYSICAL EDUCATION

Adapted physical education is an educational activity and is not a duplication or substitute of physical, recreational or corrective therapy. It is, rather, a complement to these therapies in that it provides opportunities to use the skills which the therapies help the handicapped to learn or relearn. Games, sports and play activities provide an opportunity for mental and social development as well as physical development. It is important for the physical educator to understand clearly the division between therapy and physical education. Physical education must be limited to those big muscle activities used for leisure time play and to promote body conditioning but not specifically concerned with the correction of the handicap. The physical education activity should be carefully planned in consultation with medical authorities so that the body difficulty will not be aggravated and, in the cases of those with cerebral palsy and orthopedic handicaps, so that muscles will not be incorrectly used, thus negating the therapeutic treatment.

Deviations from normal result from physical disabilities and diseases, lack of mental capacity, and emotional and social problems. Students with severely handicapping conditions will usually be enrolled in special schools; but more and more, the trend is toward placing in regular schools those handicapped youngsters who are sufficiently adjusted to their conditions and physically able to benefit from participation with their normal peers. The handicapping conditions most frequently found in today's regular schools are:

Cardiopathic conditions   Convalescence from illness and
Cerebral palsy   injuries
Epilepsy   Diabetes
Orthopedic disabilities   Asthma
Visual and auditory limitations   Hernia
Mental deviations   Dysmenorrhea

OBJECTIVES

The goal of the adapted program is the same as that of the regular physical education program—to help the student achieve optimum physical, mental and social growth. The specific objectives which promote achievement of that goal are:

1. To increase skills in the basic motor movements.
2. To achieve the highest possible level of physical fitness.
3. To stimulate a desire for continued improvement in fitness and skill.
4. To develop a variety of sport skills for participation in sports as a worthy leisure activity.
5. To improve body image.
6. To help the student acquire a feeling of value and worth as an individual.
7. To give the handicapped student an understanding of his disability and the limitations it imposes while emphasizing his potentialities.

Developing skill in the basic motor movements is fundamental to life activities. Improving the ambulatory skills such as walking and running, changing direction rapidly, balancing the body, and falling correctly are essential skills contributing to the total welfare of the student. Moreover, many of the basic motor skills are fundamental to sports: throwing and catching a ball, jumping, and so on, are motor movements that form the basis for learning many sports activities.

Physical fitness is just as important to the exceptional child as to the normal. In many cases, the fitness level of the former will be much

Figure 18–1. Table tennis is often a good activity to include in the special physical education program for those students medically excused from the regular program. (Courtesy of the Youth Service Section of the Los Angeles Public Schools.)

lower than his normal peer because of his tendency to withdraw from play activities that contribute to physical development. Furthermore, there may be a need for a high level of development of a specific factor of fitness, such as strength, in a specific part of the body to compensate for the limitations the handicap imposes on movement in another part. A case in point is the student with one arm who can, by properly exercising this arm, develop its strength for such activities as swinging a golf club, which normally requires two arms.

Handicapped students are usually well aware of their limitations but frequently unaware of their potentialities. Many possess intensified fears because they believe that their differences are so great that they are repulsive to others. Some overcompensate for this by becoming antisocial, unrestrained and obnoxious; others withdraw and escape reality through daydreams evolving around normalcy. A good adapted physical education program should provide activities that help these students to recognize and develop their potentialities, thereby restoring their confidence and self-esteem. As these students become more skilled in the execution of motor skills in games, they will feel less apart from others. Feeling a useful member of a group is an important psychological need and one which the adapted program can and should promote. Since adult hobby patterns are laid down early in life, it is vital that these students learn to do as many activities as possible with average skill and be encouraged to shop around, sampling many new interest fields. A long lonely life is ahead for those who are both hobby poor and defective.

PHYSICAL EXAMINATIONS AND EXEMPTIONS FROM PHYSICAL EDUCATION

It is recommended that all students have a physical examination given by a qualified physician every three to four years. Handicapped students may need to be examined more often than this. Those who show rapid gains in growth, sudden weight loss, or sudden signs of deviation from normal may also require more frequent examinations. A typical form for physical examination is shown on this page. The form may be adjusted to fit the situation by changing the listed activities.

It is a very unusual situation, indeed, when the school cannot provide some type of adapted physical education that will be beneficial to the special student. Schools that have inadequate teaching staffs and facilities will have to excuse some types of handicapped students from taking part in physical education. It must be recognized that under these circumstances the child is being denied an important part of his total education because of the inadequacy of the school situation.

It has been estimated that 5 to 10 per cent of the school population will be in need of special physical education. After these students have been identified by medical examination, special needs must be considered.

ORGANIZING THE ADAPTED CLASS

There are several effective ways of scheduling the classes for adapted activities; the choice is largely determined by the teaching personnel and facilities of the school. The ideal school situation is one which permits the scheduling of a separate class for the handicapped with a special teacher in charge. The time at which this class meets would coincide with a class meeting for regular physical education to permit students in the adapted activities to move into the regular program when the activities are such that they could participate with success.

However, many schools are too limited by their budgets and the size of their physical plants for such arrangements to be practical.

ADAPTED PHYSICAL EDUCATION PROGRAM
_____ School

Date _____

To Dr. _____ Family Physician for _____

Our program of physical education includes a wide variety of activities for all students in the school. The activities are adapted to fit the needs of each individual student regardless of his physical attributes, and any pupil who is unable to participate in the regular program is provided with special activities modified to meet his needs and to contribute to his welfare.

Please indicate the type(s) of activities that your patient cannot participate in and state the reason. _____
_____
_____
_____

Please state the length of time for which the patient is restricted from participation in the above activities: _____ to _____; all year _____.
A list of the activities to be presented in the adapted physical education program this year is given below. Please check those in which your patient may participate.

bowling	shuffleboard	deck tennis
badminton	weightlifting	volleyball
table tennis	*calisthenics	softball
golf	bag punching	archery
tennis	dancing, social,	swimming (no diving)
running	folk and square	swimming (regular)
walking	squash	

Please state any modifications of the above activities which may be made to permit your patient to participate in them. _____
_____
_____

* Indicate the types of movement which are contraindicated.

Form sheet for family physician. (From Fait, Hollis F): _Special Physical Education: Adapted, Corrective, Developmental._ Philadelphia, W. B. Saunders Co., 1966.)

Consequently, the program for the handicapped must be integrated with the regular program. With ingenuity and careful planning and organization the teacher can present an effective physical education program to both groups simultaneously.

Students may assemble in the same place for roll call and general instructions and then go to the areas where each group will have its own program of physical education. It is desirable to have the area in which the exceptional students are participating in the same general location as the regular class in order that the teacher may see the adapted class at all times. Most handicapped students are highly motivated by a desire to participate in the activities of their peers and to increase their limited skills and so work very well on their own, provided they know what they are to do. After starting the regular class, the teacher should check on the students to make sure they are performing successfully and to offer guidance and encouragement. Where it is possible, it is recommended that the teacher meet the adapted students during a free period in advance of the first class meeting to discuss the nature of the adapted program and to set up the individual objectives for each student and the plan for achieving them, and to establish the procedure for their working largely on their own.

Whenever possible, the adapted students should be brought into the regular program. Not only does this give these students a much needed opportunity for normal play with peers, but it eases the teacher's continual burden of dual instruction. Among the activities which may be utilized are table tennis, deck tennis, shuffleboard and horseshoes.

Thorough instruction in general safety precautions must be given to both the regular class and adapted class students, with additional emphasis on those precautions necessitated by the various kinds of disabilities in the adapted group. Lack of endurance and strength and poor coordination in handicapped students make them susceptible to overexertion and accidental injuries. Close supervision in the early months of the program is recommended. Although the students should be taught to assume responsibility for their own health and safety, the teacher must provide the best possible environment for doing so—good teaching methods, a superior program, and safe, hygienic equipment and facilities.

When the adapted students are brought into the regular class, added precautions are necessary to avoid injuries. Physical hazards, such as having nonessential equipment on the floor which normal students would readily avoid, should be removed. In addition, the teacher must promote respect among all for the playing courtesies and a regard for the abilities and limitations of others.

TEACHING METHODS

Either the direct or indirect method may be used to teach exceptional students. The indirect method is especially effective with those who are physically handicapped, because it encourages them to discover for themselves the movements they are capable of and how best to adapt these movements for execution of a specific skill.

Teaching procedures which are successful with normal students will usually be equally successful with exceptional students. Every teacher is very much aware of the individual differences which exist among the normal pupils in a class; when there are exceptional young-

Figure 18–2. Bowling is an excellent activity for some handicapped students. (Courtesy of the Lifetime Sports Foundation.)

sters in the class, the differences are simply greater in degree. A certain amount of adjustment in teaching methods is always necessary to accommodate the varying abilities, personalities and problems of the usual group of students; when there are children in the group with less than normal mental or physical capacity, the teaching method must be adapted still more.

An understanding of the limitations imposed by the handicap is of paramount importance. It is equally important to understand the potentialities of the handicapped student. Although teachers of the handicapped must rely upon medical personnel to indicate the limitations, an understanding by the teacher enables him to interpret the medical directives more fully when planning the best possible adapted program. It is highly recommended to students wishing to work with the handicapped that they become familiar with the basic etiology (see references on special physical education in *Suggested Readings*).

Below is a summary of the nature of a selected number of handicapping conditions and hints for adapting sports and activities for the particular handicap.[1]

---

[1]A more complete discussion may be found in the book *Special Physical Education: Adapted, Corrective, Developmental,* 2nd ed., written by Hollis F. Fait, published by the W. B. Saunders Co., 1972.

CARDIOPATHIC CONDITIONS

Formerly it was believed that those with cardiac disorders should never take part in physical education. It is now known that this group, with the exception of one class, will benefit greatly from participation in the less strenuous forms of team play, individual sports, dancing and recreational games. Cardiac cases are classified by physicians according to the functional capacities of their hearts, and the activities in which they are able to participate are determined accordingly. The four classes and some of the activities suitable for each are:

Class I.   Those who do not experience undue fatigue or discomfort from ordinary activity. Most activities may be offered unless the participation will be highly competitive. Suggestions include:
Softball
Paddle ball
Tumbling
Swimming
Tetherball
Badminton doubles
Handball doubles
Modified tennis

Class II.   Those for whom ordinary physical activity results in fatigue and pain. Activities suggested for moderate participation by this group are:
Archery
Bowling
Croquet
Horseshoes
Shuffleboard
Fly and bait casting and spinning
Hiking
Bag punching
Interpretative dance

Class III. Those who experience fatigue and pain from less than ordinary physical activity. Mild activities for those in this group include:
Walking
Fly and bait casting and spinning
Shuffleboard

Class IV.   Those who are unable to do any physical activity without discomfort. Bed rest during the physical education period may be prescribed by the doctor for a student in this class.

In working with the students who have heart conditions, the teacher should exercise cautious leadership, be guided always by a physician's advice and be ever watchful for early signs of fatigue. Most victims are well enough acquainted with their limitations by the time they are high school students to heed warning signs that they have played enough and should slow down. Some few, however, will push themselves too far when they are engaged in competitive activities and are urged on by their cheering peers. A good rule of thumb for detecting fatigue is that when the student begins to breathe through the open mouth, he has been working hard enough to need rest.

CEREBRAL PALSY

Cerebral palsy victims have suffered damage to motor control centers of the brain before, during or after birth. Types of cerebral palsy are:

The Spastics. The largest group, characterized by contracted, hypertonic muscles.

The Athetoids. The second largest group, characterized by involuntary, uncontrollable movements.

The Rigidity Group. Less common than the above groups, characterized by extreme muscular stiffness, usually coupled with mental retardation.

The Ataxics. Composed of 5 to 10 per cent of all cases, characterized by lack of balance, inability to control direction, multiplicity of eye movements.

The Tremor Group. Composed of approximately 5 per cent of the total, characterized by increased involuntary tremors which are often mixed with muscle rigidity.

The main task the teacher faces in working with the cerebral palsied student is to accept him, understand his condition, become aware of his educational capacities for work, play and study, assist him to gain confidence, skills and social acceptance and/or group status, and guide him toward needed personal and financial independence.

The activity program should stress (1) methods of relaxation, (2) the development of antagonistic muscles where needed, (3) body control, (4) movement accuracy, (5) the development of strength and endurance, and (6) when possible, a degree of skill in recreational games and sports. Activities for students with cerebral palsy should be noncompetitive in nature; competition tends to engender greater effort by the players, and these students become increasingly less coordinated as more effort is exerted. For this reason it is also essential for the teacher not to overmotivate.

Recommended activities are:

Swimming

Social, square, folk and tap
   dancing

Games of low organization

Horseshoes

Shuffleboard

Lead-up games to sports

Bowling

Archery

Golf

Fly and bait casting

Games requiring movement accuracy such as hitting or kicking
   stationary objects

EPILEPSY

It has been estimated that one quarter to a half million Americans are victims of epilepsy. Approximately 80 per cent of those afflicted are below 20 years of age. Epilepsy is caused by irritative injuries of the brain produced by heredity, blows to the head, physiological disturbances, personality maladjustments and environmental tension.

Seizures range from mild attacks (petit mal or "little sickness") to severe seizures lasting from one to five minutes, during which the victim has spasms or violent convulsions, bites his tongue, lapses into unconsciousness followed by stupor lasting from five minutes to several hours (grand mal or "big sickness").

Epileptic students who have mild infrequent seizures are placed in school with normal groups. Those suffering from severe attacks are usually enrolled in special schools. All should be under a physician's care. The physical educator (as well as other teachers) should be aware of the student's condition and work as a united team to help him select suitable school activities from which he can gain satisfaction, success and happiness. The controlled epileptic can benefit greatly

Figure 18–3. A modified court allows those with restricted locomotion to play tennis. (The National Society for Crippled Children and Adults.)

from many of the sports, games and dances taught in the physical education program. Swimming, gymnastics (including rope climbing) and other activities in which he would be in great danger should a seizure occur should be avoided. Combative sports such as football, in which a head injury may be possible, should be prohibited, as well as participation in highly competitive games wherein emotional tension runs high. Extreme fatigue must be avoided, so any activity that demands prolonged effort is contraindicated.

Epileptics are often fear-filled social outcasts. Many try to keep their condition secret; thus the terror of discovery is ever present. The majority are ashamed, shy and awkward socially as well as physically. Those who are busily engaged in satisfying activities are less apt to have a seizure than those who fearfully and passively anticipate them. It is important that the classmates of an epileptic be forewarned what to do and how to react should he have a seizure while in class. Should this occur, the student should be placed on his back on the floor, a coat or blanket wrapped around him, a soft object (such as an eraser or a folded cloth) placed between his teeth, and no attempt made to restrain his movements. The teacher must set a pattern of calmness for the rest of the class and keep the others occupied or away from the victim. After the convulsion, the student should be allowed to sleep or rest until he recovers from the experience.

Recommended activities for epileptics are:

Folk, social, tap and modern dance	Fly and bait casting
Bowling	Social recreational activities
Hiking	Basic sport skills
Archery	Team games in which there is
Tennis	little body contact, such as
Golf	volleyball
Badminton	

ORTHOPEDIC HANDICAPS

An orthopedic handicap is one which will not permit the individual to perform properly all normal motor movements of the body. Such a disability may be concerned with the functions of the bones, joints, tendons and/or peripheral blood vessels and nerves.

Many children with orthopedic disabilities are so severely handicapped that they are enrolled in special schools; however, many who are less seriously handicapped are able to attend regular schools. The majority of these will require adapted physical education. The specific activities in which they will be able to participate with benefit will be determined by the nature and extent of their disabilities.

Post-poliomyelitis cases, as a rule, need muscular re-education programs of some kind. Specific corrective exercises should be prescribed by the physician in charge. The selection of physical education activities should complement the exercises, giving the student an opportunity to employ his newly developed skills in play.

Students who have recovered from Perthe's disease need to avoid games and activities that put stress upon the head of the femur. Consequently, games such as basketball which require twisting and turning are contraindicated.

Those with amputated limbs or congenital deformities need to be taught ways of compensating for their losses in the performance of sport skills. As just one example, a student who must use crutches can learn to prop them against his body to give him support and at the same time free his arms to shoot a bow, toss a basketball, or volley a volleyball.

Suggested activities for those confined to wheelchairs are:

Archery	Wheelchair square dancing
Swimming	Water games
Bowling	Fly and bait casting
Wheelchair hockey, volleyball	Box hockey
and basketball	Table tennis
Modified gymnastics	Boating
Modified rope climbing	

Those wearing leg braces or using crutches can take part in:

Archery	Horseshoes
Shuffleboard	Modified softball
Fly and bait casting	Rope climbing
Tether ball	Modified gymnastics
Target shooting	

Activities suggested for those having arm paralysis are:

Social, tap, folk, square dance	Ice and roller skating
Rope jumping	Hiking
Cycling	Selected track and field events
Swimming	Modified soccer
Modified stunts	

VISUAL AND AUDITORY HANDICAPS

It has been estimated that one out of every ten Americans has some kind of hearing impairment. Special schools are provided for the most severely handicapped, but the majority are enrolled in public educational institutions. Most students with a hearing loss acquire it gradually. Turning the head to one side, cupping the ear, worried puzzled facial expressions, inattentiveness, difficulty in school, faulty posture in which the head and torso are held forward, and misbehavior may be signs that the student does not hear well, as may also poor pronunciations or other faulty speech habits.

Hearing loss is caused by excessive cerumen (wax), inherited weakness, accidents, disease, infection, a ruptured or tight tympanic membrane, mucus congestion of the middle ear, or tightness of the oval window of the cochlea. Hearing aids, lip reading classes, or moving closer to students when giving directions or talking to them all prove helpful to those unable to hear well.

Since most deaf students differ from their normal peers largely in their ability to hear, they should take part in as many regularly required physical education activities as possible. Many are shy and withdrawn; consequently, they need increased opportunities to play with others. Those wearing hearing aids are often fearful of being hit on the head or jarring the delicate instrument. Many have body balance difficulties. Activities such as dancing, roller or ice skating, modified stunts and tumbling games, track and field events, basketball, volleyball and softball are highly recommended. Tennis, badminton, handball and squash doubles increase peer participation possibilities.

Care must be taken by the teachers to give directions as clearly and simply as possible and to couple them with demonstrations as he talks. Since many lip read, it is important that all can see his face as he gives instructions. Gradually providing increased opportunities for these students to explain directions or game rules to others will give those who need it additional practice in speaking clearly.

Blind students usually are enrolled in special schools. Those partially sighted are often placed in regular schools if their vision is between 20/70 and 20/200 or there is no prognosis of progressive vision deterioration, if they are able to communicate, have behavior compatible with classroom procedure, are ambulatory and have hearing ability.

Figure 18–4. The teacher wears a blindfold while performing a skill to gain insight into the problems which the skill may present to a blind performer.

Many with impaired vision have exaggerated fears of falling and of running into objects. They usually lack social and physical skills. Many are in a weakened physical condition because of inactivity. These students will benefit greatly from contacts with normal groups. Ideally, each should be assisted in the physical education class by a seeing partner. Students can take turns for this assigned responsibility.

Suggested activities include:

Roller skating to music	Fly and bait casting
Archery	Social, folk, square, and modern
Golf	dancing
Track and field	Light exercise to music
Bowling	Marching
Modified stunts and tumbling	Body building
Basketball goal shooting	Boating
Wrestling	Swimming

THE MENTALLY GIFTED

The mentally gifted (those with I.Q.s above 130) often are the most neglected students in an entire school system. They tend to be popular and are often class leaders. Emotionally, they surpass their chronological age. Physically, they tend to be taller, heavier and more mature than their peers. Some few prefer passive pursuits such as reading, but the majority delight in highly competitive team play and rugged physical activities.

The teacher should include many marginal learning experiences for these students, such as game rules, strategy and history. Creative dance experiences, difficult stunts and tumbling activities, and advanced offensive and defensive techniques in individual and team sports should be stressed. Numerous opportunities should also be provided for the development of their great potential leadership abilities.

THE MENTALLY RETARDED

Mentally retarded is a term used to describe a condition in which normal mental growth is not possible. This occurs when the intelligence quotient is less than 75, although there are borderline cases just above and below this arbitrary number. The most severely retarded are incapable of being trained even in self-care and must be placed in special institutions. Of the others, some are capable of learning to care for their personal needs and to achieve a small degree of training for economic usefulness; they are classified as trainable. Still others have sufficient ability to achieve from second to fourth grade learning skills and are, therefore, classified as educable. Students in both the trainable and educable classifications are currently receiving instruction in special classes in the public schools. Many states have passed legislation in recent years requiring that such classes be established, and this trend will continue.

Schools providing instruction to mentally retarded students have approached the organization of physical education for them in different ways. Some schools provide separate classes, segregated from normal students, for all of the mentally retarded students together, regardless of their chronological ages. Other schools integrate these students with their peer groups in regular physical education classes, giving special consideration to planning for their special needs. The most successful organization, however, is one in which the school schedules its physical education so that segregated and integrated classes are being taught simultaneously, thereby permitting those retarded students who can profit from the instruction being given at any one time in the regular class to participate in it but enabling them to move to the segregated class when they cannot participate to their benefit. This dual scheduling, because of its greater flexibility in programming, offers the best possibilities of providing a good program suited to the individual needs of each mental retardate. Where this kind of organization is possible, it should be employed.

Teaching Methods. The benefits that can accrue to the mentally retarded student from his participation with normal peers will be realized only if he feels adequate and accepted by the class. To insure that this will be the case, the teacher should prepare the class in advance by promoting an understanding of the mental retardate as an individual who has certain strengths and weaknesses, as we all have. This requires skill and tact on the part of the teacher for he must win acceptance for his handicapped student, not merely tolerance.

The mentally retarded student will feel more secure if he is introduced to the activity in the segregated class before he joins the regular group. With some knowledge about the activity and practice on the skills, he will be sufficiently ahead of the class while it is learning the activity to feel confident of his performance and, so, to enjoy participating with the others.

The program for the mentally retarded must be carefully planned, giving full recognition to the students' mental capabilities and any restricting physical limitations. (The latter are often found in mentally retarded students.) Some students will be able to learn only the very rudimentary motor skills. Others will be capable of learning moderately complex skills, but the games, dances and other activities selected for them should require little memorization of rules, strategy and movement patterns.

In teaching skills to these students, for their comprehension it is necessary to break the movement pattern into components and to instruct how to perform each component separately before attempting the whole movement. For example, the movement pattern of the vertical jump may be broken down into these components: (1) the preparatory position with the knees flexed and arms back, (2) the vertical position with the arms moving forward and (3) the jump up with the arms fully extended.

The inability to perform complex patterns of movement must be considered when giving physical fitness tests to mentally retarded students. The importance of this consideration has been recognized only recently. However, a special physical fitness test battery, designed especially for use with the mentally retarded, has been developed; a description of it may be found on p. 564 in the Appendices.

The mentally retarded perform a skill best during their initial attempts. Therefore, the teacher should stop their practice before the students become unsuccessful and frustrated about their lack of continued success. Practice should continue in brief sessions over a long period of time. When the skills have been mastered sufficiently, the activity itself may be introduced. In subsequent periods when the activity is to be offered, the skills should be drilled on briefy to refresh the memory.

Many retardates have low physical fitness levels and, consequently, tire easily. Activities that are new or complex should be introduced early in the period while the students are fresh and alert. Injuries are more likely to occur when fatigue has set in so the teacher must be watchful for evidence of tiring.

Verbal instructions must be few in number and very clearly and concisely worded. It will likely be necessary to repeat the instructions several times; each repetition should be made in the same general word pattern as the original instructions. The teacher should speak slowly and distinctly. Replies to questions should be short and simple as the attention span of retardates is too short for complex explanations.

Demonstration is an effective method of instruction of these students. They comprehend readily through seeing the skill performed and enjoy mimicking the teacher. Kinesthesis is also very effective as a method of instruction. Leading the student through a skill, such as guiding his arms in a proper swing of the softball bat, often enables him to grasp the technique of performance when all other methods have failed.

OTHER DEVIATIONS

Other deviations likely to be found in the school population are discussed below, together with their implications for the adapted program.

Convalescence. Students returning to school after an illness, operation or injury which has kept them bedridden for a considerable length of time may need to be placed in adapted physical education until they regain their normal level of fitness. Approval for participation and recommendations for kinds of activity should be obtained from the student's doctor before he begins exercising. As a rule, any of the activities used to increase physical fitness will be suitable for normal convalescents. When a specific area of the body has been injured, special exercises to strengthen that area may be given with the approval of the physician.

Diabetes. Students with diabetes are usually able to participate in normal play activities without restrictions or adaptations and should be encouraged to do so. They are likely to become fatigued sooner than other students in the class, and the teacher should be alert to the early signs of fatigue. Activities such as relays, which allow rest periods for some of the participants while others are actively engaged, are especially good choices for those with diabetes. Care must be taken to help protect these students from injuries, such as scratches and abrasions, because diabetics heal slowly, with possible resultant complications.

Asthma. Asthmatic attacks may be triggered by physical exertion, fatigue or emotional upsets; consequently, asthmatic students often avoid physical activity, with the result that many of them score low on physical fitness. A program of adapted physical education activities designed to raise the level of fitness without causing undue exertion and fatigue is greatly needed by these students.

Students who are allergic to dust should not be required to work on dusty mats or on dusty playing fields. Substitute activities which do not arouse the allergic reaction should be provided.

Hernia. For students with hernia, all activities in which increased pressure is placed upon the abdominal area or in which a blow to the area is likely to occur are contraindicated. This includes such activities as weightlifting, boxing, wrestling and football. Running games, rope climbing and work on the bar and parallel ladders should also be avoided if the hernia is especially severe.

Dysmenorrhea. Because of pain during their menstrual period, girls often ask to be excused from physical education. Rather than being excused, these girls should be given light exercises, particularly abdominal exercises, to increase the circulation, since this will help to alleviate the pain.

TEACHING PROCEDURES

In teaching normal students a teacher relies heavily on verbalization and visualizations; but when a student fails to grasp the techniques of the skills from watching a demonstration and listening to a description, the teacher will assist the youngster by placing his hands, feet or the portions of the body involved into the proper position and guiding him through the desired movement. This is called teaching by kinesthesis, and it is a highly valuable teaching technique in that it establishes the "feel" of the correct use of the body to perform the skill successfully. The importance of kinesthesis in teaching handicapped children, particularly those with visual and auditory impairment, is obvious; and it serves as the perfect example of the fact that the methods used for teaching exceptional children are essentially the same as those used successfully with normal students.

Progress will come more slowly for exceptional students, and the teacher must be extremely patient in teaching them. Each accomplishment, regardless of how minor, should be recognized and used to help the student to gain group status and respect. However, the teacher should not permit the student to gain such approval too easily, since those in this group often tend not to try very hard and some few have learned early in life how to gain unneeded assistance quickly or have extra attention heaped upon them. The teacher needs to be especially cognizant of those to whom "I can't" comes too easily, and must seek to understand *why* it is used as well as to help the student to replace it with "I'll try."

The teacher should be ever mindful that the student has his own life to live and group problems to solve. Guidance given to handicapped students should always be geared to the development and independence of each student. Since many are lonely or social outcasts, they sometimes cling to a friendly adult as a drowning person clings to a would-be rescuer. Care must be taken not to become too close to these individuals or to become so closely identified with them that their problems become those of the instructor.

It is both challenging and rewarding to work with exceptional students. Each teacher who successfully does so is well rewarded by a newly discovered pride of accomplishment and a deeper appreciation for the miraculous courage found in these human beings.

CORRECTIVE PHYSICAL EDUCATION FOR POOR BODY MECHANICS

Corrective physical education, as the term has developed in the schools, generally refers to a program of exercises and activities designed to improve the body mechanics of standing, walking and sitting postures.

CLASS ORGANIZATION

It is usually more effective to have classes in corrective physical education small enough so that the teacher may give individual instruction to those with faulty body mechanics, especially those with severe problems. However, for general class work with those whose problems are mild, the students may be divided into groups.

For the analysis of personal posture, the class may take turns in pairs or groups of four in front of the mirrors which are available. To present postural exercises, the class may be formed into rows facing the teacher or squad leader. A certain few students may drill individually or be placed into small groups by themselves to exercise as needed, with one of the group appointed to count the cadence.

In the instruction of the correct working postures, the class may be placed in line formation parallel to the object with which they are working so that all can watch the good and faulty movements in each performance. As each student comes forward and performs the skill being taught, such as lifting, pushing or pulling heavy objects, and then returns to the end of the line, the teacher should make constructive criticisms of the performance.

TEACHING PROCEDURES

The students should be given an understanding of the objectives of the unit: improved posture, more efficient working skills, and greater proficiency in sport skills. These objectives should be presented in conjunction with each specific phase of the unit.

The posture unit may be introduced by a discussion of what constitutes good posture and how the factors that determine it will vary from individual to individual because of different body structures. To give the student the kinesthetic feeling of the posture best suited to him, have him perform the following:

1. Look straight ahead, chin in (avoid saying "Throw the head back").
2. Hold the shoulders wide (avoid saying "Throw your shoulders back").
3. Place the pelvis well under the spinal column.
4. Place the feet straight ahead.
5. Do not lock the knees.

Using a full-length mirror will help the students to get the correct concept of good carriage and may act as a motivator to work for better posture. Students working in pairs may check each other's awareness of good posture, using the above criteria.

For girls, modeling techniques are suggested as a means of creating interest in posture. Full-length mirrors, soft music to which to walk in rhythm, and the wearing of dressy clothes, including heels,

Figure 18–5. Using the silhouette graph.

are highly motivating factors. Some schools include a modeling fashion show in their demonstration to the public of the total physical education program. Others have modeling clubs as an extracurricular activity, while still others include modeling techniques in Fashion Your Figure or Weight Control units or clubs.

Taking silhouette pictures of the students helps them to realize how they stand habitually. For many this realization becomes motivation to improve their appearance through better posture. To make inexpensive equipment for taking the silhouettes, a camera is mounted on a stand. A wooden frame 6½ feet by 3 feet is covered with a sheet, and a small light is placed behind the sheet. The subject stands in front of this screen while the silhouette is snapped by the operator of the camera. A silhouette graph is also useful in helping students realize how they habitually stand or sit. Such a graph consists of a transparent plate or glass mounted on a wooden base. The plate is divided into half-inch squares. The silhouette graph is placed at a specified distance from the subject and his outline is traced upon the plate with a crayon. Care must be exercised by the one who is making the outline to maintain his eye at a constant distance from the plate so that no distortion of the silhouette will occur.

To correct poor posture the teacher must help the student to find the cause, but in making the analysis the teacher must remember that good posture is dictated by body build. Some poor posture is contributed to by muscular weakness, and strengthening the muscles may promote better posture. However, postural habits that have existed over a number of years cannot be changed by participating in postural exercises for a few minutes each day. Exercises are only an aid in creating better posture. A desire to overcome poor posture, coupled with constant awareness of what constitutes good posture, is far more essential.

A number of exercises for increasing the strength of the muscles responsible for posture are presented below:

Exercises for strengthening upper back muscles:

1. Stand with the feet slightly apart and the fists clenched. Cross the arms in front and fling them upward and backward behind the head. (As the arms are flung backward, rise up on the toes to avoid hyperextension of the back.)

2. Sit on the floor. Place the feet in front and the hands behind the body. Raise the weight of the body on the hands and feet and walk forward, backward, and/or sideways.

3. Raise the arms at the sides until they are parallel to the floor. Hold the palms up. Move the arms with moderate speed so that the hands describe a small circle, backward, downward, forward and upward.

4. Lie on the back and place the hands under the neck; inhale and raise the shoulders off the floor. Then lift the chest as high as possible. The head, elbows, hips and legs remain in contact with the floor. Avoid arching the small of the back. Exhale and return to the original position.

Exercises for strengthening the neck muscles:

1. This exercise requires a helper who will stand in front of you and lock his hands around your head. He attempts to pull your head down while you attempt to hold it back.

2. Lie on the stomach and place the hands on the neck; then turn the head from side to side.

Figure 18–6. Use of a towel for neck exercise.

3. Lie on the back and move the head from side to side, touching the ears to the shoulders.

4. Lower the head on the chest; then raise the head against an imaginary resistance, keeping the chin in (a belt or towel may be used, as in Fig. 18–6).

Exercises for strengthening the lower back:

1. Tilt the pelvis forward; rotate around and around as in hula dancing. Make a rather passive movement in tilting the pelvis backward since this will increase the sway curve. Avoid lifting the tail bone (coccyx) upward.

2. Lie on the back. Attempt to force the small of the back to the floor by rotating the lower part of the pelvis forward.

3. Lie on the back and raise both knees to the chest. Stretch both legs into the air and return them to the floor. Keep the small of the back in contact with the floor.

4. With the knees straight, bend at the hips, keeping the head up. Raise the arms as high as possible with the palms of the hands up; at the same time, bend at the waist as far as possible.

Exercises for strengthening the longitudinal arches:

1. Grasp a marble with the toes, and lift the foot so that the sole of the foot is facing the opposite knee.

2. Stand with the feet slightly apart, grip the floor with the toes, and attempt to rotate the knees inwardly to lift the arch of the foot.

3. Stand with the feet about 12 inches apart, the toes pointing straight ahead. Bend forward and place the hands 3 feet in front of the feet. Rise on the toes, move the heels outward and return to the original position.

4. Sit on the floor with the knees bent and the balls of the feet touching each other with the heels slightly apart. Draw the feet toward the body, keeping the balls of the feet together. Extend the legs with the balls of the feet together and the heels apart.

WALKING POSTURE

Correct body mechanics in walking may be checked against the items found below. Students may work in groups to rate each other, using these criteria.

Common walking faults:

Does	Does Not	
....	....	1. Leans the body forward before the leading foot strikes the ground in front of the body.
....	....	2. Exaggerates the shifting of the weight to the supporting leg which produces an exaggerated movement of the hips to the side.
....	....	3. Swings the arms in a wide arc.
....	....	4. Swings the arms at the elbows.
....	....	5. Carries the weight on the rear foot; when the lead foot strikes the ground, the body should be ready to be driven forward by the rear foot.
....	....	6. Bobs up and down, which is caused by exerting force straight up from the rear foot rather than pushing diagonally forward.
....	....	7. Looks at the feet; the eyes should be straight ahead.
....	....	8. Slumps and fails to maintain good balance.

SITTING POSTURE

The type of chair in which one sits determines the correct sitting posture for that chair. For this part of the lesson the teacher should bring in several types of chairs and demonstrate the correct way to sit in each. It should be emphasized that the best sitting posture is that which is efficient, relaxing and pleasing to the eye. Students should be given a chance to practice sitting in a straight chair, an overstuffed chair and on the seat of a car.

Instruction in good working postures should include lifting, pushing, pulling and stooping. A number of different objects of different weights and sizes should be available for demonstration by the teacher and practice by the class. Many items will be available in the school; desk, chairs, trash can, boxes of various sizes. Because many of the students will have occasion to lift younger brothers and sisters or youngsters with whom they may be "sitting," it is useful to demonstrate and explain the most efficient method of lifting children. This knowledge will also be useful to these students when they become parents.

DEVELOPMENTAL PHYSICAL EDUCATION FOR PHYSICAL FITNESS

Historically, the term developmental has been applied to physical education activities that "increase exercise tolerance of the weak and ill through individually planned and progressively vigorous programs.[2] Recently the term has also been used to refer not only to altering the exercise tolerance level but to improving low levels in motor performance.

Developmental physical education in this sense has been applied almost exclusively to programs for improving physical fitness and motor ability in children of pre-school or primary school ages. However, students reaching the secondary school without having developed a desirable level of competence in motor performance require a developmental learning experience comparable in nature to that given to young children who are in the beginning stages of learning the motor skills.

How best to provide this experience is a matter of controversy. There are those who contend that the teaching of motor skills should emphasize "movement patterns." A movement pattern is the com-

---

[2]AAHPER: *Guidlines for Professional Preparation Programs for Personnel Involved in Physical Education and Recreation for the Handicapped.* 1201 16th Street, N.W., Washington, D.C., 1973, p. 4.

bination of many specific movements, with the ability to make adjustments in the movements, depending upon the situation.[3] Many
programs of physical education today focus on the development of
movement patterns rather than on a specific skill, so that, for example,
the emphasis is on learning the pattern of hitting with an implement
rather than upon the specific skill of hitting a baseball with a bat.
Some advocates of teaching movement patterns believe that, having
learned the basic pattern, the student will be able to utilize it in all
similar motor tasks — that having learned to strike a rolling playground
ball with a stick, he is able to strike a pitched baseball with a bat. This
idea is based upon a concept that motor development skill in one
movement is automatically transferred to another movement, if both
require the same type of coordination. To accept this concept one must
accept the idea that there is a general ability of coordination. However,
the preponderance of evidence indicates that there is no such thing
as a general coordination which is basic to a number of motor activities; rather, coordination is specific to a particular motor activity.[4]
Consequently, learning to strike with a stick does not develop coordination which automatically insures skillful batting of a baseball.
There are some individuals who learn easily and perform well many
different skills requiring coordination and thereby give the appearance
that learning of one movement enhances the general ability so learning
and performing another skill is made easier. However, there is no
evidence to support this observation.

Transfer of learning in motor activity does occur from one movement to another but only under certain circumstances: when the two
movements have identical elements[5] and when the performer is aware
of the similarity of the two activities. (However, awareness is not
necessary when the movement has become habitual.) Identical elements are present, for example, in the wrist rotation used in striking
the badminton bird and the wrist action employed in hitting a squash
racket ball; therefore, the skill learning in one is transferable to the
other if the learner is aware of the likeness. Transfer of motor learning
does occur also when a principle learned in one situation can be
generalized and applied to another situation.[6] For example, learning,
while catching behind a plate in baseball, that greater stability is acquired when the center of gravity of the body is over its base (the feet,

[3]Godfrey, Barbara, B. and Kephart, Newell C.: *Movement Patterns and Motor Education.* New York, Appleton-Century-Crofts, Inc., 1969, pp. 35–40.

[4]Cratty, Bryant J.: *Movement Behavior and Motor Learning.* Philadelphia, Lea and
Febiger, 1964, pp. 40–41.

[5]Thorndike, E. L.: "The Psychology of Learning." *Educational Psychology.* New York
Teachers College, 1913, Vol. 2, *passim.*

[6]Judd, C. H.: "The Relation of Special Learning to Special Intelligence." *Educational
Review,* 1908, Vol. 36, *passim.*

when standing) may be transferred to the situation of achieving the most effective stance in the ready wrestling position.

Recognizing the limitations in the circumstances under which transfer of learning occurs, most physical educators teach many different specific skills that will provide the student with a wide variety of movement experiences, so that he has a large reservoir of skills to draw upon in performing any movement pattern. For the student with a low level of skill development, one who has a small reservoir of skills to be utilized in performing a movement pattern, the objective is to expose him to many and varied types of specific skills, so that when he is confronted with a new movement pattern he has a background of skills that he can utilize to produce the pattern successfully. In planning the student's developmental program, consideration is given to the kinds of skills he is capable of assimilating. Consideration is given also to the significance of the skill, that is, its importance in contributing to the development of a pattern of movement. Additionally, the ability and interest of the student are considered.

Generally, the development of total physical fitness is achieved through improvement of the individual components of physical fitness. Some students will evidence low levels in all of the components; a far greater number will be low only in certain of the physical fitness factors. Before a suitable program can be planned for any of these students, it is, of course, necessary to administer a diagnostic test to establish the specific weaknesses. The results of the test are used as a basis for determining the types of physical fitness activities needed to effect improvement. You may wish to refer to Chapter 11 for a complete discussion of physical fitness testing and selection of appropriate activities for improving physical fitness.

TEACHING PROCEDURES

Students with low motor performance should be included in the regular class activities even though their levels of skill and physical fitness are far below standard. Extreme cases are an exception; these students should concentrate on learning one or two lifetime sports for which they show a special interest or aptitude. If they are able to do so, they may be included in the regular class when these particular sports are being taught.

Enjoyment of the physical activity is closely correlated to success in performing it. Students with very low levels of motor performance often feel inadequate and, hence, fear and dislike physical education. It is, therefore, wise to arrange for such students to work out where their weaknesses and errors will not attract the notice of the more proficient students and, also, to allow them to compete against their own former record rather than against the performance of others. In this way they are more likely to feel secure and uninhibited about their efforts in physical activity; and, as their efforts pay off in achievement, they are very likely to begin to enjoy physical education.

The teacher must make sure that each student receives adequate instruction in the performance of the skills of the activity in which he is engaged. Then the student, if he is capable of doing so, must be encouraged to practice these skills during his free hours. He may also be referred to visual aids and reading materials that will help him to understand and appreciate his chosen activity and so enjoy it more. It is, of course, essential that he receive individual instruction to improve the techniques of performance and to overcome any errors.

DISCUSSION QUESTIONS

1. Explain the purpose of special physical education.
2. Under what conditions may exceptional students be excused from physical education?
3. Discuss methods that might be used in teaching correct standing, walking and sitting postures.
4. How can you, as a teacher, best help exceptional students to develop (a) physically, (b) socially and (c) emotionally?
5. Discuss the organization of the adapted physical education class when it must be taught by the same teacher simultaneously with a regular class.

THINGS TO DO

1. Observe a special physical education class in the local school system. Note particularly the responses of the students to the activities in which they participate.
2. Adapt one of your favorite games, dances or sports for a specific handicap.
3. Develop a list of exercises other than those listed in the chapter for postural deviations.
4. If possible, visit a hospital or special school for the handicapped to observe and talk with those afflicted with the defects discussed in this chapter. Discuss in class your conclusions concerning the physical education needs of these people.
5. Construct a silhouette graph by marking ½ inch squares on the surface of a 12 × 16 inch piece of glass with permanent ink.

SELECTED VISUAL AIDS

Choose to Live. U.S. Public Health Service.
Heart to Heart. American Heart Association.
It Takes All Kinds. McGraw-Hill Book Company.
Physical Education for the Blind. Charles Buell.
Poliomyelitis. National Foundation.
Posture and Exercise. American Film Company.
The Search. The National Society for Crippled Children.
That the Deaf May Speak. National Hearing Society.

They Live Again. Teaching Films Custodians, Inc.
Tuberculosis. Encyclopaedia Britannica Films.
The Walking Machine. State University of Iowa.
You, Time, and Cancer. American Cancer Society.

SUGGESTED READINGS

AAHPER: *Foundations and Practices in Perceptual-Motor Learning: A Quest for Under-standing.* Washington, D.C., 1971.

AAHPER: *Physical Activities for the Mentally Retarded (Ideas for Instruction).* Washington, D.C., 1968.

Adams, Ronald C.: *Games, Sports, and Exercises for the Physically Handicapped.* Philadelphia, Lea and Febiger, 1972.

Buell, C. E.: *Physical Education for Blind Children.* Springfield, Ill., Charles C Thomas, Publishers, 1966.

Fait, Hollis: *Special Physical Education: Adapted, Corrective, Developmental.* 3rd ed. Philadelphia, W. B. Saunders Co., 1972.

Lowman, Charles: *Postural Fitness.* Philadelphia, Lea & Febiger, 1960.

Vannier, Maryhelen: *Physical Activities for the Handicapped.* New York, Appleton-Century-Crofts, Inc., 1974.

PART FOUR

THE EXTRACLASS PROGRAM

The person who plans, organizes, and administers leisure programs for the future should be something more than an athlete; he should be, in fact, a fit representative of the best in our cultural life. Since it will be a part of his task to restore to human dignity the losses incurred through our present use of the machine, he should be a personality of dignified proportions, that is, an educator of the first caliber.

. . . . . Edward C. Lindeman

CHAPTER NINETEEN

INTRAMURAL ACTIVITIES

Most secondary schools provide opportunities for participation in intramural activities. To be worthy of its name, the intramural program should reach as many students, both boys and girls, as possible. The program should be set up at times when the majority can participate and may be held before and after school, during lunch periods (provided the students are allowed enough time to eat without rushing) and during the last period of the day, if such time is convenient and available.

THE PROGRAM

Activities selected for competition should be those which will serve the interests and abilities of a wide range of students. The program may well be considered as the laboratory where the skills learned in the physical education instructional class are applied in game situations, and in such circumstances, the activities taught in the physical education classes should be included in the intramural program. Participation should be voluntary. Activities high in carryover value, such as golf or tennis, should receive equal emphasis with the many team sports favored by this age group. A number of co-recreational activities, such as horseshoes, volleyball and tennis, should be included.

Suggested program offerings are shown on page 000.

Although few schools offer all of these activities, many of the larger ones do. Smaller schools usually are restricted because of lack of facilities, equipment or staff to the traditionally seasonal sports of football, basketball and softball. In such schools as many activities as possible should be included in the program and new offerings introduced as rapidly as possible. Expansion of the program can be facilitated by recruiting student and volunteer community leaders to assist the staff.

THE INTRAMURAL BOARD

Many schools provide for student representation in the administration of the intramural program through an intramural board. The board may be composed of the teacher in charge of the program, elected leaders of the Girls' Athletic Association (G.A.A.) and any similar club for boys, sport managers for each activity and a representative from each participating unit. Duties of the council may encompass determining activities to be included in the program, eligibility and playing rules, and the point award system, if one is to be used.

UNITS OF COMPETITION

There are several ways to set up units of competition for the intramural program. The method used will be determined largely by the particular circumstances of the school situation. Units frequently used are:

Homeroom teams	Activity clubs
Class teams for each school grade	Arbitrarily selected or chosen teams
Residential district teams based on geographical location	Color teams made up of groups who form own team; each is given a color
Alphabetically formed groups	Age selected group
Class teams from each physical education class	Height and weight similarity teams

Figure 19–1. "Pinnies" may be used to designate team groups. (Courtesy Darien Public Schools.)

Figure 19-2. Ladder Tournament.

TYPES OF TOURNAMENTS

Tournament drawing cards of many kinds are available commercially. The teacher or student managers, however, can make on heavy cardboard any of the following types:

The Ladder Tournament. Arrange player names on the ladder according to skill, with the best in the lowest position. Each challenges the one above; winners move up. The final winner is the player at the top of the ladder at the end of the tournament.

The Pyramid Tournament. This type is similar to the ladder, except that more players can be involved and no single one is left in lowest position. Any player may challenge any player higher on the pyramid whose name is in direct contact with his own (for example, in Figure 19-3, Jean may challenge Mary or Ted). The winner of the tournament is the player at the top of the pyramid when the tournament ends. This type of tournament is ideal for individual sports and is especially good for racquet games.

The Elimination Tournament. Although this type discourages continued participation by the losers, it has its advantage when there are large numbers competing, play-off time is short or an all-school champion is sought.

Figure 19-3. Pyramid tournament.

"Byes" (free passes to the next bracket) are unnecessary if the number of entries is a perfect power of two (4, 8, 16, 32, 64 and so on). If it is not, subtract the number of participants from the next highest power of 2 and add "byes" for the differences. For example, if there are 12 entries, 4 "byes" are needed, as is shown in Figure 19–4.

Two tournaments are recommended, instead of one lengthy one, if more than thirty players are entered. Arrange the tournament so that the best or seeded players do not meet early in the tournament. If four teams or players are seeded, numbers 1 and 3 should be placed in the first and eighth positions of the upper bracket, and 2 and 4 in the ninth and sixteenth positions.

The Double Elimination Tournament. Here no team is eliminated until it loses two games. Winners move to the right in the first elimination and to the left in the second elimination, as is shown in Figure 19–5. Note that if the winner of the first elimination loses to the winner of the second elimination he has lost but once, and another game must therefore be played by the two before a winner is declared.

The Round Robin. A revolving column is used for pairing opponents. Each team or individual is given a number; a "bye" is used if there is an uneven number of competitors. Players are moved either clockwise or counterclockwise to meet their opponents; if a "bye" is used it remains stationary and each number is moved over it to the next place. One round fewer than the number of entries is played, as is seen in the pairings and rotation series in such a tournament below. Note that the pairings are different for each round. The final winner wins the most games, and the tournament is completed when all have played each other. This type of tournament is an ideal way to increase participation and is especially recommended for secondary schools.

First Round	Second Round	Third Round	Fourth Round
1.................8	1.................7	1.................6	1.................5
2.................7	8.................6	7.................5	6.................4
3.................6	2.................5	8.................4	7.................3
4.................5	3.................4	2.................3	8.................2

Fifth Round	Sixth Round	Seventh Round
1.................4	1.................3	1.................2
5.................3	4.................2	3.................8
6.................2	5.................8	4.................7
7.................8	6.................7	5.................6

POINT SYSTEM

In many intramural programs, if the same units of competition are entered in several contests during the year, a point system is used to determine an over-all winner. Points are awarded to teams for winning

Figure 19-4. Elimination tournament.

or placing in the various contests. In some situations, only first, second and third place winners are given points; in other situations, usually where large numbers of teams are participating, the winners of the first five places are awarded points. The largest number of points is given to the first place winner and the least number to the third or fifth, depending on the number of places being awarded points. A team may also be given points for the percentage of games won in tournament play; in this case the highest number of points goes to the team with the greatest percentage of wins and fewer numbers of points to the teams with the next greatest percentages of wins. Points are also sometimes given for the number of participants each team enters in a contest, which is a good way to encourage more participation in the program. It is recommended that the same number of points be awarded to the winners in each contest, regardless of the type of activity.

Records might well be kept by a student group, elected or appointed for this responsibility, with one named chairman who is accountable for them. The group should work closely with the teacher in charge of the program; such a sponsor should serve largely in a guidance capacity.

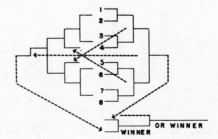

Figure 19-5. Double elimination tournament.

Intramural Sport Activities[1]

FALL

	BOYS		GIRLS		CORECREATIONAL	
	Team	Individual	Team	Individual	Team	Individual
	Cross country	Archery	Field ball	Archery	Golf	Archery
	Soccer	Bicycling	Field hockey	Bicycling	Kickball	Bicycling
	Speedball	Golf	Kickball	Golf	Modified games	Golf
	Tennis	Hiking	Soccer	Hiking	Relays	Hiking
	Touch football	Horseshoes	Speedball	Horseshoes	Tennis	Horseshoes
		Paddle tennis	Tennis	Paddle tennis		Paddle tennis
		Quoits		Quoits		Quoits
		Tennis		Tennis		Tennis

WINTER

	BOYS		GIRLS		CORECREATIONAL	
	Team	Individual	Team	Individual	Team	Individual
	Basketball	Aerial darts	Basketball	Aerial darts	Modified games	Aerial darts
	Gymnastics	Badminton	Skiing	Badminton	Skiing	Badminton
	Ice hockey	Basket shooting	Swimming	Basket shooting	Swimming	Basket shooting
	Skiing	Bowling	Tumbling	Bowling	Tumbling	Bowling
	Swimming	Deck tennis	Water games	Deck tennis	Water games	Deck tennis
	Tumbling	Fencing	Volleyball	Fencing		Fencing
	Water games	Ice skating		Ice skating		Ice skating
	Volleyball	Shuffleboard		Shuffleboard		Shuffleboard
		Table tennis		Table tennis		Table tennis
		Target shooting		Target shooting		Target shooting
		Wrestling				

SPRING

	BOYS		GIRLS		CORECREATIONAL	
	Team	Individual	Team	Individual	Team	Individual
	Baseball	Archery	Golf	Archery	Golf	Archery
	Golf	Bait casting	Kickball	Bait casting	Kickball	Bait casting
	Lacrosse	Canoeing	Lacrosse	Canoeing	Modified games	Canoeing
	Softball	Fly casting	Relays	Fly casting	Relays	Fly casting
	Tennis	Golf	Softball	Golf	Softball	Golf
	Track	Horseshoes	Tennis	Horseshoes	Tennis	Horseshoes
		Paddle tennis	Track	Paddle tennis		Paddle tennis
		Quoits		Quoits		Quoits
		Roller skating		Roller skating		Roller skating
		Sailing		Sailing		Sailing
		Tennis		Tennis		Tennis

[1]Reproduced by permission from AAHPER: *Physical Education for High School Students*. Washington, D.C., 1955, p. 378.

ELIGIBILITY RULES

There should be few eligibility rules, but all those adopted by an original planning group or current governing board should be established primarily for the protection of the players and serve as a means of reaching desired objectives. These regulations should cover participation eligibility and frequency rules, health requirements, forfeits, rule infraction penalties, and required student conduct. Rules should be established prohibiting athletes to take part in an activity in the program during the sport season in which they represent the school as a varsity team member, for these students may take part in more physical activity than is good for them, and the other students may feel that they are too skilled to be competed against on an equal basis. No student should be allowed to take part in the program if the activity will be detrimental to his health as determined by the school physician. However, all those unable to participate because of orthopedic, cardiac or other handicaps should be provided with numerous opportunities to engage in an intramural program geared to fit their disabilities such as table tennis, checkers, or other less active types of game tournaments.

AWARDS

Many schools give awards as a means of motivating and increasing participation and stimulating and maintaining interest. Some physical educators feel that extrinsic awards detract from the objectives of the program because they encourage participation for a reward rather than for the inherent values and enjoyment of play. If awards are given, they should serve only as recognition of achievement and, as such, should have insignificant monetary value. Certificates, ribbons, chenille or felt letters are appropriate awards; expensive trophies should not be given.

Awards may be given not only to team or individual winners but also for good sportsmanship. A service award might also be presented to the student who has been of the most assistance throughout the season.

Often recognition of achievement can be successfully provided by stories in the school newspaper or by means of an attractive intramural bulletin board, prominently displayed. In addition to citing individual and team winners, the bulletin board can feature pictures and records of the winners and of the highlights of the tournament.

OFFICIATING

Many intramural games will not require special officiating personnel, because the players themselves can conduct the game and do what officiating is necessary. The individual sports are easily officiated by those who are participating in the game, if a reasonable attitude has been developed in the students with respect to winning and losing so that objectivity can be maintained.

Some game situations, however, do necessitate the presence of one or more officials to insure fair play. Team sports fall in this category more frequently than other games, because it is harder for teams of several players to make exact observations and objective judgments. For example, in a game of softball or baseball, an official is needed to call strikes and balls, because of the difficulty the players have in judging the pitches fairly and accurately.

If officials are to be used in intramural play, they may be recruited from a leadership group (see discussion below) or from the student body as a whole. Training should be given these students so that they have a basic understanding of the rules of the game and the way in which it is officiated. Such training may be developed as an on-going program so that there can be several levels of skill among the officials; in such practice, beginners are limited to officiating with an advanced official and move up to advanced levels after passing officiating skill tests.

LEADERSHIP SUGGESTIONS

It is impossible to conduct a worthwhile intramural program without student aid and cooperation. Student assistants may be volunteers or may be chosen by the teacher or elected by their peers. Regardless of the way in which the membership of the leadership group is determined, it is usually the most popular youngsters or those who have demonstrated ability in the classroom who constitute the group. It is well to remember that many times, if given the opportunity and guidance, the timid or backward student or the consistent troublemakers can become effective leaders and at the same time acquire a base for continued self-development. Consequently, such students should not be eliminated from consideration.

An educational program for student leaders should be required for all who are to serve. This program should be of short duration but well planned and conducted. The major portion of it can be given by former students who have held coveted positions in the program; the teacher could serve as a guidance and consultant expert assisting those in charge of these sessions. Such a program might well include the objectives of the intramural program, activity offerings, types of tournament drawings, necessary reports to be made, organization of officials, eligibility and other rules, first-aid and accident-reporting procedures, leadership do's and dont's and methods of evaluating the results.

Each student leader might well work as an assistant leader under the teacher's or senior manager's supervision for a short period before directing a group of his own.

The secret of good leadership is to create new leaders. A good leader develops other leaders and gradually gets into the background while moving others forward into leadership position when they have been sufficiently prepared to succeed in their newly assumed group roles.

DISCUSSION QUESTIONS

1. What objectives would you as an educator endorse for the intramural program?

2. It has often been said that the school intramural program for the many should be emphasized and the interscholastic program for a few should be de-emphasized. Do you agree with this statement? If so, how can this be done? Give specific suggestions.

3. List the advantages and disadvantages of the following: the ladder tournament, the round robin tournament, the pyramid tournament, the single elimination tournament, the double elimination tournament.

4. List in order of importance to you eight qualities of leadership you believe necessary for success as either a student leader or a teacher. Which of these do you most lack? How can you develop this weakness into strength?

5. Discuss your suggestions of ways for making a school intramural program successful.

THINGS TO DO

1. Draw up a list of intramural activities you would like to include in your school. What factors must be taken into consideration as you make your list?

2. Have an interview with any fellow student in your school who is not a physical education major. Evaluate his report of previous experiences in a high school intramural program and his reactions to it.

3. Set up a double elimination tournament for nine players.

4. Set up a round robin tournament for nine teams.

5. Develop a simple point system for a hypothetical intramural program.

SUGGESTED READINGS

AAHPER: *Intramurals for the Senior High School.* Washington, D.C., 1964.

Daugherty, Greyson and Woods, John: *Physical Education Programs: Organization and Administration.* Philadelphia, W. B. Saunders Co., 1971.

Forsythe, Charles and Keller, Irvin A.: *The Administration of High School Athletics.* 5th ed. Englewood Cliffs, N.J., Prentice-Hall, Inc., 1972.

Kleindienst, Viola K. and Weston, Arthur: *Intramurals and Recreation Programs for Schools and Colleges.* New York, Appleton-Century-Crofts, 1964.

CHAPTER TWENTY

INTERSCHOLASTIC ATHLETICS

Since interscholastic athletics are a part of the broad program of physical education on the secondary school level, any discussion of the varsity sports must keep this in mind. Whereas the physical education program is organized to fulfill the needs of the entire student body, the interscholastic athletic program is designed for those students who demonstrate unusual abilities and advanced skills in certain games. The program of interschool sports might be said to be the extra-class work provided for these students whose interests and skills qualify them for work beyond that offered in the physical education classes. Some authorities refer to the program as the laboratory for the skilled students in the physical education program.[1]

INTERSCHOLASTIC ACTIVITIES FOR BOYS

Varsity sports which are commonly included in the interscholastic athletic program for boys are: football, basketball, baseball, track and field events, swimming, tennis, wrestling, golf and gymnastics. An unfortunate distinction has developed between those games which attract large numbers of fans to the box office and those which do not. The former, which in most situations include football, basketball and baseball, are commonly referred to as *major* sports while the others are relegated to the classification of *minor* sports. The distinction is entirely irrelevant from the standpoint of the objectives of these sports, and every physical educator should eliminate the terms from his vocabulary in justice to the entire interscholastic sports program. The gate receipts are entirely incidental to the contributions which the games

---

[1] See the Appendices for a checklist devised by The Educational Policies Commission for rating the school athletic program.

make to the participants. A sport should be judged on the success with which it meets these objectives:

1. Development of general health and physical fitness.
2. Development of increased skills and ability to respond in game situations.
3. Development of poise and confidence.
4. Increased personal satisfaction.
5. Increased knowledge of the game.

The physical educator who assumes the responsibility for one or more sports in the interscholastic program faces many problems of organization and administration. As he plans and carries through his program, he must never lose sight of the objectives of the program. He must never let the fame attendant upon victory obscure his sense of values. It is not an easy thing to be a *teacher of young people* when the fans, the press, and sometimes even the administration demand that you become the *coach of a winning team* at any cost. But to the degree that the temptation to win at the price of calculated overemphasis is resisted, to that degree is the interscholastic athletic program a truly educational endeavor.

SELECTING THE TEAM

Early in the season the coach issues a call for all interested students to report for practice in the particular sport that the school sponsors

Figure 20–1. All students should be made to feel welcome to try out for the team. (Courtesy of the Youth Service Section of the Los Angeles Public Schools.)

during that part of the year. The call should make clear that *all* interested students are welcome to participate in these practice sessions until the team selection is made. There are always some students who, though they are very competent and skilled, lack the self-confidence to report for practice unless they are made to feel that the chance to make the team is truly open to everyone.

After about two weeks of drilling and playing the game, the better players will begin to stand out. In selecting the varsity players, the coach should try to carry as large a number of players as is practical within the limitations of his budget and facilities. Moreover, he should organize as many teams of second choices as he can handle so that as many students as possible may benefit from the varsity program. Giving many students an opportunity to play on B and C teams has the added advantage of providing experienced replacements for the varsity squad.

PRACTICE SESSIONS

The practice periods should not be held more than five days a week, with each day's session no longer than two hours. These recommendations are based upon the physiological and psychological aspects of learning.

The coach should strictly observe any conference or association regulations about preseason practice. A conditioning period of three weeks is recommended.

The practice periods will be devoted to drill on specific skills, to the organization of team strategy and unity, and to analysis of individual and team weaknesses. The same drills taught in the physical education program may be used for varsity practice in each sport. Conditioning exercises have been presented in the chapter on body building.

Anyone who finds himself in the position of having to coach a sport in which he has had limited personal experience and preparation will benefit from reading some of the excellent books written by famous coaches and players of the sport. A list of these books has been included in the Suggested Readings at the end of this chapter.

HEALTH EXAMINATION FOR PLAYERS

Participants in varsity athletics must have a thorough health examination. It is preferable that the examination be made by the doctor who is the school's medical advisor because he will have a better understanding of the school's policies and will be more objective in

Name of School

The certification below is not valid unless signed by your family physician or the school doctor. If you wish the health examination to be made by the school doctor, the following request must be signed and dated:

....
(Date)   (Signature of parent or guardian)

Certification

I have examined the student named on the reverse side of this card and find that he is physically qualified to participate in all competitive games and contests except the following:

....

....

*Diagnosis...

....

....
Signature of family or school physician

Date...   Address...

* In case of refusal, please give brief diagnosis.

Figure 20–2. Sample form for the physician's certificate.

his examination. A sample form for the physician's certificate is shown in Figure 20–2.

PARENTAL CONSENT

It is customary for secondary schools to request written consent from parents; for a student's participation in athletics in some states this is required. A form similar to the one shown in Figure 20–3 might be mimeographed for this purpose.

Name of School

I hereby give my permission for

Name...

to participate in...
(Name of activity)

Date...   ....
Signature of parent or guardian

Figure 20–3. Sample form for parental consent.

TEAM MANAGER

A student manager who is capable and responsible can be almost indispensable in relieving the coach of his multiple responsibilities once the season gets under way. The manager may also have one or more assistants who are directly responsible to him under the supervision of the coaching staff. The managers are usually chosen from among those students who express an interest in the job. In making the selection consideration should be given to the qualities of reliability, cooperation and courteousness which the student has demonstrated in the classroom and in other extracurricular activities in which he may have participated.

The duties that the manager and his assistants perform are determined to some extent by the nature of the sport for which they are serving. Generally, the tasks in which they might be expected to assist are:

1. Taking charge of playing equipment prior to, during and after a game.
2. Cleaning and properly storing equipment between practices and games and at the end of the season.
3. Providing towels and water to players during games.
4. Helping players into sweat jackets or similar clothing when they return to the bench after participating in the game.
5. Posting notices issued by the coach of practice periods or travel arrangements.
6. Keeping records, scrapbook, and so on, as designated by the coach.
7. Attending to the needs of visiting officials and team members.
8. Officiating at practice sessions.

The coach may wish to break these general duties down into a specific list of duties for each sport. A copy of this specific checklist could be presented to the manager and his assistants and one posted in the dressing room. The managers should be asked to make recommendations for additions to this checklist on the bases of their experience during the season.

Before actual competition with other schools can begin a number of administrative details must be worked out. The care with which these matters are planned and put into operation will determine to a great extent the success of the program from the point of view of those who are involved in one way or another with interscholastic athletics either as spectators, officials, school personnel or representatives of the press, radio and television. The coach and his staff, if he has one, must make thorough preliminary plans, execute them promptly and with reasonable delegation of authority and, finally, make a last minute check on each item and person involved.

CONTRACTS

In some states it is required that a contract be drawn up between schools participating in athletic contests. This is usually a wise pro-

ATHLETIC GAME CONTRACT FOR INTRASTATE GAMES OR MEETS

The..agrees to compete with the...............
             School

....under the following regulations in
             School

....
                 Name of Contest

Date...Time...............

Place...

Guarantee...

....

....

....

and other conditions...

....

....

   Accepted for: *Accepted for:*

The...The...............
      Name of School   Name of School

By...By...............

Approved by...Approved by...............
        Principal   Principal

Approved by...Approved by...............
   Director of Health and P.E.   Director of Health and P.E.

Figure 20–4. Sample form for athletic game contract. (Courtesy of Division of Health and Physical Education, Public Schools of Baltimore, Maryland.)

cedure even when not required, unless the schools have long standing mutual agreements covering competitive athletic events. The contractual form used by one school is shown in Figure 20–4.

OFFICIALS

Officials for the interscholastic sports should be chosen with care. After some experience in watching officials on the home court or playing field and away from home, coaches become familiar enough with individual officials to be able to select them with confidence in their abilities. An inexperienced coach will have to rely on the recommendations of the school's administrators unless the state in which he teaches is one of several which has inaugurated a plan for registering, rating and classifying officials.

The contract with the official should cover:

1. The date, time and place of the game.
2. The assignment of each official for the game.
3. The amount of the fee.

The fee may be paid to the official at the half time or immediately after the game. The officials should be extended the courtesies offered to all visitors, including respect from the spectators. It may require an extensive program of re-education to achieve the latter. Cooperation of the cheerleaders might be enlisted.

SCHEDULING

The schedule for any varsity sport should be held to a reasonable limit. The following limitations of games or meets are recommended:

Football	7 or 8
Basketball	15 to 18
Baseball	12 to 14
Track and field	6 to 8
Wrestling	6 to 8
Swimming	8 to 10
Tennis	8 to 10
Golf	8 to 10

Several other factors must receive consideration in planning the schedule:

1. Whenever possible, schedule varsity contests on Friday nights or Saturdays or just before or during vacation periods.
2. Arrange the away-from-home schedule so that absences from classwork will be held to a minimum.
3. Schedule contests only with those schools which offer equal competition.
4. Agree to participate only on playing areas on the grounds of the school or those under the direct supervision of the school.
5. Observe all scheduling regulations laid down by the conference or association to which the school belongs.

ELIGIBILITY

It is the practice of schools to exchange lists (Fig. 20–5) containing the names of the players who are eligible for play in the contest well in advance of the time of the competition. The rules which govern the eligibility of players are established by the state athletic associations and have as their objective the control of those practices which result

ELIGIBILITY LIST FOR ATHLETIC COMPETITION

It is hereby certified that the following named students are eligible under the rules and regulations governing interscholastic athletics for boys in the state of

(Name) to represent..School in the

....activity to be contested as per schedule which has been submitted and approved by the Director of Physical Education and Athletics.

Name of Contestant	Birth	Date of Enrollment	Current Grade	No. of Seasons Participation	Former School

Date...

Investigated by...

Certified by...

Figure 20–5. Sample form for eligibility list.

in overemphasis of athletics in the schools. Minimum eligibility regulations in most states include these items:

1. An age limit of 19 to 20 years.
2. A limitation of the length of competition to three or four seasons in each sport.
3. A limitation of the semesters in attendance to six or eight.
4. A scholarship requirement.
5. A regulation concerning the transfer of the player to another school.
6. A rule prohibiting playing on the high school team by students below the ninth grade.
7. An amateur requirement.
8. A limitation on the value of the awards.
9. Regulations against recruiting and undue influence upon players.
10. Requirement of the physician's certificate.

TRAVEL

Playing a game away from home involves arrangements for the transportation of personnel and equipment, and possibly for food and lodging. Transportation by school-owned buses is the safest and most convenient arrangement. However, some states have regulations forbidding the use of buses for extracurricular activities. In this situation and in circumstances which make the buses unavailable for other reasons, transportation by private automobiles will be necessary. It is then of the utmost importance that public liability laws be satisfied and that the drivers be mature and competent. It is strongly recommended that private cars never be driven by students.

The players should receive explicit directions about the time and point of departure. It is a common practice to assign responsibility for personal equipment to the individual players, and for team equipment (such as balls, towels, first-aid supplies, blankets and sweatjackets) to the student manager.

If the length of the trip necessitates meals and lodging away from home, money for the expenses should be drawn in advance of the trip and the expenses paid for by the coach or person in charge of finances. In the interest of group control and efficiency in keeping the expense account, it is wise for all players to eat and sleep at the same establishment. This eliminates the necessity of collecting receipts from the players, and it enables the coach to keep a watch on the diet and hours of sleep of his team.

It may be required by the school or by the state athletic association that parental consent be obtained before a player may go out of town to participate in an athletic contest. If this is necessary, the forms should go out to the parents well in advance of the out-of-town game, and the team members should be expected to return them at an early date so that last minute collection of the slips can be avoided. The parental permission slips should state the place of the contest, the time of departure and return, the method of transportation, and place of lodging if it is an overnight trip.

Some schools will consider the parental permission for the student's participation in interscholastic athletics as an over-all consent for games played at home and away. Even when this is an accepted policy, it is courteous to inform the parents of players of the expected time of return and the name of the hotel at which the team plans to stay.

PUBLIC RELATIONS

Public relations is a matter of keeping the parents, students, faculty and friends of the school informed of school policies and events of interest to them. Because the events of the interscholastic athletic program have such wide interest appeal, the athletic staff is in a position to set the tone of the school's relationship to the public. For this reason the coaches and physical educators will want to disseminate

Figure 20–6. The school should organize as many interscholastic teams as possible to enable many students to have the experience of varsity play. (Courtesy Darien Public Schools.)

information equally to all channels of the public communications media and to maintain a professional, courteous and cooperative attitude toward all concerned.

Information to newspapers and radio and television newscasters should arrive well in advance of the deadlines stipulated by the papers or stations. The news and announcements should be issued to all competitors alike. When granting interviews to reporters, the coach should set an hour for the appointment which he is reasonably sure will be free from interruptions and will give him time not only to collect such material as he may wish to have on hand for reference but also to collect his thoughts before issuing statements for publication.

The news released to the public by the coach should observe these principles in the interest of good public relations and of sound educational practices:

1. Avoid highly emotional statements about the abilities of individual players, the team's prospects, and the evaluation of an opponent.
2. Avoid giving undue emphasis to a player's injuries.
3. Avoid making excuses for poor performance and failure to win.
4. Stress team play and the contribution of all players to the success of the team.

Representatives from the press, radio and television will require working areas in covering a game. Complimentary press cards should be made available to these people so they can move about the building with ease. The working stations assigned to them should be comfortable and should provide the best possible view of the contest. A frequent complaint of those who cover a local game is that they were stuck behind a pillar and so far back in the stands that they missed nearly all of the most exciting moments of the contest. If the game is to be covered by radio and television, certain pre-game arrangements will need to be made. If the coaching staff cannot personally assist these people as they set up their equipment, they should arrange for someone to be present to help as needed. A roster of the names of the home players, the opposing team, and the vital statistics of the game should be made available to those covering the game.

TICKETS

The entire business of the tickets from the time of printing to the counting of the receipts should be carefully administered. A sale of season tickets may be conducted a few weeks in advance of the season. In high school the sale of tickets at the gate is often a responsibility shared by the teachers in the school system. Frequently, the teachers also serve as ticket takers, although responsible students might be appointed for this duty.

Records in permanent form should be kept on the tickets received, with complete description of number and denomination, their distribution to sellers, and the receipts from sales of season tickets and at the gate.

AWARDS

The custom of presenting successful athletes with an award in recognition of their achievements has been in practice since the time of the ancient Greeks. In contemporary times the award system in some schools has become so complex that it requires much record keeping and a large expenditure from the athletic budget. This practice is extremely unsound not only because of the misplacement of educational and social emphasis but because the money would serve more students better by being spent for playing equipment.

In the granting of awards, it should be remembered that the awards are symbols of successful achievement and that every student should have an equal opportunity to earn an award. The size of the letter or the significance of the award should not be less for activities such as tennis and swimming than for sports such as football and basketball.

CLUBS FOR LETTERMEN

In many high schools those who have earned letters or awards for participation in interscholastic athletics form a club, which frequently bears as its name the letter of the school in combination with the word club, such as T Club or I Club. In some schools the club is purely social in nature; in other schools it achieves the stature of a service group and actively promotes a better athletic program. The activities may include ushering at games, welcoming and looking after the needs of officials and visitors at home contests, supporting drives to collect second-hand equipment from the public to enlarge the scope of the athletic program, and increasing participation by the student body in sports.

THE NATIONAL AND STATE ATHLETIC ASSOCIATIONS

Nearly all states have a state organization which establishes policies for the conduct of interscholastic athletics in keeping with the highest goals of education. These state associations may also be affiliated with the National Federation of State High School Athletic Associations. This organization is chiefly concerned with standardizing policies and practices throughout the country and with remedying the situations which have prompted the criticism of overemphasis which are currently being voiced against the entire program.

INTERSCHOLASTIC COMPETITION FOR GIRLS

Under wholesome conditions, competition for girls and women *can* be a rich, educational experience. However, all who wish to take part in the program should be given an opportunity to do so, and competition should not be limited to only a few, highly skilled players. The intramural program should reach the majority of students who desire to play with and compete against others, either as an individual or a team member. The extramural program, according to the recommendations of the Division for Girls' and Women's Sports of the AAHPER, should provide for competition among teams from local schools, community centers, institutions, clubs or other such organiza-

Figure 20–7. Increasingly, girls are participating in interscholastic sports that were once exclusively for males. (Courtesy Hall High School.)

tions in the form of a *sports day* (each school or other team competes as a unit); *play day* (team members are made up from all invited units); *telegraphic meets* (results are compared by mail or wire), and other invitational events (such as a symposium, jamboree, game or march).

THE INTERSCHOLASTIC COMPETITIVE PROGRAM FOR HIGH SCHOOL GIRLS

The athletic competition picture for girls and women has changed very rapidly in the last few years, mainly because of the demand for equalization of opportunity for both sexes. Women's lib has done more to bring this change about than any other factor. Pertinent questions relating to the lack of equal programs for girls and boys have been asked that reveal the appalling inadequacies of the existing operations. Girls with athletic ability who desire to compete generally are limited to participating by joining private organizations. Many public schools have not established or supported girls' athletics because of the outmoded theory that strenuous physical and mental exertion and strain are a menace to the high school girl, they cause women to become less attractive in appearance and more masculine in movement and manners, and that interscholastic contests create undesirable and possibly detrimental social influences on boys and girls.[2,3]

This attitude has been perpetuated, according to one source, because "we value in this country certain attributes in men: bravery, strength, capacity to compete in vigorous sports, but in a woman we value social graces and femininity more. These are not necessarily lost in vigorous sports, but some sports are more graceful than others."[4]

Today, one need only to observe the top women athletes to realize the fallacy of such a statement. Research proves that there are no reasons, either psychological, physiological, or sociological, for the female athlete not to participate in strenuous physical activity and that women in competitive athletics do not develop male characteristics.[5,6] According to Klafs and Lyon, "strenuous activity for the well-trained and well-conditioned female athlete results in good health and accentuates the very qualities that make her a woman."[7] The mental picture elicited when discussing the athletics of a boy or man in vigorous activity is changing rapidly. The mention of gymnastics brings about a visualization of Olga Korbutt and Cathy Rigby; in tennis, there is an image of Billie Jean King and Chris Evert.

With the changes made in the ruling of athletic governing bodies to delete discrimination of participants according to sex, the door is open for the highly skilled girl to compete. However, the changes made to meet the demand for equalization of opportunity have occurred at a very fast rate, and although cultures and society mores change, it may take longer for an acceptable code of ethics for women to become an established idea and for the acceptance of women in athletics to become a reality.

Presently, there are four critical areas, according to the Division of Girls' and Women's Sports of the A.A.H.P.E.R., that affect the growth of girls' athletic programs. These are: (1) selling the idea to the administration and the public, (2) securing quality leadership, (3) developing well-defined guidelines and principles, and (4) implementing the program in schools and leagues.[8]

Interscholastic athletic programs for girls cannot succeed without

[2]Hughes, William and French, Esther: *The Administration of Physical Education.* New York, A. S. Barnes and Co., 1954, pp. 194–207.

[3]Mann, Constance L.: "The Lack of Girls Athletics," *Physical Educator.* Vol. 29, No. 1, March, 1972, pp. 9–10.

[4]Higdon, Rose and Hal: "What Sports for Girls?" *Sport and American Society: Selected Readings.* Reading, Massachusetts, Addison-Wesley Publishing Co., 1970, p. 302.

[5]Klafs, Carl E. and Lyon, M. Jean: *The Female Athlete.* St. Louis, The C. V. Mosby Company, 1973, p. 10.

[6]Poindexter, Hally B. W. and Mushier, Carol L.: *Coaching Competitive Team Sports for Girls and Women.* Philadelphia, W. B. Saunders Company, 1973, pp. 2–4.

[7]Poindexter and Mushier, pp. 10–11.

[8]Mann, "The Lack of Girls Athletics," pp. 9–10.

the full understanding and cooperation of the school administration and the public. Teachers and coaches can bridge communication gaps by selling the program and obtaining favorable reactions. Hence, a sound philosophical statement as to the value of competitive sports is a prerequisite to developing an administrative athletic structure that will be accepted and supported.

Patsy Neal, a highly successful athlete, coach and teacher, in discussing the value of competition, states that:

> The athlete has unexcelled opportunities to live fully, give completely, make mistakes and learn quickly from them, experience winning and losing and have to take both in stride, learn to make sacrifices to achieve a goal, and feel satisfaction in achievement. In spite of fierce competition, the athlete learns how to walk off the playing field and remain friendly with the competition. Competition forces a girl to go full-speed and yet make valid on-the-spot decisions, to depend on her own initiative, and to develop the coordination needed to carry her through situations fraught with stress.[9]

The responsibility and authority for directing and coaching the girls' athletic program should be delegated to the women's physical education department. This should be a separate section within the department, much the same as for the intramural program. Although the organizational structure depends upon the size of the school, the ultimate authority in decision-making belongs to the administration which adheres to state athletic association regulations. These governing bodies are responsible for formulating policies, devising regulations, and determining rules to be used. The administrative structure of such an organization should also include provisions for input of ideas from the personnel who actually work within the prescribed program.

The growth of girls' athletics has uncovered and emphasized some problems which coaches and administrators must consider. These include: (1) athletic scholarships, (2) eligibility, (3) medical coverage and insurance, (4) travel, including meals and lodging, (5) awards, (6) financing the program, (7) scheduling, (8) use of facilities, (9) selection of coaches, (10) teaching load for coaches, (11) publicity, and (12) level of competition.[10]

Although the problems involved in administering interscholastic athletic programs are many, they can be solved through education, dedication and determination. The values of competition far outweigh the negative aspects, and the rewards, though often intangible, are worth the effort when watching a girl walk off the playing area displaying an attitude that the best was given no matter the score and knowing that there is pride in the fact that demonstrating skill ability was exhilerating.

---

[9] Neal, Patsy: *Coaching Methods for Women*. Reading, Mass., Addison-Wesley Publishing Co., 1969, p. 7.

[10] Flath, Arnold (ed.): *Athletics in America*. Corvallis, Oregon, Oregon State University Press, 1972, pp. 56–57.

STANDARDS IN SPORTS FOR GIRLS AND WOMEN*

Standards in sports activities for girls and women should be based upon the following:

1. Sports activities for girls and women should be taught, coached, and officiated by qualified women whenever and wherever possible.
2. Programs should provide every girl with a wide variety of activities.
3. The results of competition should be judged in terms of *benefits to the participants* rather than by the winning of championships or the athletic or commercial advantage to schools or organizations.

Health and Safety Standards for Players
Careful supervision of the health of all players must be provided by—
1. An examination by a qualified physician.
2. Written permission by a qualified physician after serious illness or injury.
3. Removal of players when they are injured or overfatigued or show signs of emotional instability.
4. A healthful, safe, and sanitary environment for sports activity.
5. Limitations of competition to a geographical area which will permit players to return at reasonable hours; provision of safe transportation.

General Policies
1. Select the members of all teams so that they play against those of approximately the same ability and maturity.
2. Arrange the schedule of games so that there will be no more than one highly competitive game a week for any one team or girl in any one sport.
3. Discourage any girl from practicing with, or playing with, a team for more than one group while competing in that sport during the same sport season.
4. Promote social events in connection with all forms of competition.

DISCUSSION QUESTIONS

1. Discuss the place of interscholastic sports in the total physical education program.
2. What criteria should be used in determining which sports are suitable for interscholastic competition?
3. Of what importance is the health examination for those who participate in interscholastic athletics?
4. Discuss all the details that must be given consideration before scheduling an athletic contest.
5. Discuss the D.G.W.S. standards for interscholastic competition for girls.

THINGS TO DO

1. Plan in detail an awards banquet for a high school's teams.
2. Plan on paper, using a specific theme, a sports day for 100 girls from four different high schools.

---

*Wilde, Jackie, (ed.): *Volleyball Guide*. Washington, D.C. Division of Girls and Women's Sports of American Association for Health, Physical Education and Recreation, 1971–73. Reproduced by permission.

3. Evaluate the interscholastic athletic program in the high school from which you were graduated. What were its strengths and weaknesses? How would you improve it, if you could.

4. Make a plan for practice sessions for any specific sport for one week. Indicate the time spent on each type of drill, exercise, etc.

5. Invite a physician to come to class to discuss medical problems in sports.

SELECTED VISUAL AIDS

Basketball Strategy for Girls. McGraw-Hill Text Films.
Play Ball, Son. McGraw-Hill Text Films.
Volleyball Strategy for Girls. McGraw-Hill Text Films.

SUGGESTED READINGS

Adams, Martha and Soladay, Ruth (eds.): *AIAW Handbook.* Washington, D.C., American Association for Health, Physical Education and Recreation, 1972–1973.

American Association for Health, Physical Education and Recreation. *Athletics in Education.* A Platform Statement by the Division of Men's Athletics. Washington, D.C., AAHPER, 1972.

Bunn, John W.: *Scientific Principles of Coaching,* 2nd Ed., Englewood Cliffs, New Jersey, Prentice-Hall, Inc., 1972.

Flath, Arnold (ed.): *Athletics in America.* Corvallis, Oregon, Oregon State University Press, 1972.

Handbook of National Federation of State High School Athletic Associations. 1972–1973.

Hart, M. Marie: *Sport in the Socio-Cultural Process.* Dubuque, Iowa, William C. Brown Co., Publishers, 1972.

Hay, James G.: *The Biomechanics of Sports Techniques.* Englewood Cliffs, New Jersey, Prentice-Hall, Inc., 1973.

Klafs, Carl E. and Lyon, M. Joan: *The Female Athlete.* St. Louis, The C. V. Mosby Co., 1973.

Miller, Donna Mae and Russell, Kathryn R. E.: *Sport: A Contemporary View.* Philadelphia, Lea & Febiger, 1971.

Mushick, Carole L.: *Team Sports for Girls and Women.* Dubuque, Iowa, William C. Brown Co., Publishers, 1973.

Neal, Patsy: *Coaching Methods for Women.* Reading, Mass., Addison-Wesley Publishing Co., 1969.

Novich, Max M. and Taylor, Buddy: *Training and Conditioning of Athletes.* Philadelphia, Lea & Febiger, 1970.

Poindexter, Hally Beth and Mushier, Carole L.: *Coaching Competitive Team Sports for Girls and Women.* Philadelphia, W. B. Saunders Co., 1973.

Resick, Matthew C., et al: *Modern Practices in Physical Education and Athletics.* Reading, Mass., Addison-Wesley Publishing Co., 1970.

Rushall, Brent S. and Siedentop, Daryl: *The Development and Control of Behavior in Sport and Physical Education.* Philadelphia, Lea & Febiger, 1972.

Vanderzwaag, Harold J.: *Toward a Philosophy of Sport.* Reading, Mass., Addison-Wesley Publishing Co., 1972.

Whiting, H. T. A. (ed.): *Readings in Sports Psychology.* Lafayette, Indiana, Balt Publishers, 1973.

CHAPTER TWENTY-ONE

RECREATIONAL ACTIVITIES

After-school recreational activities sponsored by the physical education department include informal games, camping and outing, social recreation, and club activities. It is but one part of the total school recreational program which, ideally, should be composed of music, dramatics, arts and crafts, nature, and other activities closely related to all subjects offered in the curriculum. The goal of all recreation programs, whether they be school or community sponsored, should be to provide individuals with meaningful leisure time activities and to help them gain enough skill to find such joy and deep satisfaction that they become recreated, refreshed and revitalized for the necessary tasks of work and daily living.

Free time and leisure are not the same thing. The former is time left after work or school every day. Leisure can only be defined in terms of what it does for a person and vice versa. In its lowest form it is mere diversion; in the highest it is creative—a developing and re-creative experience. Although we all have far more free time than we realize, only a few have found the re-creativeness of true leisure.

Americans now have more free time than any other people in world history, yet this is only the beginning of a rapidly expanding new age of leisure. The trend is toward the four-day work week of ten hours each day, with three days off, and experts predict that by 1975 most Americans will have 308 fewer work hours per year than they had in 1964. Authorities in both business and recreation claim that the three-day week of work and four of free time are soon to become a reality. The problem of the use of increased leisure time is minute today in comparison to what it will be tomorrow, for there will be not only more leisure but more people to use or abuse it. In our money and work orientated value system of life Americans are poorly prepared for leisure; too many of them are throwing away their free time in negative, detrimental, exhaustive pursuits. Youth especially needs to learn how to plan and best utilize daily free time for re-creation. Leisure, when used correctly and to its fullest, will (1) recreate the body, mind and spirit through activities which have meaning and value, and (2) bring forth renewed vigor, spirit and creative efforts. Our unrecognized incapacity to make wise use of leisure may well lead us all into what Professor Schlesinger of Harvard calls the most demoralizing factor in today's culture, "spiritual unemployment."

If the school is to raise the level of society and of value concepts and appreciations, it must prepare all its students for a life that will be well spent tomorrow, in leisure as well as in labor. The basic aim of any school educational program should be to teach students *how* to live, not merely how to make a living.

It is the teacher's responsibility to help *each* student re-examine his daily schedule and to help him to realize that he may have much more free time than he thought and then to help him plan to do recreative activities. Lifelong behavior patterns and value systems are laid down early in life, so it is the duty of the adult youth leader and teacher to help youth develop, rechannel, broaden and deepen these into moral habits and beliefs which are lasting and good. It is especially important for high school students to enjoy positive leisure daily because:

1. They are putting the final, lasting touches on the slow building of lifelong habits. Each year every boy and girl is likely to have more leisure time than the previous year. Most of them will be working 30 hours or less weekly in the near future; most will live to be 80 years old. Many will live to be over 100 years of age. Most of the girls will outlive their husbands by four or more years and will be alone in their old age.

2. "All work and no play" makes Jack not only dull but a sick, unbalanced and unhappy boy, according to medical authorities.

3. Leisure gives up opportunity to be creative, to express our basic human need to be our real selves. Work (including school) is often montonous routine. Human life should be sparkling, not drab and dull; leisure can add lasting luster to living.

4. Those who correctly balance work and play are more productive and tend to be in better physical, mental and emotional health. We play so we can work better, but work and play must each be done in proper amounts. Just as we can work too hard and too much, we can by playing too much get too far behind with our responsibilities. Balance is vital.

5. Students who are disciplined, well organized and have life goals well in mind will be the most successful.

INFORMAL ACTIVITIES

Games and activities that are frequently played informally for recreation include:

Archery golf	Checkers	Curling
Billiards	Chess	Dart ball
Box hockey	Corkball	Duckpins
Boccie	Croquet	Floor tennis

Fly and bait casting	Skiing	Touch football
Handball	Skish	Volleyball
Horseshoes	Squash	Water polo
Lawn bowling	Table tennis	Weight lifting
Paddle tennis	Target shooting	Weskit
Shuffleboard	Tin can golf	
Skeet shooting	Tenpin bowling	

Most of the skills of these activities required for recreational use are easily learned. Very little space and/or special equipment is needed. Two or three different activities can be played cross court in the gymnasium; side and end line areas can be utilized as additional game areas. Wall spots or spaces between doors or windows can be used as targets or goals. If necessary, inexpensive, discarded or improvised equipment can be used.

Suggestions for leading these activities successfully are:

1. Schedule a regular time for playing games and have all necessary equipment available so that each player can select, use and return what he needs.

2. Use student leaders to teach others to play the games. Station each helper at an assigned area and have all who wish to learn a particular game from any certain student helper go to that area.

Figure 21–1. Shuffleboard is a good recreational activity for inclusion in the recreational as well as instructional physical education program. (Courtesy of the Youth Service Section of the Los Angeles Public Schools.)

Figure 21-2. A multiple-purpose hardtop surface for tennis, handball and basketball. (Courtesy of *The Scholastic Coach.*).

3. As a friendly supervisor, rotate around all areas to help each student who seeks assistance.

4. Provide a wide variety of active and passive games.

5. Increase participation and interest through tournaments, giving recognition to winners and using as many student committees and assistants as possible.

Figure 21-3. Unfortunately, not many schools include handball in their physical education program. It is a vigorous activity that most boys find challenging. (Courtesy of the Youth Service Section of the Los Angeles Public Schools.)

6. Capitalize upon current game fads, such as Scrabble, Twenty Questions and Television Charades.

A well-organized after-school recreational program can almost run itself. The secret of success lies in careful planning, the use of student leaders, and provision of games students are eager to learn or enjoy playing.

CAMPING AND OUTING

Interest in outdoor camping, cooking and backpacking is now at an alltime popularity peak. Those eager to master campcraft skills such as axecraft, toolcraft, fire building, fishing, hiking, hunting, knotcraft, orienteering, backpacking, survival camping, lashing, outdoor cooking or shelter construction should be taught to do so at school, at a local community recreational center or at a youth-serving agency. Since the majority of students will have few opportunities to learn these skills, it is recommended that every secondary school physical education department include offerings in these areas through an after-school recreational program.

Figure 21-4. Although many of the basic campcraft activities can be taught on the school campus, students should also go on several overnight camping trips to a wooded area. (Courtesy Unified School District.)

All campcraft skills, including outdoor cooking, can be taught to small as well as large groups outdoors or indoors, and opportunities should be provided for those camping skills mastered to be practiced and used by each student in a real camping situation, even though it be a substitute one conducted at a public park. Any teacher can master these basic skills by the self-instruction method, using references listed at the end of this chapter. Services of local camp experts can be enlisted, for most real campers are enthusiastic woodsmen, eager to help others to enjoy the sheer magic of outdoor living.

Hiking, outing or hosteling clubs can also motivate student interest. Every community has unused areas and facilities for adventuresome exploration, and youth is eager for these new experiences which contain challenging and dangerous elements. Hosteling groups, whether they travel by foot, bicycle or horse, can explore other regions both here and abroad by taking advantage of the numerous opportunities now available.[1]

SOCIAL RECREATION

The purpose of social recreation is to provide for better use of leisure time, to increase social contacts, release tensions, satisfy basic needs to belong and gain recognition, and to provide self-expression, the development of leadership, and democratic experiences in group activities.

Activities that may be held in after-school or night programs include:

Games—Active, quiet, musical, table, card, low organization, relays

Informal drama—Skits, stunts, charades, guessing games, amateur nights, radio shows

Music—Community singing, mixers, guessing games, dance bands, "uke" clubs, orchestras

Dance—Social, folk, square, barn dances, folk festivals, social dance contests

Corecreational sports-Individual and team

Arts and crafts—Paper, junk, pipe cleaners, table decorations, costume design, metal-and woodcrafts, painting and sketching

Parties—Seasonal, special

Banquets and suppers—Informal, formal

Snow and ice sports—Skating and sleighing parties

Teas, coke and coffee hours

All social recreation should give each person pleasure and feelings of group worth or acceptance. School parties are often highlight

---

[1]Write to the American Youth Hostel Association, 6 East 39th Street, New York, for information.

experiences in the lives of many students. These special events should be largely student planned, conducted and evaluated with the assistance of teacher guidance. Naturally, these youth will make many mistakes while learning the necessary skills for success. The wise adult who is patient enough to let them muddle through experiences and learn from their mistakes is indeed a valuable educator.[2] However, many needless errors can be avoided by having students capitalize upon the following leadership techniques for conducting social recreation activities successfully:

1. Plan well in advance.
2. Assign or elect students to needed committees. Compose with each group a list of their responsibilities and the completion dates for each.
3. Anticipate emergencies by drawing up alternate plans (for example, plan for sunny as well as rainy weather).
4. First select a theme, then games, decorations, invitations, entertainment and refreshments to fit around it.
5. Draw up a checklist of all needed supplies and equipment, such as a record player, microphone, and so on, and be sure they are ready *before* the event begins.
6. Delegate authority and give each selected person a feeling of confi-

---

[2]See the chapter on *Learning.*

Figure 21–5. Bicycling could either be a co-educational class or after-school club activity. (Courtesy Unified School District.)

dence and responsibility. Have students direct the games and serve as hosts and hostesses, for it is *their* party.

7. Plan a well-balanced program, spacing active and quiet games properly.

8. Include numerous mixers and easy-to-do games.

9. Begin with pre-party activities that will make all feel welcome and that a big event is about to happen.

10. Plan a climactic ending. Do not drag out the event; make it short enough to be memory sweet.

11. Evaluate the results and help groups capitalize upon what they have learned from their experiences.

CLUB ACTIVITIES

Club activities are especially popular and valuable for teenagers.[3] Every activity included in the physical education program can be used as basis for a club. The chief values of these group gatherings are to learn new skills or perfect old ones, to make new friends, to learn more about others, a sport or life, to be of service and to have fun.

Types of recommended clubs include:

Archery	Hosteling
Bicycling	Judo
Bowling	Leaders
Camping	Nature
Checkers	Recreational games
Chess	Riding
Dance (square, folk, social, acro-	Service
batic, tap or ballet)	Skiing
First aid	Swimming
Fly and bait casting	Target shooting
Hiking	Teen
Health	Weight training
Hobby	Water skiing

OFFICES

All club officers should be elected, including the sponsor. Each officer should be energetic, popular, respected and capable of influencing others positively as well as possessing the ability to delegate responsibility and work democratically with others. The sponsor should regard himself as leader behind a younger developing leader and avoid superimposing his ideas or dominating tendencies upon the group. Since all clubs are miniature democratic societies, it is here that youth learn best the vital lessons and skills necessary to perpetuate our chosen way of life.

---

[3]See the chapter on *Understanding the Students.*

Each club should have a written constitution containing all governing rules, the name, purpose, membership qualifications, officers, meetings, and procedures for amendments. Meetings should be conducted according to Roberts' Rules of Order. An agenda should be planned for each meeting; this should include the call to order, reading of the minutes of the last meeting, old business, new business, announcements and adjournment. Subcommittee groups, to which as many members as possible should be appointed, will both stimulate interest and increase group identification.

The Girls' Athletic Association (G.A.A.), a Leaders' Club, or a Service Club can be almost invaluable help to every physical educator; each is a rich source for recruiting youngsters into the profession. A Gym Leaders' Club at the Wichita Falls High School in Texas has gained the attention of many physical educators. Students of both sexes are selected for membership by their teachers. Club meetings are held during the last class period of the day, and these highly skilled students receive additional instruction in physical education activities and leadership techniques. Each serves as a student assistant in the regular physical education classes. All wear special uniforms with a leader's seal on the breast pocket. The group gives a public demonstration yearly. Since membership in this select group is sought by many students, the club has been found to be a great motivator for increased effort and interest and improved attitude of all other students in the physical education program. Many of these selected club members later enter the physical education profession.

SELECTED VISUAL AIDS

All the following visual aids are available from The Athletic Institute on a rental or purchase basis:

Food and Fire. Shows 15 types of outdoor cookery and pointers on food selection, outdoor kitchens, and fire building.

Toolcraft. The selection, care and use of knives, axes, saws and other campcraft tools.

Orienteering. The use of maps, the compass, measuring heights and distances and sketch maps.

Cycling. Eight film strips showing riding fundamentals, bike safety, recreational riding, racing techniques and strategy.

DISCUSSION QUESTIONS

1. What is the difference between free and leisure time?

2. Discuss the concept given in this chapter that the basic aim of the school educational program should be to teach students how to live, not merely how to make a living.

3. Many adults consider the school recreation program to be a frill. Do you agree or disagree with this concept? As an educator, support your answer.

4. What can students learn at school through outdoor education programs that will help conserve our natural resources, rid us of pollution, and help keep America beautiful?

5. Which of the 11 suggestions given in this chapter for conducting social recreation activities successfully seems to you to be the most important? Why?

THINGS TO DO

1. Conduct a business meeting for a real or an imaginary club according to *Robert's Rules of Order*. Evaluate your results.
2. Plan an all-school party. If possible conduct it. Evaluate your results.
3. Keep a record of how you spend your free time for one week on a half-hour basis. How much free time do you have daily? Discover whether you are using your own time well.
4. Survey ten adults to find out how they spend their free time. Report your findings to your classmates.
5. There is a high correlation between increased free time and increased crime. Bring to class newspaper clippings from local newspapers printed on a weekend that illustrate this fact. What are your conclusions from this experience?

SUGGESTED READINGS

Brown, R. E. and Mouser: *Techniques for Teaching Conservative Education*. Minneapolis, Burgess Publishing Co., 1964.

Donaldson, George and Alan: "Outdoor Education: Its Promising Future." *The Journal of Health, Physical Education and Recreation*. April, 1972, pp. 23–28.

Donaldson, George and Goering, O.: *Perspective in Outdoor Education*. Dubuque, Iowa, William C. Brown and Co., 1972.

Hammerman, D. R. and Hammerman, W. M.: *Teaching in the Outdoors*. Minneapolis, Burgess Publishing Co., 1964.

Jensen, Clayne: *Outdoor Recreation in America*, 2nd ed., Minneapolis, Burgess Publishing Co., 1973.

Roberts, Dorothy: *Leading Teen-Age Groups*. New York, The Association Press, 1963.

Vannier, Maryhelen: *Recreation Leadership*, 3rd ed., Philadelphia, Lea & Febiger, 1975.

CHAPTER TWENTY-TWO

DRILL TEAMS AND PEP SQUADS

DRILL TEAMS

Drill teams composed of marching units, baton twirlers, acrobats and a drum and bugle corps are extremely popular among high school students and the general public. These colorful groups are usually service organizations for both the school and community. They perform at athletic contests between halves, at school assemblies and at community affairs. Since they are, for the most part, made up of girls they are usually sponsored by a woman physical educator. Practice hours range from one hour daily to ten or more weekly; sessions are held before or after regular school time.

Although in some sections of the country there is a waning interest in these activities, in others it remains high. This is especially true in Texas and in other neighboring states. The chief value of girls' dance-drill-baton teams is that they give needed public attention to girls' physical activities.

OBJECTIVES

The objectives of the school drill team are to:

1. Perform a service to the athletic teams, school and community.
2. Develop skills in working as a team member and in such activities as marching, dancing, baton twirling, rhythmic exercise and acrobatics.
3. Develop physical fitness, body control and beauty of movement.
4. Develop consideration for others, good sportsmanship and respect for rules.
5. Learn to be wiser, more appreciative spectators.

STANDARDS

Written policies for drill teams and related groups should be drawn up. A suggested pattern for doing so follows:[1]

---

[1]Material reprinted by permission and as a revision of that which appeared in *The Teacher's Guide to Physical Education for Girls in High School,* California State Department of Education.

GENERAL

1. Drill teams should be established primarily for the benefit of the students.

2. Whenever drill team is included in the instructional program, it should be given the same consideration as other program activities with regard to staff and facilities. It should not take precedence over or reduce other activities.

3. If a conflict exists between educational and showmanship principles, the educational ones should be the basis for making decisions regarding the structure of the activity.

4. Frequent evaluation of the activity should be made to determine whether the outcomes are educationally sound or whether the students are being exploited.

5. The establishment of drill teams at the junior high level is strongly disapproved.

6. The organization, planning, direction and execution of drill team activities should provide an opportunity for each girl to contribute in the creating of drill patterns, rhythms, dramatics and songs, under the direction of a qualified teacher.

7. Whenever drill team is included in the instructional program, other units should be included to provide instruction in a variety of physical education activities: i.e., dance, individual and team sports and mechanics of body movement.

8. Costumes should be simple, inexpensive, appropriate and in good taste. These standards should be determined cooperatively by the administration, sponsor and the participants.

9. More elaborate costumes for leaders or any related group should be avoided.

10. Drill teams should be taught and advised by women trained in physical education whenever possible because of the vigorous physical activity involved.

PERFORMANCE

1. The number of activities in which drill teams should perform during a one week period should be limited to a maximum of one competitive event plus one noncompetitive event.

2. The maximum length of marching in any parade should be limited to two miles.

3. The total time involved for competing in a parade should not exceed a three hour maximum, including formation.

4. All competitive activities should be judged by qualified personnel.

5. The value of competition should be judged in terms of the benefits to the participants rather than by the winning of awards by the participating organization or by the commercial advantage to the school.

6. Drill teams should only participate in pregame and intermission activities when they represent the home school or by invitation.

7. Drill teams should not be permitted to participate when excessive heat, undue cold or rainy conditions exist which would constitute a health hazard to those involved.

8. Choreography for all routines should be appropriate and in good taste.

PARTICIPATION

1. Selection for participation should be determined according to interest and ability.

2. The basis for selection should include health, posture, rhythmic aptitude, cooperation, reliability, dependability and scholastic standing.

Figure 22-1. Participating on a drill team is a recommended activity for high school girls. (Courtesy of the Kilgore, Texas, Junior College Rangerettes.)

3. Ability to purchase the necessary costume and equipment should in no way be used as a criteria for the selection of members.

4. Since marks are a necessary part of each class, students must understand that these are partly based on their participation in night games and all activities approved by the local administrator and advisor.

5. In the interest of student welfare, performances away from school must have educational value and administrative approval.

6. Participation in events which cause an undue amount of interference with the regular school program or cause an excessive amount of absence due to rehearsal or preparation should not be approved.

7. Participation in events which are sponsored for the purpose of commercial advertising or private gain must be consistent with the provisions as set down in the State Education Code.

8. All participants should pass periodic health exams by a qualified physician and maintain a good attendance record.

9. Prospective members should have a record which shows average or better participation in physical education.

10. All participants should be continually observed and counseled concerning their health.

11. Students should be removed from the activity when they are injured, over-fatigued or show signs of emotional instability.

12. Activities should be limited to a geographical area which will permit participants to return at a reasonable hour.

13. Safe transportation to all approved activities should be provided by the school.

14. Participation in drill team activities should not exceed twenty weeks of one school year.

15. Participation in drill team activities should be limited to a maximum of three years, each year not to exceed a twenty-week season.

PERSONNEL

To be most effective, the team should be carefully selected and well trained to work as a rhythmic unified group. Tryouts should be held for membership, and only those who meet certain qualifications should be eligible to be initiated into the group in a formal ceremony. Although membership qualifications are not standard, most of them include:

1. Scholarship (an over-all grade average of C or better).
2. Good health.
3. Height between 5 feet 2 inches and 5 feet 5 inches.
4. Good coordination as determined by tests of reaction time, body flexibility, balance and rhythm.
5. A good citizenship record at school and in the community.
6. A knowledge of the team's constitution (including the objectives, officers and their duties, rules for members, and individual responsibilities).

A girl's ability to perform cooperatively in a precision group is more important than her physical attractiveness, although this should be taken into consideration, or her skill as an outstanding baton twirler or acrobat.

THE SPONSOR

The sponsor should be selected by the group rather than appointed by the principal. She should be popular, respected and friendly with the students. Her abilities should include skill in working democratically with others, ability to lead, and a working knowledge of teaching marching, dance routines, drill formations and precision exercises. Although few sponsors have been trained to direct this extracurricular activity, courageous ones will be willing to learn the necessary techniques. The director of girls' performing groups should be allowed time within her regular teaching schedules to do the work required. Graduate students, hired dancing school teachers and others in the community may become paid assistants. Although many of these people do a fine job, some lack the skills and interest in the educational process to serve the girls to their advantage. Since few reference materials and guides have been written in this area as yet, teachers who sponsor outstanding teams and publish materials in this field quickly gain recognition and often more lucrative positions.

RULES

The group should formulate its own governing regulations. These should include rules regarding attendance at practice sessions and performances and standards of conduct before, during and after games. The sponsor should realize that group-formulated laws, drawn up with the assistance of her own experience-gained counsel, will be those by which the team will abide most closely.

UNIFORMS

There are several ways to secure needed costumes. These include having each girl buy or make her own, having the school furnish them, rental from the school for a small fee, having local civic groups supply them, and sponsoring money-raising projects by team members for their purchase. Many feel that since the club is a service group, all their expenses, including that for uniforms, should be borne by the school, as is done for the athletic teams.

The sponsor should supply a simple pattern that will be relatively inexpensive to copy if each girl is required to furnish her own uniform. The help of the home economics department might be enlisted in the project. Local merchants often will sell needed materials at cost or greatly reduced prices. For the sake of diplomacy all required items should be purchased from several local stores.

Uniforms may range all the way from satin blouses, short fringed leather skirts, cowboy hats and boots to plain blue wool skirts and white blouses, socks and sneakers. The original team should select their own name, such as the Apache Belles or The Rangerettes, select their own uniforms, and write their own governing constitution. Traditions they establish should set the pattern for following groups.

TRANSPORTATION

Ideally, the school should bear all expense for the drill team, including transportation to and from games. If this is impossible, parents or other adults can help to supply transportation. All car drivers must be covered adequately by personal, car and passenger liability insurance. The use of a bus for the transportation of both the players and the drill team is recommended. This, too, can be financed by civic organizations if the school is unable to supply it. The driver, bus and passengers must all be insured. Permission blanks, similar to those used for all athletes, should be signed by each parent.

PRINTED MATERIALS

Printed materials should be given to each team member. These should contain the constitution, marching instructions, basic step patterns used in routines, drills and formations, precision exercises, and a collection of the school songs and yells.

MARCHING

Marching commands are given in three parts: the name of the desired action, a pause and a responding action by the group. In giving commands, the instructor must face the group, stand erectly, speak in clear, concise, firm tones, and count in cadence as the group responds to the command. Cadence speed used should be in time to the step rhythm. Arms and hands should not be left hanging free while the rest of the body is being exercised but should be swung in motion as the body moves, placed on hips or shoulders, thrust to side, forward or back, or placed to the rear of the head. Correct cadence is 120 steps per minute. Double time is 180 steps per minute. To help the group "feel" cadence, the instructor might well have them count the beats aloud "one-two-three-four" with her.

In giving directions for marching, the leader should never break through ranks. This can be avoided by getting into a position where all can see her, and where she can move quickly to help each group captain. It is better to stop if groups become confused and then to start over again after clearly explaining movements desired so the group understands them. The team should be required to step lively in unison, with good posture. Small units of four or eight can be used to demonstrate more complicated movements. Group leaders for each unit should be rotated. The entire team should elect their captain and each unit its own leaders after all have tried out for these honored positions.

For elaborate drills, groups should not exceed fifty; those composed of thirty-two members are the most desirable. Shorter girls may best be blended into the line at each end and in front. Marching to lively recorded music is more exciting and fun than to group cadence or instructor command. For exhibition purposes the group should march to the music of their own school band. The sponsor should not go out onto the field while her team performs; rather she may sit in the stands watching her well-trained group perform without her and from this vantage spot evaluate their efforts realistically.

COMMANDS

Dress right . . . dress! All turn head and eyes right, straighten line. Place left hand on left hip, elbow straight out to the left. Place right arm at side, touch the left elbow of one on the right. Hold to command, "Front," all snap left arms to side, turn eyes and head front.

Right face . . . face! Face right a quarter turn by turning body on the heel of the right foot and toe of the left, then bring the left heel up beside the right.

Left face . . . face! Opposite of Right face.

About face . . . face! Always turn right. Place the toe of the right foot to rear and left of left heel, turn on the toe of the right foot and heel of the left to right, take a half turn to face the opposite direction.

Mark time . . . march! Raise left and right feet alternately in place 3 or 4 inches; on "March," move forward.

Forward . . . march! Step off on left to right; repeat with steps about 30 inches long. Step to cadence of 120 steps a minute.

Group . . . halt! Command given as either foot hits the floor. Advance and bring rear foot to forward one in two counts.

Backward . . . march! Opposite to Forward march, except that the steps are half as long.

Right step . . . march! On "march," step right on right foot, bring left over so left heel is alongside right. March in cadence. To halt, on command "Group Halt" given as feet are together, step side on right and bring left to right on two counts.

Left step . . . march! Opposite to Right step . . . march.

To the rear . . . march! On the command "March" as the right foot strikes the ground, advance and plant the left foot, turn to right about on balls of both feet, step off of the left.

By the left flank . . . march! On the command "March" given as the left foot strikes the ground, advance and plant the right foot. Turn to left a quarter turn, step off on left.

By the right flank . . . march! Opposite of Left flank.

Fours left . . . march! On the command "March" given as either foot strikes the ground, the pivot girl on left of each group of fours faces left and marks time until the extreme right girl comes abreast, then all of her group step off with her. The movement of the second, third, and fourth girls is two successive oblique movements until they arrive on a new line with the pivot girl.

Fours right . . . march! Opposite to Fours left.

FUNDAMENTALS IN MARCHING TECHNIQUES

1. Clap hands to rhythm of march music or drum.
2. Take steps in place, stepping first on left foot in time to march music or drum beat.
3. Maintain good posture; eyes straight ahead; rib cage pulled up.
4. March forward in time to music; let arms swing easily at the sides in opposition to the feet.
5. Try to keep an even spacing in relation to the person in front.
6. Keep in step and learn to do a rapid step-close-step if you get out of step.

MARCHING PATTERNS

1. In a circle formation march single file; by 2's; by 3's.

2. In a square formation march single file; by two's; by three's. Make square turns at corners; then by 2's and 3's; those on the outside pivot around inside marcher.

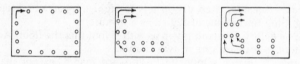

3. Up center by 2's; one file left; one file right.
4. Up center by 2's; all single file left.
5. Up center single file; all left by 2's. Pivot girl marks time as second girl marches to her right side. Both turn and march to corner.

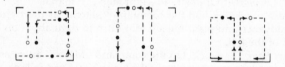

6. Up center by 2's; first couple left; second couple right; third couple left; fourth couple right.
7. Up center by 4's; form single file left and right.
8. Diagonal cross. Repeat.
9. Up center by 2's.

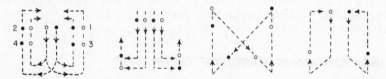

10. Up center by 4's; first four left; second right; third left; fourth right; at foot single file.
11. Up center by 8's; left and right as in figure on page 450.
12. Up center by 8's; lines 1 and 3 complete circle to left. Lines 2 and 4 complete circle to right. Leave enough space between lines of eight and take small steps on the turn to keep lines straight.
13. Break into single file and spiral inward.
14. Serpentine. One half of group wind in and out (serpentine), passing left and right of other half, who remain stationary. As first girl reaches last girl of second half all form circle and march off single file.

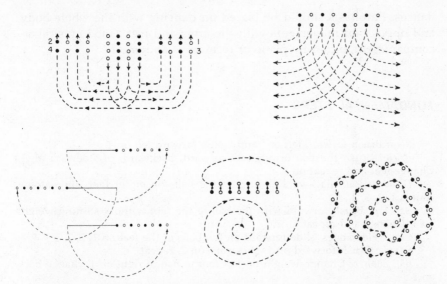

According to the proficiency of the group, many figures may be worked out using the diagonal cross by 2's, double circles moving in opposite directions, and a combination of the various figures done in sequence. The figures do not have to be complicated because, if the marchers maintain correct time and proper spacing, the movements are effective. This type of controlled rhythm is enjoyable when introduced at intervals with free-flowing movements.

DANCE ROUTINES

All forms of dance can be used for rhythmic routines by the drill team. Tap dance, however, should be stressed with this group. In some schools it is taught as an activity only for this club. Advantages of this practice are that it becomes a special treat for a hard-working but well-deserving group and is a great motivator to would-be members.

In teaching tap dance to the team the sponsor should select steps which are easily learned and can be used, with only slight variations, for many occasions. Each step should be broken down into easily imitated parts. The instructor may demonstrate the whole step, have the students say and do each part with her as in "step, step, brush, brush, ball change" as an aid to learning rhythmic timing. Next, she should add each new step sequence on to those previously learned and work for clearness of sound of each tapped beat. Creativeness among the group can be stimulated by having each tap out the rhythmic patterns to her own name, such as "My name is Betty Smith"; the patterns of popular song titles or movies for the group to guess as in "Oklahoma," or the "Rock and Roll Waltz"; and couple or small group improvised dances. Emphasis should be placed on dancing with the whole body, and opposition movements with the arms and feet. Good musical accompaniment, either by piano or records, is a must.

FUNDAMENTAL STEPS

Slap: Brush forward left on "and," step forward left on 1.

Brush: Brush the ball of one foot forward, backward, or sideward on 1. Change feet and repeat on 2.

Draw or Pull: Backward sliding on the balls on either foot, alternate on counts 1, 2, 3, 4.

Ball tap: Brush forward with the ball of the foot without shifting weight on 1. Change and repeat on 2.

Chug: Flex knees, slide forward on the balls of the feet on 1, 2, 3, 4.

Shuffle: Brush forward on 1; backward on 2, repeat.

Ball change: Change weight on left foot to ball of right on 1, change back on 2.

Threes: Brush on 1, brush on "and," step on 2.

Waltz step: Step on 1, brush forward on "and," brush backward on 2, ball change on "and 3."

Sevens: Brush on 1, brush on "and," step on 2, brush on "and," brush on 3, ball change on "and 4."

Single time step: Shuffle left on 1, hop right and hold on "2, and," step back on left on 3, brush forward right on "and," step right on 4, step back on left and "and."

Buffalo: Shuffle to side left on "and ah," step left behind right on 1, brush right to right side on "and," step right on 2.

Other suggestions for teaching routines and rehearsals include the following:

1. All rehearsal times should be carefully planned and both the director and group should know exactly what is to be accomplished by the end of each session.

2. Routines should be learned to counts and many kinds of teaching aids, such as charts, printed materials and chalkboards, should be used to help the girls visualize as well as understand what they are to do.

3. In the first meeting the entire routine should first be presented, then individual steps and various group formations shown. Sub-groups with assistants in charge of each one are then formed to practice the various parts of the routine.

4. After learning the routine indoors, rehearsals should be held on the performing area or on an area lined off exactly like it.

5. If a band is part of the performance, it and the performing group must learn to use the performing area without interrupting each other. If a pageant script is to be used, it must also be carefully interwoven into the performance.

6. The entrance and exits used in the routine should be rehearsed with live musical accompaniment, if possible.

7. In the final rehearsal the entire show should be rehearsed and timed carefully so that it does not exceed six minutes, and to insure that all staging properties, including sound effects, are in order.

THEMES

Almost any theme is suitable for a performance. Suggested ones include popular songs, states, countries, historical events, girls' names, flowers, nursery rhymes, holidays, family groups or famous people.

PEP SQUADS

Pep squads, composed of loyal and enthusiastic team rooters, are usually sponsored by the physical educator. These club groups should be operated according to previously mentioned policies for drill teams regarding membership, uniforms, transportation and regulations. The group should be led by one or more carefully selected cheerleaders who should be chosen for their personality, appearance, leadership ability and acrobatic skills. Several such carefully chosen cheerleaders of both sexes add much color to athletic contests and spectator fun.

CHEERLEADING

In assisting students to master the art of cheerleading, the instructor should stress the following points:

Use wide, sweeping movements
Keep arms flung straight out as much as possible
Face the crowd
Cheer with the group
Add slips, rolls, handsprings and other tricks often
Aim to please the fans at all times
Use psychological timing
Use a microphone, announce a yell twice before beginning it, and plant pep squad rooters throughout the audience to help put over each yell
Be enthusiastic
Use both popular and novelty yells

Pep meetings held both outdoors and indoors, team send-offs, and welcome home rallies become additional responsibilities of the sponsor, cheerleaders and pep squad. Each event should be carefully planned, publicized and conducted. Banners, flags, pennants, bands, mobile speakers and bonfires all help to heighten school spirit.

Pep squad sponsors should assist the group by guiding their desires and efforts toward reaching sought goals. Objectives should be group-formulated and progress-evaluated by each member and the entire squad at periodic intervals. All should be encouraged to make a collection of new yells for other localities. Future teachers can profit greatly while still in school by starting a card file collection of new songs and yells, tips and suggestions for successful cheerleading, as well as suggested routines for drill teams.

Figure 22-2. Drill team activities appeal to many girls. (Courtesy Los Angeles Unified School District.)

Figure 22-3. Cheerleading provides some students with an opportunity to learn the techniques of leadership. (Courtesy of Dorothy Wilson, Southern Methodist University.)

Many public schools are now sending their cheerleaders and pep squad members to Cheerleading Clinics, which are usually held in the summer for four to seven days.

DISCUSSION QUESTIONS

1. How would you convince your administrator that your school should have a drill team?
2. What rules and regulations would you set up for a drill team group to follow?
3. How can you as an educator endorse having drill teams and pep squads in a public high school?
4. What are the arguments against having them? What are your answers to these arguments as a taxpayer, future parent and an educator?
5. Someone once said that football is a pageant mainly for spectators. What is your reaction to this statement?

THINGS TO DO

1. Devise three tests for screening out the best potential drill team members.
2. Plan on paper a pregame pep rally.
3. With your classmates, practice leading and learning new school yells. Evaluate your results.
4. Direct two of the marching patterns given in this chapter in class. Evaluate your results.
5. Write an evaluation of any drill team performance you have observed. If possible, interview three of the members of the group in order to learn how much practice is required weekly, membership qualifications and other similar information. Report your findings in class.

SUGGESTED READINGS

AAHPER: *Dance Facilities; Designs for Dance.* Washington, D.C., 1913.

Broer, Marion and Wilson, Ruth: *Marching Tactics.* New York, Ronald Press Co. 1965.

Myers, Frances: "Guidelines for the Formation and Administration of Girls Dance-Drill-Baton Teams." *The Journal of Health, Physical Education and Recreation.* May, 1973, pp. 8–9.

Recommended books for Cheerleaders, all available from The National Cheerleaders Association, 11766 Valley Dale Drive, Dallas 30, Texas:

Champion Cheers, $1.00
Pep Rally Skits and Stunts, $3.00
The Gilb Book of Yells, $1.50
Cheerleading Pep Clubs and Baton Twirling, $4.50
Trampolining, $1.00
The Master Pep Book, $4.85
The Master Stunt Book, $4.25
Cheerleaders Handbook, $1.50
The Megaphone Magazine (4 issues), $2.00

RECOMMENDED RECORDS

Available from the Children's Music Company, 5373 West Pico Blvd., L.A., California, 90019

Body Contouring, $2.95
Fitness for Teens, $4.79
Music for Physical Fitness, $5.95
Marching Along With the Girls, $4.95
Majorettes on Parade, $5.00

CHAPTER TWENTY-THREE

PUBLIC DEMONSTRATIONS AND COMMUNITY RELATIONSHIPS

Since American taxpayers support subject areas in the public school curriculum in which they see real educational value, it is imperative that physical educators greatly increase and improve upon their efforts to help adults recognize that the type of physical activity program they conduct in school *is* a basic and vital part of an educational curriculum. Actually, the general public (made up of *our* former students for the most part) is greatly misinformed and confused about physical education and its real values. We in the profession must work as a unified body of teachers to restyle our present public image. Each teacher is our official representative in each class he teaches. What each *does,* what he *is,* and what he *believes in* are reflected back to us all. All of us, as professional educators, must greatly improve both our packaging (methods of selling) and our product (our programs) for our five consumer groups: our students, professional colleagues, administrators, parents and the general public. We must also stress more the "why" of exercise throughout life as well as motivate our students to the degree that they will continue taking part in physical activity when they are away from us as teachers.

PRINCIPLES OF GOOD PUBLIC RELATIONS

The following ten principles are important for carrying out a good program in public relations through our activities:[1]

1. Begin with the best program of health and physical education that you can develop for your students in your situation. Existing time factors, facilities and equipment, aided by your initiative and ingenuity, will help.
2. Use every opportunity to acquaint fellow faculty members, other

---

[1]Jackson, C. O.: Ten principles of good conduct. *Physical Education and School Athletics Newsletter,* Jan. 20, 1957. New London, Conn., Arthur C. Croft Publications.

school personnel, with your plans, your special problems. Remember, a good listener makes greater progress, so be sympathetic to their problems.

3. Take every opportunity to speak to members of the community, individually and in groups, about your program. Talks before PTA groups, civic and fraternal organizations can be of real value in putting your ideas across.

4. Dress, talk and act like a respected member of both faculty and community. Your appearance, your personality are selling the program and your profession in your classes, at school, elsewhere in the community.

5. Work with and through the administrator in getting your ideas approved and accepted. Statements by leaders in education, in medicine, and discussions of good programs in near-by schools can have nothing but good results.

6. Sell the editor of the local newspaper on the value of your program, the news value of many releases you can give him. Discuss your problems with him, keep him informed of your progress. Even better, write up your problems in short, easy-to-read form for the editor or reporter. He will meet you more than half way if the "meat" of the story is easy to uncover.

7. Arrange to use some of the educational time of radio and TV for your program presentation. The complaint in many areas is that not enough such material is available to even meet requirements set up by the Federal Communications Commission.

8. Carry on broader, more comprehensive programs of intramurals, GAA, and recreation as an outgrowth of your in-class program of physical education. This is a big step in doing something worthwhile for all students.

9. Plan and carry out demonstrations, athletic carnivals, play and sport days. Try an annual open house. Parents and townspeople are interested in what their children are doing — give them a good sample.

10. Remember that good teaching is the crux of good public relations. Your students are ambassadors of good will. If you challenge them, help them in your program, they and their parents will become your strongest supporters. Your program will grow and develop correspondingly.

Assembly programs, public demonstrations and exhibitions serve three purposes for they (1) help sell the community as well as the student on physical education, (2) offer rich opportunities for each individual youth to work democratically and creatively on a group project, and (3) provide the instructor with ways to gain recognition for his accomplishments as an educator. One reason the general public endorses interscholastic athletics so avidly is that they can observe for themselves what the students have learned. Unfortunately, they rarely have an opportunity to see the benefits of a good physical education program for the majority of students. Sponsoring these special events is well worth the time and effort spent on them, for they can pay off richly in increased interest in, enthusiasm for, and support of both the program and its leaders.

Every effort must be made to reach our many publics, which include adults in the community itself (parents, the medical profession, civic groups, etc.), school administrators and fellow teachers, pupils and others living outside the area. There are many media for reaching

Figure 23–1, A, B.   Show and sell your program with a public demonstration given at least once a year. (Courtesy The Silver Spurs, Spokane School District.)

these groups, including television, newspapers, radio, physical educators who serve as guest speakers to civic groups, school papers, handbooks for students, invitations to parents to tour the school or visit classes, projects and health contests and bulletin boards.

SHOW AND SELL!

Nothing will bring quicker and more enthusiastic support to your program than a demonstration given to the general public of what students are learning in their physical education classes. Public support to athletic programs for the minority of more skilled students is stronger than that given to the physical education program for the majority of students, regardless of their abilities, simply because the public sees what athletic teams have actually learned from their coaches. The vast majority of parents, however, rarely have opportunities to see what their lesser skilled youngsters have learned to do in the way of sports, games or dance in their physical education classes. Although it does take extra time and effort to give public demonstrations, this expenditure reaps rich dividends.

In the Spring Branch Public Schools outside of Houston, Texas, as many as 2100 youths have participated in a large demonstration given yearly at night on the lighted football field for parents, other relatives, and the general public. The many students in these programs perform a variety of activities they have learned in their physical education classes. Nothing special is planned but rather the program is an outgrowth of actual class work. Only one big rehearsal is held to put the whole show together. Students or various physical education teachers from each class introduce their own part of the program. Every student in every physical education class in every school in the district is in the program—a total of over 2100 youngsters. Parents and other relatives of each of these 2100 students, plus members of the general public, make up the audience. They watch Johnny or Susie, along with their classmates, folk dance, play squad team soccer, perform on many kinds of gymnastic apparatus or do many other kinds of activities. As many as 4000 or more spectators come away from the program enthusiastic supporters of the school's physical education program and its teachers.

Part of the professional preparation curriculum for every physical educator should be in the areas of public speaking, public relations, advertising and successful salesmanship techniques. For teaching is, among other things, winning friends and influencing people of all ages as well as "selling" wares of everlasting and precious value.

SUGGESTIONS FOR DEMONSTRATIONS

A demonstration given for the general public (preferably at night so that more can attend) should be an outgrowth of the regular class program. It may show (1) a number of activities learned during the year; (2) a typical class period for boys, girls or coeducational groups; (3) pupil demonstrations followed by participation in the activities by the parents; or (4) activities built around a general theme. For the latter, theme suggestions are colors, seasons, holidays, the wild West or other sections of the country, rivers, flowers or changing weather conditions.

Rehearsals should be held after or before the usual school hours only when essential; the majority of them should be conducted during the regular class time. It will be necessary, however, to hold some mass rehearsals before the actual demonstration. Giving each student a copy of the entire program with printed instructions for all classes will cut down this practice time considerably. Such instructions might well include the procession and recession order, large numbers, the grand finale and the specific responsibilities of each group and key persons in the whole program.

It is vastly important that as many students as possible take part in the demonstration, for each parent will thrill to seeing his child perform, even though his job is only to bend over to form a pyramid base. The teacher should keep his overall physical education and teaching objectives uppermost in mind, realizing that socioemotional growth is as important as improvement in skills. He needs to help each student select activities he can do best as his particular contribution to the program. As many students as possible should be placed on the following committees:

Program committee: Theme selections; who will participate and what each will do; featured events; procession and recession; grand finale; complete program planned on paper.

Publicity committee: Use of school and local papers; spot announcements for radio and television stations; fliers; responsible for printed or mimeographed programs.

Facilities and equipment committee: Bring and return all needed equipment; check public address system.

Hospitality committee: Welcome and seat all spectators.

Clean-up committee: Perform necessary follow-up janitorial duties.

A planning committee composed of the instructor and an elected representative from each class should be responsible for the entire demonstration. All those taking part in the program should evaluate their results with their sponsor in class the following day. Specific recommendations for improvement of future programs should be recorded and kept on file.

The arrangement of program activities should be carefully devised and students given enough time to dress between appearances. Alternating activities between the boys and girls is recommended, as is having a broad display of accomplishments; a badminton demonstration, for example, should be followed by conditioning exercises or gymnastics, rather than another demonstration of a similar sport.

The program should be well moderated and should help the audience to gain a clearer knowledge, understanding and appreciation of the physical education department offerings, objectives and accomplishments.

The following sample demonstration program shows the classwork covered by students in a semester's unit:

1. Grand entrance march   All

2. Stunts and tumbling   11th grade girls
      Handsprings
      Forward somersault
      Backward somersault
      Back handspring
      Kip to stand
      Tumbling routines
      Advanced pyramids

3. Apparatus   11th grade boys
   Parallel bars: Single and double
      leg cut-ons, shoulder stands,
      forward rolls
   Flying rings: Skin the cat, kip, full
      lever, double leg cut off and
      regress, fly-away
   Side horse: Full leg circles, triple
      dismounts
   Long horse: Jumps and vaults
   Swedish box: Squat jump, flank
      vault
   Trampoline: Back drop, front drop,
      knee landing, seat to front
      drop, jump and twist

4. Folk dancing   10th grade coeducational
   Swiss Weggis, Patty-cake Polka,
      Kavelis, Tantoli

5. Adapted activities   Students in all grades assigned to
   Modified relays, deck tennis, box   these classes
      hockey, paddle tennis, modi-
      fied individual sport skills,
      and team games

6. Team game—volleyball   12th grade girls

7. Drills and relays in basketball skills	12th grade boys
8. Mass calisthenics (done to command)	All classes
Arm circle sideward, toe touch sideward, alternate toe, sideward, alternate toe touch, jumping jack, sitting cross elbow touch, body curl, alternate leg lift, double time place marching	
9. Grand finale departure march	All classes

Costumes worn may be regular class uniforms or these may be changed slightly by crepe paper, scarfs or other means. Both the scenery and uniforms should remain secondary in importance. Student leaders selected by each class may announce or direct each activity. An informal reception following the program will enable teachers to meet a number of parents and family groups. Inexpensive refreshments can add much to the success of the evening.

The program should last less than two hours, including intermission. The numbers should be both "short and sweet" examples of a well-rehearsed plan. It should begin slowly, work up to a gradual climax, and the most spectacular activities should be near the end of the program. Other departments, such as the band, art, journalism or English, home economics, should be called upon for assistance. Such a mutually-shared project will lead to greater appreciation and understanding of the work done in each department.

The program should be given yearly, be widely publicized, and be a highlight and climactic event for both the students and their teachers of the things they have accomplished by working together in their physical education classes.

ASSEMBLY PROGRAMS

Wise teachers grasp an opportunity to be in charge of an all-school assembly wherein they will have a chance to show others what they are doing or what can be done in their specialized field. Many fellow teachers, school administrators, and even students, have gained a new respect and better understanding and appreciation for physical education through this educational avenue. Such assemblies are of two types: a general orientation and special recognition.

Ideally, the general orientation assembly should be held early in the new term. It is a wonderful way to inform the total school population of various aspects of the program—its objectives and scope or specific areas, such as creative dance or the activity possibilities on a trampoline. One quick way to show the objectives is to have them flashed on a screen or displayed on big poster cards while reference is made to them by a speaker. The program scope can be illustrated by a sports style show, during which students demonstrate the proper attire for tennis, swimming, golf, social dance and other activities.

Specific activities, such as stunts and tumbling or folk dance, can be demonstrated by a class or club group. Interest in coming events can also be stimulated in such an assembly. For instance, a creative dance club group can do much to increase both enthusiasm for and attendance at a forthcoming recital by an outstanding dance artist being sponsored by a local community organization. Outside speakers often generate high interest in physical education, especially when they couple a demonstration with verbal information fascinating to high school youth. The world-famous bow and arrow big game hunter, Howard Hill, as well as the well-known and skilled golfer, Patty Berg, and many other sport experts have done far more to motivate interest in their specific sports in a thirty-minute assembly program then teachers could in a whole semester. Such visiting champions are usually most generous with their time and willingly talk with school groups. Many are employed by leading sports equipment companies for this purpose.

The recognition assembly is one in which leaders and tournament winners are recognized by the school. Awards may be verbal recognition or in the form of inexpensive cups, pins or ribbons. Such assemblies should be student-teacher planned. The major portion of the program should be given by the former. Music supplied by choral or orchestra groups, poems written and read by individual students, short talks on sportsmanship given by the outstanding school leaders, the value of physical activity or other such appropriate subjects are suitable for this type of program. The actual awards should be presented by either a coach, a physical education teacher or the principal.

COMMUNITY AFFAIRS

Performing at community affairs is another golden opportunity for selling physical education, building a reputation for oneself as a teacher, and motivating students' drives to increase skills. Groups such as a drill team, pep squad, tumbling or other clubs are often asked to be on television programs, perform at luncheon meetings or other occasions. Although these performances take precious time and effort, they can be of great benefit to the many people called upon to be of service. They can also help adults see value in the program.

All plans regarding meeting time, transportation, equipment needed and the program content itself must be carefully worked out. Policies should be drawn up by the school principal and teachers involved covering all regulations regarding public performances of student groups during or after regular school time. These should be carefully followed as a safety precaution for all those involved. Each group should be chaperoned; no sponsor or other adult should be given the responsibility of being in charge of too large a group. Just how many students would constitute "too large a group" depends upon the age of the students, the nature of their trip, where they are going, and numerous other factors, Although high school youth usually are easily controlled, they sometimes become unmanageable when away from school or when grouped incorrectly. Some few use such misbehavior as a means of gaining peer recognition and status then or when greatly exaggerated tales are retold about the adventure later. Prevention is the best solution to such problems. The old adages "Foresight is better than hindsight" or "An ounce of prevention is worth a pound of cure" are well worth remembering.

Both the principal and the sponsor should avoid letting their various student groups perform so frequently that their schoolwork suffers from neglect. The sponsor, likewise, must learn to say "No" to too frequent requests to take part in community affairs. Each teacher must learn to emulate the wise college professor who, when asked what was the most important thing he had learned from life and his long teaching career, replied: "To separate the important from the trivial and to save my energy for the really big things that matter."

DISCUSSION QUESTIONS

1. What are the values of public demonstrations to students, teachers and the school?

2. What would you plan for the poorly skilled students in your class to do in a public demonstration of tumbling?

3. What committees are necessary to insure a public demonstration's going off smoothly? Should these be appointed by the teacher? Why or why not?

4. What school policies should be drawn up to protect each student and the teacher sponsor taking part in a public demonstration?

5. How would you handle a discipline problem which arose when you were on an out-of-school trip with a group of students?

THINGS TO DO

1. Plan on paper an assembly program for your school showing any phase of the total physical education program.

2. Through library research find out about the AAHPER's PEPI Project. Give an oral report of your findings and tell how the suggestions given in this project for selling physical education to the public can be implemented in your school.

3. Write a newspaper article on the flabby American and show how a good physical education program can help solve this problem.

4. Present in class a make-believe radio sport interview with you as moderator and

a fellow student playing the part of a physical education teacher. At the end of the program have your classmates evaluate the results from the standpoint of the use of the radio for developing good public relations.

5. Plan and present in class a five-minute talk you have prepared to give to a civic group on the place of physical education in the total school curriculum. Evaluate your results.

SELECTED VISUAL AIDS

The Flabby American. Stresses the scope of this problem and shows how a good physical education program can help solve it. Available from Text-Film Division, McGraw-Hill Book Company on a rental basis.

1967–68 Educators Guide to Free Guidance Materials. Educators Progress Service, Randolph, Wisconsin.

Gymnastics for Girls. Shows an Olympic champion demonstrating competitive floor exercises, balance beam, uneven bar and parallel bar work. Available from the Association Films in most large cities on a rental basis.

SUGGESTED READINGS

AAHPER—*Intramurals for Junior High School (1964); Intramurals for Senior High School (1964); Why Physical Education (School Packet) (College Packet); Special Events in the Girls Sports Program (1961).* AAHPER: *People Make Ideas Happen.* Washington, D.C., 1970. 1201 16th St. N.W., Washington, D.C.

Boston, Terry: *Reach, Touch and Teach.* New York, McGraw-Hill Book Co., 1970.

Daughtrey, Greyson: *Methods in Physical Education and Health for Secondary Schools.* Philadelphia, W. B. Saunders Co., 1967. New Title & Ed.

Frederick, Bruce: "The Creative Educator." *Delaware School Journal,* 1964.

Hereford, Leslie: "Creativity in Physical Education." Connecticut AHER, the *Bulletin,* 1968.

Insley, Gerald: *Practical Guidelines for the Teaching of Physical Education.* Reading, Mass., Addison-Wesley Publishing Co., 1973.

Reno, Raymond: *The Impact Teacher.* Minneapolis, The 3M Press, 1968.

PART FIVE

PUPIL AND PERSONAL ASSESSMENT

Far and away the best prize that life has to offer is the chance to work hard at work worth doing.

..... Theodore Roosevelt

CHAPTER TWENTY-FOUR

EVALUATING
THE RESULTS

The purpose of measurement in physical education is to ascertain the status of a given ability or quality. This information is essential for the proper selection of activities and teaching techniques and the best possible classification of students to insure effective teaching. Testing supplies information for determining the degree to which objectives are being met, diagnosing specific defects, analyzing effectiveness of teaching techniques, and classification of individuals according to their capacities and/or achievements. (For discussion of evaluation in contract teaching, see Chapter Four.)

EVALUATION OF ACHIEVEMENT OF OBJECTIVES

Measuring the progress made toward achieving the objectives enables the teacher to appraise the success of a program. Not all of the objectives can be measured with the same degree of accuracy, however. Success in achieving a desirable mode of conduct, because of the abstract nature of such an objective, is difficult to measure. A student's progress in running speed can be measured with a high degree of accuracy with reliable instruments, but a student's improvement in good sportsmanship must be measured more subjectively by observation. Running speed can be reported in standard measurements of minutes and seconds, while conduct must be recorded in less objective terms such as poor, average or outstanding.

To make the measurement of an abstract objective more accurate, it should be reduced to its component parts and stated as specific accomplishments. For example, the objective of good sportsmanship may be broken down into such specific attributes as humility in winning, honesty in admitting infractions of the rules of play, and so on. Evaluation of each of the components, while still largely subjective, will produce a more accurate total measurement of the student's achievement.

Figure 24–1. Evaluation helps determine teaching effectiveness as well as motivates students to master activities they are learning. (Courtesy Enrico Fermi High School.)

If behavioral objectives have been established for the unit or course, they provide the means for evaluating student achievement. Evaluation in this case is an assessment of how well the students display the behaviors described in the stated objectives. As an example, one behavioral objective in a tennis unit might be: toss and hit seven of ten serves into the proper court while standing behind the baseline and utilizing an overhead serving motion. Obviously, evaluation of achievement in this objective is determined by requiring the student to display the behavior and computing his degree of success in meeting the criteria of performance. The question of what and how to evaluate are answered inherently in the stated behavioral objective.

DIAGNOSIS OF SPECIFIC WEAKNESSES

Tests may be used to identify the specific weaknesses in an individual's performance that prevent him from achieving the desired objectives. In physical education, diagnosis involves the analysis of components of a skill, fitness quality, or behavior tendency in order to discover weaknesses and strengths. Physical fitness tests are good diagnostic tests because they point up a student's particular weak-

Figure 24–2. Physical fitness tests are good diagnostic tests because they point out students' particular strengths and weaknesses.

nesses and strengths. Having made the diagnosis, the teacher must then analyze the effect of the prevalent weaknesses upon performance. For example, a poor score in an agility test may point up the reason for a student's inability to guard well in basketball.

ANALYSIS OF TEACHING EFFECTIVENESS

Evaluation is useful in education to determine the effectiveness of both specific and general teaching methods and of the materials or activities presented. In too many cases certain activities are offered in the physical education program because they have a superficial appearance of making worthy contributions. Testing the effectiveness of all physical education offerings would help greatly to reveal their true values and to effect the elimination of those activities which are not so worthwhile.

Testing often reveals to the teacher his failure to teach a specific skill or piece of information. When a significant number of students mark a test item incorrectly or fail to perform a skill successfully, the teacher would do well to evaluate his method of presentation of the information or skill.

Along with increasing teaching effectiveness testing creates a motivation for improved performance. Students who have been given a proper orientation to the physical education program and understand evaluation procedures can be motivated by test results to put forth greater effort to accomplish desired goals.

CLASSIFICATION OF STUDENTS

Classification of students according to their abilities or capacities for learning has become a recognized educational procedure. It has been shown that more effective learning usually occurs in homogeneous groups. Such groupings are highly desirable in physical education but are rather difficult to make because of the variation in students' abilities or capacities to perform different skills. Nevertheless, a battery of fitness tests that includes several factors of fitness provides an effective basis for creating more nearly homogeneous groups. The scores of the tests are placed in rank order and the class divided into groups at the logical separation points.

According to Achievement. Testing and evaluation are fundamental to a meaningful grading procedure. Grading is used to show the degree of progress and to indicate when promotion is desirable. Unfortunately, the grades in school subjects often become an end in themselves, but the true purpose of grading remains as a means of reporting progress toward the achievement of specific goals. It is important that students be given an indication of their progress and helped to evaluate their success; grading is a useful tool for this.

There are various methods currently in use in secondary school systems for reporting accomplishment of objectives. They fall into two general categories; there can be a written statement describing the progress of the student toward achieving the various objectives or else a single symbol designating overall progress in attaining the objectives of the course. In the use of the former method, the objectives are specifically identified. In physical education these would be fitness objectives, such as strength and speed; skill objectives, such as ability to play certain games; social objectives, such as fair play and courteous conduct toward others. Comments are then made concerning the success the student has achieved in reaching these objectives. This system has several advantages: It clarifies the objectives of the course and encourages the teacher to coordinate teaching with objectives; it also enables students to identify their specific weakness for possible improvement. Its weaknesses are that it is time consuming for the teacher and, where students and parents are orientated to symbols, they expect a similar evaluation in physical education.

Various symbols are being used in school systems to report physical education grades, the most common being P and F for pass and fail or S and U for satisfactory and unsatisfactory. The use of the letter marks A, B, C, D, and F is less common for physical education but is the most common designation in other subjects.

Many physical educators feel that when physical education classes are graded with either of the two letter systems and other classes in the school are marked by the A to F scale, this is likely to cause students and parents to regard physical education as of less consequence, with the result that students are not motivated by the evaluation to perform to capacity.

Regardless of the symbols used, a teacher must relate the symbols to the objectives of the program. Since the course of study must encompass the objectives, the evaluation may be used to determine the extent to which each of the objectives is being accomplished. Each activity presented in the program is likely to have more than one objective. The percentage of class time spent in working toward the fulfillment of a given objective determines how much weight it should receive in the final evaluation. If, for example, 75 per cent of the time is spent on developing skills, the progress made in acquiring the skills should account for three fourths of the grade.

In the P and F grading system, P would be equivalent roughly to A, B, C, and D, and F to the F on the letter scale; S equates with A, B, and C, and U with D and F. The use of a two letter system tends to discourage close evaluation, and students are awarded P or S if they attend classes and demonstrate a good attitude in the assigned tasks. Unfortunately, the same lack of discrimination is also evidenced by some teachers using the A to F scale, with the result that the grades are no more meaningful than in the two letter marking. Consequently, many administrators oppose the use of any letter scale for physical education grades.

Grades in physical education may be assigned on an absolute or a relative basis. An absolute grade is based entirely upon achievement, while a relative grade is assigned on the basis of achievement in realizing potentiality. Those who favor relative grading point out that such a technique frequently fosters greater interest in improvement and will motivate the youngster who is poor in physical education because he knows that his native physical ability will not cause him to receive a poor grade if he shows improvement. Also, there are some who feel that skill in physical education cannot be likened to skill in a subject like English; and although good development of the body and in the skills of physical education are beneficial throughout life, these are not so fundamental to the educative process as the skills developed in English class. Consequently, a student who works to the limit of his physical capacity but does not achieve the desired level of performance for receiving a passing grade should not fail physical education, although one who achieves to the extent of his mental capacity without making a passing grade should fail English.

Those who oppose this line of reasoning point out that an educated person is a well-rounded person and as such should have developed some proficiency in physical education. Furthermore, assessing potentialities is very difficult and makes relative marking far from accurate.

SELECTION OF TESTS

Tests may be divided into two general types: published standardized tests and teacher-made tests, usually not standardized. Construction of standardized tests is a complex process and requires specialized knowledge of testing and measurements, a discussion of which is beyond the scope of this textbook. However, certain principles for selecting good tests will be presented; these may also be applied to teacher-made tests to determine their effectiveness as testing instruments.

In appraising a test one must consider the validity and reliability of the test. Validity refers to a test being an actual measurement of what it is supposed to test. It indicates the degree to which a measurement represents the items being considered and is expressed as a relationship between the test in question and a criterion that has been demonstrated as an accurate measurement of the item being tested. To illustrate, a valid test of ability in badminton would have a high relationship to a final ranking in a badminton ladder tournament.

There are two types of validity, statistical and curricular. The former would be indicated by figures showing relationships between two tests, one being the criterion mentioned in the badminton illustration above. The other, curricular validity, expresses the relationship of the test to an analysis of the course of study and objectives sought.

Reliability refers to the degree of consistency in the results obtained by a test administered in similar situations. To be valid a test must measure consistently each time. There may be some variation in the scores in the retesting; but, if this is minimal, the test is considered reliable.

Interpreting Results. Tests are said to be standardized when norms and specific procedures for giving the tests have been established. Scores for such tests are easily interpreted because they can be compared to scores made by large numbers of students on the same tests. The limited number of students who are evaluated by the teacher-made test does not provide a large enough sampling of scores to permit interpretation by comparison to the achievement of many others. The teacher must, for a subject matter test of his own making, analyze the questions subjectively to decide what percentage of correct answers should constitute a passing mark. This analysis is based on what amount of knowledge a student should have acquired to be considered physically educated for the age and grade level in question.

It is commonly thought that a specific percentage of correct answers to the problems or activities constitutes a passing mark. This is not necessarily so. The test must be so constructed that the percentage will indicate what is expected; in some situations correct answers to 50 per cent of the questions would constitute a passing mark.

Administrative Details. In setting up skill testing devices the teacher should use the best available space to the greatest advantage. He should keep in mind the number of students to be examined; the number of targets, high jump standards, and other equipment needed to accommodate the class so that no one need wait long for his turn to be rated; the number of student assistants needed to help give the examination, and what training they will need in order to be of greatest service. He should have the necessary equipment and score sheets ready. Since educational tests should be given primarily for the purpose of improvement, students should be informed what examination they are to take, why they are required to do so, and its relationship, if any, to their final class grade. Each should be judged individually; scores may be totaled by assistant leaders, or each student may keep his own. However, it is important that all know their test results and class standing in relationship to others. The teacher should demonstrate the correct procedure to follow. All students should be motivated to do their best.

In administering written tests, the physical conditions should be such as to insure comfort and make it possible for the student to do his best. Lighting should be adequate, a writing surface should be available, and comfortable seating in a room free from distraction should be provided.

Tests administered to more than one group should have standardized directions if the scores are to be compared. Instructions should be clear, and specific points that may cause difficulty in interpretation should be clarified before the students begin work.

SKILL TESTS

The construction of objective skill tests for use in the classroom is such a complex technique that it is infrequently performed by the teacher. Instead, standardized skill tests or rating scales, available from several sources, are used to measure achievement in sport skills.

Tests for evaluating purposes in all sport areas are available. As is shown below, these include tests for measuring speed, accuracy, power, agility and balance in:

1. The fundamental body movements (running, walking, throwing, jumping, leaping, hanging, climbing and carrying.)
2. Body mechanics.
3. Individual, dual and team sports skills.
4. Rhythms and dance skills (singing games, basic movement patterns, folk, social, acrobatic, tap and modern dance).
5. Aquatics (swimming, diving, lifesaving, boating).
6. Self-testing activities (rope jumping, weightlifting etc.).
7. Track and field events.
8. Tumbling and gymnastics.

There are numerous standardized physical fitness tests available. Teachers should consult issues of the *Research Quarterly* and the Suggested Readings at the end of this chapter for comprehensive discussions of fitness tests as well as specific skill tests. A general discussion of the aspects of physical fitness testing is given in Chapter 11. Tests for evaluating specific skills are suggested at the end of each activity chapter.

Rating scales for evaluating sport skills are subjective estimates made by a competent judge. They are employed when objective measurements are not feasible. Ratings complement objective tests; they are not valid substitutes for them. The validity of rating scales can be increased substantially by observing these basic guides:

1. The skill being rated should be broken down into its various components. For instance, in rating a player's skill in basketball, his ability in shooting, guarding, faking, dribbling and feeding should be evaluated and utilized in arriving at a final rating.

2. Observations should be recorded frequently. There is a tendency for the rater to recall only a very poor or a very good performance. Unless a record of a series of observations is kept, one or two good or bad plays may unduly affect the final rating.

3. A descriptive scoring technique should be used. Defined categories, like those given below, are very useful:

1—very poor, lacking fundamentals in the skill
2—participates with some degree of success but is below average
3—average performance
4—performs with high degree of skill in most situations
5—demonstrates superior skill in all components of the activity.

WRITTEN TESTS

Written tests include:

1. Objective-type questions which require short answers.
2. General questions requiring essay-type answers.
3. Rating scales (to be filled in by self or others).
4. Problem situation questions which require short but well thought through answers.

In physical education, written tests are often concerned with information regarding rules, game strategy, officiating techniques, game history, player and spectator courtesies, equipment and its use, and court and field dimensions.

TRUE AND FALSE TESTS

Educators claim that true and false tests are the weakest of the objective tests. Students tend to read meaning into each statement; few can distinguish between a correct or incorrect sentence or resist mentally tinkering with it, for they think, "Yes, this *would* be true *if,* etc.," and then proceed to change the simple statement before them. All students need to see test results and understand why and in what areas they made mistakes. Otherwise, they accumulate false knowledge believing that it is true; frequently no one bothers to let them know the difference.

True and false statements should be short and simple. Avoid using the words "always" or "never"; most students have been tipped off that these are sure clues that the statement is false. The use of the symbols true (+) or false (O) have been found to be the most satisfactory, in that marks + and − are difficult to distinguish between because unsure students may deliberately make them so. Other ways to score such tests include encircling T if the statement is entirely true and F if it is only partly true; or blocking out x in the first column if the sentence is correct and encircling it in the second one if it is wrong; and the use of the symbol F for false and T for true. Answer sheets speed up test grading, especially when the examination is several pages long.

Example: Write + if the statement is true, O if it is false.

Hockey

O	1. A flick is used for a long drive.
O	2. A goal counts four points.
O	3. Only a defensive player can take a free hit.
O	4. One should hold both hands close together near the top of the club when dribbling.
+	5. A bully is used to put the ball in play at the start of the game.

MULTIPLE CHOICE

This type of question is easily scored, eliminates guessing to a greater degree than true or false questions, and give students practice in both weeding out incorrect responses and selecting right ones. Questions should be short, clearly written and not copied word for word from the textbook. Care must be taken to avoid creating a pattern in which the correct response can be found by position, such as its usually being the first or last phrase given.

Example: Place the letter of the most nearly correct answer in the provided blank.

Tennis

c	1. A lob is a stroke used in (a) serving, (b) smashing, (c) sending the ball high into the air, (d) driving it directly to the net player.
d	2. The term deuce is used in (a) serving, (b) volleying, (c) rallying, (d) scoring.
a	3. A fast hard drive which "kills the ball" or "puts it away for keeps" is a (a) smash, (b) lob, (c) volley, (d) line drive.
d	4. A point made by the server after a deuce score is called (a) add out, (b) 40-15, (c) 30-40, (d) add in.

___b___ 5. A set is won by a player who first wins (a) four, (b) six, (c) eight, (d) three games, providing he has won two games more than his opponent.

MATCHING

Matching test questions are best for measuring the mastery of "where," "when" and "who" types of information. They do not develop power to interpret or to express oneself. The responses to the matched items should be placed alphabetically or numerically in the right-hand column. Blank spaces could be provided in the left column before each item to be matched. There should be at least two more answers in the right column than in the left, for this helps rule out simple elimination procedures. Clear directions should be given for matching statements, including whether or not some answers can be used more than once.

Example: Match the items in the left column with those in the right. Some answers in the latter may be used twice.

Folk Dance

___c___	1. Czardus	a. Swedish
___b___	2. La Danza	b. Italian
___a___	3. Hambo	c. Hungarian
___f___	4. Maetelitza	d. Scottish
___d___	5. Road to the Isles	e. Danish
___e___	6. Klappdans	f. Russian
		g. Mexican
		h. German

FILLING IN BLANKS

The chief drawback to this type of examination questions is that students may have difficulty filling in blanks in the exact words the teacher expects. This may lead him to give them the benefit of the doubt and to have trouble determining whether he should count as correct only those answers which are exact duplicates of his, or whether they should be given partial credit for half-correct answers. One advantage of this type of question, however, is that the student receives no hint of the correct answer as in multiple choice or matching questions.

Example: Write the correct answer in the blank provided for it below.

Tennis

1. Volleying is a stroke in which the ball is hit before it touches the ground.
2. If a person fails to get his two serves to land in the correct court, the decision is a double fault.
3. The term used to designate "no points" in a game is love.
4. The stroke used to start a game is called a serve.
5. In scoring, the server's score is given first.

ESSAY QUESTIONS

These questions are valuable in that they provide students with rapidly disappearing opportunities to write complete sentences and whole paragraphs using good grammar and to think through problems carefully. Their drawback lies in being time-consuming to read and difficult to grade objectively.

Example: Answer the following question in not less than one hundred words. Think through your answer carefully.

Physical Education Class

What seem to you to be the chief values of taking a class in physical education?

DIAGRAMS

Diagrams, although sometimes difficult to grade, are often test time-savers. Frequently, students gain a clearer picture of player position and responsibilities from being asked to show in a drawing where each team member is to be placed and his responsibilities while in that area.

Example: On the diagram below write the position of each player for team A and team B in speedball.

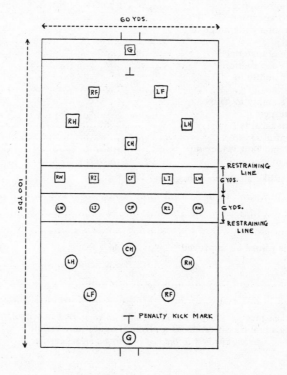

RATING SCALES

The American Association for Health, Physical Education and Recreation has splendid rating scales available for evaluating facilities, program, staff, and equipment in physical education, health education and recreation.[1] Major students as well as experienced teachers can benefit greatly from rating their own program and teaching-learning environment, as well as gain insight on how to construct such rating scales.

_____

[1]Sets for each are 50¢ per form or $1.00 for all three. They are available from this association at 1201 Sixteenth Street, N.W., Washington, D.C.

Table 24–1. PUPIL EVALUATION SHEET

Directions: Your teacher is anxious to make each course valuable. There is always room for improvement. Thoughtful student reactions can be of great value in making this course even better than it is. Rate your instructor as directed below. Add comments you wish to make on the back of this page. *Do not sign your name.*

5 – Superior   2 – Below average
4 – Excellent   1 – Marked improvement needed
3 – Average

	5	4	3	2	1
1. Value of the course					
2. Teacher appearance					
3. Teacher preparation					
4. Inclusion of a wide range of activities					
5. Coverage of material					
6. Teacher's explanations					
7. Teacher's ability to demonstrate					
8. Teacher's ability to gain pupils' respect					
9. Use of visual aids					
10. Class control					
11. Use of democratic leadership					
12. Fairness in grading					

What did you like most about this class? Why?

....
....
....

How can this course be improved?

....
....
....

Time your class meets ....Year in school.......................
Circle your general classification as a physical education student:
        among the best in the class; average; below average.

Table 24-2. TEACHER'S PERSONAL EVAULATION SHEET

	Always	Frequently	Seldom	Never
1. I like teaching.	....	....	....	....
2. I respect my students and try to understand them.	....	....	....	....
3. I am democratic.	....	....	....	....
4. I feel adequately prepared to do my job well.	....	....	....	....
5. I make the best use of student leadership.	....	....	....	....
6. I make the best use of facilities and equipment.	....	....	....	....
7. I have my own teaching objectives clearly in mind for each class.	....	....	....	....
8. I have my objectives clearly in mind for the development of each unique individual student.	....	....	....	....
9. I plan my work ahead.	....	....	....	....
10. I teach something new every class period.	....	....	....	....
11. I am cognizant of carry-over values in what I am teaching.	....	....	....	....
12. I give skill and written tests periodically and use them to evaluate my work.	....	....	....	....
13. I feel that the students admire me.	....	....	....	....
14. I have discipline trouble.	....	....	....	....
15. I try to cooperate with my administrators.	....	....	....	....
16. I feel the other teachers respect me.	....	....	....	....
17. I join professional organizations, attend their meetings, and read their periodical literature.	....	....	....	....
18. I feel that I am making a real contribution to my professional field.	....	....	....	....

Things I should do to improve myself as a teacher are

a. .... e. ....

b. .... f. ....

c. .... g. ....

d. .... h. ....

Date..

My progress on this so far has been

a. .... c. ....

b. .... d. ....

Date..

Table 24–3. SUPERVISOR'S EVALUATION SHEET

Name of teacher...Name of school..............................

Date of rating..Rated by ....

Instructions: Using a scale of 1–3, rate each teacher in each item below. Rate 3 for above average, 2 for average, 1 for below average.

This teacher:	1	2	3
1. Shows an understanding of people	....	....	....
2. Uses democratic methods	....	....	....
3. Has an understanding of the community, the school, and is aware of their relationships upon each other	....	....	....
4. Shows ability to organize and plan his work carefully	....	....	....
5. Shows ability to measure pupil progress	....	....	....
6. Recognizes individual differences	....	....	....
7. Understands group behavior	....	....	....
8. Helps groups plan, conduct, and evaluate their own program under his direction	....	....	....
9. Develops student leadership	....	....	....
10. Has ability to build group unity	....	....	....
11. Can solve discipline problems	....	....	....
12. Is respected and liked by students and fellow teachers	....	....	....
13. Can demonstrate well	....	....	....
14. Can speak well, using correct grammar	....	....	....
15. Safeguards the health and safety of all	....	....	....
16. Provides a well-balanced program	....	....	....
17. Provides definite progression in a graded program	....	....	....
18. Uses a wide variety of teaching methods well	....	....	....
19. Is attractive, neat, and looks like a leader	....	....	....
20. Is creative	....	....	....
21. Shows knowledge of the entire school curriculum and realizes the contribution of his own area	....	....	....
22. Uses the bulletin board, realizing that it is a silent teacher	....	....	....
23. Keeps adequate records and realizes their importance	....	....	....
24. Shows ability to maintain proper teacher-pupil relationships	....	....	....
25. Shows professional promise	....	....	....

Both students and teachers should evaluate their work in physical education. Some of the best ideas for program improvement often come from the former. Likewise, teachers can benefit greatly from personal follow-up conferences with their supervisors and principals after being evaluated by them.

Rating scales are often used by teachers who wish to evaluate their work, by pupils to express their reactions to the program, as well as by the supervisor or school principal.

Suggested forms for such evaluation are shown in Tables 24–1, 24–2 and 24–3.

STUDENT EVALUATION

Students should be given many opportunities to evaluate what progress they have made in relationship to the goals sought by each and the class as a whole. Teachers should appraise their progress with them, as well as be ever observant of their reactions to what they are doing and their attitudes toward him, the group and themselves as learners. Time should be taken frequently to discuss these reactions, problems which arise concerning individual or group behavior, as well as to formulate plans and chart progress objectively.

A teacher can gain valuable insight and a deeper understanding of each student if he asks the class to write on an unsigned sheet of paper the answers to the following questions at the end of each semester:

1. Did you enjoy this class? Why?
2. How many new things have you learned to do this semester? List them in order of importance to you.
3. Do you participate in any of these activities away from school? If so, which ones and where?
4. What person do you most admire in this class? Why?
5. Would you like to be like this person? How could you?
6. Did you accomplish all the things here you wanted to? What did you hope to do that you did not?
7. If you were the teacher of this class, what would you want most to accomplish?
8. What student do you think improved the most? In what ways?
9. Are students learning to be good or poor citizens here? In what ways?
10. What final grade do you think you have earned? Support your answer.

DISCUSSION QUESTIONS

1. Why is evaluation a vital part of all good teaching?
2. What factors should be taken into consideration for grading purposes? Which factor should carry the greatest weight? How can this factor best be measured?
3. Should students be given skill and written tests in physical education? Why or why not, according to the opinion of the various authors listed in the *Suggested Readings* found below?
4. How can rating scales best be used as a means of evaluation?
5. What are the advantages and disadvantages of grading in physical education?

THINGS TO DO

1. Describe the meaning of objectivity, reliability and validity in the testing program.
2. Prepare five examples each of the following types of objective questions: true-false review questions, multiple choice, matching and short answer or completion.
3. Demonstrate and give to your classmates one test (give author and source) for measuring each of the following: (a) motor ability, (b) physical fitness, (c) strength.
4. Devise a player rating scale in a team sport as well as an individual one. Include such items as: (a) use of a wide variety of skills (b) accuracy of body movements.

5. Devise a personal evaluation sheet to use to measure your own effectiveness as a student. Include such items as attentiveness in class and promptness in handing in assignments.

VISUAL AIDS

Microcards. Microcards of unpublished research materials and books that are out of print are available from the School of Health, Physical Education and Recreation, University of Oregon. They cover a wide range of research done in the areas of physical fitness, motor skill development, the physiology of exercise and many other areas of vital concern to physical educators and, especially, to graduate students.

SUGGESTED READINGS

AAHPER, 1201 16th N.W., Washington, D.C.
  Archery Skills Test Manual (Boys and Girls), 75¢ each.
  Basketball Skills Test Manual (Boys and Girls), 75¢ each.
  Football Skills Test Manual (Boys), 75¢ each.
  Personal Data and Profile Form, 3¢ each.
  Physical Growth Chart (Boys and Girls), 10¢ each.
  Softball Skills Test Manual (Boys and Girls), 75¢ each.
  Volleyball Skills Test Manual (Available winter, 1969), 75¢ each.
Clarke, Harrison: *Application of Measurement To Health and Physical Education.* 4th Ed. Englewood Cliffs, N.J., Prentice-Hall, Inc., 1967.
McCollum, Robert H. and McCorkle, Richard B.: *Measurement and Evaluation: A Laboratory Manual.* Boston, Allyn and Bacon, Inc., 1971.
Mathews, Donald K.: *Measurement in Physical Education,* 4th Ed. Philadelphia, W. B. Saunders Co., 1973.

CHAPTER TWENTY-FIVE

PROBLEMS OF THE NEW TEACHER

THE STUDENT-TEACHER AND BEGINNING INSTRUCTOR

The student studying to become a physical education teacher is preparing for a challenging and rewarding career. The study of methods for the successful teaching of physical education is but a phase of that preparation, to be followed by other courses and, in most colleges and universities, by a period of in-service training. The in-service training usually consists of observation of classes being instructed by competent and experienced teachers and actual practice in teaching physical education activities to classes of youngsters under the guidance of a supervising teacher. If the observation and student-teaching experiences are to be meaningful, the student must understand the purposes of these phases of his training and be prepared to make the most of the opportunities they present.

OBSERVATION

Observation of classes being instructed in physical education serves as an introduction to actual participation in class teaching. In watching a successful and experienced teacher work with a class, the student-observer witnesses the actual application of the techniques and methods about which he has studied. For the period of observation to be most meaningful to the student when he begins his student teaching, he must be an active observer, alert to all that occurs from the time the class enters the room or playing area until it departs for the next class. A passive observer can gain nothing more than a vague impression of the class instruction.

The observer should pay particular attention to:

1. The general behavior of the students.
2. The ways in which cooperation and effort are stimulated.

3. Opportunities provided for the students to express themselves in democratic action.

4. The use of visual aids or supplementary teaching materials.

5. The execution of routine procedures such as roll call and dismissal.

6. Planned use of different playing areas and equipment.

7. The effectiveness and clarity of the directions, demonstrations and diagnoses.

8. The operation of school policies.

9. The effectiveness of the methods used.

10. The motivational techniques.

11. The methods of evaluation.

The use of a small notebook in which to jot down the personal techniques of the teacher which have proved especially effective is highly recommended.

STUDENT-TEACHING

The student who begins a period of teaching under a supervising teacher assumes the roles of both learner and teacher. Through the process of actually teaching youngsters is gained some of the most valued knowledge any novice can acquire. Some of this knowledge will come from the guidance and suggestions made by the supervising teacher, some will come from observation and experimentation during the teaching of the class, but much of it will be supplied by the students themselves in their reactions to the class instruction.

Before the teaching begins, the supervising teacher customarily explains the school policies and the course of study for physical education. The responsibilities of the student-teacher will be discussed. Then, for a few days, in order to help the student-teacher become more familiar with the class members and the situation generally, the supervising teacher may direct the teaching while the student-teacher assists with such duties as:

Checking equipment in and out
Participating when an extra player or dancer is needed
Checking playing hazards
Giving individual help
Serving as a referee or judge
Caring for minor injuries
Helping to move equipment
Demonstrating skills as needed
Making an attractive display on the bulletin board

Because the situation of the student-teacher facing the responsibilities of teaching physical education is so nearly like that of the beginning teacher, further discussion of the two roles is combined below.

THE BEGINNING TEACHER

The beginning teacher in either the student-teaching situation or a new job would do well to realize that success is related to the ability to adjust to the school situation and to those with whom he must work. It is often disconcerting to the new teacher to find that many of the policies and practices that he was taught by his college instructors are completely disregarded by his supervising teacher, colleagues and administrators of the local program. This should be anticipated, for people differ greatly in the value and interpretation they place on the objectives of physical education; consequently, they employ different methods of arriving at their goals. The new teacher or student-teacher must be careful not to overstep his authority in trying to establish what he considers better ways of doing things. He must be careful not to contradict or antagonize his superiors or to assume more responsibilities than are delegated to him.

These remarks are not made to discourage the new teacher from making any changes or instituting new practices; no program is perfect and every physical education department can benefit from the challenge of new concepts and techniques. But the new teacher should realize that he can make a greater contribution by offering his recommendations for change gradually and in a manner of deference to established order than by attempting to convince those in charge that they are out-of-step with the times and must convert to the new ideas overnight.

Before the First Day of Teaching. The new teacher should inform himself about the regulations and policies of the school for they vary considerably from one school to another. Many schools have written guides which they provide to new or student-teachers; often, however, the general policies and regulations are passed by word of mouth from the administrators to the teachers. A beginning teacher should never hesitate to ask questions about these general procedures which he will be expected to follow. Among the things that a new physical education teacher should know are:

1. What action should be taken by the individual teacher in case of fire or other disaster involving the entire building?
2. What is the policy regarding students' leaving the school grounds at noon and between classes?
3. What is the procedure for making class or team trips to other towns?
4. What policy affects after-school practices and other uses of the gymnasium and playing fields?
5. How are discipline problems handled; which ones are handled by the principal?
6. What procedures are to be followed when a student becomes ill or is injured in class?
7. What are the features of the accident insurance policies covering the student body?

8. What is the policy governing make-up of missed classes in physical education?

9. What are the regulations concerning absences, cuts and tardiness?

10. What is the length of class periods; how much time is allotted to dressing and showering?

11. What is the policy for excusing students from physical education for religious, health or other reasons?

12. Is there an established regulation about weather conditions for outdoor class activities?

LEARNING ABOUT THE STUDENTS

Whether new or student-teacher, it is obviously helpful to know something about the students to be taught before planning the program of activities. Information which might be sought includes such things as:

1. The academic standing of each class. If the class is an accelerated one, the rate of learning skills and information may be expected to be considerably faster than in other classes. This will affect the time allotments planned for certain activities; it will also affect the need for repetition of instruction.

2. The number of exceptional students in the class. The influence of this information on class planning has been thoroughly discussed in the chapter on adapted activities.

3. The physical fitness level of the class and the extent to which they are physically educated. The need for this information is obvious.

4. The students who have behavior problems. The purpose of finding this out is to plan how these students will be dealt with if they show signs of disrupting the class. The teacher should guard against labeling these students troublemakers because this may evoke a response to them which will aggravate rather than minimize the problem.

Armed with this information the teacher may begin to plan the course of study in physical education for the year, guided by the overall plan of the administrator of the department if there is one. Students who are teaching are likely to be required to make lesson plans for daily and weekly periods. Typical methods of preparing these are discussed in Chapter 10.

Before teaching the first class, the teacher should be familiar with the indoor and outdoor facilities of the school and the location of the shower rooms and the equipment storage rooms. Information about the location, number and method of using the lockers should also be known as it will save time and embarrassment later.

WHEN SCHOOL OPENS

Until the duties which the teacher must perform before, during and after each class meeting become routine it is helpful to have a list like the one below to check against.

CHECKLIST

Before class
> Game equipment ready, including piano, records and player, instruments, charts, chalkboard, if these are required.
> Floor and wall markings made
> Roll and seating or place assignment chart ready
> Lesson plans ready
> Locker and shower rooms ready

During class
> Roll call
> Excuses, tardy slips noted
> Announcements
> Prompt dismissal

After class
> Note any suggestions for next class
> Check on locker room, equipment, etc.
> If last period, close and lock rooms and offices

The new teacher's lack of familiarity with the names of the students in his several classes presents a barrier to good relationships with

Figure 25–1. Getting all the necessary equipment ready for use before class begins is essential to well-organized and effective teaching. (Courtesy of the Hargal All-Sports Equipment Company.)

them. Names can be learned more easily if students are required to wear name tags or are given exact positions for roll call. During the first few class meetings the teacher may plan to allot a few additional moments to calling the roll so that time can be taken to associate names and faces. Another helpful technique is to require students to print their names in good sized letters on the backs of their uniforms or shirts, usually with ink markers. This is particularly helpful when the teacher wishes to call unfamiliar students by name during play.

Alertness to individual needs is important for any teacher but particularly for the new teacher; the success of physical education is measured by the total improvement of individual students. The teacher must watch for inability to perform skills, poor attitudes and lack of general good health. It is important to remember that quiet, inoffensive students may need the teacher's help as much or more than those whose overt behavior demands the teacher's attention, for these are likely to be the students who feel inadequate because of their lack of skill.

The beginning teacher usually wants very much to be liked by the students. This is a worthwhile goal, for a teacher who is liked has a distinct advantage in promoting the desirable educational objectives he seeks for his students. The inexperienced teacher sometimes makes the mistake of placing himself on the students' level in order to court their friendship. This may give the teacher a surface popularity, but actually students quickly lose respect for such a teacher. They want their teachers to be friendly but to maintain the social distance of a respectful teacher-student relationship.

DISCIPLINE AND CONDUCT WITHIN THE CLASS

The very nature of physical activity gives rise to types of misbehavior that would not ordinarily be found in the regular classroom; but on the other hand, it also reduces the kind of undesirable classroom behavior which arises from long periods of inactivity and boredom. A new teacher must learn from experience how best to deal with those whose conduct detracts from the learning of their classmates. A few very general comments about types of discipline which are sometimes employed may be useful, however.

Punishment, unless judiciously handled, frequently builds resentment and oftentimes secures only temporary good conduct. A student may change his mode of conduct for a time in order to avoid punishment rather than because he understands the reason why his conduct is unacceptable. If the teacher can impress upon students who are misbehaving the advantages to them that will be gained from good conduct, the results will be more lasting than if coercion must be resorted to. Coercion should be used only when other methods have failed. However, the punishment should never be administered in a vindictive manner and must always be judged in terms of the value to the individual student and to the group. For example, punishing students by giving them extra calisthenics or having them run laps around the gymnasium or field has doubtful value for it tends to demean one of the objectives of physical education, the development of an appreciation for strenuous activity.

Mass punishment has its limitations. Only under very special circumstances can it be used to the advantage of the group. Those circumstances would be ones in which the teacher's concept of behavior is accepted by and adhered to by most of the class, and these members are capable and willing to bring those who are misbehaving into line. This kind of group action requires a certain amount of maturity which may be beyond most high school groups. Group punishment for excessive noisiness or general disorder and confusion is seldom very effective. The teacher is more likely to be successful in restoring order by seeking out the causes and eliminating them.

EVALUATION OF TEACHING EFFECTIVENESS

The circumstances and situations that may cause problems for the beginning teacher have been dealt with in this textbook. It is suggested that you turn to these discussions, listed by topic in the index, for help with those problems that your analysis indicates may prevent you from being as successful in teaching physical education as you wish to be. The list which follows represents the most common failures and shortcomings of inexperienced teachers (new and student teachers), as observed by critic teachers and administrators of physical education. You may find it useful in analyzing your own weaknesses and strengths.

1. Ineffective organization and planning for large classes.
2. Lack of adaptability to less than ideal conditions.
3. Inadequate knowledge of testing and evaluation.
4. Insufficient skill in and information about a wide variety of activities.
5. Ineffective discipline procedures.
6. Poor communication skills.
7. Lack of consideration for students as individuals.
8. Inability to analyze weaknesses and errors in students' performance of skills.
9. Excessive discussions, leaving too little time for actual participation in the activity.
10. Failure to adapt activities to the capabilities of the students.
11. Unbalanced program: too much of one kind of activity or too frequently merely "throwing out the ball."
12. Neglect of safety precautions.

13. Failure to see physical education in its proper perspective in the total educational program.

14. Participation with the students to the detriment of class supervision.

15. Inability to develop meaningful objectives.

DISCUSSION QUESTIONS

1. Discuss the purpose of student-teaching in the preparation of a prospective physical education teacher.

2. What is the purpose of the observation period before beginning student-teaching?

3. Describe some situations that might arise for which the teacher should know school policies.

4. Discuss some of the problems of adjustment that a beginning teacher may have to make in a new teaching situation.

5. How can a student-teacher procure information about the students he is to teach?

THINGS TO DO

1. Analyze your teaching effectiveness, using the chart on p. 511 and the form on pp. 524 to 526.

2. Make a list of the factors that are involved in becoming a respected and well-liked teacher.

3. After consulting the references on methods of teaching other disciplines, make a general comparison between the teaching of physical education and the teaching of other subjects. What pitfalls are present in physical education that are not problems for teachers of other subjects?

4. If members of the class have not had an opportunity to observe a high school physical education class, make arrangements to do so. During the observation pay particular attention to the points listed on pp. 515 to 516.

5. Interview several experienced teachers about the discipline procedures they have found most effective.

SELECTED READINGS

Brown, Thomas J.: *Student Teaching in a Secondary School,* 2nd ed. New York, Harper & Row Publishers, 1969.

Cratty, Bryant J.: *Career Potentials in Physical Activity.* Englewood Cliffs, New Jersey, Prentice-Hall, Inc., 1971.

Hoover, Kenneth H.: *The Professional Teacher's Handbook: A Guide for Improving Instruction in Today's Secondary Schools.* Boston, Allyn and Bacon, Inc., 1973.

Knapp, Clyde and Jewett, Ann E.: *Physical Education Student Teaching Guide.* Champaign, Ill., Stipes Publishing Co., 1962.

Rosenstein, Irwin and Hase, Gerald J.: *Student Teaching in Physical Education.* Englewood Cliffs, New Jersey, Prentice-Hall, Inc., 1971.

CHAPTER TWENTY-SIX

PROFESSIONAL GROWTH

Preliminary professional training is a basic aspect of effective teaching. A poorly screened, inferior college student who graduates with a major in physical education and enters the teaching profession is still an inferior person, on whom precious education training hours have been spent. In spite of the fact that in some few schools "snap" courses still exist for athletes majoring in physical education, rapid advances have been made in raising both screening and professional preparation standards. Fortunately, the days of beating the bushes for major students and lowering educational standards are disappearing. The general public is awakening to the fact that professionally better prepared teachers do produce the best educational .results; these are the ones now more eagerly sought by both rural and urban communities, regardless of their fields of specialization. Preparation programs for physical educators are also improving greatly. Today, young teachers who enter this field, which has lifted itself by sheer effort and great determination up the rungs of an educational ladder, are greater in number and superior in their competencies in skills, knowledges and attitudes as leaders than those of a decade or two ago.

Three chief ways for one to grow professionally are through self-evaluation, in-service education and additional professional education.

GROWTH THROUGH SELF-EVALUATION

The teacher who engages in realistic self-evaluation can make the most progress toward becoming a better educator. Teachers are not born superior; they are made so by profiting from their mistakes and from learning how to avoid them by using better methods. Although it is difficult to "see ourselves as others see us," such soul-searching self-awareness is basic to *wanting* to grow professionally. Socrates' counsel to "know thyself" is an incomplete, life-long quest, for no college ever *gave* any student a completed education, but rather headed him down the right path toward such a desired goal. As Voeks points out when reminding us of Theodore Roosevelt's remarks, "What I am to be, I am now becoming."

As one educator has pointed out:

"What sort of person you later will be is influenced by every response you currently make. What you are like on Graduation Day depends upon all the habits you practice while in college: the way you study, the way you listen to lectures, the way you participate in other activities, the way you respond to your colleagues; in brief, the way you live each hour.[1]"

Most people wish at times that they had at least considered entering another profession than the one they did. Smithells suggests that everyone now in, or about to enter, the field of physical education give serious consideration to the following self-examining questions.[2]

Why have we chosen this profession?
What were the characteristics and abilities in ourselves that motivated us to major in this field?
Was it our own athletic prowess?
Was this the main source of ego-satisfaction?
Was it our success in adolescent leadership, as expressed in school-time popularity and influence?
Was it the enthusiasm of some teacher or coach who saw in us someone who could improve his own reputation?
Was it an unperceived desire not to mature—to be a Peter Pan, with eternal youth?
Was it a feeling that the fame we had then was something to cling to?
Was it a feeling we were a pretty important guy, or pretty smart girl?

The following self-appraisal check sheet should be filled out at least once a year by every physical educator desirous of self-improvement.

TEACHER SELF-APPRAISAL CHECK SHEET

Personal Qualities and Performance	Consistently	Frequently	Need to work on this
	3	2	1
A. *Staff Relationships*			
1. Have good intra-staff relationships with the entire school faculty.			
2. See my own program in its proper relationship to all other school subjects.			
3. Carry my fair share of out-of-class responsibilities.			

[1]Voeks, Virginia: *On Becoming an Educated Person.* Philadelphia, W. B. Saunders Company, 1957, p. 19.
[2]Smithells, Philip, and Cameron, Peter: *Principles of Evaluation in Physical Education.* New York, Harper & Row, 1962, p. 25.

	Consistently	Frequently	Need to work on this
	3	2	1

4. Accept criticism and recognition well. _____

5. Accept group decisions without necessarily agreeing; stand up for believed-in principles. _____

6. Co-operate well with my administrators and supervisors. _____

B. *Community Relationships*

7. Work understandingly and co-operatively with parents of most of my students. _____

8. Participate in and contribute to community activities. _____

9. Am a good representative for the school in the community. _____

C. *Appearance and Manner*

10. Dress appropriately; am well-dressed and poised. _____

11. Use good grammer and speak well. _____

12. Show genuine concern and interest in each student; know each student's name and something good about him. _____

13. Maintain good emotional balance. _____

14. Am worthy of the emulation of students and colleagues. _____

15. Attempt daily to correct detracting personal habits and mannerisms. _____

16. Look and act the part of a leader. _____

D. *Teaching Performance*

17. Help each student gain an understanding, knowledge and appreciation of health and physical education. _____

18. Strive to teach each individual in the class; know the emotional, physical and social needs of each student. _____

19. Use democratic methods and develops student leadership among all who show new leadership potentials. _____

	Consistently	Frequently	Need to work on this
	3	2	1

20. Plan each day's work carefully; make the most productive use of each class period.

21. Have a minimum of behavior problems.

22. Help each student to grow in physical and social skills.

23. Teach students something new and of real value in every class.

24. Work daily toward teaching the objectives of physical education in each class on each grade level.

25. Students are aware of these over-all objectives.

26. Students know the goals to be reached in each lesson.

27. Make the fullest use daily of my facilities and equipment.

28. Provide a program which has variety, meaning and carry-over value.

E. *Professional Qualities*

29. Have the refinement, character and objectivity expected of a professional person.

30. Am proud of my profession and am working toward raising its professional standards locally.

31. Am continuously growing professionally through study and experimentation.

32. Belong to my national, district, state and local professional organizations.

33. Attend one or more local, state, district or national meeting of my professional organization each year.

IN-SERVICE EDUCATION

In-service education is an on-the-job, self-improvement program. Education does not terminate when one receives his first college degree, for there are learning possibilities in every aspect of life. The old adages "Live and learn" and "Experience is the best teacher" are true only if one profits from his mistakes and finds new and better ways to succeed. Often one repeats the same methods of teaching or uses the same course materials year after year. The older and more experienced one becomes, the greater the temptation to remain in a comfortable rut rather than to try newer and better ways to accomplish desired goals. A physical educator once bragged to his class that he should know what he was doing since he had had twenty years of teaching experience. A student whispered to a seat mate that, in the final analysis, the instructor had had but one year of experience which he had repeated nineteen times!

STAFF MEETINGS

Democratically led staff meetings with fellow teachers can be a rich source of growing in understanding and appreciation. They can also lead to the development of techniques for getting along better with others and reducing professional jealousies and conflicts. Numerous studies have been made of why people lose their jobs; oddly enough, the reason most often reported is the inability to work harmoniously with others.

CURRICULUM STUDY

Increasingly, schools are providing released time of several days during the school year for teachers to work on curriculum improvements. In states where the Twelve Month Plan is in operation, all teachers are hired and paid on a yearly basis. Each summer one third of the group stays at the school working on courses of study and the general curriculum, one third is assisted financially to pursue further academic preparation, and the remaining group is aided financially to travel at home or abroad. The groups rotate roles yearly. In other schools, teachers who wish to remain on the school payroll during summer months spend four to six weeks developing a better course of study in their particular fields. The greatest benefits that can be gained from such experiences are in the growth in understanding of the professional field, the discovery of newer and better teaching techniques, the unification of the teachers as an educational team, and the increased financial security of those taking part in the program.

CLINICS

Clinics and workshops are rich sources for self-improvement. These often include opportunities to obtain new methods and materials for teaching modern, folk, square and social dance, hockey, football, tennis, archery, golf, aquatics, health and safety, outdoor education, camping and camp leadership. Although it takes precious free time to attend these meetings, such trips are a valuable means of gaining new ideas and materials and of forming worthwhile friendships.

HOME STUDY

Home study and extension courses are available in most communities. These are often sponsored by state schools and led by well-known experts. Although some teachers profit by taking correspondence courses, generally speaking, meeting with other teachers one or two nights weekly in an extension course is a better means of broadening oneself and exchanging ideas. The chief benefit of either course, however, is often found in the required reading of new materials. Many a professional worker's library has been enlarged in this way.

PROFESSIONAL ORGANIZATIONS

All teachers should be contributing members of their professional organization. In the better schools, local student physical education clubs affiliate with the American Association for Health, Physical Education, and Recreation. Increasingly, student groups are attending local, state and national meetings and conventions. The chief value is that the youth gain a deeper respect for their chosen field and stronger determination to further its cause. It is a valuable experience for them to meet their textbook authors or to hear nationally recognized leaders speak. Those who take out student memberships in this organization usually continue as professional members later. All teachers of physical education should not only join this association but realize the great professional profit to be gained from attending the meetings.

Professional organizations which physical education teachers can join are the: American Association for Health, Physical Education, and Recreation; Division for Girls' and Women's Sports; National Park and Recreation Association; American Public Health Association; American Camping Association; and the National Education Association. Each teacher should also belong to local and state physical education associations and other teacher organizations.

TRAVEL

Travel is a wonderful way to grow professionally. Aimless wandering is sometimes relaxing and fun, but to travel for the purpose of developing a newer and broadened understanding and appreciation of others is far more rewarding. Dance specialists often gather many new folk dances from the people of Spain, Mexico, Denmark and other countries. Swimming teachers profit greatly from observing techniques for training competitive teams in Japan or Australia. Every instructor with a specialized interest will return home from a trip abroad or in his own country more interested in his work and will pass on his newly gained enthusiasm to his students.

HOBBIES

It has often been said that the happiest people are those with many interests, and that those who work well also play well. Hobbies add much to one's joy in life for they lead to new friends and wider interests. Arts and crafts, music, dramatics, photography, reading, collecting and nature study are especially ideal for physical educators, for they offer contrast and relaxation to the strenuous and active life which those in this profession usually must lead.

WRITING

Preparing articles for publication in professional magazines can be a rewarding experience, for in order to contribute something of value one must profit from his experiences and the further research which is often necessary. Articles on newly discovered teaching techniques, program materials, the results of independently conducted research contribute greatly not only to the literature of one's professional field but also to increasing one's recognition and appreciation by fellow workers and improving one's attitude toward his profession.

KEEPING UP WITH PROFESSIONAL LITERATURE

This is the age of the knowledge explosion, for at no other time in history has change come so rapidly. It is imperative that today's teachers, more so than ever before, keep up to date and are not only aware of new program innovations in their own field, but in all phases of education as well. Many teachers set aside scheduled time weekly, and some even daily, for reading their professional journals and other helpful materials. Still others subscribe to such periodicals as The Physical Education Newsletter, which is published on the first and fifteenth of each school month. It is a valuable source of information of current programs and other recent changes in the field of physical education nationally. It is available from The Physical Education Newsletter Offices, 20 Cedarwood Lane, P.O. Box 8, Old Saybrook, Connecticut.

Other suggested ways of keeping abreast with current literature in education is to subscribe to *The Education Digest,* in which the best materials from hundreds of journals, papers, and speeches are condensed for the educator. Published monthly, it is available from The Education Digest, 416 Longshore Drive, Ann Arbor, Michigan, 48107.

TEACHER UNIONS AND COLLECTIVE BARGAINING

At the present time a majority of public school teachers belong either to the National Education Association (N.E.A.) or to the American Federation of Teachers (A.F.T.). Many local teacher groups or unions, however, now play a more crucial role in formulating and implementing personnel problems affecting them than either of these national organizations. It is believed by many educational experts that the most important outcome of the whole negotiation movement will be the increased political effectiveness of teachers, which will bring improvements not only in their own employment practices and working conditions but in many other facets of life which are directly concerned with the education of all children in our nation. Teacher organizations now have more political clout than ever before in our history and they are beginning to use this power most effectively.

John Dewey, the famous educator, believed that "democracy must be reborn every twenty years and education is its midwife." Just as our national professional physical education association must purge out the "ball-thrower-outers" and unproductive teachers among us, so must every other field in education rid itself of charletons, too.

In the field of education, our most urgent need is to develop a new breed of teachers of the highest quality who will work for the revitalization of the goals of our democratic society in the context of the total civilization of all mankind through the medium of education. The teachers of tomorrow will likely be more unionized and united in their efforts than their counterparts of today. They must also become giants of outspoken convictions as well as be committed to the glorification of learning and the development of students within the context of lasting human values. Under such leadership American education, of which physical education is an important part, could be entering one of its most significant decades of progress in its entire history.

FURTHER PROFESSIONAL EDUCATION

Graduate study is a costly investment that yields many rich returns. It is a must for those who aspire to self-improvement and wish to teach at advanced levels or to become leaders in their field. The Master's degree usually requires one academic year or 30 semester hours of study obtained in summer or night school at one institution (most schools will allow the student to transfer only six hours of credit earned elsewhere). In some institutions, the candidate is required to write a thesis; in others, he is given an opportunity to choose to do so or take additional course hours. Although there are certain advantages in obtaining an advanced degree from the same institution from which one received his baccalaureate, there are numerous advantages in taking further work in a different section of the country. Before starting on any graduate program, the candidate should seriously consider where he can receive the greatest profit from the investment in time and money he is about to make. Receiving a degree from a leading institution and taking work under a recognized national leader in one's professional field can be of great future value. However, the potential graduate student should use the utmost care in selecting the school he desires to attend, for graduate study is costly and some schools are superior to others. There are many advantages in going to a different institution rather than to the college from which one graduated, for the people one encounters at graduate school are second only to the coursework itself, and the opportunity to study under nationally recognized leaders in the profession.

Those who wish to receive education beyond the Master's level can, if they are qualified for admission and successfully meet all the requirements, receive either the Doctor of Philosophy degree, the Doctor of Education degree, or the newer Doctor of Physical Education degree. The Doctor of Philosophy degree and Doctor of Education degree are similar in admission standards, matriculation procedures, residence and time requirements. The Ed.D. differs largely in that it is more appropriate for those who wish to specialize in education. The Ph.D. is largely aimed at a more specific area of knowledge, and the required dissertation is written around an original contribution to some specialized field of human knowledge. The newer Doctor of Physical Education degree differs from either the Ed.D. or Ph.D. in that one specializes in some area of education or physical education. Requirements for all of these advanced degrees vary from institution to institution.

Many graduate teaching fellowships, teaching assistantships, scholarships and loans are available for those interested in advanced study.

Advanced study improves one's qualifications for professional advancement as well as increases his understanding and respect for his chosen profession. Supervisory and administrative positions increasingly require broad professional experience and a Doctor's degree. Those who are in the highest paid positions are experienced, have specialized and received advanced degrees. They usually are the recognized leaders in the profession.

Teachers are leaders of the people and help shape the future of our country by educating its citizenry. Because of this, each must be carefully selected, well prepared and anxious to grow professionally. Physical education teachers must be willing to make physical and financial sacrifices to further their chosen field. They must assist and lead others to a higher degree of fitness, skill and happiness. Through united group action much can and will be accomplished for the betterment of each individual student and teacher and, also, for society.

DISCUSSION QUESTIONS

1. Discuss ways teachers can grow as professional leaders through an in-service program.
2. Where would you like to travel as a means of broadening your interests and talents? What would you like to bring back to enrich your teaching effectiveness?
3. Discuss your future professional plans in relationship to what you are doing today.
4. What problems are you likely to encounter as a student teacher or an apprentice leader in the recreation field?
5. List and discuss, in order of importance to you, the most important things you have learned from reading (a) this chapter and (b) this book.

THINGS TO DO

1. Make a list of 25 books you want to buy first for your own professional library. Which one do you want most of all to have?
2. Consult the requirements for entrance to a graduate school you would like to attend and list their requirements for a Master's degree and the Doctor of Philosophy or Doctor of Education degree.
3. Report to your class on any local, state, district or national professional physical education meeting you have attended.
4. Make a chart showing five of your strengths as a prospective leader and five of your weaknesses. What must you do in order to reach your desired leadership goals? List five things.
5. Give a biographical sketch of any five living, nationally recognized physical educators. Summarize their educational background, service to professional organizations and their community, experience record and national listings or honors received.

SELECTED VISUAL AIDS

Careers in Recreation; Careers in Physical Education. Available from the Athletic Institute or the Association Films in most large cities on a rental or purchase basis.

Physical Education for Blind Children. Shows the use of modified sports and games for blind children. Rental from Dr. Charles Buell, 2722 Derby Street, Berkeley, California.

Teach Me! A photographic essay on the joys and challenges of learning by Carl Purcell. Available from the N.E.A., 1201 16th N.W., Washington, D.C., $8.00.

SUGGESTED READINGS

AAHPER: *Directory of Professional Preparation Institutions* (1966); *Graduate Education in Health Education, Physical Education, Recreation, Safety, and Dance* (1967); *Professional Preparation in Health Education, Physical Education, and Recreation Education* (1962). 1201 16th N.W., Washington, D.C.

Conant, James B.: *The Education of American Teachers.* New York, McGraw-Hill Book Co., 1964.

Ferm, Vergilius. *So You're Going To College.* North Quincy Publishing, Mass., The Christopher Publishing House, 1972.

Inlow, Gail: *Maturity in High School Teaching.* Englewood Cliffs, N.J., Prentice-Hall, Inc., 1963.

Jones, Ann. *Uncle Tom's Campus.* New York, Praeger Publishers, 1973.

Levine, Joel and May, Lawrence. *Getting In: A Guide to Acceptance at the College of Your Choice.* New York, Random House, 1972.

Mayhew, Lewis. *Reform in Graduate Education.* Atlanta, Georgia, Southern Regional Education Board, 1972.

Ryan, Kevin. *Realities and Revolution in Teacher Education.* Commission on Public School Personnel Policies in Ohio, Greater Cleveland Foundation, 1972.

Simons, James. "An Advanced Degree—Does It Pay To Get One?" *The Education Digest,* February, 1973.

Simpson, Ray: *Teacher Self-Evaluation.* New York, The Macmillan Company, 1966.

APPENDICES

APPENDICES

FILM SOURCES

Aetna Life Affiliated Companies
Public Education Department
151 Farmington Avenue
Hartford, Connecticut

All American Production
P.O. Box 801
Riverside, California

American Film Company
24 East 8th Street
Chicago, Illinois

American Medical Association
535 North Dearborn Street
Chicago 10, Illinois

Association Films, Inc.
Y.M.C.A. Motion Picture Bureau
347 Madison Avenue
New York 17, New York
    351 Turk Street
    San Francisco, California

Athletic Institute, The
209 S. State Street
Chicago 4, Illinois

Audio Film Center
203 N. Wabash Avenue
Chicago, Illinois

Bailey Films, Inc.
6509 de Longpre Avenue
Hollywood 28, California

Bell and Howell Company
1801 Larchmonte Avenue
Chicago, Illinois

Brandon Films, Inc.
200 West 57th Street
New York, New York
    Western Cinema Guild
    290 Seventh Avenue
    San Francisco 18, California

British Information Service
30 Rockefeller Plaza
New York, New York

Bureau of Audio-Visual Instruction
Extension Division
State University of Iowa
Iowa City, Iowa

Paul Burnford
Film Production
1413 Warner Avenue
Los Angeles, California

Castle
7356 Melrose Avenue
Hollywood 46, California

Coca-Cola Company
P.O. Drawer 1734
Atlanta 1, Georgia

Colburn Film Distributors, Inc.
P.O. Box 470, 668 N. Western Avenue
Lake Forest, Illinois

Columbia University Press
Communication Materials Center
1125 Amsterdam Avenue
New York 27, New York

Connecticut College for Women
Department of Physical Education
New London, Connecticut

Coronet Instructional Films, Inc.
65 E. South Water Street
Chicago, Illinois

Duckpin Bowling Council
1420 New York Avenue, N.W.
Washington 5, D.C.

Eastman Film: Eastman Kodak Co.
Informational Films Division
343 State Street
Rochester 4, New York

Encyclopaedia Britannica Films, Inc.
Wilmette, Illinois

General Motors Corporation
Department of Public Relations
Film Distribution Center
3044 W. Grand Boulevard
Detroit, Michigan

Internation Film Bureau, Inc.
Chicago 4, Illinois

Johnson and Johnson
Promotion Department
New Brunswick, New Jersey

McGraw-Hill Book Company
Test Film Department
330 West 42nd Street
New York 18, New York

Modern Talking Picture Service, Inc.
45 Rockefeller Plaza
New York 20, New York

Museum of Modern Art Film Library
11 West 53rd Street
New York, New York

National Film Board of Canada
1270 Avenue of the Americas
New York 20, New York

National Foundation, Inc.
120 Broadway
New York 5, New York

National Society for the Prevention of
    Blindness
16 East 40th Street
New York 16, New York

Official Films, Inc.
Grand and Linden Avenues
Ridgefield, New Jersey

Official Sport Film Service
7 S. Dearborn Street
Chicago, Illinois

Perry-Mansfield
15 West 67th Street
New York, New York

R. K. O. Pictures, Inc.
Rockefeller Center
New York, New York

State University of Iowa
Iowa City, Iowa

Teaching Film Custodians, Inc.
25 West 43rd Street
New York 18, New York

Educational Film Department
United World Films, Inc.
7356 Melrose Avenue
Hollywood 46, California
    1445 Park Avenue
    New York 29, New York

University of Michigan
Audio-Visual Education Center
4028 Administration Building
Ann Arbor, Michigan

Wholesome Film Service, Inc.
48 Melrose Street
Boston, Massachusetts

Young America Films, Inc.
18 East 41st Street
New York 17, New York

ADEQUATE STANDARDS FOR A PUBLIC SCHOOL HEALTH AND PHYSICAL EDUCATION PROGRAM*

THE PROGRAM FOR THE SECONDARY SCHOOL

I. PROGRAM CONTENT
A. Health
   1. Examination by a qualified physician at entrance and at least twice thereafter with consistent follow-up for correction of remediable physical defects by physicians, nurses, teachers, and parents.
   2. Periodic dental examinations with referral to family dentist.
   3. Chest x-rays of 11th and 12th grade children.
   4. Provision through the school administration for aid to indigent children.
   5. Health instruction, emphasizing personal health, community health, home care of the sick, family relations, first aid, safety, and nutrition, one period a week for four years *or equivalent* of a one-year two-semester course meeting five times per week or one period a week for four years.

B. Physical Education
   1. An opportunity for the promotion of vigorous normal growth through a wide range of large motor activities such as the natural activities of daily life, free and individual play, sports and games, self-testing activities, relaxation and rest, remedial and adapted activities, coeducational and corecreational activities, dance, and wherever possible camping, hiking, and outing.
   2. Specific activities including
      a. Individual sports and games, free play and squad play activities adapted to age levels.
      b. Stunts and tumbling, achievement tests in sports, and fundamental skills tests
      c. Swimming and lifesaving
      d. Prevention of fatigue through rest and relaxation taking into consideration physical status, emotional stability, and intellectual capacity
      e. Rhythmic fundamentals, movement fundamentals, dance composition, folk dancing, and social dancing.
   3. Adequate program of intramural athletics for junior high school boys and girls. Intramural and interschool athletics for senior high school boys. Interschool physical education activities for girls consisting of sports days, playdays, and invitational games; championship-type activities not approved.

II. FACILITIES AND EQUIPMENT
   A. Gymnasium — one for boys and one for girls depending upon size of school
      1. 65' × 90' floor space
      2. 18' ceiling acoustically treated
      3. Smooth walls
      4. Hardwood floors
      5. Recessed lights
      6. Recessed radiators
      7. Well-screened windows

   B. Health service room
      1. Approximately classroom size
      2. Equipped with first-aid materials and lavatory
      3. Functionally planned for private examinations, eye tests, etc.
      4. One cot per 100 pupils for rest
      5. Waiting room adjacent

   C. Supplies
      One piece of material per 8 pupils

   D. Health instruction room of classroom size

   E. Locker and dressing room
      8 square feet of floor space per child at peak load exclusive of lockers

---

*Reproduced by permission of the AAHPER. 1201 16th St., N.W., Washington, D.C.

539

F. Lockers
  1. Unit type combining large dressing locker (12" × 12" × 72") with box or basket storage lockers (24" × 6" × 12")
  2. Number of lockers established on basis of number of pupils served at peak load

G. Shower and shower room
  1. Fourteen square feet of floor space for each shower head
  2. Showers arranged at shoulder height in batteries and thermostatically controlled with master valve
  3. Allowance for three pupils per shower at peak load with number of showers planned accordingly
  4. Two individual shower booths and two dressing booths for girls in addition to gang showers

H. Toilet rooms in connection with locker or dressing room including:
  1. 5 boys' urinals per 100 boys
  2. 4 boys' water closets per 100 boys
  3. 7 girls' water closets per 100 girls
  4. 2 lavatories for each toilet room

I. Swimming pool
  30' × 75' varying in depth from 3'6" at the shallow end to 9' or 10' at the deep end

J. Outdoor court and field area
  1. Junior high school 10 to 20 acres
  2. Senior high school 15 to 30 acres

III. TIME ALLOTMENT
  A. One period per week for four years for health instruction or equivalent of a one-year two-semester course meeting five times per week. Health coordinator recommended for each school.

  B. One period per day for physical education, length of period to be consistent with the established length of periods in the individual school.

IV. TEACHER EDUCATION
  Bachelor's degree with major in health and physical education for full-time teaching. A minor for part-time teaching.

V. TEACHER LOAD
  A. One teacher per 50 pupils in physical education
  B. One teacher per 35 pupils in swimming
  C. One teacher per 35 pupils in health instruction

CHECKLIST ON SCHOOL ATHLETICS*

PURPOSES OF SCHOOL ATHLETICS

1. Does your school have clearly defined goals for its athletic program?
   Y......... N......... U......... A......... D......... U.........
2. Do other teachers, as well as coaches and teachers of physical education, have a part in formulating the purposes of athletics in your school?
   Y......... N......... U......... A......... D......... U.........
3. Do lay citizens have opportunity to express themselves with respect to the purposes of athletics in your school?
   Y......... N......... U......... A......... D......... U.........
4. Are athletics recognized by your school as an integral part of complete education?
   Y......... N......... U......... A......... D......... U.........
5. Are athletic activities in harmony with the objectives of the total educational program?
   Y......... N......... U......... A......... D......... U.........
6. Does your school's athletic program encourage participation in satisfying play by *all* pupils?
   Y......... N......... U......... A......... D......... U.........
7. Does your school in its athletic program seek to contribute to the development of wholesome personalities?
   Y......... N......... U......... A......... D......... U.........
8. Does your school conduct athletics in ways intended to help participants develop health and physical fitness?
   Y......... N......... U......... A......... D......... U.........
9. Does your school seek to conduct athletics in such a way that participants develop enduring play habits, skills, and attitudes?
   Y......... N......... U......... A......... D......... U.........
10. Does your school encourage athletic activities which aid development of desirable social growth and adjustment?
    Y......... N......... U......... A......... D......... U.........
11. Does your school conduct athletics in such a way as to avoid excessive emotional strains and tensions on the part of both players and spectators?
    Y......... N......... U......... A......... D......... U.........
12. Does your school take steps to prevent athletic practices which might be detrimental to the welfare of pupils as individuals?
    Y......... N......... U......... A......... D......... U.........

HEALTH AND WELFARE OF ATHLETIC PARTICIPANTS

13. In determining policies and procedures for athletics in your school is the health and welfare of participants considered paramount?
    Y......... N......... U......... A......... D......... U.........
14. Does the school provide adequate protective equipment and other health safeguards for all participants in athletic contests?
    Y......... N......... U......... A......... D......... U.........
15. Are all games and practice sessions conducted in facilities that are hygienic, clean, and safe?
    Y......... N......... U......... A......... D......... U.........
16. Is adequate training and conditioning required for all types of athletic competition?
    Y......... N......... U......... A......... D......... U.........
17. Has the approval of a physician been secured for the practices of your school's interscholastic athletic program which involve conditioning, training, and health?
    Y......... N......... U......... A......... D......... U.........

---

*Permission granted to reprint this checklist from *School Athletics: Problems and Policies,* Educational Policies Commission, Washington, 1953.

18. Is a thorough health examination required of all participants in both intramural and interscholastic sports before they take part in vigorous athletic competition?

    Y......... N......... U......... A......... D......... U.........

19. Is a postseason health examination required of athletes?

    Y......... N......... U......... A......... D......... U.........

20. Is emergency medical service available during all practice periods, intramural games, and interscholastic contests held under school auspices?

    Y......... N......... U......... A......... D......... U.........

21. Are athletes who have been injured or ill readmitted to participation only with the written approval of a physician?

    Y......... N......... U......... A......... D......... U.........

22. Does your school have a written and well-publicized policy regarding the legal and financial responsibilities for injuries incurred in athletics?

    Y......... N......... U......... A......... D......... U.........

23. Even when not legally responsible, does your school have a plan for making financial provisions for the care of injuries incurred in school athletics?

    Y......... N......... U......... A......... D......... U.........

24. Does the school seek to prevent injury to the personality development of star athletes from overattention and ego-inflation?

    Y......... N......... U......... A......... D......... U.........

ORGANIZATION AND ADMINISTRATION OF SCHOOL ATHLETICS

25. Are all athletic activities in your school recognized as the responsibility of the school and under its control?

    Y......... N......... U......... A......... D......... U.........

26. Are all athletics in your school administered as part of the school's total program of physical education?

    Y......... N......... U......... A......... D......... U.........

27. Is your school (if a high school) a member of your state high school athletic association or similar organization?

    Y......... N......... U......... A......... D......... U.........

28. Does your school accept the aid of your state's department of education (or public instruction) in establishing and maintaining high standards in the conduct of school athletics?

    Y......... N......... U......... A......... D......... U.........

FACILITES FOR SCHOOL ATHLETICS

29. Does your board of education provide adequate facilities in athletics for *all* students?

    Y......... N......... U......... A......... D......... U.........

30. Are physical education facilities in your school available to all phases of the program, including required activity classes and intramurals?

    Y......... N......... U......... A......... ...D......... U.........

31. Do girls share equally with boys in the use of your school's athletic facilities?

    Y......... N......... U......... A......... D......... U.........

32. Does your school provide a standard field, court, or play space for each team game and individual sport most popular in your section of the country?

    Y......... N......... U......... A......... D......... U.........

PERSONNEL FOR THE ATHLETIC PROGRAM

33. Are all who coach athletic teams in your school competently trained and certified as teachers?

    Y......... N......... U......... A......... D......... U.........

34. Do the athletic coaches have professional training in physical education equivalent to a minor or more?

     Y......... N......... U......... A......... D......... U.........

35. Do the athletic coaches consistently set good examples in the matter of sportsmanship and personal conduct?

     Y......... N......... U......... A......... D......... U.........

36. Do athletic coaches use their influence with students to help them with personal problems?

     Y......... N......... U......... A......... D......... U.........

37. Are those members of the school staff whose chief work is coaching athletics generally regarded by other faculty members as fellow teachers of comparable professional status?

     Y......... N......... U......... A......... D......... U.........

38. Does the school provide sufficient personnel for the proper instruction and supervision of all participants in the required activity classes, in co-recreation, in intramural sports, and in interscholastic athletics?

     Y......... N......... U......... A......... D......... U.........

39. Do school authorities seek to maintain at all times a balance in the amount of staff time and instruction given to all phases of physical education, including required activity classes, co-reaction, intramural sports, and interscholastic athletics?

     Y......... N......... U......... A......... D......... U.........

INTRAMURAL PROGRAMS

40. Does every student in your school system have opportunity for participating in a variety of intramural sports?

     Y......... N......... U......... A......... D......... U.........

41. Is the intramural sports program conducted as an integral part of the total program of physical education and not as a "feeder" system for interscholastic athletics?

     Y......... N......... U......... A......... D......... U.........

42. Does the intramural sports program serve as a laboratory where students can test the things they are taught in physical education classes?

     Y......... N......... U......... A......... D......... U.........

43. Do most of the students in your school find the intramural program sufficiently interesting, diverse, and convenient that they voluntarily participate in it?

     Y......... N......... U......... A......... D......... U.........

44. Does the school provide opportunities for co-recreation (that is, for boys and girls to play together) through intramural sports?

     Y......... N......... U......... A......... D......... U.........

45. Does the intramural athletic program have good equipment rather than handed-down equipment, worn-out balls, unmarked fields, and poorly organized game situations?

     Y......... N......... U......... A......... D......... U.........

JUNIOR HIGH SCHOOL POLICIES AND PROGRAMS

46. Is the athletic program for junior high school pupils suited to the needs of children who are undergoing rapid changes in physical growth?

     Y......... N......... U......... A......... D......... U.........

47. Is the athletic program of your junior high school planned cooperatively by teachers, pupils, and parents?

     Y......... N......... U......... A......... D......... U.........

48. Does your junior high school provide a broad athletic program for every boy and girl in the school?

     Y......... N......... U......... A......... D......... U.........

49. Does the athletic program in junior high school consist primarily of sports organized and conducted on an intramural basis?

      Y......... N......... U.........   A......... D.........' U.........

50. Are junior high school pupils given opportunities to develop responsibility through the athletic program by participating in the planning, by organizing groups, by holding office, and by helping with equipment?

      Y......... N......... U.........   A......... D......... U.........

51. Is tackle football prohibited as an athletic activity in your junior high school?

      Y......... N......... U.........   A......... D......... U.........

52. Does your junior school refrain from participation in varsity-type interscholastics?

      Y......... N......... U.........   A......... D......... U.........

53. Are the leaders of athletic activities in your junior high school competently trained teachers?

      Y......... N......... U.........   A......... D......... U.........

INTERSCHOLASTIC ATHLETICS FOR BOYS IN SENIOR HIGH SCHOOL

54. Are interscholastic athletics conducted primarily to serve the needs of students with superior athletic skills?

      Y......... N......... U.........   A......... D......... U.........

55. Are games and practice periods for interscholastic athletics worked into the school schedule with a minimum of interference with the academic program?

      Y......... N......... U.........   A......... D......... U.........

56. Are interscholastic games played only with schools that maintain acceptable principles and policies in their conduct of interscholastic athletics?

      Y......... N......... U.........   A......... D......... U.........

57. Are interscholastic games played only on school or public property?

      Y......... N......... U.........   A......... D......... U.........

58. Does the school observe the rules of its state high school athletic association?

      Y......... N......... U.........   A......... D......... U.........

59. Does the school refuse to participate in all postseason tournaments and postseason championship games?

      Y......... N......... U.........   A......... D......... U.........

60. Is the board of education adequately informed regarding the interscholastic athletic program?

      Y......... N......... U.........   A......... D......... U.........

61. Is the board of education adequately informed regarding the rules and regulations of the state high school athletic association?

      Y......... N......... U.........   A......... D......... U.........

62. Are athletes engaged in interscholastic sports held to the same standards of scholarship as other students?

      Y......... N......... U.........   A......... D......... U.........

63. Are boys who participate in interscholastic athletics required to attend regular classes in physical education (except during the actual period of their interscholastic participation)?

      Y......... N......... U.........   A......... D......... U.........

64. Does the school try to prevent solicitation of its athletes by colleges and universities through tryouts and competitive bidding?

      Y......... N......... U.........   A......... D......... U.........

65. Does the school make an effort to develop high standards of good sportsmanship on the part of all students?

      Y......... N......... U.........   A......... D......... U.........

ATHLETICS FOR GIRLS

66. Does the school athletic program for girls provide opportunities for all girls to participate according to their needs, abilities, and interests?

      Y......... N......... U.........   A......... D......... U.........

67. Are facilities for girls' athletics provided in accordance with the requirements of the girls' program and not on the basis of causing minimum inconvenience to the boys' program?
Y......... N......... U......... A......... D......... U.........

68. Is the school athletic program for girls under the direction of a competent woman leader who is professionally trained in health and physical education?
Y......... N......... U......... A......... D......... U.........

69. Does the school include in its girls' athletic program such dual, individual, and recreational sports and games as archery, badminton, bowling, croquet, horseshoes, golf, riding, shuffleboard, skiing, swimming, table tennis, and tennis?
Y......... N......... U......... A......... D......... U.........

70. Does the school include in its girls' athletic program such team sports as basketball, field hockey, softball, soccer, speedball, and volleyball?
Y......... N......... U......... A......... D......... U.........

71. Does every girl in the school have an opportunity to compete in team games?
Y......... N......... U......... A......... D......... U.........

72. Is participation of girls in athletics based on an appraisal of the health status of each participant which takes into account quality and extent of participation, type of activity, individual differences, and general organic condition?
Y......... N......... U......... A......... D......... U.........

73. Are girls prevented from participation, under school auspices, in sports which involve rough and tumble body contact?
Y......... N......... U......... A......... D......... U.........

74. Are girls provided opportunities for athletic competition with girls of other schools through such means as play days and sports days?
Y......... N......... U......... A......... D......... U.........

75. Are all school athletic contests for girls conducted in accordance with girls' rules?
Y......... N......... U......... A......... D......... U.........

76. Is the school's athletic program for girls conducted in conformity with the policies and recommendations contained in *Standards in Sports for Girls and Women?*
Y......... N......... U......... A......... D......... U.........

FINANCING ATHLETIC PROGRAMS

77. Does the board of education control the financing of the athletic program?
Y......... N......... U......... A......... D......... U.........

78. Is the welfare of participants considered more important than financial gain in determining the athletic policies and practices of your school?
Y......... n......... u......... a......... d......... u.........

79. Is the size of the budget for athletics in sound proportion to the size of the budget for the rest of the school program?
Y......... N......... U......... A......... D......... U.........

80. Is balance maintained in the financial support of all phases of the physical education program, including required activity classes, co-recreation, intramural sports, and interscholastic athletics?
Y......... N......... U......... A......... D......... U.........

81. Are the salaries of other teachers equitable in comparison with the salaries of coaches?
Y......... N......... U......... A......... D......... U.........

82. Are all athletic moneys, including gate receipts, considered as school funds with records accurately kept and audited?
Y......... N......... U......... A......... D......... U.........

83. Is the intramural sports program of your school financed entirely by appropriations from tax funds?
Y......... N......... U......... A......... D......... U.........

84. Is your school district moving toward complete financing of the athletic program from tax funds?
Y......... N......... U......... A......... D......... U.........

COMMUNITY RELATIONS

85. Is the school actively concerned with providing adequate community athletic facilities for children and youth?

    Y......... N......... U......... A......... D......... U.........

86. Does the school staff study your community to determine how to use, to improve, and to increase available space for wholesome play for the students enrolled in your school?

    Y......... N......... U......... A......... D......... U.........

87. Is the school actively interested in providing community athletic programs for children and youth during vacation periods?

    Y......... N......... U......... A......... D......... U.........

88. Do community organizations look to the school for expert counsel and advice regarding athletic programs?

    Y......... N......... U......... A......... D......... U.........

89. Does the school assume responsibility for informing the community regarding the standards of good sportsmanship that should be observed at all athletic contests?

    Y......... N......... U......... A......... D......... U.........

90. Is the conduct of spectators at interscholastic games such as to reflect favorably on the school?

    Y......... N......... U......... A......... D......... U.........

91. Does the board of education enjoy as much freedom from outside pressures in the selection of a coach as it does in the selection of other teachers?

    Y......... N......... U......... A......... D......... U.........

92. Does the community support the coach of a boys' varsity team that has a losing season?

    Y......... N......... U......... A......... D......... U.........

93. Do local newspapers, radio stations, and television stations support clean athletics and have a high regard for standards of good sportsmanship?

    Y......... N......... U.....!.... A......... D......... U.........

94. Are the schools comparatively free from undesirable activities on the part of outside organizations primarily concerned with winning teams in interscholastic games?

    Y......... N......... U......... A......... D......... U.........

NEW YORK POSTURE-RATING CHART*

Grade | 4 5 6 7 8 9 10 11 12
Rater's Initials
Date of Test

Row 1:
5 — HEAD ERECT GRAVITY LINE PASSES DIRECTLY THROUGH CENTER
3 — HEAD TWISTED OR TURNED TO ONE SIDE SLIGHTLY
1 — HEAD TWISTED OR TURNED TO ONE SIDE MARKEDLY

Row 2:
5 — SHOULDERS LEVEL (HORIZONTALLY)
3 — ONE SHOULDER SLIGHTLY HIGHER THAN OTHER
1 — ONE SHOULDER MARKEDLY HIGHER THAN OTHER

Row 3:
5 — SPINE STRAIGHT
3 — SPINE SLIGHTLY CURVED LATERALLY
1 — SPINE MARKEDLY CURVED LATERALLY

Row 4:
5 — HIPS LEVEL (HORIZONTALLY)
3 — ONE HIP SLIGHTLY HIGHER
1 — ONE HIP MARKEDLY HIGHER

Row 5:
5 — FEET POINTED STRAIGHT AHEAD
3 — FEET POINTED OUT
1 — FEET POINTED OUT MARKEDLY ANKLES SAG IN (PRONATION)

Row 6:
5 — ARCHES HIGH
3 — ARCHES LOWER, FEET SLIGHTLY FLAT
1 — ARCHES LOW, FEET MARKEDLY FLAT

Total Page One

*Reproduced by permission.

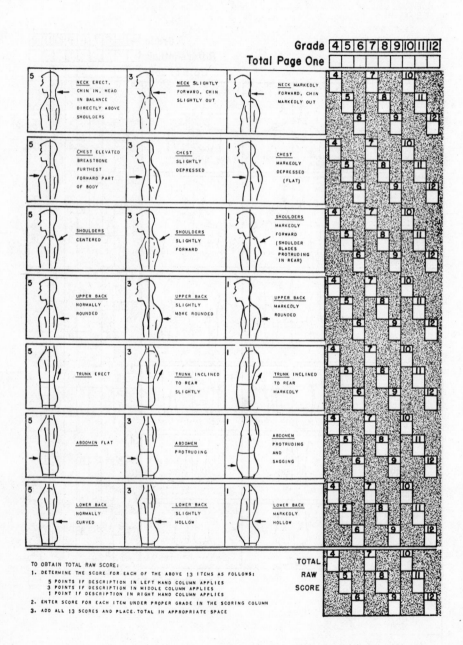

Grade 4 5 6 7 8 9 10 11 12

Total Page One

| 5 | NECK ERECT, CHIN IN, HEAD IN BALANCE DIRECTLY ABOVE SHOULDERS | 3 | NECK SLIGHTLY FORWARD, CHIN SLIGHTLY OUT | 1 | NECK MARKEDLY FORWARD, CHIN MARKEDLY OUT |

| 5 | CHEST ELEVATED BREASTBONE FURTHEST FORWARD PART OF BODY | 3 | CHEST SLIGHTLY DEPRESSED | 1 | CHEST MARKEDLY DEPRESSED (FLAT) |

| 5 | SHOULDERS CENTERED | 3 | SHOULDERS SLIGHTLY FORWARD | 1 | SHOULDERS MARKEDLY FORWARD (SHOULDER BLADES PROTRUDING IN REAR) |

| 5 | UPPER BACK NORMALLY ROUNDED | 3 | UPPER BACK SLIGHTLY MORE ROUNDED | 1 | UPPER BACK MARKEDLY ROUNDED |

| 5 | TRUNK ERECT | 3 | TRUNK INCLINED TO REAR SLIGHTLY | 1 | TRUNK INCLINED TO REAR MARKEDLY |

| 5 | ABDOMEN FLAT | 3 | ABDOMEN PROTRUDING | 1 | ABDOMEN PROTRUDING AND SAGGING |

| 5 | LOWER BACK NORMALLY CURVED | 3 | LOWER BACK SLIGHTLY HOLLOW | 1 | LOWER BACK MARKEDLY HOLLOW |

TO OBTAIN TOTAL RAW SCORE:

1. DETERMINE THE SCORE FOR EACH OF THE ABOVE 13 ITEMS AS FOLLOWS:

    5 POINTS IF DESCRIPTION IN LEFT HAND COLUMN APPLIES
    3 POINTS IF DESCRIPTION IN MIDDLE COLUMN APPLIES
    1 POINT IF DESCRIPTION IN RIGHT HAND COLUMN APPLIES

2. ENTER SCORE FOR EACH ITEM UNDER PROPER GRADE IN THE SCORING COLUMN

3. ADD ALL 13 SCORES AND PLACE TOTAL IN APPROPRIATE SPACE

TOTAL RAW SCORE

FORMS FOR USE IN PHYSICAL EDUCATION DEPARTMENT

LONG BEACH UNIFIED SCHOOL DISTRICT
Wilson High School • 4400 East 10th Street
GEneva 3-0481

WARNING OF FAILING WORK

Student's Name _____ Grade 10 11 12

The above named Student's work in _____ PHYSICAL EDUCATION _____
is failing at the present time. A final failing grade in this subject will result in the loss of credit and may cause delay in graduation.
We are asking your help in correcting this situation. For complete details, telephone the school number during my conference period (_____ to _____).
If you do not reach me at the time of your call, please leave your number with the switchboard operator and I will return your call.

Pupils Acknowledgment of Notice | Signature of Teacher

OCT 26 1975
Date

Courtesy of the Long Beach Unified School District, Long Beach, California.

Long Beach Unified School District
REGULATIONS PERTAINING TO THOSE WHO WEAR GLASSES

PUPIL'S NAME

THE WEARING OF GLASSES DURING CERTAIN PHYSICAL ACTIVITIES CAN BE HAZARDOUS.

IN THE INTEREST OF SAFETY, ONE OF THE FOLLOWING PRECAUTIONS MUST BE TAKEN WHILE PARTICIPATING ACTIVELY IN PHYSICAL EDUCATION, RECREATION, OR OTHER ATHLETIC ACTIVITIES:

    _____ 1. REMOVE GLASSES AND LEAVE IN SAFE PLACE.
    _____ 2. WEAR GLASSES GUARD. [THESE GUARDS ARE AVAILABLE AT THE SCHOOL WITHOUT COST.]
    _____ 3. WEAR TEMPERED GLASS LENSES OR OTHER APPROVED SAFETY LENSES: PLASTIC, CONTACT, ETC.

I HAVE READ THE ABOVE SAFETY PRECAUTIONS.
My child is instructed to follow the one checked above. Attached is a verification indicating lenses are safety type if number 3 is checked.

DATE _____ PARENT'S SIGNATURE _____
NOTE TO PARENT: PLEASE FILL OUT AND RETURN TO SCHOOL.

Courtesy of the Long Beach Unified School District, Long Beach, California.

FORM 116 5M L. C. COOK PTG. CO. 1957-58

DADE COUNTY PUBLIC SCHOOLS
Physical Exemption Card — SECONDARY

Family Physician's Certificate of Physical Inability of

Name_____Address_____
           (Last)   (First)

School_____Grade_____Home Room_____

To Participate in (Please check x)

STRENUOUS ACTIVITY		MODERATE ACTIVITY	RESTRICTED ACTIVITY
BADMINTON	SOFTBALL	ARCHERY	SUN BATHING
BASKETBALL	TOUCH FOOTBALL	BOWLING	RELAXATION PERIOD
BASEBALL	TENNIS	DECK TENNIS	PASSIVE RECREATION
FOOTBALL	TUMBLING AND APPARATUS	HORSESHOES	(CHECKERS ETC.)
GYMNASTICS	TRACK AND FIELD	SHUFFLEBOARD	
HOCKEY	VOLLEY BALL	PING PONG	
SOCCER		CROQUET	

Rest period advised for a period of...................weeks.

Please underline any of the above activities or write in others that are particularly suited to the student's condition.

My diagnosis is (be specific)_____

_____

Date_____19____   Signed_____M. D.

Signed_____
                        (Parent or Guardian)

TO THE PARENTS OR GUARDIANS AND TO THE FAMILY PHYSICIAN:

Beginning with the school year 1941-42, all students are required by the Dade County School Board to take physical education unless the family physician considers such activity to be detrimental to the student's health.

We shall appreciate your full cooperation in helping us carry on a worthwhile program of health and physical education.

JOE HALL, Superintendent.

Courtesy of the Dade County Public Schools, Dade County, Florida.

Gen. No. 1 100M-1-54-3181   **WAIVER FORM**   Long Beach, California
                            LONG BEACH PUBLIC SCHOOLS   Date_____

We,_____, are the parents or guardians

of_____, and in consideration of the special benefits
of the extracurricular activity being afforded the student by the Long Beach Board of Education and
the school districts whose school the aforementioned child attends, hereby permit_____

_____to participate in_____

and we hereby release and discharge the said Long Beach Board of Education, the said school district,
and each and all their agents and employees from any liability whatever to the undersigned resulting from or in any manner arising out of any injury or damage which may be sustained by

the said_____, on account of his participation in

_____or in the transportation in connection therewith.

We further agree that in case of any action being brought for, or on behalf of the aforementioned child on account of any injury received during his participation in the above mentioned
events, or in the transportation connected therewith, that we will be personally responsible to the
school district, the Board of Education, and any of its officials or agents concerned, and will repay
to them and hold them harmless against any judgment recovered in any such action against them
or either of them.

Signed this_____day of_____, 195____

_____   _____
   Signature of Parent or Guardian   Address

_____   _____
   Signature of Parent or Guardian   Address
NOTE: Parents or Guardians, read the reverse side of this form.

Courtesy of the Long Beach Public Schools, Long Beach, California.

```
CONDUCT REPORT:

Name_____ Period_____ Teacher_____ Date_____

____  Lock ____ on wrong locker              ____  TAKE THIS SLIP TO THE EQUIPMENT
            ____left off locker                     ROOM AND PICK UP MISSING
            ____unlocked on locker                  ARTICLES.
____  Gym clothes left out of locker
____  Purse left out of locker               **** A DUPLICATE OF THIS SLIP HAS
____  Misplaced articles (_____)            BEEN GIVEN TO YOUR TEACHER.
____  Locker room  ____late leaving
                   ____unauthorized presence
                   ____eating
____  Misuse of cot room
____  Swim cap borrowed, not returned
____  _____


      ATTITUDE:  _____
                 POOR    SATISFACTORY   COOPERATIVE
```

Courtesy of the Compton Union High School District, Compton, California.

G.A.A. RECORD OF ACTIVITIES
COMPTON UNION HIGH SCHOOL DISTRICT

Name _____ (Last) _____ (First)

Constitution Test _____ Student Body _____ Inition Mock _____ Formal _____

ACTIVITY	7-10th	8-11th	9-12th	10 Hike	10 Bicy.	10 P.Day	11 Hike	11 Bicy.	11 P.Day	12 Hike	12 Bicy.	12 P.Day
Archery												
Badminton												
Baseball												
Basketball												
Bicyling												
Bowling												
Dance												
Hiking												
Hockey												
Officer												
Playday												
Speedball												
Swimming - Fall												
Swimming - Spring												
Tennis - Fall												
Tennis - Spring												
Volleyball												
TOTAL										Tot.		

Awards - Numerals _____ Letter _____

Sweater _____ Star _____

Courtesy of the Compton Union High School District, Compton, California.

Compton Union High School District
HEALTH INFORMATION SHEET – SENIOR HIGH SCHOOL

Counselor _____

Student's Name _____ Grade _____
              (Last)   (First)

Address_____ Date of birth _____

Father's name _____Mother's name _____

EMERGENCY PROCEDURE

     There is need many times for contacting parents at work when they cannot be reached in the home. Will you please list home phone and business phone where you may be reached in an emergency.

Home phone _____

Where does father work _____ Phone _____

Where does mother work _____ Phone _____

Where does guardian work _____ Phone _____.

     In case parent cannot be reached please write the names of *two other persons in this district* who will assume responsibility for this student.

     1. Name _____ Address _____ Phone _____

     2. Name _____ Address _____ Phone _____

Family Physician_____ Address _____ Phone _____

Family Dentist_____ Address _____ Phone _____

What injuries or operations has student had? Give dates _____
_____

Does student wear glasses? _____ Constantly? _____When were lenses last changed?_____
_____

Does student have a hearing problem?_____ Punctured ear drum? _____

Ear discharges? _____

Does student have headaches?_____ Occasionally? _____ Frequently? _____

Give the approximate dates and results of the following tests and immunizations:

        Smallpox _____Tuberculosis _____

        Polio (1)_____ (2) _____ (3)_____

        Other_____

Underline the following illnesses that student had: Rheumatic Fever, Epilepsy, Asthma, Heart trouble, Scarlet fever,

Polio, Appendicitis, Hay fever, other _____
_____

Give any special health information that we should know_____
_____
_____
_____

Signature of Father_____ Signature of Mother _____

Signature of Guardian_____ Date_____

Form 212 5M 10/60

Courtesy of the Compton Union High School District, Compton, California.

DADE COUNTY PUBLIC SCHOOLS
DEPARTMENT OF HEALTH AND PHYSICAL EDUCATION

SENIOR HIGH SCHOOL
SPECIAL RECOGNITION AWARD

SPORTS & ATHLETICS

INTRAMURALS

PHYSICAL FITNESS

PHYSICAL EDUCATION

This is to Certify that

HAS SHOWN EXCEPTIONAL ACHIEVEMENT and/or PROGRESS IN
THE ACTIVITIES HEREIN LISTED DURING THE SCHOOL YEAR
196 - 196

Date:_____ School:_____

Physical Education Instructor   Principal

ABILITY · EFFORT · TEAMWORK · SPORTSMANSHIP · LEADERSHIP · CONDUCT

Courtesy of the Dade County Public Schools, Dade County, Florida.

DUE DATE: October 1   P.E. 15
           February 15 (If changed from first semester)

BALTIMORE PUBLIC SCHOOLS
BALTIMORE 18, MARYLAND
Division of Physical Education

-oOo-

INDIVIDUAL TEACHING SCHEDULE

Name_____ School_____ Date_____

In the spaces below indicate the following:
   1. In Period Column: Time (i.e. 9:05 to 9:50)
   2. In Day Columns: a) Grade and group (i.e. 10B6-22B or 9A10-20G)
   3. If no class in Physical Education, indicate assignment, by periods.
   4. If no assignment, leave space blank.
   5. In small square put total number in class.
   6. Different pupils refers to those assigned to each instructor.
   7. Assembly day is_____ period is_____.

	Time	Monday	Tuesday	Wednesday	Thursday	Friday
1. From To						
2. From To						
3. From To						
4. From To						
5. From To						
6. From To						
7. From To						
8. From To						
9. From To						

Teaching Periods per week_____   Number of different pupils assigned
                                   to teacher per week_____
                                   Total in all classes per week_____

Courtesy of the Baltimore Public Schools, Baltimore, Maryland.

DOMINGUEZ HIGH SCHOOL

Girls' Physical Education Department

Dear Parent:

We are anxious to work with you to help your daughter profit from her physical education class.

The following is a brief summary of our requirements in obtaining the fullest cooperation from the students.

Costume
A regulation costume is desired of all students because it permits freedom of movement in the various activities. This costume may be purchased at many of the local stores.
1. White socks
2. White tennis shoes
3. White cotton blouse with short sleeves
4. White shorts
The blouse, shorts and socks should be washed once each week and be clean on Monday for weekly inspection.
All articles should be marked with full name so that each girl will wear her own clothes and clothes that are lost may be quickly returned.

Showers
Showers are required every day after physical education activities, and towels will be furnished.

Lockers
Each girl has an individual locker furnished with a combination lock. This lock must remain locked at all times. A girl who leaves her locker unlocked will receive a low grade in citizenship.

Dressing for Physical Education
Girls are required to dress for activity daily.

Grading
1. The subject achievement grade will be based on skill tests, rhythms, written knowledge tests, playing ability, showers and a complete costume every day.
2. The citizenship grade will be based on work completed on time, promptness for class, cleanliness, neatness in the shower room, class conduct, keeping her locker locked, and not borrowing other girls' clothes.

Physical Education Excuses
California State Law states that there are no permanent excuses from Physical Education. However, if your daughter is physically unable to participate, she may secure a printed form from the nurse to be filled out by your doctor.

If there are any questions, please call NEwmark 9-4321, Ext. 396 and we will be glad to help in any way we can.

Sincerely,

GIRLS' PHYSICAL EDUCATION DEPARTMENT

Courtesy of the Dominguez High School, Dominguez, California.

SPRINGFIELD PUBLIC SCHOOLS
Springfield, Massachusetts

PHYSICIAN'S RECOMMENDATION FOR MODIFICATION OF THE REQUIRED CLASS PHYSICAL EDUCATION INSTRUCTION PROGRAM

This is to certify that in my professional opinion _____, a pupil in _____ School, should have his or her required physical education program modified as indicated below.

Check with an X the total program and the individual activities in the selected program in which you wish the pupil to participate.

☐ NORMAL PROGRAM

☐ Body mechanics (posture)
☐ Gymnastics
☐ Apparatus
☐ Tumbling and stunts--self-testing activities
☐ Individual and dual sports
☐ Swimming
☐ Dancing: modern, folk, square
☐ Team Sports--intramural and class Examples: soccer, basketball, track
☐ Shower baths
☐ Fundamental rhythms
☐ Relays
☐ Rhythmic activities

☐ ADAPTED PROGRAM

☐ Mild exercise--lying down or sitting
☐ Body mechanics--modified as to need
☐ Mild rhythmic activities
☐ Square dancing
☐ Ball skills--little running
☐ Shower baths
☐ Simple recreational games-- little running

☐ RESTRICTED PROGRAM

☐ Relaxation--quiet table games
☐ Helper or managerial duties such as recorder
☐ Shower baths
☐ Complete rest

These recommendations shall apply from _____ 19 _____
to _____ 19 _____

Date _____ 19 _____

_____
Signature of physician

Courtesy of the Springfield Public School System.

FIELD AND COURT DIAGRAMS

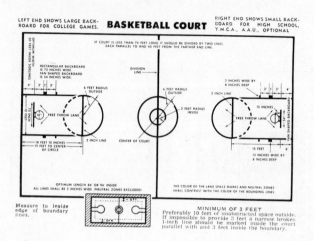

BASKETBALL COURT

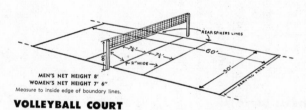

VOLLEYBALL COURT

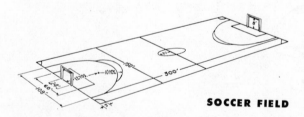

SOCCER FIELD

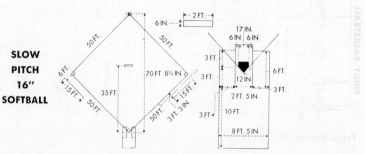

**SLOW
PITCH
16"
SOFTBALL**

From *Athletic Field and Court Diagrams.* Courtesy of Wilson Sportings Goods Co.

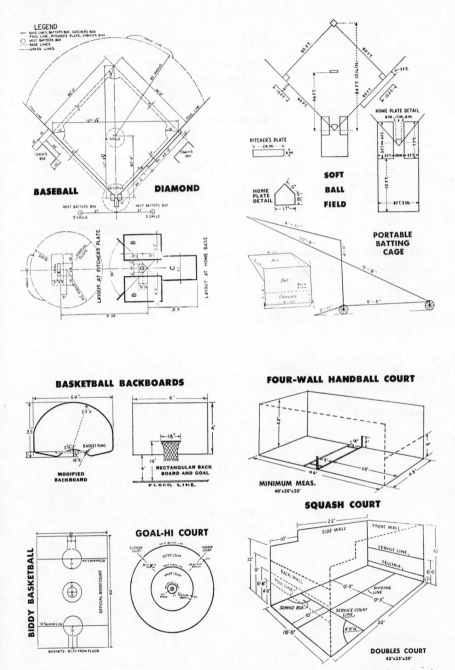

From *Athletic Field and Court Diagrams.* Courtesy of Lowe and Campbell Athletic Goods Co., Kansas City, Missouri.

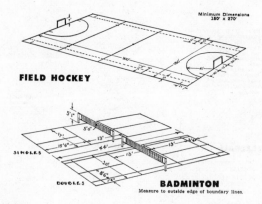

Minimum Dimensions
180' x 270'

FIELD HOCKEY

BADMINTON

Measure to outside edge of boundary lines.

HOW TO LAY OUT A TENNIS COURT

First spot place for net posts, 42 feet apart. Measure in on each side 7½ feet and plant stakes 27 feet apart at points A and B in diagram.

Then take two tape measures and attach to each peg—one tape 47 feet 5 inches, the other 39 feet. Pull both taut in such directions that at these distances they meet at point C. This gives one corner of the court. Interchange the tapes and again measure to get point D. Points C and D should then be 27 feet apart. Put in pegs at C and D and measure 18 feet toward net and put in pegs to denote service lines.

Proceed in same way for the other half of court and add center line from service line to service line—distance 42 feet. Then add 4½ feet on each side for alleys. Alleys should then be 3 feet inside posts on each side. Put in permanent pegs to mark all corners.

Measure to outside edge of boundary lines.

LAWN TENNIS
Singles and Doubles

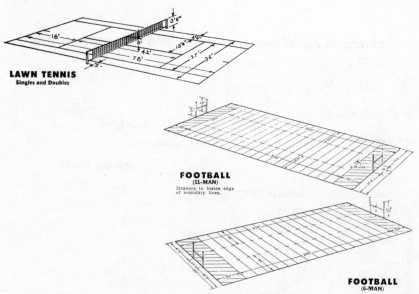

FOOTBALL
(11-MAN)
Measure to inside edge
of boundary lines.

FOOTBALL
(6-MAN)

From *Athletic Field and Court Diagrams.* Courtesy of Lowe and Campbell Athletic
Goods Co., Kansas City, Missouri.

QUARTER-MILE TRACK

Approved by the National Federation of State High School Athletic Associations

Note: It is recommended that the straightaway of the track be made 22 feet wide to allow for six lanes of 42-in. hurdles; and that the curves and back side of the track be 18 feet, allowing six lanes of 3 feet width each.

As alternate locations for the Broad Jump and Pole Vault pits and runways both may be placed parallel to each other across the end of the track opposite the High Jump pit.

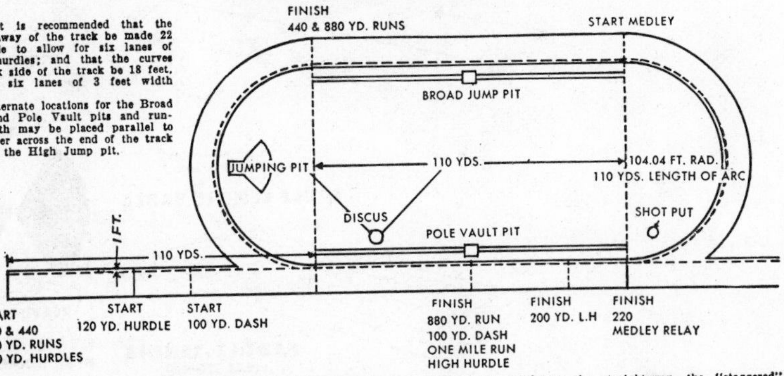
FINISH
440 & 880 YD. RUNS
START MEDLEY
BROAD JUMP PIT
JUMPING PIT
110 YDS.
104.04 FT. RAD.
110 YDS. LENGTH OF ARC
DISCUS
SHOT PUT
POLE VAULT PIT
1 FT.
110 YDS.
START
220 & 440
880 YD. RUNS
200 YD. HURDLES
START
120 YD. HURDLE
START
100 YD. DASH
FINISH
880 YD. RUN
100 YD. DASH
ONE MILE RUN
HIGH HURDLE
FINISH
200 YD. L.H
FINISH
220
MEDLEY RELAY

HANDICAPS—When races, run in lanes, start on the straightaway and relay exchanges are made on the straightaway, the "staggered" distance may be determined from the following tables. These figures apply to all tracks which are laid out with semi-circular turns, regardless of the number of laps to the mile.

For 30-Inch Lanes

No. of turns to run	4	3	2	1
Hdcp., Lane 2 over 1	27′ 2⅛″	20′ 4⅞″	13′ 7¼″	6′ 9⅝″
Lanes 3, 4, 5, 6, 7 & 8 over next inside lanes	31′ 5″	23′ 6¾″	15′ 8½″	7′ 10¼″

For 36-Inch Lanes

No. of turns to run	4	3	2	1
Hdcp., Lane 2 over 1	33′ 6″	25′ 1½″	16′ 9″	8′ 4⅛″
Lanes 3, 4, 5, 6, 7 & 8 over next inside lanes	37′ 8⅝″	28′ 3¼″	18′ 10¼″	9′ 5⅛″

For 42-Inch Lanes

No. of turns to run	4	3	2	1
Hdcp., Lane 2 over 1	39′ 9⅛″	29′ 10⅛″	19′ 10¾″	9′ 11⅝″
Lanes 3, 4, 5, 6, 7 & 8 over next inside lanes	43′ 11¾″	32′ 11⅞″	21′ 11⅞″	11′

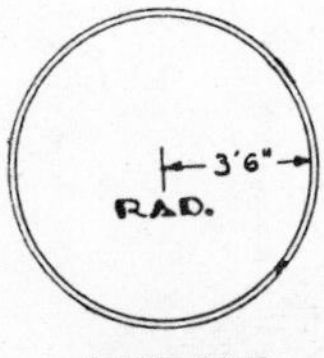
3′6″
RAD.

SHOT PUT and HAMMER THROW CIRCLE

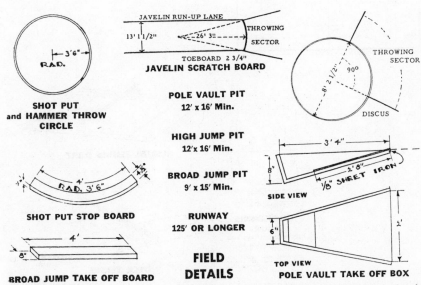

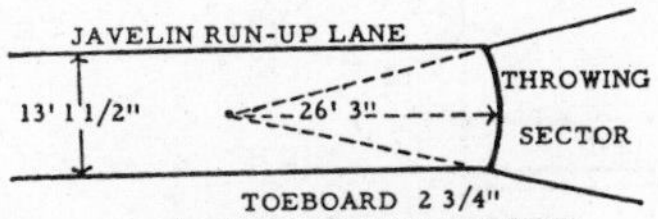
JAVELIN RUN-UP LANE
13′ 1 1/2″
26′ 3″
THROWING
SECTOR
TOEBOARD 2 3/4″

JAVELIN SCRATCH BOARD

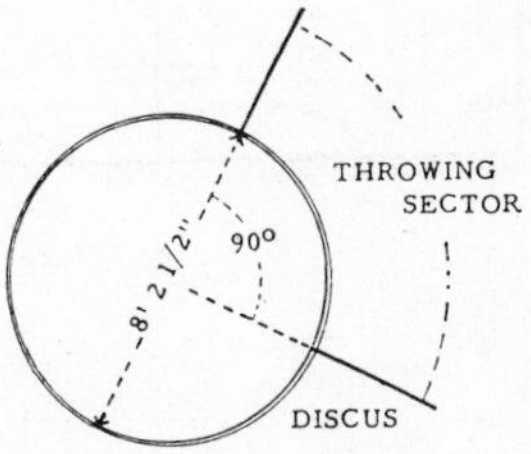
THROWING
SECTOR
90°
8′ 2 1/2″
DISCUS

POLE VAULT PIT
12′ x 16′ Min.

HIGH JUMP PIT
12′x 16′ Min.

BROAD JUMP PIT
9′ x 15′ Min.

RUNWAY
125′ OR LONGER

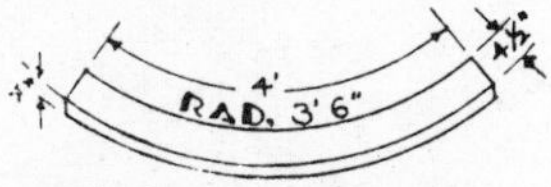
4′
RAD. 3′6″

SHOT PUT STOP BOARD

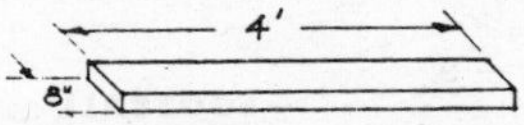
4′
8″

BROAD JUMP TAKE OFF BOARD

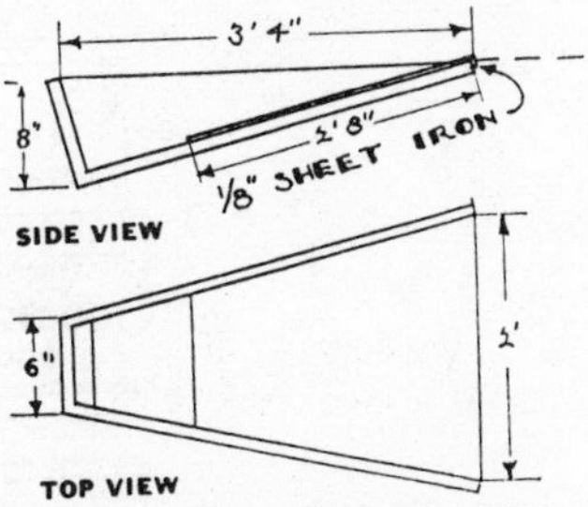
3′ 4″
8″
2′ 8″
1/8″ SHEET IRON
SIDE VIEW
6″
2′
TOP VIEW

POLE VAULT TAKE OFF BOX

FIELD DETAILS

From *Athletic Field and Court Diagrams.* Courtesy of Lowe and Campbell Athletic Goods Co., Kansas City, Missouri.

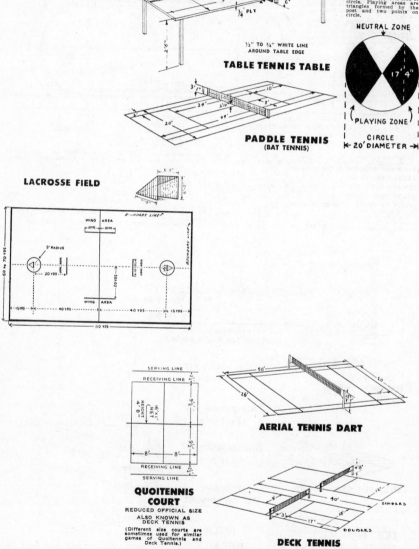

From *Athletic Field and Court Diagrams.* Courtesy of Lowe and Campbell Athletic Goods Co., Kansas City, Missouri.

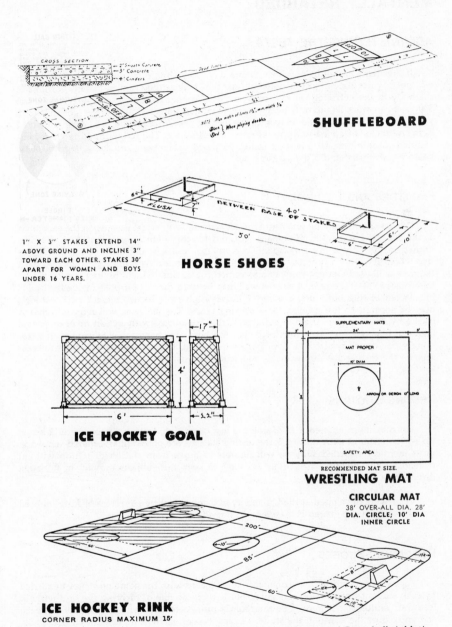

SHUFFLEBOARD

HORSE SHOES

1" X 3" STAKES EXTEND 14"
ABOVE GROUND AND INCLINE 3"
TOWARD EACH OTHER. STAKES 30'
APART FOR WOMEN AND BOYS
UNDER 16 YEARS.

ICE HOCKEY GOAL

WRESTLING MAT

CIRCULAR MAT
38' OVER-ALL DIA. 28'
DIA. CIRCLE; 10' DIA
INNER CIRCLE

ICE HOCKEY RINK
CORNER RADIUS MAXIMUM 15'

From *Athletic Field and Court Diagrams.* Courtesy of Lowe and Campbell Athletic
Goods Co., Kansas City, Missouri.

PHYSICAL FITNESS TESTS FOR THE MENTALLY RETARDED

ADMINISTERING THE TESTS

If the items are all to be given in one day, they should be placed in an order that will not require the subject to perform tests that may fatigue him in certain portions of the body to the detriment of his score on the following item. For example, running the 300 yard run-walk test item is likely to create enough fatigue to affect the score of the 25 yard dash if it is run immediately after the former, even though one is basically involved with the factor of speed and the other with endurance. The following order is recommended to eliminate fatigue as a factor: 25 yeard dash, bent arm hang, leg lift, static balance test, thrust and 300 yard run-walk.

FACILITIES AND EQUIPMENT

The test items may be given indoors or outside with equal ease, with the exception of the 300 yard run-walk. The space required for this item is such that it can be performed inside only if the participants run in laps, and keeping track of the number of laps which have been run may create confusion. The administration of the 25 yard dash requires a 35 yard straight runway and something against which the foot can be placed for a brace to start the race. A cleared wall may be used for this purpose inside the building. When testing outdoors, a board 2 inches high by 4 inches wide 2 or 3 feet long may be secured to the ground for a starting block. The leg raise will require a mat at least 6 by 4 feet in size. If a mat is not available, a mattress with a clean cover or several layers of blankets may be substituted. For the bent arm hang a bar is needed. If a stationary bar is not available, a door bar may be used. Other items of equipment necessary for the testing are stop watches and scoring cards.

TESTING STATIONS

For maximum efficiency in giving the test items, five testing stations should be set up with a tester at each station. If the testing stations are placed in an ordered sequence, most mentally retarded subjects will be able to move from station to station without difficulty. It is helpful to have an assistant to keep the subjects moving in the right direction to the next station.

Tests were developed at the University of Connecticut by Dr. Hollis F. Fait, financed by a grant from the Joseph P. Kennedy Jr. Foundation.

RECORDING SCORES

For ease in recording the scores, a 4×6 inch card with his name on it may be carried by each student from station to station. Students incapable of carrying the card without losing or mutilating it may have their cards pinned to their shirts. The tester at each station records the score on the student's card as soon as he completes the test.

PERSONNEL

Only one person is required to administer the 25 yard dash if he serves as both timer and starter. He will need to stand at the finish line and give the command to start from there. One person is able to administer the bent arm hang, static balance test, and thrust. An assistant will be needed for the leg lift. The 300 yard run-walk should be the last test item given. Three people will be required to administer the test: a scorer, a timer, and an assistant to keep the students in line after they have finished.

UNIFORMITY IN TESTING

In administering the test items, extreme care must be taken to ensure that each item is performed uniformly by all the subjects. Unless this is done, the comparison with norms will not be meaningful nor will the comparison of one student's scores with another's have any valid meaning. If a subject is unable to perform in the prescribed manner, his score, however, need not be discarded entirely as a measurement of the fitness factor being tested. The score may still be used as a basis for comparison of his future scores on that item to determine the extent of improvement achieved by the subject.

DESCRIPTION OF TEST ITEMS

TWENTY-FIVE YARD RUN (MEASURES THE SPEED OF RUNNING SHORT DISTANCES)

The subject places either foot against the wall or block with the foot parallel to it. He then takes a semi-crouch position with the hands resting lightly on the knees. His forward foot and trunk are turned in the direction he is to run. His head is held up so that he is looking toward the finish line. At the command of "Ready . . . Go!" the subject begins the run. The watch is started on the "Go" and is stopped as the subject passes the finish line. However, the subject is directed to run to a second line, which is about 5 feet beyond the finish line, to prevent his slowing down as he approaches the true finish line. The time of the run is recorded to the nearest one-tenth of a second.

BENT ARM HANG (MEASURES STATIC MUSCULAR ENDURANCE OF THE ARM AND SHOULDER GIRDLE)

A horizontal bar or doorway bar may be used for this test. A stool approximately 12 inches high is placed under the bar. The subject steps onto the stool and takes hold of the bar with both hands, using a reverse grip (palms toward the face). The hands are shoulders' width apart. The subject brings his head to the bar, presses the bridge of the nose to the bar and steps off the stool. He holds his position as long as possible. The timer starts the watch as the subject's nose presses to the bar and the body weight is taken on the arms. The watch is stopped when the subject drops away from the bar. The tester should be ready to catch the subject in the event that he falls. The number of seconds the subject held the position is recorded on the score card.

LEG LIFT (MEASURES DYNAMIC MUSCULAR ENDURANCE OF THE FLEXOR MUSCLES OF THE LEG AND OF THE ABDOMINAL MUSCLES)

The subject lies flat on his back with his hands clasped behind the neck. A helper should hold the subject's elbows to the mat. The subject raises his legs, keeping the knees straight until they are at a 90 degreee angle. Another helper, who stands to the side of the subject, extends one hand over the subject's abdomen at the height of the ankles when the legs are fully lifted. This serves as a guide to the subject in achieving the desired angle and encourages him to keep the legs straight. He should be instructed to touch the shins against the helper's arm. The subject is to do as many leg lifts as possible in the 20 second time limit. He begins on the command of "Go" and ceases on the command of "Stop." The score is the number of leg lifts performed during the 20 seconds.

Static Balance Test (Measures Ability to Maintain Balance in a Stationary Position)

The subject places his hands on his hips, lifts one leg and places the foot on the inside of the knee of the other leg. He then closes his eyes and maintains his balance in this position as long as he can. The watch is started the moment he closes his eyes. As soon as the subject loses his balance, the watch is stopped. The score is number of seconds, to the nearest one-tenth of a second.

Thrusts (Measure the Specific Type of Agility That is Measured by the Squat Thrust or Burpee)

The subject takes a squatting position with the feet and hands flat on the floor. The knees should make contact with the arms. At the command "Go," the stop watch is started. The subject takes the weight upon his hands so that he may thrust his legs straight out behind him. The legs are returned to the original position. The score is the number of complete thrusts the subject is able to perform in 20 seconds. One half point is awarded for completing half of the thrust.

300 Yard Run-Walk (Measures Cardio-Respiratory Endurance)

In taking a starting position, the runner should place one foot comfortably ahead of the other. A semi-crouch position with the hands resting lightly on the knees is taken. At the command to go, the stop watch is started. The subject runs the prescribed course. He is allowed to walk part of the distance if he is unable to run the total distance. The time required to complete the run-walk is the score.

ACHIEVEMENT SCALES OF PHYSICAL FITNESS TESTS FOR MENTALLY RETARDED YOUTHS

25 Yard Run

Boys
(Score in seconds)

Age	Trainable			Educable		
	Low	Av.	Good	Low	Av.	Good
9–12	7.0	6.0	5.2	6.2	5.2	4.4
13–16	6.5	5.5	4.7	5.4	4.7	4.2
17–20	6.0	5.0	4.2	5.1	4.4	3.9

Girls

Age	Low	Av.	Good	Low	Av.	Good
9–12	7.4	6.3	5.3	5.8	5.4	5.2
13–16	6.7	5.6	4.7	6.1	5.2	4.3
17–20	7.3	6.1	5.1	6.4	5.4	4.7

Bent Arm Hang

Boys
(Score in seconds)

Age	Trainable			Educable		
	Low	Av.	Good	Low	Av.	Good
9–12	2.0	10.0	16.0	3.0	19.0	33.0
13–16	11.2	22.0	30.2	5.0	25.0	43.0
17–20	23.0	23.0	31.0	8.0	30.0	50.0

Girls

Age	Low	Av.	Good	Low	Av.	Good
9–12	2.0	8.0	12.0	3.0	9.0	13.0
13–16	4.0	14.0	22.0	5.0	15.0	23.0
17–20	3.0	9.0	13.0	4.0	12.0	18.0

Leg Lift

Boys

Age	Trainable			Educable		
	Low	Av.	Good	Low	Av.	Good
9–12	6	9	12	7	10	13
13–16	6	9	12	8	11	14
17–20	7	10	13	8	11	14

Girls

Age	Low	Av.	Good	Low	Av.	Good
9–12	6	10	14	6	10	14
13–16	7	11	15	7	11	15
17–20	6	10	14	6	10	14

Static Balance

Boys
(Score in seconds)

Age	Trainable			Educable		
	Low	Av.	Good	Low	Av.	Good
9–12	3.0	4.4	5.8	4.0	5.0	6.0
13–16	3.1	4.5	5.9	5.0	6.0	7.0
17–20	3.2	4.6	6.0	5.0	10.0	15.0

Girls

Age	Low	Av.	Good	Low	Av.	Good
9–12	2.2	3.2	4.2	2.5	3.5	4.5
13–16	5.1	6.1	7.1	8.6	9.6	10.6
17–20	4.9	5.9	6.9	5.2	6.2	7.2

Thrust

Boys

Age	Trainable			Educable		
	Low	Av.	Good	Low	Av.	Good
9–12	4	8	10	6	12	14
13–16	4	8	10	8	14	16
17–20	5	9	11	8	14	16

Girls

Age	Low	Av.	Good	Low	Av.	Good
9–12	4	8	10	5	9	11
13–16	4	8	10	8	12	14
17–20	5	9	11	5	9	11

300 Yard Run-Walk

Boys
(Score in seconds)

Age	Trainable			Educable		
	Low	Av.	Good	Low	Av.	Good
9–12	145	115	95	105	80	60
13–16	111	86	66	95	75	55
17–20	104	79	59	74	59	39

Girls
(Score in seconds)

Age	Low	Av.	Good	Low	Av.	Good
9–12	198	148	108	143	113	83
13–16	158	108	65	125	91	61
17–20	159	107	66	142	102	71

INDEX

Page numbers in *italics* indicate a figure; page numbers followed by a t indicate a table.

569